WILSON

WILSON

The Authorised Life

of Lord Wilson of Rievaulx

PHILIP ZIEGLER

Weidenfeld & Nicolson · London

First published in Great Britain in 1993 by
Weidenfeld & Nicolson
The Orion Publishing Group Ltd
Orion House
5 Upper St Martin's Lane
London WC2H 9EA

ISBN 0 297 81276 9

British Library Cataloguing in Publication Data is
available for this title.

Typeset by Selwood Systems, Midsomer Norton
Printed in Great Britain by Butler & Tanner Ltd, Frome
and London

Contents

Contents

Illustrations

Unless otherwise stated all photographs come from the collection of Lord and Lady Wilson and are reproduced with their kind permission.

Illustrations

Abbreviations used in text

AEU   Amalgamated Engineering Union
ANF   Atlantic Nuclear Force

BBC   British Broadcasting Corporation
BMA   British Medical Association

CBI   Confederation of British Industries
CIA   Central Intelligence Agency
CIR   Commission for Industrial Relations
CLPD   Campaign for Labour Party Democracy
CND   Committee for Nuclear Disarmament

DEA   Department of Economic Affairs

EDC   European Defence Community
EEC   European Economic Community
EFTA   European Free Trade Area

FAO   Food and Agriculture Organisation
FCO   Foreign and Commonwealth Office

GATT   General Agreement on Tariffs and Trade

IMF   International Monetary Fund
ITN   Independent Television News

MI5   Military Intelligence 5 (The Security Service)

Abbreviations

MLF	Multilateral Force
NATO	North Atlantic Treaty Organisation
NEB	National Enterprise Board
NEC	National Executive Committee (of the Labour Party)
NFFC	National Film Finance Corporation
NHS	National Health Service
NIBMAR	No Independence Before Majority African Rule
NOP	National Opinion Poll
NUM	National Union of Miners
NUS	National Union of Students
OECD	Organisation for Economic Cooperation and Development
PLP	Parliamentary Labour Party
PPE	Philosophy, Politics and Economics
SAS	Special Air Service
SDLP	Social Democratic and Labour Party
SNP	Scottish Nationalist Party
TGWU	Transport and General Workers' Union
TUC	Trades Union Congress
UDI	Unilateral Declaration of Independence
UN	United Nations

Foreword and acknowledgments

The phrase "authorised biography" arouses suspicion in the reader. What price has been paid for exclusive access to the subject's papers? When he agreed to my writing this book Lord Wilson provided that he should "be given the opportunity to read the text in typescript form" and that the author should "take into account any observation he might make specifically on matters of fact when he believed these to be incorrect". The contents of the book, he concluded "will be entirely at your discretion". That is precisely what has happened. Neither Lord Wilson nor anyone acting on his behalf has caused me to modify my judgments or omit uncomfortable material.

If they had done so with any success this book would have been markedly different. There is much in it with which Lord Wilson would disagree. Still more is this the case with Lady Falkender. She has spoken with me for many hours, and I am painfully aware of the fact that she feels she has been ill-rewarded for her trouble and that my portrait of her is in many ways unfair. My gratitude to her and to Lord and Lady Wilson is unfeigned.

I have done my best to eliminate any political bias from my writing, but it still seems only fair that the reader should have some idea of my political opinions. Probably over the years I have voted Labour more often than Conservative but the balance must be a fine one; I am one of nature's floating voters. When I told Harold Wilson, before I took on the book, that I was far from being a committed socialist, he replied with some satisfaction, "That's lucky. Nor am I!" He was joking; but there was enough truth in the joke to make me feel that, on political grounds at least, I was not unsuitable as a biographer.

Wilson has been the subject of two other biographies within the last eighteen months. With the first, that by Austen Morgan, I disagree fundamentally; he has, however, done much valuable research and his book has suggested lines of enquiry which I have followed with advantage.

Ben Pimlott's impressive biography unfortunately, or perhaps fortunately, came too late for me to be able to pay it more than cursory attention. It is almost a third again as long as mine, in spite of the fact that I have had access to many extra papers. There is no right or wrong length for a biography: Professor Pimlott could easily have made his book considerably longer; I, though with greater difficulty, could have made mine shorter. The difference, however, does make direct comparison less easy. In general, he deals more fully with internal Labour politics; I concentrate more on foreign affairs and Wilson's relationships with international statesmen. This reflects partly the materials that were available to us, but more, I suspect, our personal predilections. The same is true of Pimlott's extensive verbatim reporting of those to whom he has spoken and my preference for quoting from the reports of foreign, mainly American, diplomats. But though we tread widely different paths, it seems to me that our conclusions are in essence similar. I would not seriously dispute any of Professor Pimlott's major judgments or conclusions.

Whether or not I have quoted from them verbatim, a host of people have talked to me about Harold Wilson, or have helped me in other ways in my research. I am most grateful to Lord Armstrong of Ilminster, Mr Robert Asprey, The Hon David Astor, Mr Harold Atkins, Mr Correlli Barnett, Miss Nora Beloff, Mr Tony Benn, Lord Bridges, Professor Arthur Brown, Sir Michael Butler, Sir Robin Butler, Lord Callaghan, Mr William Camp, Lord Chalfont, Lord Charteris, Mr Winston Churchill, Esme Countess of Cromer, Mr Ivor Crosthwaite, Lord Donoughue, Sir Antony Duff, Sir Richard Faber, Miss Peggy Field, Mr Tony Field, Mr Michael Foot, Sir Edward Ford, Mr John Freeman, Mr Martin Gilbert, Lord Glenamara, Lord Glendevon, Lord Goodman, Lady Greenwood, Mr Joe Haines, Professor Nigel Hamilton, Lord Harris of Greenwich, Mr Roy Hattersley, Councillor Norman Hazell, Lord Healey, Sir Edward Heath, Sir Nicholas Henderson, Sir James Hennessy, Dame Wendy Hiller, Mr Anthony Howard, Mr David Humphrey, Lord Hunt of Tanworth, Mr Graham Ison, Sir Kenneth James, Lord Jay, Baroness Jeger, Lord Jenkins of Hillhead, Mr Paul Johnson, Mr Gerald Kaufman, Dr Leon Kaufman, Lord Kissin, Dr Helkn Langley, Lord Lever, The Earl of Longford, Lord Lovell-Davis, Lord Marsh, Mr Peter Meyer, Mr Harry Middleton,

Mr John Miller, Sir Derek Mitchell, Mr Charles Monteith, Sir John Morgan, Dr Kathie Nicastro, Dr Frederick Nicole, Lord O'Brien of Lothbury, Dr John Orbell, Lord Owen, Sir Michael Palliser, Mr Barrie Penrose, Lady Antonia Pinter, Sir Peter Ramsbotham, Sir Robert Rhodes James, Mrs Stella Rimington, Mr Kenneth Rose, Mr Edmund de Rothschild, Mr Neville Sandelson, Mr Mark Savage, Lord Shackleton, Mr Peter Shore, Sir Sigmund Sternberg, the late Mr Michael Stewart, Lord Thomson of Monifieth, The Hon Mrs Frieda Warman-Brown, Lord Weidenfeld, Miss Marjorie Wilson, Dr Robin Wilson, Dr Ruth Winstone, Sir Oliver Wright, Lord Wyatt of Weeford, the late Lord Zuckerman.

Of the above, I owe a special debt to Lord Weidenfeld since it was he who first suggested I should write this book. I have never for a moment regretted accepting his invitation; I hope that he feels the same. Ion Trewin has proved himself a scrupulous and sensitive editor while Morag Lyall has picked up innumerable inconsistencies and infelicities of style. Douglas Matthews has contributed greatly; both as Librarian of the London Library and indexer of infinite skill and conscientiousness. My agent, Diana Baring, has been, as always, a stalwart support when needed and admirably reluctant to bother one at other times. First and foremost she has been a cherished friend.

In the acknowledgments to my biography of King Edward VIII I wrote that my wife Clare, by her wisdom and generosity of mind, had brought to my understanding of my subject a depth that would otherwise have been lacking. I cannot improve on this except to say that my consciousness of my debt to her continues to grow from year to year.

Philip Ziegler

I

The Child and the Boy

1916–1934

Harold Wilson was a very ordinary small boy. His origins were equally unremarkable. Alec Douglas-Home, irritated by Wilson's repeated references to him as the fourteenth Earl, retorted that the Labour leader was presumably the fourteenth Mr Wilson. If ancestors be taken to exist only from the time at which they were recorded, Harold was in fact the eighth, or perhaps ninth, Mr Wilson. There had been Wilsons for many generations before that, however, in the little Yorkshire village of Rievaulx from which the family hailed, and there is no reason to doubt that Harold Wilson's forbears were amongst them.

The first about whom anything much is known is Harold's great-grandfather. John Wilson was born in Rievaulx and at first worked there as a cobbler. In 1850, however, he migrated and was appointed master of the workhouse at Helmsley. He seems to have done the job well; at least the seventy or so inmates were given their own privy during his period of office and were even promised a bath. After three years he was promoted and moved on to a similar job at York. By 1877 there were nearly 500 people in the workhouse and Wilson's salary had been increased from an original £60 to £135 a year. Almost the only blemish on his record arose in 1861 when he was accused of flogging a boy so severely that "his back was as black as a coal." Wilson explained that the boy had broken three panes of glass, thrown stones into the pump, destroyed a brass top and frequently fought with his companions. The guardians of the workhouse found this justification entirely convincing and on Wilson's retirement recorded that they were "highly satisfied with the very efficient manner" in which he had discharged his duties.[1]

Harold Wilson's grandfather, James, was born in 1843. He was apprenticed to a draper in York and while still thus engaged married a Miss Thewlis from Huddersfield. In so doing he moved perceptibly into a higher class; his brother-in-law, Alderman Herbert Thewlis, had an umbrella factory in Stockport – "the best place in the world for such an enterprise", as Harold Wilson remarked[1] – and flourished to the point of becoming Lord Mayor of Manchester. No doubt encouraged by this connection James crossed the Pennines to Manchester, thus introducing a Lancastrian element into what had hitherto been a solidly Yorkshire background. He was modestly successful and became a pillar of the Congregationalist chapel and vice-president of a brotherhood hopefully called the PSA – Pleasant Sunday Afternoon.[2]

James had six children: Jack, the eldest son, was the first Wilson to play any notable part in politics, acting as Keir Hardie's election agent when the first Labour member lost his seat in 1895 and regained it in 1900. H. A. L. Fisher, as President of the Board of Education, appointed him HM Inspector of Technical Colleges. Jack's younger brother, Herbert, Harold Wilson's father, was born in 1882. He excelled in chemistry but did not do well enough in other subjects to win a scholarship to university. The best he could hope for was to become an Associate of the Institute of Chemistry. This he duly achieved, but he never lost the belief that he had been robbed of a golden opportunity and he resolved that his children should not be similarly deprived.[3]

Herbert was a kind and generous man, volatile, impetuous, with a strong awareness of his responsibilities as a member of society and of the Congregationalist church. His somewhat forbidding rectitude was relieved by a vigorous enjoyment of life: time was not to be wasted, duty must always come first, but there was no reason why one should not have a lot of fun along the way. One characteristic in particular he passed on to his son. An essay by a fifteen-year-old schoolgirl on "The Most Remarkable Person I Have Ever Met" took Herbert Wilson as its subject and referred to his "wonderful memory, for he remembers in detail things which occurred many years ago".[4] He shared his elder brother's enthusiasm for politics, distributed handbills for the Liberals when he was only ten years old, canvassed for Winston Churchill as Liberal candidate for North-West Manchester in 1908 when there was no Labour candidate standing, and switched allegiance to the Labour Party as soon as the possibility existed.

Herbert chose a wife who was as committed a radical and a

Congregationalist as he was himself. Ethel Seddon, though notably tranquil and good-tempered, was a powerful personality who expected great things from her children. She was a founder and organiser of the Women's Guild, a Girl Guide captain, a Sunday School teacher, but this daunting probity was mitigated by an infectious giggle and as strong a capacity as her husband's for getting fun out of life. She came from much the same background as Herbert but basked in the reflected glory of an elder brother who had emigrated to Australia, conspicuously made good, and drawn other members of the family – including eventually Ethel's father – in his wake.

Herbert and Ethel married in 1906, their daughter Marjorie was born three years later, and in 1912 the family moved to Milnsbridge, a town in the Colne valley a mile or so from Huddersfield. There Herbert worked for Leitch and Co and subsequently for the dye-stuff company of L. B. Holliday and Co – a firm in which, Harold Wilson later wrote bitterly, he was expected to sack a quarter of the employees every month so as to keep the others on their toes. He was earning about £350 a year, an income which enabled him to maintain his family in the modest comfort to which he aspired.

The Wilsons, in short, were low church, low-living, lower middle class and proud of it. In a *Sunday Times* profile of Harold Wilson, Godfrey Smith described the family as being "middle class" and living in "a pleasant, wide avenue two miles from the centre of town".[1] "It is not," Wilson wrote indignantly against the words "middle class", and "nonsense" against the description of the avenue.[2] He no doubt felt it advantageous to stress the lowliness of his origins, but his identification with the respectable and industrious poor was more emotional and deep-seated than mere political expediency could explain. It contained an element of self-deception. His world was far removed from the public-school privilege enjoyed by some of his future colleagues, such as Gaitskell or Crossman, yet almost as remote from the grinding proletarian poverty endured by Ernest Bevin. Short of money without being penurious, socially conscious, reverent of learning, addicted to hard work, Harold Wilson's family provided a background which offered no easy road to glory but from which any boy of talent and application would have the opportunity to make his way in life.

Harold Wilson was born at 10.30 a.m. on Saturday, 16 March 1916.

He was christened James Harold, "Harold" after a maternal uncle, an electrician. The "James" seems rarely to have been used. He always wanted to be called Frank, his sister remembered: "Perhaps it's just as well he wasn't. After all, he wasn't always very frank."[1] As a Congregationalist Harold had no godparents, but his father's sister stood as sponsor. The ceremony was performed by the Reverend Robert Sutton who had presided at the wedding of Harold's maternal grandparents as well as at his parents' and at the christening of his mother and his sister Marjorie.[2] Shortly after Harold's birth the family moved into a new house, 40 Western Road, which provided a bigger garden and a large attic which was made over to the children. Harold's earliest clear recollection was of the peace celebrations at Huddersfield in June 1919 when he was taken to hear the bands parading through the streets. But even before this he remembers his mother answering difficult questions with a phrase which clearly had its genesis in wartime. Harold would look up at the crescent moon and ask: "When will the moon be mended?" "When the war's over," his mother would reply. "But perhaps the phrase was being used after the war, just out of habit," Wilson told Martin Gilbert, anxious not to seem improbably precocious.[3]

He grew up in the shadow of his sister. Marjorie was as powerful a personality as her mother but considerably bossier. She treated Harold as a cherished possession; to be looked after, cosseted, but subjected to rigid discipline. Occasionally her brother would revolt, as when she was being particularly exigent over packing for a holiday and he went on strike and refused to put in anything at all, but usually he was happy to accept her bidding. He was, indeed, somewhat frightened of her; fifty years later he still remembered how she had made him go into the sea at Scarborough wearing a sailor suit, with the result that he was drenched by an unexpectedly large wave and had to be taken back to the boarding house to dry out.[4] He never wholly rid himself of a slight awe of her; it was said that one could always tell by the Prime Minister's attitude whether or not his sister was in town. She was not the only dominant and powerful woman to play a significant role in Wilson's life.

Every summer the family would pile on to a motor-cycle – Marjorie on the pillion, Ethel Wilson and Harold in the sidecar – to spend a holiday at Old Byland, a Yorkshire village a mile or so from Rievaulx where their relations still lived. It was there that Harold Wilson heard of the formal signing of peace in the summer of 1919. His tastes as a child seem to have been similar to, if perhaps a little more utilitarian than, those of others of his age. "I hope you will come to our house this year," he wrote to Father Christmas in 1922, "and please will you bring me a tool-box, a pair of compasses, a divider, Tiger Tim's annual, a joiner pencil and the Playboy Annual if you can. With heaps of love and kisses from Harold Wilson."[1]

When aged four and a half he began to attend the New Street Council School in Milnsbridge. At first he hated it. His teacher was a Miss Oddy, who was "either incompetent or a sadist, probably both", Wilson recollected.[2] She seems to have tormented him but he bore it stoically, saying not a word to his parents to indicate his unhappiness. They for their part were well aware what was going on but felt it best to leave it to their son to sort out for himself. He survived, escaped Miss Oddy's clutches and, in due course, throve. The competition does not seem to have been particularly imposing, but he excelled academically and was usually at or near the top of his class. Though he was not considered by his teachers to be especially brilliant or original he impressed them by his tenacity, his eagerness to learn and the first indications of his prodigious memory. Wilson himself regretted that he could never remember a face or memorise poetry or the features of a map, but his appetite for facts or figures and his power to retain them was extraordinary. Even at the age of six or seven he could, without apparent effort, reproduce whole pages of a textbook or complicated lists of figures. A good memory alone is not enough to achieve academic distinction but it is a useful tool and at a primary school is enough to guarantee success.

As important to Wilson as his life in class was his membership first of the Cubs, then of the Boy Scouts. His father was a Rover Leader, his mother a Guide captain, Marjorie an enthusiastic Guide; it was hardly surprising that Harold when a child should long to become part of this enchanted fellowship. He joined the Cubs at the first possible moment and was in no way disappointed by what he found. His strongly romantic instincts relished the rituals, the oaths, the ceremonies around the fire; his urge to be practical and perpetually busy was indulged by the tying of knots, the building of camps, the preparation of maps and all the other arcane lore with which the good Cub is required to acquaint himself.

His ardour was redoubled when he became a Scout. His Group Scout master was the Reverend W. H. "Pa" Potter, who ran his troop as an extension of the Baptist church over which he presided. All

Scouts were required to attend Sunday School, every meeting ended with a prayer. Scouting and religion fused in Harold's mind, scouting taking on a semi-mystical significance, religion being a matter of practical good deeds, the theological equivalent of knots and fire-making. "I don't care how high tha climbs, Harold, tha'll always be one of my Cubs," his Cub master is alleged to have said.[1] The remark sounds improbably picturesque but there turned out to be considerable truth in it. One side of Harold Wilson was a perpetual Boy Scout. At twelve he won a *Yorkshire Post* competition in which he had to say, in less than a hundred words, who was his greatest hero. He selected Baden-Powell. Fifty years later he might well have made a similar choice.

To Wilson's more sophisticated colleagues this was to seem either intolerably naïve or consummately hypocritical – no doubt both. "No man can be the kind of boy scout Harold is and read aloud Kipling's *If* as often as he reads it to me without a great deal of self-deception in his make-up," mused Crossman. "It's because he is unreflective and unphilosophical ..."[2] Certainly he was neither reflective nor philosophical, but when he declaimed *If* or extolled the values of the Scouts, he was speaking from the heart. Those were the standards by which he felt he and everybody else must ultimately be judged; whether he lived up to them is another matter. He told Kenneth Harris that the Fourth Scout Law – "A scout is a friend to all and a brother to every other scout" – had been one of the guiding principles of his life.[3] As leader of the opposition he spoke at the Scout Commissioner's dinner in London. "In a world where there is a growing emphasis on materialism," he said, "there is a danger of a loss of individual, and above all of moral purpose, especially among young people. And that is why the values taught by the Scout Movement are not only as relevant but are even more relevant today ... I think it is important that the Scout Movement gives them some basic elemental truths which, once absorbed, are never forgotten throughout their whole lifetime."[4]

After these glories, the conventional religion of the Congregational chapel, though very much part of his life, must have seemed a little tame. The two sermons which he most vividly remembered and which he claimed provided the basis for his religious views were both preached by Rover Scouts. The texts were: "He hath made of one blood all nations of man for to dwell on the face of the earth," and "I am come that they might have life, and that they might have it more abundantly." His religion was more that of the social worker than the mystic; in his early twenties he took part in a debate in the correspondence columns of the *Christian World*, arguing vigorously that the Church was insufficiently preoccupied with evils such as poverty and unemployment.[1]

All this must make him sound solemn or even priggish; in fact, though his less motivated contemporaries may have found him something of a sobersides, he shared the interests and enthusiasms of the ordinary small boy. He played games with energy and enthusiasm if not much skill, he was a reliable team member rather than a star. His strengths were determination and stamina, not dexterity; confronted long afterwards with a photograph of his class in the gym he remarked with a shudder that the setting revived many unhappy memories.[2] He was more in his element as a fan than a participant. These were the great days of Huddersfield football and Harold went to almost every home match with his father; when his team won the League for three years running and the Cup Final in two of those years, "we felt," he wrote, "we were the Lords of Creation."[3] At home the Wilsons were not great games players; they might indulge in a little whist or knockabout bridge but were more likely to talk and argue, the men being notably more vociferous than the women. Their greatest collective enthusiasm was for Gilbert and Sullivan – "G and S" they referred to it, as if an unholy compound of gin and soda. The church choir gave a performance every year: Harold was in the chorus, Marjorie sold programmes, Herbert handled the cash. By the age of six, Harold Wilson subsequently claimed, he was word-perfect in *The Pirates of Penzance*, and he could say as much sixty years later.[4] Another passion was for toy trains and Meccano; he was an ardent reader of the *Meccano Magazine* and a founder member of the Meccano club at the New Street Primary School. He once set out to make a model of the Sydney harbour bridge but ran out of material and had to settle for the Forth bridge instead. Not surprisingly, the first book he could remember reading was *Engineering for Boys*.[5] Pets were another enthusiasm that endured all his life. His first was a guinea-pig called Gerry which died while his master was in hospital recovering from appendicitis. His parents procured another one, as similar as possible, but Harold quickly saw through the deception and was briefly but noisily inconsolable.

The extraction of his appendix, which happened when he was seven, was significant because during his recovery he devoured the historical sections of Arthur Mee's *Children's Encyclopaedia* and acquired a taste for history that he never lost. Political history particularly appealed to him; not surprisingly, since politics were the subject of endless debate at home. Though Keir Hardie had to some extent replaced him, Gladstone was the traditional family hero: a reproduction of Millais's full-length portrait hung in Harold's bedroom and a prized possession was a Gladstone tablecloth embroidered in black to commemorate the great man's funeral.[1] He was infected by his parents' ardour. They visited him in hospital on the day of the 1923 general election. The invalid insisted that they should leave early so as to be in time to vote for the Labour candidate, Philip Snowden. Snowden won, but no thanks to the Wilsons, who got lost in the fog on the return journey and arrived after the closing of the poll. For months they did not dare admit to their partisan son that they had thus let down his champion.[2]

But though Harold's childish enthusiasm for the Labour Party was genuine, it was no more significant than his support for the Huddersfield football team – in fact, if the choice had been between Labour in office or Huddersfield for the Cup, he would probably have plumped for the latter. It was on a visit to London shortly after his operation that a photograph was taken of Harold on the steps of Number 10 Downing Street. This happy snap has entered Wilson's iconography and is regularly cited as evidence that he dreamed of becoming Prime Minister from his early childhood. It would be as sensible to assume that every Japanese tourist photographed in front of St Peter's harbours a secret ambition to become Pope. Harold first wished to be an undertaker, then poet laureate, then – during the Meccano phase – a civil engineer. By the time he was approaching the point where a decision on the subject was required he had relapsed into the state of bemused uncertainty which is the lot of the majority of teenagers. He was in some ways precocious, certainly, but, though public affairs were very much part of his family background, any suggestion that he felt himself dedicated to a career in politics while still a boy is far from the mark.

Two years later Harold widened his horizons drastically when he accompanied his mother on a six-month trip to Australia. Ethel Wilson wanted to see her father once more before he died; Marjorie said she was perfectly ready to look after her father during Mrs Wilson's absence but baulked at accepting responsibility for a ten-year-old brother as well; Harold went along as much to resolve this difficulty as to further his education. Godfrey Smith, in the *Sunday Times* profile mentioned earlier, remarked that Herbert Wilson was "a shrewd man who had obviously managed to save", witness the fact that he could afford to send his wife and son to Australia on a holiday. "Ridiculous," wrote Wilson in the margin,[1] but unless the Seddons in Australia had contributed it is hard to see where else the money came from. The Seddons could probably have afforded to; Ethel's brother Harold was about to take his seat as a member of the Legislative Council in Western Australia and finally, as Sir Harold, was to become President of the Council.

Harold derived enormous pleasure from his visit to Australia and used subsequently to maintain that it had laid the foundations for his future enthusiasm for the Commonwealth. He set up as an expert on his return, lectured his schoolfellows with alarming self-confidence and at great length, and wrote a series of articles on the subject. His early journalistic efforts met with only limited success. His description of a visit to a gold mine was turned down by the *Scout* on the grounds that it was not of sufficient interest to its readers, and by *Meccano Magazine* because it had recently published two pieces on a rather similar subject. The editor of the latter, however, commented: "For a boy of your age the article is remarkably well written and I am sure that with a suitable subject you can write an article of the required standard." Encouraged, Harold persisted. His article on Mundaring Weir, near Kalgoorlie, was rejected as being unsuitable and needing good illustrations, while his account of Rievaulx Abbey was "not quite on the right lines for the *Meccano Magazine*" (it is hard to imagine what the right lines would have been for such a journal). The only consolation he gained came in January 1929 when the editor of the *Scout* wrote to tell him: "I should like to use your little hint for strengthening a signalling flag in my column, 'Things We Should Know', and I am sending you the enclosed pencil-case as a small reward."[2]

In 1927, along with four other boys from his class, Wilson won a County Minor Scholarship to Royds Hall Grammar School in Huddersfield. The item which clinched the award was an essay on a drunken farmer, touchingly describing the price which his family paid for his delinquency,[3] a theme of which his personal experience must have been limited. Royds Hall was an excellent school, opened only six years before, with unusually good facilities for sport and a reputation for encouraging its pupils to act, sing and play music. Of this last opportunity Wilson did not avail himself but, resplendent in brown blazer with pale blue piping, he flung himself into almost every other activity. His headmaster, E. F. Chancy, wrote much later that he had liked "the bright-eyed way he looked me straight in the face". Wilson, Chancy remembered, showed no signs of academic brilliance and his record was "no better than that of the average intelligent lad", but, "He was alert. He was cheerful. He had an enquiring mind. He was determined to make a success of anything he tackled; and, above all, he was popular with his colleagues."[1]

History was now his strongest subject. He was on the committee of the school Historical Society and lectured on such themes as "The Ark to *Aquitania*" (resourcefully borrowing slides from the Cunard Company) and "The Romance of Modern Transport". Told to write an essay on the position he would like to achieve in twenty-five years, he chose Chancellor of the Exchequer and gave the details of his first budget. An element was a tax on gramophones, as being a luxury enjoyed only by the idle rich. One teacher, more rosy in his recollections than the headmaster, remembered him as being "in all academic subjects ... brilliant. He excelled at French, Latin, Greek and displayed more than a passing interest in Esperanto."[2] He found the school paper, the *Roydsian*, more amenable than the *Meccano Magazine*, and wrote for it frequently. His "Diary of a Choir Boy" is typical of the rather lumbering humour which marked the majority of his contributions: "For the first time in history the Choir turns up in full force, to do justice to the *free* train trip and tea, on the occasion of the annual choir picnic to Hope Bank Pleasure Grounds, Henley. Unaccountable loss of water from the 'lake' during afternoon – for solution ask the winners of the splashing bout. Choir attempts descant while singing grace and fails miserably. The tea, together with the roundabouts and swings, create disturbance in the interior of choir boy."[3]

He proved more distinguished as a debater. His first effort, according to the *Roydsian*, was marked by a "brilliant opening sentence", which proved to be the closing sentence as well since the speaker abruptly sat down as soon as it had been delivered. Excessive brevity, however, was not for long to be a feature of Wilson's oratory. Usually the problem was to stop him talking. One of his more successful performances came in a debate on the duty of the citizen to fight for his country in time of war. Wilson spoke up for pacifism and carried the day. Probably he believed in what he was saying at the time, but he could almost as convincingly have argued the other way. Certainly his speech had as little relevance to his attitude when war actually came as the vote by Oxford undergraduates that they would not fight for king and country.

In his fourth year at Royds Hall his education was cruelly interrupted. He caught typhoid from milk which he drank while on Scout camp. There were thirteen boys in the group; one Wilson saved by accidentally knocking over his glass; the others all caught the fever, six of them died. Wilson was very seriously ill, seemed to be recovering, then suffered a relapse and was almost despaired of. When he finally emerged from hospital he was emaciated, his weight at one point down to a mere four and a half stone. His family never forgot the horror. In December 1963 Herbert Wilson wrote to George Brown to condole with him on being in hospital: "Family separations I always think are much worse at Christmas. My wife, daughter and I experienced that at Christmas 1930 when Harold was in hospital recovering from Typhoid Fever and did not come home till early in January."[1]

The home to which he did finally return was in disarray. While he had been in hospital the economic depression had got out of control and Herbert Wilson had lost his job. It was to be sixteen months before he found new employment, sixteen months of demoralising idleness for him and privation for his family. Mrs Wilson managed well with what little there was but their standard of living declined drastically; Harold remembered his chagrin when he was denied 3s 6d (17.5p) to buy a sheath-knife. He bitterly resented what he felt to be the injustice of his father's plight and the irrationality of a system which could waste the talents of a man of such ability and probity. At one point it seemed as if the family's position was so dire that Harold would have to leave school at the age of sixteen and find a job that would contribute to their income. Plans were made for him to join his uncle, James Thewlis, now in charge of the umbrella factory in Manchester, but fortunately Herbert Wilson was back at work in time to make this sacrifice unnecessary.[2]

Another problem was that his long illness had left Harold academically behind at least the brighter of his contemporaries. That he quickly made up the lost ground was largely thanks to one dedicated teacher, F. S. Wilmut, who coached him in mathematics after the school closed every day. Wilmut was not only an inspiring teacher but an ardent socialist who had suffered for his convictions and at one time been dismissed from his job for his support of a teachers' strike. Wilson liked, admired and was grateful to him: "The idea that I had forgotten you or your connection with the movement is most fantastic," he replied many years later when Wilmut wrote to congratulate him on his election to the House of Commons.[1]

Herbert Wilson's new job was in Cheshire and the family moved house to the Wirral in November 1932. It was clear that Harold, now sixteen, would need a new school, and a good one if, in spite of the vicissitudes of his education, he was to win the sort of award to a university which would make it economically possible for his family to maintain him there. The Wirral Grammar School at Bebington had opened only a year before and Jack Wilson urged his brother to send Harold to it on the grounds that they had their name to make and would therefore take special trouble over someone who might prove a star pupil.[2] Wilson was not merely a star, in the sixth form he was the only pupil and the deputy headmaster, P. L. Norrish, was to all intents his private tutor. Norrish later said that Wilson was a "whale for work" and "kept *him* up to scratch".[3] The Scout master recorded with amazement that this prodigious youth could recite the names and dates of all the British Prime Ministers; the history master was evidently less impressed by this feat since he doubted whether Wilson stood much chance of getting an Oxford scholarship.

The lack of other sixth-formers meant that there could be no team games for Wilson at the Wirral Grammar School and debates, theatricals and other such distractions were also a rarity. He took up rugby union with a neighbourhood club and played, he remembered with satisfaction, a thoroughly dirty game. With greater distinction he also went in for running, winning the junior three-mile cross-country championship of the Wirral Athletics Club and captaining the team in the Merseyside championships. Not surprisingly, given his solitary eminence, he became captain of the school, thoroughly enjoyed the exercise of authority, and organised lunchtime soccer matches so as to counter certain unspecified "unwholesome tendencies" which he thought he had detected among the fifth-formers.[4] Thirty-five years later he must have wished he could ordain some similar therapy when he detected still more unwholesome tendencies in the Parliamentary Labour Party.

The Wirral also witnessed Harold Wilson's maiden public speech when, as captain of the school, it fell to him to propose a vote of thanks to the distinguished chemist and future chairman of the British Overseas Airways Corporation, Sir Harold Hartley.[1] The event passed off unsensationally, but among the audience was the father of the philosophy tutor at Jesus, Oxford. The link seems tenuous, but Wilson himself believed that it was instrumental in securing him an award at that college. Whether it was or not, in 1934 he was accorded an Open Exhibition in Modern History. The award was worth only £60 a year, but after a certain amount of pressure from his headmaster the county Director of Education agreed to make a special grant which would fill almost all the gap between the income from the Exhibition and Wilson's minimum needs. The news of this success, says his sister Marjorie, for the first time brought home to his family the fact that Harold Wilson was anything out of the ordinary.[2] Previously they had thought him bright and assiduous enough, but no more than that; now they came to the conclusion that they had fostered a boy of limitless potential. In what way Harold would succeed they had no idea, but that he would succeed, and would succeed dramatically, they henceforth believed to be inevitable.

II

Oxford

1934–1939

Harold Wilson's Oxford was as remote from that of Evelyn Waugh's Lord Sebastian Flyte as can well be imagined; indeed, even the austere existence of a Paul Pennyfeather seemed extravagant in comparison. The most obvious reason was that he was extremely short of money. His parents were having to subsidise him to an extent which he knew they found difficult and he was determined to put them under no greater pressure than was essential. The easy course would have been to run up bills with the Oxford tradesmen, who were used to waiting for their money for inordinate lengths of time, but Wilson abhorred debt and would not have contemplated spending money unless he knew he could afford it.

His letters home show how anxious he was to scrimp and save. He sent the bulk of his washing to his mother to deal with: "I'm trying the laundry for shirts and pyjamas: I'll let you know how much they cost, then we can see what to do." She used to send him meat too, which was cheaper than the beef in college, and he pleaded for "any spare butter-currant biscuits you have -- you know the kind I mean". He managed to buy a cap and gown for 3s (15p) from one of the college servants and announced proudly at the end of the first fortnight: "So far, I've kept minute accounts of expenditure and am correct even to the nearest ½d ... The book says battels should be kept below £2.5.0 (£2.25) by avoiding extravagance, but I expect we shall be a long way below that – probably under £2 – because the £2.5.0 appears to include cigs and beer as well as college lunch and breakfast." A few weeks later he was able to announce in triumph that he had kept his battels down to a mere £1.5.0½ (£1.25): "You see, absence of beer and cigs and entertaining and afternoon tea and toast takes a lot off battel bills."[1]

Even if he had enjoyed a lavish allowance it is unlikely that his way of life would have been very different. He did not think smoking and drinking wicked, but he felt them weaknesses to which he had no wish to succumb. Even the modest revelries of the Jesus Junior Common Room seemed to him a pointless distraction from the important things of life; the high living to be found in some of the smarter colleges was so alien as to be incomprehensible. He viewed the fellows gossiping over their port with the same puzzled suspicion as forty years later he would observe Roy Jenkins indulging his taste for good claret and gracious dinner parties; these were serious people, how could they waste their time and befuddle their minds in such frivolous pursuits? "If I had a choice between smoked salmon and tinned salmon, I'd have it tinned. With vinegar," he once declared. The boast, if boast it was, was true when he made it in Downing Street; it was still more the case at Oxford in 1934.

He was fortunate to belong to a college which had no pretensions to elegance, and to share his room with a kindred spirit. A. H. J. Thomas was the son of a Welsh plumber from Tenby: "an exceptionally nice fellow, and we get on well. We seem to have similar tastes – both keen on running, neither on smoking or drinking, and have similar views on food, etc."[1] Thomas was as impecunious and as keen to economise as Wilson. Once when the two friends were together at a lecture, Thomas fainted. Wilson relished the opportunity to exhibit his Boy Scout skills. "I immediately rendered first aid while everybody else was clucking and fussing about," he wrote proudly. "I jolly well took charge of the affair; no one else knew any first aid ... lucky I took that Ambulance Course last year, or I wouldn't have known the difference between a 'white' faint and a 'red' one."[2]

Wilson and Thomas presented a united front against the blandishments of those who sought to involve them in the innumerable time-consuming pursuits that seduce the freshman undergraduate. They refused to join the Officers' Training Corps or the College Dramatic Club. Wilson was flattered by an offer to enrol him in the Oxford University Dramatic Society – the membership of which was limited to 200 – but this too he rejected. "Rugger, hockey, boat club were also unlucky with us, altho' if there is time *next* year we might learn rowing." Almost the only sport in which he indulged with any regularity was running. He ran for the University Second Team against Reading Athletics Club and finished seventh out of sixteen, the third Oxford man to finish, and won his heat of the freshmen's quarter mile. Momentarily he was dazzled by the suggestion that he was likely to gain a half-blue – "very good news", he told his family – but even if he had been ready to sacrifice the time he lacked the necessary ability. Many years later he told the Tory MP and distinguished athlete Lord John Hope that they had run together at Oxford. "I don't think I remember," replied Hope unkindly. "You must have been behind me." "*Touché*," said Wilson ruefully.[1] His career as an athlete died away except for occasional fitful appearances with the college football team: "My methods are very unorthodox, and not exactly soccer. Just dashing in from the wing at top speed and trying to beat the back."[2]

His life was not as austerely rigorous as this litany might suggest. He told his family that he had been to see the D'Oyly Carte company in the *Yeomen of the Guard* and *The Pirates of Penzance*: "by queueing could get in for 6d." He squandered twice as much on a gramophone record of Gracie Fields singing Toselli's "Serenade" and "Laugh, Clown, Laugh".[3] But though Wilson had a fair number of friends, some of whom he grew to know well, he chose on the whole to lead a solitary life. "I am not wasting time going to see people and messing about in their rooms," he recorded.[4] All his life he was to deplore disorder of any kind, and "messing about" was the sort of ill-organised and unproductive activity which most offended him. Sometimes friends would invade his rooms whether he welcomed it or not. David Lloyd Jones, also at Jesus, one day brought A. H. Atkins to tea so that he could show off this ornament to the college – "He's a remarkable man here – what a brain!" Atkins was impressed by Wilson's energy and the immense speed of his mind: "What most stood out were the powerful clarity and economy of his thinking." He seemed not to be lonely or hostile to the society around him but had no apparent need of company; he was "self-contained, detached and perfectly balanced ... immensely content with his own life ... and showed no envy of anyone else".[5]

Sharing a room with Thomas had one disadvantage: "I hope I don't," he told his family, "but now and again I catch myself speaking with a slightly Welsh intonation."[6] It has been suggested that one of the reasons he scarcely ever spoke in the Oxford Union was that he feared he would be mocked for his north-country accent.[7] This seems unlikely; he never made any attempt to conceal his background and indeed frequently showed himself proud of his Yorkshire origins long before he realised that they could be a useful electoral asset. It is more probable that he was deterred by the time and expense that would have been involved in playing an active role in the Union, and also by a suspicion that that institution was dominated by a group of upper-class sophisticates with whom he would have been ill at ease. He felt more at home in the newly founded Jesus Debating Society, named the Sankey Society after the Liberal politician and old Jesus man, Lord Sankey. He made his first speech in a debate on war and "soon made my presence felt. I tried to counteract the Labour element with the Christian line of argument, so to speak, advocated closer cooperation with the Churches, etc."[1] In 1970 a fellow member of the Sankey Society, G. V. Harries, wrote to congratulate him on his intervention in a private members' debate on hare coursing. Wilson reminded Harries that he had been the first secretary of the Sankey Society and that he had said very much the same things then. He rarely spoke on a private members' bill, he added, "but sometimes my natural instincts get on top of me. The question of blood sports gave me the chance to let fly."[2]

At first it seemed as if the Oxford Group might also seduce him from the strict path of academic duty. A second-year undergraduate called Vickery took him up and invited him to several meals so as to explain what the group was trying to achieve. Wilson had already experimented with the Student Christian Union and found it "shallow and, more important, definitely run by the Anglican element, and worse than that, by the Anglo-Catholics at Pusey House".[3] The Oxford Group, with its evangelistic insistence on personal reconstruction through honesty, purity, love and unselfishness, was at first more appealing. Wilson attended several meetings – "it's the only thing I've seen more than skin deep [sic]"[4] – but his enthusiasm seems soon to have faded. He never wholly lost interest in Moral Rearmament, but it does not seem that it played any large part in his thinking after his first few months at Oxford.

Nor were politics allowed to distract him seriously from his studies, except in so far as the two coincided. Bernard Miles wrote to him in 1987 to record that his old tutor, "Ronnie McCallum, told me that when you came down from Oxford you knew more about *Elections* and how they work than anybody else in Europe".[5] It seems unlikely that Wilson in 1937 conceived that such esoteric lore might one day prove of practical importance. As an undergraduate he at first was not committed to any party, though he knew, at least, that he had no sympathy with the Conservatives. His instinct was to follow the family bent and join the Labour Club: "the sub's 2/6d [12½p]. I shan't go to many meetings, just to those addressed by G. D. H. Cole and Stafford Cripps."[1] He quickly decided, however, that the membership was "very petty; squabbling about tiffs with other sections of the Labour party instead of getting down to something concrete".[2] It was a complaint that he might have reiterated at almost any point of his career, nor did he ever see much reason to revise his judgment that many of the most vociferous and influential members of the Labour Party were simultaneously too middle class in origin and too Marxist in conviction to suit his taste. Wilson at that time had no particular objection to Marxism but he distrusted any sort of rigid economic or social theory, remarking with some pride that he had never managed to get beyond "that whacking great footnote on the second page of *Das Kapital*".[3] What was important was not to devise some blueprint for grand policy over the next twenty years but to solve the immediately pressing problems. He was flattered when invited to become college secretary of the Labour Club and reckoned it might provide a useful chance to get to know G. D. H. Cole but in the end he decided against it; the reasons being, he told his family: "(a) Lloyd George; (b) the Labour party; (c) am much more interested in foreign affairs than Labour politics."[4]

By this time he was anyway becoming involved with the University Liberal Club. "The mean, sentimental, elitist Liberalism fostered by the PPE school exactly fitted Wilson's political attitudes," wrote Paul Foot in his highly intelligent, entertaining and frequently perverse study of Harold Wilson.[5] Without endorsing Foot's choice of adjectives, it is certainly true that the mild and pragmatic radicalism to be found among the Liberals at that time suited Wilson better than the doctrinaire orthodoxy of the left-wing Labour Club. Wilson in his memoirs recorded that he had joined the Liberals in the hope that he would convert them to "a middle-of-the-road Colne Valley* standpoint".[6] He does not seem to have made any strenuous efforts to achieve this end. Frank Byers, who was one day to become chairman of the national Liberal Party and was a contemporary of Wilson's, could not remember "his taking any strong political line at any time and certainly I had no indication that he was likely to join Labour".[7] Wilson became a member of the Liberal Club in October 1934, was college secretary and finally became a most competent treasurer: "I went to the Liberal Club dinner: it was really fine – Herbert Samuel,"

* A traditional Lib–Lab stronghold.

he told his family in March 1935. "I'm getting a few new members."[1] But he never allowed such activities to absorb a significant amount of his time and energies. Far from indicating a resolve to make his way in national politics, his support of what, in the mid 1930s, was clearly a failing if not lost cause, shows just how low he rated his political future in his scale of values.

He was far from partisan in his political opinions. In the election in November 1935 the result that pleased him most was the success of the strikingly independent-minded A. P. Herbert.[2] One of the few books that survives from his Oxford library is John Morley's *On Compromise* in the "Thinkers' Library". In it Wilson sidelined the passage in which Morley argued that compromise, though not always desirable, was to be commended if it involved "a rational acquiescence in the fact that the bulk of your contemporaries are not yet prepared either to embrace the new idea, or to change their ways of living in conformity to it". It was a thesis which he would have defended throughout his life.

His statement that he was more interested in foreign affairs than Labour politics was unsurprising at a time when Europe was careering towards war. Wilson was alarmed by Germany's growing assertiveness and revolted by its persecution of the Jews. He was particularly impressed by a lecture by Mendelssohn-Bartholdy: "V. good. I think he's a non-Aryan refugee ... he is certainly a German and, I expect, a Jew if it's possible nowadays for anyone to be both." He was attending a series of lectures on Germany between 1918 and 1935 by a young New College don called Richard Crossman which "seem good. I've only been to the first one."[3] But he was reluctant to accept that any happening on the continent, be it never so outrageous, should be allowed to drag Britain into war. He laid out 1s a year (5p) as his subscription to the No-More-War League and, though not a committed pacifist, came closer than at any other point in his life to rejecting violence as a means of solving problems. "What of the international situation?" he asked in March 1936. "It all depends on France, doesn't it? Mad if they try to use sanctions v. Germany. Why don't they recognise her and get her back into the League?"[4]

But nothing – not religion, politics, war – was allowed to stand between Wilson and his prime objective at Oxford: to cover himself with academic glory. He arrived in October 1934 as one of many bright but unproven freshmen who had shown no striking sign of incipient greatness; by the time he had taken his Finals in the summer of 1937 he was accepted as one of the finest scholars of his generation. This he achieved partly by sheer, grinding assiduity. He was uncertain how successful he would be in Moderations – the examinations which an undergraduate sits after his first year – but told his family, "If I don't [pass] it won't be shortage of work that lets me down. I've done $7\frac{1}{2}$ to 9 hours a day several days this week and 6 yesterday. But the French and Latin seem such a waste of time. I'll be glad when I've finished with them and can settle down to History or something worthwhile."[1] These hours were those which he worked alone in his room or the libraries and did not include the lectures and tutorials. A few months later the pace was still harder: "I worked very hard last week; touched ten and a half hours one day and eight on several days. Total: forty-six hours for the week," and plaintively a few weeks later, "I *still* don't like the idea of working Saturdays."[2]

But all work and no play did not make Harold a dull boy. More and more he was picked out by his teachers as a future star. Typically he first impressed his tutor in constitutional history, J. G. Edwards, by a feat of memory. Edwards wanted to send a telegram to the Northern Matriculation Board but could not recall the address. "None of the tutors nor freshers knew, until I brightly remarked '315 Oxford Road, Manchester', which sent J. G. E. into rhapsodies of joy, appreciation and thanks."[3] Not all the dons were so quickly convinced of his ability. It was 1936 before Professor Fraser told the Principal of Jesus that Wilson was "a born economist ... He said my essays were not only of first-class quality, but a very high first!"[4] The applause of his tutors speaks well for their tolerance as well as their perceptiveness. Wilson must often have been an irritating pupil. With Professor Knox he argued about Locke: "Knox began defending him, and we worked through chemistry to geometry and back to philosophy, and in the end he said there was a lot in my criticism. He thinks I have 'a penetrative mind'." G. D. H. Cole equally found himself worsted – at least in Wilson's view. Wilson pointed out a fallacy in one of Cole's definitions, "and he admitted it too ... he said it was a good point. So that's one up. He's a very nice chap!"[5]

Wilson complicated his progress by deciding that he wanted to switch from History to the relatively new course of PPE – Philosophy, Politics and Economics. The Principal, presumably to deter him, said he would only agree if Wilson passed an examination in German at the end of the Christmas vacation. The language was virtually unknown to Wilson but he bought a Teach Yourself manual and settled down. Six weeks later he passed, though only just, and aided by the fact that he was set an unseen which he had prepared a few days before.[1]

His reputation began to spread. Christopher Mayhew proposed to enter for the George Webb Medley Junior Scholarship but was told he was wasting his time because an undergraduate from Jesus called Harold Wilson was already a candidate. "The name meant nothing to me, but Wilson duly won."[2] But the greatest challenge was the Gladstone Memorial Prize for an essay of between 12,000 and 18,000 words. Wilson chose as his subject "The State and the Railways in Great Britain 1823–63" and devoted a large part of two terms' work to its preparation. "I wish I had a chance – it *would* be worth winning," he told his family. He claimed to have read between 300 and 400 books on the subject and, while working at Gladstone's old home at Hawarden, had unearthed a draft bill for nationalising the railways prepared by Gladstone when he was President of the Board of Trade. "Surely the amount of reading should affect the quality of the material? Still, we never know. It's all luck. Anyhow, whatever the net result it's been worth it."[3]

Luck was with him. His paper began with a flourish – "Into the unsettled England of the eighteen-twenties the locomotive burst its way" – but thereafter lapsed into the sound but pedestrian. He ended with a plea for an integrated transport policy for road and rail – that holy grail for every minister concerned with transport which proved as elusive when he was in Downing Street as it had done for any of his predecessors. "Neither *laissez-faire* nor glib talk of nationalisation will solve the problem. Measures of control must be evolved which will secure for the public the maximum advantage from both modes of transport."[4] His lucidity, grasp of his subject and obvious hard work (there were more than 400 footnotes) impressed the examiners and he was adjudged the winner. One of those present at the Encaenia when he read a page from the winning entry was Anthony Eden, then a young Foreign Secretary awaiting the award of an honorary degree.

With such credentials it seemed a foregone conclusion that he would get a First in his Finals. The economist Redvers Opie taught both Wilson and Edward Heath at Oxford and left notes on his pupils. Heath was usually given a beta mark and criticised for trundling out run-of-the-mill views; Wilson, however, had exceptional intellectual ability and a remarkably comprehensive mind. Wilson did not disappoint his admirers. He was awarded seventeen alphas or alpha minuses and one beta ?plus plus plus. In economic theory he got an alpha plus – the first given since the PPE school had been established. It was, as he never ceased to assure anyone who would listen to him, the most distinguished First in PPE awarded that year, perhaps even that decade. It meant more to him than almost any other of his many achievements. Henceforth he could never quite treat as an equal any man or woman who had failed to secure First Class honours at Oxford or Cambridge. Whether or not his point of view was intellectually tenable, it was unlikely to lead to harmony in the Labour Cabinets in which he served.

One way of spending time and money which Wilson almost entirely eschewed was the pursuit of women. Austen Morgan, in a recent biography,[1] has discovered an early girlfriend, Doreen Richmond, whom Wilson courted when more important pursuits allowed the time and to whom he confided his current ambitions – he thought the foreign service might provide quite a good career, he remarked, after going with Doreen to see a film about the Congress of Berlin. He seems to have been obsessed with the belief that some of the other boys were trying to break up their relationship: "Above all don't believe anything they tell you," he wrote to Doreen in October 1933, "it will be as far off the truth as the tripe they tell me." It is disconcerting to find that the suspicion everyone was plotting to do him down – so marked a feature of his prime-ministerial career – was rampant at this early stage. Whether or not the conspirators contributed, Miss Richmond slipped out of his life not long afterwards. She was soon replaced. The new object of his affections so much monopolised him that he felt no urge to stray from the celibate path which was still easily followed in the largely monastic Oxford of the 1930s.

He was in love, and the object of his love was far from Oxford. While still at school and revising for his examinations he had one day gone with his father to a competition in mental arithmetic (where Herbert, incidentally, won a prize). On the way back he stopped for a few minutes to watch a game at the local tennis club. One of the players caught his eye. "It suddenly became blindingly clear to me that life was not designed for cramming the words of long dead poets, but that there was another world."[2] He established that the girl was called Gladys Mary Baldwin, at that time still known as Gladys but later to be called Mary and referred to as such hereafter. Promptly Wilson invested 15s (75p) in the purchase of a racket and £1 on becoming a member of the tennis club. Three weeks or so later, on 4 July 1934, he told Mary he was going to marry her, a statement which she received with some caution but without noticeable protest. He also told her that he was going to become Prime Minister. If she had believed him she would have said his two objectives were incompatible – no husband of hers was going to be a politician, still less Prime Minister. As it was, she very reasonably ignored the second of his predictions and concentrated on the first.

Mary Baldwin came from much the same background as Harold Wilson – her father was a Congregationalist minister at Penrith, held the same beliefs and worked by the same scale of values. Less dedicated to the crusade for personal success, she was no less exigent in the demands that she made on herself and the standards that she observed. But she was gentler and more approachable. Robert Lusty, the publisher, worked closely with her many years later and wrote: "I quickly found that Mary Wilson possessed all the virtues of charm, modesty, frankness and humour, guided by compassion and an acute awareness of life's realities. She was at once immensely kind and friendly and a human being to whom one instantly warmed."[1] But there was an unexpected quality about her. Within that Roundhead exterior, that stern recognition of an overriding duty, a Cavalier was longing to escape. In her private pantheon lurked Rupert of the Rhine, Bonnie Prince Charlie and other dashing but notably disreputable heroes. She had a soft spot for cads and a penchant for the romantic, a weakness that made her no less resolute a character but rendered her incomparably more endearing. Wilson showed striking good sense in so quickly deciding that he wanted to marry her.

Mary for her part responded to his determination, energy and obvious affection. He was far less demonstrative than was the case with her own, more extrovert relations, but she was shrewd enough to sense the profound feeling that lay below the cool exterior. She was not ready yet to commit herself to a formal engagement but neither she nor Wilson had much doubt that in the end they would marry. Nor could Wilson's parents have been in the dark: his letters home from Oxford were peppered with injunctions to keep in touch with her and make her feel part of the family. "Do you ever see G. M. B. now?" he asked. "How many walk her home from chapel?

Why not give her a lift home some night? It will help to preserve the link. I believe she was going to the dance at Highfield last Thursday. *Don't forget* about the lift home now and again; it's a good idea." A few months later her father was to preach in Chester: "Are you going to ask them along for an evening?" asked Wilson.[1] Mary preferred Shelley to Gilbert and Sullivan and had no time for politics or economics but in general they enjoyed doing the same sort of things. The theme tune of their courtship was "I'll See You Again", from Noël Coward's *Bitter Sweet*. Harold Wilson chose it, sung by Peggy Wood and George Metaxa, when he featured in 1977 in the BBC *Men of Action* programme; Mary repaid the compliment on *Desert Island Discs*.

At one time it seemed likely that they would marry soon after Wilson's triumphant success in Finals launched him on what seemed destined to be a successful career in academic life. To be married to a don struck Mary as ideal. "There's nothing I would have liked so much," she told Kenneth Harris, "... very old buildings and very young people. There is everything anyone could want, music, theatre, congenial friends, all in a beautiful setting, and within a four penny bus ride. It symbolised so much for me."[2] Delay was forced on them, however, when Herbert Wilson again lost his job while his son was taking his Finals. Wilson never doubted that he must be prepared to help out and repay some of the sacrifices his parents had made for him over the past years. Fortunately at this point he was awarded the George Webb Medley Senior Scholarship worth £300 a year for two years. It might have provided a starting point for married life; instead a large part of the income went to pay the rent on his parents' flat. Thoughts of marriage were regretfully postponed. It was the end of 1938 before Herbert Wilson found another job.

In other ways too Wilson was discovering that everything did not always run as smoothly as it had so far done in his academic life. Before he sat his Finals he applied for lectureships at St Andrews University in Scotland and at Christ Church College. His tutors furnished him with the most glowing references – "far and away the ablest man I have taught" as well as being "a very pleasant and entertaining person" – but the jobs went elsewhere.[3] The University of London advertised for a Fellow in Economics at £400 a year. Wilson contemplated putting in for it but was advised to wait for a year or two.[4] In the autumn of 1937 he and the future Professor Arthur Brown were rival candidates for a Fellowship of All Souls.

Brown won. Wilson tried again the following year, submitting a paper based on his Gladstone Prize essay, but was again unsuccessful.[1] It probably did him no harm to be reminded that he was not invincible; certainly these setbacks do not seem seriously to have dented his self-confidence. He made overtures to the *Manchester Guardian* and was offered a job writing leaders for a probationary period. He worked at it for a week and found the work uncongenial. Each day he was given an office to sit in and a subject to write about; when he had finished he handed in his copy, was gravely thanked, waited hopefully for some comment or any kind of human intercourse, found none, and went back to his hotel until the next day when the same procedure would unroll. He would have found life in a Trappist monastery more inspiring.[2] Fortunately, before he had to decide whether or not to resort to journalism, the Webb Medley Scholarship and the consequential opportunity to work with the social reformer and economist, William Beveridge, convinced him that for the immediate future at least he should stay at Oxford.

Beveridge was one of the most influential figures of his generation, an acolyte of the Webbs, who had graduated through the civil service and the directorship of the London School of Economics to University College, Oxford, of which he became Master in 1937. His intention was to devote himself to the study of unemployment and a statistical survey of the history of prices. Tactless, autocratic, with a streak of quixotic generosity, he infuriated most of his fellow dons but won the total loyalty of a small group of disciples and assistants. Prominent among these was Harold Wilson. Beveridge wrote to Raymond Fosdick, President of the Rockefeller Foundation, to report that he had got a first-rate new research student working under his supervision. His particular lines of enquiry were to be: "Why are there so many thousands of unemployed in all the prosperous parts of the country?" and, "How many 'unemployed jobs', i.e. unfilled vacancies, there are, and of what kind and why?"[3] To find the answers Wilson was required to visit employment exchanges all over the country and to study many thousands of job applications, convincing himself in the process, and in the end convincing Beveridge as well, that hardly any of these applications led to the offer of jobs and that there was an army of unemployed in search of work.[4] He would subsequently claim also to have opened Beveridge's eyes to the economic theories of Maynard Keynes as set out in the seminal *General Theory of Employment, Interest and Money*. If he achieved this at all the effects must have been fleeting; Beveridge rejected what he saw as Keynes's empty theorising and pinned his faith on the accumulation of statistics and hard facts. A Namier to Keynes's Toynbee, he would have given short shrift to any assistant who preached the latter's dangerous and insidiously fashionable doctrines. Wilson in fact seems to have paid little attention at this time to the precepts of Keynsian economics and would certainly have hesitated to propound them with any vigour in the company of his employer.

Wilson did not much enjoy research – he would have preferred setting to work to solve the problems rather than seeking to establish their exact dimensions – but he recognised that the opportunity to work for Beveridge and the specialist knowledge he would acquire could be invaluable to him in any future career. Besides, he liked and admired Beveridge and shared his ability to dedicate himself totally to the work in hand. At first they worked on slide rules, then a hand-operated calculating machine was procured and the Rockefeller Foundation paid for a girl to operate it. At one time it was intended that Wilson and Beveridge should cooperate on a book about the trade cycle, but only the first nine chapters had been completed by the time war aborted the enterprise.[1] Perhaps it was just as well: Wilson confessed to finding Beveridge "a devil to work for" and the hazards of joint publication would have tested their relationship. As it was, even Wilson's devotion to duty was strained by summer "holidays" with the Beveridges at their country cottage in Wiltshire. Beveridge would swim in the open and unheated pool at 6.00 a.m., then he would bring Wilson a cup of tea and the two would work together till breakfast and again till 12.30 p.m. A light luncheon, a bathe, and two hours' brisk walk or work in the garden would be followed by a return to the trade cycle between tea and dinner. Finally came the most demanding part of the day, bridge with Beveridge's cousin and future wife, the formidable Jessy Mair.[2]

Beveridge could afford to pay his research assistant no more than expenses so Wilson applied for a lectureship at New College. The Warden of New College, H. A. L. Fisher, asked Beveridge whether he thought Wilson was the right man for the job. "He has a good head, is extremely methodical, and is prepared to work really hard," replied Beveridge. He hoped that his assistant would not be seduced into teaching when he was both being more useful and doing better for himself by "applying his economic training to the study of concrete problems".[1] Fisher had no intention of offering Wilson more than part-time work, at £125 a year. Encouraged by Beveridge's good opinion, he summoned the potential lecturer to tea so as to take a closer look at him. The French poet and novelist, Jean Giraudoux, was also there and Fisher decreed that the conversation should be in French. This challenge reduced Wilson to total silence; fortunately it seemed that the inspection was no more than a formality and that the job was already his. He found himself responsible for Richard Crossman's pupils – Crossman having recently been cut off from all tutorial work because of a matrimonial escapade. They were a mainly Wykehamist group who revered Crossman, resented Wilson as an inferior substitute, and thought that they were cleverer than he was. It was not a happy period.

Fortunately it only lasted two terms. In September 1938 Beveridge offered him a junior research fellowship at University College. It was worth £400 a year with free rooms and food, and since he was also allowed to take pupils from Jesus, it represented for Wilson something close to affluence. He had "some teaching duties", Beveridge recalled[2] but the Master was in no doubt that Wilson's principal role was to continue to act as his research assistant. The other dignitaries of the college were not always in complete accord with this view. Arthur Goodhart, then Professor of Jurisprudence, remembered Wilson as being "like a lively fox terrier",[3] and much liveliness was called for if he was to meet the demands of the college as well as its exigent Master. His formal function was to support the reader in economics, G. D. H. Cole. Cole was a committed socialist and Fabian; a regular contributor to the *New Statesman* and author of such popular and influential books as *The Intelligent Man's Guide Through World Chaos* and *What Marx Really Meant*. Wilson found him "most congenial"; he would have preferred it if Cole had asked him to teach economic history instead of theory, which he disliked, but he gladly accepted whatever was on offer.[4] He was later to give Cole much of the credit for convincing him that the Labour Party deserved his loyalty, but though he helped out in some work for the Fabians, he had neither the time nor the inclination to devote himself at all seriously to politics. One of the most dramatic of inter-war by-elections came in Oxford in October 1938 when A. D. Lindsay, the Master of Balliol, opposed Chamberlain's champion, Quintin Hogg, on a platform confined almost exclusively to the issue of appeasement. Richard Crossman, Roy Jenkins, Frank Pakenham, Denis Healey,

Edward Heath were among the young sympathisers who canvassed –
unsuccessfully – for Lindsay; G. D. H. Cole was involved; Wilson
played no part.

The time was soon coming, however, when it would no longer be
possible to remain isolated from outside events. At the beginning of
September 1939 Wilson was driving in Scotland in what was then his
most cherished possession, a seven-year-old, ten-horsepower Wolsey
Hornet which had cost him £25; "very noble," commented Beveridge,
when introduced to it.[1] On behalf of Beveridge, he was to present a
paper on trade cycles to the British Association. The conference was
interrupted by the news that Germany had invaded Poland. Wilson
hurried south, appeared before the University Military Recruiting
Board and registered at the local employment exchange under the
Military Service Act. Rationally, he can have been in no doubt that
he could do more valuable work for his country in some civilian role
than with the armed forces. Emotionally, he must have asked himself
whether it was not his duty to enlist. He was not yet in a reserved
occupation and no serious obstacle would have been put in his way
if he had chosen to do so; his qualifications for work with the civil
service, however, were so obvious that unless he made strenuous
efforts to follow another course he was bound to end up with a job
in London. He made no such efforts. Whether he felt relief or regret
when it became clear that he would not have to fight remains
unknown; probably, as would be true of most people, a bit of both.
Certainly it is unfair to say, as some have done, that he took steps to
avoid being called up; the most that can be said is that he made no
effort to escape the current that bore him unprotesting into the maw
of the civil service.

On the way south he had spent a day with Mary Baldwin and her
family and they had decided that the uncertainty of what lay ahead
made it all the more desirable that they should quickly marry. Wilson
worked frantically to clear the decks before the ceremony. On 31
December he sent Beveridge the fruits of his work on the eighteenth-
century industrial index and correlations: "although I worked solidly
through the Xmas period ... apart from Xmas day itself, I have only
just finished my stuff."[2] The wedding took place in Oxford on 1
January 1940. The weather was foggy and cold, both protagonists
had heavy colds, but "it was a delightful ceremony", remembered

Arthur Goodhart. "She looked so pretty and charming. They were both very young looking, but terribly attractive." Mary wanted to omit the promise to obey, something which her future husband thought entirely reasonable, but was overruled in her wish for "Here Comes the Bride". The organist rather snootily pronounced that the music was not good enough and substituted "Gaudeamus Igitur". Best man was Patrick Duncan, a friend of Wilson's who was waiting to join the Indian civil service and was killed on the North West Frontier shortly after the war. Nobody wore morning dress or top hats – an omission which Mary regretted – and there was fruit cup instead of champagne, but otherwise all was done in fine style. Beveridge could not attend but sent two red Venetian glass bowls as a present.[1]

Because of the fog and the incipient snow, the man who was to drive the Wilsons to their honeymoon hotel in the Cotswolds insisted on leaving before the reception was over. As they drove off one guest noticed that the back of the car was stacked with books. If Wilson had picked them they were probably official publications or volumes of statistics. They did not have much time to read, however. Before they had been there a week there was a telegram from Beveridge demanding Wilson's urgent return. They had not long been back in Oxford before Wilson was on the move again. The first few years of their marriage, when the young couple should have been growing together, were to be beset by many such interruptions and by long and frustrating partings. It was a far from ideal start to a relationship which, even at the best of times, was likely to have its difficulties.

III

The Civil Service

1940–1945

Wilson's first wartime job was hardly glorious. Within a few days of his registration he found himself despatched to the Potato Control Board in Oxford as a temporary clerk Grade 3 at £3 a week. The only redeeming feature was that Mary was given a job in the same organisation. A few weeks later he was summoned to an interview in the Ministry of Supply. The Director of Statistics, who interviewed him, tried to assess his awareness of current issues by cross-examining him on an article in that week's *Economist* on the mobilisation of the national economy. Since Wilson was able to admit coyly that he had actually written the article himself, he not surprisingly got the job.[1] Beveridge claimed the credit for the appointment: "I was successful in introducing younger colleagues and friends to departments," he wrote. "... Harold Wilson to the Ministry of Supply."[2] Wilson saw no cause to be particularly grateful. The work proved arduous but unstimulating and he was relieved when within a few months he was head-hunted by members of the Cabinet Secretariat. Their first proposal was that he should join Professor Stanley Dennison's Anglo-French Coordinating Committee. He took up the task in April 1940, hardly a propitious moment for Anglo-French coordination, and found his efforts superfluous within a couple of hectic months, though not before he had sat in on a meeting between Churchill and de Gaulle and – or so he says, at least – had impressed the Prime Minister by the lucidity of his memoranda.[3] The British members of the committee were merged with the War Cabinet Secretariat, and with what must have been a slightly dispiriting sensation of *déjà vu* Wilson found himself, after some toing and froing, once more working for Beveridge on manpower problems.[4]

It was Ernest Bevin who had originally recruited Beveridge to carry out a survey of the government's problems in making best use of the available manpower. In December 1940 Beveridge was slotted in as under-secretary at the Ministry of Labour. Wilson duly followed him there and was appointed secretary of the Manpower Requirements Committee, of which Beveridge was chairman. Douglas Jay in January 1941 attended a meeting of the committee. He was told by Oliver Franks that Beveridge had enlisted as his assistant "a very young and very clever statistician from Oxford called Harold Wilson. There they both were across the table ... rather like an owl and a sparrow: Beveridge, august, white-haired, venerable and dogmatic; and Wilson diminutive, chubby and chirpy."[1] The committee's primary duty was to establish what resources in manpower were available and then to relate them to the needs of the individual departments. To do this properly involved much interrogation of officials from the various ministries and probably provided as accurate and detailed a picture of what actually went on in Whitehall as could have been acquired by a decade of training. One thoroughly sensible recommendation which the committee made and which Bevin accepted early in 1941 was that the rate of call-up for the armed services should depend not solely on the arbitrary demands of the navy, army and air force but should take account of the availability of munitions.[2] Wilson claimed to have acquired during this period "a solid antipathy to the over-whelming power of the Treasury".[3] In later life he was more often to be accused of undue deference to the Treasury mandarins but it is possible to see in these early years in Whitehall the genesis of the Department of Economic Affairs and his fleeting attempt to break the stranglehold which the Chancellor of the Exchequer and his officials enjoyed on the British economy.

At the Ministry of Labour Wilson, still aged only twenty-four, was appointed head of the Manpower, Statistics and Intelligence Branch. At New College, in an unavailing attempt to look older than some of the undergraduates whom he was teaching, he had grown a mous-tache. He managed only to look like a schoolboy made up to play an adult role. At the Ministry of Labour, where virtually without excep-tion his colleagues and subordinates were years, sometimes decades older than him, the problem was even worse. Only a sublime con-fidence in his own ability protected him from a feeling of almost intolerable exposure.

After a few months Beveridge was made chairman of a committee to investigate the misuse of skilled labour in the services. Here too

Wilson served as secretary. The job involved much travel and the making of many enemies – more by the abrasive Beveridge than by his comparatively emollient assistant. The army came out particularly badly when the committee's report was published in February 1942. Bevin accepted the resultant furore with equanimity but he took it less kindly when his own feathers were ruffled by Beveridge's truculence and extravagant pretensions. Soon he shifted him into what was intended to be a backwater, an enquiry into the coordination of social services. Wilson was offered the chance to accompany his master, but decided against it. If he had known the influence that the Beveridge Report was to exercise in post-war Britain he might have changed his mind, but he probably served his own long-term interests best by escaping from Beveridge's shadow and making his own name in a field that was more immediately relevant to victory in war.

In August 1941 Wilson was transferred to the Mines Department, a semi-independent body operating under the suzerainty of the Board of Trade. The deputy under-secretary responsible, W. G. Nott-Bower, had heard that other ministries were after this promising young statistician and was keen to grab him at once. "Personality decidedly good; extremely alert mentally and not afraid of tackling anything in the statistical line," he reported, and though only twenty-five seeming far more mature than his years.[1] Wilson's new post was a responsible one. Britain depended on coal for by far the largest part of its energy, demand had soared, production fallen, a dire crisis threatened. Andrew Duncan, President of the Board of Trade, had been involved with the coal mines at the end of the First World War but had recently been concerned with iron and steel and was happy to leave the Mines Department largely to Wilson and to another Oxford don, John Fulton. Wilson's main responsibility was to establish the statistical base without which the problems of the industry could not be tackled, let alone resolved. "Much of the credit ..." wrote W. H. B. Court, the official historian of the wartime coal industry, "must go to the young Oxford don, Mr J. H. Wilson, who was, for a long time, their official head."[2] At first his main tool was "a cylindrical wooden slide rule, too heavy to hold in the hand, mounted at an angle on a spiky base like a Crimean War mortar, and equivalent to a flat rule eighty-three feet four inches long". There were supposed to be two of these devices; only after prolonged search was the second discovered, still in its box, propping up Wilson's desk.[3] Soon, less antiquated instruments were procured and order imposed. Under his management weekly production figures, which had traditionally only been available a month after the event and were then often inaccurate, were presented every Saturday at noon, valid up to Friday night. With the information he procured it became possible to identify log-jams, monitor progress or the lack of it, plan sensibly for the increasing needs of industry and the demands of winter. Within a few months a faltering and demoralised group of men had been transformed into an efficient and highly active unit.

It was one thing to identify problems, another to solve them. Wilson established, and soon satisfied Duncan, that it was shortage of skilled labour in the right places that was impeding production, not laziness or absenteeism as the colliery owners maintained. His information, and still more his interpretation of it, prepared the way for a radical rethinking of Britain's coal industry. When Hugh Dalton took over from Duncan as President of the Board of Trade he received a rapturous report on Wilson from a high-flying young Wykehamist on his staff called Hugh Gaitskell. Wilson was described as "extraordinarily able. He is only twenty-six or thereabouts, and is one of the most brilliant younger people about ... he has revolutionised the coal statistics ... The great thing about him is that he understands what statistics are administratively important and interesting. We must on no account surrender him either to the Army or to any other department."[1] "He really got things under control," wrote another colleague, Donald MacDougall. "The quality of papers emanating from the department improved out of all recognition."[2] Aneurin Bevan once asked Wilson what his son was studying at university. Wilson replied that his subject was pure mathematics. "Just like his father," said Bevan, only half in fun, "all facts, no bloody vision."[3] In the Mines Department, at least, Wilson showed that facts and vision were not incompatible; indeed, that the second without the first would serve little useful purpose.

With the statistical service soundly established Wilson had time to extend his range of duties. Discontent in the mining industry and a flurry of strikes led Dalton to set up a Board of Enquiry under the chairmanship of the Master of the Rolls, a Chancery lawyer and formidable scholar, Wilfrid Greene. Wilson was one of the two joint secretaries of the board and Lord Greene looked to him for guidance on the facts and figures. Without too much difficulty Wilson persuaded him that the miners had a case, that they deserved a rise of half-a-crown (12.5p) a shift, and that it would also be desirable to establish a national minimum wage for the whole industry. Rather nervously he pointed out that it would be difficult to go back on this once the war was over. "It means the nationalisation of the whole coal mining industry," said Greene, "but I'm not afraid of that."[1] William Lawther, the miners' leader, told Paul Foot that Wilson had done "a tremendously good job"; a view shared by Sidney Ford, the union's chief administrative officer. But Ford saw no evidence that Wilson had any particular political axe to grind or was out for anything except a settlement that would bring stability to the coal miners: "If you'd asked me at the time, honestly, I'd have said he was a Liberal."[2]

By then the Department of Mines had escaped from the Board of Trade to become the core of a new Ministry of Fuel, Light and Power. Wilson was appointed Director of Economics and Statistics with a salary of £1,150 a year and a staff of 350. His new minister was Gwilym Lloyd George, a son of the former Prime Minister and himself a Liberal of markedly right-wing leanings, though with little respect for the private colliery owners. Under him Wilson's responsibilities widened still further. Early in 1943 he became joint secretary of a subcommittee of the Combined Chiefs of Staff, the supreme Anglo-American body responsible for allied strategy. His task was to build up coal stocks at the main invasion loading ports and to ensure that all consumers had twenty weeks' stock. The work involved him in negotiations with the Americans and in October 1943 he paid the first of what were to be innumerable visits to Washington. The flying boat in which he flew was the last to take off before bad weather closed the route for a week and he found the journey too hazardous for his taste: "Having now flown the Atlantic twice since I last wrote," he told his family proudly on his return, "(the feat they fussed about so much when Lindbergh did it) I don't quite know where to begin."[3]

Like most British visitors to the United States at the time, he indulged in an orgy of shopping and eating. He only had $40 plus an allowance of $9 a day but he somehow managed to buy himself "a new suit (dark blue tweed), a lightweight imitation gaberdine made of spun glass, five good shirts, eight pairs of pants, three pairs of socks, four ties," not to mention an umbrella, two pairs of sandals and some stockings for his wife. As for food, he gorged himself contentedly on all the delights that were unavailable in London:

"Loads of eggs, bacon, steaks, chops, tomato juice, orange and grape-fruit juice, oranges, lobster, oysters, shrimp cocktails."[1]

All his life Wilson tended to assume that everyone he met was favourably impressed by his talents and personality and he cherished a firm belief – not always borne out by the facts – that the Americans in particular responded well to him. On this occasion at least he seems to have been right, though his account of his dealings with them is characteristically self-satisfied. "I had a good time with the Yanks I met ... They seemed to think I got on OK with them: the day I left I was shown (very unofficially) a memo from the American head of CPRB [Combined Production Resources Board] to the head of the British Supply Mission saying that the British really ought to send far more like me, and less Old School Tie wallahs. He said my Yorks accent was a great asset and also my direct manner: both much more understanded of [*sic*] the Americans. He said my handling of the Americans was 'superlative' – and some of them very difficult. What he said to *me* was that it was a good thing they hadn't gold fillings in their teeth, or else I'd have had them as well as the $4 million of mining machinery and a US commitment for the Mediterranean."[2] He was relieved to find that the renowned American statistical machine in fact produced results markedly less useful than those he had obtained in London; he returned from Washington "more in favour of British methods than before".[3]

As the war drew towards its close the long-term future of the coal mining industry became a matter of debate. Wilson himself had no doubt that public ownership in one form or another was essential if the progress made during the war was to be maintained, a view that was shared, at least tacitly, by a surprising number of politicians from the right as well as the left. He was responsible for preparing a digest of information about the industry for the use of MPs who wanted to take part in a debate on the coal industry in the House of Commons. The document was purely factual and contained no recommendations but it included most of the material Wilson needed for a book on the subject which he planned to write once time permitted. He did most of the work on it while still employed at the ministry, though he did not put the finishing touches or try to get it published until after he had left the civil service. *New Deal for Coal*, which was published by George Weidenfeld and thus initiated an association which was to last throughout his life, ran to 264 pages and was packed with statistics but was still a trenchant call for nationalisation presented in terms accessible to the layman. He did not claim that to take the industry into public ownership would solve its problems but argued that, without such a preliminary, those problems would be insoluble: only nationalisation would create the conditions in which the skill and experience of the miners could be used to best advantage. Public ownership of the mines would show not only "that socialism and efficiency are compatible but also that socialism, properly applied, is the only means to full efficiency".[1]

Paul Foot, though conceding that *New Deal for Coal* was probably the best book Wilson wrote, argued that it was elitist in that it envisaged no role for miners in the regional or national councils which it was suggested should be set up.[2] The omission was unsurprising. Wilson was not preoccupied by theoretical concepts of equality or industrial democracy; what he was seeking was a plan which would work and would put the coal industry on to a new footing with a minimum of complications. If that was compatible with giving the miners a greater say in the control of the mines then he would be delighted, but workers' power was not the object of the exercise. "There speaks a Socialist without illusions and without obsessions," commented the *Observer*. It was a judgment that must have seemed to Wilson both unequivocally laudatory and eminently well deserved.

His last months with the Ministry of Fuel were not entirely tranquil. His reiterated demands that he should be given more staff to support him in his new directorate and that his present subordinates should be promoted stung Nott-Bower to fury. Angrily he denounced Wilson's "unreasoning prejudice" and his "usual over-weening desire to boost individual members of his staff and his Directorate generally".[3] The establishment triumphed: Wilson did not get what he wanted. Quite why Nott-Bower was so tetchy about what seem on the face of it to have been excessive but not outrageously extravagant demands is hard to say. Probably it was more a question of tone than substance. Wilson was pleased with himself and apt to show it; such bouncy self-confidence from a mere temporary civil servant would have seemed deeply offensive to his career superiors. It was not a serious setback but it tarnished an otherwise impeccable performance.

Wilson had enjoyed what any objective observer would have considered "a good war". He had done a series of difficult and responsible jobs with notable success, had built up a solid reputation in Whitehall and beyond, had acquired an understanding of the machinery of government which was to serve him well in future years. "I know more than anyone else about how Britain's Government works," he boasted in one of his last interviews as Prime Minister.[1] The OBE which he was awarded in the New Year's Honours of 1945 was a merited recognition of his achievements. What had not gone so well was his family life. The Wilsons had become used to being much apart and had developed in different ways. Wilson's unremitting dedication to the needs of his work, largely unavoidable in view of the wartime demands made upon him, confirmed what was already a pronounced cast of his mind. His vocation had become all-important to him. He was never to deny that other responsibilities existed, and he did a reasonable job of carrying them out, but in the scale of his values nothing came before the demands of his career. He would have been hurt and surprised if accused of being a bad husband or father – "bad" is indeed too pejorative a word – but he had it in his power to be exemplary in both these roles and he excelled in neither.

When Wilson started work in Whitehall Mary came to London with him. At first they lived in rooms in Earl's Court, then moved to Dolphin Square in Pimlico, and finally took a two-roomed flat in Twickenham and furnished it at a cost of £150 on hire purchase from the Times Furnishing Company. When the blitz began Mary for a time stayed with Wilson's parents in Cornwall where Herbert Wilson was now working, then moved to Oxford; Wilson as often as not slept in a shelter beneath his office or spent the nights on the roof fire-watching. Often he would share this duty with his colleague and fellow exile from Oxford, John Fulton. They used to grumble together about the amateurishness of the civil service and the need for an injection of professional skills. Twenty-five years later Wilson was to invite Fulton to conduct an enquiry into the workings of the civil service.[2]

The Twickenham flat was on the top floor and there was still danger from air-raids when Mary came back to London. After a few months they crossed the river to Richmond and set up in a flat on the Little Green. There Mary conceived her first child. "Gladys quite well and going on fine," Wilson wrote to his parents. "Her doctor has told her he thinks Bogus is a lady. I brought Bogus (lady or gent) some nappies and two sets of clothes (very nice) from Washington."[3] The doctor was wrong, Bogus was a boy and was born in December 1943. He was christened Robin, and when the flying bombs made life in

London unduly perilous for a mother and baby Mary took him to her parents' home at Duxford in Cambridgeshire. In theory Wilson was to join her there every other night but in practice a week would quite often go by without a visit.

It was time to give thought to the future. Mary had always assumed, or at least hoped, that Wilson would return to Oxford after the war. University College would have welcomed him back with enthusiasm, indeed when he briefly reappeared there in 1945 he was at once appointed Domestic Bursar. Another possibility was to remain in the civil service. Though no direct offer was made, it was hinted to him that if he wanted it a permanent job in the Treasury would be available. Much later he was asked if he regretted not having taken it up. "Heavens, no," said Wilson. "I couldn't have stood the intrigue!"[1] His reply was disingenuous; Wilson would have found the intrigue positively congenial and have indulged in it with great skill. He rejected the civil service because his time in Whitehall had convinced him that, however great the officials' influence might be, the power to get things done rested with the minister. And Wilson wanted to get things done.

In 1940 a cousin of Wilson's, Norman Adamson, suggested to him that after the war he would go into politics. Wilson insisted that he would return to academic life.[2] At that time he clearly had no other definite plan in mind. Gradually, however, his work made him more concerned with political issues. In the summer of 1943 he allowed himself to be nominated for the executive committee of the Fabian Society. By October he was playing a prominent role. He appeared on a platform with Herbert Morrison and Ellen Wilkinson: "I met Morrison before and after lecture," he reported with some pride.[3] Soon he was drafting papers of considerable importance for the Labour Party's future: one, unsurprisingly, was on the coal industry; another on the financing of railway nationalisation – a long remove from his Gladstone Prize essay in which he had deplored "glib talk" about the nationalisation of the railways. Wilson favoured compensation in cash to the existing proprietors; there were "strong political and psychological arguments against perpetuating a class of persons who could be regarded as railway shareholders, no matter how impotent they would be in the matter of control". Compensation should be "the minimum compatible with fairness and political practicability in order to avoid placing an excessive debt and interest burden on the new Authority".[4]

In December 1943 Wilson told Beveridge that John Parker, the

General Secretary of the Fabian Society, was anxious to put his name on the Transport House list of potential parliamentary candidates. Beveridge urged him to accept. Gwilym Lloyd George gave him the same advice. By early 1944 the National Executive was busily making up lists in case Churchill decided to call a snap election as soon as the war with Germany was over. Wilson agreed to let his name go forward and was formally nominated by Tom Smith, a miner MP who was parliamentary secretary at the Ministry of Fuel and Power. His reputation had spread far enough to ensure that a gratifying number of invitations to appear on the short list of candidates was soon before him. Most of them were for seats held at the time by Tories but two, Edmonton and Ormskirk, seemed potentially winnable. Edmonton was electorally the more promising and conveniently close to Westminster but Ormskirk was in Lancashire, where he felt he would be more at home and enjoy the appeal of a local boy. He might well have settled for Edmonton none the less but by the time that the selection committee there had told him that his nomination was a near certainty he had already been offered Ormskirk and had accepted.

Ormskirk was a large and sprawling constituency, the greater part of it agricultural land but with a few mining villages and some 37,000 voters concentrated on the fringes of Liverpool. Potatoes were the principal crop and Wilson's only serious rival as Labour candidate had been a farmer. The constituency chairman, Fred Sayer, a self-made baker, told Wilson that he had supported the other contestant, but the party secretary and treasurer, Leslie and Hettie Last, were vigorous Wilson fans and the party machine was enthusiastic and, by the standards of the times, remarkably well organised.

Ormskirk had been won by Labour in 1929 but the member had supported Ramsay MacDonald's national government. When he retired early in the war he had been replaced by a "National Labour" candidate, Stephen King-Hall. King-Hall, who was eventually to be created a life peer by Harold Wilson in 1966, was a maverick figure who found any party yoke intolerable. In 1942 he styled himself an Independent and he now wished to fight under that banner as a supporter of Winston Churchill and with Tory support. The Tories preferred to run their own official candidate and a delighted Wilson found that the vote against him was thus likely to be split. In his campaigning he struck the note that was to become his trademark over the years, the need for an industrial and technological revolution:

"We are living in a totally different world. The Government is made up of tired old men."[1] His performance was more conscientious than inspired; his speeches, in his own words, were "painfully dull, factual and over-weighted with statistics".[2] His electoral address was equally colourless though sensible enough; his principal theme was an unexceptionable "Peace Abroad and a New Deal at Home".

He had made one serious misjudgment. Though the gods of the civil service were prepared to tolerate its temporary members putting their names forward as parliamentary candidates they insisted that, once they had been officially adopted for a constituency, they must resign. Wilson had counted on remaining in his job until the campaign began; now, as he rather peevishly complained in a speech in Blackheath in January 1945, he had been sacked.[3] Beveridge offered him a refuge in University College, where there were enough undergraduates to keep him decently employed and he was able to finish his book on coal and his report on railway nationalisation. He thought it probable that he would have to stay there for the next few years. Even with the split in the Tory vote Ormskirk was very much a marginal seat and the received wisdom of the time was that a convincing Tory win in the general election was a near certainty.

By the time of the election in July 1945 Wilson was beginning to hope. Though he had no idea of the likely national picture he seemed to detect a tide of opinion running in his favour in his own constituency. His meetings were consistently well attended, pledges of support came from some unexpected quarters, the official Tory candidate professed total confidence but was said to be secretly disquieted. After the poll there was a three-week gap while the votes came in from the servicemen overseas. Wilson returned to Oxford to wait with as much patience as he could manage. On 26 July he was back in Ormskirk for the declaration of the poll. The unfortunate King-Hall had secured only 12,000 votes, the official Tory 23,000, Wilson 30,000. His exact majority was 7,022. If the right-wing vote had been combined he would have been defeated, but a narrow win was good enough. At the age of twenty-nine Wilson had become a member of the House of Commons.

IV

Junior Minister

1945–1947

Harold Wilson in 1945 seemed formidably well equipped for success in politics. His academic training, wide knowledge of the British economy, understanding of the workings of Whitehall, all gave him advantages that were denied to most of the new entrants. But it was in his character that he seemed most obviously destined to success. All the qualities that were to mark his political career were apparent in these early days; frailties – in particular his paranoiac suspicion that all his colleagues were seeking to undermine and eventually replace him – for the most part only became evident at a later date.

"His image of himself," wrote Richard Crossman in 1965, "is as a gritty, practical Yorkshireman, a fighter, the Britisher who doesn't give in, who doesn't switch, who hangs on."[1] Any gritty Yorkshireman who knows how to play his role must appear phlegmatic and eschew all signs of extravagant emotion. To Wilson this was not so much image building as second nature. "In a long public career," he wrote in his memoirs, "I do not think I have ever lost my cool except on rare occasions for specific effect."[2] He overstated his case: to his credit there was at least one issue – that of racism – about which he felt so passionately that he was several times betrayed into unguarded and tactically injudicious outbursts. In general, however, his self-control was formidable; he rarely showed himself to be more than mildly irritated and preserved an impressive calm throughout the most alarming crises. Leo Abse, in his tendentious but entertaining analysis of Wilson's character, described this as a deformity, a "regressive schizoid phenomenon" which was positively damaging to his career.[3] It is hard to accept this judgment: Wilson's capacity to bide his time; to gauge exactly when a show of indignation would be of value; to keep his head when all about him had not merely lost theirs but were having a good stab at removing his as well, was not perhaps always endearing but equipped him with some formidably effective armour for battles in the corridors of power.

Gritty Yorkshiremen are also expected to be pragmatic and to distrust, if not invariably avoid, flights of fancy or reflective theorising. Henry Kissinger marvelled at Wilson's indifference to abstract ideas; "He was fascinated by the manipulation of political power; he relished the enterprise of solving definable problems. Longer-range objectives elicited from him only the most cursory attention. He saw no sense in planning, because he had complete confidence that his many skills would see him through any tight spot."[1] Generally he was proved right, in the short term at any rate. The accusation that Wilson was a superb tactician but no sort of strategist has been levelled at him so often and so unthinkingly that it deserves to be treated with grave suspicion. It is possible to find plenty of occasions on which Wilson acted rashly and foolishly; one can even find instances of his evolving a long-term strategy and sticking to it successfully. But these are the exceptions. For the most part the conventional and hackneyed judgment is correct. Any successful politician must be a skilled tactician, but he does not need to limit himself exclusively to that horizon. To be able to surmount each obstacle as it arises is a transcendent virtue but it helps too to have some idea in which direction one is going. Wilson all too often lacked that knowledge, did not feel it necessary or desirable. He was "essentially a pragmatist," judged an ardent supporter, George Wigg, "and pragmatism, if you are constantly below deck having a chat with the crew, is dangerous in rocky seas".[2]

An ability to avoid immediate and ignore distant dangers breeds a sometimes alarming optimism. Optimism is often a strength, a sturdy flame of hope when things are blackest, sustaining morale and feeding the will to continue the fight. Wilson's colleagues, however, saw it as more often perilous; at the best a minor irritant, often breeding an illusory and ill-justified assurance. Crossman referred to the "interminable self-defeating optimism of Harold Wilson",[3] while Barbara Castle, when the unemployment figures fell slightly and Wilson proclaimed that the corner had been turned, groaned: "That optimism again. It could be fatal."[4] Yet Wilson's rosy certainties about the future were in fact rarely translated into rash actions. He was, indeed, remarkable for his caution. At the Board of Trade his staff complained that he would take twice as long as Stafford Cripps to make up his mind on any issue, though they conceded that, when finally arrived at, his decision was more likely to be the right one.[1] At the worst this indecision amounted almost to a paralysis of will which would preclude any action until it was too late. Wigg, again, complained that "he tended to wait on the march of events before taking the decisions which his own research and acute intelligence had already revealed to him as being the right ones."[2]

Caution went with moderation. Though occasionally forced to endorse extremist policies, his instinct always was to avoid them if he could and to mitigate them if he could not. It made no difference whether the extremes were of the left or the right; he was repelled by them. "Very much middle-of-the-road, slightly right of centre and ... generally conservative in his views", Richard Marsh judged him.[3] "Slightly left of centre", was Michael Stewart's verdict.[4] It depends where one puts the centre; the key word in both cases was "slightly". Wilson believed that absolute truth was rarely if ever to be found; the nearest one could hope to come to it was by seeking between two points. Any extreme or dogmatic position was almost certain to be ill-chosen. The primary function of a leader was to keep the show on the road, and to do this endless compromise was necessary. "To bridge a deep political chasm without splitting a party or provoking dramatic ministerial resignations is sometimes regarded as something approaching political chicanery," Wilson complained. "The highest aim of leadership is to secure policies adequate to deal with any situation ... without major confrontations, splits or resignations."[5] It was a doctrine which he followed faithfully: "In all the hundreds of meetings over which I saw him preside," wrote Edward Short, "I never knew him fail to find some area of agreement between different – often overtly hostile – points of view."[6]

What to one man is pragmatism is to another lack of principle. "If there were a word 'aprincipled', as there is 'amoral'," remarked John Freeman, "it would describe Wilson perfectly."[7] Any irrevocable move was to be eschewed, however worthy the cause; no position should be taken up unless a line of retreat had first been established. He enjoyed, wrote Richard Crossman, "a really elegant ability to be imprecise, to steer a non-committal hedging course and to say things which aren't quite right in order to avoid any commitment".[8] "Devious" is one of the words that occurs most often in assessments of his character: "I think Harold is rather devious and I must be careful to keep myself covered," wrote Tony Benn.[1] James Callaghan told Benn that Wilson was "extremely devious" and would not believe a straight line was ever the shortest way between two points.[2] When levelled at him by his enemies, such criticism dismissed Wilson as a dishonest and unprincipled schemer: "There are two things I dislike about Wilson," said one hostile critic. "His face!"[3] Yet even when at his most deceitful there was an element of playfulness about Wilson's cozenage; he was as much delighting in his own cleverness as seeking to achieve an end. "The devious machinations of Tsarism found an echo in Wilson's own personality; he is openly fascinated by Rasputin,"[4] wrote Anthony Howard and Richard West in their admirable study of Wilson's march to Downing Street. The Yorkshire tyke and the Mad Monk may seem to have little in common but Wilson was capable of seeing himself in a multiplicity of roles. Another might have been Iago, chuckling to himself at his extreme cleverness as the gullible Othello brooded balefully over the incriminating handkerchief.[5]

At least as important an element in Wilson's evasiveness was a wish to avoid painful confrontations. Time and again subordinates who had reason to expect a resounding rebuke found instead that nothing was said to them; they heard at second hand that Wilson was displeased, the light of his countenance might be withdrawn, but the direct censure never came. Anthony Crosland rushed back from Japan because he was told on all sides that Wilson was threatening to dismiss him, yet when he finally saw the Prime Minister he was assured that it was all nonsense.[6] He "cannot say no to a man's face", George Brown told Cecil King. Even though he had offered Roy Jenkins Frank Soskice's job as Home Secretary he could not bring himself to sack the latter.[7] He wanted to be liked and was perpetually concerned about the impression that he made on other people. "Touchingly eager for approval," Kissinger found him, "especially from those he respected. This category generally included men of power or academics."[8] For a man who enjoyed a reputation for toughness he had an extraordinarily thin skin. Tom Williams made a joke about being ruled by economists, heard that Wilson had been hurt by it and went to apologise. "I have spent all my life doing things for other people," said Wilson sadly, "going out of my way to help them. And then I find, so often, that they act as if I had no feelings."[9]

When he claimed that he went out of his way to help people, he said no more than the truth. On the political plane he was inspired by a wish to help the poor and under-privileged, but it was at a personal level that this generosity was most marked. "Kind" is a word that occurs as often as "devious" in accounts of Wilson. He was a man "of outstanding kindness, charm and generosity", concluded Gerald Nabarro, after abusing Wilson roundly on many other points;[1] "a very nice, in particular a very kind man," wrote Frank Pakenhem. "Much of the idealism that he acquired as an active Boy Scout has stayed with him";[2] "an extremely kind man", said Tony Benn. When Benn's father, Lord Stansgate, died, he received from Wilson "without any doubt the nicest letter that I had and the most understanding".[3] Any civil servant who worked under him in the Board of Trade or at Number 10 attests to his extraordinary consideration and the trouble he would go to so as to ensure that their conditions of work were tolerable and their family life not too brutally disrupted.

His loyalty to those subordinates or to his friends was equally remarkable; "strong and enduring," Michael Stewart found it, "even if his judgement in making friends had been at fault".[4] If he had been Prince Hal he would undoubtedly have created Falstaff a peer at his accession. No one who served under him had cause to complain that he let them down when there was trouble, wrote George Thomas: "Loyalty to his colleagues was one of his strongest points."[5] But he expected the same treatment himself. In the first draft of his study of Wilson[6] Ernest Kay wrote that his subject "deep down could not countenance disloyalty" and "passionately regarded disloyalty to himself as disloyalty to the Party". "Not true. Delete," wrote Wilson in the margin. But his ministers never doubted that he would find it hard to forgive any transgressions of which they might be guilty. "I suspect Harold will never really trust me again," wrote Barbara Castle after she had opposed him in Cabinet. "Behind that blandness he never forgets."[7] Robert Armstrong, when private secretary, once mentioned a former junior minister whose name had been omitted from the new administration in March 1974. "He's done nothing for me," expostulated Wilson. "Rather the opposite in fact." Armstrong suggested that the time had come to forgive and forget. After all, the garden at Number 10 was filled with buried hatchets. "I put a lot of them there myself," said Wilson with some satisfaction. "But I always leave a label so I know where I can find them again if I need them."[8]

The mildly self-derisive note of that last remark is not unusual. Wilson did not take himself too seriously and could accept with equanimity any amount of criticism provided it was kindly meant.

He was, indeed, a remarkably good listener, always ready to consider arguments that conflicted with his own opinion though not necessarily treating them with great respect. Crossman's remark that he fancied himself as "the Britisher who doesn't ... switch" was partly true – he could be obstinate and he did conceive himself as possessed of the bulldog's tenacity and determination – but he was in practice one of the most flexible of politicians. Few indeed were the positions which he would not swiftly abandon if he became convinced that they were unlikely to prove tenable. He could afford to listen to others, to act unassumingly, to profit by advice, because of the rocklike self-confidence which underlay his tentativeness and uncertainty. Wilson was a man entirely content with his own personality and way of life. He had no aspiration to change or improve himself. He suffered from no kind of inferiority complex, wrote Crossman, but led his own "real, natural life".[1] The result seemed sometimes like complacency but it was also a source of inner strength.

To his more cultivated colleagues – Crossman, Roy Jenkins, Denis Healey – this "real, natural life" seemed sometimes pitifully narrow. Writing about Herbert Morrison, Patrick Gordon Walker remarked, "he lacked the element of ultimate greatness ... He was a professional politician to the fingertips – living for nothing else. In politics the big men are usually those who have other interests as well."[2] He would have argued that, *a fortiori*, Wilson failed the same test. "His idea of recreation was to sit around with his kitchen cabinet and one or two congenial ministers mulling over the events of the day," wrote Roy Jenkins. "He never wanted to go out to dinner or even much to eat it at home."[3] Food for the mind was equally sparse. He had in his time read and professed admiration for most of the more obvious classics, but by the time he was a politician he had little time for reading and when he did usually opted for detective stories (Dorothy Sayers's *The Nine Tailors* being a favourite and a most well-chosen one too) or popular history. Carl Sandburg's *Abraham Lincoln*, Arthur Bryant's *English Saga* and J. B. Priestley's *English Journey* were among the titles which he most often cited when asked to name his preferred literature and he read and re-read the political novels of Disraeli.[4] But this was holiday reading, and even on holiday he was more likely to be found with a White Paper or some other official publication.

His choice of music for the *Men of Action* programme was equally predictable, though it contained some splendid things: "The Trumpet Shall Sound" from the *Messiah*; "Forty Years On", because it had been adopted as the school song at Royds Hall; Stanley Holloway reciting, "Good Old Yorkshire Puddin'"'; "Poor Wandering One" from *The Pirates of Penzance*; "I'll See You Again"; "England, arise, the long, long night is over" sung by the Glasgow Socialist Singers; the Battle Hymn of the Republic; one of Dvořák's Slavonic Dances and "The Day Thou Gavest, Lord, is Ended" as "an expression of the essential unity, or togetherness, of our Commonwealth of Nations".[1] No list could have been less pretentious or more true to the personality of the chooser. He usually went to the ballet while in Moscow and impressed Frederick Ashton by his knowledge of the leading Russian dancers and his comments on some unusual features in a performance of *Swan Lake* – "He is the first politician who has seen a ballet and remembered anything about it after" – but he would never have put himself out to go to Covent Garden or Sadler's Wells.[2] He enjoyed but rarely visited the cinema and had little use for the theatre. Once, at a gala evening, he was forced to sit through extracts from a number of plays: *The Rivals, Henry V, The Importance of Being Earnest*. In the interval he was heard to ask – it seems guilelessly – "Do you think anyone has ever seen any of these plays all through?"[3] He had the least speculative of minds and was almost entirely incurious about any developments outside his immediate sphere of activity. "Even his taste in paintings reflects his 'Englishness'," wrote Marcia Williams. "His favourite painter is Lowry – because Lowry's world is a world Harold Wilson understands."[4]

Tony Benn, in his diary, quotes Antonia Fraser as saying how her mother, "who lived in Hampstead, bitterly hated Harold Wilson, how contemptuous she was of his style of life in Hampstead Garden Suburb. This explains a great deal of Wilson's dislike for that snobbish Hampstead establishment of upper middle-class socialists and Fabians."[5] The dialogue does not ring wholly true – "bitterly hated" is pitching, it rather high – but it was certainly the case that Wilson not merely did not aspire to upper middle-class standards but actively rejected them and that some of his socialist neighbours made it very clear they had no wish for his company. Neil Kinnock is supposed to have said that Wilson was "a petty bourgeois, and will remain so in spirit, even if they make him a viscount".[6] The remark was presumably meant to be offensive; Wilson would have taken it as a compliment.

Wilson's political career almost ended before it had properly begun.

After the initial party meeting to endorse Clement Attlee as leader, Wilson hastened north to his constituency. He gave a lift to a group of fellow members, including George Tomlinson, who had already served as a junior minister and seemed likely to get promotion in Attlee's future government. His car broke down and he hired a replacement, only to discover when he had got well on the way that the brakes could scarcely be said to work at all. At the best of times Wilson was an inept and clumsy driver; in the circumstances his passengers resigned themselves to probable death. It was 2.00 a.m. before he delivered a shaken Tomlinson at his destination, 4.00 a.m. before he reached his agent's house in Ormskirk.[1]

By the time he got back to London, Attlee had begun to announce his appointments. The enormous influx of new entrants and comparative shortage of seasoned old hands among the 393 Labour members made it inevitable that many people would be in office for the first time, but with his twenty-ninth birthday only recently behind him and no parliamentary experience Wilson had little hope that he would be among them. Attlee, with his public-school background, would presumably wish to reserve some of the best jobs for people from the same class; on the other hand he would want to compensate for this by favouring the 150 or so Labour members who had been passed by the socialist writer Margaret Cole as "genuine working men and women".[2] Wilson, with his lower middle-class roots and Oxford education, seemed to fail on both counts. Though the fact that the new Prime Minister had been at University College seemed a modestly hopeful augury, the best that Wilson felt he could reasonably hope for was to be picked as parliamentary private secretary to one of the senior ministers.

Nevertheless he knew that he was already ahead of the pack. Harold Nicolson bemoaned the fact that he was no longer in the House of Commons: "I want to see how the new people fit in. I want to see how the brilliant Harold Wilson really does. He is only twenty-two [sic]."[3] Harold Lever remembered him as "a smart boy with a moustache" who had the reputation of being admired by Attlee.[4] The press selected him as a man to watch: in the *Daily Telegraph* he was referred to as "a coming President of the Board of Trade or Chancellor of the Exchequer", while in the *News Chronicle* Ian Mackay remarked that "Outstanding among the really 'new' men on the Labour benches I would put the brilliant young civil servant, Harold Wilson."[5] When, on 30 July, Dalton gave a dinner at the St Ermin's Hotel for some of the more promising among the new entrants, Wilson was there with Crossman, Woodrow Wyatt, Kenneth Younger, Christopher Mayhew, John Freeman, Evan Durbin, George Brown and Hugh Gaitskell (whom an earlier heart attack had temporarily removed from consideration for a job in the new government). Mayhew was dazzled by the company, which seemed to him to be composed almost entirely of future ministers with perhaps a Prime Minister or two thrown in as well: "I expressed myself badly and no one seemed to agree. Everyone else sparkled brilliantly." He found Wilson particularly daunting: "I watched his bulging cranium with anxiety as he talked, expecting the teeming brain within to burst out at any moment."[1] Gaitskell considered that Wilson, Crossman and Durbin made "the best contributions to the debate".[2] One remark that Wilson made stuck in the memory of at least one listener; when asked which of the new MPs was eligible for immediate office he said emphatically that no one should serve in a government without previous experience of the House of Commons.[3]

Sure enough, Emanuel Shinwell upon appointment as Minister of Fuel and Power invited Wilson to become his parliamentary private secretary. This was the slot that had been allotted him in Attlee's first rough list of appointments, though the same list included him with a question mark as number two to George Tomlinson at the Ministry of Works.[4] He accepted Shinwell's offer gratefully, went to Oxford for the weekend, and returned from a shopping expedition to be told that the Prime Minister had been asking for him on the telephone. Their conversation was characteristically brief. I have a job for you, said Attlee. "George Tomlinson will be your Minister. Said you tried to kill him but doesn't hold it against you. Report to him."[5] He was the youngest office-holder in the government, at a salary of £1,500 a year. The only other new members to get jobs were Hilary Marquand and George Lindgren.

The Ministry of Works was one of those departments that had expanded greatly under the stimulus of wartime demands. Before the war the Commission of Works and Public Buildings had employed 6,000 people; by 1945 its staff had swollen to more than 20,000 and it was responsible for vast programmes of housing, schools, training colleges and buildings required to meet the needs of the Atomic Energy Bill. The allocation of scarce resources within these programmes, and the elimination of bottlenecks that would prevent those resources being used to best advantage, were to be Wilson's main responsibilities over the next two years.[1] He could not count on his minister to provide more than the most generalised support. Tomlinson was kindly, honourable and loyal but even his benevolent biographer had to admit that his "genius did not lie in the direction of statistics" and "no one would contest that organisation was one of George Tomlinson's strongest points".[2] Observers quickly concluded that, if the ministry was to do all that was needed, the parliamentary secretary would have to carry the burden. Wilson, reported the American Embassy, had "made a reputation during the war as a statistical wizard and as an aggressive, fearless and imaginative civil servant ... He furnished the drive in the Ministry of Works which Tomlinson was unable to supply and was largely responsible for the success of that Ministry."[3]

The permanent under-secretary at the ministry, Sir Percival Robinson, was dismayed to find that this whippersnapper, barely half his age, not only knew his way around the Whitehall jungle but was resolved to impose his will on his civil servants. Robinson lectured him on a minister's role – in effect that of a mouthpiece for a policy which had been evolved by his permanent staff – and protested bitterly when the brash young parliamentary secretary ignored the usual channels and insisted on talking to the responsible officials who actually knew the answers to his questions. To be fair to Robinson, Wilson must have been an infuriating minister to have around: a bumptious know-all who took no trouble to spare the older man's dignity and reputation. But Wilson was right on every major issue. Though Tomlinson would not have done it himself, he acquiesced gratefully when Wilson so engineered matters that Robinson retired to become a director of the Suez Canal Company.[4] "I do not want to go into the question of the personnel of the Ministry of Works," Wilson told the House of Commons with some satisfaction early in 1946, "except to say that it is a very different place now from what it was in August."[5]

"Concern about housing has not been forefront country's attention in recent weeks," the State Department in Washington was told in October 1945, "but this will be Government's biggest domestic headache before long."[6] It had been Wilson's biggest headache from the moment he joined the ministry. His main problem was that the Conservative government had promised that within a year of victory in Europe 200,000 temporary and 300,000 permanent new dwellings would be provided. In the electoral campaign Labour leaders had derided these targets as being shamefully inadequate for the nation's needs. Now Wilson realised that there was no hope of doing anything like as well. The main difficulties, he told a contact at the American Embassy, were "slowness of Government in preparing sites after approval, failure to make decisions about types of houses, failure to make firm contracts for housing and supplies, and labour shortage".[1] One way to alleviate the problem was to improve houses which existed already, many damaged during the war but still usable. Wilson was largely responsible for piloting through the Building Materials and Housing Bill, which increased the powers of the ministry and raised the level of advances which a local authority might make for the repair of houses.[2] Another was to streamline the procedure for building prefabricated houses. Wilson told the House of Commons in March 1946 that "the planning of the temporary housing programme was inadequate and amateurish in the extreme ... This so-called military evolution was almost totally unplanned."[3] For each house some 2,500 to 3,000 parts were needed, made in 165 different factories; to ensure that the right parts were in the right place at the right time was an undertaking that would have taxed the most adept administrator but the officials charged with it at the outset of the programme seem to have been paralysed by the immensity of their task. It was the sort of work at which Wilson excelled. New blood and expertise were imported from outside, obstructions ruthlessly removed, production speeded up and standardised. The problems did not vanish overnight, indeed they never vanished, but they were enormously reduced. Wilson was regarded by his civil servants – at least the younger and less hidebound of them – as something of a magician; and by his fellow politicians as a coming man.

He was notably less effective in the House of Commons. His maiden speech, on 9 October 1945, dealt with the amenities available to back-bench members in the Palace of Westminster. On this particular issue no minister has ever done right, and in 1945, with much war damage to be repaired, the situation was peculiarly horrible. Wilson began his speech from the front bench by saying that he was unsure whether "in making a maiden speech from what is, I think, an unusual part of the House, one is entitled to ask for its indulgence".[4] Entitled or not, he did not receive it. He was interrupted four times and left in no doubt that the back-bench members felt they were being asked to put up with intolerable conditions. He did not speak again until December and then only briefly. It was 1946 before George Tomlinson felt it fair to ask him to speak at length in debates on housing.

For ten years, Wilson himself said, he was "one of the dullest speakers in the House of Commons".[1] He was never to become an orator of the first flight. "Technically Mr Wilson is a terrible speaker," commented the political correspondent David Watt, "he gabbles his words half the time as if he himself were bored of them. He builds cliché on statistic on cliché in mountainous sandwiches of tedium; he has no gestures to speak of and very little variety of inflection."[2] Though he was to become brilliant in his handling of hecklers or any unscheduled interruption, he always found it necessary to prepare his speeches in meticulous detail; indeed, until he became Prime Minister and the pressures of time made change imperative, he was unhappy unless he had written out any important speech in his own hand. Without copious notes, at least, he would lose the thread of his argument and become wordy and repetitive.[3] But he did soon achieve a level of competence and by April 1946 was stirring satisfactory enthusiasm among his own backbenchers with a vigorous attack on the Conservative record in 1918, contrasting the way Labour were concentrating on the needs of the homeless poor with the indulgence which the Tories had shown at the end of the last war to the rich who wished to build themselves palatial houses.

Housing was a good job and he knew that he was lucky to have it, but he still rejoiced when in September 1946 Attlee detached him from the Ministry of Works to attend a conference of the Food and Agriculture Organisation (FAO) in Washington. John Boyd Orr, the British Director-General, had ambitious ideas for a world food board which would buy and hold stocks for distribution to the needier nations. He was anxious that his fellow countrymen should set a good example by sending as delegate a minister of ability who would be taken seriously by the other participants. Attlee was ready to oblige, but wanted a man who could be trusted not to become over-enthusiastic and commit his government to undertakings that might prove unacceptably expensive. Wilson was chosen, and Douglas Jay, Attlee's personal assistant, was charged with keeping his seat warm at the ministry until the conference was over.

Wilson spent three months in Washington, working twelve hours a day on problems of food and agriculture. It was, he said, "one of the most valuable training sessions in my life"[4] and gave him a lifelong concern for the problems of the under-developed world. For Boyd

Orr the conference ended in disappointment, since the Americans were not prepared to finance his grandiose schemes and no one else could afford to. Wilson had never thought they would; he too was disappointed but bore the blow with equanimity. He defended the government's position in the House of Commons early in 1947, to such good effect that the Tory spokesman, Richard Law, praised his exposition highly, calling it "lucid" and even "reasonably objective".[1] He had left behind a good impression in Washington. Lord Bruce, the former Prime Minister of Australia, who was one of Boyd Orr's strongest supporters, told Attlee that Wilson had been an "admirable leader" for the British team.[2]

Douglas Jay noted that when Wilson left for Washington he briefed his surrogate copiously on his views on architecture, building standards and so forth. When he got back, however, and Jay expected to be called on to give a full account of his stewardship, he found that Wilson seemed to have little interest in what had happened. Probably his mind was already on new horizons. He had been given reason to believe that a move might be in the offing. As early as May 1946 Tomlinson had told him that he was to be moved to serve under Shinwell at Fuel and Power and that Gaitskell was to take his place at Works. "I suspect," wrote Gaitskell, "that Shinwell objected to this and chose me because he did *not* want anyone who was supposed to know about mining to be his Parliamentary Secretary."[3] This seems unlikely: Shinwell had been eager to secure Wilson's services as parliamentary private secretary the year before and later said that he never even knew that the name had been suggested for a job at a higher level.[4] Whatever the reason, Wilson stayed where he was. A few months later Dalton proposed to Attlee that he should "be given a third minister at the Treasury, preferably Harold Wilson".[5] With characteristic indiscretion, Dalton let word of this proposal get back to the potential beneficiary. Once again Wilson was disappointed. But no one doubted that it was only a question of time. "The most promising of the younger Ministers are Hector McNeil, John Strachey, Geoffrey de Freitas, J. H. Wilson and Hugh Gaitskell," reported the American Embassy, though adding cautiously, "Except for McNeil, it is impossible to say yet which of the others have the capacity to develop into astute and wise political leaders to complement their ability."[6]

While awaiting the call, Wilson struggled with the problem of reconciling the duties of minister and constituency MP. Ormskirk was not the sort of constituency that even the best-established member could take for granted and Wilson, who had had no chance to get to know his voters before being pitchforked into office, felt particularly vulnerable. "I well understand the feeling in the Division about my not being able to be there more and I am sure you realise that this has been through no lack of effort on my part," he wrote to his local chairman. "To be quite honest, there have been several days when there has not even been time to eat and I am getting about half the amount of sleep one ought to have."[1] When he was elected he had promised to visit the constituency at least once a month and on any other occasion that there was an urgent need; on average he managed nearer three times every two months but the demands of his work in Whitehall meant that the gaps between visits were sometimes longer than his constituents thought proper. Nor did he always go down well when he did get there; he had not yet learned the knack of hobnobbing affably with people with whom he had little in common, and he battered party meetings, which would have been well content with some homely chat about local problems, with complicated statistics and his views on international politics. "Can't you talk down to people, so they can understand what you're talking about?" demanded his agent in something near despair.[2]

If it was difficult to combine the jobs of minister and constituency member, to be minister, member, husband and father must sometimes have seemed impossible. These were not easy years for his marriage. It is not necessary to accept the more lurid speculation about his problems to realise that a woman bringing up a small child, who sees little of her husband at the best of times and sometimes virtually nothing for several weeks, is likely to become unhappy and embittered. Mary was rarely bitter but she felt let down. Wilson had begun his parliamentary career spending the weekends with Mary and their child at Oxford and the weekdays with his parents, who had taken over the flat in Richmond. He hoped he could maintain the balance. "I am still continuing in some connection with Univ," he wrote in the late summer of 1945, "and I hope it may still be possible to continue with the supervision."[3] It was not possible, and the demands of Ormskirk and his ministerial duties meant that his weekends in Oxford became, if not infrequent, at least erratic. When he reappeared briefly in the middle of his stint in Washington, Mary's distress was obvious. He responded by taking her back to the United States with him, but it was not until the couple settled together into a house in London that the marriage was re-established on a sounder basis.

* * *

Though Wilson owed his original appointment to Clement Attlee and depended on the Prime Minister for any hope of promotion, his personal hero among the Labour leaders was Stafford Cripps. In many ways the two men were very different: Cripps was patrician, rigidly austere, with little sympathy for Wilson's homespun moralising, yet when Wilson assured a meeting of 800 Baptists that: "No one should be in a political Party unless he believes that Party represents his own highest moral and religious ideals,"[1] he was expressing himself in language that Cripps would have found congenial. One was high church, the other low, but both men believed that religion and politics were closely linked and that hard work and dedication to duty were the privilege rather than the burden of mankind. Talking about Cripps to Wilson a few years later, Attlee once remarked: "Stafford, political goose!"[2] Wilson would have accepted the justice of the comment, but he felt that Cripps was also a moral swan. He had no intention of being a goose himself but he could admire and respond to the swan in others. He recognised in Cripps a quality to which he aspired, even if he did not propose to emulate him in all his doings.

Cripps must have had a hand in his new appointment when it came, for in March 1947 Wilson was told that he was to join the team under Cripps's suzerainty as President of the Board of Trade: Shinwell at Fuel and Power, John Wilmot at Supply, George Isaacs at Labour, Alfred Barnes at Transport and Wilson himself as Secretary for Overseas Trade. It was not technically promotion, but it was an immeasurably more important job than he had previously done and brought him into the inner circle of governmental policy-making. His first task was to appoint a parliamentary private secretary and he chose the woman who had served Cripps in the same role, the young – though several years older than him – Barbara Castle. Mrs Castle was colourful, even flamboyant, with a sharp mind, endless persistence, and feminine charm which she used without scruple to achieve her ends. Her new minister's mind was as sharp and his persistence as endless but otherwise the contrast was complete: "I was a bit of a pudding at the time," Wilson would admit ruefully.[3] The two complemented each other admirably and, with occasional vicissitudes, made a team until the end of Wilson's political career.

On the day that Wilson took up his new office, Cripps in a broadcast declared that exports were "a matter of life and death" to the country; Britain would need to export £30 million more a month to pay its way.[1] It was a daunting preamble to what promised to be an uphill task. Nor did Wilson have time to ponder his problems at leisure. Almost at once he was involved in intensive negotiations at the General Agreement on Tariffs and Trade (GATT) conference in Geneva, paying five visits in July and August alone. So pressing were his various responsibilities that he only managed to get home to Oxford for two weekends out of the first fifteen in his job. Crossman judged that he was admirably suited for his new role: "In top-level negotiations ... he displays neither the intellectual arrogance of the public school socialist, nor the chip on the shoulder of the working-class politician without higher education."[2] He had stamina and patience; essential qualities for anyone involved in those interminable meetings where a readiness to miss lunch, dinner and the last train home might be factors quite as important in winning the day as logical skill or debating power.

His main task was to ensure that Britain imported its needs as cheaply as possible and maximised its exports. He believed that Russia offered a promising field under both these heads. In this he was strongly supported by Stafford Cripps but had greater problems with Ernest Bevin and the Foreign Office, who viewed the communist bloc with a suspicion which was as well justified as it was occasionally disadvantageous to the country's trading interests. His problems were compounded by American doubts about any overtures to the East. Dalton in his diary quotes Bevin as believing that Cripps was "intriguing to keep open a door towards cooperation with the Russians rather than the USA", while Sir William Stephenson was reporting from New York that "in the U.S. Cripps is regarded as a dangerous half-communist".[3] Wilson's encouragement of East–West trade led to a legend that he was "soft on" or even actively sympathetic towards communism. The label stuck, and seemed to become more prominent with every year. In fact he had little interest in the theories and no time for the practice of communism but he saw nothing in that to prevent the making of advantageous deals. He was as pragmatic about East–West trade as any other subject; if he had been offered the chance to promote the export of pitchforks to Hell he would certainly have wished to investigate the possibility and would probably have embraced it.

One issue which prompted dark surmises in intelligence services on both sides of the Atlantic was the export of advanced British jet engines to the USSR. The Nene and Derwent engines had come off the secret list in December 1945, but the RAF considered that political developments since that date made any exports east of the Iron Curtain undesirable if not potentially disastrous. Cripps was principally responsible for deciding that, nevertheless, the engines should be offered to the Russians: Wilson did little more than implement his instructions and present them as an extra bargaining counter when he judged the moment was right. It was Wilson, however, who was identified with the policy in the public mind. In the event little came of it – Bevin made sure the deal was aborted after only a handful of sample engines had been delivered – but the damage to Wilson's reputation lasted far longer.[1]

Wilson's main preoccupation, however, was the importation of cheap grain from Russia. Laborious discussions went on during a preliminary visit in April 1947 and then again for a longer period in June. His principal counterpart was the Deputy Premier and Minister of Foreign Trade, Anastas Mikoyan. The two men seem to have conceived not merely respect but even a certain affection for each other. They kept up the relationship when they had no immediate business to transact. In this case, however, they got nowhere, or rather got almost to the end, only to fall at the last fence. They had successfully reached what Wilson felt to be "a really magnificent Agreement",[2] whereby Britain would have secured more wheat at a lower price than had seemed likely or even possible, only to see the talks break down on the issue of Russian debts. Russia owed Britain substantial sums for power stations and other non-military goods supplied during the war. Mikoyan wanted the down-payment on the debts which was now due to be substantially reduced and credit extended. Wilson was authorised to go some way to meet him, but not far enough. The issue was significant but need not have been all-important. Left to himself Wilson would have settled for a lower figure, but Bevin was determined to make no concession in the face of growing Soviet aggressiveness. "When an Armenian is dealing with a Yorkshireman, what chance is there of an agreement?" Mikoyan had once asked.[3] The answer in this case was probably that they would do well enough if left to themselves but could manage no better than anyone else when confronted with the *force majeure* of international politics. Wilson was eager to show his colleagues that he could be as robust in defence of British interests as anyone might ask of him, referring proudly to "an extremely tough but for me a very enjoyable two hours clouting one another all over the room, in the course of which he [Mikoyan] was told a number of things designed to improve his educational development".[1] Such swaggering may give a poor impression of his diplomatic skills, but the minister in the British Embassy in Moscow, Frank Roberts, in a letter not meant to be seen outside the Foreign Office and thus not tailored to please Wilson, reported that the Secretary for Overseas Trade had "conducted the talks with great skill and firmness and proved himself fully a match for that redoubtable and much more experienced negotiator, Mikoyan".[2]

On landing after the return journey from Moscow, the pilot misjudged the touch-down point, pulled hard on the brake cable which then snapped, and ended up in a V-shaped ravine fifteen feet deep. The plane was a converted Wellington bomber – a fortunate chance since a less toughly constructed aircraft would have disintegrated. As it was, enough harm was done: there were no seat-belts or facilities for storing hand baggage and "luggage, seats and passengers were thrown in one big heap." The passengers were extricated by ladders in the light of torches; Wilson made himself unpopular by insisting that someone go back to rescue his briefcase, a demand that was put down to shock until he managed to convince his rescuers of the importance of the contents.[3] Wilson, black and blue and with cracked ribs, limped back to London. "The things some ministers will do to get publicity," was Cripps's comment.[4]

Considering the talks had ended in failure, Wilson was greeted as something of a hero. "Courage and strength of character must be added to his proved gift of a quick and brilliant mind," declared the Observer.[5] Attlee was equally impressed. In September 1947 he included Wilson's name in a list of candidates for early promotion which he sent Herbert Morrison. Wilson, he suggested, might take over the Board of Trade; Arthur Bottomley – then at the Dominions Office – could replace him in his present job. "Wilson is right for Board of Trade and Gaitskell for Fuel and Power," replied Morrison, "(I warmly support both) but they are the type needed for Overseas Trade. What about Jay?"[6] Attlee paid no attention and Bottomley it was. The Prime Minister realised that Wilson's appointment needed some justification when he recommended it to George VI: "Although he is the youngest member of the Government he has shown great ability in trade matters and has done exceptionally well at international conferences."[7] In fact Wilson's selection caused little surprise and still less disapproval: "What do Messrs Mayhew, Wilson and

Gaitskell know of the Trade Union struggle?" demanded the communist leader, Harry Pollitt, but only the most doctrinaire left-winger believed that a knowledge of the trade union struggle was a necessary prerequisite for success at the Board of Trade. On 2 October 1947, indicated in the minutes as "President of the Board of Trade (Designate)", Wilson attended his first Cabinet meeting. He made a modest intervention in a discussion of the Steel Distribution Scheme, urging that priority should be given to export orders, but otherwise seems to have remained discreetly silent.[1] At the age of thirty-one and seven months, the youngest President of the Board of Trade and one of the youngest Cabinet ministers ever to be appointed, even a man of Wilson's self-assurance must have felt that a little decent reticence would be in order.

V

President of the Board of Trade

1947–1951

"I shall see less of him than ever," Mary Wilson commented mournfully on her husband's latest appointment. "He works sixteen hours a day already. I saw him for two weekends only during the summer."[1] She was unduly gloomy. Wilson worked no less hard in his new role, but while the Secretary for Overseas Trade was often required to be overseas the President of the Board of Trade presided usually at home. Furthermore, with an income of £5,000 a year the Wilsons were able to afford a London home large enough for their purposes. With the help of a mortgage they bought for £5,100 No. 10 Southway, a pleasant if undistinguished house in Hampstead Garden Suburb. They stayed there till 1953, when they moved next door to No. 12, which had one more bedroom. No. 10 was eventually sold for £4,550 – some 10 per cent less than they had paid for it. The possession of a London house meant that nights apart were far less frequent, though ominously enough Wilson had an austere bedroom fitted up next to his office in the Board of Trade, with canvas folding bed, sheets and army blankets.[2]

Shortly after the move their second son was born. They called him Giles after his godfather, Giles Alington, Dean of University College, one of their closest friends. Alington appealed to a side of Wilson's character which he rarely allowed to be seen. He had "the largest of hearts and the largest of personalities," wrote another friend. "He was uproarious fun."[3] He was also a dedicated if sometimes eccentric Christian. His early death from cancer removed what would have been a splendidly robust and apolitical influence from Wilson's life. Attlee was another godfather. Wilson wrote to thank him for his congratulatory telegram. "You will be glad to know that she and the baby are both very fit. He for his part, although about the size and general appearance of a small trout, would, if he were capable of it, wish to be associated with me in writing to thank you for your message."[1] Robin, the small trout's elder brother, was soon going to day school. Another boy told him that his father was very important. "Is this true?" he asked his mother. "*All* fathers are important," answered Mary firmly. Wilson was a supportive if inevitably distant parent. He encouraged Robin to join the Wolf Cubs but did not reproach him when he retired from the Scouts after acquiring only a badge for stamp collecting; took him to *The Mikado* and *The Pirates of Penzance*; played somewhat amateurish chess with him and joined in such traditional – if capitalist – family games as Monopoly. He gave his son a Meccano set for his fifth birthday and inevitably spent all the time he could spare playing with it himself. Sunday evenings were as sacred as any time could be: the family ate cold meat and salad – Wilson always had a meat pie with HP Sauce – and listened to *Sunday Half Hour*. The children went with their mother to the Free Church in Hampstead; Wilson usually stayed at home and Robin was also encouraged to decide for himself about matters like church attendance. On their drives to school or on Sunday walks Wilson would talk about Robin's work and interests, but heart-to-heart dialogues about religion, the facts of life or, for that matter, politics were not at all their style.[2]

As if being a political widow were not bad enough, Mary faced a new threat when, late in 1948, Wilson played his first game of golf. His reasons were at first more therapeutic than sporting, but he soon developed a passion for the game. He took lessons and by the summer of 1949 felt competent to challenge his replacement at Overseas Trade to a match during the party conference at Blackpool. They did not finish the round – after fourteen holes Wilson had taken 112 strokes against Bottomley's 122 – but he could still claim a moral victory.[3] Golf remained an important part of his life for thirty years. Inevitably it was to some extent subordinated to the needs of work – matches with colleagues or foreign potentates tended to be punctuated by political exchanges – but he also played with old friends for nothing except the pleasure of the game. It provided both good exercise and badly needed relief from total concentration on the business of the day.

Hampstead at that time was home to a plethora of Labour's coming stars – the Gaitskells, Pakenhams, Gordon Walkers and Jays all lived within half a mile or so of Southway – but Wilson hardly mixed with them.[1] Partly this was because he was ten years younger than his neighbours, partly because he disliked socialising and casual conversation and felt ill at ease in the upper middle-class surroundings of his richer colleagues. Nor would he have been particularly welcome; he had the reputation of being a ponderous dry-as-dust whose idea of dinner-party chatter was to lecture whoever was next to him on the balance of trade. It was not just the Hampstead set who found him heavy going. At a New Year's Eve party, when he was holding forth about the statistics of nylon stocking importation, Eva Robens, wife of the Labour MP and future minister Alfred, burst out: "You come from north of the Trent, don't you? Surely you know how to behave! and then proceeded to fling her arms around him and kiss him passionately, to his very great embarrassment."[2] But he could at times show himself light-hearted, even when in alien surroundings. He was asked by Attlee to dinner to meet Princess Elizabeth and the Duke of Edinburgh. Gaitskell was also there. "While waiting we all became very frivolous," Gaitskell recorded. "We had been talking about capital punishment. Harold reminded us that it was still a capital offence to rape a Royal Princess!"[3]

Gaitskell was quick to congratulate Wilson on his promotion to the Cabinet. "I have no doubt at all in my mind that you will be a great success," he wrote. "It is a grand thing both for the Party and the country."[4] Other such messages flooded in: "I feel like someone who has been given proof of the efficacy of prayer," wrote Harold Laski.[5] Philip Noel-Baker struck a much-needed cautionary note: "Don't kill yourself. REST IS A PART OF WORK – that is a rule that should be put in the Bible of every Minister ... And by working too hard in the thirties you may damage your powers when you reach the fifties, and when it may be in your power to reorder the world as you desire."[6] A more dispassionate note was struck by outside observers. Reporting the changes to Washington the political officer at the American Embassy commented: "Infusion of new blood in Cabinet is confined to appointments of Woodburn* and Harold Wilson. It is not expected that they will play any very prominent role in Cabinet deliberations."[7]

As President of the Board of Trade, Wilson was not to inherit the full mantle of Stafford Cripps. Cripps was the chief beneficiary of the

---

* Arthur Woodburn. Secretary of State for Scotland, 1947–50.

reshuffle; he had been appointed Minister of Economic Affairs and as such would be in overall charge of a personally hand-picked team that would include Wilson, Gaitskell at Fuel and Power and George Strauss at Supply. "Cripps wants to run the whole thing ... He made this quite plain to us," noted Gaitskell in his diary.[1] But even if not completely independent, Wilson's responsibilities were still awesome. The Board of Trade was in charge of all industries which were not specifically allocated to other ministries – as coal, gas and electricity to Fuel and Power or iron and steel to Supply. It reigned over the vast and complex empire of controls, constructed piecemeal during the war and now affecting almost all public and private consumption. It looked after, or was intimately concerned with, insurance, prices, censuses. It boasted a permanent under-secretary, three second secretaries, nineteen under-secretaries and eighty-three assistant secretaries. Altogether it employed more than 14,000 civil servants and received more than a million letters a month. No department generated more paper, spawned more statistics, was governed by more intricate and detailed legislation. No department would have suited Wilson's talents better. Yet the perils were obvious. What was needed above all was a capacity to delegate, to ignore or take for granted detail, to see the wood in spite of the trees. Wilson loved details, and though he could appreciate the shape of a wood as well as any other minister, he found the individual trees almost unbearably enticing. Civil servants notoriously seize every chance to drown an over-zealous minister in paper. Wilson needed no encouragement.

As in his last post, his task was above all to build up British exports. He pursued this goal with a single-mindedness which alarmed some of his colleagues who believed that higher priority should be given to developing industries at home. Wilson had no doubt that his strategy was the right one. He supported it, explained Paul Foot, with language that was "unabashedly capitalistic and chauvinist", extolling the spirit of the "merchant venturer" and the successes of private enterprise under Labour.[2] The point was a fair one. Wilson always believed in a mixed economy and was notably more ready than many of his colleagues to accept the mixture more or less as it was and not to press too vigorously to increase the nationalised element. He was perfectly happy to work with private industry provided it played its part efficiently. State direction, he believed, was often necessary and even desirable but its justification was that it produced better results, not that it represented the working out of some abstract principle.

On the whole he was well satisfied with the way British industry was adapting itself to peacetime conditions and his presentation of the statistics, though characteristically optimistic, showed that there was a lot to be optimistic about. When in October 1947 there was pressure from Cripps and the Chancellor of the Exchequer, Hugh Dalton, to reduce imports, Wilson pleaded that the estimates of exports to the United States were unduly cautious while the timber import figures were too high.[1] He had infinite faith in the capacity of the USA to absorb British exports and urged Cripps to agree to the setting up of a special export target for North America.[2] As the monthly export figures continued to increase Wilson's "pronouncements to the Commons," wrote Kenneth Morgan, "became almost triumphant".[3] By early 1949 he could proudly tell the Cabinet that January's exports were £12 million higher than November's figure – itself a record – and in volume 60 per cent above the level recorded in 1938. Not surprisingly the Cabinet noted his statement "with approval".[4]

Another responsibility was to ensure that essential imports were bought from the cheapest source. By mid 1948 Wilson was able to tell the Cabinet that Britain had successfully switched a large part of its buying to producers in non-dollar countries. (Unfortunately other countries had done the same, with the result that prices had risen and Britain could no longer afford to import as much.)[5] This operation served a double purpose: it saved dollars but also, since many of the new suppliers were members of the Commonwealth, it strengthened the ties of that amorphous body. To Wilson this was an end in itself. He had nourished an affection for the Commonwealth ever since his visit to Australia as a boy; now he firmly believed that it could be developed into a great political and economic force for good. By 1949 45 per cent of all British imports came from the Commonwealth against 36 per cent before the war. Some part of this change reflected the efforts and predilections of Harold Wilson.

One of Wilson's attractions to Attlee was said to have been that he belonged to no group and owed no obvious allegiance to any factional leader. In Cabinet he usually sat between A. V. Alexander and Chuter Ede, but had little in common with these unglamorous and slightly superannuated figures. In so far as he was the protégé of anyone it was of Stafford Cripps, but Cripps was a diminishing force, his intellect as sharp as ever, his spirit indomitable, but his body visibly weakening. With Herbert Morrison Wilson never felt any close rapport. Dalton had been initially a champion, but he had become suspicious of his young colleague's readiness to make concessions to the Russians and had grown less enthusiastic with the years. Dalton's favoured candidate for rapid promotion was, anyway, Hugh Gaitskell. Bevin, too, had initially supported Wilson but had become doubtful of his judgment and feared that he might have improperly left-wing sympathies. He showed signs of becoming a crony of Aneurin Bevan; and nothing, in Bevin's view, could be much worse than that. It was indeed almost inevitable that, with the older generation of Labour leaders visibly spluttering out, Wilson should be drawn towards that brilliant, turbulent, generous-hearted Welshman, the Charles James Fox of Ebbw Vale. Bevan was deservedly Wilson's hero for the skill, energy and unflagging zeal with which he had pushed through the creation of the National Health Service; more unexpectedly Wilson was fascinated by the rich rhetoric, the temper, the bombast, which made Bevan one of the most formidable and yet uncontrollable parliamentarians of his age. It was the appeal of the opposite. Wilson knew he was no Bevan, nor did he wish to be, but a part of him hankered for the recklessness and flamboyance that he himself eschewed.

Dalton's resignation after a budget leakage in November 1947 strengthened Wilson's position: a champion of Gaitskell had departed, at least temporarily, while Cripps's move to the Treasury meant that the President of the Board of Trade was left much more to his own devices. "I have rarely been so upset by any event during my parliamentary life," wrote Wilson in his memoirs.[1] No doubt it had been a shock at the time, but it would have been surprising if he had not found some consolation in his new independence. A month later he was leading a delegation to Russia to follow up the two visits he had already paid while at Overseas Trade. Promotion in no way dimmed his enthusiasm for trade agreements with the Soviet bloc: "The healthy development of trade between Eastern and Western Europe is an essential part of the programme for European recovery," he told the Fabians. "Politics do not enter into it."[2] Ernest Bevin did not accept this last point at least. In Cabinet he hoped that "no undue publicity would be given to any new trade agreement with Russia. It was embarrassing for him that the Press should give so much more prominence to our trade with Russia and her satellites than they gave to our trading arrangements with friendlier countries."[3] Even with Dalton departed, a strong group in the Cabinet looked with little favour on Wilson's activities in Moscow in December 1947. Ministers knew, however, that Britain was desperately short of grain and that there would have to be mass slaughter of cattle if supplies were not quickly made available. Russia was equally short of manufactured goods, so the bargaining was far from onesided and the energetic haggling over prices ended with a deal which both sides could represent, with some conviction, as a victory. Wilson's difficulties with his own party were eased by the ferocity with which the agreement was assailed by the Tories. Wilson had returned with "a balalaika and a bad bargain", sneered Oliver Lyttelton; he had surrendered on every contentious point.[1] Any doubts the Labour leaders might have had were stifled. They had anyway no legitimate grounds for complaint. Wilson could claim with justice that he had secured the grain for a price markedly lower than the Australians had almost simultaneously received for grain of a similar quality – a circumstance which satisfied his wish to give the Commonwealth preference as well as his determination to secure a good bargain.

This brush with the Tories was the preamble to a far more cantankerous clash a few months later. In July 1948, speaking in Birmingham, Wilson declared that, when he went to school, "more than half the children in my class never had any boots or shoes to their feet". He claimed that he went on to say that, instead, they wore clogs – rough wooden shoes – which were cheaper and longer lasting than their leather counterparts. Either he omitted the qualifying phrase or it was ignored by the press; whoever was to blame, Wilson found himself saddled with the assertion that half the children in his class had gone to school barefoot. The Mayor of Huddersfield was quoted as saying that Wilson was a liar, and then denied ever having uttered or even harboured such a view. Wilson's attempts to explain what he had meant were confused still more by doubts as to whether he had spoken of the period "before the war" or "during the war". From all over the north of England veterans recounted horror stories of their bare and bleeding feet or, if they happened to support the opposition, described the rows of smart leather shoes which could have been seen in every schoolroom. Wilson's personal archive contains a folder – the "Bootless File" – bulging with letters from people who had been to school without shoes, or seen others doing so, or heard of others doing so. It was one of those futile but – for the public and press at least – enjoyable altercations which fill the newspapers but contribute nothing to any serious debate. It worried Wilson at the time – more seriously than it should have done – but did him little harm. The public were left with the impression that he was not above bolstering his arguments with detail that was more picturesque than accurate, but since they took it for granted that this was to be expected of politicians, it made not much difference to his reputation.[1]

The Monopolies Act of 1948 was one of the more important pieces of legislation for which the Board of Trade was responsible. It was a cautious measure; in general extolling the merits of competition though admitting that the overriding demands of the export drive might sometimes make a measure of monopoly essential. It could as well have been drafted by a liberal-minded Tory. "Its sponsor's predilection for efficiency, investment and technology," wrote Paul Foot, "took preference over the promise in Labour's manifesto of 'public supervision over monopolies and cartels'."[2] Herbert Morrison was equally disappointed. He found Wilson "moderate in his views – at times too moderate for my liking. His Anti-Monopolies Act was something of a compromise and therefore not too effective."[3] Wilson would have retorted that only a compromise could hope to be effective. His approach to the problem was as always pragmatic; not, were monopolies in principle right or wrong? but, in each case what would produce the best result? Some two years later Dalton complained that Wilson was "*very* weak and disappointing" on retail price maintenance. Gaitskell agreed, saying that Wilson was "weak, ambitious and over-worked". If Wilson was ambitious, asked Dalton, "why doesn't he try to hit a headline against monopoly?"[4] Wilson was never loath to hit a headline, and if in opposition would probably have denounced with vehemence the legislation he had put through when in office; but he had a job to do and his intention was to do it efficiently without devoting too much time to considerations of principle.

Wilson had the good fortune to preside over the Board of Trade at a time when economic conditions were improving and the supply of goods returning to something nearer normality. His two and a half years in office were marked by the steady increase in food and other rations and the liberalisation of controls (this last phrase, incidentally, caused the Cabinet some problems – in June 1949 it was agreed "some alternative words should be substituted for 'liberalisation' and 'liberalising' in future papers").[5] The opposition, of course, greeted each new concession as inadequate and belated, but the fact remained that Wilson was associated in the public mind with an improvement in material comforts and a loosening of the bureaucratic grip. This suited him admirably. He recognised that some controls would be necessary, perhaps for ever, certainly so long as the need to divert resources into the export industries remained so urgent. But it was the maintenance of the control that had to be justified rather than its abolition and Wilson was, in the eyes of his left wing, exaggeratedly sensitive to the likely reactions of the consumer. When Dior's "New Look" led to demands for longer skirts and thus the use of more material, Wilson ruled firmly that it was not the role of the Board of Trade to interfere in matters of high fashion. The customer must decide.[1]

In May 1948 children's shoes were taken off the ration, in July all shoes and certain furnishing materials followed. October provided a setback, when the Board of Trade felt compelled severely to restrict the supply of nylon stockings for the home market but in November came the celebrated "bonfire of controls", in which more than 200,000 permits and licences a year were made unnecessary. Morrison accused Wilson of deriving "inordinate pleasure" from this exercise[2] while his left-wing critics complained that he was scrapping the armoury of state direction without any glimmer of a national plan to put in its place. The propriety of intervention by the government in the course of industry and commerce is an issue which will never be resolved. Fashion will change and change again and the demarcation line between over-officious meddling and irresponsible indifference change with it. What seems demonstrably true, however, is that by the end of 1948 a great number of wartime controls had lost their usefulness and were obstructing rather than promoting the growth of Britain's manufacturing industry. Certainly the move was popular. To win a few extra headlines Wilson fixed the operation for 5 November – Guy Fawkes' Day. By the time he went back to Hampstead to eat treacle toffee and home-made parkin (a peculiarly indigestible form of gingerbread) by his own family bonfire, he knew that he had achieved a considerable public relations success.

In March 1949 came the end of clothes rationing. "I found out the black market price of coupons," Wilson recollected; "when they dropped from half a crown to three pence in the East End, I knew I was safe. I didn't even take it to Cabinet. I should have done."[3] Price control for clothing was retained and in September the price of all utility clothes, footwear and textiles was arbitrarily cut by 5 per cent, the cost to be borne by the retailer. The trade was not surprisingly aggrieved at this new impost, but they were to some extent appeased by the abolition of a fresh batch of controls. Big business did not love Wilson – it rarely loves any minister, let alone a Labour one – but he was considered, on the whole, to be reasonable, approachable, and certainly no dangerous radical. "He is quick on the uptake," wrote the chairman of the Cotton Board approvingly shortly after Wilson's appointment, "too well versed in economical and civil service work to rant or rave like a soap-box journalist ... Wilson feels no duty to his party to take a political line ... He is less aloof than the men of austere principles, fanaticism and Christian ideals with whom we had dealt since 1945."[1] Hostile confrontations between the President of the Board of Trade and business leaders were sufficiently unusual to be noteworthy. One came when he addressed the annual dinner of the Institution of Production Engineers. When the heckling became intolerable he snapped angrily: "It seems that whatever else is short in this country, the supply of wine is not restricted."[2]

His first years at the Board of Trade were intensely active. He travelled constantly, visiting industries in every part of the country. Undeterred by the occasional show of bad temper, he attended innumerable business lunches, dinners and conferences. Apart from his negotiations in Russia he led long trade tours abroad, notably a twenty-day visit to Canada. He was responsible for a string of bills: as well as the Monopoly Bill, he took through the House of Commons the Export Guarantees Bill, the Distribution of Industry Bill, the Development of Industry Bill and – with particular personal commitment – the Cinematograph Film Production Bill. All were dutifully assailed by the opposition, though it was not until the nationalisation of iron and steel came on to the agenda in 1949 that Wilson found himself involved in any really acrimonious and sustained debating.

There were agreeable interludes of triviality. Shortly after Wilson became president, Arthur Goodhart, Professor of Jurisprudence at Oxford, lobbied him about the importation of two sea lions from the United States for the Dudley Zoo. Wilson hoped that some donor would be found to put up the necessary dollars, "sea lions, in spite of their cultural and aesthetic value, having a very low priority in this connection". Goodhart assured him that this could be arranged but that help over the transportation was needed if the workers of Dudley were to be given "that fuller life which is at present denied them". As an extra inducement one of the sea lions ("I have insisted on two sea lionesses in order that I may not be faced with this problem on a subsequent occasion") was to be called Harold. Wilson succumbed, only to find that the sea lions were to cross the Atlantic on the same boat as himself. He believed, or professed to believe, that it was intended the beasts should travel under his protection. Goodhart was able to relieve his fears: "I would have found some embarrassment in having them share your cabin, however docile and companionable they might be personally," he wrote.[1]

The Cinematograph Film Production Bill of 1948 was of interest as demonstrating both the limits of Wilson's enthusiasm for public ownership and his zealous interest in this particular industry. The making of films, though not insignificant, was hardly central to Britain's economic survival. Wilson, however, found the glamour and the effervescence of the industry irresistible. He devoted to it a wholly disproportionate amount of his energies and remained concerned by it throughout his life. The background, familiar both before and afterwards, was one of crisis among British producers. The inflow of American films caused an undesirable expenditure in dollars and stifled any attempt to develop the local product. Shortly before Wilson took over at the Board of Trade Cripps sought to rectify the situation by clapping a 75 per cent duty on imported films. This in effect shut them out altogether; a result which, since the Rank Organisation, the only British producer of any size, was quite unable to make up the shortfall, threatened dismal consequences for British cinemas and the public. Something had to be done, and in March 1948 Wilson concluded a deal with Eric Johnston, President of the Motion Pictures of America, whereby the 75 per cent tax would not be taken by the Inland Revenue but left available to be spent on the production of films in Britain. Almost simultaneously, to the indignation of the Americans, who felt with some reason that they had been double-crossed, he increased from 20 per cent to 45 per cent the proportion of films shown in British cinemas which had to originate in local studios. The outrage of the Americans, combined with the patent inability of the national industry to increase its production so as to make up the shortfall, quickly convinced Wilson that he must modify his policy. In 1949 the quota was reduced to 35 per cent – a target which Rank and its few rivals still found it hard to hit. The net result of these manoeuvres was disastrous for the industry they were supposed to succour. While the import tax and the high British quota had limited American competition, Rank had hurriedly produced a variety of second- or, more often, third-rate films. These now had to compete with the best of the American films which had been stockpiled while the British market was inaccessible. By the end of 1948 the Rank Organisation was in a mess.[1]

The Cinematograph Film Production Bill was an attempt to tackle this problem at the root and build up a healthy national film industry. Referring in 1976 to the Report of the Official Group on the Film Industry, which contained several cautious references to the risks involved in governmental investment, Wilson wrote wearily that he had read it all three times before: "The first was in the 1940s when an almost identical document proved that the National Film Finance Corporation [NFFC] project could not possibly work. In fact it saved the film industry for a period of nearly thirty years at very little cost to the taxpayer – far less than had been estimated."[2] He was rating his achievement rather higher than it deserved. The NFFC was endowed with a capital of £5 million to subsidise independent producers. Alexander Korda and British Lion were the principal beneficiaries. They achieved some notable successes. Korda, who had a misplaced enthusiasm for extravagant epics, outlined to Wilson his current masterpiece, *Bonnie Prince Charlie*. Wilson groaned and said that it would lose money. When told that the next film was to be set largely in the sewers of Vienna, he groaned again and predicted renewed disaster.[3] Though the *Bonnie Prince* sank on the way to Skye, *The Third Man* became and has remained one of the most profitable of British films. But the industry did not take off as Wilson had hoped. To the Cabinet, when in March 1949 he announced his intention to reduce the quota of home-made films that had to be shown in British cinemas (at that time only to 40 per cent rather than the eventual 35 per cent), he complained that the manufacturers had failed to take advantage of their opportunities. His aim, he said, was to build up a healthy industry, not to reduce unemployment. "The industry was overstaffed at present and undesirable restrictive practices were supported both by employers and workers."[4] Ten or twenty years later much the same accusation might have been made and with equal justice: "If he had been a real socialist," wrote Nicholas Davenport, "he would, of course, have nationalised or municipalised the two great cinema circuits."[5] One can accept Davenport's view of Wilson's socialism without agreeing that such a drastic measure would necessarily have proved the salvation of the British film industry. What was certain, however, was that the gingerly administration of first aid, which was Wilson's policy, though a useful palliative, was not going to provide a lasting cure.

*   *   *

71

Towards the end of 1948 an unpleasant scandal afflicted the Board of Trade. The culprit was John Belcher, a junior minister, who, it was alleged, had received bribes in exchange for granting import licences and other favours to private businessmen. Wilson first heard the rumours in August 1948, in connection with an allocation of paper to Sherman Football Pools. He had been concerned about Belcher's heavy drinking, but otherwise liked and trusted him. Still, he felt bound to send for him and quickly realised that, though there might not be much fire beneath the smoke, there was enough substance in the allegations to make investigation necessary. He reported the matter to Attlee, who in turn referred it to the Lord Chancellor. A tribunal was set up under Mr Justice Lynskey and, on 15 October, Wilson told the Prime Minister that Belcher had agreed to go on indefinite leave.

The work of the tribunal was enlivened by the evidence of a flamboyant rogue called Sydney (or sometimes Sidney) Stanley, "The Spider of Park Lane" as Hartley Shawcross somewhat melodramatically described him, who had claimed to Sherman Pools that for £5,000 he could ensure that their prosecution for exceeding the paper ration was abandoned and had distributed lavish gifts and hospitality to anyone he felt might be of use to him. Belcher had been the recipient of a holiday in Margate, a gold watch and a suit; favours which he had in no way repaid but which had so obviously been offered with a view to corruption that the minister's naïvety and folly almost pass belief. Stanley busily dropped hints that if he chose to name names he could bring down the government; Bevan and Dalton were among those whom the allegedly well-informed whispered were likely to be incriminated. "It was further stated that three Cabinet Ministers are involved and also some Americans," reported an alarmed American Embassy. "If true, the scandal is expected to break in about ten days."[1]

It was not true, no scandal broke, no corruption was discovered, the tribunal in due course found Belcher guilty of extreme indiscretion and he duly resigned. Even Stanley never seems to have tried to pretend that Wilson had been drawn into his web and on the whole the president emerged with his reputation enhanced by the firmness and speed with which he had acted. Churchill grumbled that the head of a department ought "to know pretty well how his immediate Parliamentary subordinates are carrying on". How could either he or Cripps have known, protested Wilson to Attlee, unless they had started from the hypothesis that Belcher was untrustworthy and had had him spied on? The only industry with which he had known Belcher to have any connection was that of cosmetics; he had watched the minister's decisions in this field with particular care but in so far as any bias was evident they had seemed generally to be contrary to the interests of the manufacturers.[1]

Wilson was genuinely distressed by the fate of his subordinate, and in 1960 interceded with the Inland Revenue to prevent them prosecuting Belcher over delays in settling arrears of tax. He was successful, and an arrangement was worked out which allowed Belcher to pay off the arrears over several years.[2] By intervening in this way Wilson risked being accused of misusing his influence so as to help a former colleague. There was no possible benefit to him in the operation. Yet it was not uncharacteristic, and no one who knew him well would have been surprised. In June 1963 Belcher wrote to thank him for a kindly reference Wilson had made to him in a debate in the House of Commons. "The treatment you suffered years ago has always given me very great concern," replied Wilson, "and it is not the first occasion I have spoken as I did."[3]

Tradition has it that Wilson, during his visit to Canada in the spring of 1949, became convinced that British prices were too high and that devaluation was essential.[4] The evidence suggests that he was by no means so sure. That something needed to be done was increasingly evident. After the payments surplus of 1948 the balance had moved dramatically against Britain. The abolition of controls had fanned demand for imports; recession in the United States had taken its toll of exports. But was devaluation the best, or an acceptable solution? The issue was far from clear-cut. To an extent which it is hard to realise today, the pound sterling was a symbol of national virility. To devalue would represent humiliating defeat. Sterling was also an international currency; arbitrarily to reduce its value would throw world trade into disorder and grievously harm the numerous countries, notably in the Commonwealth, which kept a substantial part of their reserves in sterling. Finally, though this was not so much argued at the time, there was no certainty that devaluation would achieve the results intended. By making it easier to sell exports it might merely perpetuate the antiquated work patterns, inadequate investment in new equipment and self-indulgent staffing which had become endemic in British industries in those halcyon years after the war when there was little or no effective competition. Wilson was right to hesitate. But there is a fine yet distinct line between justified hesitation and nervous dithering. At the crucial moment, Wilson dithered.

The champions of devaluation were Hugh Gaitskell, Minister of Fuel and Power, and Douglas Jay, the Economic Secretary to the Treasury. Its most implacable opponent was Stafford Cripps, who felt himself in honour bound to retain the parity of sterling and pinned his hopes on fierce austerity at home. Cripps far outgunned his junior adversaries, but he was a sick man and on 19 July was forced to leave for medical treatment in Zurich. Management of the economy was put into commission, with Wilson, Gaitskell and Jay in effective day-to-day control. On 21 July the three men met. Without a transcript of their meeting it is impossible to know what was decided, and with how much clarity, but both Gaitskell and Jay left in the belief that Wilson had "agreed to support our view and to recommend it to Attlee and Morrison".[1] The question of timing was the only point of difference. Jay was for immediate devaluation, Wilson "favoured devaluation *fairly* soon but not before the Washington talks" (the meeting of the International Monetary Fund – IMF – in September), Gaitskell was uncertain.[2] When the three men met again this point was apparently resolved; Jay says that Wilson "took refuge in ambiguity" but Gaitskell was clear that he "had appeared to accept" the earlier date.[3] Yet he was still evidently in some doubt. At the end of July Dalton recorded: "Gaitskell and Jay both explain distrust of Wilson. They don't know what he's up to. They think he's currying favour with Bridges and Treasury officials."[4]

When Gaitskell and Wilson were summoned to Chequers on 19 August they were confronted by Attlee, Bevin and Cripps, who had returned briefly from his sick-bed. Cripps, said Gaitskell, was "quite out of touch"; Attlee "did not intervene at all but sat at his desk doodling"; Gaitskell argued forcefully for early devaluation; Wilson, to Gaitskell's dismay, pleaded for delay.[5] What had led to his change of heart, if change of heart it was, is hard to decide. It can hardly have been a wish to curry favour with Bridges, as Gaitskell supposed, since Bridges himself was in favour of devaluation, though he would probably have agreed that the susceptibilities of Britain's allies made it worth waiting until after the Washington conference. What is certain is that Jay and Gaitskell felt let down if not betrayed. It seems likely that they had some justification for their feelings. By the end of the month Wilson had lost the day, and accepted the decision with reasonably good grace, volunteering to visit Ernest Bevin and Cripps, who had returned to Zurich, so as to explain to these two ailing patriarchs what the Cabinet had decided. His recantation did nothing to appease his critics. "He turns and wavers and is thinking more of what senior ministers – and even senior officials – are thinking of him than of what is right," wrote Dalton in his diary. "Jay wonders what he said to Cripps and Bevin when he took messages to them on the Continent."[1]

In fact he seems to have said nothing to which his colleagues could have taken exception, and when devaluation was debated he defended the government's action vigorously, giving, said Michael Foot, "the first hint the Commons had seen that he might wish to abandon his civil service brief and engage in the wider political argument".[2] But he now compounded his iniquities in the eyes of Gaitskell and Jay by seeming to take the credit for something which he had, at the best, unenthusiastically accepted. By November 1949, says Jay, when it was becoming evident that, in the short term at least, the operation had been a success, stories began to appear in the press suggesting that Wilson had advocated devaluation, Gaitskell had opposed it, and Wilson had won the day by enlisting Cripps's support when he visited him in Zurich. "Cripps's press officer investigated the source and found it was the Board of Trade."[3]

Wilson was certainly not above briefing the press to ensure that favourable stories about himself appeared. Whether he did so on this occasion will probably never be fully established. If he had thought he could get away with it he might well have done so, but on the whole it seems unlikely that he would have taken the risk of propagating a version of events which so many people knew to be at variance with the facts. However innocent he might have been, however, the fact remains that his handling of the devaluation crisis had put Gaitskell and Jay in a frame of mind where they were ready to place the worst possible interpretation on his motives. Neither man had had much against Wilson before, and they had considered him on the whole to be a strong and dependable ally. Now, says Jay, "they never fully trusted him again."[4] The civil servant mandarins too were unimpressed: "H. Wilson is no good, ought if possible to be shifted from the Board of Trade and certainly ought not to succeed SC," was the opinion recorded by Robert Hall after a discussion with Oliver

Franks, Roger Makins and Edwin Plowden.[1] Worse still, Dalton –
who was still a major force in Labour politics – had been left with
grave doubts about Wilson's suitability for the highest offices. Morrison too, or so Jay claimed at any rate, "used some unsympathetic
expressions about Wilson".[2] Most serious of all, Attlee had been
favourably impressed by Gaitskell's handling of the devaluation crisis
and contrasted it with what he saw as Wilson's shilly-shallying. His
reaction was to cost Wilson dear when the time came to reshape the
Cabinet.

One of the more disagreeable features of the Belcher affair had been
the wave of anti-semitism inspired by the extravagant Jewishness of
Sydney Stanley. Wilson was abnormally free of racial prejudice except
in so far as it was a racial prejudice to find Jews generally more
attractive than the rest of mankind. In 1951 he was to be involved in
the selection of Arthur Goodhart as Master of University College.
Possible objections were said to be that Goodhart was Jewish, American and a Cambridge man. "We found the first interesting," Wilson
later told Goodhart, "the second amusing, but the third objection
gave us a lot of trouble."[3] There is no saying whether his affection
for Jews or his support for Zionism came first, certainly the latter
was a potent force in his life from a very early date. He never forgave
Bevin for adopting an anti-Zionist foreign policy, and though he
usually took care to keep his feelings to himself, the Foreign Secretary
must have known that he was a strong critic of his views, something
which may have contributed to the estrangement between the two
men. Many years later Wilson praised Bevin to the skies in a speech,
then murmured to his companion as they left the platform: "The only
good thing I ever heard about Bevin was when they told me he was
dead!"[4]
    Stalin's persecution of the Jews was an extra factor in Wilson's
dislike of communism, which his advocacy of increased East–West
trade and his frequent visits to Russia did little to weaken. He saw
communism as a constant and potent threat. In the spring of 1948,
he told Martin Gilbert many years later, he had made a critically
important contribution to the defence of the West. The Foreign Office
had put forward figures which appeared to prove that Berlin could
not be supplied by air for more than a few days. Wilson announced
in Cabinet that he was convinced the figures were wrong. Attlee

questioned him, and Wilson, after making some rapid calculations, was able to satisfy the Cabinet that he was right. The Foreign Office was overruled and the Berlin airlift became a reality.[1] The incident sounds a little too colourful to be entirely true, certainly no trace of it survives in the Cabinet minutes of the time. Wilson, however, did believe that communist pressure must be resisted. In June 1949, in a curious preview of what was to be one of his more controversial pronouncements as Prime Minister, he denounced the role played by the communists in a dockers' strike in Liverpool. They were, he told George Isaacs, the Minister of Labour, offering "large sums of money to the Liverpool strike committee to continue the stoppage".[2] But though he deplored the activities of the communists, he recognised that they could not thrive unless the circumstances were right. The strikers had genuine grievances; the surest way to confound the communists would be to put the matter right.

In spite of his patent moderation, however, he was beginning to acquire in certain circles the reputation of being a hardline supporter of the left, or at least a particularly ferocious hater of the Tories. His House of Commons manner, though still staid and sometimes maladroit, was becoming notably more belligerent. In March 1951 he enraged the opposition and upset his own front bench by suspending negotiations with a group of trade associations, who were seeking increases of prices, on the somewhat specious grounds that the harrying tactics adopted by the Conservative Party in the House made the transaction of ordinary business impossible. Unfortunately for him his gambit, injudicious at the best of times, cut across the negotiations which the Home Secretary, Chuter Ede, was conducting privately with the opposition. Wilson was forced to beat a humiliating retreat, leaving the Tories with the conviction that he was their most malevolent enemy, his own front bench with doubts about his judgment, and Wilson himself with a marked sense of grievance.

The reality, yet also the limitations of his radicalism, were well demonstrated in a paper which he and his deputy, Christopher Mayhew, prepared for a group of senior ministers in 1950.[3] Wilson had been on a visit to Washington and had returned preoccupied by the recession that had recently afflicted the American economy. In his covering note to Attlee he stressed that his paper contained only political ideas prepared without the help of officials (though in fact the contribution of civil servants from the Board of Trade must have been considerable).[4] His concern was the relationship between the state and private industry, a partnership which he took for granted would continue for the foreseeable future even though some further limited nationalisation might take place (ICI was among the few businesses he recommended for inclusion in the public sector). He was as critical of reactionary trade unions as of inefficient or selfish management and urged potent intervention by the state as a third party in all serious negotiations. Among the devices he recommended were development councils for different sectors of private industry (though shorn of most of the powers with which the left wing had wished to vest them), consumer consultative councils to regulate the state industries, a consumers' charter, a war on monopolies and restrictive practices, and government-appointed directors on the boards of public companies. All these assumed a more actively inter-ventionist attitude on the part of the state – though characteristically an attitude concerned more with the nuts and bolts of making things work better than with any theoretical debate about the rights and wrongs of central control or nationalisation.

To the far left these proposals fell short of the cherished objective, whereby the commanding heights of the economy would be wholly taken out of private hands. To Jay and Gaitskell, on the other hand, the paper seemed dangerously extreme, a reversion to the worst kind of primitive collectivism from which they were seeking to rescue the Labour Party. On the whole it was the right which took greater alarm; their hostility to Wilson's ideas was one of the main factors which steered him towards the Bevanite wing in Cabinet and prepared the way for his eventual resignation. In the light of their criticism he prepared a watered-down version of his ideas, which kept his recommendation to take the chemical industry into public ownership but placed more emphasis on the value of the mixed economy. The document was pol-itely forwarded to Transport House for use in drawing up a future manifesto, but Wilson was not left with the impression that his ideas would find much favour among the party *apparatchiks*. By the time that he quit office his ideas had been further diluted. His cherished development councils had already run into trouble. To industry they represented a threat to the right of management to handle its own affairs and the thin end of the wedge of state control. To some of his own colleagues they seemed to presage a nightmare world where unions and management might present a united front to force the government into unwise policies.

*   *   *

While fighting his ministerial battles Wilson had constantly to keep a nervous eye on his constituency. At the best Ormskirk would never have been more than marginal; with the revision of boundaries which was due to come into force before the 1950 election it gained a large, affluent and probably Conservative district and lost two industrial areas to the neighbouring constituency of Huyton. To stand and fight on this unpromising terrain would have been quixotic. By good chance the sitting member for Huyton, Christopher Shawcross, decided not to contest the next election. A deal was quickly done and on 27 November 1948 Wilson told his Ormskirk Labour committee that he would be deserting them – pleading the difficulties of combining his work as minister with the demands of a geographically huge constituency. The excuse was as good as any other; the wisdom of his decision was shown in 1950 when the Conservatives won Ormskirk with a majority of over 14,000.

Not that Huyton was in any way a sure thing. It was a town of phenomenally rapid growth; a mere 5,000 in 1931 had swollen to 34,000 by the beginning of the war and doubled again by 1964. The birth-rate, Anthony Howard pronounced in 1965, was "said to be the highest outside Red China, and the crime rate is one of the highest in Britain".[1] No doubt coincidentally, so far as the second feature was concerned at least, it had the highest proportion of Roman Catholic voters of any constituency in the British Isles, an element which Wilson was to woo assiduously but had had little opportunity to get to know by the time the election came early in 1950. It would have been an easy seat to win in 1945; by 1950, with what seemed certain to be a substantial overall swing against Labour, it looked hazardous. Attlee had almost gone to the country the year before, but his natural caution led him to prefer postponement. According to Gaitskell "only three Ministers – Cripps, Bevan and Harold Wilson – spoke in favour of the early election."[2] Dalton describes Wilson as being only "half against" postponement.[3] Half-hearted or not, he always subsequently maintained that Attlee missed his chance.

Certainly the result when the election did come was catastrophic from Labour's point of view. Their immense majority of 186 was reduced to a mere six. As a minister Wilson had to speak for the party all over the country and was not able to give Huyton the attention it deserved. It was a rough campaign and the Tories took pleasure in attacking both Wilson's supposed softness on communism and the contrast between his promises and his performance: "The

Walter Mitty of the Socialist party", the leader of the local Conservative Party described him;[1] a reference to James Thurber's fantasising self-glorifier with whom Wilson was in the future often to be compared. Wilson did his best to combat the Tory propaganda by himself stoutly denouncing communism whenever an opportunity arose, but the accusation still did him harm. The Roman Catholics swung violently against him in the last three days, he told Dalton[2] – though the supposed readiness of the Tories to support Catholic schools was probably a more important factor than any doubts about Wilson's soundness on communism. The result was that he scraped home by a mere 834 votes. It was not a disaster, but it was near enough to being so to convince Wilson that he must never again take his own constituency for granted.

The election made no difference to Wilson's duties; he remained at the Board of Trade. There were not many other changes among the leadership but one appointment was particularly significant: Gaitskell was made Minister of State for Economic Affairs with a place on the Economic Policy Committee of the Cabinet. Dalton had persuaded Attlee that the ailing Cripps was in need of support and, furthermore, "we agreed that Gaitskell was better for this than Wilson (though he was doing very well), or Jay, who though very able, had not always good judgment, and wasn't very personable."[3] Hitherto Wilson's political career had been one of almost unbroken triumph. He had been the first of his generation to be promoted to the Cabinet, had been a conspicuous success at the Board of Trade, and was privately convinced that succession to the chancellorship was his by right. Only the devaluation crisis had marred his reputation, and that merely in a little inner circle of the elite. Gaitskell's appointment, not over his head but to a position strategically of great importance, came as a sharp disappointment to him. He still believed the succession to Stafford Cripps would be his, but for the first time since he had entered politics he felt insecure. He would have been disconcerted however, even outraged, if he had read the American Embassy's prophecies about the future of the Labour Party. Gaitskell was signalled out as a possible Chancellor: "He is competent professional economist and Attlee has highest regard his ability." Hartley Shawcross, James Griffiths, Hector McNeil and even the civil servant, Oliver Franks, were picked out as likely contenders for top office. There was no mention of Harold Wilson.[4]

In October 1950 the blow fell: Cripps finally succumbed to ill-health and resigned as Chancellor. Even before Dalton had had a chance to put in a word for his protégé, Attlee had appointed Gaitskell as his successor. "There is no doubt in the minds of any of us that you were the right man for the job," wrote Wilson. "You know you can rely on me."[1] In fact there was great doubt in Wilson's mind; or perhaps rather no doubt that if justice had been done he would have been the choice himself. In spite of his generous letter to Gaitskell, he found it impossible altogether to conceal his feelings. Wilson was "inordinately jealous, though in view of his age there is really no reason for it", wrote Gaitskell.[2] In Wilson's view there was excellent reason. He had been supplanted by a man who was, it was true, ten years older than him, but who he also believed to be manifestly less well equipped for the job which he coveted above all others. This, perhaps, he could have tolerated if he had found Gaitskell sympathetic but, on the contrary, he actively disliked him. Wilson and Gaitskell – both socialists, both economists, both highly educated – were antipathetic to each other. "It is a pity that Harold Wilson, whom I regard as extremely able and for that reason alone most valuable to the Government, should offend so many people by being so swollen-headed," Gaitskell wrote in his diary in February 1950. "What is depressing really is ... that he is such a very impersonal person. You don't feel that you could ever be close friends with him, or in fact that he would ever have any close friends. How different he is, for example, from John Strachey, with whom one may often disagree, but who is a real person with interests and feelings rising above politics."[3] If Wilson had kept a similar diary he would have accused Gaitskell of being a snob, a bigot and a prig. But an indication of the difference between the two men is that Wilson kept no diary, rarely expressed his thoughts on paper unless they were immediately relevant to the job in hand, confided little in his friends, had – as Gaitskell remarked – few if any close friends in whom to confide. His instinct was to keep his own counsel; he loved gossip but was neither given to speculation about the characters of his colleagues nor disposed to share with others whatever reflections he might have. He knew that Gaitskell considered him to be limited, low-brow and boring, and he resented it; he knew too that if Gaitskell were to become leader of the Labour Party, though he might not be able to keep Wilson out of office, he would promote him with little enthusiasm and would favour others at his expense. Gaitskell's appointment to the Treasury was a blow both to Wilson's *amour propre* and to his career prospects.

Though Wilson himself would have denied the fact, was perhaps even unconscious of it, Gaitskell's promotion was one of the main factors which drew the President of the Board of Trade towards the left wing and eventual resignation. German rearmament was the first issue on which this realignment became noticeable. Bevin, and most of the heavyweights of the party, concluded that the threat from Russia made a measure of German rearmament essential. Aneurin Bevan felt as strongly that it was unacceptable. "H. W. is clearly ganging up with the Minister of Labour," wrote Gaitskell, "not that he cuts very much ice because one feels that he has no fundamental views of his own."[1] In this case he did his rival an injustice. Wilson felt strongly opposed to anything that might lead to a revival of German militarism. But he neither felt nor argued his case with the passion of Bevan, and Gaitskell could be forgiven for believing that his position owed more to expediency than to principle.

It was the Korean War, however, which turned Wilson from a dissenter into a rebel. Attlee pressed moderation on the Americans with some success, but was forced to agree that he would increase the British defence budget from £3,400 million to £4,700 million. Wilson believed that this was literally impossible – the material and men were not available – and that any attempt to reach the target would be disastrous to the British economy. Gaitskell dismissed this as playing politics; Wilson, he believed, was looking for a stick with which to beat the Chancellor and was preparing an alibi "in case exports dropped catastrophically".[2] Bevan's attitude was equivocal. On German rearmament and later on health charges it was he who took the lead and Wilson who followed; on the defence budget he expressed doubts as early as August 1950 but subsequently appeared to acquiesce in the proposed expenditure.[3] It was not till the end of January 1951, when Gaitskell's budget was imminent, that he restated his objections, and then only as a secondary issue.[4] In Barbara Castle's diary Wilson was quoted as saying that Bevan did not "latch on to the rearmament issue" until late in the day.[5] A researcher from the London School of Economics in 1984 asked Wilson how he reconciled that statement with the line Bevan had taken in Cabinet early in 1951. "There is no discrepancy," retorted Wilson. The statement to which the researcher referred had been made one month before the resignation. Wilson had by then been arguing the case for six months or more. "The other resignations, of John Freeman and myself, related very specifically to a view of rearmament which we had taken for a long time."[1]

It was not the cost of rearmament, however, which was the immediate cause of the Cabinet crisis, except in so far as the need to rearm forced Gaitskell to press for a stringent budget. One of his favoured methods of raising money was by imposing charges on false teeth and glasses acquired under the National Health Service. The figure at stake was £23 million. This was not the first time the possibility of levying such charges had been suggested; Cripps had made similar threats late in 1949. On that occasion Bevan had announced that he would resign rather than accept any such impost on his beloved Health Service. Wilson decided that he meant what he said; hastened to Cripps to explain how passionately Bevan felt about the issue; hastened back to Bevan to stress that Cripps was old, ill and needed careful handling; and finally negotiated a compromise under which no direct charges were levied but a ceiling was placed on the grand total of National Health expenditure.[2] Even if he had been disposed to approach Gaitskell in the same spirit it is unlikely that he would have achieved anything: Gaitskell abominated Bevan and a report that the Minister of Labour was showing himself intransigent would merely have fortified the Chancellor's determination to make no concessions.

By March the battle lines had been drawn up. "Hugh said that he expected main opposition from Nye with support from Harold Wilson," Dalton noted in his diary. "I asked why Wilson? Hugh said he was always intriguing with Nye and was hoping to get Hugh's job if *he* had to resign."[3] Dalton professed to believe that Wilson was Bevan's poodle, barking only at his bidding – " 'Nye and the Dog', I call them." There was no doubt that Bevan was the senior partner, but Wilson took pains to distance himself from his ally, emphasising whenever opportunity arose that it was the defence budget, not the relatively trivial issue of the health charges, which caused him the gravest disquiet.

By the eve of the budget it was clear that, though George Strauss, Chuter Ede and one or two other ministers were sympathetic to the case on rearmament, Bevan, Wilson and perhaps John Strachey were the only senior members of the party seriously contemplating resignation. Increasing pressure was put on potential rebels to stay in line; John Freeman, parliamentary secretary at the Ministry of Supply, was more or less explicitly offered Wilson's place in the Cabinet if he would stay loyal;[1] while Wilson was said to have been promised Ernest Bevin's safe seat at East Woolwich. Wilson stuck by his guns, arguing in Cabinet on 22 March that the sums allocated to defence could not possibly be spent and that "the abandonment of the symbol of the Welfare State" would make bad publicity in the United States.[2] Gaitskell, who had lobbied assiduously among other members of the Cabinet, did not even bother to talk to Wilson before the meeting, "because I knew quite well that he was likely to side with Bevan".[3] When Dalton warned him that his attitude might lead to Strachey and Wilson following Bevan into resignation, the Chancellor retorted brusquely: "We'd be well rid of the three of them!"[4] Herbert Morrison, for his part, spoke only once to Wilson during the crisis, and then to "warn him savagely that if he resigned he would be finished in Labour politics for twenty years".[5]

The Cabinet on 9 April was the last chance for the rebels to persuade Gaitskell to change his mind. They failed. It was suggested that the charges might be deferred for six months while it was seen whether the money allocated for defence could in fact be spent, but there was no real enthusiasm for this compromise on either side.[6] The cause of the rebels was weakened by the fact that there was no sign of a grass-roots revolt in the party which might compel the Chancellor to relent. On the contrary, it was the rebels who were isolated. James Callaghan told a contact at the American Embassy that he saw their point of view but "had no sympathy whatsoever for Bevan's allowing his disagreement with Gaitskell to become public and for his threatening to resign from the Government. He indicated that there was virtually no sympathy within the party for Bevan in this regard."[7] Callaghan's judgment was proved correct; when Gaitskell announced the charges "there was no outcry," recorded Dalton, "hardly an audible reaction on either side of the House."[8] Dalton was by no means an objective observer but all reports suggest that the only notable sign of dissent came from Bevan's wife, Jennie Lee.[9] Within the Cabinet also Bevan's support melted away: "We are told on good authority that he is completely isolated ..." reported the American Embassy, "with the exception of Harold Wilson (Wilson has reportedly been miffed that he was not made Chancellor)."[10]

Bevan had been defied, but it was still uncertain whether he would resign and, if he did, who if anyone would accompany him. Consulted in hospital, where he had retreated before the storm blew up, Attlee remarked sardonically that he had only heard of one other minister resigning over a budget issue: that had been Randolph Churchill – and look what happened to him.[1] If Attlee had been in day-to-day control of the situation it is possible that it might never have got so far out of hand. Even if Bevin had played an active role he might have secured a settlement – but he was a dying man. Without them, there was no hope of appeasing Bevan. Wilson met Dalton on the way to a meeting of the Parliamentary Labour Party (PLP). "Good morning, Mr Dalton," said Wilson nervously. "I hope we're still colleagues. I've been trying to persuade Nye not to resign." "I've heard different," said Dalton grimly.[2] He was convinced that Wilson was intent on making mischief and was egging Bevan on to be yet more obdurate. "I made no effort to persuade Harold Wilson from resigning," he wrote in his memoirs. "In contrast with the other two, he did not seem to have much warmth or strength of character."[3]

In fact Wilson did feel that Bevan was ill-advised to resign and, up to within a few days of the event, made some, though not very vigorous, efforts to dissuade him. But he had no doubt that if Bevan *did* resign he was bound to follow him.[4] Bevan argued – though one suspects without great conviction – that this was unnecessary: "He has been very loyal and I release him."[5] He said the same to John Freeman, who had made greater efforts than Wilson to keep Bevan in the Cabinet, telling him that there would be "amazement as well as anger" if he resigned and that he ought to bide his time.[6] Left to himself Freeman would probably have accepted Bevan's offer and stayed in his job, but Wilson stood firm – he would quite understand if Freeman decided differently, he said, but he himself felt that he was in honour bound to go.[7] Freeman was left with little option but to do the same. Solly Zuckerman called on Bevan, who told him that he was going to resign and that " 'young Harold', who was lolling on a sofa in Nye's sitting room, beneath a gloomy picture by Michael Ayrton – it seemed to reflect the gloom on his face – was going with him".[8]

The gloom was real; whatever Wilson's motives for resignation he did not come lightly to that conclusion. It was, he said later, one of the very few occasions in his life when he had lost sleep worrying over what to do. He stood to forfeit a great deal. Most immediately there was his ministerial salary and a job which, if not all he aspired to, was interesting and responsible enough. In the longer term he would make powerful enemies in the party, in particular sacrificing the favour of Clement Attlee, who could see no point of principle involved which could possibly justify his behaviour: "I was surprised when Harold Wilson took Nye's line," Attlee wrote. "He ought to have had more understanding of the economic position."[1] Wilson knew too that he would quite possibly annoy his constituency and imperil his anyway fragile majority. His future as a minister and politician would be in peril.

In the longer term, though, there were arguments on the other side. John Freeman at first thought Wilson's behaviour "quixotically honourable and public-spirited" but later concluded that it offered him the best chance of one day getting to the top. If Gaitskell became leader there would be only limited opportunities for advancement; if Wilson backed Bevan, and Bevan won, then the succession was his.[2] Woodrow Wyatt claims that Wilson told him he resigned because he thought it would help his career: "It would win him backing from the rank and file of the Labour Party activists." Till then, commented Wyatt, he had admired Wilson and thought him sincere; "now his attitude shocked and disappointed me greatly."[3] For "activists" read "left wing": his resignation, wrote Paul Foot, "disguised his political attitudes for the previous six years in a cloak of left-wing principle".[4] Till 1951 Wilson lacked any substantial power base in the Labour Party; from the moment of his resignation he became crown prince to Bevan's shadow king. And though the loss of office was unpleasant it was not the sacrifice that it would have been two or three years before; in the eyes of most political pundits the government's days were numbered and he would anyway probably have been out of a job within the next twelve months.

Whatever his calculations, however, he had not left himself much room for manoeuvre. Perhaps in the belief, certainly in the hope, that Bevan's threat to resign would force Gaitskell to retreat, he had committed himself unequivocally to the Bevanite cause. Now he could not withdraw without a loss of prestige and credibility that he found unacceptable. It was clear that no one else from the Cabinet would follow his example; on the evening the final decision was reached, wrote Jennie Lee, "John Strachey sat squirming by our sitting-room fireside enjoying exquisite thrills, but he had no intention of resigning."[5]

The departing ministers made their ritual resignation speeches in the House of Commons on 24 April. Bevan was polemical, cantankerous and intemperate; Wilson, said Harold Macmillan, "was more in the classical style – modest and mournful. The House and the Labour Party liked it."[1] He based his argument above all on the size of the defence budget; he was, he said, "strongly in support of an effective defence programme ... But if the titanic programme for rearmament runs beyond the physical resources which can be made available, then rearmament itself becomes the first casualty." It was not a narrow issue, he insisted, "not a matter of teeth and spectacles". Indeed, he mentioned almost in passing that one consequence of this exaggerated commitment to defence had been that "the principle of the free health service had been breached and I dread how that breach might be widened in future years". This was a symptom of the malaise rather than the malaise itself; it was his inability to support the proposed level of defence expenditure that had led him to resign. His final message was one of reconciliation.

Although a matter of principle, as I believe it to be, now severs me from my colleagues in the Cabinet, I should, at the same time, wish to express my deep sense of the privilege it has been to have had an opportunity of serving with them and in however modest a way to have played a part in the real and great achievements of the Government in these past few years. Achievements in our economic and social life I believe without parallel in our history.[2]

It was the speech of a man who wished to leave no bitterness behind, who was already envisaging a return to the fold which he was temporarily deserting.

He was not entirely successful in disarming criticism. Gaitskell and his followers dismissed as hypocrisy the blandishments of a man whom they believed to be fundamentally dishonest. Emanuel Shinwell, for the older guard of loyalists, dismissed Wilson as "highly ambitious", an attribute which was admirable in itself but was not "improved by insincere gestures of alleged idealism". Wilson's disloyalty, Shinwell believed, cost Labour the 1951 election.[3] But on the whole the statement was well received and did much to appease the indignation of those who resented any attempt to rock the parliamentary boat. As evidence accumulated that the defence budget had, indeed, been set impossibly high, so Wilson's stock rose and the left wing of the party, even some of the moderates, considered him more and more as prescient sage rather than traitorous rebel.

"His resignation left us speechless with surprise," wrote Herbert

Morrison. "Was the move from ardent conviction? Or was it because he felt that Bevan's resignation would in due course bring victory?"[1] It is possible to construct two plausible scenarios: the first featuring Wilson as a gallant young idealist sacrificing his job and risking his future for the sake of a principle and in support of a cherished leader; the second portraying him as a cynical schemer, calculating the course of action that promised him greatest advantage in the long term and inflicting grave damage on his party in the pursuit of his individual ambitions. Anyone who believes that either of these versions presents the entire truth would be better employed designing puppets for *Spitting Image* than in the craft of biography. Wilson did look before he leapt; he did make calculations about his political future; but equally he did feel strongly about the burden of defence and the health charges; he did admire and feel loyalty to Aneurin Bevan, one of the few politicians admitted by Mary to the family home as a friend; above all, he was taking a serious and avoidable risk. He may not have been impulsive or idealistic but his resignation was an act of political courage, a gamble which fits ill with the image of cautious and devious time-server which has won such wide acceptance.

VI

Opposition Under Attlee

1951–1953

Any dispossessed minister is likely to suffer withdrawal symptoms, if only from the vanished perquisites of office. If one is a poor man, with a mortgage to pay and two children to educate (both Robin and Giles went to schools which required a proportion of the fees to be paid by the parents) this deprivation could become disaster. Wilson knew that he could command a substantial income from private business if he so desired. The night after his resignation he told a friend that he had already been offered directorships worth £22,000 but "had turned them all down because he did not like the way the companies were run".[1] Though he later denied that he was ever offered an executive position in the film industry, part of this at least must have been accounted for by an unspecified post, said to have been worth £13,000 a year, offered him through the good offices of Alexander Korda. But though he could afford to be selective he could not reject every offer. Both by personal taste and political discretion he wished to avoid anything too aggressively capitalistic or which might involve him in conflict with the unions. Foreign trade seemed the obvious solution, and there was no field where his connections and his knowledge of the workings of Whitehall were likely to be more valuable than that of East–West trade.

Montague Meyer, the timber importer, was the first and most long-lasting of Wilson's connections in this world. Russia was one of its principal sources of timber, and the firm was happy to offer Wilson £1,500 a year, an office, a car, and to take his secretary on to its staff in exchange for part-time attendance and regular availability to give advice or act as go-between. He had first got to know the family through Ernest Bevin, who got on well with Montague Meyer, the eponymous chairman of the firm. He was invited to join the board, but refused, since he did not know for how long he would be available and preferred a more detached relationship. He would work there most mornings, often lunching with Meyer at the Savoy before moving on to the House of Commons. He had no fixed job but was used as a sounding board and adviser and charged with particular assignments from time to time. His usefulness was exhibited when British Railways tried to withdraw the cheap rate which covered deliveries to Meyer's timber yard at Widnes. He was the only man who thought of consulting the original Act of Parliament, and he was able to establish that they had no such right. But his principal value lay in his access to ministers in the Soviet Union and other countries behind the Iron Curtain. Meyer's wanted to sell in Russia new equipment for manufacturing a kind of chipboard; Wilson accompanied the inventor to Moscow, secured an interview at the highest level and brought off the deal. On another occasion he persuaded the Romanian government to grant a bigger discount on the hardwood that Meyer's was importing from that country.[1]

Meyer's would have been happy to continue the relationship indefinitely; they liked having him around as well as valuing his experience, good judgment and wide range of contacts. A residual loyalty to his old employers always remained. When Alexei Kosygin, Chairman of the Council of Ministers in Moscow, was being entertained at Number 10 in 1967, Wilson asked Barbara Castle to keep his guest in play for ten minutes. The Prime Minister then 'surfaced with an odd-looking chap who had something to do with timber'.[2] Wilson, Kosygin, and the chairman of Montague Meyer reminisced happily about timber deals while the other guests watched in some perplexity. He withdrew from his work with Meyer only when he found that other demands on his time made it impossible for him to do a proper job. It had suited him well. There had been a little sniping from critics on the left, who felt that it was improper for a socialist to accept a salary from a capitalist organisation, but nothing which caused him more than transitory embarrassment. On the other hand he had been able to use his visits to Moscow to make new political contacts and to establish himself still further as a leading authority on relations with the communist bloc. When he visited Russia in May 1953 his old friend Mikoyan arranged for him to be received by Molotov (the Soviet Foreign Minister), and to discuss with him Churchill's proposals for top-level talks. On the return journey he stopped at Budapest to see if he could help over the incarceration of the English businessman, Edgar Sanders. In neither capacity did he play any official role but an aura of officialdom seemed to cling about him. Not everyone took his claims to expertise altogether seriously. After the Moscow visit a special meeting of the PLP was held to hear his report: 'He did a magnificent job of blowing out his information so that he could tell us everything that was happening in Russia,' wrote Crossman. 'All his little jokes went down well and Attlee congratulated him on a magnificent inside report.'[1]

Even more than when in office he became identified with the cause of East–West trade. His *Tribune* pamphlet, *In Place of Dollars*, which was published in September 1952, was an urgent plea that Britain should free itself from the domination of the dollar and make possible a truly independent foreign policy. ('I find these words odd,' remarked Solly Zuckerman, 'in relation to the policies which the realities of politics forced on its author when he became Prime Minister some twenty years later.')[2] Apart from proposing more nationalisation and higher taxes on the rich, the pamphlet urged that strategic controls on exports should be relaxed and American objections to such a policy ignored. It was the high-water mark of Wilson's radicalism, described by the *Daily Express* as an 'anti-American blueprint for a Bevanite Britain', but so far as East–West trade was concerned it was only the most conspicuous element in a protracted campaign; at a meeting at Rochdale, for instance, shortly after the Russian trip, Wilson called for the export of tin-plate to China and of 'penicillin and other healing drugs' to Eastern Europe.[3]

His reputation led other would-be exporters to seek his help and advice and over the years Wilson became involved with a number of businesses. Marchon Products, the manufacturer of detergents, was one such firm. Frank Schon, the founder and chairman, wanted to expand his exports to Russia; Wilson helped arrange the contract and became a consultant at a fee of £1,000 a year. Lewis and Peat, the metal and rubber dealer, was another client: 'I am getting on with the Czech enquiries and also hope to have something to report from the East Germans,' wrote Wilson.[4] They contributed £500 a year for secretarial services. By 1963 Kagan Textiles was paying him £100 a month 'for consultations and technical advice ... in respect of Gannex sales to the USSR'.[5] His earnings from such sources were erratic but averaged about £5,000 a year during his period in opposition. To some, at least, this seemed unduly modest. In 1960 Wilson cried off a trip to the United States because some Russian officials were visiting

London and his advice was needed by a British group who retained him as consultant. Senator William Benton feared he was not making enough out of it for himself. If a £10 million contract was in question, Wilson should charge £100,000 – 1 per cent. "All right, I'll make it £20,000. But this should be an absolute minimum. You should come out of this deal as a man who is 'comfortably well off'."[1]

It was no fault of Benton's that Wilson never approached what the senator would have considered a decent minimum of comfort. He was constantly urging Wilson to undertake lucrative lecture tours of the United States or to contribute to the Annual Year Books of the *Encyclopaedia Britannica*. Sometimes Wilson accepted, more often he did not; he averaged about five lectures a year in the United States in the decade after his resignation. Journalism proved a useful source of extra income, as well as giving Wilson a chance to keep his name before the public. In May 1953 *Life* offered $3,000 for an article on Russia to include an interview with Stalin's successor, Georgi Malenkov; in the event the project was aborted and Wilson had to settle for the guarantee of $1,000.[2] He wrote regularly for *Tribune* – hardly a noticeable source of income; for the *New Statesman* – little better; and less frequently for the *Economist*. He kept meaning to write a book but never found time; his correspondence with his agent, David Higham, was a litany of excuses: "One or two ideas do keep occurring to me, but I do not see any immediate prospect of getting down to one, particularly as I have rather a lot of drafting and redrafting to do on my report for the Cotton Trade Unions"; "I am afraid that I am now so fully occupied with Party organisation work ... that there is no hope of my thinking about starting a book in the foreseeable future"; "my experiences of the last few months have robbed me of any hope that I could get down to writing a book. Ever since January I have been waiting to put pen to paper on a quite short report for the Film Trade Unions."[3]

One project which did reach book form was *The War on World Poverty*, which began as a 25,000-word report for the Association of World Peace. The association had been inspired by the publisher, Victor Gollancz, who recruited a high-powered committee to support him. Wilson was an early recruit. "For the vast majority of mankind the most urgent problem is not war, or Communism, or the cost of living, or taxation. It is hunger," were the opening sentences of his book, and its contents, mainly factual and often statistical, nevertheless are suffused by a real sense of outrage at the miseries to which the world's poor were subjected. His major purpose, wrote *The Times*, was to advocate "that much more should be done and that there must be an International Development Authority to do it".[1] Wilson suggested that 3 per cent of the national income of the richer powers should be devoted to an aid programme: "It is a moral imperative. We are rich and they are poor, and it is our duty to help them." It was a message he preached consistently while in opposition; that he failed to practise what he preached when he came into office says more about the realities of exercising power than the sincerity of his protestations at the time that he uttered them.

These extra occupations rapidly filled the time made available by his liberation from office. He saw a bit more of his family, often cooked the breakfast, drove his sons to school, was more frequently at home at weekends, but he remained a man preoccupied by his work. As a son, husband and father he was dutiful, affectionate, but detached. In June 1957 he executed seven-year covenants of £90 per annum in favour of his father and his mother, and £50 for his mother-in-law.[2] Relatively prosperous though he was, the provision – worth, say, £1,500 at current prices – was a generous one, given his other responsibilities. In fact his mother died the following year in Cornwall. Wilson had loved her fervently if undemonstratively; his sorrow at her death was no different. Only those who knew him best would have detected any sign of his feelings and even to them he shied away from expressing overt grief.

Those who knew him best, or even well, were a tiny number. George Caunt, an official attached to the Parliamentary Labour Party, described him in 1955 as, "An unknown quantity in a crumpled suit prowling about the corridors and committee rooms on his own, not particularly friendly and suspicious and lonely."[3] In the House of Commons he would consort with Barbara Castle, Crossman, Arthur Skeffington, Leslie Plummer, but none of these was what Gaitskell would have considered an intimate. Outside the House there were even fewer; one of the handful of people who called regularly at his home in Hampstead was the Oxford don Thomas Balogh, who with Nicholas Kaldor, another Hungarian-born economist, rampaged around Whitehall in the 1960s and 1970s. "Buddha and Pest", Dalton nicknamed Kaldor and Balogh – most people liked the first but disliked the second – "Suspicious and conspiratorial where Nicky was genial and expansive", Healey found Balogh.[1] But he was also courageous, energetic and a man of many ideas, all original and eloquently expounded, some of them sound. Wilson admired him, shared his expansionist ideas, and was ready to endure the storm clouds which so often seemed to herald Balogh's arrival for the sake of the stimulation and intellectual challenge which he provided. Sometimes he was provoked almost beyond endurance by an act of churlishness or some outrageous demand – "Those awful Europeans," he would say, "and intellectual Europeans are the worst of all!" – but he could endure almost endless affront if he thought the offender basically well disposed and worth listening to, and he remained loyal to Balogh for many years.

One unpleasant by-product of Wilson's activities in the field of East–West trade was that the reputation he had already acquired as a communist sympathiser took on a new and sinister significance. There were powerful forces in official circles in London, still more in Washington, who considered any trade with Russia to be dubious if not reprehensible. The export of many items was forbidden; inevitably a grey area grew up in which trading might or might not be illegal. Some of Wilson's associates strayed into that area or even beyond it. In the Foreign Office a blacklist was kept, and by association Wilson's name figured on it. Partly it was Wilson's fault; for a man of high intelligence and considerable cunning he could be startlingly naïve and he rarely stopped to wonder whether people whom he found agreeable and who were prepared to reward his services handsomely might not break the law if they thought they could get away with it. More to blame was the paranoiac suspicion of MI5, who were too ready to assume everyone a traitor unless they could be proved innocent. When the Russian defector Anatoli Golitsin in 1963 denounced Wilson as a tool of the KGB, the suspicions of certain sections of the security services were confirmed. When Golitsin was discredited, the suspicions were hardly allayed. No one of any import-ance believed that Wilson had personally been involved in breaches of the law; no one in their senses imagined he was a Russian agent, but in the shadow world where nods and winks and covert hints were the accepted means of communication the belief that he was a dangerous man took root and proved almost impossible to extirpate.

Fortunately for Wilson the man in the street, still less the voter in Huyton, knew nothing of such rumours. Wilson had feared that his resignation might incur the displeasure of his constituents. The contrary proved true; he was given an enthusiastic reception when he next visited Huyton and left in no doubt that his independence of mind had been appreciated. It was perhaps as well that they did not know their member had only a few months before been sounding out Transport House about the possibility of moving to a safer constituency. With Herbert Morrison's support, Dalton scuppered that idea. "Harold Wilson must not be helped to find a better seat," he told the National Agent vengefully. "If Huyton is to be lost, let *him* lose it."[1]

It was clear that Wilson could not expect any vigorous support from the party machine when Attlee called a general election for 25 October 1951. The Bevanites agreed on a policy of self-help. Freeman and Tom Driberg were both defending marginal seats, but with a majority of only 834 Wilson was in the most precarious position. Bevan visited Huyton and, unlike the previous election when he had spoken only fifteen times in his own constituency against thirty-five times outside it, Wilson concentrated almost exclusively on his domestic battle. Things looked hopeful; the area had benefited by the fact that Merseyside had been designated a development area, the industrial estate was thriving and since the last election Wilson had cut the first sod of a large new housing estate. More than 1,000 new voters, expected to be predominantly Labour, had moved into the constituency. But the national swing was believed to be towards the right and nearly 2,000 former Liberal voters were wondering which party to support. The Tory candidate, Francis Neep, made great play with Wilson's links with the extreme left while the Roman Catholic Archbishop also denounced "crypto-communists", though subsequently denying that he had had Wilson in mind. Wilson indignantly retorted that he detested communism and was a staunch member of the Parliamentary Christian Socialist Group. "I would not make quite so much of this, only that Mr Neep is trying any kind of poisonous slime to try to discredit me with people whose approach to politics comes from the religious side."[2] His protestations were well received; against the national trend – the Tories under Churchill won a majority of seventeen – Wilson not merely maintained but increased his majority to 1,193.

The election over, Wilson settled down to what would certainly be several years in opposition. Since the moment of his resignation he had been confronted by the problem of defining where he stood politically and, still more critically, where he wanted to end up. He had resigned with Bevan; did that make him a Bevanite? Were there, indeed, such animals? Driberg described them as "not so much a party within a party as a Smoking Room within a Smoking Room",[1] a group of convivial hard drinkers, mainly intellectual and middle class, loving conversation and by no means exclusively concerned with politics. Wilson could never have been at home in such company. They rarely met to plan their strategy, still less to fix their tactics; Bevan, as his biographer, John Campbell, has remarked, did not want a coherent bloc so much as "a group of compliant followers to amplify his own concerns".[2] They impressed the rank-and-file Labour member as a bunch of irresponsible mischief-makers: he was not interested in the Bevanites, Callaghan told a friend in the American Embassy, "He was disgusted with their arguments and quibbling about the past, feeling this was sterile and pointless."[3]

Peter Clarke has aptly described the conflict within the Labour Party as being on three related but distinct levels: "Bevanites versus Gaitskellites, left versus right, and fundamentalists versus revisionists".[4] On none of these levels did Wilson feel himself unequivocally in one camp or the other. Subsequently he rejected the Bevanite label; he was a co-belligerent, not a satellite, he was fond of saying: "a bunch of us were in the wilderness together and, since Moses was there and overshadowed the rest of us, we should have been more conveniently dubbed Moses-ites".[5] He wore the label, remarked John Freeman, like a poppy on Remembrance Day – for form's sake.[6] His closest ally within the group, Richard Crossman, saw the role of the Bevanites as being to move the party towards the left but not necessarily to make Bevan leader. He wanted to make bridges with the party leadership. He and Wilson, he remarked, formed a sub-group, left of centre but well to the right of the Bevanite devotees.[7] Wilson would have been put out by a comment which, though in essentials accurate, did not take account of the vigorous efforts which he was making in 1951 and 1952 to assert his radicalism. Paul Foot cites as evidence of Wilson's alienation from the rest of the group a rousing affirmation of his support for the monarchy – "I believe it essential to democracy as we know it" – and an occasion when he made a Bevanite meeting stand and sing the national anthem.[8] The scenario, though quaint, is not inconceivable. Wilson held certain institutions sacred: the monarchy and the Boy Scouts among them. But at the same time he was calling for a capital levy, increased death duties, a price freeze, further nationalisation. He relied on the support of Marxists and extremists, wrote Woodrow Wyatt, and that involved "obligations and concessions to their viewpoint".[1] His object was to establish himself as Bevan's natural successor on the left, though without sacrificing the lines which he kept open to the main body of the party. It was a delicate and dangerous path to tread, and one which from the start necessitated his distancing himself from the hard core of the Bevanites, if not from Bevan himself. Wilson had become "a deviationist from the Bevan line", Carol Johnson, the secretary of the PLP, declared as early as December 1951. He realised he had little future in the party if he became part of a splinter group, his speeches within the PLP had been moderate and he was "successfully re-establishing himself" within the parliamentary party.[2] The American Embassy approvingly noted that, alone among the Bevanites, he welcomed American aid to support the defence programme, provided that aid was not granted unilaterally but as "the result of NATO 'burden sharing' negotiations".[3] By January 1952 Wilson was sounding out Bevan and Crossman about a proposal that he should go back on the front bench. It was much too early, he was told; Wilson could not return without Bevan, and, with the United States threatening to spread the war from Korea to China, there was no way Bevan could contemplate such a move.[4]

The "Keep-Left Group" had been launched in November 1946 in reaction to Ernest Bevin's pro-American and anti-Zionist policies. Its membership by mid 1951 numbered twenty-two, including such left-wing stalwarts as Tom Driberg, Stephen Swingler, Ian Mikardo and Jennie Lee, with a few more maverick figures like Fenner Brockway and Richard Acland. The three resigning ministers were welcomed enthusiastically, bringing in their wake George Wigg, who had resigned from the group a few months earlier but now recanted.[5] Crossman mused on the resultant mixture. "What a mysterious thing 'the left' is"; the old Keep-Left Group had worked out a certain homogeneity, but now they had superimposed on it "Nye Bevan and Harold Wilson who have virtually nothing in common".[6] There was a general feeling that the group should expand further but some dispute as to who should be asked to join: Tony Benn was deemed suitable, Kenneth Younger not; Wilson suggested he might recruit

Lewis Silkin, others proposed Harold Lever.[1] In December Wilson was elected chairman. He was "as neat and competent as ever," noted Crossman. "Whenever an idea is put forward, he remembers without fail an occasion on which he did it ... when he was at the Board of Trade. His complacency must be unique, but he has a good mind, is an excellent member of a group and is likeable into the bargain."[2]

What was in effect the group's manifesto, *One Way Only*, appeared in July 1951. Bevan, Wilson and Freeman, who jointly contributed a preface, were the only signatories and though they did not specifically endorse all that followed it can be assumed that they broadly accepted it. It was not an explosive document – "an essay in qualified judgments", Michael Foot described it[3] – but the fierce attacks on American foreign policy and German rearmament caused some excitement. The other proposals – price control, public ownership of cement, sugar and mineral workings, a capital levy – were all measures that Wilson had espoused in other forums and which were not wholly at variance with official Labour policy. The press treated the pamphlet with some disdain. Fine rhetoric but muddled thinking, the *Manchester Guardian* concluded: "If this is really what Mr Bevan and Mr Harold Wilson believe, the country is to be congratulated on having lost their services."[4]

In the autumn of 1951 Wilson decided to stand for the National Executive Committee (NEC) of the Labour Party. The election showed a remarkable swing to the left: Bevan and Barbara Castle led the poll for the constituencies' section – the litmus test for popularity within the party as a whole; Driberg and Mikardo retained their seats; Wilson just failed, with only Shinwell as a closer runner-up. It was a good result but not quite as good as he had hoped for; some believed his relative failure occurred because Transport House cunningly disguised him on the ballot paper as "J. H. Wilson".[5] The Bevanite successes were enough to alarm the right, notably the trade unionists under the rigidly reactionary Arthur Deakin, whose fierce denunciations of any schismatic tendency within the unions or the Labour Party were a constant threat to anyone of even mildly heretical opinions. Deakin's indignation was redoubled in March 1952 when Bevan, Wilson and fifty-five other Labour members – inevitably christened "The Heinz Group" or the "Fifty-seven Varieties" – defied the party whip. The leadership, afraid of being branded as pacifists, wanted the party to abstain in a vote on the Tory arms programme but to support an amendment of no confidence in the capacity of the government to carry out its policy. Wilson warned the PLP that the country would be left bankrupt if the present spending plans were forced through and insisted he would vote against the Tory motion. Even if the party leaders sympathised with his position they were stuck with the fact that the Tory programme was little different from what they had earlier espoused themselves. The Chief Whip ordered members to abstain; the rebels ignored him. In the subsequent turmoil the Chief Whip, Morrison and other hardliners wanted all fifty-seven members expelled; Attlee demanded a vote of censure and an instruction that all Labour members must sign and in future obey the Standing Orders which had been suspended since 1945; in the end all that happened was that the Standing Orders were reimposed. It was a warning to the rebels not to offend again but not as severe a reprimand as the hardline disciplinarians would have liked. A few months later the Keep-Left Group made a conciliatory gesture when they threw open their meetings to all members of the party. Bevan and Wilson had committed themselves to this line, and even written articles for the *New Statesman* and *Tribune* expounding the new policy, before consulting the other members of the group. Luckily the group approved the line and were never told that the pass had already been sold. Personally, wrote Crossman in his diary, "I had a distinctly uncomfortable feeling about diddling forty colleagues in this way and I said so to Harold Wilson. He was baffled, which shows what good politicians he and Nye are."[1]*

Wilson at this time rarely missed a chance, in public or in private, to reaffirm his loyalty to Attlee and to emphasise his belief that the unity of the party must be restored and maintained. If he could manage it without alienating his new allies he would have been more than ready to reintegrate himself with the leadership. He was coming to terms with the fact that Gaitskell was likely to take over when the old guard departed, but was still meditating ways by which he could maintain his position in the race until the decision was finally made. One idea, which he nursed until he himself became Prime Minister and was able to put it into practice, was to deprive the Treasury of its control of economic planning and transfer this to a separate ministry, which he would be eminently well qualified to lead.[2] The

---

* Crossman's diary entries are always incisive and intelligent and often irresistibly quotable. They tend, however, to reflect what he thought happened rather than actual events, and are coloured by his volatile and capricious personality. They need always to be treated with discretion.

concept of what was one day to become the Department of Economic Affairs was not conjured up solely as a device for clipping Gaitskell's wings, but this was certainly an important element in his calculations. Such thoughts, however, were kept for a few cronies; to the world at large he spoke only of reconciliation. Even that he needed to do with some circumspection. "He is an amphibian," remarked the press magnate, Max Beaverbrook, "sometimes on Mr Bevan's water, then on Gaitskell's land. He may end up in the mud!"[1]

The elections for the NEC at the party conference at Morecambe in 1952 proved to be a Bevanite triumph. Bevan came top, Castle and Driberg followed, Wilson was fifth with 632,000 votes – nearly double Gaitskell's total. Even more satisfying, the election of Wilson and Crossman forced Morrison and Dalton off the committee. His success was only marred by the tepid reception given to his speech; "in part," surmised an American observer, "because as one of the victors in the National Executive elections, he was taking himself more seriously than usual".[2] Dalton took his rebuff philosophically. It was not unreasonable, he thought, that two elderly has-beens should be replaced by younger men of undoubted ability and promise. "And these two, if one had to have two more Bevanites, were much abler and much more likely to render good service than Driberg and Mikardo."[3] Mikardo did not agree. He found it ironical that Morrison and Dalton had been replaced by their exact equivalents on the left. Both Crossman and Wilson were "operators, wire-pullers, bargainers, persuaders, dealers". But Crossman did it for fun, Wilson "had eyes for nothing but the goal, and his goal was to become Leader of the Party and then Prime Minister".[4]

Even before Morecambe the right wing were stepping up their campaign against the Bevanites. They were, said Patrick Gordon Walker, "a deliberately organised party within a party"; they "concert their own line and choose their own spokesmen", accused Frank Pakenham.[5] The swing to the left at Morecambe caused something near panic and led to yet more furious assaults from Gaitskell and the trade union leaders. Attlee's response was to push through a resolution in the PLP calling for the dissolution of all groups within the party. Wilson presided at a meeting of Bevanites and sympathisers in which he protested that the ban was illiberal and damaging to party unity, and reiterated his view in a letter published in the *New Statesman*. The letter, which appeared shortly before the elections to the Parliamentary Committee – precursor of the shadow Cabinet –

did nothing to soften the hearts of the right. The rules were changed for this election, so that each Labour MP could vote only for twelve candidates. Those who got 50 per cent of the total vote were elected first time round; the rest went back into the melting pot for a second ballot. It was generally believed, by the Bevanites at any rate, that the object of this innovation was to make it harder for them to be elected. Wilson described it as "califugling" (a word unknown to the *Oxford English Dictionary* but clearly not meant to be complimentary).[1] Though success in the NEC elections was no reflection of a member's popularity in the PLP, the results of the ballots for the Parliamentary Committee seem to support his view. Bevan scraped in in last place the first time round while Wilson was eliminated in the second ballot. When Bevan contested the deputy leadership of the party with Herbert Morrison he secured eighty-two votes to Morrison's 194.

With Bevan back on the front bench and the old guard, as Crossman hoped, having "got their revenge out of their system by disbanding the Group and organising the Shadow Cabinet elections", there seemed reason to hope that the schism was a thing of the past. Crossman looked forward to a tranquil session, "and I think that Harold Wilson feels it too. He said this afternoon, 'Well, I'm going to get on with my book.'"[2]* But there were issues which still divided the party. One was German rearmament. The Americans insisted that this was essential if the Russian threat were to be confronted and Attlee was disposed to agree; the dispute grumbled on through 1952 and 1953 and finally erupted in 1954. Wilson was a signatory of the *Tribune* pamphlet *It Need Not Happen* which dismissed as derisory the safeguards which would keep the proposed twelve German divisions securely under the umbrella of the European Defence Community (EDC). "The twelve divisions will be Nazi-led and Nazi-trained." What was needed instead, the pamphlet argued, was an accommodation with the Russians which would recognise and appease their justified fears of German revanchism. The dispute transcended the usual left–right dichotomy; Dalton for one was a fervent opponent of German militarism. When Wilson moved a motion opposing German rearmament in the PLP on 25 February 1954 he as near as nothing carried the day. Even with the help of Labour peers the leadership won only by 111 votes to 109. If Wilson had won and Attlee resigned the cause of party unity would have been damagingly set back; Wilson

---

* Presumably *The War on World Poverty.*

must have found his disappointment at his narrow defeat tempered by some relief that a crisis had been avoided.

But despite the stresses created by this issue, in the course of 1953 Bevan and Wilson, freed from the pressure to which the Keep-Left Group had subjected them, moved with some relief towards a reconciliation with Gaitskell. In April Crossman remarked how, in the House of Commons, Bevan, Wilson and Gaitskell "as the cartoonists soon spotted, were a happy trinity".[1] "Happy" was perhaps an overstatement, but compared with the storms that had gone before the atmosphere was noticeably peaceful. In this process Crossman himself played a significant part. He was no friend of Gaitskell's. The two men were Wykehamists, with all that that implied in the way of arrogance and self-righteousness, but otherwise were widely different. Gaitskell was a man of resolute principle; Crossman considered that ideas were worth advancing only for the sake of challenging and that to believe in a principle was as absurd as to believe in God or the hereditary monarchy. He was not so much an intellectual playboy as a perpetual, extremely clever undergraduate, holding that politics consisted of a long, acrimonious and enjoyable debate. Like a bishop who denies the Virgin Birth, he considered that his periodic tilts at the socialist shibboleths were in the best interests of his party and the nation, but he got great fun out of them as well. In this he differed as widely from Wilson as from Gaitskell, but for the former, through long association, he had acquired a real esteem and even affection. His friendship with Wilson lasted, he once wrote, because both knew that "friendships in politics are best kept cool and detached."[2] Certainly it never stopped him being sharply critical, both to Wilson's face and behind his back. But in the last resort he felt a loyalty towards Wilson stronger than towards any other politician.

It was Crossman who acted as Wilson's second in the battle which broke out within the Bevanites in 1954. The stage had been set the previous year when Wilson missed by only one place election to the shadow Cabinet. According to the party constitution this meant that he would automatically become a member if a vacancy arose through death or resignation. In April 1954 this duly happened, though not in a way Wilson would have chosen. Bevan had been growing increasingly restive about what he regarded as the Labour leadership's failure to stand up to American bullying, whether on German rearmament, the boycotting of communist China or Vietnam. It was this last which provoked the explosion. Attlee, in the House of Commons on

13 April, cautiously defended the American intention to create a South-East Asian counterpart of the North Atlantic Treaty Organisation (NATO) to guard the area against communism. Bevan angrily thrust his leader to one side and denounced the policy as barely cloaked colonialism. In the shadow Cabinet next day the row was resumed and Bevan stormed out. Attlee criticised him sharply at a meeting of the PLP the same evening. Bevan then resigned from the shadow Cabinet. He had consulted none of his Bevanite allies and picked his quarrel with Attlee on an issue which had barely been discussed with them.

Wilson believed, and stated publicly, that Bevan was right on the South-East Asian question,[1] but it was not an issue about which he felt strongly. Certainly he would not, left to himself, have contemplated resignation in protest at Attlee's attitude. Yet that in effect was what was now expected of him; Wilson did not have to decide whether to take the vacant seat but whether to renounce what was automatically his by succession. He was indignant with Bevan for putting him in such an invidious position. "As the philosopher Confucius observed, 'No annihilation without representation'," he remarked to Crossman. If he followed Bevan to the back benches he would once again be labelled as Nye's little dog: "I agree with his policy stand, of course, but not with this tactic and with no consultation."[2] A compromise, in which Bevan might have acquiesced, would have been to reject the automatic succession but instead contest a new ballot for the vacant seat. This was Wilson's preferred solution, but proved impossible; if Wilson refused to join the shadow Cabinet his seat would pass immediately to the next person on the list. In spite of this, Bevan made it plain that he would regard Wilson's taking his place as black treachery. Nearly all his followers supported him; when Wilson told a Bevanite meeting that he wished to take over the vacant seat he was assured that to do so would "inflict serious damage not only on Nye but on the left as a whole".[3]

For several days Wilson agonised. He discussed the matter lengthily with his father, who was so concerned about the pressure being put on him that he said to Mary, "If I were Harold I would give up, do something else."[4] Crossman urged him to hold fast, telling Bevan that he had behaved abominably and that Wilson had every right to feel himself freed from all responsibility towards him. Bevan, who had already drawn a parallel between Wilson and Ramsay MacDonald, predicted balefully that his former disciple would destroy himself if he acted with such reckless opportunism. Crossman retorted that Wilson was far more likely than Bevan to be Attlee's eventual successor. "If he's that kind of man, I don't want anything to do with him," grumbled Bevan. "Don't be silly," Crossman replied. "You've always known that he's that sort of man."[1] In the end, as was predictable from the start to those who knew him best, Wilson accepted the seat. There are no scales in which one can weigh up the pros and cons and conclude that he was right or wrong. To have retreated with Bevan to the wilderness would have been the more obviously noble course, but it might have done irreparable harm to Wilson's own career and it is hard to see that such a sacrifice could reasonably have been expected of him. That he was actuated largely from self-interest is clearly true; equally he could and did argue convincingly that he was justified in the long-term interests of the party as a whole. "What matters in the last resort is the unity and strength of the party," he told the secretary to the PLP. "My conclusion is that in the party's interest it is impossible for me to refuse co-option."[2]

For him the all-important factor was that he should not forfeit the standing he had gained with the left wing. A. J. Irvine, destined to become Solicitor-General in 1967, was one Bevanite who was so outraged by his future Prime Minister's behaviour that he cancelled an engagement to speak at Huyton.[3] Bevan himself remained estranged and "furiously refused" when Wilson asked to be allowed to say that he had joined the shadow Cabinet with the former member's blessing.[4] But though most of those who associated with Bevan resented Wilson's action, they were almost equally indignant with their leader for precipitating such a crisis. The group did not disintegrate and Wilson was not formally evicted. Freeman pleaded with Bevan not to allow "Dick's folly and Harold's ambition" to cut him off from his supporters, and Bevan heeded the appeal.[5] But the Bevanite morning, never particularly glad or confident at the best of times, had clouded over. Political observers in the American Embassy speculated on the possibility that Wilson might bid to take over the leadership of the left wing. He had hesitated before taking his seat in the shadow Cabinet, they concluded, not out of concern for Bevan's feelings but so as to listen to "the ground swell from the party". Once satisfied that this was in his favour, he grasped the prize.[6]

That he had read the portents correctly was shown at the party conference when Wilson came top of the constituency section with

Barbara Castle second. Bevan, who contested with Gaitskell the election as treasurer, was defeated by two to one. Wilson's triumph, in Crossman's gnomic judgment, arose because "he was Bevanite, and he wasn't purely Bevanite".[1] The impurity of his Bevanism became ever more apparent. When asked on television by Malcolm Muggeridge whether he was still a Bevanite he refused to answer yes or no but insisted he had not changed any of his ideas about politics.[2] To Crossman, in October 1954, it seemed that he was palpably seeking to take over the leadership of the left from Bevan's faltering grasp.[3] But though his position had been strengthened he still lacked committed, popular support either to left or right. For every Mikardo who distrusted him on the left, there was a Jenkins or a Healey in the main body of the party. "Harold Wilson is unpopular," this latter pair told an American diplomat in November. "Jenkins criticised his aloofness from the rank and file by alleging that he would speak to no one but Ministers or Ambassadors."[4] Wilson, the embassy's political report concluded a few weeks later, "is generally disliked in the Party despite his efforts to avoid personal differences".[5]

In the same report it was noted that Wilson's relationship with Gaitskell had improved. When they get together as economists, observed Crossman, "Harold Wilson and Gaitskell get on fine."[6] Wilson had by now accepted that Gaitskell was almost certain to be the next Labour Prime Minister and was determined that when that happened the post of Chancellor of the Exchequer should be his. Gaitskell respected Wilson's ability and realised that he needed his support in the interests of party unity. No real rapport had been achieved but an uneasy alliance existed which would survive so long as both men felt it to be in their best interests.

In March 1955 another issue widened still further the rift between Bevan and Wilson. Unlike Mary, who was a passionate unilateralist and once threatened to vote Liberal unless the party policy was changed, Wilson believed in the need for a nuclear deterrent. Hugh Jenkins remembered disputing the point with him in 1955: "I was at that time arguing that Britain should not manufacture her own hydrogen bomb. You did not agree with me and in the discussion showed yourself to be a firm Western alliance man."[7] When Attlee, in the defence debate, tabled an amendment which accepted the need for a deterrent, Wilson was happy to endorse it. Bevan, at the head of sixty-two Labour MPs, not exclusively from the left, defied the party line and spoke in terms extremely offensive to his own front bench. The right wing clamoured for instant retribution. Many thought that Wilson would support or at least acquiesce in it. Bevan faced expulsion, the American Embassy reported: "Crossman and Wilson in particular have been increasingly unhappy with Bevan's actions ... partly because they thought them illogical and stupid politically and partly because they foresaw the political wilderness looming ahead."[1] Crossman found Wilson prepared "so blithely to accept the removal of Mr Bevan that I could hardly stand him".[2]

In fact in the shadow Cabinet Wilson was one of only four members – James Griffiths, Alf Robens and Dalton being the others – to vote for censure rather than expulsion. He refused Bevan's plea that he should resign from the NEC in protest at the shadow Cabinet's decision – a reluctance he shared with the other Bevanites[3] – but claimed that he was ready to argue against expulsion when the matter was discussed by the PLP. No doubt to his considerable relief he was not put to this test; the meeting was deferred because of Bevan's illness and when the PLP finally met on 16 March he was able to plead a long-standing engagement in Paris. Sobered by the thought that a general election was imminent and that the expulsion of Bevan would hardly strengthen party unity, the PLP endorsed the shadow Cabinet's ruling with something less than enthusiasm – a majority of only 141 to 112. Attlee concluded that this unimpressive mandate was insufficient, Bevan was cajoled into making a qualified apology, and the whip was restored to him after only a fortnight – to the satisfaction of everyone except a few hardliners. At a party meeting at Huyton Wilson pleaded for moderation in the exercise of majority power but distanced himself still further from his former ally: "In a democratic party it is essential for the minority to accept majority decisions democratically arrived at."[4]

The general election which followed Churchill's resignation in favour of Anthony Eden came at the end of May 1955. Labour, still riven by dissension and led for the last time by an ageing Attlee, fought a lamentable campaign. One of the redeeming features, though it hardly appeared so to the participants at the time, was Wilson's first appearance on television for the Labour Party. He had made his debut in the United States when interviewed by Ed Murrow and had been given three pieces of advice: "Never attack a man for his race; never attack a man for his religion; never sweat." The first two points were easily met, since Wilson and Edith Summerskill were concerned with more mundane issues, being cast as a married couple deploring the high prices of a range of food products which had been set on a table in front of them. The third was harder, since the studio was a furnace, the butter melted, the cheese dribbled. Edith Summerskill kept getting the butter and the cheese mixed up, thrusting the price labels into the wrong one, while Wilson, who had reluctantly agreed to cut out a lot of his points during the rehearsal, put them all back in again and was left desperately shouting his final lines over the swelling background music. Morgan Phillips, the Labour Party secretary, who was sulking because he had not been allowed to take part, said that it was the worst political programme ever made but William Pickles, from the London School of Economics, insisted it was the best such programme he had seen. Pickles seems to have spoken for the housewife in the street; the public response was excellent.[1]

It was not enough to reverse the national trend, however; the Tories increased their majority to fifty-nine. At Huyton Wilson had little problem. He could fairly claim to have done well by his constituents: 200 surgeries held, 10,000 letters answered, nineteen local issues raised in the House. The inflow of likely Labour voters had gone on as well, with the result that he doubled his majority to 2,558. Huyton could still be described as marginal, but with the redrawing of boundaries that took place after the election it gained a substantial section of Liverpool's seedier suburbs and became established as one of Labour's safer seats.

The election was followed by a post-mortem and the setting up of a small subcommittee under Harold Wilson to examine the state of the party's organisation. He seized the opportunity joyfully, toured the country for two months, held 144 meetings and produced a report of 105 pages with eight appendices. The report concluded that there was too much centralisation; too few voluntary workers; too few full-time agents, especially in marginal seats; inadequate pay for constituency officials; but its presentation was almost as important as its recommendations. "Very tough in tone, almost nasty," Wilson described it.[2] The party machine, he found, was still "at the penny-farthing stage in a jet propelled era and, at that, is getting rusty and deteriorating with age". "After what we have seen of Party organisation throughout the country," he concluded, "our surprise is not that the General Election was lost but that we won as many seats as we did." Crossman thought the report sensational, while Attlee was said to have commented: "Absolutely first-rate! Superb job!"[1] Morgan Phillips, on the other hand, was unsurprisingly offended by a report which so disparaged the work of Transport House, and Shinwell felt that it was all that could be expected of a dyed-in-the-wool *apparatchik* and ignored the fact that "if the causes of disillusion were eradicated the traditional zeal of voluntary Party workers would revive."[2] Bevan agreed; when the report came before the party conference he sabotaged Wilson's hopes of commanding the limelight by launching a ferocious attack on the right wing, particularly the union leaders, whom he claimed had cost Labour the election.[3] Preparing the report, however, had given Wilson unrivalled understanding of and contact with the grass-roots of the party; his role as chairman responsible for implementing the reforms that followed ensured that this proved more than a fleeting advantage.

Inevitably Bevan's hostility strengthened the relationship between Wilson and the right. In the economic debate of October 1955 Gaitskell and Wilson worked harmoniously and successfully together. Some of Gaitskell's followers were less than pleased. "I asked Hugh about Wilson as No. 2," wrote Gordon Walker in his diary. "He had made no deal with him ... We must break up the Bevanites, but Wilson was quite unreliable – an envious enemy of Hugh."[4] Some of the more doctrinaire trade union leaders were equally ill at ease. But Attlee, observing with satisfaction this new cooperation, remarked to the Chief Whip: "Now those two are working together, I can go, leaving the party in good hands."[5]

He duly went, retiring on 7 December 1955. Bevan, Gaitskell and Morrison contended the succession. Wilson contemplated standing but calculated that he would only have got about fifty votes and would have infuriated the other candidates. He let it be known that he favoured Gaitskell, to the indignation of a Tory backbencher who accused him of betraying his former champion. It would have made little difference if he had stood by the Bevanites: Bevan got 70 votes, Morrison a mere 40, Gaitskell 157.

The following day Wilson wrote to Gaitskell pledging his fullest loyalty. "In my view the issue of the leadership is settled for twenty years ... We cannot afford during those years the intrigues and 'Attlee-must-go' type of manoeuvres that have characterised the past. I think that those of us who will be closely associated with you really owe you a pledge that they will have none of it or be associated with backstairs intrigue. For my part you have that pledge."[1]

Gaitskell's reply was equally effusive.

Thank you so much for your very kind and penetrating letter ... Somehow, Harold, we've *got* to replace the suspicions and hatreds and jealousies of these last few years with teamwork and tolerance and friendship among us *all*. This is not just the sentimental utopianism of a new leader! It really is not possible to govern the country unless in the cabinet and in the government there is loyalty from each to all. You and I know that from experience. We know that the business of governing in a Labour government is a pretty desperate affair in which we need, to succeed – as we must – not only brains and judgment – important as these are – but courage and loyalty too. We just can't afford boat-rocking. Part of the job of the next three years is precisely to prepare ourselves for government – and I count this positive working together and confidence among each other as the most important way of doing this.[2]

Kind words cost nothing. Even as they wrote these letters both men must have had their reservations. But there is no reason to doubt that in December 1955 they had the most excellent intentions.

Opposition Under Gaitskell

1954–1963

Gaitskell presided over a shadow government from which the old guard had almost entirely disappeared. Cripps and Bevin were dead, Attlee and Dalton retired, Morrison an embittered has-been. At forty-one Wilson was no longer a child among veterans but in age he was still among the junior members of the shadow Cabinet. In every other way he was one of the most senior, by no means heir apparent but certain to be a strong contender if a vacancy at the top unexpectedly arose. Under Attlee Wilson's role on the opposition front bench had been confined to trade; with Gaitskell promoted he took on the vacant role of shadow Chancellor of the Exchequer. Almost simultaneously, Harold Macmillan took over the Treasury from R. A. Butler. The stage was set for a protracted confrontation that was to enliven the House of Commons and make Wilson's reputation as a parliamentarian.

Almost overnight his style, his attitude, it seemed his personality, fundamentally changed. Many people have turned themselves into orators; Wilson, says Gerald Kaufman, achieved the far more difficult feat of deliberately acquiring a sense of humour.[1] He was still capable of being boring and repetitive – "I don't think that he can do very much work on his speeches," remarked with some disdain the Treasury mandarin Robert Hall in 1957[2] – but more often he was sharp, lucid and brilliantly witty. He set out to be destructive, but then he saw his role as being to destroy the government's handling of the economy rather than devote too much time to propounding his own philosophy. He developed with his Conservative counterpart a rumbustious double act in which a lot of economic argument was dressed up as a highly entertaining dialogue. Whatever Macmillan really thought of Wilson – and some of those who knew him best maintain that he privately viewed the shadow Chancellor with distaste as a vulgarian and a trickster who debased the House of Commons – it suited both men to present themselves as the best of friends. "After a gladiatorial exchange," wrote Wilson, "each of us illuminating economic problems in personal terms, the Chancellor would pass me a note, usually suggesting a drink in the smoking room, occasionally congratulating me on my attack on him ... Of such is the camaraderie of the House of Commons at its best."[1] Macmillan for his part paid tribute to the brilliance of Wilson's attacks on him: "Epigram followed epigram, and the continual flashes of wit were from time to time relieved by more serious arguments."[2]

Wilson's contribution on the budget in 1956 was certainly acrimonious enough to test to the uttermost whatever goodwill existed between them. He dismissed Macmillan's speech as "shambling, fumbling, largely irrelevant and, at one point, degrading". Premium Bonds, a device which was to prove strikingly popular and which Wilson made no attempt to abolish when he found himself in power, were a "squalid raffle. The Tory party used to have the slogan 'Land of Hope and Glory'. They will be fighting the next Election on 'Honest Charlie always pays'." The government's explanation that its cuts in food subsidies accounted for only a seventh part of the current price rises was "as convincing as the defence of a man who gives his wife a gentle push over the cliff and then says that her death was to be explained as to one-seventh the push and six-sevenths gravity".[3] The press in the next few days must have satisfied him that he was following the right lines: the *Daily Telegraph* praised his wit and dexterity: "He hit hard, as clowns tend to do, and with the clown's uncanny knowledge of when his blows are going to tell"; the *Manchester Guardian* hailed "his wittiest and most effective debating speech"; while the *Express* declared that he had emerged as "one of the major figures" of the Labour Party. Gaitskell applauded his efforts. "He managed to combine a good deal of hard argument with considerable wit, and he also adopted a really responsible line," he wrote in his diary. "I am delighted that he should do this, because if he is to be Chancellor in the next Government, it is essential that he should build up a store of confidence in the country generally."[4]

Badinage and headline-catching repartee were fine as far as they went, but by 1959 some of the party faithful had begun to fear that there was little substance behind it. The party had no economic policy, grumbled Kaldor, because Gaitskell took little interest in the subject and "Wilson has completely failed to lead and has retired into himself." Crossman agreed that Wilson was unlikely to make a Chancellor.[1] But Wilson established himself as a serious potential leader in 1961 when he prepared the economic section of the party's new manifesto, *Signpost for the Sixties*. In this he called for a national plan for economic growth, a capital gains tax, public ownership of building land, a takeover of public schools and the raising of the school leaving age to sixteen. The emphasis was on growth as the solution to almost every problem: "if the Chancellor wants to stop this sudden, sharp increase in costs and prices and if he wants to hold it," he declared in the House in July 1961, "the way is not by restricting production but by expanding it."[2] In an article in the *New Statesman* on a "Four-Year Plan for Britain", he argued that the first priority was to increase investment – for which purpose he proposed to set up a National Investment Board. Production must be channelled into exports by "purposive planning" and the state must intervene more vigorously in British business by a system of guaranteed orders for progressive firms, taxation for the slothful and increased public ownership – though not necessarily by a programme of mass nationalisation.[3] Already the dominating *Leitmotivs* of his first government were becoming apparent: wages must be related to economic growth, "Economic awards cannot for long outstrip national production";[4] technology was to play a large part in the new revolution – a "Group of Three", comprising Wilson, Patrick Blackett and Vivien Bowden – were carrying on the work of Gaitskell's Science Committee and planning the technological breakthrough and the new polytechnics that would follow a Labour victory.[5] The growing and dangerous dependence on imported oil must be reversed; Wilson was head of a TUC/Labour Party team which in September 1960 called for a tax on fuel oil, the reconversion of some oil-burning power stations to coal and the regulation of oil imports.[6]

Meanwhile he had to consolidate his position in the shadow Cabinet and work out a *modus vivendi* with the new leader. Their relationship was superficially amiable enough but even at its best had little real warmth. Wilson was "a cold fish", wrote Gaitskell within a few weeks of the affectionate exchange of letters quoted at the end of the last chapter, but "I thought he knew the need for loyalty."[7] It was hardly an ardent affirmation of approval, any more than his remark that Jim Griffiths was the only member of the NEC with courage and intelligence. Wilson had "plenty of intelligence and a little courage".[1] Wilson was "inevitable", he told George Brown;[2] Wilson might have said the same of him; it was an excellent reason for cooperation. The price Wilson paid for this cooperation was still sharper estrangement from Aneurin Bevan. When Wilson dropped to third place in the National Executive elections Crossman mused that "by openly breaking with Nye Harold Wilson and I have done ourselves no good. Harold had gone further and antagonised the agents [by his attack on party organisation] but, on the other hand, had not had an open quarrel with Nye, as I had done."[3] The party conference that year was at Blackpool. Determined to end up with some dramatic footage the television cameramen cut briskly from speaker to audience and back again. Sometimes they got their sequences a little confused. One section had Wilson orating on the platform, cutting to the audience where Wilson was to be seen applauding enthusiastically.[4] Wilson would happily have clapped himself if given half a chance, but even a man as quick on his feet as he was could hardly have contrived to be simultaneously on the floor and on the platform.

By the time of the conference the Suez crisis was breaking. As the most pro-Zionist member of the shadow Cabinet Wilson was not particularly disturbed by the alleged collusion with Israel, but he had no difficulty in joining in condemnation of the Anglo-French intervention. He doubted, however, whether this attitude would win the party much popularity in the country. Remembering the hostility that Lloyd George had encountered when he visited Birmingham in 1901 and put forward his pro-Boer views he told the shadow Cabinet that he hoped he would not have to go to Birmingham himself. In fact he soon found himself addressing a large audience there; he told them "millions yet unborn may rue this week and curse the Government," and to his great relief was well received.[5] To a constituent he wrote: "No one will ever know whether or how far Britain's action in Suez influenced the Russians in their decision to make their ruthless and brutal attack on Hungary. My own view is that the Russians would have taken such action in any event. But our earlier action in Suez made it much more difficult for us to play the part we should have been doing in condemning them."[6] He somewhat intemperately declared that Eden bore part of the responsibility for the loss of "hundreds, perhaps thousands of lives" in Hungary, was taken to task in the press and received several hundred letters from the public, 90 per cent of which were in his favour. But on the whole he behaved with marked moderation during the crisis: "Harold Wilson made a very good speech, as helpful as he could have been in all the circumstances," wrote Robert Hall appreciatively, after Wilson had spoken in the Commons on the economic measures made necessary by Suez.[1]

His moderation was less evident at the end of 1957 in his handling of the curious bank rate scandal – or lack of scandal as it turned out to be. Shortly after the government raised the bank rate from 5 per cent to 7 per cent Wilson, on grounds which at the time seemed plausible though later they were shown to be decidedly flimsy, wrote to the Financial Secretary, Enoch Powell, to complain that someone, clearly benefiting by a tip-off, had made an illicit profit dealing in gilt-edged stock. A "thorough-going and impartial enquiry" was essential. When this was refused Wilson, professing astonishment, wrote to the Prime Minister saying that he had evidence of a leak from a political source. Macmillan invited him to submit his evidence to the Lord Chancellor, which he duly did, only to be told again that no enquiry was called for. "Wilson's detective instincts had now been aroused to an intense pitch of excitement," wrote Macmillan. "He was not to be thrown off the trail by any denials, official or unofficial."[2] He continued the battle, and made it more bitter by suggesting that Oliver Poole, the deputy chairman of the Conservative Party and a City figure, had cognisance of the leak even if he had not himself profited by it. In view of the personal attack, the Prime Minister set up a tribunal which duly found that there had been no irregularities and that, in particular, Poole had not been privy to the information he was supposed to have passed on.[3]

When the House of Commons met to debate the affair early in 1958 most people, including some of his own colleagues, thought that Wilson had put himself in an impossible position and would only be able to extricate himself by a grovelling apology. Instead he took the fight to the government. In a brilliant debating performance lasting an hour and a half, he conceded that his original suspicions had proved unfounded but maintained that the tribunal had exposed many malpractices in the City and that his attitude had been more than justified.[4] His speech was "the cleverest I've ever witnessed in the House of Commons", said Paul Johnson;[5] a "tremendous show", thought Crossman, not just a "brilliant forensic performance" but a display of "sheer guts in battling his way through the entrenched hatred he had engendered among the Tories".[1] The Labour benches had come prepared for an embarrassing debate and stayed to rejoice at what was far more nearly a victory than they had believed possible. Wilson had been lucky, reflected Robert Hall: "The things he *thought* were wrong turned out to be all right, while the City end of the transactions, about which he knew nothing, have at least seemed to be questionable."[2]

It was in some ways a Pyrrhic victory. That he incurred the ferocious enmity of the Tories caused him little concern but the City magnates, who felt that they had been unfairly pilloried and in particular resented his failure to apologise to Poole, were still more vengeful. If Labour won the next election and Wilson took on the Treasury, he would have to work with those men, yet "they will not cooperate much when he is Chancellor," wrote Hall.[3] In fact memories are short and bankers, like anybody else, are well able to cooperate with the uncongenial if there is no alternative. But this was not evident to Gaitskell in 1958 and the affair put a question mark over the role Wilson would play in a future Labour government. Crossman, always ready to stir up mischief, hastened to Wilson with the news that the Labour leader had told him that he did not see how he could have as Chancellor a man so loathed by the City.[4] No doubt Crossman put the worst possible interpretation on Gaitskell's words, but Wilson had little doubt that the gist of it was true. On the other hand, his pugnacious assault on the City won him back-bench approval and to some extent restored his position as standard-bearer of the left. He had already emerged from Bevan's shadow, now he had produced a performance worthy of Bevan at his best – or worst, as the Tories would have seen it.

Bevan was less than enthusiastic about Wilson's claims to take over his role. Crossman, in December 1958, discussed with him what would happen if Labour won the next election. Bevan said that he despaired of Gaitskell's entourage: "of course there's Harold Wilson. He's much more dangerous than Gaitskell because he isn't honest and he isn't a man of principle but a sheer, absolute careerist, out for himself alone." Gaitskell rarely met Wilson because "Hugh doesn't trust Harold any more than I do."[5] Whether this was true or not, Gaitskell knew that he could not do without Wilson in the electoral campaign. He wrote in September 1959 to apologise for having been "a bit rough" in recent discussions in the NEC and went on: "I do want to suggest that any time you can spare from your speaking tour and your own constituency ought really to be devoted to keeping a close eye on organisation. I realise the difficulties of doing this; nevertheless it remains absolutely vital."[1] According to Woodrow Wyatt, Gaitskell asked him to teach Wilson "how to look trustworthy on television". It went against his inclinations, said Wyatt, but "I made Wilson sound sincere and reliable."[2]

Labour started the 1959 election with high hopes. Probably they were exaggerated from the start; the average Briton was noticeably better off after three and a half years of Macmillan's leadership and it would have taken a remarkable *volte-face* on the public's part to unseat him. Gaitskell, however, was a formidable opponent and he was much to the forefront in the Labour campaign. He seemed to be making a real impression, then rashly went too far in promising lavish new government spending with no increase in taxes and the abolition of purchase tax on certain items. "They are turning the election into a mock auction," accused Macmillan; they were insulting the intelligence of the British people. From that moment the tide turned.[3] Gaitskell certainly blundered; when Bevan heard of his leader's pledge he announced angrily: "He's thrown it away. He's lost the election."[4] Wilson was also inculpated. Gaitskell spoke to him on the telephone and told him what he planned to say. Driberg and Crossman concur that Wilson accepted even if he did not welcome the idea; Wyatt even states that he planned to say something similar himself.[5] Marcia Williams, however, who was in the lobby of the Adelphi Hotel in Liverpool when Gaitskell telephoned an hour before his fateful broadcast, says that Wilson's attitude was "very doubtful". He did not say that he thought the proposal folly, since he believed that Gaitskell could not be deflected, but he left little doubt that he was ill at ease.[6] It would have been surprising if he had had no doubts but his failure to convey them forcibly to his leader means that he must accept some responsibility for the débâcle that followed. For the third election in a row the Tories increased their majority. There was some consolation in the fact that in Huyton, where Wilson benefited by the continuing inflow of potential Labour voters and his ever-growing reputation as a diligent constituency member, his majority once again doubled to a comfortable 5,927.

No party can lose three elections in a row without indulging in some serious soul-searching. The left took it for granted that the matter could only be put right by the adoption of full-blooded socialist principles; the right were equally convinced that it was the socialist baggage that was dragging the Labour Party down and that this must be dumped if they were to win over the electorate. At a meeting at Gaitskell's house the Sunday after the election the leader's inner circle – Jay, Gordon Walker, Roy Jenkins, Herbert Bowden, Anthony Crosland, John Harris – agreed that Clause IV of the party constitution, which called for the "nationalisation of the means of production, distribution and exchange", should be abandoned. Jay went even further and advocated that the name of the party be changed as well, or at least the word "Radical" be added.[1] When word of their deliberations filtered out, Wilson was genuinely horrified. At the Cambridge University Labour Club, though naming no names, he denounced as cynical and opportunistic those who sought to abandon "essential and fundamental parts of our creed" to meet the needs of political expediency.[2] He had no particular affection for Clause IV himself, describing it irreverently as "the Party's equivalent of the detailed architectural passages of the Book of Revelation",[3] but he knew that to many of the party faithful it possessed almost mystical significance and he had no wish to strain their loyalty by treating their susceptibilities with cavalier indifference. He told John Junor that he thought Macmillan was a genius: "He's holding up the banner of Suez for the Party to follow, and he's leading the Party away from Suez. That's what I'd like to do with the Labour Party over nationalisation."[4] Wilfully to pull down the banner of Clause IV and trample it in the mud, however bedraggled it might have become, was to commit what was, in Wilson's book, the worst of crimes: to imperil party unity. His resentment was heightened by what he saw as an attempt to saddle him with the blame for electoral defeat. The *Daily Mail* assured its readers that Wilson was being held responsible for his failure to reform the party machine and to warn his leader of the dangers in making rash economic pledges.[5] Crossman made things worse by passing on hints from Gaitskell that the shadow Chancellor was about to be moved to another job – news which Crossman was entertained to see stung Wilson to passionate anger.[6]

The party conference was cancelled in 1959 because of the election, and a weekend meeting at Blackpool substituted. Gaitskell chose this occasion to thrown down the gauntlet, urging the party to accept the principle of a mixed economy and admit that public ownership was only a means to an end, and far from the most efficacious means at that. Bevan threatened resignation and an immediate challenge to Gaitskell for the leadership. Wilson helped to restrain him; he was convinced that Gaitskell must be opposed but saw nothing to be gained by conducting a violent quarrel on the Blackpool platform. His common sense told him that a compromise between the reformers and the fundamentalists not merely could but must be arrived at, and that Blackpool was not the place to do it. For the moment he bided his time and said as little as he decently could.

He caused some surprise at this time by seeking the chairmanship of the Public Accounts Committee, a body responsible for examining how the money voted by parliament had been spent. This gruelling and time-consuming task was usually taken on by a more drudge-like figure, with no aspirations to reach the top. For Wilson it provided both the detailed and statistical labour that were his meat and drink and a priceless education in the workings of the Treasury. The demands the job made on his time led him regretfully to give up his work at Montague Meyer.[1] His Uncle Jack, for some reason, had been given the idea that Wilson was moving the other way and might soon abandon politics altogether. "There was never any question of my deserting politics for industry," wrote Wilson. "Indeed, I am giving up my job with Montague L. Meyer's and shall be able to devote a good deal more time to politics as a result."[2] The decision was made the easier because his new job carried with it that rare perquisite, a room in the House of Commons. This meant that Wilson could abandon his office at Meyer's without undue anguish and, incidentally, bring with him to the House of Commons his secretary, Marcia Williams.

It is difficult to overestimate the importance of Marcia Williams in Wilson's political career. Wilson, other things being equal, preferred women to men and could relax with them more easily, possibly because he felt they provided less of a threat to his position. But he did not want a woman for dalliance or talking of Michelangelo. He wanted to discuss politics or to gossip about politicians; not political theory or gossip for gossip's sake, but the nuts and bolts of who would vote for whom, how X could be persuaded to do this, Y prevented from doing that. If Mary had wanted it, her husband would have been happy for her to fill the role, but though concerned with political issues, she hated the political world. She was prepared to smile loyally at election times, to rejoice in his triumphs and lament at his disasters, but endless late-night debate about the state of the party was not for her. Wilson needed a supplementary, a political wife. His specifications for such an adjunct were unusual. Perhaps as a legacy of his childhood, Wilson relished assertive and bullying women. Mary was strong but tranquil, she abhorred rows and regarded the making of scenes in public as vulgar and distasteful. Marcia, whose temper was explosive and self-control so wayward as to be at times non-existent, seemed to consider scenes a necessary part of life. Wilson, equable himself, viewed her excesses with mingled tolerance and admiration. She was prepared to tell other people the things Wilson would have liked to have told them himself but could not bring himself to say aloud. He was frightened of her – for she was formidable in her ferocity – but frightened with the delighted glee of one to whom a frisson of terror adds savour to a relationship. Those who marvelled at the patience with which Wilson endured Marcia's threats and insults missed the point: it was those very threats and insults which enhanced her value in his eyes. Wilson was not a weak man, he was perfectly capable of ignoring Marcia's objurgations and continuing along his chosen route indifferent to her protests. Often he did so. But he was incapable, chose to be incapable, of shutting her up and cutting off the lava flow of protest in midstream.

Largely this was because he had confidence in her loyalty and dedication. She might sometimes be obstreperous, perverse, but she was on his side. The relationship was sexual, in the sense that it could only have existed between man and woman, but there is not the slightest reason to believe that it ever contained any element of physical sexuality in it. The affinity between them was more that between parent and child: "doting father and spoiled daughter", said Joe Haines; "father and caring daughter", was Sigmund Sternberg's verdict.[1]

Sometimes the roles were reversed, and it was Wilson who seemed the child – mischievous, provocative – and Marcia the mother. Usually, though, it was Wilson who played the protective role. Crossman described him arriving forty-five minutes late for dinner: "he melted my heart when he explained that this was because he had been with his secretary, who had just had a nervous breakdown ... All this was really endearing, since afterwards he said, 'Take my mind off her, for God's sake, by discussing pensions.' "[2] Whether or not Wilson's words or Crossman's rendition of them were unduly colourful (Lady Falkender today denies that she had anything approaching a nervous breakdown at the time and feels Crossman must have been confused), the fact that Wilson had spent valuable time trying to comfort her when she was in distress is typical of his attitude towards her over the next quarter of a century.

Those who try to assess Marcia Williams's significance in Wilson's career must realise that the relationship evolved and her own performance within it varied greatly. First there was Marcia in the years of opposition: young, ardent, relatively ingenuous, feeling her way. Then came Marcia in the first years at Number 10, preoccupied with problems of her own status and a drawn-out guerrilla campaign with the permanent civil service. Finally there was Marcia at bay, hounded by the media, seeing enemies behind every desk. The contribution that the first Marcia made to Wilson's climb to the top can hardly be overestimated. Extremely hard-working, with a good brain and outstanding administrative skills, she organised his political life and freed him to conduct his campaigns without needing to concern himself about the logistic back-up. A "competent, hard-working shorthand-typist" without any special talents, George Wigg pronounced her;[1] an absurd misjudgment by one who had time and again been put to rout by that shorthand-typist in skirmishes in the Downing Street corridors. At the very least she was a superlative personal assistant; but in fact her shrewdness, common sense and knowledge of the Labour Party made her far more than that. Callaghan remarked that her knowledge of the party was limited – "She didn't have the root of the matter in her"[2] – but she understood well the workings of the party *apparatchiks*, and could tell Wilson with almost unfailing good judgment how far he could go in attacking the sacred cows of socialism and how best to manipulate the complex and antiquated machinery of the Labour Party headquarters. But she gave him more than that. "I doubt very much," wrote the political journalist James Margach, "whether Harold Wilson would ever have become Party leader and Prime Minister but for the ambitious thrust provided by Mrs Williams."[3] Marcia herself put her contribution more modestly. "I helped to encourage and build the enthusiasm that he already felt," she said. "I couldn't have put it there. But I did keep him going through difficult times."[4] That was already a great deal.

Marcia Williams got into politics with some help from James Callaghan, who met her when he addressed the Queen Mary College Labour Club and was so greatly charmed that he rang up Morgan Phillips, the national secretary of the Labour Party, and told him that he had a promising recruit for Transport House. Under Phillips the party headquarters was a staid, even reactionary institution. Marcia did some temporary work for Callaghan but wanted something permanent and more stimulating, preferably by the hitching of her wagon to some convenient star. "It could have been me," Callaghan mused, though he suspects she would have moved on pretty soon.[1] She was asked to work for Gaitskell, wondered if that might be her destiny, then decided that he was both too autocratic and too right-wing for her taste.[2] When attempts were made from within Transport House to frustrate Wilson's reform of the party organisation, she wrote him anonymous letters warning him what was being done. Soon she had satisfied herself that he offered the best chance that the Labour Party would develop in the way she hoped – a less heroic figure than Bevan but, to her mind, incomparably more likely to prove effective. She had got to know Arthur Skeffington, a member of the NEC whose son was Wilson's godchild, and it was through him that she was offered the job when Wilson's secretary became pregnant. She joined him in October 1956, just in time for the Suez crisis, and worked by day in the Montague Meyer office, taking the post over to the House of Commons in the evening. At first she was overawed by his reputation as a tough-minded intellectual, but reverence did not come easily to her and within a few months she was speaking her mind with the sometimes brutal frankness which was to mark their whole relationship.

She had married, when still very young, an engineer who had been Chairman of the Conservative Association at Queen Mary's College and encouraged her in her political activities. It was the need for a larger income that led to her husband's decision to work for Boeing in Seattle. Absence, as usual, made the heart less fond and Mr Williams eventually fell in love with an American girl and asked Marcia for a divorce. Two years after this she was contemplating leaving politics and going to the bar. Wilson reluctantly agreed and she was taking the preliminary steps when Gaitskell died. Marcia found herself working for the man who was likely to be the next Prime Minister. By the time they went to Number 10 she was political secretary and a crucial member of the entourage.

Inevitably there was gossip, and as her role in Wilson's office grew, so the gossip became more vengeful. When she worked at the Montagu Meyer office she was said to be a dangerous *éminence grise*, when she appeared more often at the House of Commons she was flaunting her power. She did not help her own cause: tact was never one of her stronger points, and though she could keep a secret, other forms of discretion were hardly known to her, and she was ruthless in protecting her employer from those whom she thought unworthy of him. She did not yet earn any attention in the press, but there was no shortage of quidnuncs in the House who surmised darkly about the extent of her duties. Nor did she always handle Mary discreetly. On the whole the two women co-existed harmoniously, each with their own sphere and content to leave the other in possession of what they held, but Marcia had no doubt that hers was the more important share, and sometimes she let this show. Mary had deliberately cut herself off from her husband's political life, but a wish not to be part of something does not necessarily preclude resentment at being excluded. From time to time she was made to feel that she was neither needed nor wanted, and there were those who told her that she had been brutally pushed aside. At the end of 1959 there was as yet little overt criticism of Marcia's role but the possibility existed. The relative indifference of the press was not likely to endure if the shadow Chancellor and his personal assistant were one day to become Prime Minister and political secretary.

Gaitskell's challenge on Clause IV meant that his disagreements with Wilson, hitherto in the main personal, springing from rivalry and differences of temperament, now became doctrinal. Towards the end of 1959 stories were rife that Wilson, either under the aegis of Bevan or by himself, was plotting some kind of coup. "The whole leadership of the Party is now stinking with intrigue and suspicion," wrote Crossman with characteristic hyperbole, "since everybody knows that Bevan is now manoeuvring against Gaitskell and that Harold Wilson, who doesn't forgive easily, is going to take his vengeance for Gaitskell's vague plot to oust him from the Shadow Chancellorship."[1] Wilson was sufficiently disturbed by such rumours to make a statement at the weekly meeting of the PLP more or less explicitly disavowing them. Bevan was the only man who might have contemplated overt revolt against Gaitskell at this point, and by Christmas 1959 he was a dangerously ill and probably dying man.

The knowledge that Bevan could not last much longer gave Wilson cause for much agonised reflection. He told Crossman that he would stand for deputy leader. Half jokingly Crossman questioned the desirability of two Oxford economists at the head of the Labour Party: "Then I realised that Harold was in deadly earnest and won't let anybody step ahead of him."[1] When Bevan died in July 1960, Wilson felt bereft at the loss of one who had been for so long a heroic figure in his life, and isolated by the disappearance of a man with whom he held many positions in common, but also he was excited and filled with a sense of new opportunity. There was no shortage of people to tell him that Bevan's heritage was now rightfully his and that he must prepare to do battle for it. Bill Davies, an old friend of Herbert Wilson and future Lord Arwyn, wrote to thank Wilson for the "truth and sincerity" of his tribute to Bevan and urged him to take on the sacred charge, "or the Party and its ultimate aims will die". The banner Bevan had held so high, Davies insisted, "must not be allowed to be besmirched by the dust of decay".[2]

If dust was not so much a sign of decay as of disuse, then Wilson asked nothing better than that it should be spread liberally on the controversies that divided Labour. On Clause IV he achieved a fair measure of success. In the NEC the trade union leaders seemed resolved to continue the fight, and with Jay and Gordon Walker on one side and Crossman on the other, ready and apparently eager to stir things up, it was only too likely that the row would erupt again at the party conference in Scarborough in 1960. According to Tony Benn, however, Gaitskell decided that trade union support was not to be counted on.[3] In the NEC in July a compromise formula emerged which Gaitskell accepted and Wilson agreed to move at the conference. *Labour in the Sixties*, the document which enshrined this doctrine, in Wilson's words "embodied the Saint's prayer 'Lord give us chastity but not yet'. Clause IV was repeated as an ultimate objective, in God's good time but not in ours."[4] Wilson's masterly obfuscation, crystallised above all in the phrase "common ownership substantial enough to give the community power over the commanding heights of the economy", satisfied nobody completely but left everyone thinking that the party had moved in their direction.[5] It was a victory for pragmatism over ideological extremism, or for time-serving over principle, depending on whether you were a Wilsonian or a Gaitskellite.

One of the reasons Gaitskell gave way was that he saw another battle ahead in which there could be no such concession. The seeds had been sown in 1957, when the Conservatives agreed with President Eisenhower to test the British hydrogen bomb on Christmas Island.

Next year the Campaign for Nuclear Disarmament (CND) was launched, supported by most of Labour's left wing but by neither Bevan nor Wilson. Wilson was the more emphatic of the two. "I have never said that I support the campaign, never ..." he later told Richard Marsh. "I have frequently and specifically said that I have never been opposed to Polaris."[1] But specific though he might have been, he never considered the matter one on which it was necessary to take a dogmatic line, claiming once that he could draft "at least seven defence policies" on which the party could unite.[2]

In April 1960, with the cancellation of the Blue Streak missile project, the so-called British "independent" nuclear deterrent became even more of an illusion. Gaitskell was abroad when the matter was debated in the House of Commons and Wilson and George Brown took advantage of his absence to modify the party line. "From now on, there is no sense in any defence talk about independence," stated Wilson. He derided the Prime Minister as being "Like so many other rather pathetic individuals whose sense of social prestige outruns their purse". Macmillan reminded him of "the man who does not admit that he cannot afford a television set and who knows that he cannot afford it, and who just puts up the aerial instead". Unilateral disarmament was still not the right solution, but there was scope for placing what was left of the British deterrent under the umbrella of NATO.[3] Wilson claimed that he and Brown had formulated the new policy together; Brown maintained that he had done it single-handed and that Wilson's role had been confined to a respectful readiness to follow his instructions;[4] whatever the truth, Gaitskell returned to London to discover that the pass had to a large extent been sold and that his chief lieutenants had formed a united front against him.

It did not last for long. Though Gaitskell did not specifically reject the new party line, he made it clear that his interpretation of it was different from that of Wilson. Even his staunchest followers became alarmed at his apparent determination to reopen an issue which it seemed might have been safely buried. "I begin to fear that Gaitskell has the seeds of self-destruction in him," wrote Gordon Walker after a discussion in Roy Jenkins's flat on pacifism in the unions. "He is becoming distrustful and angry with his best friends and wants to take up absolute and categorical positions that will alienate all but a handful."[5] He seemed in danger of being isolated; James Callaghan reported that Brown and Wilson had done a deal, that Brown was to be leader with Wilson as his deputy. No one took the story particularly seriously, if only because Brown and Wilson would be improbable partners for such a plot: "If we have to die in the last ditch," Brown had said a few days before, "Harold won't be there. He will have scrambled out."[1] But, though the party was fragmented and no clear alternative was generally acceptable, for a time Gaitskell stood almost alone in his opposition to anything that conveyed even a hint of unilateral disarmament.

It was a tribute to his courage, obstinacy and persuasiveness that, when the party conference began at Scarborough, the leadership had once more rallied behind Gaitskell. Brown was loyal, even Wilson seemed prepared to acquiesce in the shadow Cabinet line, though still casting around for some compromise that would avert a clash with the unions, led by a belligerently unilateralist Frank Cousins of the Transport and General Workers. "If the Labour Party ends this week facing two directions," remarked the *New Left Review*, "it is certain that the figure of Mr Wilson will be there at the end of both of them."[2] But though he was not intending to indulge in overt revolt he allowed his disapproval of his leader's line to become more and more apparent. When Gaitskell vowed that, if the unions imposed upon the conference a defence policy that he felt unacceptable, he would "fight and fight and fight again to reverse it", Wilson sat in a hostile silence and conspicuously failed to join in the ovation. Shinwell even claims that Wilson was absent from the platform throughout his leader's speech.[3] He perhaps lost sight of him in the cloud of smoke that hung around his place; "Never," reported the *Sunday Times*, "have so many matches been struck in such a short time on one small pipeful of tobacco as there were by Mr Wilson during Mr Gaitskell's speech."[4] Subsequently he made no attempt to conceal his disapproval, telling the *Guardian* that he believed the "crisis of confidence arises from the feeling that some of our leaders do not unequivocally reject the idea of the British bomb, and that they are waiting for Skybolt or Polaris to come along, with the idea of returning to the notion of a separate British deterrent, with an American rocket to deliver it".[5]

But that was as far as he felt disposed to go. Left to himself he would have returned from Scarborough and worked diligently behind the scenes to find some formula which would reconcile Gaitskell and the union leaders. He would have contested the election for deputy and continued to serve with consistent if not particularly ardent loyalty, content in the knowledge that if Gaitskell lost another election or in some way stumbled, the succession would in all probability be his. He was not left to himself, however. He knew that his position was still vulnerable. He was a favourite target of the right wing. There had long been rumours that Gaitskell proposed to replace him as shadow Chancellor by Roy Jenkins;[1] now Wilson was told that Callaghan had been promised the job as a reward for his loyalty.[2] George Brown, too, expected a reward; he had reason to believe that Gaitskell would support him in the contest for deputy. If Wilson simply sat tight, how long would it be before his enemies on the right destroyed him or at least before he was displaced in the party pecking order? From the left came clamour that he should challenge Gaitskell for the leadership. Jennie Lee, Bevan's widow, urged him to pick up Nye's sword and join the battle. "You must come out from behind your bush," insisted the journalist and adviser to the Labour Party on press affairs, Trevor Lloyd-Hughes. "Harold hadn't even known he *was* behind a bush," remarked Marcia Williams;[3] if it had occurred to him he would certainly have chosen to stay there. But the pressure to emerge was hard to resist. Crossman described him as "desperately worried. Poor little man, he has really cornered himself this time. He knew he would be pressed to stand against Hugh, in which case he would be committing political suicide, and he wants to stand as Deputy Leader instead. But he also knows that, if he doesn't stand against Hugh, he will be accused of cowardice and he may well be defeated for Deputy Leader, now George Brown has jumped on the band-wagon again and has Hugh's backing. Here is an object lesson in the master-tactician and the super-opportunist who is so clever that his tactics are disastrous and he destroys his opportunities. But what can I say about somebody who, throughout all these talks, has been utterly trivial, complacent and vain?"[4]

Crossman must have been in an exceptionally bilious mood when he made that diary entry, but Wilson knew that the left as a whole would think that he had let them down if he allowed Gaitskell to get away with his defiance of the party conference. He would have still felt that this was the lesser evil, however, if Anthony Greenwood had not announced his intention of himself resigning from the shadow Cabinet and challenging for the leadership. Greenwood stated subsequently that he had put forward his candidature not with any serious intention of standing but so as "to put some fire into Harold".[5] Certainly he had even less chance than Wilson of posing a serious threat to Gaitskell. Whatever his motives, he put Wilson in an awkward dilemma. If Greenwood stood and did badly then Gaitskell would be strengthened, if he did well then Wilson would be eclipsed as a natural centre of revolt. The pressure redoubled from those, headed by Barbara Castle, who felt that Greenwood's decision made it even more necessary for Wilson to stand. Michael Foot alarmed him still more by arguing persuasively that, provided Wilson made his support manifest, Greenwood would prove an excellent candidate for the championship of the left.[1] "It was the most difficult and upsetting decision I have ever had to take in my political life," Wilson remembered. "In office or in opposition I have never been one to lose sleep over any problem. When I was faced with this one I lay awake night after night."[2]

In the end he announced that he was ready to stand, and Greenwood, with some reluctance, withdrew. In the election that followed, said Anthony Crosland, the overriding object must be to keep Wilson's vote as low and Gaitskell's as high as possible; "to achieve this we must resort to any degree of chicanery, lying, etc, etc".[3] It is charitable to suppose that Crosland's language was more colourful than his real intentions, but Gaitskell's strongmen still went to considerable pains to ensure that the election result was not embarrassing to the leader. The final figures, 166 to 81, gave Gaitskell a convincing enough victory but were by no means humiliating to his opponent. When Wilson fell from first to ninth place in the shadow Cabinet elections, with eight loyal Gaitskellites ahead of him, he may have hoped that honour was now satisfied and the affair could be forgotten.

Some people had thought that he would do better to stand aside from these elections and give time for the dust to settle. He had given the matter a lot of thought, said Wilson, but had concluded that defiance was the best policy. "The Nye parallel was never far from my mind, but I don't intend to become a prisoner of any hatchet men, and I certainly intend to keep my freedom of action in speeches I make in the country."[4] His behaviour was more conciliatory than these words suggested. His main preoccupation was now to be accepted back as a full member of the team. The team itself, or some members of it, were less ready to forgive and forget. Except by a group of the fiercest partisans, it was generally felt that it was better to have Wilson in the shadow Cabinet than loose outside – "he would be safely tied up, we did not want to split the party too badly, etc", wrote Gordon Walker[5] – but there seemed no reason not to make him suffer for his disloyalty. Gaitskell at one moment contemplated demoting Wilson from shadow Chancellor to the charge of the colonies: "Wilson might take over 'darkest Africa'," suggested Dalton hopefully.[1]

Crossman had gone too far when he said that Wilson would commit "political suicide" if he opposed Gaitskell, but it had still been a dangerous and damaging exercise. The two years after the leadership election, said Marcia Williams, were "the worst of Wilson's political life, because he was really sent to Coventry for that period. He was avoided everywhere and treated like a leper."[2] She used to lunch regularly with him in the Members' Cafeteria, just to make sure that he was not left to eat alone. The tradition in the Labour Party was that a leader once elected was there for life and must be supported loyally. Wilson's challenge to Gaitskell had defied that rule; it had guaranteed the support of the left but had alienated moderates and right alike: "Wilson was *loathed* by the right wing," said Tony Benn.[3] It was not only a Gaitskellite elite who felt lasting rancour, much of the rank and file concurred: Fred Williams and his mates at the Hammersmith Bus Garage wrote to tell Wilson "what a dirty, treacherous, back-stabbing Bastard we think you are. You sit on the fence to see which way the cat jumps, and then you try to stab Hugh in the back."[4]

The majority of the shadow Cabinet might not have expressed themselves with quite such crudity but their views would have been broadly similar. Fred Lee, not one of its livelier members, was said to be the only one to have voted for Wilson in the contest with Gaitskell. It was a lonely position for the shadow Chancellor and he could only hope to retain it by reminding people of his value. Like Lewis Carroll's Red Queen, he had to run twice as fast if he was to stay in the same place. He achieved it by his mastery of his subject; by sheer hard work – almost single-handed he wrote the economic sections for the new draft Labour manifesto; and by a series of coruscating performances in the House of Commons. His attack on Selwyn Lloyd's budget in the summer of 1961 put heart into a demoralised opposition.[5] Macmillan was still his principal target – he had been "degrading, debasing and debauching our national life by preaching the gospel of the free-for-all, the gospel of grabbing all one can"; Lloyd was treated with some disdain as the organ-grinder's monkey, who grimaced to order but did not have the talent to do it well. "Not since the days of Nye Bevan have the Commons heard louder Labour cheers than greeted Mr Wilson after his brilliant knock-about performance," reported the *Sunday Telegraph*. But it noted too that

Gaitskell "had apparently not forgotten the 'Shadow' Chancellor's clumsy attempt to snatch the leadership last year. He sat hunched over his notes, sparing neither a word not a gesture of praise."[1]

That the body of the party quickly forgave Wilson was shown when he was once again returned at the top of the constituency section at the party conference; that the leadership still had serious reservations was equally evident. In November 1961 Gaitskell moved Wilson to become shadow Foreign Secretary. It is possible to see this – as Douglas Jay does – as a routine reshuffle intended to widen a minister's experience and not necessarily related to the role that he would play when Labour came to power.[2] Equally it could be presented as a malign manoeuvre designed to move Wilson from a role in which he shone to one to which his talents were unlikely to be suited. Probably Gaitskell had a complex of motives. Callaghan was known to covet the Treasury and Gaitskell was glad to be able to reward him for his loyalty: as Marcia Williams perhaps over-colourfully put it, Callaghan demanded "St John the Baptist's head on a charger. He wanted Harold Wilson's job and, like Salome, he got what he wanted."[3] And then Gaitskell was anxious to see Wilson in a place where he would find it less easy to renew the leadership challenge; he told Alastair Hetherington, editor of the *Guardian*, that, in office, "he would prefer to have Wilson as Foreign Minister where he could keep a close eye on him. He'd have less independence of action there."[4] And, finally, there is no reason to doubt that he genuinely believed it was a good idea to shift shadow ministers around, so that they would have a greater understanding of the wider picture when the time came for them to move from Westminster to Whitehall.

Crossman and others of Wilson's intimates ensured that the most malign of these interpretations were presented as being the most significant. Wilson, Crossman maintained, was being invited to step into a trap where he would be destroyed at leisure. He should refuse the offer. "I don't mind walking into a trap, provided I'm packing a Luger," Wilson told Anthony Howard,[5] but in fact he was not sure that his Luger was loaded, or even that he knew how to use it. Some time before, he had been warned that he might become shadow leader of the House of Commons; that would have suited him far better because of the contact it would have given him with members of the party. Foreign affairs were another matter, and he had little doubt that the task was thrust upon him as belated punishment for his challenge for the leadership. At one point he told Marcia Williams that he intended to follow Crossman's advice and refuse the posting. Yet it was, after all, one of the great offices of state; to shadow it would give him good experience in a field which would be of the utmost importance if he ever found himself at Number 10; he was quite confident enough of his powers to believe that he could do the work, at the least, with competence. In the end he accepted. Christopher Mayhew was made his deputy, Gaitskell explaining candidly to him that "he wanted me 'to keep an eye on Harold'."[1]

Wilson was not a conspicuous success in his new role. Harold Macmillan noted that his first speech was "so violent as to make many even of his own side feel somewhat ashamed. Although brilliant and witty, his jibes and insinuations failed in their purpose."[2] The criticism of his subsequent performances was more often that they were lacklustre and ponderous; the sparkle of his performance as shadow Chancellor seemed to have been extinguished by the need to digest a mountain of new information. The lot of the opposition spokesman, confronting a minister formidably well briefed and backed by the full resources of his department, is always a difficult one. When the field of debate is as vast as foreign affairs, and the opposition spokesman as inexperienced as Wilson, then the disparity becomes almost intolerable. Given this, Wilson did better than had been expected – or, perhaps, hoped – by certain of his colleagues. He was fortunate in that several of the most lively issues during this period had a strong economic content – notably the crisis in the Congo with its vast mineral resources, and the future of Britain's relationship with Europe. Here he was in his element. He found, too, that when he went to Washington, some of his former pupils from his years at Oxford had risen to high places in the administration and were eager to welcome him. He had never been anti-American, though many Americans had thought him so because of his views on East–West trade and their policy in South-East Asia; now his speeches were notable for their praise of almost every aspect of American foreign policy.

But his year as shadow Foreign Secretary was above all important for the opportunity it gave him to establish a line on Europe – a subject that was to dominate British foreign policy throughout his time as Prime Minister and leader of the Labour Party. On this, as on so many issues, his prime concern was that it should not be allowed to breach party unity – it *must* be possible to establish a consensus which would be broadly acceptable to the great majority of members. But he started with a powerful emotional prejudice against the entry of Britain into the European Community. Partly this was because he was an ardent supporter of the Commonwealth, and any strengthening of the ties with Europe must in the long term be damaging to the Commonwealth connection. Partly he was influenced by the fact that the Eastern bloc was hostile to the concept, and saw a united Europe as a potential tool for German revanchism. Then too, as a devoted parliamentarian, he looked with unease at anything that might encroach on the free exercise of its powers by the House of Commons. And finally – though the point may seem trivial – the fact that Britain would be acceding to the Treaty of *Rome* jarred against his nonconformist instincts. "The end will be mass being said in the streets of Geneva," a Labour stalwart announced balefully in the House of Lords. Wilson knew that such an attitude was absurd, but he would still have found it easier to stomach if the treaty had been of Copenhagen or The Hague.[1]

Wilson enunciated his doctrine with considerable skill in the House of Commons in August 1961.[2] Macmillan described his speech as being the most brilliant of the debate: "Its only fault was that it seemed to come down too much against the European plan, but he retrieved this at the last moment and climbed back upon the official party fence by wishing well to the government in their endeavour."[3] A few weeks earlier Crossman had complained how shocked he had been by Wilson's "bumbling fence-sitting and by his anxiety to postpone decisions by any kind of excuse".[4] Fence-sitting, yes, but there was nothing bumbling about Wilson's performance on 3 August. One of his few intemperate comments came when he spoke as defender of the Commonwealth: "We are not entitled to sell our friends and kinsmen down the river for a problematical and marginal advantage in selling washing machines in Düsseldorf." Otherwise his speech was balanced and reasonable, reflecting the genuine perplexity of a man who loved the traditional institutions of his country yet saw the attractions of a new, resurgent Europe. On the whole, as Macmillan approvingly noted, he gave a cautious green light to negotiations for British entry: "The whole history of political progress is a history of gradual abandonment of national sovereignty." To the full-blooded Europeans like Roy Jenkins it seemed that he hedged his approval around with conditions that he knew would never be accepted; ardent little Englanders like Shinwell felt that he had sold out to those who would betray national sovereignty; the fact that both wings were discontented at his posture convinced Wilson that he was broadly right.

But Gaitskell was moving against the concept, and if Gaitskell could take the party with him then Wilson was quite ready to be borne along by the tide. At first Gaitskell's attitude had been that the controversy over Europe did not involve any serious matter of principle but was "a bore and a squalid nuisance".[1] He held this line throughout 1961 and the first half of 1962, but when the Commonwealth leaders met in September 1962 he seems for the first time fully to have taken in what was proposed. Wilson had prepared "a carefully balanced draft" for the final communiqué, Gaitskell rejected it and "insisted on rewriting it much more critically".[2] By the time of the Brighton party conference later that year, the leader's opposition to British entry had grown still more emphatic. With Wilson as that year's party chairman listening with mingled approval and consternation, Gaitskell denounced the European Community and all its works and declared that the Labour Party should never cooperate with any attempt to join it. It was not how Wilson would have handled the matter but he saw no particular reason to quarrel with the speech's purport; if Gaitskell could neutralise the ardent Europeans, who were concentrated in his own wing of the party, then good luck to him. Wilson referred appreciatively in his summing-up to "this historic speech" and proposed that it be "immediately printed and made available to every Party member in the country".[3]

The conference was on the whole a success for Wilson; he presided with skill and avoided the most obvious pitfalls of prolixity and bossiness. It provided one moving moment when an elderly and unfamiliar figure rose to second the vote of thanks to the chairman. "I have to pay a respectful tribute to the seconder of the motion for his maiden speech," replied Wilson, "and that is not the only thing I have to thank my father for."[4] But his performance did not do much to improve his standing within the parliamentary party. In November he challenged George Brown for the deputy leadership. With the full weight of the Gaitskellites behind him, Brown won comfortably; Wilson only got twenty or so more votes than when he had opposed Gaitskell for the leadership in 1960. It was a question of personalities, Hetherington reported Gaitskell as explaining: "Wilson was not trusted. That wasn't only his feeling (though it *was* his feeling) it was also quite commonly shared in the Party." Brown, particularly when the worse for drink, could be very disloyal, "but it was a very different thing to the kind of disloyalty encountered in Harold Wilson".[1] Wilson himself was not surprised by the voting figures, though he had hoped to do better, especially since Brown had recently disturbed much orthodox opinion by his ardent advocacy of the Common Market. George Caunt described him as "a little hurt and resentful".[2] He did not take the result tragically, he was still very evidently an indispensable element of the little group at the head of the party and it was hard to see how he could be discarded. But he knew that he was there on sufferance; if ever for any reason he ceased to be indispensable, he would be dumped at once and ruthlessly.

At the end of 1962 Gaitskell fell suddenly and mysteriously ill. On 4 January 1963 he was moved to the Middlesex Hospital. He was expected to recover but nobody knew how long he would be incapacitated. The Chief Whip, Herbert Bowden, summoned what the *Guardian* described as a Regency Council, which concluded that things must carry on, so far as possible, as normal. In particular Wilson should go ahead with a lecture tour of the United States on which he was just about to embark. But Gaitskell continued to deteriorate. "I hear very disturbing rumours about Hugh's real state of health," Henry Brandon, the *Sunday Times* correspondent, wrote from Washington to George Brown. "A. Schlesinger believes that because of the conflict between you and W. Calahan [*sic*] would be chosen as a more neutral chap, but I cannot believe that Labour would not want a more forceful person, and I mean you." Brown replied that he still hoped for Gaitskell's recovery: "It is much too early to talk about the succession." But Arthur Schlesinger should be told not to believe everything he read in the *Sunday Telegraph*.[3] Already hopes were growing dim; on 17 January the Chief Whip telephoned Wilson in St Louis to give him the latest bulletin. He advised him not to rush back, no doubt calculating that there was no point in starting a scramble for the succession before it was forced upon the party.[4]

Gaitskell died the following day. Wilson heard the news in a car while on the way back from a visit to the United Nations in New York. He reached his hotel to find Marcia Williams on the telephone urging him to return at once and the *Daily Express* asking for a tribute to the late leader. The latter he provided promptly. The *Express* then tracked down Roy Jenkins, who was also in the United States, and asked him to do the same thing. Jenkins refused. The *Express* commented in surprise that Wilson had been able to supply a most moving tribute. " 'Yes,' I said bitterly," wrote Jenkins in his memoirs, " 'but you have to remember that he was very fond of Gaitskell,' and rang off. The silly little incident expressed both my shattered dismay and my revulsion from the prospect of a Wilson leadership ... whom, since 1951, I had deeply distrusted."[1] If that was the reaction of one of the more level-headed Gaitskellites then Wilson's task would not be easy.

Wilson was back in London on 19 January. "He had no expectation, no confidence, that he would bring it off," Marcia Williams said later, "but he thought he'd a good chance."[2] He had no particular reason for confidence. It was only a few months since Brown had beaten him soundly in the election for deputy. But Brown had a marked talent for making enemies, drank to excess – or, to be more precise, drank far more than his curiously weak head would stand – and was felt by certain moderates to be too closely identified with the right to be able to unite the party. There must be a chance. Wilson was met at the airport by Mary and Marcia Williams and rushed to Balogh's house in Hampstead where Crossman was waiting. A few decisions were quickly taken. Wilson would stand, there would be little or no canvassing, Brown would be given all the rope he needed to hang himself. In a draft of his biography of Wilson, Ernest Kay wrote that the campaign was to be run by Crossman with the help of George Wigg. In the margin Mrs Williams wrote: "Not true. Delete. Damaging."[3] Her protest was partly at the suggestion that there was any sort of organised campaign, partly at the idea that Wigg played a large part in it. On the latter point at least she was on strong ground. Wigg convinced himself that he masterminded Wilson's strategy and that he excluded Crossman from the operation for the reason – soundly based – that the latter could never keep his mouth shut.[4] In fact his own role was largely confined to picking up gossip and bringing it home in triumph to his master; a useful function, but neither indispensable nor particularly constructive. In so far as there was a centralised campaign it was run by Wilson himself with his old friend and confidant, the MP for Deptford, Leslie Plummer, as ADC.

Both sides in the campaign maintained that the other conducted itself with conspicuous unscrupulousness. "It was not a nice election

..." wrote Brown. "I discouraged active campaigning on my behalf, but that didn't prevent a bitter campaign from being waged against me."[1] "I kept out of it," Wilson told William Benton "– no canvassing, no Press interviews, I refused even to discuss it with my Parliamentary colleagues."[2] His only preoccupation, he maintained, was to curb any possible intervention by his supporters. It would be amazing if an electoral campaign in which Crossman and Wigg were concerned did not generate some mischief but Wilson does seem genuinely to have tried to keep the debate as low-key as possible. Wigg called on him when the crisis was at its height to find him drafting a speech for a Boy Scouts' meeting: "a desirable enough objective but, as it seemed to me, a bit off-beam in relation to the business in hand". Wigg asked sharply whether Wilson wanted to be Prime Minister or Chief Scout. Wilson's concern was not overtly to try to win votes but to project the image of a moderate man of good faith who would unite the party. He was anxious to play down his links with the left, nervously asking the editor of *Tribune* whether he was going to come out in support of him and obviously relieved that the answer was "no".[3]

Whether or not with Brown's acquiescence, a disagreeable smear campaign was levelled at Wilson and his entourage. Rumours circulated about Wilson's Russian links, about the incipient break-up of the Wilsons' marriage with Marcia cast as *femme fatale*, even about Wilson's atheism.[4] George Thomas heard stories about Mrs Wilson's unhappiness in her marriage and reported them to Wilson, who insisted that he repeat them to Mary. She responded by accompanying her husband when he went to Hugh Gaitskell's memorial service the following day.[5] Dirt of this kind probably had little effect; what damaged Brown more were the tactics which he and his henchmen adopted in trying to ensure support. "George Brown's arm-twisting produced a strong reaction and helped to contribute to Harold's success," judged Tony Benn.[6] Sam Watson, the Durham miners' leader, gave his group of MPs peremptory orders to vote for his close ally, Brown. All voted for Wilson, some at least to show their resentment at such overt bullying.[7]

But what scuppered Brown was not Wilson's appeal – "We have to choose between a man we don't like and a man we don't trust," remarked one Labour MP gloomily[8] – but the intervention of Jim Callaghan. To his dismay Brown learnt that Callaghan was considering standing and thus splitting the anti-Wilson vote. He urged him not to. "I am sorry that I cannot give you a reply about standing yet," replied Callaghan. "People whose opinion I respect believe that I should do so."[1] The people concerned were among those on whose support Brown had been counting. The hard core of the Gaitskellites were concerned above all with stopping Wilson, and Crosland for one believed that Callaghan was the best man for the purpose. Many people, Robens included, felt that Alfred Robens would have been the ideal standard-bearer for the right, but Robens had opted out of politics in favour of the Coal Board;[2] failing him the anti-Wilson lobby dithered and Callaghan decided to stand.

The voting on the first ballot was 115 to Wilson, 88 to Brown and 41 to Callaghan. It is possible, though on balance unlikely, that if Brown had had an unimpeded run the Callaghan vote would have gone almost entirely to him and Wilson would have been defeated.[3] Since an absolute majority was required, Callaghan now dropped out and his supporters had time to reflect on the long-term prospects of the party. Wilson had to win over only a handful of Callaghan's votes to secure victory. Though he was too cautious to attach great importance to such assurances, he had been led to believe that twelve votes were already pledged to him. Victory was not in the bag, but it seemed a much better than even chance. Wilson was "exhilarated and excited," Crossman recorded, "but he was also extraordinarily professional and sensible. Though vain, he is certainly not conceited. Though enormously intelligent, he is certainly not an intellectual. He is a supremely professional politician – in this he resembles Kennedy. But he is also an agile manoeuvrer and something of a demagogue, and therefore a wonderful listener who can pick the brains of skilful people, qualities he shares with Lloyd George."[4] It was agreed that Crossman would give a supper after the first ballot for a few of Wilson's personal friends. "I was interested to find who Harold meant by personal friends," he wrote. They turned out to be Marcia Williams, George Wigg, Leslie Plummer and Anthony Greenwood. Greenwood may to have been asked partly because he could have put paid to Wilson's chances if he had stood himself and done for Wilson what Callaghan had done for Brown.[5]

Wilson boasted that he had not lost a moment's sleep during the contest. Probably this was true; he was remarkably good at relaxing if nothing was to be gained by staying alert. But the last hours before the second ballot must still have been anxious ones. So few votes were involved, and so little was needed to make them slip away. Michael Stewart for one, who had voted for Callaghan the first time round, said openly that he proposed to switch to Brown: "I had no doubt that Harold was the most talented of the three, but I had not liked what seemed to me his equivocal attitude during the C.N.D. dispute, nor his hostility to Hugh."[1] How many more would think the same way? Harold Lever had abstained because he could not bring himself to betray Brown but felt he was unsuitable to be leader. Would his doubts survive? However phlegmatic he may have contrived to appear it must still have been an overwhelming relief for Wilson when the final figures were announced: 144 to Wilson against 103 to Brown.

Shortly before the second ballot Wilson received a letter from a prominent member of the Labour Party protesting that if only he had not been in the United States he would have been canvassing vigorously for the better man. The only trouble was that by ill fortune this communication came to be compared with an identical letter addressed to George Brown.* This somewhat *nuancé* support was the best that Wilson could expect from the upper reaches of the PLP. The Conservatives were more emphatic. "I think he will do," Driberg wrote to Beaverbrook; "I think Wilson will do wonderfully," replied Beaverbrook.[2] "Wilson is an able man, far more able than Brown," wrote Macmillan in his diary. "He is good in the House and in the country – and, I am told, on T.V."[3] Able was the word that occurred most frequently in the letters of congratulation. Lord Hailsham's message was delectably equivocal: "I thought you would win, and you did. I am sure your followers chose their ablest man. I hope that history will also say you were their best."[4]

For Wilson, for the moment at least, the attitude of his colleagues or of the Tories was almost equally unimportant. He knew what hostility he had to overcome, with time he felt sure that he could succeed. What mattered was that the possibility was now open: at the age of forty-six he had become leader of the Labour Party; only an election stood between him and Downing Street.

---

* With some magnanimity Wilson gave the writer of these letters high office in his administration. It was *not* Callaghan, as Tony Benn suggests in his diary entry for 10 September 1975.

VIII

Leader of the Opposition

1963–1964

"I was elected without ties, commitments, promises or any obligations to any individual or group," wrote Wilson exultantly to
William Benton. "Now I am free to do the job my own way."[1] Even
Wilson can hardly have believed that he was as free from commitment
as this letter suggests. There was virtually no section of the Labour
Party whose susceptibilities he did not feel it essential for one reason
or another to consider; the only question was which group he would
disappoint. The left, the bloc which had provided his most solid
support, took it for granted that they would now inherit the promised
land. Except for a few personal allies Wilson had little sympathy with
their aspirations; yet he could not afford overtly to abandon them
and he wanted to reward their loyalty. But almost all the high ground
of power was in the possession of the right, and it would be difficult
to dislodge them without destroying the fragile unity of the party.
"You must understand that I am running a Bolshevik Revolution with
a Tsarist Shadow Cabinet," he told his left-wing intimates: Crossman,
Barbara Castle, Michael Foot, Greenwood.[2] They must be patient,
their time would come. For the moment he must conciliate the right;
but which right, the right of Jim Callaghan and the trade union
barons; the right of Brown; or the right of Jenkins and the Gaitskellite
rump?[3] "All three," was the only answer he could afford to give, but
to keep everyone happy between January 1963 and the general election was going to call for great dexterity. For the moment he tried to
propitiate everyone while making as few firm promises as possible as
to what would happen after the election had been fought and, with
luck, he had to form a government.

The first demand on his tact and agility was the accommodation
of George Brown. Brown had accepted Wilson's victory with tolerably

good grace but was not prepared immediately to offer to serve under the new leader. "I am of course thinking very hard about that," he told the editor of the *Daily Herald*.[1] To Gordon Walker he said that he had heavy debts and needed a job; Wilson, he handsomely conceded, was not weak or bereft of principles; it was just that the principles he had were the wrong ones.[2] He retreated to Scotland where he brooded for a few days, then returned and said that he was ready to serve as deputy leader but must be shadow Foreign Secretary as well. Wilson had anticipated this demand and was determined not to give way to it; he disliked Brown's pro-Arabist views and thought him temperamentally ill-suited for the work. He skilfully stymied Brown by appointing Gordon Walker instead, a right-wing nomination to which Brown could hardly object and which reassured the Americans that they need not fear any dramatic swing in foreign policy if Labour came to power. Brown was offended; Gordon Walker realised that this was inevitable but reflected that he could not "forever be GB's loyal No 2".[3] According to Crossman Wilson's avowed reason for picking Gordon Walker was that: "He is so stupid that, by appointing him Shadow Foreign Secretary, I need not commit myself to my real Foreign Secretary when I form my Government."[4] The comment sounds more as if it were made by Crossman than by Wilson and certainly reads oddly in the light of what was to happen in October 1964, but it is true that Wilson had some reservations about Gordon Walker's talents and would probably not have put him in so important a place if he had not wished to frustrate his new deputy. To one colleague he described Gordon Walker as a "good house master", and said that he planned to run the economy and foreign affairs himself.[5] Brown was appeased with the assurance that he would have some role of great economic importance when the time came: Chancellor of the Exchequer perhaps. Since Callaghan was at the time shadow Chancellor and Wilson on several occasions showed himself critical of his performance, this hint was admirably designed to spread unease and ensure that his two principal competitors did not make common cause.

In an essay on Ramsay MacDonald, Wilson wrote that any Labour leader's task would be complicated "by the week by week and, at times, almost hour by hour requirement to keep his Party together and driving to the same goal ... Even if the broad strategy of policy is agreed, there will be those who want to move more rapidly and others who will want to move more slowly to the desired objective."

A still deeper division would exist between "the ideologists and theologians who seek a fundamentalist approach, and the more moderate, pragmatic group, no less idealistic but less prone to determine the reaction of any situation in terms of its relevance to some ultimate state of society".[1] In that dichotomy there was no doubt where Wilson placed himself but in January 1963 his preoccupation was that no one – left or right, ideologue or pragmatist – should feel excluded. Crossman was the only ally whom he promoted within the shadow Cabinet, but he took pains to appear "extremely faithful to his friends, seeking them out for advice, giving them his time, and even taking care to smooth down Barbara Castle and Tony Greenwood".[2] Within a few months he had managed to secure the restoration of the party whip to the little band of rebels who had been expelled two years before for their attitude on unilateralism. But it was the right whom he was at still greater pains to appease: Gaitskell's PPS, Joe Slater, was kept on and became a "staunch and comforting ally";[3] the press officer, John Harris, offered his resignation on the grounds that it was well known he had opposed Wilson, only to be told that the new leader had total confidence in him. Roy Jenkins called on Wilson to discuss whether he should accept the editorship of the Economist. He was received with "immense consideration. I cannot pretend that Gaitskell would have been nearly as nice to, say, Barbara Castle in similar circumstances."[4] In fact Jenkins could have found no better way to improve the already high regard which his new leader had for his intelligence and ability – to edit the Economist was a task demanding just the combination of donnishness and administrative skills which would appeal to Wilson, who was anyway always ready to be impressed by a politician who could shine in a different sphere. From whatever wing of the party people came, they were made to feel that their opinion counted; Tony Benn, who at that date had hardly begun his leftward progress, remarked in wonder: "What a change from Hugh! That man knows how to get the best out of people."[5] Even Crosland observed that he still thought Wilson a shit, but that he now considered "he has done very well and would like to help in any way he could".[6]

On each issue he made it his business to take up a position which almost everyone could accept if not actually share. On nationalisation he admitted himself no more than modestly enthusiastic but insisted that support of Clause IV was "the position of the whole party". On defence he argued for support of NATO and the retention of bases east of Suez, but urged acceptance of the fact that the independent deterrent as such was a mirage and – a sop to the left – insisted: "We are completely, utterly and unequivocally opposed now and in all circumstances to any suggestion that Germany ... directly or indirectly, should have a finger on the nuclear trigger."[1] On labour relations he called for a partnership between the TUC and the government, in which wage restraint would be matched by radical legislation – a rathe primrose heralding the summer of the Social Contract. On Europe, he professed admiration for the European ideal but laid down five conditions for British entry; the most important being safeguards for the Commonwealth and for British agriculture. Never again, he proclaimed in a line designed for the edification of the little Englanders, "must a British minister be put in a position of sitting in a cold antechamber while six European nations decide the fate of his country".[2] On this issue, indeed, he more nearly took up an identifiably committed position than on any other. His opposition to British entry seemed clear enough for that doughty champion of national sovereignty, Arthur Bryant, to write to him, "I wish you every success in the battle you are waging for our country's future."[3] But he still managed to hedge his bets to an extent that gave even the most ardent Europeans grounds for hope that if things went well with the negotiations all might yet be all right on the night.

On the eve of his election Wilson declared that he was not going to waste his time on interviews with the press: "And no social life either. That was another of Hugh's mistakes. A leader cannot afford it. Mary and I will have none of it whatsoever. We have a serious job to do."[4] On the second point he was as good as his word. By personal taste as well as on grounds of discretion he had no use for dinner parties, general conversation, all the *convenances* of social existence. He would have an inner core of intimates with whom he could discuss issues and exchange political gossip but not a coterie: as leader he insisted that his door was open to every member of the party and on the whole he kept himself remarkably available. As for the press, however, he not only devoted much time to them but courted them with an assiduity and skill that few others had matched. "The Lobby" – that inner group of privileged political correspondents – he wooed with especial ardour; studying not merely their personal idiosyncrasies but their wives' and children's names as well, confiding in them, flattering them subtly. "He described the Lobby as the 'golden thread' in Britain's parliamentary democracy. He became very adept in pulling it."[1] His hard work laid the foundation for what should have been, but was not, an extraordinarily happy relationship with the press and other media when he became Prime Minister. On every occasion he sought to demonstrate that he was the ordinary man: decent, concerned, unfettered by prejudice or ideology, seeking a practical approach to practical problems; "neither a Bevinesque robust proletarian nor a Crippsian conscience-stricken toff", as Peter Clarke has neatly summed it up.[2] He did not always hit the mark. On one occasion he went to Cardiff to address Labour students and struck the chairman as "indescribably pompous". The chairman's future wife, who was also there, was so incensed that "she put her thumb to her nose and wiggled her fingers." He ignored the students, and only bothered to speak to the cameras. "It was the first of many disappointments from Harold Wilson," recalled the future Glenys Kinnock.[3]

Wilson concealed his determined immobility on all doctrinal matters under a cloak of hectic activity. In opposition, he wrote, the Labour Party was like a stagecoach: "As long as you keep it rattling along at a quick pace, the occupants are either too exhilarated or too seasick to cause any trouble."[4] The pace he set was brisk enough to satisfy anyone: in his first six weeks as leader he made twenty-two major speeches, gave eighteen talks on radio or television and gave eleven press conferences. In part this whirlwind progress was dictated by his conviction that the Tories would go to the country in the autumn of 1963. When this hope was disappointed, he decided that May 1964, the date said to be favoured by the Conservative Chancellor, Reginald Maudling, was the most probable alternative. This misjudgment caused him some concern. By the time that the general election was eventually called in October 1964, he was seriously alarmed lest he had exposed himself too early and would have nothing new to say. "I've played every trick I've got," he remarked despairingly.[5] In the event he had little to worry about. If he was forced to play the same trick several times the electorate never noticed, while the vigour and resourcefulness which he displayed in the spring of 1963 did much to convince the remaining doubters in his party that they had made the right choice.

But Wilson's greatest contribution to the unity of the party and its electoral prospects was to transfer its main thrust from the scorched earth of nationalisation and Clause IV to the brave new world of science and technology. When asked with what he associated socialism in the modern age, he wrote: "I answer that if there was one word it was 'science'. The scientific revolution would affect everyone, bring everyone wider opportunities; it would be a revolution of all our people."[1] Through science would come expansion, the generation of new wealth, new hope for the under-privileged. Only under Labour could the technological tide be harnessed to best advantage, so that it benefited not just a selfish capitalistic fringe but humanity as a whole. The doctrine was politically expedient, distracting attention from issues that were best ignored and offering a future to which it seemed that the Tories did not aspire. It does not follow from this, however, that Wilson saw it as being no more than a political device. On the contrary, he believed every word he said and preached his doctrine with a messianic zeal that could have left only the most cynical in any doubt of his sincerity.

He had for many years advanced the claims of science as the spearhead of the new Britain, but it was at the party conference at Scarborough on 1 October 1963 that he exposed his ideas with the greatest impact. For forty-five minutes he kept a hard-boiled, sceptical and jaded audience enthralled as he set out his vision of the future. Under Labour there would be a second industrial revolution, creating ten million new jobs by the mid 1970s by: "Planning on an unprecedented scale to meet automation without unemployment; a pooling of talent in which all 'classes' could compete and prosper; a vast extension of state-sponsored research; a completely new concept of education; an alliance of science and socialism." Only by central planning could the full potential be realised: "Because we are democrats, we reject the methods which Communist countries are deploying in applying the results of scientific research to industrial life but, because we care deeply about the future of Britain, we must use all the resources of democratic planning, all the latent and under-developed skills of our people, to ensure Britain's standing in the world." The Tories had proved themselves incompetent to meet this challenge. They said Britain would have all the scientists it needed by 1965: "of course we shall – if we do not use them. We shall have all the bull-fighters we need by 1965." They believed in amateurism: at a time when even the MCC had abolished the distinction between amateurs and professionals, "in science and industry we are content to remain a nation of Gentlemen in a world of Players." But Labour too must be prepared to rise to new challenges: "There is no room for Luddites in the Socialist Party ... The Britain that is going to be forged in the white heat of this revolution will be no place for restrictive practices or for outdated methods on either side of industry."[1]

The speech has been much mocked in the decades since its delivery. "'Change', 'technology', 'automation', 'the scientific revolution' – these were the glittering slogans of the new crusade," wrote Christopher Booker in his brilliant polemic, *The Neophiliacs*. "No mention of Clause Four or nationalisation or the dead mottoes of revisionism; the eyes of the faithful were lifted to new hills, misty, far-off, and shining in the dawn."[2] Given Britain's history since 1963, a touch of derision seems justified. Yet at the time it was heady stuff, as vibrant and appealing to the speaker as to his audience. It struck a nerve in the public's consciousness and identified Wilson in their eyes with all that was hopeful and adventurous. "Harold Wilson will not just be a good Prime Minister," wrote James Cameron in the *Daily Herald*. "He may well be a great one ... Harold Wilson's startling essay into political science-fiction may well be held by experts to be the most vital speech he has ever made. Here at last was the twentieth century." It was, said *The Times*, "the most immediately successful conference speech Mr Wilson had ever delivered, and the audience showed a fervour that hardly knew any bounds when he sat down".[3]

Scarborough set the pattern for Wilson's most effective electioneering in the next twelve months, a theme rubbed in with especial relish in Birmingham in January, when he contrasted the forward-looking vigour of the Labour Party with the "grouse-moor conception of Tory leadership". It was a promising line of attack, for by the beginning of 1964 the Conservative Party was in sad disarray. Things had begun to go badly wrong in the spring of the previous year. A few months earlier Wilson had received a letter from a society osteopath and part-time artist, Stephen Ward, reporting his disquiet about the government's behaviour during the Cuba crisis. Through his friendship with the Russian naval attaché, Eugene Ivanov, Ward had been privy to an offer by the Russians to stop the ships taking the missiles to Cuba and to discuss the removal of the Soviet bases if a summit conference was at once convened in London. The offer had been ignored, though Ward was convinced that it was "a genuine effort to get out of an ugly situation without any victory being claimed by either side". Wilson wrote to thank Ward for the information: "The event you describe was completely unknown to me; there has been nothing in the Press and I have not heard it from any other sources."[1] He seems to have shown the letter to Macmillan and to have been satisfied with assurances that the Foreign Office had good reason not to attach much importance to Ivanov's approach.

In March 1963 Ward called on George Wigg at the House of Commons. Ward knew that a scandal was about to break concerning an affair between the Minister of War, John Profumo, and a strikingly beautiful call-girl, Christine Keeler; that he had been instrumental in fomenting the relationship; and that Ivanov was also to some extent involved. In view of this he had decided to get his story in first. Wigg already knew quite a lot about the business and was delighted to learn more. "In my opinion Profumo was never, at any time, a security risk," he wrote on 29 March 1963,[2] but his behaviour at the time hardly seemed to reflect that conviction. He wrote down all he knew about the affair and showed it to Wilson and Brown. "The more I think about it, the more I feel that we ought to keep out of this," wrote Brown. Wilson should pass on the papers to the Prime Minister but no more. "If we 'blow it up' in the light of that correspondence I have a somewhat uncomfortable feeling we may share in the unpleasantness that may follow."[3]

On 4 June Profumo, who knew that he was on the point of exposure as having lied to the Prime Minister and the House of Commons about his relationship with Christine Keeler, resigned both as minister and MP. Wilson, who was in the United States, was telephoned to ask what line he felt the opposition should take. "No comment – in glorious Technicolor," he replied. "And that's what I'm telling you; no comment in wide screen."* On the whole Wilson had followed the cautious line suggested by Brown, though he had gone further than his colleague would have thought wise in urging the Prime Minister, in view of the security implications of Christine Keeler's simultaneous relationship with the British Minister of War and the Russian naval attaché, to set up a judicial enquiry into the affair. One problem for Wilson was that, though he wanted to discredit Macmillan, he had no wish to destroy him. He told Crossman that he wanted to keep Macmillan in Downing Street as "our most valuable asset ... The one thing I am really frightened of is Maudling."[4]

* This comment, which was originally quoted in Wayland Young's *The Profumo Affair* (London, 1963, p 26), was dismissed as an invention by Gordon Walker in the House of Commons but never disavowed by Wilson. Lady Falkender confirms that this is more or less what he said.

The other thing was Iain Macleod: either man, he felt, would make a far more dangerous opponent at the general election.

"No comment – in gorgeous Technicolor," was therefore the keynote of his speech when the Profumo affair was debated in mid June; not too gorgeous either, rather a chill and dispassionate restraint which led Macmillan to pay a tribute to his "complete propriety".[1] But it was still a damning verdict, inspired not just by political expediency but by his puritanism and revulsion from the seamier side of political life, of the sort of society and standards that could breed such a scandal. "There is something utterly nauseating", he said, "about a system of society which pays a harlot twenty-five times as much as it pays its Prime Minister, 250 times as much as it pays its Members of Parliament, and five hundred times as much as it pays some of its ministers of religion." He concluded by asserting that "The sickness of an unrepresentative sector of our society should not detract from the robust ability of our people as a whole to face the challenge of the future." But there had to be inspiration and leadership and that had to come "here, in this House".[2] During the course of the debate the historian Professor Barraclough wrote to Wilson to tell him that in 1938 Profumo had befriended a woman called Gisela Klein, who had been under surveillance by MI5 and had fled the country before the war. "It is only now that we are learning something of the men who were chosen to rule over us," responded Wilson bitterly.[3] Almost by the same post Stephen Ward wrote to him from prison to protest that Ivanov had been monstrously maligned: "He was genuinely interested in achieving some sort of greatness in this country as a balance to American aims that he believed endangered us all." Ivanov and Ward had together tried to avert war over Cuba: "So far I am the only person who has had the courage to lay bare the bones of the situation."[4]

Wilson's speech on the Profumo affair, judged Crossman, was "absolutely magnificent, the best I've ever heard him make, better than I thought possible".[5] It is satisfactory to be able to drag one's opponents in the mud while striking a note of resounding rectitude oneself, and the affair had certainly been of benefit to Wilson personally and to the Labour cause. His most important consideration, however, was to establish himself as a responsible heavyweight, a man of prime-ministerial calibre who would be at home in Number 10 and in the higher reaches of international statesmanship. When the affair of the "Third Man", Kim Philby, threatened to erupt into a

1a. (*Above*) A family group with neighbours. Harold stands between his paternal grandparents with his mother on the left of the picture.

1b. (*Right*) Harold as a midshipmite in *HMS Pinafore*.

1c. (*Below*) With his sister Marjorie – as powerful a personality as his mother, but considerably bossier.

1d. (*Below right*) Patrol leader in the Colne Valley Milnsbridge Boy Scouts – a role in which he saw himself throughout his life.

2a. (*Left*) Harold and Mary Wilson in 1944, shortly after the birth of their elder son.

2b. (*Right*) A firework party at the Wilsons' home in Hampstead attended by Aneurin Bevan, one of the few politicians who visited the house as a friend.

2c. (*Below*) At play with his son Robin – Wilson was a fond if inevitably distant father.

3a. At the Ministry of Works in 1945 with his private secretary.

3b. (*Below*) With President and Mrs Truman in Washington in 1950.

4a. With King George VI, Queen Elizabeth and Princess Margaret at the British Industries Fair in 1948.

4b. (*Below*) With the film star Stewart Granger. Wilson's enthusiasm for the film industry first became apparent while he was at the Board of Trade.

5a. Harold Wilson with his father at the Labour Party Conference at Margate in 1953.

5b. (*Below*) With the Leader of the Opposition, Hugh Gaitskell. Their relationship oscillated between distrust and overt dislike.

6a. The Leader of the Opposition in Red Square.

6b. (*Below*) In Moscow in 1963 with, from left to right, John Harris, Michael Stewart, Patrick Gordon Walker and the Soviet Trade Minister, Anastis Mikoyan.

7a. (*Left*) Electioneering in 1964.

7b. (*Right*) Mary Wilson carries the toy panda which became the Wilsons' election mascot and which they still possess today.

7c. (*Below*) On the way to Buckingham Palace with Mary and Robin to receive the invitation to form a government.

8a. (*Left*) Thomas Balogh.

8b. (*Right*) Marcia Williams.

8c. (*Below*) A staff party in Number 10. Harold Davies is on the left, George Wigg on the right.

scandal that would do serious harm to the security services he found himself reacting in three guises: as a patriot required to put the interests of his country before those of his party; as an outsider impressed by the glamour and supposed omniscience of those charged with great secrets; and as a would-be Prime Minister who enjoyed the sense of importance fostered by confidential briefings at Number 10. He responded as Macmillan had hoped and expected, urging the House of Commons not to press for a debate on the affair.[1] "Thank you so much for the way you dealt with the Philby Questions this afternoon," Macmillan wrote. "I hope you will allow me to say, with all respect, that your contribution was a great help to the cause of national security. I am most grateful." Wilson was duly flattered and appreciative. "We shall have, no doubt, a number of other exchanges on this and other security subjects," he replied, "and I hope we shall be able to handle them in this way."[2]

Part of the process of establishing one's credentials as a potential national leader is to be received by one's putative peers abroad. A visit to Washington is essential for any leader of the opposition, particularly for a Labour leader who has to show that his advent to power is not going to damage Anglo-American relations or cause a run on the pound. Wilson was particularly anxious to go, since the advent of President Kennedy to power, at forty-six a year younger even than he was himself, seemed to herald a new age for the West, with youth on the prow and, if not pleasure, then at least exhilaration at the helm. He was convinced that the American administration would greet him with real enthusiasm; a view not wholly shared by that prince among British correspondents in Washington, Henry Brandon of the *Sunday Times*. "The feelings towards Wilson are mostly on the negative side," Brandon told George Brown; "the lack of trust in the man's word that is reflected in the British press is even stronger here."[3]

Wilson arrived at the end of March and spared no pains to appear responsible and sober. His speech to the Chamber of Commerce could as well have been delivered by any Conservative of moderately radical ideas; it was, felt Goodhart, "particularly useful ... as a means by which to persuade them that a Labour Government would not necessarily be anti-American or very far on the Left".[4] To the Press Club he stressed his conviction that Britain still had a role to play east of Suez. "We stand firmly by N.A.T.O. and the Western Alliance. We are not a neutralist party and neutralism has no part or place in our policies."[1] He met Kennedy that same evening, backstage at a visiting British production of *School for Scandal*. Kennedy at once referred to the Press Club speech: "He seemed very pleased with it and said he wanted to discuss it when we met the next morning." At the White House they were alone together for more than an hour. Kennedy went straight in – "like a bomb", wrote Wilson – on the problems of world liquidity, moved on to American ideas for a mixed-manned force armed with nuclear weapons, discussed the GATT and Britain's relationship with Europe. On the negotiations with de Gaulle on British entry to the Common Market Wilson said that "we shouldn't do too much appeasing; we should recognise that we had some very strong cards in our own hand; while we shouldn't play them, we should at any rate start brandishing them." Wilson was impressed by the tremendous speed of the President's mind: "One never had to explain anything, never had to go back over the previous sentence ... We were both talking shorthand. Behind each point was a paragraph or a chapter that didn't need to be said."[2]

He was sublimely confident that he had made an excellent impression on the President and he left in a flush of optimism about their future dealings: "I felt there would be a new kind of relationship between heads of government." Brandon was more realistic; Kennedy had been impressed by the breadth of Wilson's knowledge but "did not take to him as a person". Still, Brandon conceded, it had been "quite an exceptional physical as well as mental feat to have accomplished as much as he did in such a short time". He had favourably impressed the Senate Foreign Relations Committee and the State Department and had struck all who met him as a "shrewd, intelligent and able politician and most of them have said: 'So far, so good' ".[3] Almost the only point of difference with his hosts had been on the nuclear deterrent; Wilson reaffirmed Labour's determination to phase out the unilateral deterrent and regretted the deal done between Kennedy and Macmillan at Nassau, which had given Britain the Polaris submarine armed with nuclear missiles. He told the Press Club that he did not intend to repudiate the Nassau agreement but that Labour would rectify the "shambles" of British defence policy. He felt that Kennedy had not realised what he was getting into at the Nassau talks, recording later, "I think he was more surprised than anyone when Macmillan returned to this country and put the whole thing in terms of Britain having an independent nuclear potentiality."[1]

Some of the good done by the Washington visit was undone a few weeks later when Wilson and Gordon Walker went to Moscow. John Cronin, the Labour MP for Loughborough, had previously conducted a fact-finding mission to the Soviet Embassy. The main object of the visit, he explained, would be for Wilson and the Soviet First Secretary, Nikita Khrushchev, to reach a "friendly understanding", though if it was as obviously successful as the Washington trip "it would also fulfil a useful electoral purpose". He was told that the degree of cordiality and confidence shown by Khrushchev would depend on Wilson's attitude; "a repetition of your good wishes for the N.A.T.O. Alliance ... would not help the success of your visit." In some alarm, Cronin told the Russian Ambassador that Wilson could hardly be expected to denounce the Western Alliance: "Any advantage which the Soviet Union might derive would have to be after and not before he became Prime Minister."[2]

In spite of this alarmingly broad hint, Wilson found Khrushchev in truculent mood, insisting that if Western forces were to remain in Berlin it should be under United Nations command. Wilson said that he favoured a UN presence in Berlin but not their assuming command of the Western forces. Khrushchev threatened "to put locks on the doors" to Berlin. "We know what would happen if that situation arose," said Wilson. "And we know what would happen to London," retorted Khrushchev. "If you threaten us with war, then we shall retaliate." Wilson contented himself with insisting rather feebly that he had not been threatening anyone. When Khrushchev said that Western Germany was revanchist and that the reunification of Germany could never take place, Wilson replied: "We have no respect either for Adenauer or for Ulbricht." This sentence, which suggested that Britain equated East with West Germany, caused special offence to Kennedy's senior adviser, McGeorge Bundy, who had secured a transcript of the talks. He sent a copy to George Brown with an acerbic commentary. "I cannot pretend that on the document as a whole we come out particularly nobly," replied Brown, "but since the exercise was to establish relations and good will I suppose he could defend that in a rational way." If *he* had been there, he commented drily, it "would have been questionable as to whether the meeting would have gone on as long as it did". Brown told Bundy that Wilson had returned from Moscow speaking proudly of the "flaming row" he had had with Khrushchev over Berlin. His own idea of a flaming row, said Brown, was something a little more robust.[1] Bundy accepted Brown's somewhat half-hearted apologia for his leader's diplomacy: "I incline to agree with you that the more serious problem is the underlying tone on both sides, although I must say I still think it strange to equate Adenauer and Ulbricht in the way it was done."[2] The incident was closed, but it did nothing for Wilson's credibility in the White House. It is a curious commentary on the relationship between Brown and Wilson that the two men seem to have had no further discussion of the Moscow visit, even though Brown clearly had serious reservations about Wilson's handling of the talks.

On 21 October 1963 Wilson was due to lecture in Chicago. He was to be paid $5,000. He had to cancel at short notice, Brown taking his place at a fee, Wilson was not displeased to note, reduced to $1,500.[3] The reason for the change of plan was the unexpected resignation of Harold Macmillan. In a draft of his biography of Wilson, Ernest Kay described his subject that summer as rejoicing at the thought of his coming electoral victory. Everything seemed to be going right: "He had become the nation's man. And he loved it." Against this Wilson scored an irritated: "This is absolute rubbish, rubbish, rubbish."[4] He disliked the implication that he was complacent or certain that he would win the election. But in fact two months later everything did seem to be going right and Douglas-Home's selection to replace Macmillan was one of the righter factors. When he heard of the appointment, wrote John Harris, he was "almost ecstatic with pleasure".[5] It was not that he underestimated Douglas-Home, still less despised him, but he saw immediately how the contrast between the two men could be exploited. Wilson was lower middle-class against aristocratic, innovator against traditionalist, statistician against self-avowed innumerate, golfer against keen shot and fisherman, technocrat against territorial magnate, Montagu Burton against Savile Row or scruffy tweeds, professional against amateur, the future against the past. When Marcia Williams found in an *Observer* interview a casual reference by Douglas-Home to the fact that he did his sums with matchsticks, Wilson's cup flowed over. Nothing could encapsulate more neatly his superior claim to be the man who could tackle Britain's economic problems. The white heat of the technological revolution never glowed more brightly than in the months between Douglas-Home's appointment and the election.

Not all went so well, however. Kennedy's assassination came as a profound shock to Wilson, both because he had genuinely admired the young President and because the rapport between them – real or imaginary – would have been a major asset in the election. Lyndon Johnson was an unknown quantity, and though he continued stoutly to maintain that a Democratic America would admirably complement a Labour Britain, he had some doubts how well his ideas would go down in the White House that existed after 22 November 1963. The assassination caused more immediate embarrassment when a very obviously drunk George Brown appeared on television to broadcast an incoherent and over-emotional tribute to the dead President, with whom he unexpectedly claimed close friendship. It was a considerable vexation to the Labour Party and Wilson made little effort to conceal his disapproval; to a correspondent he remarked pointedly that it was not the case "that if a Labour Government were formed and anything happened to the Prime Minister, the Deputy Leader would auto-matically become Leader".[1] Brown was contrite and apologised to all and sundry: "This is not a matter on which explanation will help," he told the American Ambassador, "but I hope it will when I tell you that I have had the most miserable week of my life in consequence."[2] Characteristically he contrived to be apologetic and belligerent at the same time, accusing Wilson, more or less explicitly, of exploiting the scandal to his disadvantage. "I strongly deprecate the suggestion that the incident has been seized on and used," protested Wilson. "The only people who have seized on it have been one or two Tory papers."[3] Brown was unconvinced. The "broo-ha" over the Kennedy broadcast was much exaggerated, he told Brandon: "Some of my own colleagues lent themselves to it."[4]

Wilson was capable of making his own, though less serious, gaffes. In March 1964 he unwarily told a journalist that he saw no objection to British ships being contributed to a UN force. Promptly he found himself quoted as saying that the Royal Navy should be placed under UN command. Irritated denials merely gave the story more life. Wilson was worried about his remarks, recorded Benn: "For my part I found it a very exciting idea and was rather sorry to see him back-tracking so fast."[5] Wilson reflected apprehensively that in election year even the most innocent observation was likely to cause a furore.

The planks of Labour's, or at least Wilson's, platform were laid in place in 1964. *Purpose in Politics*, edited by Marcia Williams and published in March, was a collection of his speeches and writings selected to set out his personal faith as a socialist. In his preface he reiterated the message he had preached at Scarborough and Birmingham and would shortly carry all around the country: Labour rejected "the dead Marxian generalisations about the proletariat as we reject aristocratic patronising about 'the people' ". Socialism was about growth, opportunity, investment, prosperity, purpose. "Purpose" and "purposive" were the keywords that echoed throughout the text: "They erupt quietly, flatly but continuously into his discourse, like hiccoughs," commented Colin Welch unkindly.[1] "The Relevance of British Social Democracy", an article for the *Britannica Book of the Year*, called for greater international efforts to increase liquidity, harness the industrial capacity of the advanced countries, draw up commodity agreements and a world food plan, and generally ensure a vast increase in aid to the poorer parts of the world.[2] A more curious item in the Wilsonian armoury was a hagiographic study of the leader of the Labour Party, heavily adorned with pictures, which was said to be "compiled and edited" by John Parker MP and Eugene Prager but was signed by Michael Foot.[3] Wilson was described as a "dedicated person ... meaning sacredly, solemnly or formally devoted, wholly given up". He was the "professional *par excellence*", but was loved by the rank and file in spite of his sophistication because of his deep-rooted "native affinity with the Labour movement". He was no opportunist, no automatic backer of the big battalions. "Whatever else he did, Wilson did *not* play safe." But he was resolved to heal the rift in the party: "A measure of his insight may be seen in the much more substantial unity which Labour has attained under his Leadership." Michael Foot's vision of Wilson would have been very different even two years later but he still feels that the potential for being a great radical leader existed in him in 1964 and never wholly died.[4] As it was he had achieved a competent piece of propaganda. Robert Maxwell wrote to Wilson to report that he had printed 10,000 copies; W. H. Smith had taken 3,000 and a further 5,000 were already being printed. "I expect this little booklet to sell well."[5]

The Labour Party, and indeed most Conservatives, thought May 1964 the most likely date for the general election. All planning was on that basis, and a vigorous campaign launched in the spring. Once it was clear that the autumn was Douglas-Home's preferred date then Wilson – haunted by his conviction that Gaitskell had peaked too early in 1959 – tried to put the party's effort into cold storage for the summer. He was no more than half successful. In effect the first ten months of the year were dominated by the incipient election.[1] Douglas-Home's decision to defer polling day, in fact the source of much vexation to Labour, was hailed by Wilson as proof of panic: "It must be the only recorded occasion in military history," he declared on 1 April, "of a tattered and demoralised army being united in its unfeigned relief at being blessed with a general whose one quality was his ability to run away."[2] It was the first shot of a sustained attempt to belittle the Tory leader and emphasise Wilson's superior attractions. Early in 1964 Wilson gained some attention for his intervention in certain industrial disputes. Lord Blakenham chided him for behaving as if he were Prime Minister. "Well, thank God somebody is!" Wilson retorted.[3] It was an effective line, as the opinion polls bore out. In Gallup polls Wilson was never approved as leader by less than 61 per cent, Douglas-Home never by more than 48 per cent. An NOP survey in April showed 71 per cent thought Wilson "brilliant" and 80 per cent "tough" compared with 53 per cent and 54 per cent for Home. But Wilson did not want to push his luck too far. He shied away from a direct confrontation on television with the Tory leader. "Some small thing might have gone wrong. I might have got hiccups from smoking a dusty pipe," he explained.[4] He was as much, perhaps even more concerned by the thought that possibly nothing *would* go wrong. Gratifying though it might be to outsmart his rival, Wilson saw the dangers. The spectacle of the slick professional outwitting at every turn the obviously decent and honourable amateur might have led to a wave of sympathy for the underdog; and Wilson was far too shrewd to underestimate Alec Douglas-Home's appeal to the general public.

Through the spring of 1964 the two leaders stumped the country, trying to establish themselves as the nation's favourite. Wilson thought Douglas-Home made a mistake in taking to the hustings rather than remaining in London governing the country: "He should have allowed me to go on and on making speeches, probably boring people in the process."[5] George Brown had no doubt Wilson's over-exposure was harming the party's prospects. "I frankly think that we are making a mistake in nationally concentrating only on the Leader's tours," he told Transport House, "when it is quite obvious at this moment that my visits around this country could be used to much greater advantage as well."[6] In fact, in their different styles, both Douglas-Home and Wilson were quite proficient enough at putting themselves and their policies across to ensure that they did no damage to their prospects. But Wilson was the winner. His appeal, as Kenneth Morgan has perceptively expressed it, was something fresh and infinitely attractive, with "his call for expansion and innovation, coupled with a commitment to growth and articulated with a kind of Coronation Street folksiness and lack of pomposity ... For a moment it seemed to change the national psyche and with it the electoral landscape."[1]

From the moment the campaign proper began, Wilson took charge. He did not, said Marcia Williams, suffer from the delusion that he must "hog the whole show", but he distrusted the ponderous and antiquated machinery of Transport House and believed it essential that he should handle his own affairs. Some months earlier Len Williams, the General Secretary, had objected strongly when Wilson proposed to set up a committee, independent of Transport House, to discuss electoral advertising. Wilson brushed him aside with some brutality: "I have never seen Harold being tough before and it was impressive," noted Benn.[2] He carried on as he had begun. It seemed to him entirely reasonable that the media should concentrate on him rather than his colleagues: he was the leader, the only one with Cabinet experience and, incidentally, the most competent to survive in the blaze of publicity.[3] He appointed no *ad hoc* campaign committee and gathered almost all the threads of power into his own hands. For the most part it worked well, but the policy militated against central planning. Wilson, so often regarded as prudent and calculating to a fault, in the electoral battle showed himself bold, intuitive and determined to make up his policy as he went along. "I'm not a Kennedy," he said. "I'm a Johnson. I fly by the seat of my pants."[4] His failure to consult his colleagues or to abide by the strategy that had been previously worked out caused surprise and some offence. "Of course, we've all been downgraded because Harold's so absolutely determined to be the sole man," grumbled Crossman. "I honestly think that I had more influence on Hugh than I have on him."[5] It was a high-risk strategy. If it worked his position would be greatly strengthened, if he failed he had cooked his goose. A few days before the polls Harold Lever predicted a majority of sixty for the Tories. "In the Labour party," read a CIA report, "there is unanimity that Harold Wilson is to blame, and the consensus appears to be that he is finished if Labour loses this election."[6]

Crossman's bile was in part due to the fact that he felt the role of senior counsellor to Wilson was his by right and yet he seemed in part at least to have been supplanted by Tony Benn. Wilson greatly enjoyed Benn's enthusiasm and endless stream of new ideas – some dotty, all of interest – and valued also his experience of television. In December 1963 he had "more or less" asked Benn to become his principal speech-writer and adviser. What about Crossman? asked Benn. "Dick is going through one of his moods," replied Wilson.[1] Wilson was sensitive about any suggestion that he did not write his own speeches. "Harold doesn't want any people to know that anyone helps him at all," wrote Benn in his diary. "He wants it all to be his show ... It's very silly but I know that my capacity to influence him depends upon total self-erasure."[2] In fact it usually was Wilson's show; he much preferred to write his own speeches, "in my kind of shorthand ... on pieces of large House of Commons paper".[3] For a long campaign he would prepare a master speech, divided into sections, and would take out the relevant passages for each occasion, slotting in new material as need arose. But as leader he eventually realised he could no longer cope unaided and set up a group chaired by Benn and with Peter Shore and Balogh also members to prepare a set of keynote speeches. Benn was in particular responsible for anything connected with industry or technology; he drafted the speech delivered at Swansea in which Wilson acknowledged that Labour's social programme and reformist dreams depended on the success of its economic planning.[4]

Whatever the elements that went into Wilson's electioneering, the results were usually happy. In the House of Commons his speeches sometimes seemed almost too exquisitely crafted. Macleod congratulated him on a speech which was "as always witty, cogent and polished [pause] and polished [pause] and polished". Wilson had said that Macleod had brought a fresh mind to the subject: "I wish that *he* would bring a fresh speech."[5] On the hustings, however, the smoothness disappeared: he was vigorous, blunt, radiating honesty and down-to-earth practicality. He spoke for Edward Short in Newcastle and was "in top form, and Harold at his best was superb. His ability to make everyone present feel confident that we were winning was one of his many gifts as Party Leader."[6] He handled hecklers as well as anybody in the country and revelled in their interruptions, being genuinely disturbed if they were ejected. He even enjoyed it on the rare occasions that hecklers got the better of him. At a meeting near the naval dockyards at Chatham he held forth on the deficiencies of the Tory defence policy and demanded rhetorically: "Why do I emphasise the role of the Royal Navy?" "Because you're in Chatham!" came a bellow from the back of the hall. Wilson laughed almost as much as the rest of the audience.[1]

The fact that the press was largely Tory-owned gave television particular importance in Wilson's eyes – let the right-wing journalists denounce him as much as they liked as a dangerous ogre, he could confound them by appearing on the screen in the voters' sitting rooms as a pattern of moderation and good sense. Tom Driberg was charged with improving his performance and wrote recommendations after each broadcast: "Last one a great improvement on previous one," he reported about halfway through the campaign; "far more assured and calm, no sign of your eyes following the tele-prompter. When you glanced down at your notes it might have been better to let the paper be seen ... otherwise this perfectly natural and acceptable gesture may look slightly furtive."[2] His performance was a sharp contrast to that of Douglas-Home. They appeared on consecutive nights on *Election Forum*. Grace Wyndham Goldie remembered that Wilson arrived early, "polite, wary and prepared, with a posse of advisers". He ate cold ham and salad with the production staff and went to the studio "with the air of a serious politician dealing with an important situation". Douglas-Home arrived only a few moments before the programme started with a solitary escort. "He looked so exhausted that his skin appeared to be drawn tightly over his skull. His answers to the questions ... seemed completely unprepared."[3] Wilson was resolved that his final broadcast should be a resounding success and refused to wear spectacles in case his youthful image was impaired. As a result he could not read the autocue, fluffed his lines and became more and more bad-tempered. Finally they broke for tea. Wilson had a glass of brandy, scraped some minestrone off his suit with a pair of scissors, and went back to work with a will. All went well. Watching the run-through, Wilson punctuated his performance with a muttered commentary: "Who's that chap? He looks like the pig we've just seen on children's television! No, I don't like the look of him. I wouldn't vote for him myself."[4]

It can be taken for granted that every British politician believes the BBC to be prejudiced in favour of the other party. Wilson's sense of persecution was as strong as any, but in the 1964 campaign it did not run rampant. The Labour Party pressed for the political element of the daily programme *Today's Papers* to be suspended during the election period, on the ground that the papers were predominantly Tory. Lord Normanbrook, the chairman of the BBC, replied that this would be dereliction of duty on his part: he would, however, ensure that the material was impartially selected and presented. "Not enough," Wilson wrote, "because the raw material is unbalanced. We want it in writing that the political balance will be six of one and half a dozen of the other."[1] He got no joy on this and probably expected none, but he did better when he protested to the Director-General, Hugh Greene, that the immensely popular *Steptoe and Son* was being screened an hour before the polls closed. *Steptoe*-watchers, he believed, were likely to be Labour voters. Greene asked what Wilson wanted shown instead. *Oedipus Rex*, Wilson suggested. When Greene postponed *Steptoe and Son* by an hour Wilson telephoned in gratitude: "Thank you very much, Hugh. That will be worth a dozen or more seats to me."[2]

The party manifesto was scrambled out just before the campaign began. Wilson wrote the section on defence and took a keen interest in the rest of it, which was mainly drafted by Peter Shore. Its general tenor was predictable. "Let's Go With Labour", was to be the slogan, and Britain going with Labour was the overriding theme, with the emphasis on policies that would appeal to the middle classes and those who were more concerned with national prosperity and an efficiently run economy than with abstract justice or the application of egalitarian principles. "Not at all good, absolutely flat," grumbled Crossman, the reason being: "Harold's such a natural conservative that he does everything in an Establishment way, through the proper channels, all that sort of thing."[3] Randolph Churchill took the same view though from a different angle. On the eve of the election he sent Wilson a pink tie with a good luck message:

> The Leader's tie is palest pink,
> It's not as red as people think.[4]

The manifesto was launched at a mass rally at the Empire Pool, Wembley, with turns by Humphrey Lyttelton, Harry H. Corbett, Vanessa Redgrave and the Grimethorpe Colliery Band to add savour to the occasion. "We need men with fire in their belly and humanity in their hearts," declared Wilson. "The choice we offer, starting today, is between standing still, clinging to a tired philosophy of a day that is gone, or moving forward in partnership and unity to a great society, to a dynamic, expanding, confident, and, above all, purposive new Britain." It was rich rhetoric, though the American Embassy, in a slightly snooty report on this "huge vaudeville-like rally", was more concerned with what Wilson did *not* say. There was virtually no mention of defence or foreign policy, subjects which the embassy assumed were considered "impolitic to stress in party circles". Hugh Gaitskell was not once referred to; Bevan, on the other hand, was much invoked and the appearance of his face on a screen "aroused frenzied applause".[1] Electioneering was electioneering, the report implied, but this was going a little far.

Every party leader in a general election knows that some issue, often entirely unexpected, is likely to explode with disconcerting violence and mar the smooth progress of the campaign. Wilson lived with the knowledge that the rumours linking his name with Marcia Williams, which had circulated during the leadership contest, might at any moment be revived. They were, but without much conviction. The trouble started with an extempore outburst from Barbara Cartland which was then picked up by the national press and at one point threatened to become prominent in the run-up to polling day. Arnold Goodman was consulted and concluded, as he was often to do over the next decade, that the whole thing was most deplorable and a *prima facie* case of libel existed, but that to take any action would be injudicious. The press lost interest, or found nothing new to say, and the matter died. But it caused much distress to Mrs Williams, particularly when Quintin Hogg (who had renounced his title as Lord Hailsham the previous year), evidently without having her or Wilson in mind, remarked that there were quite as many adulterers on the Labour front bench as the Conservative. Marcia Williams locked herself in her bedroom and, according to the baggage-master George Caunt, emerged "tearful, red-faced and slightly hysterical". Wilson drank the best part of a bottle of brandy in the course of that night and the next morning and expostulated to Caunt that Marcia was "pure as the driven snow".[2]

George Brown was harder to dispose of. At his best he was one of the most effective propagandists in the Labour camp but it was only a few months since the Kennedy affair had shown how disastrous he could be at his worst. Wilson tried to persuade him to concentrate on defence questions; since Douglas-Home planned to make the nuclear deterrent a major element in most of his appearances would

Brown "take charge of the whole strategy campaign"?[1] But Brown was not to be so easily corralled. Even before the campaign started he had had a confrontation with Edward Heath on television to debate nationalisation, in which he struck many viewers as being rude, silly and unconvincing. A deluge of letters urged Wilson to gag his unruly deputy, to which Wilson replied cautiously that he "appreciated the spirit" in which the criticisms were made.[2] In the event Brown's only serious indiscretion came when he was goaded into asserting that Labour intended to get the cost of mortgages down: "something in the order of 3 per cent" was a probable target. So incautious a pledge to halve the existing mortgage rate could have proved dangerous, but Brown claimed he was misrepresented, Wilson dismissed it as a typical *Express* stunt, and little harm was done.[3] Brown's gusto and energy on the whole far outweighed his occasional indiscretions.

Wilson contributed his own blunder. A strike at Hardy-Spicer, the manufacturers of motor-car propeller shafts, threatened to disrupt the entire motor industry. Wilson alleged that the trouble was due to right-wing troublemakers seeking to damage Labour's electoral chances. "I must say that's a rum one," commented Maudling. "Tory shop-stewards going around sabotaging Mr Wilson's election! Really!"[4] The nation found Wilson's accusations equally far-fetched and his credibility might have been seriously damaged if the chairman of Hardy-Spicer, Herbert Hill, had not distracted attention by some still worse-judged remarks, dismissing the strikers as "people who are not of very high intelligence ... I feel very much they are poor dears and am very sad for them." Wilson attacked Hill so ferociously for these comments that a writ was issued for slander, and the whole question went *sub judice* until long after the election was over.[5]

Throughout 1962 and 1963 opinion polls had shown Labour comfortably in the lead over a Conservative Party which seemed to be in terminal disarray. In the summer of 1964 the Tories were clearly on the way back, and though Labour still started the campaign as favourites nobody imagined that it was a sure thing. The Hardy-Spicer affair coincided with the blackest moment for Labour when NOP gave the Conservatives a lead of 2.9 per cent. Then the portents changed again and a week before polling day it seemed as if Labour had once more a commanding lead. Wilson, who felt he had neglected his own constituency, decided to spend the last few days in Merseyside. To some members of his party this seemed a serious error: so completely had he dominated the campaign that his virtual disappearance from the national stage left a hole which nobody else could fill. Probably the damage done was overestimated but it is incontestable that there was a swing back to the right in the last few days and Wilson was never again to risk so long an absence from the centre of the stage. By election day there was a cautious consensus that Labour was likely to win narrowly but that the race was still very much an open one.

"Anyone, especially a foreigner, would be extremely foolish to try to predict, with any assurance, its result," wrote the American Ambassador, David Bruce. The local soothsayers, "usually emphatic in drawing conclusions, have sought refuge in ambiguity and whisky". The Liberals might hold the balance of power. Wilson had presented himself admirably, "emanating self-confidence, impressive diction, ready and caustic in suppressing hecklers, passing easily from dispassionate economic announcements to rough-and-tumble vituperation". Yet there were still doubts whether "he has popularly overcome the animus against him engendered during past battles within his own party that he is tricky and unreliable". The result might turn on the women's vote, believed Bruce, and there were some indications that this might favour Douglas-Home.[1]

Election day was a protracted torment for both party leaders. The first result, at Cheltenham, showed the Tory majority halved, but Billericay, the first marginal to be announced and generally held to be a sign of what was to come, was held by the Conservatives with a comfortable majority of 1,592. The key Midland seats were proving disappointing, with even a swing away from Labour in some cases. Elsewhere the party did better. Wilson had said that if he looked like winning he would return to London by the 8.30 a.m. train on Friday 16 October. He did not finally make up his mind until 3.10 a.m. On the way up to London he listened to the results, whenever the reception was good enough, on his portable radio. Little by little Labour's anyway thin lead was whittled away by the inevitable Tory wins in the rural constituencies. By the time he reached London he still felt confident enough to tell Len Williams that only the size of the majority was in question, but to the press he said no more than that it was too early to comment on the results. It was not till Labour won Meriden in Warwickshire after a recount that they were sure of half the total seats. The final results did not come in until Saturday: given that two out of the three non-voting jobs in the House of Commons were held by the Tories, Labour had an effective overall majority of five. By the time that this was finally established Wilson was already Prime Minister; at three minutes past four on Friday, 16 October 1964, he was called to Buckingham Palace and invited to form a government.

In the next few days Wilson received more than 4,000 letters to congratulate him on his victory.[1] Some took longer to arrive; Leonard Miall's because he carelessly put it in the wrong envelope and sent it instead of a cheque to pay his telephone bill. "It is a reflection on the type of acquisitive society in which we live," wrote Wilson sympathetically, "that a letter of that kind is not accepted in settlement of a telephone account." A. J. P. Taylor was one of many who urged him to throw off the legacy of Hugh Gaitskell: "It was wished on us by the capitalist press" (a subject on which it might be thought that Taylor could speak with some authority). Lord Faringdon spoke for the left when he rejoiced that, "my belief in the party is restored and all those emotions and faith which were the reason why one joined it are again valid. It is a kind of political rebirth." Helen Wheeler struck a more cautious note, advising Wilson, "Don't let Lord Acton have a look in as far as you are concerned." What Acton should have said, Wilson retorted, was: "All power corrupts, but too long out of power corrupts absolutely."

But was it such a famous victory? Given the state of the Tory Party at the beginning of 1964, the unpromising economic situation, the comparative lack of popular appeal of Alec Douglas-Home, should not Labour have won by a larger margin? Fewer people had voted Labour in 1964 than in 1959, even though the electorate was a larger one. A revived Liberal Party had secured some two million extra votes, some from Labour, more from the Tories. The Liberals in a sense had won the election for Harold Wilson. An overall Tory majority of almost a hundred had been overturned, to be replaced by an overall Labour majority of five. That was not an achievement to be belittled. But it was not all it might have been.

Harold Wilson was as conscious of that as anyone. He knew how much he had done, but he was quite as aware how much there was still to do. He had convinced the electorate that Labour was fit to govern. Now remained the far more difficult task, to convince them that Labour was the natural party of government.

IX

The Making of the Government

1964

If it had been necessary to construct a model Labour Prime Minister for the 1960s, his *curriculum vitae* would have been very similar to that of Harold Wilson. His Yorkshire accent and lower middle-class credentials made him acceptable to the proletarian elements of the party; his Oxford record won him the respect of the intellectuals. He was only forty-eight years old. As Wilson himself was accustomed to point out whenever opportunity arose: since the Reform Bill of 1832 the average age of new Prime Ministers had been fifty-nine; only three – Peel, Rosebery and now Wilson – had been under fifty. As President of the Board of Trade, shadow Chancellor and shadow Foreign Secretary, he had wide-ranging experience of the great fields of government. He had evolved into a brilliant speaker and debater: "the most accomplished parliamentarian of them all," wrote James Griffiths, "... a superb politician and a master of the debating forum".[1] His memory, always formidable, had been honed into a fine-edged weapon for the wonder of his friends and the confusion of his enemies: at Number 10 he quoted to John Freeman a long extract from some speech. That is exactly what I feel, said Freeman. It's exactly what you wrote, retorted Wilson, and cited the *New States-man* reference from six or so years before.[2] He had mastered the tricks of the media and established a remarkably close and friendly relationship with the press. "Even his most rabid critics," Griffiths continued, "... have to admit that he comes over well on television and presents himself and his policies with consummate skill."[3] In his first months in office he proved himself "stupefyingly able", said Healey – a man whose opinion of Wilson was, in general, far from idolatrous;[4] the "most competent and best informed of them all", judged Shinwell – whose admiration was tinged by the same dislike and distrust as Healey's.[1] Benn was dazzled by the speed of his mind and his ability to get to the heart of a problem: "His interrogation when you'd explained your problem – his interrogation to see if *you'd* understood it – was always rather frightening."[2]

It is interesting to note the qualities that Wilson singled out in his essays on his predecessors at Number 10. Liverpool was no mediocrity. He was "the strongest Prime Minister since Pitt ... He put his foot down hard on cabals and splits." Melbourne had "that indefinable quality of leadership and unification which some Prime Ministers have and some do not". Writing of Rosebery he extolled those who keep their subconscious under close restraint: "No one should attempt the role of Prime Minister who cannot fall asleep the moment he is in bed." With Baldwin he sympathised: "A healer does not usually get a good press; Fleet Street thrives on confrontations ... If he uses his political skills to keep the Cabinet together, he is condemned as devious, if he forces splits and public recriminations then, as long as he takes the right side in the division, he is a hero. But his Cabinet disintegrates."[3] A Prime Minister who is calm and strong, a leader, a unifier, a healer: this was the role that Wilson extolled, that he planned to play, and for which he felt himself eminently well qualified. But it was his energy and exuberance which most vividly impressed those who saw him in the first weeks at Number 10. There was an atmosphere of fizzing, said Oliver Wright, the Foreign Office private secretary who had been left over from the old regime. Wilson's "sheer enjoyment" was delightful to see, he kept breaking off from whatever he was doing to dash over and wave to the crowds outside.[4] "I do feel that this job ... is a tremendous adventure," he told Goodhart. "John Reith once told me that one should never take on a job that one could not describe as 'fun' and I am certainly not the worrying type."[5]

"Delighted to see that Resident of Duchy of Cornwall is new tenant of Downing Street," the Duke of Edinburgh telegraphed to Wilson when he heard the result of the election. "Thanks to the generous attitude of the Duchy," Wilson replied, "my residence within the Duchy of Cornwall is a freehold against the tied cottage status of my tenure of Downing Street."[6] It was the tied cottage aspect which caused greatest pain to Mary Wilson. To be asked to leave the home which she had built up lovingly over the years was bad enough; it was worse to move into a house which was theirs temporarily, perhaps only for a year or two, and on which she could leave no imprint except by permission of the appropriate authorities; worst of all was to live in a house which was primarily an office and in which everything took second place to the demands of business. Crossman told her that "the most important thing she could do in Downing Street was to keep Harold's home life absolutely separate in the top flat and feel no compunction about not doing much social activity".[1] It was excellent advice, but, like most excellent advice, more easily given than acted on. How was it possible to keep home life separate when private secretaries imposed their endless and wearisome demands; when her husband rejoiced in his work and wanted to eat it, drink it, breathe it, take it to bed and dream it? "It is going to alter my life considerably," she said gloomily at a press conference after the election. "I shall have to go out more. I am a bit overwhelmed, but I shall do my best to help Harold as much as I can."[2]

She did do her best, but it was at the expense of her peace of mind. When a libel action was in progress against the author of a biography of Wilson which, *inter alia*, alleged that she had cut herself off completely from his political life, counsel maintained that she had fully supported him at elections, had accompanied him to twenty-six out of the twenty-seven party conferences which he had attended, went fifteen or so times a year to meetings of party members, gave regular tea parties at Number 10 for ministers' wives.[3] All this was demonstrably true. George Wigg for one paid tribute to her ability to create "friendly relations among the wives of members of the Government";[4] an achievement which, it might have been hoped, would be only a preamble to the more challenging project of creating friendly relations among the members of the government themselves. She was one of the few people who could soothe down George Brown when he was in a tantrum and threatening resignation.[5] She subjected herself to the agony of interviews, though not always to the total satisfaction of the more solemn political counsellors, some of whom were disconcerted to read in the *Observer*: "When Harold is worried, he does not get angry or anything like that. He just hums as he walks around."[6] But she hated it all. She wanted to live a normal life, talk to a few close friends, read, write poetry, behave like the wife of the Oxford don whom she thought she had married. The first six months at Number 10 were among the unhappiest of her life. Wilson could be remarkably unperceptive. Once he told Crossman that he thought Mary should be used more at electoral meetings. Crossman remarked that she would hate it. Oh no, said Wilson, she had thoroughly enjoyed the meeting of the night before. Crossman repeated this to Mary. " 'Enjoyed it!' she said, with agony on her face. 'Who told you that? That man?' "[1] But even "that man" could hardly fail to sense her discontent at the pattern of their lives. It tarnished the pleasure which he took in his work, but was very far from ruining it. Crossman was fascinated by their relationship. "I am sure they are deeply together," he wrote in his diary, "but they are now pretty separate in their togetherness. It is one of those marriages which holds despite itself because each side has evolved a self-containedness within the marriage."[2]

By now Robin Wilson was twenty-one years old, a pure math-ematician who was largely wrapped up in music and his studies and featured rarely at Downing Street. When he did he occasionally played "Onward Christian Soldiers" with such vigour on the family harmonium that it was clearly audible in the Cabinet Room below. Giles, aged sixteen, who had followed his brother to University College School in Hampstead, was more often at home, but though both boys liked and admired their father, the relationship between them was not a particularly close one. Neither son had any enthusiasm for politics, and though their mother's poetry meant little more to them, they sympathised with her when she revolted at the invasion of their private life by the demands of her husband's career.[3] Other members of the Wilson family felt very differently. His father, in particular, revelled in his success and wished to share the limelight as far as he could contrive it. He could rarely resist a chance to give an interview. In 1967 he gave the *Daily Express* a lot of details about Wilson's christening. His son wrote to say that he *must* submit all such queries to Number 10: "This is an absolute imperative in present circumstances."[4] Herbert was contrite, but the penitence did not last for long. At the Durham miners' gala he stood on the balcony beside the Prime Minister and, when autograph books were thrown up, had to be restrained from signing them himself and throwing them back again.[5] He could at times be a nuisance who tried his daughter almost to breaking point. "He's as nasty as can be ..." Marjorie had complained some years before. "I shall never forget or forgive his behaviour."[6] But they always did forgive if not forget because of his real warmth and generosity. When Heath was elected leader of the Conservative Party, Herbert Wilson wrote to his father to say how pleased he was to think of the elation that William Heath must be feeling at his son's triumph. "I look back on Harold's years as a boy,

a Boy Scout, etc. etc. and remember with joy his youthful enthusiasm."
Heath's biographer wrote to ask if he could quote the letter. It would
be churlish to refuse, Marcia commented: "My only regret is that
Granpa always feels moved to do these things without telling us
first."[1]

Becoming Prime Minister was an expensive business. In the tax
year 1964–5 Wilson had earned £944 as an MP, £1,458 as leader of
the opposition, £3,971 as economic consultant and £804 as author
and broadcaster, a grand total of £7,177. As Prime Minister his
income from politics rose to £3,686 but in 1966–7 – the first full year
in Downing Street – his earnings from other sources fell to £1,581,
leaving him with £5,267 or a drop of nearly a quarter. There were,
of course, some rich perquisites to ensure that his way of life became
more affluent, but in terms of available cash he was worse off.
Except in so far as this created problems for his family, Wilson was
untroubled by the loss. The only non-essential of which he would
have hated to be deprived was alcohol, and even in that case his
demands were relatively modest. Gaitskell once remarked that Wilson
"liked the drink rather too much". "I know Harold far better than
Hugh does," wrote Crossman, "and though Harold quite likes a drink
he is nothing like the drinker Hugh himself is." Wilson took some
pride in the fact that he did not know the difference between hock and
burgundy, but "he is good at drinking either," Crossman commented a
year or so later.[2] That was in 1960. Four years later the intake –
mainly of brandy or whisky – had become greater, an occasional
stimulant had become a need. But politicians as a group do tend to
drink heavily and Wilson was far from being among the worst of
them. Only rarely, when safely at home relaxing with his cronies, was
he noticeably the worse for drink; partly because he had a strong
head, more because he was too much the professional: "I don't drink
too much because I am like a man who is always driving," he once
remarked to an official.[3]

Apart from that, his only modest luxury was to join the Elles-
borough golf club close to Chequers and play a round there most
weekends. He bought few books and no pictures; rarely had time to
go to concerts or theatres even if he had wanted to; abhorred dinner
parties, whether as guest or host. His suits were cheap and ready-
made: he could afford no better, had no wish to look elegant, and
anyway had the knack of reducing the most finely crafted suit within
a few days to something more fit for a tramp than a Prime Minister.

Food, preferably plain, was something to be shovelled down as time permitted. Roy Jenkins recalls with a mixture of amusement and exasperation the normal pattern of his bilateral meetings with the Prime Minister. They would often run from 7.00 p.m. to about 9.30 p.m. There was never any suggestion of eating but plenty of inadequately diluted whisky. However, at the price of missing dinner and mild intoxication, the satisfactory disposal of an agenda of points could usually be achieved. Arnold Goodman used to plead to be allowed to come after 8.30 p.m. at the earliest so that he would have a chance of dining first.[1] When they were there they talked business interspersed with much gossip and political reminiscence; Wilson had no use or time for the sort of discursive conversation which contributes to no immediate problem but builds up mutual understanding. His social patience was limited; he was never intentionally rude but he switched off; at a banquet for a foreign dignitary he would look into space during his guest's after-dinner speech, "not even feigning interest, peacefully emptying his wine glasses one by one".[2] Almost the only times he would appear animated when not engaged in political talk were when stars from the world of show business came to Number 10. Wilson took a childlike delight in the presence of celebrities from other walks of life, particularly the stage or television. It was the time at which the television series, *The Forsyte Saga*, was enjoying phenomenal success, and its stars, Eric Porter and Susan Hampshire, were frequent guests; so much so that Porter once remarked: "You know, I think I ought to bring my bed and sleep here."[3] Even on such occasions, however, Wilson rarely took his eye off the political ball. After a few minutes' conversation with a particularly delectable film star he remarked disapprovingly that her views on taxation seemed most reactionary. Except for such minor divagations, life in Number 10, as Crossman disdainfully put it, "was deeply *Petit bourgeois*". It was caricatured in *Private Eye*'s column "Mrs Wilson's Diary". Mary objected to the inaccuracies in this – she *never* drank Wincarnis, Harold did *not* favour HP but Worcestershire Sauce – but recognised that the underlying tone was mild, even affectionate. When the column was developed into a book, Benn argued that this was going too far and that legal action should be taken. Wilson, who knew only too well how much worse the press could be, said that *Private Eye* was now so scurrilous that nobody read it or took it seriously. It had best be ignored.[4]

The flat in Number 10 was somewhere to sleep, to grab a hurried lunch, to eat a cold supper of sandwiches or meat pie and salad. Try as Mary might it was not much of a home. She found Chequers, the country retreat of most Prime Ministers, almost equally unacceptable: large, gloomy and isolated; Wilson's romantic instincts, however, were kindled by this fine Elizabethan house. He loved to show off its treasures – Napoleon's despatch case, Elizabeth I's ring, Nelson's pocket-watch – and to air his theories about Shakespeare's associations with the neighbourhood. He was delighted to find the initials W. H. in several parts of the house and assured Tony Benn that "the mysterious W. H. of the sonnets was really a friend of whoever owned the place at the time."[1]

The Isles of Scilly, where they went regularly at Easter and for the summer holidays, was the place where the Wilsons felt most at ease. They first visited them in 1952 when they went to stay with their friends, the Kays, and enjoyed themselves so much that they vowed in future always to holiday there. In 1958 they bought a small plot of land on the main island, St Mary's, for £200 from the Duchy of Cornwall. There they built a three-bedroomed bungalow, 300 yards from the sea, on what was then the fringes of town and is still near the open country. The rooms were poky, the architecture unambitious, but it was exactly what they wanted. Mary paid off the mortgage with the profits from her first book of poems, and the ownership was then transferred to her. At Marjorie's suggestion it was called Lowenva, an old Cornish word meaning House of Happiness. It was a base from which they could take long walks – the eight miles circuit of St Mary's was an Easter Saturday ritual – bathe in the coldest weather, make occasional expeditions in fishing boats, garden desultorily. Wilson played rustic golf on the local course. By the time he became Prime Minister he was an accepted feature of the island, boasted of as an additional tourist attraction but otherwise left in peace. An informal press conference and photo session were held early each visit, after that it was accepted that he would not be bothered except in crisis. The security was perfunctory, and though by 1966 he had been equipped with a walkie-talkie, which gave him immediate communication with London from anywhere on the island, he used it as rarely as possible. There were occasional excitements. Lord Moynihan arrived, carrying a gun and vowing vengeance for some unknown affront. Giles Wilson, who happened to be at the landing strip, obligingly helped him park his private aeroplane and sped him on his way, but luckily the police, warned of his advent, intercepted him and returned him to the mainland. A Russian trawler, supposedly on surveillance duty, was often spotted near the Isles of Scilly while the Prime Minister was there and since they were presumably monitoring his phone calls Wilson would amuse himself by passing cryptic messages – "The fox has a black cloak," or some such gibberish. The Isles of Scilly, indeed, seemed to bring out a fine vein of schoolboy humour. Once, after bathing, the zip on Wilson's shorts jammed. "You can tell the Russians there are no flies on the British Prime Minister," he announced.[1]

When he told Frank Pakenham that he was to be leader of the House of Lords, Wilson concluded: "We should have a lot of fun together."[2] The greatest source of fun, he calculated, would be the formation of his government; he enjoyed giving good news as much as he disliked being the bearer of bad tidings and expected the handing out of offers to be a protracted Christmas. But, optimistic though he was, he saw the risks ahead. By sacking a minister, Wilson once said, you make twenty enemies: the victim, and the nineteen people who think they should have taken his place.[3] By appointing a minister you make only nineteen enemies, unless, of course, the appointee thinks he should have had a better post. To satisfy everyone would be impossible. His only advisers were Edward Short, the future Chief Whip, and Herbert Bowden, Short's predecessor. Marcia Williams and one or two other members of the entourage undoubtedly had views and had already expressed them, but they played no part in the actual work of drawing up the lists. On entering Number 10, wrote Short, Wilson went straight to the Cabinet Room, lit his pipe, "that malodorous instrument which dominated the hundreds of meetings we sat through during those years, produced a copy of the Labour Manifesto and placed it in the stationery box in front of him where it remained, a cynic would say unread, until the next General Election; took out his pen and started to appoint a government".[4]

As always, options were limited. Only two of the possible candidates for the Cabinet – Patrick Gordon Walker and James Griffiths – had served at that level before. In theory this should have given Wilson more room for manoeuvre, but when it came to selecting ministers he felt bound to give priority to the existing shadow Cabinet even though "I had not voted for all of them and even fewer had voted for me in the leadership contest."[1] There was therefore certain to be a heavily Gaitskellite flavour about the new Cabinet, too much so for the left, who were disconcerted to find the old enemy preferred to them by their chosen champion. "I think Harold's problem is that at bottom he just hasn't got faith in himself, despite all the air of bubbly india-rubber self-confidence," was Barbara Castle's regretful judgment.[2] It would be equally true to say that, apart from Castle herself and Crossman, there was not much talent at the highest level on the left. The biggest guns were Gaitskellites or at least right-wingers and the disposition of the two biggest of them was Wilson's first problem.

Wilson's most important innovation in government-making met so precisely the needs imposed by the personnel available that if he had not mooted it long before it would be easy to believe that he had contrived it especially for the occasion. The belief that the nation would never prosper so long as the grip of the ultra-cautious Treasury impaired the reconstruction and modernisation of British industry had been a prominent dogma of the left for many years. "Take economic planning away from the Treasury," Bevan had urged in his resignation speech. "They know nothing about it."[3] Shortly after he became leader Wilson acted on this advice by charging Balogh with the task of planning the division of the Treasury and turning half of it into an independent Ministry for Expansion.[4] In his visit to Washington as leader of the opposition, Wilson had spoken of this plan to create a Department of Economic Affairs (DEA) and added, with a wink in the direction of Eric Roll, then serving as Economic Minister in the embassy, "and we have even picked the Permanent Secretary".[5] Jay tried vigorously to dissuade Wilson from what seemed to him a potentially disastrous venture and urged Callaghan to take the same line. Wilson "listened politely" but showed no signs of changing his mind.[6] Callaghan dutifully seconded Jay's efforts, though not as vigorously as his ally would have wished. He did not dispute the need for a Department of Economic Affairs in principle but believed that it was unnecessary in 1964 when the Treasury under William Armstrong was ready to countenance an expansionist policy. Instead the creation of the new, hyperactive department – the Department of Extraordinary Aggression, as the Chancellor's private secretary unkindly christened it[7] – drove the Treasury back into a defensive laager.[8]

Wilson believed in the doctrine of "creative tension"; friction between the two great departments would generate an extraordinary dynamism of its own. "This was not my experience," wrote Callaghan gloomily, though accepting that Wilson genuinely believed he was on to a winning idea and was not just trying to neutralise two of his principal rivals.[1] Jay was less charitable. For him it was "a prime example of creating bad organisation in order to appease personalities ... Wilson, I am sure, knew the scheme was ill-judged, but for some reason put personal appeasement first."[2] Wilson did *not* know the scheme was ill-judged but he did see it as a solution to the problem of what was to be done with George Brown. Brown, in Marcia Williams's words, believed that he was "not so much a Deputy Prime Minister as the alternative Prime Minister".[3] He had been denied the Foreign Office, partly on political but still more on temperamental grounds. Wilson believed that Brown's drunkenness would be a liability in such a conspicuous position. In the first few months of the new government Castle and Crossman in their respective diaries record thirteen occasions on which Brown was incapably drunk in public.[4] At a Buckingham Palace reception Wilson was heard to murmur nervously: "Tighten your seat-belts. Here comes George!"[5] In the Department of Economic Affairs Brown would be able to exercise his formidable energy, enthusiasm and persuasive powers in a forum in which the occasional brick could be dropped without doing damage to Britain's international relations.

The appointment would also cause tension – creative or not – between Brown and Callaghan, and render more remote the possibility that the two might make common cause against their Prime Minister. Brown was the first minister to be appointed and had the status, if not the formal title, of Deputy Prime Minister. Callaghan had his appointment in Downing Street two hours later but enjoyed the effective power. Roy Jenkins has been quoted by Crossman as saying that he knew no one who "combined such a powerful political personality with so little intelligence".[6] The second half of the judgment – probably more Crossman's than Jenkins's – is uncharitable; Callaghan was no intellectual nor wished to be but his common sense and cunning were remarkable and he had a capacity to grasp complicated ideas and to expound them lucidly to fellow laymen. Wilson had no doubt at this point that he was his most dangerous rival; the only man apart from the Prime Minister who had contrived to be acceptable both to the right and left while not committing himself to either camp. All he lacked was a power base, and that in time the unions were to supply. As Chancellor of the Exchequer he could be relied on to do nothing silly and, quite as important, to make sure that Brown did not do anything silly either.

Wilson's other striking innovation was to create a Minister of Technology, to encourage productivity and efficiency and to ensure that scientific methods would in future be applied to industrial production. It was to be the realisation of the dream he had preached so frequently over the last few years. He invited Frank Cousins to leave Britain's most powerful union, the Transport and General Workers, so as to lead the ministry; thus, he hoped, signifying the unity of government and unions in the new crusade and, incidentally, disarming a potentially dangerous enemy. Cousins had made himself a suspect figure to the right by his clashes with the leadership over unilateral disarmament, but towards the end of Gaitskell's life there had been something of a reconciliation and there had even been talk of his joining a future Labour government as Minister of Transport.[1] Now the offer became reality. Jack Jones, who was eventually to fill Cousins's seat at the union, urged him to accept and to act as Wilson's ally in the Cabinet: "Roy Jenkins and George Brown were particularly suspect as right-wingers and in my view potentially disloyal to Wilson. Harold would need strong support if he was to pursue socialist policies."[2] Wilson argued the same point. He needed help if he was not to be overwhelmed by the right: "I want you to be close to me, Frank. There is no one else I can trust as I can trust you. That is because I know you are the one man who doesn't want my job."[3] Even as he spoke he must have doubted whether this would provide sufficient basis for a harmonious relationship. Cousins had his doubts as well. Both were right. To bring in a union leader was a good idea, but he would have had to be either a lesser or a greater man; a tractable minion or an Ernest Bevin. Cousins was vain, arrogant and unable to appreciate what government was all about. He had been a good if, in the eyes of some, over-political union leader; as a minister he proved truculent, tetchy and incompetent to develop his ministry in the way Wilson had hoped; in the House of Commons he was disastrously out of touch.

The need to find him a seat in the Commons proved embarrassing, especially as it was coupled with the search for a vacancy for Patrick Gordon Walker. Gordon Walker had been selected as Foreign Secretary for the same reasons as he had been picked for the shadow job the previous year: to thwart George Brown and because Wilson wanted "a donnish, quiet, acquiescent figure" who would let the Prime Minister make his own foreign policy.[1] The plan went wrong when Gordon Walker, one of the least demagogic members of the Labour front bench, fell victim to an unpleasantly racist electoral campaign and lost his seat at Smethwick. Wilson rallied nobly and at once telegraphed: "Deeply regret this result ... This will make no difference, and have broadly hinted so to the Press."[2] Gordon Walker would still be Foreign Secretary and another seat would be found him. To provide for Cousins and Gordon Walker, however, meant persuading two sitting members that they would be happier in the House of Lords. Reg Sorensen, who was asked to make way for Gordon Walker at Leyton, was particularly recalcitrant: "Heavens above! God forbid!" he was said to have exclaimed when offered a peerage. Sorensen's patent displeasure, the feeling on the part of the constituency party that both he and they had been treated without proper consideration, and some characteristically lacklustre electioneering by Gordon Walker, together produced catastrophe. He turned the 8,000 majority of his seventy-three-year-old and not particularly charismatic predecessor into a loss by 205 votes. Cousins got in at Nuneaton with a sharply reduced majority but Gordon Walker's defeat reduced the government's effective overall majority from five to three.

To replace Gordon Walker, Wilson promoted another donnish, quiet, if not invariably acquiescent figure, Michael Stewart, from the Ministry of Education. Wilson trusted him because he always knew where Stewart would stand, which was usually somewhere to the right of any but the most immoderate Tory. He was a friend from the Isles of Scilly, where he too took regular holidays, was safe, sensible, lacking in popular appeal and no possible threat to Wilson's position in Number 10. To Barbara Castle this was yet one more example of Wilson's determination to surround himself with potential or actual enemies. She deplored this weakness to Marcia Williams, who vehemently agreed: "Doesn't he see that this is his most dangerous rival? I keep telling him but he won't listen."[3] He was right not to listen, as Mrs Williams would subsequently have agreed. Whether or not Stewart was a good Foreign Secretary depends on the point in the political spectrum from which the judgment is made, but as a Cabinet colleague he was totally dependable and turned a deaf ear to the plotting that went on around him.

Gordon Walker's defeat at Smethwick was of particular interest because it provoked one of Wilson's strikingly few unpremeditated outbursts of temper. In the House of Commons he referred to the "utterly squalid" campaign waged by the local Conservatives and then, when further stimulated by some brisk heckling, said that the new member should be treated as "a parliamentary leper".[1] It was a major political blunder, judged Alan Watkins in the *Spectator*. He was still behaving like a leader of the opposition; he must learn to be a Prime Minister.[2] Short, whose preoccupation as Chief Whip was to establish a relationship with the Tories which would make it possible to keep things going in the House of Commons in spite of the minuscule majority, was horrified by what seemed a wanton attempt to stir things up. Wilson must have known what result he would achieve, Short considered, since, "unless the case was almost unique", he never spoke without first calculating the effects.[3] Even the former Archbishop of Canterbury, Geoffrey Fisher, weighed in with a measured rebuke. Wilson's reply to Fisher was defensive yet unrepentant. His remarks had indeed been inexpedient, he admitted, and had distracted attention from his main point, but "a month from now all that will be remembered is that there was a major explosion, that it was on the question of racialism and that we were on the side of the angels". He had been appalled and angered by the Smethwick campaign, he went on:

The undercurrent, backlash or whatever is the fashionable phrase has become too strong to be ignored and unless this problem is dealt with head on, I am afraid that it will foul our politics not only in the next Election but over a very considerable period of time. We want, as we said in the Election, to concentrate attention on the constructive problems of housing, education and integration of the immigrant population, and we are already working hard on this. Our Bill against racial intolerance I hope will help to counter some of the slimier activities. I believe that the major explosion I caused will help in all this.[4]

That the explosion was not a contrived effect was obvious to those closest to him. He returned to Downing Street looking distinctly sheepish and wondering whether he might not have gone a little too far. His staff assured him that he had.[5] No one, including Wilson, had expected such an outburst. As on at least one other occasion,* it

* See p 234 below.

was racialism which had provoked him; and nobody near him in either case doubted that his anger was as uncontrolled as his revulsion was sincere.

It was the same spirit which led to his appointing Barbara Castle Minister of Overseas Development with a seat in the Cabinet. Hastings Banda wrote from Malawi to congratulate him: "She is well known to most of us in Africa and in Asia. She is not, of course, as you know, popular with the Europeans in the Rhodesias, but she is very popular with the Africans. And in Africa, Commonwealth Development means Africans really, because Europeans can very well take care of themselves."[1] Economic and political pressures were to ensure that Banda was largely disappointed, but Wilson meant Castle's appointment to be a rousing assertion of the government's intention greatly to increase the scale and commitment of Britain's aid to the under-developed world. It also gave him a friendly face around a largely Gaitskellite Cabinet table. Another belonged to Richard Crossman; but though Wilson knew that Crossman was basically on his side he found irritating the latter's habit of treating Cabinet as an undergraduate seminar in which it was the good don's duty to provoke discussions by playing devil's advocate or advancing preposterous theses. Crossman was made Minister of Housing and Local Government, a job which kept him more than busy but not to the extent of preventing him from expressing an opinion on almost every subject however little he might know about it. Denis Healey, at Defence, was similarly uninhibited but disdained Crossman's intellectual pyrotechnics. His weapon was the bludgeon, and he used it against the Prime Minister with as much relish as against any other of his colleagues.

There were some nice individual touches in Wilson's selection of the lesser ministers. Hugh Foot, who had resigned from his post at the United Nations in protest at the Tory policy in Africa, was created Lord Caradon, Minister of State in the Foreign Office, and permanent representative at the United Nations – another affirmation of Wilson's good intentions towards the poorer and less developed countries. A vigorous effort was made to persuade Solly Zuckerman to join the Foreign Office team as minister responsible for disarmament. Zuckerman would have none of it and, when Wilson asked for the name of another internationally respected scientist who would be acceptable to the Americans, proposed John Cockcroft. Cockcroft refused too, and at Wigg's suggestion Wilson had recourse to Alun Gwynne

Jones, defence correspondent of *The Times*, who renewed life as Lord Chalfont.[1] Barbara Castle called the appointment a "dangerous gimmick";[2] whatever danger there was seems to have been endured by Chalfont himself, who was noticeably ill at ease in a Labour administration. C. P. Snow, novelist and pontificator about "The Two Cultures", was brought in, also ennobled, to support Cousins at Technology. When Wilson told Zuckerman that he was forming a "ministry of all the talents", Zuckerman remarked that he supposed Snow was one of the talents referred to. "Oh, that's public relations," said Wilson. "That's not serious."[3]

The government was noteworthy, too, for who was *not* included. The left-wing dissidents were excluded almost to a man. The whip had only just been restored to the group recently expelled from the party, but the left – and for that matter the Chief Whip[4] – had still hoped that Foot and Mikardo at least would find jobs. Wilson later claimed that he had not offered Foot a job because he thought he would prefer to remain free of the constraints of office. Wigg more cynically thought that Wilson reckoned Cousins was certain to resign sooner rather than later and did not want to give Foot the chance of resigning at the same time.[5] In a few cases personal prejudice seems to have played a part. Edward Short, for instance, believed that Arthur Blenkinsop was excluded because he had been at the Ministry of Health in 1951 but had failed to resign with Aneurin Bevan.[6] Certainly Wilson made no secret of his dislike for Blenkinsop. On the whole, however, it was felt he had been strikingly forgiving. Of one appointment an astonished Chief Whip exclaimed: "Don't you remember all the horrible, defamatory things he has said about you since you became leader of the party?" Wilson "smiled with that impish but enigmatic smile of his, which made me wonder whether he was being magnanimous or very crafty, and said, 'Life is too short to worry about things like that.' "[7]

Wilson's Cabinet was "predominantly moderate" reported the American Embassy, "probably last homage of kind to old order if Wilson survives next few precarious months without upset". Wilson's few left-wing appointments were no doubt intended to "tie them down, neutralise them", an insurance policy rather than a "testimony to personal standing or vitality of left in party councils".[8] The comment was not unfair; Wilson had done a neat balancing act with the right having decidedly the better of it but not to the extent where the scales tipped dangerously in their favour. In Crossman's view there were two main weaknesses: the foreign affairs team was sub-standard (he was referring to Gordon Walker but would have said the same *a fortiori* of Michael Stewart) and the relationship between the parliamentary party and the Cabinet was in the hands of Bowden and Short, two "unimaginative disciplinarians".[1] To some it seemed too Oxonian a government; Shinwell complained that Wilson's links with Crossman, Crosland, Healey, Castle and Longford were "apparently based on their university background rather than on their abilities and parliamentary experience".[2] To Longford it was one of the last "Christian family Cabinets in modern times"; he counted eleven committed Christians – including Wilson, Callaghan and Brown – among his colleagues.[3] The Christianity did not extend far beyond this inner group of faithful. In 1964 Wilson told the Chief Whip to organise "a private service of dedication at the beginning of the session". Short laid on a Labour bishop, Mervyn Stockwood, and the Methodist Donald Soper, but less than a third of the ministers turned up. In 1966 and 1974 there were similar services with even smaller attendances.[4] "The whole idea makes me cringe," complained Barbara Castle. "Is he really a believer or is he doing a Mary Whitehouse?"[5] Why the reality of Mrs Whitehouse's belief should be questioned is not clear, but there is no doubt that Wilson's was real enough.

The need to cram in his own supporters as well as the mass of the Gaitskellites meant that he grossly overshot the limits on the size of the government laid down by the Parliament Act. "I am not going to allow Queen Anne to tell me how to appoint my Government," he announced grandiloquently when Burke Trend, the Secretary to the Cabinet, pointed this out to him, only to be deflated when Trend rejoined that the Act in question had been brought in by Attlee's government.[6] An Act had to be rushed through increasing the possible total of ministers in the House of Commons from seventy-three to ninety-one. By the time he finished, the administration numbered 110, against Home's eighty-four.

The big three were undoubtedly Wilson, Callaghan and Brown; anything which they agreed on was likely to be accepted by Cabinet. But Wilson was nervous of establishing any sort of inner Cabinet, however informal. Gordon Walker, before his electoral disaster, convinced himself that he was part of an intimate cabal which would meet from time to time at Chequers or Number 10,[7] but the existence of this clique seems shadowy and certainly it had ceased to function within a few months. Instead Wilson depended for informal political discussion on a group of congenial advisers. Crossman, Castle and, from a lower level, Benn were members of the government who might be included in this amorphous assembly, but the minister whose presence was most invariable, who saw more of the Prime Minister even than the Chief Whip or Herbert Bowden, the leader of the House, was the egregious George Wigg.

Wigg's favoured role in politics, which he played with distinction, was that of the soldier's friend; but his passion was secrets, the more malodorous the better. He was at his happiest in the twilight world of spies, counter-spies and Chapman Pincher and viewed his fellow MPs with the same ferocious suspicion as he would have lavished on an accredited agent of the KGB. His office was that of Paymaster-General, one of those convenient sinecures which enable a Prime Minister to employ ministers on any odd job that occurs to him. Wigg's odd job was to keep an eye on the intelligence and security services and report to Wilson anything which he felt the Prime Minister ought to know about – a duty which he interpreted with some extravagance. Justifying Wigg's existence to the head of the civil service, Laurence Helsby, Wilson claimed that "he was able to give me immediate warning not only when there had in fact been a security incident but also when there was even a breath of suspicion in this field. In addition he was able, by constant prodding, to keep certain Departments up to scratch in their security organisation and arrangements."[1] To breathe suspicion and to prod constantly are not the most endearing of occupations. Wigg was heartily disliked, both in Number 10 and in the rest of Whitehall. Bowden and Short were constantly protesting about his trespassing on their territory in the areas of party discipline and the business of the House.[2] He told Chalfont that he was responsible for all intelligence matters; a view which the heads of MI5 and MI6 conspicuously did not share.[3] He had his uses; one of his harshest critics, Edward Short, admitted that his "dog-like devotion" made him valuable to Wilson and that he sometimes "discovered things before they happened and averted a lot of potential trouble in the Party".[4] But most of those who observed him closely felt that he was more of a nuisance than an asset. By nature an alarmist, detecting conspiracies behind every innocent discussion or casual encounter, he aroused false suspicions in the mind of the Prime Minister more often than he drew attention to real perils. Wilson had a taste for gossip and an incipient dread of betrayal; Wigg indulged the first and fanned the second into a state which was soon close to paranoia. He contributed more than anyone else to the miasma of suspicion and uncertainty which hung around the Downing Street of Mr Wilson.

Even without his activities Number 10 would never have been a comfortable place. This was largely the work – though by no means exclusively the fault – of Marcia Williams. Mrs Williams had a battle on her hands. Derek Mitchell, the private secretary inherited from the old regime, was outstandingly able: intelligent, quick, conscientious, a consummate professional, "one of the most brilliant civil servants I encountered", Marcia Williams herself described him;[1] but his view of his profession did not encompass the invasion of Downing Street by a group of political attendants with no formal official status. Jay urged Wilson to retain Mitchell but noted regretfully that, after a time, the private secretary's "attempt to preserve his idea of the proprieties of the system apparently proved unacceptable".[2] What to Mitchell were proprieties were to Marcia Williams an intolerable interference with the right of the Prime Minister to consult whom he liked whenever he liked in the way he liked. There was a real difference in principle between them – Mitchell believed it would be disastrous to have two separate and uncoordinated lines leading to the Prime Minister and wanted to establish a common approach; Marcia was determined jealously to guard her right of personal access – but there was nothing which two people of goodwill could not have sorted out, or which was not sorted out in future years as the idea of a political office in Number 10 became accepted. There was precious little goodwill between Marcia Williams and Derek Mitchell, however. George Wigg maintained that they were too alike to get on together, they were both "feline". Certainly, having made what he felt to be a generous gesture of welcome, Mitchell did not exert himself to ensure that the relationship worked more smoothly. He tried to "freeze out the political staff ", claimed Gerald Kaufman.[3] When Marcia wanted to travel with the Prime Minister's party to Washington, Mitchell said that the only way it could be done would be if she were listed as Mary Wilson's lady's maid. The remark, he maintains, was no more than a joking aside, but it rankled none the less.[4] But though neither side was wholly innocent, Marcia Williams was the main aggressor. Mitchell claims that she openly stated her first priority was to purge the civil service, starting in Number 10, and though the words may not be exactly quoted, the spirit sounds much what might have been expected. Urged on by Wigg, she harried the "garden girls", the predominantly middle- or upper middle-class shorthand-typists who worked in the garden room, and denounced treachery when one of them was found to be telephoning an old friend who happened to work as secretary to a Tory MP. By the end of 1964 Edward Short was recording a "minor upheaval in No 10". After a row with Mitchell "Marcia downed tools and walked out. Tommy Balogh ... was sent to persuade her to come back, which she did in her own good time."[1] A year later things were no better; Marcia told Tony Benn that "Mitchell had tried to knife her and that Harold intended to get rid of him".[2]

The importance of all this did not lie in the effect it had on the two principal protagonists – who may even rather have enjoyed it – but its impact on the running of the office and on the Prime Minister himself. Wilson had a remarkable capacity for insulating himself from the rows around him and remaining impassive as the emotional pressure cooker threatened explosion, but Marcia Williams was not one to suffer her woes in silence. Her constant and strident protests, her demands for protection, must have ruffled even his tranquillity and distracted him from more important issues. Nor was she the only disturber of the peace. Though Balogh had been accommodated in the Cabinet Office rather than Number 10 – in itself a source of grievance – his tantrums, when they occurred, were no less ferocious. Once Balogh minuted Wilson on the desirability of inviting an expert on cost-effectiveness to a forthcoming Chequers weekend devoted to defence. Mitchell brushed him off in a way that was sensible but decidedly disobliging. "I do not think Mitchell is entitled to lecture me in this tone," protested Balogh. "I agree with Thomas that this is a disgraceful way in which to write to him," Marcia weighed in. "Better if Tommy raises these with me," was Wilson's cryptic summing-up.[3] The civil servants, who thought Balogh an irresponsible mischief-maker, kept as many papers away from him as they could decently contrive. Balogh for his part dismissed the civil service as a Victorian relic and argued that its radical reform was "one of the most essential and fundamental preconditions" for a successful socialist government.[4] Wilson, who on the whole admired the civil service and was not at all sure that he wanted a successful socialist government, did not pay much attention to Balogh's views on this point. Indeed he often differed from Balogh, but he found his views stimulating and of interest, and though he would sometimes pretend not to read the endless papers with which the economist bombarded him, in fact he always looked at them and usually studied them with care.

In mid 1964 Wilson is said to have discussed with Norman Brook his plans for reorganising Number 10. "He had very inflated schemes for a greatly expanded Prime Minister's office," said Brook. "I think I pricked that balloon all right. If so, it was a really good afternoon's work."[1] The balloon may have been slightly deflated but it was still airborne by the time Wilson reached Number 10. His importation of Marcia Williams, Thomas Balogh, Trevor Lloyd-Hughes for the press, as well as parliamentarians like Peter Shore and Wigg, showed that he intended to provide himself with a political machine which, while not offering an alternative to the civil service, would furnish additional advice and information. Marcia Williams was at the heart of this inner group and without her it could hardly have functioned. The exact parameters of her influence took some establishing. Bowden and Short were disconcerted to find that she was to be present as Wilson's political secretary at the regular meetings – "Prayers" – which were held to discuss the day's business. They showed their displeasure and, at the end of the meeting, Bowden pointedly said that he had a private matter to discuss. Mrs Williams retired in moderately good order and thereafter rarely if ever appeared.[2] But within her bailiwick she reigned supreme and allowed herself complete freedom of expression in setting out her views. She went through the list of the Prime Minister's appointments with derisive criticisms. Lunch at the Baltic Exchange: "What is this for and why was it thought good?" Outstanding Young Businessmen of the Year: "Where did this come from and why was it accepted?" IXth Assembly of European Municipalities: "In God's name what is that all about and why is a P.M. involved in it?" Open World Cycling Championships: "I can think of nothing less virile looking than that – motor cars, yes, not bicycles. And even worse, it is excessively old fashioned. Please get out of it."[3] Her comments were always frank. A draft letter was put up by the Foreign Office. "This draft is appalling. I enclose a redraft which I have dictated," wrote Wilson. "The draft was *not* appalling. Your redraft is," Marcia Williams retorted. "I do not approve of the redraft as it is either meaningless or the same thing as the earlier draft," she told the secretary responsible.[1]

Whatever its expression, the advice was generally sound. The accusation levelled at her by successive civil servants who worked with her was not that she gave bad advice but that she wasted time with her tantrums and demands for attention. Crossman said that she had more influence with Wilson than any single man.[2] Up to a point that was true. Wilson would have paid little attention to her views on the international aspects of Vietnam or devaluation, nor would she have been likely to proffer them; but when the question was what the average party member expected from him on such questions, whether he ought to open a cycling championship, which minister was planning to stab him in the back, he would listen carefully. It was not the quality of the advice alone which mattered, it was the fact that it was offered with total honesty. Some Prime Ministers have wives who will share their political lives and point out the realities with a bluntness that no private secretaries or colleagues could normally permit themselves. Mary Wilson had neither the inclination nor the experience to play such a role. In a sense Marcia Williams was his political wife. "She was essential to Wilson and her resignation would have been more disastrous than that of any cabinet minister,"[3] said Tony Benn. The relationship between wife at home and wife at work is seldom wholly easy. Marcia had excellent intentions. "Dear Mary," she wrote, "I thought I should let you know that Harold has invited Senator Benton to Chequers on 7th May to dinner and to stay overnight. I have, however, not yet sent off the letter, in case you wanted to have a word with him since I know it is Giles's birthday."[4] But such consideration was far from invariable; though she did much valiant work for Wilson's family and friends her first priority was always the next move in the political battle.

A constant source of grievance was the selection of official papers which she and the others in the political office were authorised to see and whether they read by stealth what they were not allowed to have by right. "No member of my Political Office ever had access to classified documents," said Wilson firmly,[5] a denial which Lady Falkender today stalwartly endorses. Even if "classified" were interpreted to mean only secret or top secret – a definition which would have been unacceptable to Mitchell or Burke Trend – it seems still unlikely that none of Wilson's closest advisers was ever privately shown Cabinet or other secret papers. "If anybody claims that Mrs Williams did not see secrets, he's a liar," Wigg told Chapman Pincher.[1] Trend told Solly Zuckerman that he was sure all the papers in the Prime Minister's box were riffled through by unspecified members of the political staff.[2] Certainly the opportunity was there and, given the fact that the value of their advice would depend on how well they were informed, it would have been astonishing if they had never availed themselves of the opportunity.

Whatever the meaning of the term "kitchen cabinet" – and there were several – Marcia was at the heart of it. "A more or less self-formed group of Balogh, Shore, Kaufman, Marcia Williams and the other Parliamentary Private Secretaries of the time", Short defined it,[3] and that, with the occasional addition of Wigg and the maverick presence of Crossman, is as good a description as any. Crossman referred to "our little group" as comprising exactly the same people, while Benn referred to Wigg, Balogh and Marcia Williams as being "the three favourites at the court of King Harold".[4] How much the existence of the group mattered and the extent of its influence are other questions. Shore supposed the kitchen cabinet to be a group of thinkers who debated long-term as well as short-term policy and to some extent filled the gap which was left by Wilson's failure to undertake strategic planning.[5] Kaufman, who in 1965 was brought from the *New Statesman* to reinforce Lloyd-Hughes, took a less sanguine view of the group's significance. He felt that Wilson did not take them particularly seriously, especially when they turned to the long-term issues about which he cared so little.[6] Wilson was anxious to avoid their having anything approaching official status and banned any resumption of the lunches they used to hold before the election,[7] but he enjoyed having them around, and though he probably got more satisfaction from the political gossip than the policy discussions, the influence of this talented group should not be discounted.

Lloyd-Hughes, the press secretary, was one of the inner circle, who had worked closely with Wilson and Marcia Williams in the constituency. He was said to be a most successful ventriloquist's dummy – "If you disagreed with Trevor, you were almost certainly disagreeing with the Prime Minister himself"[8] – but though this made him invaluable to the press his influence in Number 10 did not extend beyond his immediate concerns. Solly Zuckerman was a frequent visitor. Wilson admired his mind and enjoyed his mischievousness, but there was never any question of his claiming, or for that matter desiring, a place in the kitchen cabinet. And there were other callers who dealt directly with the Prime Minister or Marcia Williams. Some were old business contacts. Roy Jenkins was practically run over by a little sports car late one morning when he was walking along Downing Street to Number 11. A stocky figure parked at the end and hurried to the door of Number 10, which was automatically opened for him. Finding the face faintly familiar but unable to place its owner, Jenkins walked back to Number 10 and said to the policeman, "Who was that?" "Oh, don't you know, sir," was the almost reproachful reply, "that's Mr Kagan. He's *very* well known here."[1] Arnold Goodman was in and out, advising on the perils of libel actions or other aspects of the Prime Minister's affairs. "The original Pooh Bah", Wilson described him – the description broke down in that Goodman eschewed any formal or honorific title, but the range of his interests and extent of his influence conceded nothing to his Gilbertian counter-part.[2] Siegmund Warburg, the merchant banker, was frequently con-sulted and Harry Kissin and Sigmund Sternberg were other former business associates. Such conspicuously capitalistic figures might seem curious companions for a Labour Prime Minister but they had been helpful to Wilson in the past, he liked them, was interested in their views and saw no reason why he should drop them now that he was in power. It was an attitude which was to earn him much criticism over the years, some of it justified, but at least one that could not be described as calculating or ungenerous.

But the man who probably influenced Wilson most during his first administration was neither a Jewish financier nor a Hungarian economist, neither a government colleague nor a member of his kitchen cabinet. Burke Trend, the Secretary to the Cabinet, was the best civil servant he had ever known, Wilson told Barbara Castle.[3] He was the ultimate mandarin: academically distinguished, cool, reserved, omniscient, with sound judgment and total calm in the face of crisis. If asked to advise Sir Humphrey Appleby – the hero of *Yes, Minister* – he said he would urge him to remember that he was not the Prime Minister's exclusive servant: "He's the servant of the full Cabinet. He's got to have no truck with the idea of a Prime Minister's Department, a 'Kitchen Cabinet'."[4] He had no truck with the kitchen cabinet himself but he established with Wilson a relationship so intimate that the Crossmans and Castles were left resentful and excluded. Wilson was too deferential to senior civil servants, Marcia Williams considered: "He felt he could understand them."[5] He *did* understand them, because at heart he was more than half mandarin himself. His years in Whitehall had been among the most formative of his life and he never forgot them. He described himself as being "to some extent, in a Whitehall phrase, 'house-trained' ",[1] and that training was nowhere more evident than in his handling of the civil service. His reverence for order and hierarchy, his admiration for academic prowess, his respect for people who made things work rather than pontificated about principles, all made it certain that he would find his relationship with Trend both comfortable and rewarding. It was appropriate that this most conservative of socialists should draw his closest counsellor from the very heart of the establishment.

X

The First Administration

1964–1966

"Your policy should be to keep your government by a strong majority," the Duke of St Bungay advised his Prime Minister, the Duke of Omnium. "After all, the making of new laws is too often but an unfortunate necessity laid on us by the impatience of the people. A lengthened period of quiet and therefore good government with a minimum of new laws would be the greatest benefit the country could receive."[1] A strong majority must have been fancifully remote in October 1964 but the rest of St Bungay's counsel would have seemed sensible to Wilson. His prime objective at that moment was not to pass new laws or to reform society but to win the election that must come in the not too distant future and turn his tiny majority into something more substantial. If laws and reforms could be got through the two Houses and help to win the election, then that would be a bonus; but legislation that might prove unpopular or produce an election at the wrong moment was to be eschewed. "You can't keep a Government going by the skin of your nose," protested James Margach, who was interviewing him at the moment it became clear he had won the election. "I'll pilot it by the seat of my pants then," retorted Wilson. "The main thing is to get in there, form a Government and then control events and time the next election."[2]

To control events, with a majority down to three, called for good nerves and much agility. Just before the election Wilson told Richard Neustadt of Harvard that "he meant to take all decisions into his own hands. He wants not only to make ultimate decisions but to pass issues through his own mind early, sitting at the centre of a brains-trust, with himself as the first brains-truster, on the model, he says, of J. F. K. ... Also, more importantly, he has to keep one step ahead of all his colleagues in the precedent-making first encounters and arrangements which set tone and style for their relationships. 'I shall be Chairman of the Board, not President,' he says, 'but Managing Director too, and very active at it!' "[1] This view of himself as being, if not an autocrat, then at least very much *primus inter pares*, was one he never abandoned. Writing about Lord John Russell, he criticised him for having gone too far in deferring to his colleagues: "You cannot ignore your party, or the particular views of individual ministers, but equally you cannot put the Prime Minister's position into commission."[2] He was resolved to impose his views upon his Cabinet, not by compelling them to accept some visionary long-term strategy, but by ensuring that they were all harnessed to the medium-term goal of establishing Labour in the voters' minds as the natural party of government which should be returned with a proper working majority at an election in 1965 or 1966.

To achieve this the first essential was that the party should remain united. Harold Wilson's supreme gift, judged Richard Marsh, "was his ability to keep the Labour Party together. It has been called two-facedness, trimming and all sorts of other things, but it is an essential and honourable skill."[3] He had the right temperament for such a task. Judith Hart saw him as possessed by a "profound inferiority complex" inherited from his years in a minority in the shadow Cabinet and NEC,[4] but Hart was a disappointed left-winger who felt that Wilson had surrendered to his former enemies. Wilson reckoned that there were few if any issues that were worth a serious Cabinet split, a compromise acceptable to everyone could almost always be found, it was healthier for Labour's prospects that he should unite the party on the second best rather than do battle for the best. He raised expediency to the level of a political philosophy. In so doing, at first at least, he disarmed even his fiercest critics. "I am very struck by how well you have treated me ever since I came to see you to discuss the *Economist* offer," wrote Roy Jenkins early in 1965. "Each time you have been a little better than your word. May I also be permitted to say what a great pleasure it is to work closely with you on a problem?"[5]

Wilson's extraordinary amiability was indeed his greatest asset in his dealings with his colleagues or party followers. He took endless trouble over his personal relationships, was almost invariably courteous, remembered the names of people's wives and children, managed their susceptibilities with tact, appeared to be interested in their opinions. This, of course, reflected well on the briefings he received from Marcia Williams and others, but the briefings only worked because Wilson genuinely liked people and wanted them to like him. He was, said Patrick Cosgrave in the *Spectator*, "the nicest Prime Minister we have had since Baldwin".[1] To secretaries, civil servants, chauffeurs, he was considerate and appreciative. After the hectic reorganisation of Whitehall that followed the formation of the new ministries, he wrote to the head of the civil service, Laurence Helsby, to tell him that never had he seen "anything so impressive as all you have done in the past few days".[2] He would have taken as much trouble to thank a typist who had worked all night or a driver who had turned out in the early hours of the morning to take him to his destination. William Armstrong claimed that he was a nicer man before he became Prime Minister: "Absolute power did corrupt him, but not in the normal sense – bribes and so on. I mean *folie de grandeur*."[3] Few Prime Ministers can be immune to such temptations. Wilson's Mr Toad-like vainglory will be referred to hereafter. But with it all he never lost the common touch; at the end of 1964 he was astonishing in his readiness to listen to and consider the views of others.

Niceness alone was not enough to handle a Cabinet of talented and ambitious *prima donnas*, still less to dominate it in the way he had claimed he would. Crossman told him he could not pretend to have introduced a Kennedy-style regime. "I suppose you're right, Dick," admitted Wilson. "You can't really sell a Yorkshire terrier as a borzoi hound."[4] American observers watched with interest his efforts to establish a White House in Downing Street. "Wilson is trying to draw more power into his hands and combine more of the powers of the Presidency, US style, with the advantages of the Cabinet System," Lyndon Johnson was informed. "He's got a start, especially through George Brown's new Economic Ministry, but he won't break all the Ministerial monopolies overnight."[5] He knew he never would; the best he could hope for was to modify the system. After meeting Johnson, Wilson remarked to Frank Pakenham that total disaster might ensue if the President went round the bend. "If *I* begin to go round the bend, there would always be the Cabinet to stop me." Pakenham reminded him of Eden at the time of the Suez crisis. " 'Ah', he replied cryptically. 'I am not Anthony Eden.' "[6] But he established his personal authority to an extent far greater than would have at first seemed likely or even possible. After the first six months Crossman reckoned that he had completely dominated defence and foreign affairs and, by arbitrating between Brown and Callaghan, had played a leading role in economics too.[1] To dominate defence, with a minister as assertive as Healey in command, was no trivial achievement. "No prime minister ever interfered so much in the work of his colleagues," wrote Healey, adding truculently, "Unfortunately, since he had neither political principle nor much government experience to guide him, he didn't give Cabinet the degree of guidance which even a less ambitious prime minister should provide."[2]

His tactical skill in handling Cabinet meetings was remarkable, knowing when to press and when to ease off, when to defer a decision, when to take a vote and when to sum up in a way patently at variance with the drift of the discussion. His favourite tactic was to allow the argument to drift on interminably until he got his way through the confusion and frustration of his opponents. Barbara Castle complained that it must be "the most talkative Cabinet in political history". It was Parkinson's law at work: words expanding to fill the time available.[3] Wilson's contribution was as long-winded as anyone's; politicians are a prolix lot but, said Leo Abse, he was "the most incessant talker of us all ... When he speaks at you it is not a rapport that is being established: rather you feel he is relating to you by the only way open to him, by way of oral discharge."[4] Roy Jenkins was grateful for the way Wilson supported him in Cabinet on certain controversial issues, "though I did not admire the way he got the package through ... His own patience being apparently limitless, he allowed the Cabinet to bore itself into exhaustion."[5] The technique was not heroic, perhaps, but it was certainly effective, and that was the criterion by which Wilson would have judged it.

On 16 October 1964 Wilson broadcast to the nation, affirming that the size of their majority would not affect his ministers' will or ability to govern. They would carry out their mandate. Already the difficulties in the way of doing so were becoming evident. The most immediate problem was the trade deficit, which seemed to be running at £800 million a year, twice as bad as Wilson had deemed likely in his most gloomy moments. Keith Middlemas has argued that the figure could only be substantiated by adding the current and capital account deficits together, but Wilson himself believed in its reality and convinced not only his colleagues but the foreign bankers and investors that Britain was in a desperate plight.[1] There were various ways of tackling the problem. The most dramatic would have been devaluation. Before the election this option had firmly been excluded. When a group of left-wing economists met Wilson and Callaghan, Kaldor had argued for immediate devaluation. "There will be no devaluation. You would water the weeds as well as the flowers," said Wilson. Callaghan characteristically remained silent.[2] But if the economy were really in as dire a state as now appeared, it seemed clear that the possibility would have to be reconsidered. It was, but only to be dismissed again by Wilson, Callaghan and Brown in a summit meeting held immediately after the election. The civil service mandarins, William Armstrong, Eric Roll and Donald MacDougall, were also in attendance. Of the six only MacDougall advocated devaluation.[3] Brown and Callaghan subsequently claimed to have had reservations but they barely voiced them at the time. Wilson said that he thought the certain risks were greater than the possible gains and that Balogh had convinced him that "socialist" policies could cure the balance of payment problem (a position which Balogh himself had abandoned within three weeks).[4]

It has often been maintained that the rejection of immediate devaluation, when it could plausibly have been presented as the result of thirteen years of Tory misrule, was an egregious blunder; a naïve failure to understand that expansion could not otherwise be achieved, wrote the Labour right-wing rebel Desmond Donnelly; an error which "put the Government in a strait-jacket for the next three years", felt Barbara Castle.[5] At least as many doubt whether devaluation would have achieved the hoped-for result; indeed some maintain that the J-curve effect, by which the rise in the cost of imports precedes the rise in the volume of exports, would have exacerbated the disaster.[6] The Bank of England opposed the move both in principle and because it feared that a Labour government would squander whatever benefits there might be.[7] To the layman it seems as if the balance of economic argument tips narrowly in favour of devaluation but that the point was anyway academic since politically such a step was inconceivable. Wilson was haunted by the fact that he had been involved in the last devaluation and felt that if he did the same thing in 1964 Labour would be for ever stamped as the party of the easy option. All the arguments which had made him so reluctant a devaluer in 1949 now recurred at least as forcibly. He saw sterling, said Healey, "as a sort of virility symbol"; to let its value fall would be a proof of British weakness.[1] It would also be to let down those Commonwealth countries who still kept their balances in sterling. Most conclusively of all, while still in opposition the Labour leadership had promised the New York Federal Reserve Bank that they would not devalue if support for sterling were forthcoming. The undertaking was not quite so categoric as Edward Short has suggested,[2] but the Americans would have had reason to feel let down if the first act of the new government had been to go back on it. Certainly they could see no immediate justification. "Wilson is an impressive, take-charge, no-nonsense, non-stuffy Prime Minister," Walter Heller told the President. "He's in a tight economic box, but he's got a tough, sensible program that gives him a fighting chance to get out of it without devaluation."[3] Devaluation "would strike a severe blow at Britain's standing within the sterling area and in the O.E.C.D.," concluded a State Department memorandum. "Psychologically, it could be ruinous for the fortunes of the Labour party ... This measure is, however, definitely not in prospect, if only because Britain's reserves are now many times above their 1949 level."[4]

Wilson can hardly be blamed for reaching the decision not to devalue; he is however guilty of then enshrining the level of sterling as the most sacred Ark of the Covenant. To Heller he said: "It was the first day or never ... we looked at it hard that first day, but now it's never." Every politician should know that "never" means "not just yet", but Wilson seems to have at least half deluded himself that his decision would rule for perpetuity. Discussion of the issue was banned, even in the most privy conclave. The concept seemed so outrageous that, when he wrote to Lyndon Johnson, he could not bring himself even to mention it. There were two courses of action which had been ruled out, he told the President: the second was higher interest rates; "The first, with all its repercussions on the international exchanges, will be obvious to you, and this we have rejected now, and for all time."[5] To make such protestations publicly is the distasteful duty of any national leader who wishes to protect his country's currency; to write them in secret letters to one's peers, still worse to believe them oneself, is to make the most dangerous and unnecessary commitment for the future. It was to cost Wilson and Britain dear.

If Britain was not to devalue it must deflate; that at least was the judgment of the Treasury and the Bank of England. Up to a point Wilson accepted the logic; but he could not tolerate the price that society would have to pay, particularly in unemployment. He sought a third way, in the words of Sam Brittan, the economic journalist, "some mysterious kind of 'direct physical intervention'", which would obviate the need for a move so much at variance with the government's promises and aspirations.[1] To hold the line in the meantime the government elected to curb imports by levying a surcharge on everything except food, raw materials and tobacco (the last exemption reading oddly in the light of contemporary morality). The measure was ill received at home – "a flagrant violation of the E.F.T.A. treaty", said Crossman; "blatantly illegal", stormed Jay[2] – and worse abroad. Britain's Scandinavian allies in the European Free Trade Area were particularly incensed but some of the sourest protests came from those very countries whose interests Wilson had been seeking to protect when he refused to devalue. "You have been in power just over ten days and one of your first acts is detrimental to Jamaica's exports," complained the Jamaican Prime Minister, Alexander Bustamante. "On behalf of my government and my people I protest most vehemently."[3] Wilson airily assured Johnson that the measures had been well received: "There have, of course, been some squeals from overseas, but these are mostly for the record."[4] He soon had to revise his opinion. Resentment in EFTA was growing, reported the Foreign Secretary, Gordon Walker, three weeks later: "It would be misleading you if we were to give the impression that we have been able to do much to restore the loss of confidence."[5] Within a few months Wilson was ordering plans to be made so that the surcharge could be replaced by a system of import quotas.[6] In the view of Oliver Wright, the Foreign Office secretary in Number 10 at the time, the outraged reaction in Scandinavia was one of the factors that moved Wilson towards acceptance of the need to join the EEC.[7]

As a contribution towards balancing the books, the government was looking for ways of cutting back on unnecessary expenditure. Concorde – or, as it was then still spelt in London, Concord – seemed a hopeful target. Wilson wrote to Pompidou, the French premier, to suggest an urgent review. The British were, he said, "profoundly concerned by the magnitude of the problems that lie ahead"; they did not believe that the financial outlay involved in developing a supersonic airliner was acceptable in the present economic situation.[8] Pompidou's response was so unforthcoming that Wilson hurriedly retreated. There had never been any question of "unilaterally abrogating the Anglo-French agreement", he protested. The British still had doubts but, since the French did not share them, "I confirm our readiness to proceed with the project."[1] Baulked on that front, he had to look for savings in the area under his sole control. Ministers going to an unofficial meeting at Chequers were told that they must use their own cars, redecoration of ministerial offices was kept to the essentials. "We were all so constrained by this puritan streak in Harold ... that we felt considerable guilt if we had a room or corridor done out with emulsion paint," complained Short.[2] Wilson accepted with some reluctance that the pay increase put forward for MPs by the Lawrence Committee must be met but proposed that the recommended increase for Cabinet ministers should be halved and deferred while he himself would take nothing at all. George Brown led a revolt and the Cabinet concluded that all the increases should be paid in full.[3] Since they took effect immediately, while for technical reasons the increases in old-age pensions, which were announced at about the same time, could not be implemented until March 1965, the opposition were able to exploit the contrast between greedy socialist MPs grabbing their quick gains while letting the elderly wait for theirs.

Morale was still high, however, when the Queen's Speech on 3 November laid out the pattern for the forthcoming session's legislation. Prescription charges were abolished, the iron and steel industry was to be nationalised, a major review launched in the field of social security. It was a full and popular programme, with most of the questions about paying for it awaiting Callaghan's autumn budget the following week. Arthur Schlesinger was in London at the time and reported that euphoria was the dominant mood from Wilson down, but he feared, he added grimly, "that he may be having his Bay of Pigs sooner than he expected".[4]

By the time Johnson got that letter Wilson's Bay of Pigs had come and – almost – gone. Callaghan's budget of 11 November, with its increases in social benefits and national assistance and the introduction of capital gains tax, caused alarm in the international banking world. The White House was disturbed as well. When Johnson saw Wilson in December he "spoke frankly but kindly to the Prime Minister about the troubles which the latter had already given the President". The heavy emphasis on social security in the budget and consequent pressure on the pound had put the Americans in difficulties: "The British decision had shaken us some."[5] Its consequences had shaken the British some, as well. A hectic run on sterling

followed Callaghan's budget statement and the reserves fell dangerously low. Wilson appealed to Johnson for support in securing an
additional standby of $1,000 million from the IMF but received a
reply that was no more than politely non-committal.[1] The Governor
of the Bank of England, Lord Cromer, who was a man steeped in the
traditions of the City and convinced of the need for the most rigid
balancing of the books in the nation's accounts, called for deflation
and deep cuts in government expenditure. He found Wilson slippery
and unsound and made little attempt to hide the low opinion he held
of the Prime Minister; Wilson for his part found Cromer hectoring
and bigoted, a wolf from the capitalist pack determined to thwart
socialist policy if not actually destroy the administration. The differences between them were in fact not so great as both men imagined,
but variants in style and in political rhetoric exacerbated what would
anyway have been a difficult relationship. To Cromer's insistence that
cuts were essential, Wilson countered with a threat to float the pound
and go to the country. "The Queen's First Minister," he declared
with rare grandiloquence, "was being asked to ring down the curtain on parliamentary democracy." If the international financiers
would not allow him to carry out his manifesto, then he would call
an immediate election on the platform of "The bankers against the
people".[2]

"The wily Yorkshireman," rejoiced Michael Stewart, "spreadeagled
Cromer's stumps with a googly."[3] "You know, Barbara, he's tough,"
said Callaghan admiringly to Mrs Castle, "much tougher than you
and I. You should see him handling the Governor of the Bank. The
Governor comes in breathing fire and slaughter. Harold does all the
talking and he goes out like a lamb."[4] It is reasonable to suppose that
Cromer's account of the relationship would have been somewhat
different, but on this occasion at least Wilson seems to have got the
better of it. Cromer accepted that Wilson's bluff, if bluff it was, could
not safely be called. In a night's hectic telephoning to his colleagues
around the world he succeeded in raising a massive guarantee of
$3,000 million to protect sterling. "As the situation was potentially
a dangerous one," Wilson wrote in relief to the Queen, "I am taking
this first opportunity of letting Your Majesty know that the position
has been restored."[5] By any count it was a remarkable achievement
on the part of Cromer: "If it had not been for your personal acting,"
the Governor of the Belgian National Bank paid tribute, "the Bank
of England would never have got the support she was given in 1964."

Wilson admired the Governor's skill – "There is no better Cromer than Cromer," he once remarked[1] – but was confirmed in his belief that the international bankers hung together and would be well pleased if Wilson were hanged alone. For the moment, anyway, the Governor had done all that Wilson could have asked from him. When Douglas-Home and Maudling visited Number 10 on 26 November, in Paul Foot's words "oozing bonhomie and promising Wilson all support in a coalition Government in the nation's hour of crisis", Wilson was able to "wipe the smiles off their faces" with the news of the loan.[2]

Lord Rothschild argued that the first few months of any new government, when it was still haunted by "the promises and panaceas which gleam like false teeth in a party manifesto" and possessed by the desire to prove itself, though without the knowledge to do so competently, were dangerous both for the party in power and for the country. "This prolonged festival, a mixture of the madness of Mardi Gras and Auto da Fé ... can be a great nuisance to put it at its mildest ... There should be a period of purging and purification, a kind of political Ramadan."[3] He must have had Wilson's first administration very much in mind. The "Hundred Days of dynamic action", which Wilson had promised in emulation of John F. Kennedy, would not run out till 24 January 1965, but the Prime Minister chose the party conference at Brighton in mid December 1964 to proclaim how much had been already done. He took as his text a cartoon by Vicky of a blimp in a West End club exclaiming angrily: "I always said you couldn't trust that fellow Wilson – he is doing exactly what he said he was going to do."[4] He *had* done what he had said he was going to do: increased old-age pensions and social benefits, abolished the restrictive rules about widows' earnings, reformed the Conservative Rent Act. It was, in fact, not at all a bad record, though his speech was not improved by a call to Britain to show the spirit of Dunkirk, an appeal which he had in the past mocked when made by Churchill or other Tory leaders.

The party received his address well, with some complaints about the slowness with which the machinery could be made to work; that the country was not entirely convinced was shown when Gordon Walker was slaughtered and Cousins savaged in the January by-elections. Much of the blame for these setbacks could be put on the special circumstances but they could not be considered encouraging for the prospects of the party. John Whale claims they led Wilson to dismiss the idea of a March election and to spend "the next twelve months wondering whether he had been right".[1] It does not seem that he had in fact thought seriously of a spring election, but if he had any such fancies had now been brutally dispelled. In Cabinet Cousins complained that the government had been too high-minded and must now be more political. Wilson responded that in the future he was going to reduce the time he had been devoting to travel abroad and foreign affairs and concentrate on domestic issues, most notably the economy.[2]

His attention was badly needed. The much vaunted Department of Economic Affairs was failing to produce results. The sceptics were being proved right: a ministry that had neither operational control like the spending departments nor the grasp of the purse strings enjoyed by the Treasury, could in the end do little except issue pious exhortations.[3] Its energies were too often dissipated on demarcation disputes, in particular clashes with the Board of Trade and Treasury over responsibility for overseas economic policy, and problems of prices and incomes, which Brown had made his particular charge. Callaghan later reproached Wilson with failing to intervene decisively and lay down the law as to what was expected of the new department: "In his personal relationships Harold is a kindly man who does not enjoy knocking heads together, nor does he easily ride roughshod over his colleagues' feelings."[4] Whether it was due to kindness, the fact that it suited him to see his principal lieutenants locked in combat, or his preoccupation with other matters, Wilson certainly failed to sort matters out during those first, vital months, and thus doomed the DEA to eventual impotence.

He had, or chose to put, a great deal else on his plate. Inspired, perhaps by wartime memories of the Churchillian style of government, he bombarded his colleagues with peremptory memoranda beginning: "I have been thinking a little", "I have been considering", "I have thought pretty carefully about". Nothing escaped his attention: water resources, owner-occupiers, Parliamentary Counsel, international liquidity, the rating system, blood sports, the Farm Price Review. No one could be sure what would catch his eye; an inconspicuous memorandum from the Board of Trade about machine tools inspired an outburst: "It is shattering to find that the value of production over the last ten years has risen only from £56.6 million to £75.5 million on current prices ... I feel, therefore, that machine tools should be transferred to the Ministry of Technology as the one hope of giving the industry the shake-up which is required."[1] A traffic jam in Parliament Square caused by heavy lorries was equally provocative: "What about establishing zones through which lorries can only pass if granted a permit?"[2]

He was particularly anxious to find "useful and constructive employment" for his backbenchers; a concern which pre-dated the 1966 election after which this particular species became more numerous and hence potentially more mischievous. "I simply do not accept," he told Bowden, "that all wisdom and human knowledge ... necessarily resides either in the members of the Government or in the departmental machines." There should be more select committees, more opportunities for members to work on the preparation of bills – though he prudently excluded those bills which involved heavy financial commitments, "since Members might be more prodigal with the tax-payers' money than the Chancellor would be likely to be". His objective, he maintained, was not only to make parliament more effective, "but to return in some measure the initiative to Parliament which in the past half century has certainly been 'usurped' by the Executive".[3]

The Prime Minister as informed gadfly can play a useful role provided he does not allow himself to be distracted from the most important things by peripheral diversions. For a time Wilson fell into this trap. For the first few months in office he took too much pleasure in playing the international statesman and in interfering in the tasks of his ministers. The fact that he thoroughly enjoyed it, though perhaps endearing, did not excuse his aberration. His restless activity extended even to the arrangements made when his great role-model, Winston Churchill, finally died. Please ensure, he told Bowden, that from 2.30 p.m. "Sir Winston's traditional seat below the gangway on the Government side be left unoccupied, and very obviously unoccupied".[4] It was a nice thought, but if he had had rather less time to deliberate on it, he might have been doing a more effective job. He spent as much time preparing his tribute to Churchill in the House of Commons as he had devoted to many speeches of critical importance to his career, and on the last night of Churchill's lying-in-state in Westminster Hall he, the Speaker, Harold Macmillan and Alec Douglas-Home mounted guard in place of the regular servicemen. "That was the longest ten minutes of my life," he told Martin Gilbert.[1]

Wilson was apt to represent his period in government as showing a clean break with the past, a cleansing of the Augean stables of Tory misrule and a bold start along the paths of righteousness. With the benefit of nearly thirty years' hindsight, the continuity of policy is quite as obvious as the new departures; in Keith Middlemas's words, the "overhang of progressive Conservatism can be explained partly because, in its march away from messy and inconclusive civil war after 1959, Labour had spent its intellectual energy on very similar projects ... and partly because of the way the Macmillan Government had responded to Wilson's own criticism in 1961".[2] Butskell – that egregious compound of left-wing Tory Butler and right-wing socialist Gaitskell – might have been long dead but there were traces of MacWilson to be found in Number 10 in 1964 and 1965. Financial problems and the slimness of his parliamentary majority gave Wilson an excellent alibi against charges that he was neglecting his radical mission, but the fact is that none of the more extreme features of the party manifesto particularly appealed to him and he allowed them to languish without more than a passing pang.

A prime example was the nationalisation of steel. This piece of legislation was enshrined in the manifesto and Wilson could therefore not discard it, but privately it seemed to him unlikely that it would contribute much to the nation's prosperity. Certainly it was not worth going to the stake for. His handling of the affair showed well how he gained his reputation for deviousness. The problem was that a handful of Labour MPs, notably Desmond Donnelly and Woodrow Wyatt, were strongly against the project. In normal circumstances they could have been ignored, or crushed if they stepped out of line. With a majority of only three, however, the rebels, if they persisted in their opposition, could bring down the government. The rank and file assumed that nevertheless the government would press on with the legislation, but when the White Paper was debated in the House of Commons, George Brown startled his backbenchers by assuring Wyatt that he was ready to listen to proposals from the industry which would concede the principle of state control but stop short of outright nationalisation. What did a promise to "listen" amount to? Was this the prelude to a sell-out? And, if so, was Wilson party to it? Castle thought the Prime Minister had been as much taken by surprise as any other minister.[1] Short claimed Wilson had told him he had seen Brown's formula in advance but subsequently, when a storm blew up in the party, chose to keep quiet about his complicity: "Was he a party to the manoeuvre? I suspect he was, but we shall never know."[2] Wilson's own record of events is obscure on this point.[3] Since, if he had *not* anticipated Brown's overture, he would almost certainly have said so, it can safely be assumed that he was warned in advance. It does not seem probable, however, that either he or Brown intended to do more than defer confrontation while seeking a way round the obstacle.

Certainly he did his best to work out a compromise with Wyatt throughout 1965; a thankless task which earned him little credit with any party. Wyatt claimed to have found him "totally cynical". Wilson kept repeating that he was a pragmatist and insisting: "I don't think there are ten votes in the country in steel one way or another but I'm stuck with it."[4] When Wilson told the Cabinet what he had been doing, Crossman accused him of being "without a touch of vision – no Kennedy touch, not even the dynamic of Lyndon Johnson".[5] Wyatt claimed that he had been offered a peerage if he would come into line;[6] the offer may have been dangled in front of him as a distant prospect, but Wilson would hardly have courted disaster by holding an unnecessary by-election in 1965. The Queen's Speech of November 1965 omitted any reference to steel; proof that no compromise had been discovered. In the eyes of much of the PLP this omission meant that the government had shirked its clear responsibility.

The need to impose some sort of control on prices and incomes also increasingly poisoned relations with the left as 1965 wore on. It was American pressure and a series of alarmingly generous wage settlements that forced the government to consider statutory rather than voluntary restraints. To make this acceptable to the left and the unions called for deft salesmanship. "We must move craftily," said Wilson, when the matter was discussed at Chequers in September.[7] No amount of craft would have made such measures palatable to doughty left-wingers like Eric Heffer, who dismissed Wilson's "obsession" with a prices and incomes policy as being based on an elitist conviction that he "knew what was good for the people even if the people themselves rejected the proposals".[8] Nor was it likely to appease Frank Cousins, who threatened resignation throughout the winter of 1965–6. Wilson tried to convince him that the measures would be mere "window dressing" to impress foreign opinion.

Cousins was unmoved. It was a matter of principle, he said. If his defection brought down the government, then so much the worse for it.[1]

Immigration was another issue on which the left felt that Wilson took no account of their susceptibilities. The increasing tide of immigration, much of it illegal, caused concern to the Home Office and Frank Soskice, the Home Secretary, pressed for legislation to restrict entry. Wilson played for time by sending Mountbatten around the Commonwealth to try to persuade the individual governments to impose their own controls and to sell to them in advance the idea that restraints were going to have to be applied in Britain. The Commonwealth governments were more easily persuaded than Wilson's own left wing; there was remarkably little protest from abroad when the restrictions on entry were in due course applied, but there was an indignant revolt at the party conference in September 1965 and 1.5 million votes were cast against the government's line. Wilson had considerable sympathy with his left wing on this issue. He disliked the legislation and would have liked at least to accompany it by measures that would ensure that those immigrants who were allowed in were treated properly. He argued for a law that would prohibit any sort of racial discrimination. He soon ran up against the opposition of the Home Office. Such legislation, they maintained, would do no good and might well exacerbate the very prejudices that it was intended to frustrate.[2] Wilson was unconvinced, but he had to await the advent of Roy Jenkins at the Home Office before race relations became a legitimate field for government intervention. Nor could he point to any conspicuous increase in aid to the undeveloped world to appease those who felt that the black and brown Commonwealth was being unfairly treated. The fierce cuts that followed the economic crisis in July 1965 fell particularly heavily on Overseas Development. Wilson made a rather weak attempt to increase Barbara Castle's allocation but was opposed by Brown and Callaghan, who argued that there could be no exceptions and, said Crossman, "leapt on Harold like wolfhounds in at the kill".[3] When Castle was moved away to Transport towards the end of the year it was clear that much of the impetus had gone out of Wilson's crusade to better the lot of the under-privileged overseas. Certainly overseas aid got short shrift in Brown's much heralded National Plan, which was at last published in September 1965. This, in some ways admirable, document set out schedules for action in many fields of industrial activity but based all its proposals on a hypothetical surplus in the balance of payments which, even when the plan was published, seemed disturbingly unlikely to be achieved. The TUC had little faith in it from the start and, by the time the DEA itself decayed and disappeared, the plan had been almost forgotten by all except the economic historians.

There was one achievement in which every section of the party could take satisfaction. The Open University was a bold attempt to give a chance of higher education to those who had missed out on university. Wilson had cherished the concept since he had first spoken of it publicly in 1963. He told Callaghan even before he became Prime Minister that this was going to be one of his priorities and that he would need money for it,[1] and he jealously defended it when almost every other sacred cow was suffering in the crises of 1965 and 1966. Bevan's widow, Jennie Lee, was put in charge of the enterprise. Without her energy and enthusiasm it would have got nowhere, but without Wilson's continued support she would have had no chance to do what she did. It is easy to see why it appealed so strongly to Wilson: his reverence for academic achievement and his genuinely egalitarian instincts both attracted him to a project which would extend the joys of Oxbridge – however much diluted – to a class which had hitherto been denied them. The fact that the most conspicuous beneficiaries turned out to be under-employed middle-class house-wives surprised and mildly disappointed him but never led him to doubt that his initiative had been worth while.

The honours system was another field in which, though professing to find the whole thing trivial, Wilson took great pains to demonstrate his radical intentions. Hereditary peerages were eschewed; sport, entertainment and the arts more liberally recognised. His object was to make the lists less stuffy; a goal which he achieved with a vengeance when in June 1965 he made the Beatles MBEs for services to exports. On the whole the gambit was dismissed as a silly gimmick: an "appalling mistake", thought Benn, Wilson was trying to buy popularity but was "ultimately bolstering a force that is an enemy of his political stand"; "This ploy of Harold's seems to have boomeranged," wrote Barbara Castle. "He seems to have a streak of vulgarity which is also part of his strength."[2] It was, of course, a bid to buy popularity; it was also a reflection of his admiration for the astonishing achievements of those young men – his constituents among them – and the pleasure he had derived from their music ever since Bessie Braddock had first introduced him to the Cavern in Liverpool in the early

1960s. Another departure was to abolish, or at least severely cut down on, political honours. Wilson originally proposed to implement this immediately after the election, but was persuaded to drop the idea by Transport House and did not finally achieve his object till 1966. Even then it was at the price of a considerably increased allocation of honours for local government.[1] He had quicker results with his scheme for honours to encourage industrial innovation and exporters. Early in 1965 he invited the Duke of Edinburgh to chair a committee which would make awards in this field: "You have great knowledge of industry throughout the country and I rather hope that the whole idea of stimulating enterprise in this way will appeal to you."[2] It did, and the Queen's Award for Industry was launched later the same year.

But Wilson's real achievement, as he had foreshadowed in October 1964, was to "form a Government and then control events and time the next election".* "Harold is a bastard, but he's a genius," Crosland told a young Labour MP who was criticising the Prime Minister. "He's like Odysseus. Odysseus was also a bastard, but he managed to steer the ship between Scylla and Charybdis."[3] If Scylla and Charybdis were left and right, Wilson not merely steered between them but managed to present to the general public, as well as to the crew, the image of an intrepid mariner remaining calm and resolute as the storms beat furiously about him. He fostered this impression by enterprising public relations and manipulation of the media. No Prime Minister can have taken greater trouble to present himself as seemed most advantageous. He was once shown the draft text of an interview with him in which one of his weaknesses was described as "talking to the Press too much". Against this Wilson wrote: "Offensive to Press. I think should come out."[4] He did not say that it was untrue, though in fact he could well have argued that he talked to the press a great deal but not too much, in that his words were usually well chosen to create the effect he wanted. He selected as his press secretary one of the Lobby correspondents but took him from the *Liverpool Post*, thus ensuring that the new recruit was known to him and trusted and also – so he hoped at least – avoiding the jealousy which the metropolitan journalists would have felt if one of their number had been preferred above his rivals. He read the papers with avid interest and was always badgering his staff, or sometimes the cor-

* See p 186 above.

respondent or editor direct, to secure better coverage in future. Once he telephoned the assistant press secretary, Henry James, from the Isles of Scilly and complained that a certain story had been running too long. "Get it off the front page, Henry! I don't care how you do it, but get it off the front." Later that day a grisly sex murder in Shepherd's Bush swept everything else out of the headlines. Wilson was on the phone at once: "Henry, you've gone too far this time!"[1]

The honeymoon could not last for ever. The Lobby correspondents began to feel that they were being used and reacted critically. Wilson expected that they would be properly grateful for his attentions and was resentful when their reporting was less than adulatory. But throughout the first eighteen months of his government his relationship with the press remained excellent. The same was true of the BBC. In the first eighteen months he had five long interviews on *Panorama* and six ministerial broadcasts – a far higher hitting rate than the Prime Ministers before and after him. A satire programme had John Bird appearing as Wilson and saying: "Good evening. It is more than a day since I last talked to you. I am sure you have been wondering ..."[2] But the BBC was as anxious as the Lobby not to appear to be in the Prime Minister's pocket. Wilson objected to the Director-General's determination to give the opposition equal time; the BBC took exception to barely veiled hints that the size of the licence fee on which it depended for its revenue would be decided on the basis of its readiness to cooperate. The remarkable thing is not that Wilson eventually fell out with the BBC but that it took so long for him to do so.

Another of his obsessions matured more rapidly. On 21 December 1964 he addressed a minute to the President of the Board of Trade about a story in the *Sunday Times* on aids for exporters. The measures, he complained, were not due to be announced till January.[3] The minute is noteworthy as being the first time Wilson formally complained to one of his ministers about a leak. A second minute followed a few weeks later. The constant complaints in Cabinet about the delinquencies of his colleagues did not gather force till after the crises of 1966 but he always took it for granted that his fellow ministers were seeking to use the press for their own advantage with the same energy if not the same skill as he employed himself. Quite often his suspicions were justified.

In spite of a few such tremors of incipient trouble the first months of 1965 passed placidly enough. Callaghan's first proper budget, however, was causing apprehension outside Whitehall as rumours of devaluation began once more to circulate. The chairman of the Governors of the Federal Reserve System wrote to Johnson to urge him to call Wilson to order. The budget must be a tough one: "The United States has a vital interest in this and I just want you to know how concerned we are."[1] In fact the budget was tough enough to satisfy most people, with taxation increased by some £475 million. Johnson's worries were temporarily allayed; Wilson told Lester Pearson, the Canadian Prime Minister, at the end of April that the President's "earlier anxieties about sterling had now been completely set at rest".[2] The rest, at the best fitful, was rapidly disturbed. Bad trade figures in May led to a loss of gold reserves which in its turn set off another run on sterling. Callaghan visited Washington to seek support but was given a cool reception. Johnson was advised to offer little or nothing. Any deal must be "in terms of our overall interests ... political and economic as well as monetary. None of us expects this sort of deal can be made with Callaghan. It will have to be a bargain at a higher and broader level."[3] In the meantime Callaghan came up with what even the American Ambassador, David Bruce, admitted to be a "drastic program of cuts". Public expenditure was cancelled or postponed, mortgages and hire-purchase curbed, defence economies announced. If such measures proved ineffective, Bruce believed, "we will witness almost immediate terrifying run on the pound with presently incalculable consequences. US would then probably be faced with alternatives of British devaluation or full support of pound by ourselves."[4]

Wilson would have been delighted to know that Johnson's blood was thus being made to run cold by his ambassador. He himself spared no pains to stress to the Americans the immensity of the demands he and the Chancellor were making on their followers. "Politically this has been a very difficult operation indeed," he told the President. "Many of my colleagues were resistant to what I considered necessary and since the announcement there has been a lot of unrest among our supporters in Parliament and outspoken opposition by the Trade Union Congress. The support of the Confederation of British Industries [CBI] and the recognition by our *Financial Times*, with its specialised readership, that the measures showed the Government's determination to put the strength of sterling before politics, are things that count both ways for a Labour Government – particularly when it is far from certain that there is a case on objective economic grounds for more than a minor degree of deflation."[1] The measures, Wilson claimed, were already producing good results. They were, but not good enough, nor were they fast enough in coming. It was clear that American support on a formidable scale would be essential if sterling were to survive.

Johnson was receiving two kinds of advice. The hard line, from the majority of his advisers, was that the British must be told bluntly "under any and all circumstances devaluation of the pound is unthinkable and cannot be permitted".[2] The Americans must find ways of propping up sterling but they must exact a price for their help. George Ball of the State Department said that aid should be subject to two conditions: "(a) That the British agree to maintain fully their worldwide defense commitments; (b) that they agree to take whatever additional measures are necessary to make possible multi-lateralising a rescue effort."[3] McGeorge Bundy, Johnson's principal adviser, went still further. When Burke Trend was about to arrive in Washington, Bundy minuted the President: "We want to make very sure that the British get it into their heads that it makes no sense for us to rescue the Pound in a situation in which there is no British flag in Vietnam, and a threatened British thin-out both east of Suez and in Germany. What I would like to say to Trend myself, is that a British Brigade in Vietnam would be worth a billion dollars at the moment of truth for Sterling."[4] But not everyone was advocating such overt bullying. Francis Bator of the Treasury pointed out the risks. If Wilson were pushed too far he might "cut loose", devalue, withdraw troops from Germany and east of Suez. The United States should decide what was the most that Wilson would consider reasonable and stick out for that. To ask for more might mean getting nothing.[5]

The deal that was in the end done between Wilson and Johnson was not of the sort that was enshrined in formal documents. Largely it was a matter of nods, winks and tacit understandings. Its exact details will probably never be known; were, indeed, hardly known to the negotiators.[6] The American offer, Wilson told Brown in mid August, was "to raise round about two billion dollars", not in the form of a loan, but as "an operation reserve to deal firmly and brutally with any speculator who rears his head". This would enable Britain to deal with the increase in unemployment and to bring down interest rates. The only price that Wilson admitted to having paid was "positive action to reinforce our prices and incomes policy". This, he maintained, was no more than the government itself thought necessary. It could be presented to the TUC as only one element in a daring new enterprise, an effort to right Britain's economic problems once and for all by "a sustained attack on everything which is impeding productivity ... be they restrictive, labour-wasting practices, or be they lack of imagination or lack of investment on the management side".[1] Of other commitments there was no mention. There never was. All that is certain is that the Federal Reserve and other central banks entered into a massive operation in defence of sterling which effectively silenced the speculators until the middle of the following year. In return Wilson made various commitments, implicit or explicit, about the deflationary policy to be pursued at home and about Britain's defence and foreign policy. As will appear later on, some at least of these were to embroil him with his own left-wingers and to expose him to accusations that he was betraying the principles on which he had been elected.

Meanwhile he remained preoccupied by his main consideration: how and when to win the next election. Early in June 1965 he told George Brown he was concerned at the way in which the government's various economic measures "add up to a pretty dismal and gloomy set of squeezes". Something positive was needed "of a popular and heart-warming character, and from every point of view – not least our pre-Election emphasis – this would seem to be housing ... Just as in the War the idea of a common purpose, winning the War, had a dynamising effect, so possibly the launching of a great housing plan could have a similar effect today."[2] There is no indication how Brown received this reminder that he was not the only minister specialising in woolly but high-sounding proclamations; long before such a crusade could be evolved the economic squalls of the autumn of 1965 made it injudicious even to talk about expensive undertakings.

Almost simultaneously Wilson made it known that there would be no election in the autumn. The Tories took advantage of the breathing space to replace Douglas-Home by Heath as leader. Maudling was the man whom Wilson feared most but any change was to be regretted. After the Tories had lost a by-election at Roxburgh to the Liberals in March he had been so worried lest this might induce them to ditch the previous Prime Minister that he told Lloyd-Hughes to spread the rumour that a general election was a probability for May. "He was grinning like a mischievous schoolboy," wrote Barbara Castle.[1] Heath, he feared, would be more difficult to beat. He decided to minimise the threat as far as possible by ignoring the new incumbent; Heath was never referred to by name but only, if at all, as the leader of the Conservative Party.[2] It did not at first seem as if there were serious cause for anxiety. Particularly in the House of Commons Heath was slow to establish himself and Wilson time and again outmanoeuvred him with insolent ease: "I have witnessed many confrontations between rival leaders in Parliament," wrote James Griffiths, "but none which was so uneven as that between Wilson and Heath."[3] These easy victories bred false confidence and an ill-judged contempt for the ponderous but formidable Heath; it was not till the general election of 1970 that Wilson fully appreciated the calibre of his opponent.

The death of the Speaker, Sir Harry Hylton-Foster, in June at one time seemed to make an election imminent. The Tories refused to oblige by allowing any of their members to take on one of the three non-voting jobs and would thus have reduced Labour's exiguous majority still further if an obliging Liberal, Roderic Bowen, had not been found to fill the gap. Not surprisingly, the jostling for position generated talk about a Lib–Lab pact, a proposition which the Liberal leader, Jo Grimond, had long been advancing, though with conditions attached that made it unappealing to Labour. For a man who relished conspiracies and compromises, Wilson was surprisingly forthright in his denunciation of anything smacking of a coalition, even if it were merely to involve accepting Liberals in a few of the less important jobs. He seems, however, to have been forced to consider the possibility rather more seriously than he would have wished. In August 1965 Gerald Kaufman was despatched to take soundings among backbenchers. His findings, broadly, were that three were against a Lib–Lab pact for every two in favour of it and one uncommitted.[4] The discrepancy was not overwhelming but enough to convince Wilson that he could safely dismiss the possibility. The following month he said as much to the Cabinet. Even if they wanted to respond to Grimond's overtures, he asserted, the PLP would never let them get away with it.[5]

A socialist Prime Minister, faced with the need to impose spending cuts, will tend to think first of defence. This would certainly have been the course advocated by Labour's left wing. In other circumstances Wilson might not have demurred. But however imprecise the promises he had made to the Americans he knew that he could not afford to take any step which would expose him to the wrath of the White House. One possible field for economies which might win favour both with his own supporters and in Washington was the "independent" nuclear deterrent. While in opposition Wilson had indicated that he was resolved to take drastic action in this respect. When he visited Washington in March 1964 he had told Robert McNamara, the Secretary of State for Defense, that one of his first acts as Prime Minister would be to renegotiate the Nassau Agreement. He was not, he took pains to point out, a unilateral disarmer, but he was all for integrating the British deterrent with a common, European effort. The trouble was, he said, that the issue had become "highly electoral" and the idea of a British deterrent "had an emotional appeal to the man in the pub".[1] Once he was in power it soon became apparent that the issue remained "highly electoral", in his eyes at least and, what is more, that when it came to the point he shared with the man in the pub an emotional attachment to that ultimate virility symbol, the national deterrent. He genuinely wanted to ensure the non-proliferation of nuclear weapons and was ready to contemplate some sacrifice in sovereignty for such an end, but he was going to have to be very sure that the price was right before he agreed to dismantle his heritage. When it came to negotiations with the Admiralty he showed himself disconcertingly ready to be convinced that the Polaris submarine programme had advanced too far to permit any cancellations. The mathematics of the proposition were, to say the least, questionable.[2] It subsequently transpired that the Admiralty, resigned to losing its deterrent, had made plans to eliminate the section of the hull where the missile tubes were situated and so to produce a truncated hunter-killer submarine which they proposed to christen the "Wilson Class".[3] Nevertheless, it suited Wilson and Healey to accept the protestations of the experts without too much examination. Quite whom the independent deterrent was intended to deter was not clear. Wilson never deluded himself that it should be used by Britain in isolation against the Russians. The nearest he got to expressing his real view was probably when he told the political journalist Peter Hennessy: "I didn't want to be in the position of having to subordinate ourselves to the Americans."[4]

That, of course, was exactly what the Americans *did* want. Johnson's brief for a visit Wilson paid to Washington at the end of 1965 set out the American ambition: "The essence of our position is to encourage the British in any action which 'lowers the status' of their 'independent' deterrent."[1] The favourite device to achieve this end was the MLF – Multilateral Force – a mixed-manned fleet which, it was hoped, would bury the British deterrent in an "international" body effectively under American control. The Tories, with some qualifications, had opposed what would have been, both in political and military terms, a rickety and artificial creation; any hope that Labour would prove more cooperative was quickly dispelled. Their counter was to propose the ANF – Atlantic Nuclear Force – under which Britain's nuclear submarines and an equivalent number of American would be loosely assigned to NATO. Reactions to this in Washington varied widely. Ball indignantly rejected any tampering with the American concept: "We have been working on the mixed-manned surface ships proposal for two years and the British are johnny-come-latelies ... Wilson has been told ... that agreement in principle on British participation in surface ships is a *sine qua non* for the successful outcome of these talks."[2] Bundy, however, urged that the MLF should be allowed to "sink out of sight"; otherwise the Alliance would be left with a "deeply reluctant and essentially unpersuaded" Great Britain in its midst.[3] Bundy's advice prevailed. The MLF gradually slipped into oblivion; the ANF, as a concept, lasted a little longer but, since the Americans had no real interest in it and the British had only advanced it as a device to frustrate the formation of the MLF, this too soon perished. The ANF, commented Franz-Josef Strauss cynically, was "the only fleet that had not been created that torpedoed another fleet that hadn't sailed".[4]

The Washington talks had been "very successful", Wilson assured Brown. The Americans were "very ready to consider our new proposals".[5] He did not escape entirely unscathed, however. Kosygin wrote indignantly to complain that, though Labour had set their face against the principle of the MLF while in opposition, they had now espoused it. The change of name made no difference; there would still be German participation; non-dissemination of nuclear arms was the vital issue. Exactly, replied Wilson. Non-dissemination was what the ANF was designed to achieve; no German, indeed no new finger would be on the trigger.[6] In the House of Commons he was accused by the Tories of betraying the principle of the unilateral deterrent and had little difficulty in defending his position; in the PLP he was accused of defying the manifesto by retaining nuclear weapons, an accusation he found it harder to rebut. The fact was that, by the middle of 1965, he, Brown, Stewart and Healey, with precious little consultation with other members of the Cabinet, had determined to retain four out of the projected five Polaris submarines under the same conditions as had prevailed under the Conservatives. When he explained this to the Cabinet, wrote Short, "I got the impression of a highly skilled conjuror who had thrown his silk handkerchief over our Polaris submarines and, hey presto, they had gone – but he still had them up his sleeve or behind his coat-tails. It was sheer wizardry. He was the cleverest politician for many a long year – by far!"[1] In the House of Commons he defended his position with equal dexterity. He had prepared a closely argued speech which, his private secretary knew, was timed to last twenty minutes. He then said he would need half an hour. The explanation came when, in the last ten minutes, he indulged himself in knockabout invective which enraged the Tories and appeased all but the most hardened of his own left wing.[2] Regretfully the Americans accepted the inevitable. The British deterrent had escaped the economy axe, the President was told in mid 1966: "The reason is simple: The nuclear deterrent is the most important of the great power symbols still in British possession. Although Wilson is committed to give it up, he has so far shown no disposition to do so."[3]

If there were to be no economies to be made over the deterrent, it remained to look elsewhere. In the opinion of most Labour MPs an obvious way to save money would be by withdrawing from Singapore and other bases east of Suez. This, however, would have been considered almost treasonable in Washington. In March 1964 Wilson had talked to McNamara of building up British conventional forces in the area, with "highly mobile fire brigade forces" to keep the peace.[4] McNamara may have been privately sceptical about British credentials as fire-fighters but he felt that their presence in South-East Asia was essential on political as well as military grounds. There was no formal link between a British presence east of Suez and American financial support, Wilson assured the Cabinet early in 1966, but he also made it clear that the first would facilitate the second.[5] Lee Kuan Yew, who was probably closest to Wilson among the Commonwealth leaders, was equally emphatic. "Singapore is the linchpin of South-East Asia," he told Wilson. "If your bases are out of Singapore,

Democratic Socialists are out also. We have no death wish."[1] Nor did Wilson. The Prime Minister viewed any retreat from imperial responsibilities with regret and distaste. He once pronounced grandiloquently that Britain's frontier was on the Himalayas. This made his pretensions sound more extravagant than in fact they were, but he did believe firmly that Britain was still a world power, that the world was a better and safer place because of the British presence far beyond Europe and that that presence should therefore be maintained whenever it was humanly possible. To abandon a Commonwealth ally like Singapore might one day prove inevitable, but only as a last resort. Little persuasion was needed from McNamara. Three years later Wilson was to say that he felt clinging on to the east of Suez role had been one of his worst mistakes as Prime Minister: he was, he said, one of the last to be converted, "and it needed a lot of hard facts to convert me. Others of my colleagues, left-wing and pro-European alike, were wiser in their perceptions."[2] In 1964 and 1965 conversion was still far ahead.

Since troop reductions in Germany were also at this point ruled out on political grounds, it was clear that Britain's defence commitments were not going to be substantially reduced. This in its turn limited the cuts that could be made in manpower and equipment. Healey's decision to phase out aircraft-carriers, so controversial that it drove the First Sea Lord and the Navy Minister, Christopher Mayhew, to resignation, did not come till just before the 1966 election. The chief victim of the first economy drive was the TSR2, a new bomber designed to replace the obsolescent Canberra and deliver Britain's nuclear bombs. Development costs were already huge and would shortly become prodigious, and it was clear to most of the Cabinet that the project would have to be abandoned. The trouble was that, taken in conjunction with other cuts in military aircraft and the possible threat to Concorde, the cancellation of the TSR2 put Britain's aircraft industry in jeopardy. Cousins thought that Wilson would support the retention of this project and felt badly let down by the final outcome; it convinced him, wrote Cousins's biographer, that "his Prime Minister was not a wholly dependable ally".[3] Healey accepted the logic of the decision but for his part was not in the least pleased when he was required to keep development going at a cost of £4 million a week so that it could be buried with other items in the April budget rather than relinquished in conspicuous isolation: "I was deeply conscious of what could have been done with that £40 million for more useful purposes."[1]

The last few months of 1965 promised to be troubled ones. One worry, minor but potentially dangerous, was the incipient defection from the Labour camp of the chairman of Daily Mirror Newspapers, Cecil King. In August 1965 Wilson had offered King a life barony and a post in the Board of Trade in charge of exports. King was outraged at the suggestion that he might serve as an "understrapper to Douglas Jay" but told Wilson he would accept an earldom. Wilson explained that this was impossible since he was only giving life peerages and there was no provision for a life earl. King said that he was sure that it was possible.[2] Within a week he was describing Wilson as a man whose "days look to be numbered" and who was "a very short term tactician" who could not even look forward as far as the next election.[3] By October he was telling a senior civil servant that Wilson would be ill advised to count on the automatic support of the Daily Mirror and the following spring he was announcing to all and sundry his intention to break loose from the Labour Party.[4] The confrontation was yet to come, but with the press dominated by the Conservatives even the possibility of a change of heart on the part of Labour's traditional ally was seriously alarming.

Then things began to look up. Even as King was muttering about sinking ships, the government seemed suddenly more buoyant. Partly this was the result of a particularly well-judged speech by Wilson in a censure debate at the end of July.[5] He "remoralised his own Party – gave them back their faith", wrote Crossman. "This is an example of how one speech can really transform a situation."[6] The mood seemed to communicate itself to the nation. The opinion polls in mid September showed a sudden resurgence in Labour popularity; the National Plan proved popular; the party conference at Scarborough went well; the economic cuts of the summer, if not forgotten, were at least no longer at the forefront of people's minds. It was against this relatively tranquil background that Wilson was able to plan his first government reshuffle in December 1965. When he had appointed Benn Postmaster-General Wilson had apologised for not putting him in the Cabinet: "My real Cabinet will be made in 1966," he said, "just as Clem's was made in 1947."[7] It was almost 1966 but there was still no place for Benn; indeed the most significant change was the promotion of Roy Jenkins to the post of Home Secretary, Frank Soskice being put out to grass as Lord Privy Seal. Jenkins had been told this was to happen some months before but the change had been deferred because the press had been prophesying the move and Wilson was determined not to seem to be succumbing to external pressure.[1]

The appointment proved a striking success; Jenkins's energy, ability and liberal ideas made him popular with the party and, less fortunately in Wilson's eyes, turned him into a plausible candidate for the succession to Number 10. The other most noteworthy move was equally successful, if at first less well received. Wilson told Barbara Castle that his "two incubi" were Soskice and Tom Fraser, the Minister of Transport. With Fraser in office there would never be an integrated transport policy: "I must have a tiger in my transport policy and you are the only tiger I've got."[2] Castle, who was anxious to stay with Overseas Development, asked for time to consult her husband and returned in triumph to announce that there was a fatal obstacle which could not be overcome. "I know," said Wilson, "you don't drive," and went on to explain why this was one of the reasons he had thought of her for the job.[3] Short remonstrated with Wilson, saying that she was totally unqualified. Wilson replied that "she always got her own way and would be able to control those so-and-so Civil Servants."[4]

Another change in personnel meant as much or more to Wilson, if only because it promised to end the turmoil which the battles between Marcia Williams and Derek Mitchell had caused in Downing Street. Early in 1966 it became possible to move Mitchell to a new job and look for a successor. Wilson told Helsby that he would like to appoint Michael Halls, a civil servant who had worked for him years before in the Board of Trade. Helsby doubted whether Halls would be the right man for the job. Wilson said that was for him to decide. Helsby suggested such an appointment would be an improper use of prime-ministerial patronage and asked Wilson at least to see five other candidates. Wilson agreed to meet them and then wrote:

If I am told that this is a question of patronage and challenged to choose between Prime Ministerial patronage and patronage exercised by a small, self-perpetuating oligarchy of Permanent Secretaries, I have no alternative but to say that patronage, if patronage it be, must be exercised by me.

I certainly cannot accept the implied suggestion that such an appointment would imply a deterioration of standards since the arrival of the present administration. I do not know whether the system you extol was responsible, or whether there was at work a system not merely of Prime Ministerial patronage, but Prime Ministerial *Political* patronage, but the fact remains that of four secretaries in post up to October 1963, the two most senior are now on the short list for adoption as candidates in safe Conservative seats, a third, recruited direct from Conservative Central Office to Mr Macmillan's Private Office, now takes the Conservative whip in the Upper House. My suggested appointment has no political implications, I have not the slightest idea of the political views, if any, of the five I saw.

But I do not regard the appointment as patronage, reward for past services, or as a promise for the future, still less an intellectual accolade comparable to a Fellowship of All Souls. I regard it as the means of ensuring that my office will work ... as efficiently, smoothly and agreeably as possible. What I want is a Private Secretary, not either a Presidential Assistant nor a Permanent Secretary, actual or in embryo. No. 10 is an office, not a Government Department; it is also a small and necessarily intimate community – it is also a home.[1]

It was a splendid put-down of an importunate bureaucrat and one which engages one's sympathy. Unfortunately Helsby was right and Wilson wrong. Halls was not big enough for the job. He struggled with the work, read papers slowly, was befuddled by complex issues, overworked ferociously, became tired, fretful and demoralised, grew jealous of colleagues who picked up parts of the burden he could not bear himself. A kind and generous man, for whom Wilson had good reason to feel affection, he was made to feel inferior, cracked under the stress, and died, after a heart attack, early in 1970. He was a painful example of the dangers of promoting people above their merit, taking them from a role which they filled competently and with pleasure to heights whose rarefied atmosphere they could not support.

One other change which Wilson contemplated before the 1966 election was based on the hypothesis that Frank Cousins would be bound soon to resign. In such a case, he asked, would Michael Foot be prepared to take his place? Certainly not, said Foot; on every issue on which Cousins disagreed with the government, he was of the same mind.[2] His response was a disturbing reminder of the chasm, skilfully covered over but still menacing, which divided left from right in the PLP. Benn noticed with disapproval how Wilson was perpetually looking over his shoulder and concentrating only on the weaknesses of his colleagues. Callaghan, he felt, was an enemy but he did not dare make him leader of the House of Commons because then "he would conspire against [him] and weaken his position."[1] Brown he longed to sack but, he told Barbara Castle, if he did "he would only make cause with Wyatt and Donnelly to destroy us".[2] Cousins complained that Wilson had sold out to his former enemies: "Why on earth did Harold insist on surrounding himself by right-wingers at the key points?"[3] Sometimes it seemed that only the fact that an election was round the corner prevented a full-scale revolt by the left.

Almost the only person with whom Wilson felt he could properly discuss matters of high policy and who was clearly not after his job was the Queen. In awe of the monarchy as an institution, he soon felt affection and respect for her as an individual. He attached great, some felt exaggerated, importance to his weekly audience, which grew longer and longer as his period in office wore on. Though his personal staff at Number 10 tried valiantly to find out what had been said on these occasions when he returned from the palace, he took delight in preserving the mystery; almost the only topic of discussion which he ever divulged to Marcia Williams was the style of a new riding habit which the Queen had just had made for Trooping the Colour.[4] He would come back, however, in euphoric mood, and sometimes seemed noticeably to have modified his opinions as a result of what had been said. When he resigned she sent him a photograph of the pair of them in the rain at Balmoral, which he thereafter carried in his wallet.

Whenever the size of the Privy Purse or other royal issues were in question, Wilson proved himself a most loyal supporter of the monarchy. Towards the end of 1965 Benn, as Postmaster-General, produced designs for a new series of stamps that set a precedent in that they did not carry a picture of the Queen's head. The Queen seemed acquiescent but subsequently told her private secretary, Michael Adeane, that she disapproved of the innovation. Adeane wrote to Mitchell at Number 10, who in turn spoke to Wilson. The King asked the Queen, the Queen asked the Dairy maid and the Dairy maid duly approached the Cow. "She is a nice woman," Benn quotes Wilson as saying, "and you absolutely charmed her into saying yes when she didn't really mean it."[5] On paper the Prime Minister was more emphatic. Through the private secretary network Benn was told that he should not commission experimental designs without the Queen's head. If such designs already existed, then on no account were they to be shown to the press without the Queen's prior approval.[1]

A month before the official announcement of the election the Queen was told that the Prime Minister would shortly be formally asking for a dissolution on 11 March and the State Opening of the new parliament on 21 April. "The fact that the first of these dates is my birthday and the second is Yours is purely coincidental," he told her. "My colleagues and I are loath to inflict on the Nation a further electoral contest so soon after the last one, but we believe it to be essential. In our mind there is the need for an urgent grip on the industrial situation, particularly so far as prices and incomes, and productivity are concerned."[2] Theoretically the royal prerogative would have entitled the Queen to turn down the request. There have been occasions in the twentieth century when the monarch must have at least considered the alternative of sending for the leader of the opposition and giving him a prior chance to form a government. In this case, however, Wilson had kept the government on the road with a fragile majority for far longer than had seemed likely in 1964, and there was no doubt that his request for a dissolution would be granted. Wilson had resolved that he was not prepared to see through another winter, with all the strains that managing the House of Commons with a tiny majority imposed on ministers, backbenchers and, above all, whips. The choice was between the spring and the autumn, and of the two he reckoned that the spring was more propitious. The date of Easter and various arcane calculations about wakes weeks, the new electoral register and the budget made 31 March the chosen date.

His plans were almost thrown out by a threatened train strike on 14 February. George Brown intervened, but failed to avert a strike which the Cabinet was convinced could be catastrophic for their electoral prospects. It was agreed that the union leaders should be summoned to Number 10 in the hope that the august surroundings and Wilson's blandishments might soften their resolve to reject the government's final offer out of hand. Crossman felt certain Wilson would bring it off and also that he would claim full credit for doing so, to the indignation of George Brown.[3] He was proved right, on both counts, but in this case at least Wilson, and even more Barbara Castle, deserved the credit. The meeting nearly turned sour when the Government Hospitality Fund's wafer-thin sandwiches proved wholly inadequate to the appetite of the union representatives. "Harold was furious," recorded Barbara Castle, "sent the women scattering to raise more food and barked at the junior official that he was tired of having his instructions ignored." Soon bottles of beer, thick sandwiches, sausages and pies were on the table in profusion, Marcia Williams having sent messengers to all the nearby pubs and even raided the larder of the Chancellor of the Exchequer next door at Number 11.[1] Either the beer, or the promise of jam tomorrow in the form of pay increases related to a hypothetical improvement in productivity, led to a change of heart on the part of the union leaders. The strike was called off. Beer and sandwiches at Number 10 entered political mythology as the Prime Minister's favoured recipe for any sort of union trouble. He complained that this was unjust; there were only five occasions between 1964 and 1970 when such revelries took place. Certainly it was a device that depended for its effectiveness in part at least on its flattering rarity. Prime-ministerial intervention is a weapon to be deployed only as a last resort. On this occasion, however, it proved markedly successful and provided an encouraging overture to the forthcoming electoral campaign.

It was a campaign that Wilson could deservedly face with confidence. His first government had no earth-shaking legislation to its credit, no National Health Service or major extension of public ownership, but it had done well. The poor and old were better off, the Housing Subsidy Act had reduced the burden on those living in council houses, the Rent Act gave security of tenure in most rental property. There had been economic crises, but the government had weathered them; the trend of exports was upwards and the balance of payments seemed to be on the mend. Whatever the stresses within, to the outside world Wilson was in command of a united administration. Perhaps as significant as anything, on the two most troublesome areas of foreign affairs, Wilson had conducted himself with notable dexterity. On Vietnam he had avoided outright condemnation by either the Americans or his own left wing; on Rhodesia he had won almost universal respect for the combination of restraint and yet firmness with which he had handled the rebellious colony.

XI

Foreign Affairs

1964–1966

To describe the events in Rhodesia and Vietnam as they actually made their impact on Wilson, interspersed with twenty other crises and spread out over several chapters, would be to render them almost impossible to follow. To treat them in isolation, however, is to risk misrepresenting the atmosphere in which such problems were considered and decisions made. On any given day Wilson might have to give priority to negotiations with Ian Smith while grappling simultaneously with a run on sterling, a furious Minister of Defence complaining about a projected cut in spending, a left-wing revolt over the nuclear deterrent, an American President demanding support for his policy in Vietnam, not to mention a row between his political and his private secretaries, a scandal involving an MP's improper use of inside information and all the routine matters that by themselves fill the life of a Prime Minister to overflowing. Worse still, these problems were interrelated: if he made no concessions to the left wing over the deterrent they would be more likely to revolt on Vietnam; if he did not do as the American President wanted over Vietnam the run on sterling might become a stampede. To give the Rhodesian negotiations the calm and concentrated attention which they deserved against such a tempestuous background was beyond the powers of any except the superhuman.

It could be said that this was what Foreign and Commonwealth Secretaries were for; to give to crises like Vietnam and Rhodesia the careful consideration which the Prime Minister could not afford. Even if they intended to at the start, however, few Prime Ministers have been able to resist playing a large part in all the most important international problems. Wilson never even intended to. Lord Lansdowne, he said, could never have achieved what he did in foreign affairs but for "the constructive mind of Balfour and the constant support he gave him, not only in executing his foreign policy, but in conceiving and shaping it". The same, he added, should "be true equally of every Prime Minister in his relations with his Foreign Secretary".[1] When considering whether Wilson interfered too much in international affairs Michael Stewart concluded that it would have been even worse being Foreign Secretary under Macmillan.[2] It can fairly be said that Wilson devoted a disproportionate part of his time and energies to a problem like Vietnam, in which the British interest was no more than peripheral. It is harder to criticise the time he devoted to Rhodesia, which was pre-eminently a British responsibility. At the end of 1965 Crossman estimated that in the previous months more than half the Prime Minister's working time had been devoted to this single issue; a few months later John Freeman found Wilson obsessed by the subject and was kept at Number 10 for two hours on a Saturday morning while Wilson held forth compulsively. He never entirely took his eye off the political ball, however; as Freeman went out into Downing Street Wilson shook him dramatically by the hand and put an arm around his shoulders, murmuring as he did so: "This'll be good for forty seconds on TV tonight. Ted Heath's speaking at Gravesend and I haven't got an engagement."[3]

Two underlying considerations were always in Wilson's mind: the need to keep the Commonwealth united and the vital importance of the Anglo-American alliance. That these aims sometimes seemed incompatible was an additional, vexatious strand in a complex web of responsibilities and commitments. His love for the Commonwealth was romantic and traditional: he relished the idea of Britain at the heart of this great international network; believed that it represented the surest way by which his country could remain among the foremost powers; and was convinced that the British role in Africa and Asia was essential for world peace. Defending a British presence in the Indian Ocean, Wilson challenged the PLP: "Perhaps there are some members who would like to contract out and leave it to the Americans and Chinese, eyeball to eyeball, to face this thing out ... It is the surest prescription for a nuclear holocaust I could think of."[4] He has been ridiculed with some justification for his extravagant illusions about the contribution Britain, and he personally, could make if the great powers fatally fell out. But he was right in thinking that there was a real contribution to be made, if only as a conveniently positioned honest broker, and that the potential to serve in that role should not lightly be discarded.

In fact there *was* an important part for Britain to play, though less dramatic than the single-handed averting of nuclear war between the United States and China. Wilson's readiness to take a hand in the affairs of India and Pakistan was highlighted when he sent John Freeman as High Commissioner to New Delhi; an indication, Freeman thought, that he did not believe the Commonwealth Office was to be trusted with anything as important as the Commonwealth.[1] In June 1965 the American Secretary of State, Dean Rusk, told Lyndon Johnson that Wilson had been working like a Trojan "to hammer out with the Indians and Pakistanis an agreement on the Rann of Kutch. Personal congratulations to Wilson would be in order."[2] They were duly despatched, and from the Indian Prime Minister too, who told Wilson that his contribution to the negotiations had been invaluable: "I write to thank you most warmly for your initiative and your friendly patience and tact."[3] A few months later he was urging restraint over Kashmir on Ayub Khan of Pakistan. "I believe that while he is basically sound," he told Johnson, "he is subject to strong pressures from his advisers, particularly Bhutto, whom I regard as one of the most evil men God ever created."[4]

He was less successful in averting the break-up of the Malaysian Federation. When he was told, with twenty-four hours' notice, that the Tunku, Abdul Rahman, proposed to announce that Singapore would be leaving the federation, he responded indignantly. "Have you really thought out the implications of what you propose to do," he demanded, "or considered the difficulties which this will create for us, who have done so much in so many ways to uphold the integrity of Malaysia?"[5] Lee Kuan Yew, Prime Minister of the newly independent Singapore, wrote to stress that the collapse of the federation was no fault of the Labour Party; it was the Tories who had been complacent; "But for the Labour Party's victory in last September's general elections, the whole of Malaysia would have disintegrated, and with it a Communist victory in S.E. Asia complete and final."[6] It was a mark of how tragically Wilson took the setback that he abstained from scoring a party point but instead responded that the Tory leaders "share with us feelings of sympathetic concern over the problems facing your part of the world. It would be of no help to Singapore to become involved in domestic politics here."

The Americans were constantly reassessing the importance which they attached to a substantial British military presence in South-East Asia. "We place higher value on Far Eastern British commitment than European," McNamara advised the President at the end of 1965.[1] Wilson must be persuaded to stand firm on this front. Six months later Rusk was reporting that the British had no intention of joining in any military effort anywhere north of Malaysia and hoped even to pull out of there at the earliest possible moment. "We must explain to Wilson the importance of staying in Asia in Britain's own interest," commented the President's adviser, Walt Rostow; adding gloomily that, if that failed, there would be nothing for it but to try to build up an Asian security structure without British participation.[2] Rostow's doubts chime curiously with Crossman's conviction that Wilson was determined to "recreate the Anglo-American axis" at the expense, if necessary, of Britain's links with Europe, and that it was in pursuit of that objective that he was resolved to keep British forces in Asia. In the eyes of certain Americans, even that would not have been enough; to recreate the Anglo-American axis it would be necessary for the British to give military support to the American effort in Vietnam.

When Wilson had first visited Lyndon Johnson early in 1964 as leader of the opposition the President was given some distinctly cautious advance briefing by his staff. Wilson was "not a man of strong political convictions himself", said Rusk, though he now probably represented the consensus of Labour Party opinion. "Somehow, he does not inspire a feeling of trust in many people. It has led some to say that in the next election, the British are faced with a choice between 'smart aleck and dumb Alec'." Bundy told Johnson that he would find Wilson "interesting, affable, persuasive and seemingly sincere (although he is widely accused of opportunistic insincerity) ... He is a cold man."[3] On that occasion Wilson had been intent merely to demonstrate his respectability and the fact that the Americans had nothing to fear from a Labour victory. There was little serious discussion of South-East Asia. In December of the same year he returned as Prime Minister. Economics and the MLF were top of the agenda but Vietnam soon came up. In Wilson's words, the President, "without excessive enthusiasm", raised the question of some form of British cooperation in the area. According to John Harris,

Johnson took Wilson for a walk in the rose garden and in these seductive surroundings pressed him to send the Black Watch to Vietnam; even a few pipers would be better than nothing. Wilson did not respond.[1] The talks had been "very successful", he told Brown; he had accepted no new commitment as regards Vietnam. But this was far from satisfying his left wing, indeed many Labour moderates, who believed that it was not enough to abstain from helping American operations in Vietnam, they should be roundly denounced as well. Wilson, in Castle's view, had "developed a close friendship with President Johnson, which was later to bedevil the Government's policy over Vietnam".[2] His efforts to reconcile the expectations of his new friend, the President, and of the Labour Party were to involve him in some of the most tortuous manoeuvrings of his time in office.

He quickly discovered that Johnson was more than a little touchy on the subject. In February 1965, when both sides were increasing their stakes and there was some reason to fear that the Americans might be contemplating the use of nuclear weapons, Wilson telephoned the President to suggest that he fly over to Washington to discuss the question. Since he had stayed up to 3.30 a.m. so as to catch Johnson at a convenient moment, he was rather hurt to be greeted by a blast of invective. Johnson clearly considered that the Prime Minister was intent on playing to his left-wing gallery and was sticking his nose into what did not concern him: "If you want to help us some in Vietnam send us some men ... Now, if you don't feel like doing that, go on with your Malaysian problems."[3] Undiscomfited, Wilson continued to hold his line. When the Cabinet showed signs of restiveness, Wilson assured them that he was in constant touch with David Bruce, the American Ambassador, and that he hoped the matter could be left to him and the Foreign Secretary.[4] He assured Bruce that Britain "solidly supported" US policy in Vietnam, though hoping that military action would be matched by willingness to negotiate.[5] But the solidity of that support proved ever harder to maintain, as the American use of napalm and gas as well as their heavy bombing of North Vietnam raised the temper of the PLP. Wilson cabled to Michael Stewart, who was visiting Washington, that Rusk

should be left in no doubt about the strength of feeling here and about the difficulties which we are facing. There is a danger of widespread anti-Americanism and of America losing her moral position. Should the President try to link this question with support for the pound I would regard this as most unfortunate ... If the financial weakness we inherited and are in the process of putting right is to be used as a means of forcing us to accept unpalatable policies or developments regardless of our thoughts this will raise very wide questions indeed about Anglo-American relationships.[1]

Johnson did not on this occasion make any overt link between the pound and Vietnam, but the threat was always implicit. Wilson continued to support American policy and to blame the North Vietnamese for refusing to negotiate but, as he told Stewart, he was finding it ever harder to resist the jibe that he was "the tail-end Charlie in an American bomber". In fact he made a good job of muting the worst complaints of his critics. Bertrand Russell bombarded him with angry letters complaining that he was backing the worst kind of old-fashioned imperialism but Wilson responded with his standard reply that the Americans were ready to negotiate, it was the North Vietnamese who refused to do so unless the Americans first withdrew. "Inept brush-offs and bureaucratic responses", stormed Russell, but they worked for the time being.[2] The American Embassy reported that left-wing opposition had been "temporarily driven underground, although its bitterness and resentment at what it views as Wilson's betrayal will almost certainly well up again". The debate in the House of Commons on 1 April had "left strong impression Prime Minister undisputed master in his own house who can count on bipartisan support for his current South-East Asia policy".[3]

He could not expect the same support from Britain's European allies. General de Gaulle wanted British backing for a Franco-Soviet initiative to get a conference going on Vietnam, and treated Wilson's reluctance to cooperate in this doubtful venture as proof that London was no more than a satellite of Washington. De Gaulle had been "very friendly and forthcoming", Wilson told Johnson, but he had refused to accept that the United States had any part to play in Vietnam.[4] Wilson had stuck up stoutly for American interests both in London and Paris and, in the view of most of Johnson's advisers, deserved some thanks when he visited Washington in April 1965. They were not at all confident that he would get them, however. Johnson was still in a somewhat truculent mood. "We are trying to keep in close touch with the Prime Minister and we recognise his problems," he told J. K. Galbraith. "What is just as important is that he should recognise ours."[5] In a telephone call to follow up this letter Bundy added that Wilson's visit would certainly be counter-productive if he pressed the President to open negotiations on whatever terms the North Vietnamese might offer.[1] But Bundy himself was under pressure from his colleague David Klein, who argued that the "firmest support from any government on our policy in Vietnam has come from the British. This despite the fact that Vietnam is a difficult issue for any British Government, and especially a Labour Government. I think I understand the reasons for some of the pique with the Prime Minister here. But I honestly doubt that this in itself is sufficient justification for the way we are handling the Prime Minister." Bundy minuted that he agreed and that he had made the point "with *some* effect for the time being".[2] His efforts were reinforced by Dean Rusk, who pleaded that Wilson be invited to lunch. "We have had an excellent degree of understanding and coop- eration in crucial foreign policy matters from the Labour Government in Britain. Anything we can do to maintain this state of affairs is in our best interests."[3] Wilson, for his part, was coached for the meeting by that panjandrum of economic theorists, Eliot Janeway, whom the businessman Harry Kissin had tried to call in as special adviser on American matters to Number 10. Wilson, Janeway advised, should "show himself in a serious academic atmosphere during his stay here". His image would project greater strength in that area and Johnson was "most susceptible to demonstrations of strength".[4]

Whether it was thanks to Wilson's seriously academic air or the intervention of Rusk and Bundy, the meeting passed off well. Johnson, according to Wilson, had expressed "very deep appreciation" for the British line on Vietnam. Wilson had contributed to the love-feast by speaking with approval of the Australian decision to send a battalion to Vietnam and even implying that he would have done the same if he had not had "to give priority to our Malaysian task".[5] His reward was an undertaking by the President that he would back any British initiative which seemed likely to lead to constructive peace talks.[6] He had not been back in London long before he realised that he must take such an initiative at once, if only in self-defence. The Labour government had a real problem, Bruce reported. "The pressure on Wilson comes not just from the Left but from Labor moderates and from the general public as well. He must be sorely tempted to buy some political credit at home by criticising American policy. Wilson has not done so and I do not think he will. If nothing else, self-interest dictates that he must risk no serious split with the Americans."[7] But he could not hold the line indefinitely, especially if the bombing of North Vietnam were stepped up.

Wilson's response was a dazzlingly ingenious attempt to achieve his three main policy objectives in a single stroke: to maintain the Anglo-American alliance, to fortify the unity and standing of the Commonwealth, and to keep his left wing quiet. At the Commonwealth conference of June 1965, having first got the blessing of Johnson and privately sounded out Robert Menzies of Australia, Wilson proposed that a mission of Commonwealth leaders should visit all the capitals concerned and see whether a basis for a peaceful solution in Vietnam existed. The idea was well received; only Julius Nyerere of Tanzania made any serious demur. His concern was that the North Vietnamese would be made to feel that they were being put in the dock if they were urged to negotiate by the Commonwealth leaders at a time when they were refusing to do so without prior American withdrawal. "If they won't negotiate, that's where they ought to be," retorted the Prime Minister of the Gambia.[1] Even the other leading radical, Kwame Nkrumah of Ghana, supported the idea, provided it was understood that North and South Vietnam should be treated on equal terms. Nkrumah felt it essential that Wilson should lead the mission because of the influence he possessed in Washington. There had been suggestions, he said darkly, that Wilson had consulted Menzies before the other Commonwealth leaders; he hoped this was "merely a malicious rumour".[2]

"Poor old Harold. George Wigg has committed him to yet another of his stunts," was Crossman's bilious comment on this new initiative.[3] Wilson for one believed it was more than just a stunt. Menzies told him that it was "the most important peace initiative in his experience", and the Prime Minister proudly repeated the remark to all and sundry.[4] The Americans were sceptical. "We expect the British to move ahead even though no Communists give them the time of day," Bundy reported, making it clear that in his view communist approval was the last thing to be expected.[5] He was right; Russia and North Vietnam turned the idea down out of hand. Wilson was disappointed, though he assured Johnson that he had never been optimistic. At least, he reflected, it had deflated some of the more extreme African members of the Commonwealth. It had also, though he did not make the point to Johnson, temporarily disarmed his own left wing. Nor did he despair of rescuing something from the wreck. Before the grave had even closed over the corpse of the Commonwealth mission, he was sending his future parliamentary private secretary, Harold Davies, to try to persuade the North Vietnamese to change their position. The idea was far-fetched but not as idiotic as has often been claimed. Davies had known Ho Chi-minh in Paris and was believed to be trusted by him; it was unlikely but not impossible that he could achieve something through face-to-face talks. In the event he never got face to face; news of the mission leaked – through the malign indiscretion of the Foreign Office, Wilson believed – and Davies was received only by officials. If the North Vietnamese had really been interested in talks it seems unlikely they would have let a premature leak deter them, but Wilson was at least able to present himself once more as the man who had spared no pains to bring about a peaceful settlement.

For a few months the heat went out of the Vietnamese War so far as domestic politics were concerned. In August 1965 Wilson was still protesting to Johnson his admiration for "the careful balance you have throughout maintained between determined resistance to aggression and a patient insistence on your readiness to negotiate an honourable settlement ... I wish there was more we could do to help you ... I am urgently examining the feasibility of doing something to make still more manifest our support for your patient and courageous policy."[1] The indignation of his left wing if they had known of this letter can hardly be imagined; as it was, when Wilson arrived in Washington in December 1965 he found awaiting him a telegram signed by sixty-eight Labour MPs demanding an immediate end to the bombing. It was believed by some that Wilson had inspired the telegram himself – "A very skilful operator had organised it," wrote Short, "and the daddy of them all lived in No. 10 Downing Street."[2] Even if he was not directly responsible, it probably came as no surprise to him; the telegram was a useful means of reminding Johnson of the pressure he was under. When he saw the President he talked of "the raps he was taking from within his own party" but insisted that his support for the American position was unshakeable. He and Wilson got along beautifully, Johnson declared. "He was wonderful in every respect and very fair and very eloquent."[3] Wilson was equally enthused, telling Menzies that the talks could hardly have been "more friendly, more open, and more generally satisfactory".[4]

Shortly after Wilson's visit the Americans called a halt to the bombing, in the hope that negotiations might be started during a Christmas truce. The truce was prolonged until the end of January,

but no talks began. When the bombing resumed the Foreign Office –
without his prior approval, claimed Wilson[1] – issued a statement
supporting the decision. A large section of the PLP was outraged and
ninety MPs signed a telegram to Senator Fulbright in Washington
applauding his condemnation of the action. Wilson may have inspired
the earlier telegram but he certainly had nothing to do with this one.
He told Stewart that he was "extremely angry"; the recalcitrant MPs
seemed to be unaware "of all we have done to try and secure peace
in the last six weeks, and of the fact that the whole world must now
have seen who is responsible for a continuation of the fighting".[2] He
confronted the PLP with considerable spirit, complaining that none
of them had thought fit to send a telegram to Ho Chi-minh demanding
that *he* open negotiations or to parade with "Peace in Vietnam"
banners outside the Chinese Embassy.[3] Left to himself he might
have gone further still; it was about this time that he remarked to
the union leader, Jack Jones, how much greater his influence in
Washington would be if Britain sent even a token contingent to
Vietnam. Jones firmly replied that to do this would be to split the
party.[4]

Wilson's worst worry was that the Americans would extend their
bombing of the North to the cities of Hanoi and Haiphong. He had
always said publicly that this would be the point at which his support
for the United States would end: "This reservation has for long been
his stock in trade for fending off left-wing attacks," reported David
Bruce. Bruce reckoned, however, that even if such bombing took
place, Wilson would dissociate himself from it but would continue to
support American policy as a whole.[5] He hoped the Prime Minister
would be favourably impressed by a presentation given by a Colonel
Rogers at Number 10. It was "superlative", said Bruce, but though
Wilson could see the military arguments for extending the bombing,
he was "gravely concerned over what he believes will be unfavourable
political repercussions in Britain".[6] Johnson urged him to maintain
solidarity as far as possible and, if he felt he had to wash his hands
of the American action, at least to stress its limits and the military
needs. Having sent the letter, he began to hesitate over the wisdom
of a visit Wilson was due to pay to Washington a few weeks later.
Rusk felt it would be damaging to withdraw the invitation but
accepted the Americans must "make bloody clear ... that (1) the visit
must be very carefully prepared; (2) the Prime Minister, whatever his
pressures at home, should not come unless what he says here in public

and in private reinforced your position on Vietnam; (3) if this is impossible for him, he must find an excuse for the visit not to take place."[1]

The furore in the Labour Party when Hanoi and Haiphong were bombed was fearful and prolonged; members who had previously been conspicuous for their moderation now demanded that Britain dissociate itself totally from American policy in Vietnam. Wilson was by no means unsympathetic to this point of view. His opinions, said Bruce, were held "very firmly, as party commitment, and to significant extent as question of personal conviction. He has never believed in possibility of clear cut military decision in VN."[2] But he was still no less convinced that a breach with the United States must be avoided. His next ploy was to visit Russia. The Americans, cynically but probably correctly, assumed that his main reason for the trip was to give himself "the aura and glamor of confidante and go-between between East and West". The visit was not exclusively motivated by the need to appease his left wing, "but the home front is a dominant factor in his mind".[3] After an earlier visit Wilson had told Johnson how hard he had tried to persuade Kosygin that his views of "the Americanski" were based on ignorance. But on Vietnam it had been "to quote the Iron Duke, 'hard pounding' ". No progress, he had said, would be possible until the next party congress had been got out of the way: "These people, like us, are politicians and he and Brezhnev ... are as nervous about their forthcoming Congress ... as any Western politician."[4] Now the congress had come and gone, but the Russian position seemed unchanged. The only new development Wilson had to report was that the Russians had tried to make his and thus Johnson's flesh creep with prophecies of massive Chinese intervention in Vietnam. It was on this visit that Wilson decided to illustrate his special status in Moscow by making a speech entirely in Russian. The embassy staff worked all night translating what he planned to say and then transcribing it into a phonetic form which they hoped would help him pronounce the text correctly. Their efforts were unavailing; when Wilson came to rehearse the speech next morning his rendering was striking but totally incomprehensible. Regretfully Wilson settled for a few introductory sentences which he learnt painstakingly by heart.[5]

In London Wilson found himself more and more isolated. In May Frank Cousins had berated him for subservience to America. Why had he not taken a firm stand over Vietnam? "Because we can't kick our creditors in the balls," said Wilson furiously. "Why not?" asked Cousins.[1] Now even a right-winger as staunch as Brown was asking, "Why not?" Brown told Barbara Castle on 18 July that he was sickened by what he had to defend in the House of Commons. Wilson was incorrigible. "I know what he'll say this time: Let's go over this again, then he'll go to Washington and cook up some screwy little deal."[2]

The "screwy little deal" was even more necessary because when Wilson arrived in Washington at the end of July Britain was in the throes of yet another financial crisis. American support was essential, yet Wilson feared his criticism of American bombing policy and reiterated refusal to send even the most token force to Vietnam might have poisoned his relationship with Johnson. He had no reason to fear. The President had been assured that Wilson had gone as far as he could possibly have contrived in support of the American position and he deserved support.[3] Johnson responded generously. In a lavishly hyperbolic after-luncheon speech he tossed in references to Milton, Shakespeare and Churchill and congratulated Britain on being blessed "with a leader whose own enterprise and courage will show the way. Your firmness and leadership have inspired us deeply in the tradition of the great men of Britain."[4]

The allusion to Churchill caused some derision, and an alarmed Johnson asked an aide exactly what he had said. There had been no direct comparison with Churchill, came the reply, the two men had not even been mentioned in the same paragraph. The White House line should be that Johnson thought very highly of Wilson but had never compared him with Churchill and "the whole thing is a silly tempest in a teapot, cooked up by reporters who didn't read the text very carefully."[5] Wilson was more than happy with the speech, even if he had not been directly compared with Churchill, or for that matter Shakespeare and Milton. He recognised that Johnson's praise would not do him much good with his left wing in London, but it was cheering all the same.

If Vietnam was the international issue which involved Wilson in the most intricate manoeuvring at home and abroad, it was over Rhodesia that he felt the closest personal involvement. The disintegration of the Rhodesian Federation had left the former Southern Rhodesia, with its minority white-settler government, as a belated colony, in many ways more advanced than its newly independent neighbours but obstinately reluctant to take those steps in the direction of multiracial democracy which the British government insisted on before it could be admitted to the Commonwealth as a self-governing state. Winston Field, whose Rhodesian Front had captured power in April 1963, was content to play it long. When he met Wilson in London the two men agreed that there could be no grant of independence in present circumstances; a "slow evolution of political power" was the way forward, with the emphasis on the "slow".[1] After a year, however, Field was replaced by the fiercer Ian Smith. Smith insisted that Rhodesia should become independent on the basis of a constitution which would be approved by a plebiscite among the white settlers and an "indaba" or council of black chiefs. Since almost all the chiefs were servants of the government the Tories had dismissed this proposition and insisted that independence could only be granted on a basis "acceptable to the people of the country as a whole". When Labour came to power, the situation remained deadlocked. Wilson could count, initially at least, on a bipartisan approach to the problem, but he was uneasily conscious of the fact that Conservative support might waver if it seemed that he was treating Smith with undue harshness. The white Rhodesians were "kith and kin", many of whom had fought for Britain in the Second World War. The great majority of the British would have opposed surrender to their racist doctrines but many fewer would countenance the bullying of the white minority into acceptance of immediate black rule.

Among the telegrams of congratulations that flowed in after Wilson's election victory in 1964 was one from Ian Smith. "I trust that the relations between my Government and the Government of Great Britain will remain friendly," wrote Smith, more in faint hope than expectation, ". . . and that Rhodesia's determination to take her rightful place among the independent nations of the world will not be impeded."[2] To reinforce this somewhat sanguine proposition, he persisted with his idea of an indaba and soon announced triumphantly that his preferred constitution had been approved by an overwhelming majority of the white sixteenth of the population and his 622 henchmen in the assembly of chiefs. Even before the plebiscite rumours were rife that Smith proposed to declare his independence without waiting for Whitehall's approval, so the possibility of a Unilateral Declaration of Independence – UDI – was soon at the centre of Wilson's mind. When Smith refused an invitation to talks in London and seemed to be preparing to announce UDI at a forth-coming meeting of the Rhodesian parliament, Wilson decided to deliver a pre-emptive strike. He ostentatiously summoned the Chief of Defence Staff, Earl Mountbatten of Burma, to a meeting at Number 10 just before an emergency meeting of the Cabinet at which it was known Rhodesia was on the agenda – thus fuelling stories that preparations were being made for military intervention – and published a stern warning that UDI would be an act of illegal rebellion which would leave Rhodesia "isolated and virtually friendless in a largely hostile continent".[1] Proudly he told Crossman that he had called Smith's bluff. He "had made him try to run for cover and climb down", he announced. Crossman was duly impressed – "This I reckon is Harold's first big success."[2] Nkrumah was equally admiring, congratulating Wilson on the "firmness, realism and good sense" which he had shown.[3] Whether Smith was in fact daunted is less clear; at least the danger date passed without the Rhodesians taking the fatal step.

They proved no more amenable, however. When Wilson proposed that Arthur Bottomley, the Commonwealth Secretary, should visit Salisbury, Smith insisted that it would be impossible for him to meet any of the nationalist leaders who had been imprisoned: "I am shocked that a man in his high position should want to see these people when he knows of their evil and criminal conduct and of the subversive and violent behaviour of their followers."[4] Wilson continued to try to persuade Smith to visit London; striking, indeed, a rather more conciliatory note than Nkrumah or his own left wing would have approved. "I assure you that we have no pre-conceived plan that we wish to impose on your country. We want to look for any line of negotiation that may lead to a satisfactory solution."[5] He stopped short of compromising British insistence on eventual enfranchisement for the Africans as a whole but insisted: "We have an open mind on the timing of independence in relation to progress towards majority rule."[6] Here was an opening – a sign of weakness Nkrumah would have said – which Smith could well have tried to exploit. Instead he became more intransigent, complained that since the advent of the Labour government the relationship between Great Britain and Rhodesia had seriously deteriorated, and threatened that, unless there was a change of heart in London, "relations between us will become more and more strained until eventually a break will become inevitable".[1] Three weeks later he was accusing Wilson of economic blackmail and "immoral behaviour" which made it impossible for him to continue negotiations "with any confidence that our standards of fair play, honesty and decency will prevail".[2] When he visited London for Churchill's funeral at the end of January 1965 he tried to avoid talking to Wilson and subsequently denied to Pearson and Menzies that any meeting had taken place.[3]

At least Smith agreed that Bottomley and the Lord Chancellor, Gerald Gardiner, should make an exploratory visit to Salisbury. They achieved something. Wilson told Lester Pearson that there had been a hardening of positions all round – the whites more reluctant to accept any move towards early majority rule, the blacks more determined that it must come immediately – but that Smith had hinted that some concessions might be offered, making it impossible for the white settlers to block the progress of the Africans towards majority rule if independence were granted before this was achieved.[4] "I believe that the suggestions which you made privately offer the germ of an idea," Wilson told Smith, "but we should of course have to carry our Cabinets and Parliaments with us."[5] A potential – and in the minds of Wilson's left-wing critics, dangerous – distinction was appearing between the African demand for NIBMAR, No Independence Before Majority African Rule, and the last of the five principles enunciated by Gardiner and Bottomley, that the basis of independence must be "acceptable to the people of Rhodesia as a whole". The possibility that Britain might settle for a test of acceptability which the independent African states would find inadequate was at the forefront of everybody's mind when the Commonwealth conference discussed the matter in June. As usual the most vociferous sceptic was Nyerere; he was indeed the only Commonwealth leader openly to voice doubts about British goodwill. Two months later he wrote to Wilson to say that his suspicions had only been fortified by subsequent events. He could not dismiss the "frightening possibility" that Britain might hand over power to a minority regime. Would Wilson deny that this was his intention?[6]

Wilson would not. On the contrary, if he could get terms that could plausibly be presented as protecting the long-term interests of the Africans he would hand over to a white regime immediately. But the prospects of such a dénouement grew ever more remote. In October Smith returned to London. The talks, Wilson told Michael Stewart, were sober and candid. "Indeed, Smith's frankness and obvious sincerity are two of his most engaging characteristics. At one point he started to discuss how, in the event of UDI, we might minimize by agreement the messy consequences of treason. It was a shame, in a sense, that I had to pull him up very sharply at this point."[1] Wilson convinced himself that he had rattled Smith with his talk of UN intervention and possible military action. "Smith's nerve may fail," he told Pearson optimistically; or his followers might decide the game was too dangerous and push him out of power. "My hope is that if a u.d.i. can be avoided during October it will not take place at all."[2] Smith, however, had stronger nerves than Wilson anticipated; indeed, according to his chief of intelligence, Kenneth Flower, he never expected or intended the talks to succeed.[3] As soon as he was back in Salisbury he briskly dismissed any idea of a Commonwealth mission, even if led by a man as likely to be sympathetic to the white regime as Robert Menzies. The matter was one "for settlement between Britain and Rhodesia alone".[4] The countdown to UDI seemed to have started again. A dramatic flight to Balmoral to persuade the Queen that Mountbatten should head a mission to Salisbury was Wilson's next effort to avert the crisis; the fact that this headline-catching enterprise thoroughly disrupted the Tory conference was an enjoyable by-product, but not the reason for it. The Queen was cautiously acquiescent but Wilson thought better of it. He himself would go to Salisbury and make one last effort to reach a settlement.

He knew that this foray would arouse suspicions in the African Commonwealth. He told Nyerere that he would never have forgiven himself if he had failed to take the initiative: "U.D.I. would be a disaster for Rhodesia, a disaster for her neighbours, it would mean the end of the Commonwealth as we know it, it would have ghastly repercussions on race relations the world over." There was no length he would not go to avert it, save betraying the basic principles of democracy.[5] Some members of the Cabinet were as doubtful as Nyerere – a majority, Crossman thought – but they were presented with a *fait accompli*. Most people, however, accepted his good intentions and put to the back of their minds any fear that he might be contemplating a sell-out. Lester Pearson congratulated him warmly: "I strongly hope that this very timely personal intervention will result in some real progress."[6] Wilson's hopes were more faint than strong but there was still a jubilant, almost holiday atmosphere as the party took off from Heathrow. It took only a few hours at Salisbury to dispel this spurious euphoria. "The Government are impervious to argument and are collectively like a suicide on a windowsill waiting to jump," Wilson told Johnson. "Moderate European opinion is paralysed by a sense of helplessness before impending doom." He had tried to play for time by proposing the setting up of a Royal Commission to establish the terms on which independence could be granted.[1] To Brown he said that perhaps his visit had restored a little fluidity to the situation but "I cannot honestly claim that we have done more than to delay UDI for a few days."[2]

The visit produced one memorable outburst when the African leaders, Joshua Nkomo and Ndabaningi Sithole, summoned from prison to meet him, were kept for several hours without food or water in an airless police van in the sun outside Government House. "This was the first time I had ever known what 'seeing red' could mean," he later wrote. "On going in to harangue the Governor, I was unable to see him because of red flashes before my eyes."[3] He had met both the Africans as prominent socialists at various international gatherings and he was outraged and disgusted by their treatment. If his visitors were not given a meal at once, he said, he would himself go out into the streets of Salisbury to buy them food. He found Nkomo and Sithole almost as intransigent as Smith, with the obvious difference that they were powerless to enforce their views. He returned disconsolate from Salisbury but managed to turn an unsuccessful venture into a personal victory. His statement in the House of Commons was "really a triumph", thought Benn. He could now claim with justice to have done all that was humanly possible to avoid a break.[4]

The break was not long in coming. On 11 November 1965 UDI was declared. Wilson condemned the action vigorously in the House of Commons and to the nation – "the best television broadcast he had ever made", said the Tory MP Nigel Fisher[5] – but had little idea what to do next. In the United Nations the non-aligned nations clamoured for military intervention to quash the racist rebels; at home Edward Heath demanded assurances that nothing of the sort would be undertaken; Wilson wanted to sound sympathetic to the first while conforming to the wishes of the second. Military action would have been expensive and hazardous, quite apart from private doubts as to whether British troops would be ready to shoot down their white compatriots. He told Hugh Cudlipp, the editor of the *Daily Mirror*, that, while a threat to use force before UDI was declared *might* have been successful, it was certainly too late now. It would be opposed and the fighting would involve Rhodesia's neighbour, Zambia, where 40 per cent of Britain's copper was produced.[1] If this supply was cut off there would be heavy unemployment in Britain and almost equally unfortunate results in the United States; a thought which led the State Department to ask that no action should be taken which might affect Zambian supplies.[2] In fact Wilson had categorically ruled out the use of force even before UDI both privately to Smith and in a broadcast on 30 October. Healey considered that this was "a classic strategic blunder"[3] and certainly Smith's task was made easier by his knowledge that he did not need to fear armed attack. Almost the only direct action that was possible was to send Javelin fighters to Zambia so as to guard against any Rhodesian air attack – or perhaps, more realistically, to pre-empt any attempt on the part of the Russians to send units of their air force there on the same excuse. At one point Wilson played with the idea of despatching a force of British, Canadian and Australian troops to Zambia to occupy the Kariba dam and power station,[4] but even if the Canadians and Australians had been ready to cooperate, the Prime Minister of Zambia, Kenneth Kaunda, was extremely sceptical about the desirability of such a move. Wilson was left in the familiar posture of trying to look as if he were doing a great deal while in fact remaining largely inactive. His Cabinet colleagues were not greatly impressed. Callaghan called for "a quick kill", without specifying with any precision how so happy an end was to be achieved, while Castle could not decide whether "Harold's aims are tactical or ready for a compromise on principle".[5] Bruce McKenzie and another former Rhodesian minister suggested one way of making a quick kill, which was to spread a virus that would wipe out Rhodesia's cattle. Wilson admitted to having been briefly tempted but quickly dismissed the idea.[6]

He took *some* steps. Shortly before UDI he sent for Lord Cromer and asked for details of the private and official sterling holdings of Rhodesians in London. Cromer refused to supply them. Did he realise that he was dealing with the Prime Minister? demanded Wilson. Cromer replied that he did, but that in his view the City of London's reputation for integrity must be his first consideration. The City would live with its reputation long after Mr Wilson had ceased to be Prime Minister. Wilson brooded over this rebuff then, two days later, sent for Cromer again and said that he proposed to pass legislation requiring banks to give such information. Would Cromer obey such a law? Of course. Then would he give the information now on the basis of an assurance that such legislation was on the way? Certainly not. By the time the law was passed, Cromer recorded with some relish, Rhodesian balances had been run down to practically zero. He was no more cooperative when, after UDI was declared, the Bank of England official who had been Deputy Governor of the Reserve Bank of Rhodesia made plans to return to London. Wilson wanted him questioned on his return about the state of Rhodesian finances. Cromer judged that this "would have put him in an intolerable position of conflict of interests between the Reserve Bank and H.M.G.". He put his man on the slowest possible boat for the return passage so as to ensure that his information was out of date by the time he got back.[1]

In the last weeks before UDI Wilson held several meetings with City or commercial dignitaries to discuss the possibility of sanctions. Unsurprisingly, he was told that they would do little harm to Rhodesia but would seriously damage Britain.[2] He was unconvinced. "I was tremendously impressed by what you had done in getting the oil embargo ... to such a high state of readiness and so quickly," he congratulated Brown,[3] while in Washington he boasted that the Smith regime was tottering. He did not commit himself to an exact date, but his private secretary spoke of "a matter of weeks" before it collapsed.[4] All the indications are that he was succumbing to his natural over-optimism, though only after having been fed with thoroughly misleading data from the intelligence services; early in January 1966 he assured Barbara Castle that sanctions were really beginning to bite; "our hand had turned out to be much stronger than we thought and Smith's weaker."[5] His object was to involve the United States so far as possible in his operations. The Americans were publicly supportive but determined not to be drawn in too far: "We must keep them [the British] in front or else this whole matter will be in our lap," warned Ball.[6]

While the black Commonwealth demanded stronger action, Wilson's reputation remained high in more moderate or right-wing circles. Menzies assured Wilson of his "unlimited admiration for the way in which you have handled this problem. I have admired, and admire, your firmness, your tact, and your longsighted view. Two years ago, I would not have thought it possible that two people so traditionally opposed in political theory could have understood each other so well."[1] It remained to be seen whether Menzies's voice would be heard above the clamour of abuse when the Commonwealth leaders met at Lagos in January 1966.* The background was unpromising. At a meeting of the Organisation for African Unity (OAU), members had been called on to sever diplomatic relations with Britain if Ian Smith's regime had not been crushed by mid December. Nobody paid much heed except for Nyerere and Nkrumah, but the real disquiet of the more moderate members of the Commonwealth was voiced by Bustamante of Jamaica when he asked, "Is the British lion dead under your Government? It must be remembered that the negroes ... helped England and made it a great power and they expect and demand protection."[2] Kaunda said that he well understood Wilson's problems at home but, "You must decide which is worse, political confusion within Britain or a bloody war that might end with the big powers destroying the entire world with their dangerous weapons."[3]

"H.M.G.'s heart is not in proposed Commonwealth Conference," reported the American Embassy.[4] They could have put it more forcibly. Wilson viewed the prospect with extreme distaste. When it came, he only averted a disastrous breakdown of the discussions by his categoric assurance that sanctions – in particular oil sanctions – were working and that the regime might well fall in "weeks not months". He probably believed it when he said it, but within a few days of his return to London he was asking how economic and financial sanctions were to be stepped up, and by the middle of February he was talking of a "long haul ... which it will require all our courage and determination to keep up".[5] He had underestimated the strength of the Rhodesian economy, the readiness of the South Africans to keep it afloat, and the resistance of the Zambians to measures which would involve their participation in a possibly suicidal economic *Blitzkrieg* against Rhodesia.[6] There were some who doubted whether Wilson himself had the courage and determination that was needed. Benn noted suspiciously that the Prime Minister was always insistent on being left "as much freedom for manoeuvre and discussions with Smith as he possibly could".[7] Discussions about what? Driberg, on behalf of the NEC, demanded that there should be no talks which could be taken as implying recognition of Smith's new status. Have no fear, replied Wilson, "there can be no question of our talking to

---

* In fact he wisely stayed away and sent his High Commissioner to represent him.

Smith in order to 'legalize the swag'."[1] But doubts remained among his colleagues.

What were doubts in London became the grimmest certainties in Africa. If Lagos had been purgatory for Wilson, the Commonwealth conference of September 1966 was hell on earth. It was devoted almost exclusively to Rhodesia, and the discussion of Rhodesia consisted largely of personal attacks on Wilson. The fact that his promise about quick results from sanctions had so conspicuously failed to be fulfilled left him in an exposed position and he was accused of weakness, incompetence and cowardice. It seemed that only a categoric commitment to NIBMAR would prevent the Commonwealth breaking up. The majority of the Cabinet were ready to pay this price but Wilson was convinced that such an undertaking would finally extinguish any hope of a negotiated settlement. It was, as he told the Queen, "a deep and at times agonizing debate" but at the end of the day he had won a respite. He had been given three months more in which to reach a settlement with the rebels; after that, all proposals would be withdrawn, NIBMAR would become a firm condition and sanctions would be stepped up. "To sum up, I believe that we have retained control of the Rhodesian problem and kept the Commonwealth together. Of course, no one can say what mad decisions may be taken hereafter."[2] He had got his way, against the will of the majority of the Commonwealth leaders and of his own colleagues. In Cabinet Brown had insisted that NIBMAR must be the basis for British policy. "Harold was prosy and repetitive and unimpressive," wrote Crossman. "George was dynamic, clear and giving leadership." But Wilson won. "The P.M. may not be a very dominant leader, but he's certainly very pertinacious."[3]

To produce results that would match his pertinacity was to prove more difficult. Comings and goings by various underlings achieved nothing. "There can be no question of my meeting Smith or any of his colleagues for so long as they persist in their illegal action," Wilson had assured the Governor of Rhodesia.[4] Now he was determined to do just that. He justified his *volte-face* by saying that things had changed. Smith, he told Cabinet, was "a frightened, worried man ready to accept our terms". Wilson could not lose by negotiations, it must be "either a victory or a draw".[5] Barbara Castle, with Judith Hart's support, tried to fix limits on the concessions that he might make, but had little hope of success: "He is implacable when he has made up his mind to a compromise ... If only he would be as stubborn in *not* compromising."[1] Sir Elwyn Jones, the Attorney-General, was to attend the talks. As he left Cabinet the Lord Chancellor handed him a note which read: " 'Remember, you are our conscience.' He and others feared that the Prime Minister was so determined to achieve a settlement ... that excessively favourable terms might be offered to Smith."[2] Wilson prepared carefully for the fateful meeting. Hearing that Kaunda would shortly be calling at the Vatican he telegraphed the Pope to tell him of the forthcoming conference, "because I am confident that Your Holiness will wish for – and may perhaps be willing to pray for – an honourable and just settlement". If the Pope could say a word to Kaunda to predispose him to accept some compromise deal, then it would also be most useful.[3]

The talks were staged on HMS *Tiger* at Gibraltar, the choice of a naval vessel being partly theatrical, partly for the sake of privacy and security. At first it seemed a propitious venue. Both sides made important concessions; the most significant on the part of the British being the drawing-up of the electoral roll in a way that would defer majority rule for a decade at least, into the next century thought the former Prime Minister, Edgar Whitehead.[4] The terms were nothing to rejoice over, Wilson told the Cabinet, but they were worth accepting so as to secure the return of Rhodesia to legality.[5] Elwyn Jones thought the agreement went too far to meet Smith's demands.[6] If he was right, the subsequent behaviour of the two governments was perverse indeed. The British Cabinet had reservations but accepted the terms unanimously; the Chief Whip estimated that there would be at the worst fifty left-wing abstentions when they were put to the vote. A group of ministers gathered at Number 10 to await the response from Salisbury. First, a Reuter's flash reported that the terms had been rejected. Wilson looked incredulous. Then ITN reported that they had been accepted. Wilson remarked how extraordinarily accurate ITN always was. Finally came confirmation that Smith and his government had turned them down.[7]

Wilson had prepared two speeches for the House of Commons, one for success, one for failure. Barbara Castle and Callaghan were nervously awaiting his arrival in the chamber. Castle grew irritated at the delay. " 'He is making us look indecisive again. It's no good acting like Superman if you end by falling short.' Jim replied gravely, 'He *is* a Superman. I couldn't do what he has done.' In the end H came dashing in, head down. To my utter relief there was no indication of running away in his statement. His control of the detail and the House was masterly. Jim's right: there is a touch of the Superman about him."[1] It was, indeed, one of his most effective speeches; he contrived to savage the opposition while preserving a position of noble rectitude, with the invocation of Abraham Lincoln and much talk of moral principles. At the end the Labour benches rose, cheering and waving their order papers. Crossman rose too, but typically could not bring himself to wave his order paper. "But there's no doubt about it. Harold had roused the Party which is a moralistic party and which disliked the idea of any settlement."[2]

One by-product of the traumatic Commonwealth conferences of 1966 had been to induce Wilson to look with greater favour on Britain's links with Europe. The indignation of Britain's partners in the European Free Trade Area (EFTA) at the import surcharges similarly made him think more kindly of the EEC. He was still far from being converted to Britain's entry, however. His instinct was to look for a compromise; to retain the existence of the EFTA but to build bridges with the EEC so as to reduce the differences and trade barriers between the two. He was so apt to say different things to different people and to conceal his real feelings that it is impossible to chart the course of his thinking with any confidence, but the first two years of his government seem to have been marked by a gradual and reluctant acceptance of the impossibility of finding a halfway house and his recognition of the fact that, if this were true, Britain's future would probably be safest as part of the EEC. He had certainly not moved as far as this by the summer of 1966. When Cousins resigned he told Benn: "The little man actually asked me to stay in the Government in order to help him to keep Britain out of the Common Market."[3] In May, when Chancellor Erhard said that he did not think the time was yet ripe for British entry, Wilson neither felt nor expressed distress but merely indicated British willingness to enter negotiations if the chance did present itself.[4] On 19 May he agreed with Brown that a high-level working party should examine the Treaty of Rome with a view to establishing how far it was compatible with British interests. Without a positive recommendation from the party, he concluded, "I am bound to say that ... I should be reluctant to invite the political controversy which would undoubtedly be aroused if we gave any public indication that we were prepared formally to accept the Treaty."[1] His doubts were reinforced by his belief that Jenkins and Callaghan were plotting to remove him: "You know what the game is," he told Castle; "devalue and get into Europe. We've got to scotch it."[2] If his rivals wanted something, it was surely a good reason not to want it himself.

But part of him felt differently. He could see the attractions of a greater Europe based on common ideals more significant than mere economic advantage. Would it not be a noble feat to be the architect of a united and socialist Europe? What did the price of butter matter in the eye of eternity? "High heaven rejects the lore of nicely calculated less or more," he had quoted grandiloquently in Strasbourg.[3] Such inchoate romanticism would not have been enough in itself, but other factors also worked on him. For one thing, the Americans were anxious for Britain to enter Europe, and American opinion was not something he would lightly ignore. Only a week after Wilson spoke so decidedly to Barbara Castle, Ball recommended to the President that he should urge Wilson to "sign the Treaty of Rome with no ifs and buts".[4] Johnson in the event seems to have been less categoric but he made his views abundantly clear. The conversion of Michael Stewart to Europe was another factor that played a part in the evolution of Wilson's thoughts. Douglas Jay considers that Cecil King was even more important an influence; as early as April 1966, according to King, Wilson had admitted that he thought Britain would be a member of the EEC in two or three years.[5] Wilson himself told Wigg that he had seen the light as the result of an article in the *Economist*;[6] the piece in question seems convincing enough but it is hard to believe that it was conspicuously more illuminating then any of the other beacons that marked his road to Europe. The process was set back by a disastrous visit paid to London by the French Prime Minister, Georges Pompidou, in July 1966. Wilson was not only compelled to cancel a meeting at short notice but cut a dinner given in his honour at the French Embassy. "Ham-fisted and most uncharacteristic discourtesy," Jenkins called it:[7] in fact Wilson had had a debate on Vietnam forced upon him and it would have been hard for him to escape. He could have grovelled more vigorously however; according to Heath, Pompidou returned to Paris disgusted and "convinced that Wilson does not mean business over joining the Common Market".[8] Even if Pompidou had been better disposed, it is unlikely that he could markedly have influenced de Gaulle on the central issue of Britain's entry, but certainly the contretemps made things no easier when a few months later Wilson showed that he did, indeed, mean business.

The only other overseas issue which preoccupied him seriously in these first two years (if to be across the Irish Channel is to be overseas) was the future of Ulster. Terence O'Neill, the Prime Minister of Northern Ireland, had first called on Wilson in July 1964. "I fully expect to dislike him but instead I find a lot of charm as well as the expected intelligence," he wrote. "I feel that if he wins we shall get on well."[1] He did win and they did get on well. O'Neill came back to London in 1966 to find Wilson "relaxed and happy and unmoved by world events". When he showed his visitor out into Downing Street Wilson called for his pipe. "The shaking of hands ... was a professional affair ... but then Harold Wilson is a professional through and through. If physical vigour and enjoyment of office were sufficient to sustain him, then he was going to be at No. 10 for a long time to come."[2] O'Neill's main point was that he had set such a hectic pace on fostering human rights in Northern Ireland in the last two years that a period of consolidation was essential if he were not to be destroyed by his reactionaries. Wilson was very ready to be convinced. Britain must keep up pressure for progress, he told the Liberal, Eric Lubbock, but "at the same time it is important to recognise that Captain O'Neill has by local standards a very 'liberal' outlook and is, I think, genuinely concerned to improve matters in Ulster." Wilson was anxious "not to undermine his position and deliver the six Counties to the extremists".[3]

Meanwhile he had made a gesture towards the South. The Irish had long pleaded for the return to Ireland of the body of Roger Casement, the traitor/hero who had been executed for high treason in 1916. Wilson felt that here at least was one irritant that could be disposed of. Casement's grave had been identified, he told Sean Lemass, the Taoiseach, and the remains would be returned, though, he added cautiously, it would be impossible to identify them with certainty. "Our understanding would therefore be that their return would be taken as the gesture which we intend to the people of the Republic of Ireland, and we would hope that no question would arise as to their authenticity."[4] Lemass had no intention of looking this gift skeleton in the mouth: he replied warmly that the British move had received a "universally favourable reaction"; it had been "yet another step towards the establishment of the closest and most friendly relations between our two countries".[1] With such harmony on both sides of the border, Wilson could be forgiven for imagining that Ireland would not be one of the most pressing problems during his period in office.

Triumph and Disaster

1966

George Caunt, a Transport House official who was Wilson's baggage master for his first three electoral campaigns, has left a diary of *grand guignolesque* horror in which he describes the atmosphere as the cortège moved around the country: Marcia Williams raving, raging, weeping; accusations of arrogance, treachery, incompetence flung freely to and fro; two members of the staff coming to blows on a provincial railway station; rows, rows, rows; only Wilson "above it all and as calm as a cucumber".[1] Though no other accounts have quite so melodramatic a flavour, it is clear that the atmosphere of the touring party was not notably harmonious; Marcia Williams describes the occasion when Ron Hayward, then the party's Southern Regional Organiser, turned on her and called her "a bad-tempered old bitch". She wasn't old, she protested.[2] Caunt was a prejudiced reporter and, if things were really as bad as he suggests, it is hard to see how anyone survived the election, let alone won it. His remarks say more about the pressure-cooker nature of an electoral campaign than the personalities involved: the overwork; the endless fears that something has gone, is going or shortly will go wrong; the difficulties of operating from railway carriages or cramped hotel rooms; the impossibility of establishing contact with other senior figures in the campaign when all of them were almost constantly on the move; the need perpetually to monitor press, radio and television; the knowledge that one injudicious remark could lose an election overnight yet that the unforgivable is not to say anything. To survive successfully called for calm, patience and a sense of humour: qualities, fortunately, which Wilson possessed in good measure.

The pressure on his staff varied between the outrageous and the intolerable. Eight hundred and fifty letters a week were received in

Downing Street in January 1966; 1,210 in February; 1,570 in March; while in the weeks of the election the figure rose to over 10,000. Many of these could be ignored or put into a pending tray, but all had to be looked at and often a vote would be lost if no reply was sent. Marcia Williams, who was suffering from shingles and should really have been at home in bed, was particularly vulnerable. The press rarely missed a chance to make snide remarks about her role in Wilson's life and she overreacted with some spectacular displays of bad temper. Those close to Wilson saw her value: very loyal, Crossman thought her, "intensely critical of anyone who criticizes Harold"; "infinitely the most able, loyal, radical and balanced member of Harold's personal team", wrote Tony Benn.[1] But others saw only the disruption she could cause and the demands she would make on the Prime Minister when he should have been concentrating exclusively on the campaign.

The campaign proper began on 11 March. Labour began as 4–1 favourite with a 9 per cent lead in the polls. The surest way to retain its commanding position was to avoid giving hostages to fortune by stirring up the controversial issues which might cost them votes, yet to wage too passive a campaign would invite apathy and lead to the Labour voter staying at home. Certain issues were eschewed. Nothing was said about trade union reform and as little as possible about Europe. Wilson dealt with this last topic in one speech at Bristol. He contrived to tread a delicate tightrope, emphasising for the sake of the Europeans that Britain would be ready to join if the terms were right while placating the anti-Europeans by assuring them that Britain would enter only "with head high, not crawl in". Douglas Jay was exultant over Wilson's insistence that he would have no truck with supranationalism or submit to being cut off from the Commonwealth markets,[2] but in fact every pledge was qualified and it was possible to read more or less what one wanted into the speech. Nationalisation was another subject which, if not taboo, was certainly not featured prominently; nothing was to be introduced that might mar the image of a moderate, competent and united Labour Party quietly getting on with the job of running the country.[3]

Wilson's personal performance was tailored to this need. He told Sean Lemass shortly after the election that his object had been to look like a family doctor, "the kind of man who inspires trust by his appearance as well as by his soothing words".[4] The original plan had been for him to remain aloof from the hurly-burly until the last week or so of the campaign, but to no one's surprise he found the role too unobtrusive for his comfort. "Every night he has spoken somewhere," complained Crossman, "and so he has hogged most of the available Labour publicity."[1] Barbara Castle was disappointed by his performance: "I knew he was tired before he started but he failed to strike any new notes – not even the old note about modernization."[2] New notes were not at all what Wilson wanted to strike. He played the international statesman, the man who had handled the Rhodesian crisis with firmness yet moderation, the man who knew the answers. It was not to everybody's taste; Benn reported meeting a former supporter who found the Wilson of 1966 "phony and without principle". The more successful Wilson was, Benn reflected, the less he appealed to those who had campaigned most actively for him as leader.[3] The criticism was fair enough, but Wilson knew that those who had campaigned for him in the past had nowhere else to go; what he needed was the floating vote that in 1964 had gone to the Conservatives or Liberals.

Just by looking prime-ministerial, a Prime Minister can enjoy a head start over a leader of the opposition. Heath featured even more prominently in the Tory campaign than Wilson in the Labour, taking up 70 per cent of the television time as opposed to Wilson's 56 per cent. In direct comparison, however, Wilson fared better: 54 per cent thought he had a "strong, forceful personality" as opposed to 28 per cent for Heath; an astonishingly high 95 per cent of Labour supporters were satisfied with Wilson, only 70 per cent of Tories with Heath.[4] Wilson was far better at handling hecklers, and demonstrated his technique night after night while the Tory leader talked to tamer assemblies confined to the accredited faithful. The approach had its dangers, as was shown when Wilson was hit in the eye by a stink bomb thrown by a boy in Slough. He could have been made to look a fool, but his quick comment – "With an aim like that, the boy ought to be in the England eleven" – instead won him respect and sympathy. His most effective attack on Heath came in his Europe speech when he jeered, "One encouraging gesture from the French Government and he rolls on his back like a spaniel," going on to appease dog-lovers by explaining that some of his best friends were spaniels. Heath's best joke misfired. The panda at London Zoo had been packed off to Moscow to mate. "No doubt in a month's time we shall see Mr Wilson having tea at Number 10 with a pregnant panda," said Heath; a pleasing image, but one which conceded that Wilson would still be Prime Minister when the election was over.[1]

His mastery of the media was well demonstrated by his handling of a mass meeting at the Bull Ring in Birmingham on 16 March, the forum where Alec Douglas-Home had been shouted down in 1964. For twenty minutes he indulged in knockabout politicking, stirring the audience into a frenzy of protest and counterprotest; then, at the instant that he knew the ITV cameras were due to start their coverage, he switched mood and became the sober statesman. "At home the audience saw the Prime Minister seeking to expound his policy to the country, being shouted and yelled at but battling on in the face of uproar," wrote the Editor of Independent Television News, Geoffrey Cox. "It provided some of the most remarkable television ever seen in a news programme."[2] The press were in two minds next day as to what had happened – the *Daily Worker*'s headline was "Wilson gets the better of Tory hecklers" while the *Sketch* concluded "Hecklers drown Wilson" – but the television audience were left in no doubt at all.

Even though he felt pretty confident that he could outshine his rival, Wilson was still less ready to confront Heath on television than he had been with Douglas-Home in 1964. Why take the risk of giving Heath exposure as a potential Prime Minister? Heath was probably little keener, but was bounced into expressing his willingness as an off-the-cuff reaction to a last-minute question from Alastair Burnet.[3] Wilson ingeniously countered by saying that any such meeting must also include the Liberal leader, Jo Grimond. Heath was as unwilling to share the limelight with Grimond as Wilson with Heath and the idea was dropped. The BBC annoyed Wilson by continuing to press for the confrontation long after his reluctance to undertake it had been made obvious. It offended him still more by failing to give live coverage to his Birmingham or indeed to any other campaign speech, and compounded its crimes by showing a particularly popular programme, *The Man from UNCLE*, while the polls were still open on election day. Always ready to suspect the worst of any element of the media, Wilson convinced himself that the BBC was prejudiced against him and his government. He contrasted Hugh Greene's refusal to change the schedules on polling day with his readiness to do the same thing in 1964 and assumed a change of political attitude as the explanation – not admitting the possibility that the BBC felt it indispensable to emphasise its independence of whoever might be in power at the time. It was the beginning of a feud that was to continue for several years.

It was a dull campaign in that, though there were minor fluctuations, Labour's victory never really seemed in doubt. Wilson paid only two brisk visits to his constituency before the final stages of the campaign but his agent, Arthur Smith, was as energetic as ever and a massive majority was assured. Everything went well; even the balmy spring weather was ideal for a party which traditionally had the use of many fewer motor-cars to get its supporters to the polls. Wilson's final broadcast struck the same note as he had achieved throughout the campaign: statesmanlike, calm, professional, calling for patriotism and stability and leaving it to his Conservative rival to demand radical change. The result was little short of triumph: a majority of three was turned into one of ninety-seven. It was Wilson's victory; Labour owed it, Callaghan wrote generously, "to his tactical skill, his determination, his orchestration, and the confidence he conveyed to the electorate".[1] Now, surely, he would at last be master in his own house.

The journey south from Liverpool gave him peculiar pleasure. The BBC had installed an electronic studio on the train and expected to interview him. Wilson refused, telling the would-be interviewer that there was nothing personal about it "but I'm going to teach your masters a lesson they won't forget in a hurry". The effect of his gesture was blunted when the BBC sent Desmond Wilcox to interview him at Euston. Wilson spoke to him for five minutes under the impression that he was still working for ITV.[2] Back at Number 10 he got into the lift and "in a very tired voice" remarked, "Now we can have a rest from politics. Now we can just govern."[3] From a man whose life was politics, the sentiment was anyway unconvincing. In fact the election ushered in three years of the most relentless political in-fighting in Wilson's life.

The trouble was that Wilson had done too well. The last thing Labour needed was a crop of new seats which might be filled by left-wing militants, David Bruce reported. "Majority of 25–35 seats would be dandy, quite enough to manage business and keep M.P.s in line. P.M. almost certainly shares this view."[4] PM did. Ayub Khan visited Chequers shortly after the election and found Wilson practising his putting on the carpet in the great hall. "How's your handicap?" he asked. Wilson groaned: "Gone up from three to ninety-seven!"[5] The size of the majority ensured that the government would be unlikely to fall even if the backbenchers stepped out of line and thus gave potential rebels more scope for making mischief. Wilson cast around for some way in which the rank and file could be kept "active, busy and happy". More meetings of the PLP and more committees in which members could air their views and perhaps practise their drafting skills on such issues as health, pensions or education, seemed a promising device.[1] In the House of Commons he spoke of the need for some sort of congressional committees. "He has dozens of new members; we are told they are all very clever," Iain Macleod commented, "... so the Prime Minister had decided to keep them busy as squirrels in a cage and give them the illusion of occupation and importance."[2]

The major Cabinet reshuffle which many had anticipated did not take place: a few elderly ministers were put out to grass and there was some switching around of portfolios; "niggling" changes, Crossman described them.[3] Wilson wrote to Gordon Walker to apologise for not bringing him back into the Cabinet, but only two slots had come free: one was Wales, "which is hopeless", and in the other, "I shall be under the heaviest criticism if I don't bring in one under-50 to bring down the very high average age."[4] The two most interesting changes were made for specific purposes. Richard Marsh, a former civil servant, was the under-fifty – indeed, under forty – who joined the Cabinet as Minister of Power, with responsibility for the long-delayed nationalisation of steel, while George Thomson was made Chancellor of the Duchy of Lancaster in charge of Britain's relations with Europe. Thomson told Wilson that he felt he might be unsuitable since he had no strong convictions on Europe. "That's why I'm appointing you," retorted the Prime Minister.[5] But the two appointments were an indication of Wilson's priorities over the coming year. He told Gordon Walker that he hoped to have a more radical reshuffle in the autumn.

He therefore ignored the central problem of his Cabinet: the failure of the DEA to achieve what was expected of it and the far from creative tension between the new department and the Treasury. His only contribution to this imbroglio was to set up a new Cabinet committee under his own chairmanship to take over some of George Brown's responsibilities in the field of trade. In Callaghan's view this made things even worse.

I have slept on your new proposed arrangements, but I do not like them any more this morning. Basically my objection is that they involve too much interference with the job of a Chancellor. He has executive responsibility but in future he will have to cope with the Deputy Prime Minister's initiatives, and also with your new Group which is to be set up to oversee the Board of Trade. I don't believe the Chancellor's job can be done successfully in this way. He should have greater freedom of action than you propose ... With the Deputy Prime Minister's coordinating role, and your own ... Committee, we shall find that action will be smothered by compromise and delay. Therefore, with great personal regret, I prefer not to continue if these are your final arrangements.[1]

A private secretary minuted that Wilson and Callaghan met and the resignation was withdrawn. The new committee seems to have been withdrawn too; if it survived it was remarkably unobtrusive. Callaghan had talked of resigning just before the election and at that time Wilson had contemplated replacing him by Jenkins or Gordon Walker.[2] He knew, however, that he could not afford to let Callaghan go, for the moment at any rate. Two months later he told Barbara Castle that the Chancellor was "in a bad state. Getting too arrogant." Castle said that Wilson ought to get rid of him. "He smiled a cunning smile, 'That thought had occurred to me. But not a word to anyone.'"[3]

To the outside world, indeed to the average backbencher, the signs seemed propitious for the Labour Party in April and May 1966. Wilson had a majority sufficient to get things done; the economy seemed stable; exports were rising; now at last the faithful could expect the radical social legislation which they had been awaiting so long. A start was made in some directions. In spite of last-minute pressure for compromise from a few ministers, the nationalisation of steel featured in the Queen's Speech of 21 April and it was made clear that any halfway house had been ruled out. The enquiry into the staffing and organisation of the civil service, under the chairmanship of Lord Fulton of the University of Sussex, got under way on the two-year stint that was to lead to the Fulton Report of 1968. But the real meat of the reformist programme was still to come.

It was the seamen's strike which threw the government off course, or perhaps more accurately exposed the shallow roots of its new-found confidence. The National Union of Seamen (NUS) was better placed than any body of similar size to bring the country's economy to a halt. The rights and wrongs of the dispute were hotly argued but most people agreed that the seamen had genuine grievances. The relationship between employers and employed was so bad that common sense and moderation were singularly absent from the negotiating process. For Wilson, a settlement which would give seamen no more than a modest pay increase seemed of vital importance for the policy of wage restraint which he was trying to persuade the unions to accept. He realised that it might be necessary to confront and face down some major union if his policy were to work and he wished to convince both the British public and the international bankers that, if need arose, a Labour government could be as tough as any Tory. He would not have chosen the merchant navy as a battlefield, but since it had been forced on him he did not propose to shrink from it.

On 13 May Wilson summoned the seamen's leaders to Number 10 in a last-minute attempt to avert the strike. The meeting was a disaster; the seamen were a turbulent lot and singularly unimpressed by their surroundings; they abused the employers and berated Wilson for supporting the capitalist against the working man. The TUC proposed concessions; Wilson rallied a majority of the Cabinet to the view that nothing should be offered the seamen beyond the recommendations of the Pearson Court of Inquiry. "The fact is that Harold is out to smash the seamen's union," Crossman noted gloomily;[1] a comment which was over-dramatic but not entirely unjustified. The fact was that Wilson had convinced himself that the NUS, or at least a powerful element in it, was a menace to national security. He had been briefed by MI5 – "the gentlemen in raincoats and black boots", as he called them – to the effect that the union was effectively controlled by a group of communists who considered the interests not of their members but of Moscow. The briefings were not recorded and conducted in great secrecy – the only time that the door between the offices of Marcia Williams and the Prime Minister was locked was when representatives of MI5 or MI6 were visiting – but Wilson found the evidence conclusive.[2] After the strike had dragged on for six disastrous weeks he denounced the union leaders in the House. A "tightly knit group of politically motivated men", he said, were hoodwinking the seamen and holding the country to ransom for their own nefarious ends.

The far left were naturally outraged. Why shouldn't trade unionists be politically motivated? asked Ian Mikardo. Was it a crime?[3] "I couldn't find anyone in the Cabinet who thought it very clever," said Barbara Castle of Wilson's declaration. "Bonkers," said Peter Shore;

"Wiggery-pokery," said Crossman; "It made me sick and reminded me of McCarthyism," recorded Benn, when Wilson went further and named the individuals he had in mind.[1] Within the union, however, Wilson's outburst either achieved better results or, perhaps more probably, coincided with a change in mood. The moderates among the leaders rallied their forces, the extremists were voted down, at the end of June the strike was called off.

But by then grave damage had been done to sterling. A run on the pound had started when the strike was on, had been temporarily checked by its conclusion, but resumed when the American bombing of Hanoi caused panic in world markets. A serious financial crisis suddenly threatened, and it happened against a background of political instability caused by the resignation from the Cabinet of the Minister of Technology, Frank Cousins, in protest against the government's income policy. Basically, Cousins believed that while it was acceptable to control prices, which would inevitably lead employers to be cautious in wage settlements, it was wrong to curb the rights of trade unionists to put forward their members' claims. Any legislation, therefore, which sought to limit pay settlements was out of order. During the electoral campaign he threatened to resign if the prices and incomes policy was not reconsidered. Wilson, Cousins claimed, replied that "there are many things that can be consigned to the incinerator – that included."[2] Wilson denied having made any such commitment and both the manifesto and the Queen's Speech foreshadowed legislation. It was the publication of the Prices and Incomes Bill on 4 July which provoked Cousins to resign. He was egged on by Michael Foot, who claimed that Wilson was losing all his friends. "Didn't he realise that he was now strong enough to stand up to the Right? He ought to have set a new tone after the Election, with a 'soak the rich' Budget."[3] In his letter of resignation, Cousins maintained that the bill was "fundamentally wrong in its conception and approach". To restrict wage increases was no substitute for an economic policy. Wilson replied mildly, agreeing in principle but reminding Cousins that wage increases must be related to productivity if national bankruptcy were to be avoided.[4] He neither changed Cousins's mind nor expected to. Tony Benn was given Cousins's job; the Chief Whip, Edward Short, was moved to the Post Office; and John Silkin, Short's deputy, was promoted to be Chief Whip. Silkin was reputed to be more liberal than Short, and the left wing of the party hoped that his appointment heralded happier days for those who wanted greater freedom to criticise government policy.

These changes had not even been contemplated before the financial storm broke. It was triggered by some ill-considered remarks by Georges Pompidou who was quoted, correctly or not, as suggesting that Britain would have to devalue before it could be considered for entry into the Common Market. Devaluation had never been altogether out of people's minds. Robert Neild, the economist, told Benn that during the 1966 election he and a group of other mandarins had produced a paper recommending devaluation. When he returned to Downing Street Wilson ordered all copies of it to be collected and burned. "It was quite medieval," commented Neild. Balogh confirmed that the story was true.[1] But by mid 1966 the danger seemed to have receded. On 1 July Callaghan had dismissed the idea as wholly unnecessary. He was satisfied that British prices were competitive.[2] Jay at the Board of Trade agreed; only a measure of restraint in wage demands and the end of the seamen's strike were needed to put the balance of trade healthily back into the black.[3] The loss of gold shown in the reserve figures published on 4 July had shaken confidence but the damage would probably only have been fleeting. Pompidou's remarks turned a rivulet of losses into a raging torrent.

Within a week Callaghan had concluded that the pound was indefensible and that devaluation must come at once. The Governor of the Bank of England, he said, had just returned from a meeting of the Central Bankers at Basle and fully shared his view. The new Governor – Leslie O'Brien, the former Deputy Governor, who had taken over from Cromer – denied that this was the case. Callaghan and Brown persisted that the only course for Britain was to devalue, enter the Common Market and endure the wrath of the Americans.[4] Brown for one believed that it was only Wilson's promise to Johnson not to devalue which made him now hold back. "God knows what he has said to him," he told Castle. "Back in 1964 he stopped me going to Washington. He went himself. What did he pledge? I don't know; that we wouldn't devalue and full support in the Far East? But both those have got to go ... This is the decision we have got to make: break the commitment to America."[5] Certainly the American attitude was an important element in Wilson's mind, but not as all-important as has been suggested.[6] He had other reasons, in his own mind equally forcible, for rejecting devaluation: pride in his own reputation, fears as to the effect it might have on the Labour Party, doubts whether it was needed or would be efficacious. The American attitude also was not as unequivocal as it had been in 1964. The Secretary of the Treasury, Joseph Fowler, suggested that the United States could not both block devaluation and insist on a British presence east of Suez. If a choice had to be made he would favour accepting a British withdrawal from Asia. Ball and Dean Acheson agreed but the Secretaries of State and Defense both felt that devaluation would be the lesser evil.[1] American opposition would be strong but not, perhaps, adamantine.

Brown and Callaghan accepted that a decision could wait till after the visit that Wilson was due to pay to Washington at the end of the month, then two days later reverted to their belief that the matter was too urgent for such delay. Wilson and Brown met privately, to the annoyance of Callaghan, and Brown, in another bewildering *volte-face*, "said that as Leader and Deputy Leader we should link arms ... We agreed that if Jim would not agree and insisted on resigning we should accept the resignation and that I [Wilson] should take over the Treasury for three or four weeks, at the end of which George might become Chancellor." Callaghan did not resign, and at Cabinet next day Wilson said that a deflationary package would be hurriedly put together and announced before his Washington visit, so as to ensure he did not appear "as a suppliant not having put our own house in order". This time it was Callaghan who sided with the Prime Minister against George Brown. Brown argued passionately against announcing the cuts before Wilson had visited Washington and, on the phone that night, recorded Wilson, was "not at his best" and accused "Jim and me of going back on our word".[2] Observing with some cynicism the activities of the three great men, Harold Lever posed a riddle: "If Harold, George and Jim were in a small boat in mid Atlantic and it sank, who would be saved?" His answer was "The British people".[3]

While his officials were busily putting together the deflationary package, Wilson paid a brief visit to Moscow. His main reason for going had been to sound out the Russian leaders on Vietnam; he persisted in the plan in case cancellation made the financial crisis seem even worse than in fact it was. When he returned on 19 July he found that the devaluation lobby had re-formed and strengthened in his absence. The Europeans, notably Brown, Jenkins and Crosland, had made common cause with the left, Crossman, Castle, Greenwood and Benn: the former thinking devaluation was the key to Britain's entry into the Common Market; the latter hoping it would obviate, or at least reduce, the need for fierce deflation. Both groups knew the alliance to be temporary and confined to this solitary issue, but it was clearly going to present Wilson with some formidable opposition. If Callaghan swung back again and joined the devaluers then the Prime Minister could find himself in a minority in the Cabinet. There was uncertainty too about the long-term future. What were the cuts *for*? demanded Brown and Crossman. If they were just to appease the bankers, it was not good enough. "Time and again Harold has promised that, if we will only let things through, we really will discuss long-term remedies, but we never do," Crossman complained to Castle. "I'm not going to take that any more. We mustn't get drawn into discussion of details on the package until we have had this out first."[1]

Given the disparate nature of his opponents, it was unsurprising that Wilson got his own way. The Prime Minister had "been forced to make some important concessions", said Crossman,[2] but it is hard to see that he had given much away. He agreed that, in certain circumstances – for instance, if unemployment rose markedly above 2 per cent – he would consider devaluation and that a Cabinet committee should deliberate on the virtues of either floating or moving to another fixed rate, so that a contingency plan would exist if need arose. At the end of the day, however, devaluation had been indefinitely postponed and the cuts Wilson wanted had been accepted. George Brown at first refused to agree to the decision. "It is my firm conviction," he told Wilson, "that what the Cabinet has now accepted – if it works – can only lead Britain back to industrial stagnation and therefore to economic disaster."[3] He promised to explain what was intended to the TUC and the CBI, changed his mind and left the task to Wilson, resigned, and finally allowed himself to be persuaded graciously to stay on. Next day Wilson presented the proposed cuts to the House of Commons. He insisted that he should do the job himself rather than leave it to the Chancellor and a rough time he had of it; he "was a fighter who never lacked courage when his back was to the wall," wrote Callaghan, "and he needed every ounce of will power, for the anger and noise of the Opposition exceeded anything I had heard since the terrible Suez debate ten years before".[4] The Tory fury helped him with his own backbenchers who might otherwise have shown their discontent more audibly. They were being asked to endure a lot, for the package contained a startling crop of restrictive measures. Hire-purchase controls were tightened, indirect taxes and post office charges raised, a surtax surcharge introduced, public investment cut and, most dramatic of all, incomes and prices frozen for six months to be followed by a further six months of severe restraint. To put it in a nutshell, Wilson told the Indian Prime Minister, "we are asking the country to accept the severest economic measures that any government has had to bring in since the war, and this is the beginning of a continuing effort to put our balance of payments to rights, once and for all."[1] It was also, though Wilson would never have admitted and was perhaps hardly aware of the fact, the end of the National Plan and of all the proud dreams of controlled and purposive expansion.

One of Wilson's principal objectives had been to impress the Americans. In this he was successful. "The British Government," Johnson was told, "for the first time since 1950, has faced up to the United Kingdom's economic problems taken as a whole. The politics of pulling it off will continue to be tough. But the fiscal and monetary instruments available to a modern government ... are very powerful."[2] Wilson paid a high price in terms of his personal standing, not just with his left wing, who felt betrayed, but in the party and country as a whole. He seemed temporarily to have lost heart. Barbara Castle watched him enter the House of Commons "with his now customary stance: a hunched Churchillian prowl accompanied by a brooding bulldog look", but "he seems strangely to have lost his grip of things. Is it his health?" Cecil King's wife Ruth noticed "a marked deterioration – fatter, worried, more bewildered, and so *small*". His myth had been destroyed, thought Crossman: "I suppose it is the most dramatic decline any modern P.M. has suffered."[3] But few thought that he was finished. He hardly seemed the same man as the brilliant tactician who had mastered the House of Commons in 1964 and 1965, Dean Rusk told Johnson. "Events seem to have become his master and he is rushing from one fire to another without ever really putting any of them out." But he was fighting back. He still had "the will to take difficult decisions and the determination to see them through". What he needed from Johnson was friendly advice and encouragement, Rusk concluded. Both were provided.[4]

Wilson himself accepted that the press and much of the Cabinet and the House of Commons were against him but was convinced the people loved him still. He had been cheered by the enthusiastic welcome he received when he had recently called in on that Mecca of Beatledom, the Cavern in Liverpool, he told Crossman proudly: he has "a deep natural survival instinct which enables him to deceive himself as a protection against collapse".[1] But his temporary vulnerability was well illustrated when the Cabinet debated the controversial clause 4 of the Prices and Incomes Bill which introduced the possibility of punitive measures to enforce the wage freeze. The powers were only to be held in reserve, to be used if the voluntary system broke down, but they represented a new and, to many of those present, frightening precedent. It was obvious that it would be impossible to get it through the House of Commons without a backbench revolt. In Cabinet Brown presented and championed the measure; Wilson did little more than tot up the votes at the end of each part of the discussion. At one point there was a tie. "What shall I do?" Wilson asked. "Be a Prime Minister," Crossman muttered. But for the moment Wilson found that hard.[2]

"There was no plot, no conspiracy, no cabal, no organisation," Wilson wrote in his history of the 1964–70 government.[3] He was probably right but he certainly did not believe it at the time. When the battle was at its height he told Barbara Castle that "there was a great plot on by George and Jim to get rid of him". Some time later he urged her to find out who had attended a weekend party at Anne Fleming's – a celebrated hostess and former close friend of Gaitskell's – which had taken place while he had been away: "He said he knew what the ploy was – to make Jim Callaghan Prime Minister, Roy Jenkins Chancellor and form a Coalition Government."[4] He voiced his suspicions about the same weekend party to Arnold Goodman and seemed wholly unconvinced by Goodman's answer that he had been one of the guests and the principal occupations had been scrabble and croquet.[5] Peter Shore reported that the Prime Minister was "shaken to the core" and convinced everyone was plotting to get rid of him, while Callaghan was told by Wilson that Jenkins and Crosland were behind the conspiracy, which had been organised while he was in Moscow.[6] His suspicions lingered on; at the end of the year George Brown put forward the names of various young backbenchers whom he felt deserved promotion. "Wilson replied coldly that they had all been involved in the 'July plot'."[7]

What is evident is that, while Wilson was in Moscow, various members of the Cabinet discussed the desirability of devaluation and formed a rough-and-ready alliance to force it through. If they had succeeded and Wilson had felt so strongly on the issue that he had resigned rather than accept, they would not have been unduly concerned. The Prime Minister was not beloved or even trusted by a Cabinet which was still largely composed of people who had never been his supporters. But to oust him was not the prime object of the rebels. Crosland spoke for most of the former Gaitskellites when he told Benn that Wilson was gimmicky and had no idea of strategy but was "probably as good a peacetime P.M. as this country ever gets".[1] As was to be still more evident in 1967 and 1968, there was no one candidate behind whom an anti-Wilson faction could unite. Jenkins would never conspire to make Callaghan Prime Minister, nor Callaghan Jenkins; and neither man viewed with enthusiasm the possibility of putting George Brown in Number 10.

Callaghan told Benn that he was "extremely upset" at the suggestion that he had been conspiring to get rid of Harold. "I personally believe Jim: I just don't think he was conspiring," wrote Benn.[2] Brown knew he would never get anywhere. When urging Barbara Castle to join him in forcing devaluation through the Cabinet, he challenged her directly: "You wouldn't have me for Leader, would you?" "No," answered Castle emphatically.[3] Jenkins was the nearest approach to a credible alternative and the threat which Wilson took most seriously. When George Blake escaped from jail Wilson exclaimed rancorously: "That will do our Home Secretary a great deal of good. He is getting complacent and he needs taking down a peg."[4] Things even reached a point where, when Jenkins was about to address a Socialist Commentary meeting, "Marcia Williams and Gerald Kaufman . . . marched in looking like ill-disguised Special Branch officers at a subversive meeting, sat in the front row and opened their notebooks." After that, Jenkins tackled Wilson directly and was told that it was not him but his entourage of young MPs, notably Roy Hattersley, who were causing the Prime Minister concern.[5] But however active such dissidents might have been, Jenkins had no effective power-base within the party and Wilson knew, or should have known, that only the most improbable realignment of forces could at that point have turned him into a serious challenger for the leadership.

His reshuffle in the late summer of 1966 was designed to make that realignment yet more unlikely. It was provoked by an article in the *Guardian* on 23 July, stating that Callaghan intended to leave the Treasury for the Foreign Office; that, at Callaghan's insistence, the DEA would be wound up, and that Jenkins would go from the Home Office to the Treasury, to be replaced by Michael Stewart. Wilson was convinced that the story came from Callaghan and that, "if I carried out the *Guardian*'s instructions I would no longer be Prime Minister but taking orders from one of my colleagues". The article had assumed that Brown would be dismissed or pushed into some gilded sinecure; a step Wilson had contemplated after Brown's disastrous speech when winding up the economic debate on 20 July but which he now deferred. Instead he decided to move Brown to the Foreign Office as "a chance, a last chance, to rehabilitate himself and even put himself in the running for ultimate preferment". The fact that Brown was an ardent advocate of the Common Market made him no less suitable in Wilson's present mood. If he had made a success of his new job Wilson would have been surprised but not displeased; if, as seemed more likely, he made a spectacular botch of it, then the Prime Minister would axe him without any sense of guilt or fear that he was making a formidable enemy. Callaghan would be left where he was to expiate his sins. The DEA would not be wound up, but Michael Stewart would be sent there so as to ensure it was more closely under Wilson's control.[1]

Another striking change was the replacement of Bowden by Crossman as leader of the House of Commons. The appointment was "peculiar", said Shinwell, and "made on impulse"; Attlee had described Crossman to him as being a "clever fool ... no judgment, no common sense, no idea of how to deal with men".[2] He knew how to deal with Shinwell anyway, quickly manoeuvring him out of the chairmanship of the party, but was uncertain what else he was supposed to do. Wilson spoke vaguely of the need for "inventiveness and iconoclasm" in devising ways to keep the backbenchers busy,[3] but though Crossman was quite as inventive as and more iconoclastic than any of his colleagues he did not have much material to work with. Marcia Williams saw the dangers of a Crossman with time on his hands and little to do except make mischief. Since Wilson refused to let Crossman take over the chairmanship of some of the Cabinet committees, she suggested that he should be used to coordinate information from departments: 'I know you feel this makes him William Deedes, but clearly you will have to give way on some point ... Please don't let this be another in a long series of things you have started off and then lost interest in. You may particularly regret this one if you take that attitude. While Dick can be very usefully employed to bring all branches together, Government, Parliament and Transport House, if under-employed he could bring you down."[1] Beyond writing a terse "No" against Mrs Williams's suggestion Wilson does not seem to have responded directly to this minatory message. With John Silkin now installed as a liberalising Chief Whip, Crossman soon settled down to an active if not particularly constructive role. The only other change of moment was the replacement of Bottomley by Bowden at the Commonwealth Office. Bottomley's relationship with Smith had reached a level where he would be a liability if or when the time came to reopen negotiations over Rhodesia. Bowden would start from scratch and was anyway more emollient. The left viewed the change with some apprehension but otherwise it escaped attention in the excitement of the more dramatic moves.

"Really, I sometimes think Harold moves people around the chess board with complete frivolity," wrote Barbara Castle tartly.[2] Cynicism perhaps, frivolity no: Wilson's reshuffle was calculated to move Brown into a field remote from domestic politics and to isolate Callaghan. "What this would do would be to end a situation in which a Crown Prince was developing," he wrote with satisfaction. "There would now be six, Brown, Stewart, Bowden, Callaghan, Crossman (at least in the minds of the more imaginative Lobby correspondents) and Jenkins. Safety in numbers ... The doubt at the moment would be Callaghan's reaction since every move on the chess board meant check-mate for him."[3] Callaghan's immediate reaction was to revert to his complaints of a few months earlier about the uneasy demarcation between the Treasury and the DEA. He tackled the Prime Minister and found him still resentful of what he saw as the Chancellor's attempt to bounce him into giving him the Foreign Office, but ready to acquit him of taking part in the plot to depose him. If he fell under a bus, Callaghan would succeed him, said Wilson, adding, "Mind you, I take good care not to go near a bus nowadays." He promised that he would help work out a concordat between the two departments, but in the end did nothing about it. It was left to Stewart and Callaghan to work things out for themselves, a task which proved a great deal easier than when Brown had been involved. "Perhaps that was what the Prime Minister intended all along," reflected Callaghan.[4]

If Wilson had temporarily lost his grip after the economic crisis, he seemed to have recovered it by the autumn. He confronted the trade unions at Blackpool with an honesty that was almost brutal, ramming home the need to increase productivity and eliminate restrictive practices. It was "a difficult tight little speech," wrote Crossman, with no histrionics or playing to the gallery. "This time he was a Prime Minister coming to the Congress to put the fear of God into them, telling them what jolly well had to be done, making them acquiesce, asserting his authority."[1] The party conference a month later was a similar story. Wilson was not triumphantly acclaimed but he escaped without being severely mauled and he hit the headlines with a bravura display when he took on a mob of hostile demonstrators, mainly from the car industry. Wilson seized a microphone, harangued the protesters, persuaded them to send in a delegation to discuss their problems peacefully, listened with courtesy and argued his point of view with determination. It was the kind of confrontation at which he excelled. He left the conference to shouts of "Good old Harold" from those who had booed him earlier. Hugh Cudlipp found him "as always full of confidence; but I got the impression this time that the confidence was more solidly based". Cecil King accused Cudlipp of having fallen victim to Wilson's spellbinding – "He usually *says* the right things. His problem is that he does nothing"[2] – but the American Embassy was closer to Cudlipp than King in its assessment. Wilson, they reported, had recovered from the collapse of support in mid 1966. His position now seemed "reasonably if temporarily secure". He was "in effect on probation with the Party and the people", but the most immediate danger had been surmounted.[3]

Taking stock at the end of 1966, Wilson could legitimately congratulate himself that he had weathered the worst of the storm. Things had not gone well. The bright illusions of the immediate post-electoral period had faded; the National Plan had run aground; the social revolution to be financed by an industrial renaissance had strikingly failed to come about. But not all had been lost; Wilson could still point to solid achievements in education, regional development and the distribution of the national wealth. He was still very much at the helm; now it remained for him, if not to steer the ship in a radically new direction, then at least to prepare himself for the stormy and uncharted waters that lay ahead.

XIII

The Road to Devaluation

1967

When Wilson became Prime Minister, Crossman remarked, Mary had seemed "embittered and unhappy". Since then she had become one of the successes of the government and had created her own independent image in a way which never inspired her husband's jealousy because she was always "cool, collected and determined not to go beyond herself".[1] Whether she would have recognised herself in this rosy picture is doubtful; she still disliked life in Number 10 with its pomposity below and lack of privacy above, and looked forward with longing to her eventual liberation. But she had contrived to make her own life and resolutely refused to be overawed or even affected by her surroundings. Crossman, having late-night supper after a ministerial meeting, was confronted by tinned salmon emptied into a potato dish with the tin still on the table, with toast and apricot jam to follow.[2] When Crosland lunched in the flat the cooking was done – badly, he considered – by the Wilsons' housekeeper. It consisted of pork chops dished up with a mountain of vegetables. Marcia was also there and Mary popped in once or twice. "No one could say that Harold is the most elevated conversationalist ... Really all he wants to do is chitter-chatter."[3]

Wilson enjoyed every aspect of Number 10, relished the formality of the state rooms but had no intention of adapting his personal tastes to suit the ethos of the building. He appeared almost invariably relaxed and affable. One morning he sent for his detective and complained that a policeman had been singing on Horseguards Parade at 5.00 a.m. that morning: "I know a policeman is on duty there. I know no policeman would desert his post. I know a policeman would stop anybody else singing. Therefore it was the policeman singing. I've nothing against singing policemen. Mary and I have seen *The Pirates of Penzance* many times. But not at 5 a.m." Later on a police car with flashing lights raced by: "Late for choir practice, I assume," said Wilson.[1] He was unruffled when the not unequivocally laudatory obituary of him written by Tom Driberg for *The Times* was leaked and appeared in *Private Eye*. The editor, William Rees-Mogg, wrote to apologise. It was of no importance, said Wilson, "although naturally I hope that this particular obituary will require further up-datings over many years to come".[2]

He enjoyed sharing Number 10 with constituents or other visitors. Barbara Castle arrived to find a flag-seller for the blind and a blind former soldier talking to the Prime Minister in the hall. "They were delighted with their few words with him, and since there were no press or photographers there, it *must* mean that he has a naturally kind heart."[3] He continued to adorn official receptions with celebrities from the world of sport or show business; at one party in 1970 attended *inter alia* by Cliff Michelmore, Iris Murdoch and More-cambe and Wise, he was heard to say proudly: "There are people here from all walks of life – artists, musicians, sculptors. Jack Kennedy's parties at the White House had nothing on this."[4] Sometimes such enterprises turned sour. He refused an invitation to dinner from David Frost, minuting crossly: "Last time I accepted it was on strict understanding no publicity. Yet Press had it before I was back at No. 10 and ran it as Wilson giving it."[5] In spite of this he had no intention of breaking off his relationship with Frost, nor would Marcia Williams have let him do so without a fight. When the Yugoslav Prime Minister visited London, Marcia wrote: "I wish him [Frost] to remain friendly and I wish him to be at the Yugoslav Reception – even dinner if possible ... Clearly Wednesday or Thursday are better for him and I shall be grateful if the office could make sure that the Yugoslav No. 10 function takes place during that part of the week." Wilson saw the point: "Yes, but can't change date," he replied. "I tried Wed but he is already booked."[6] So vigorous an effort to accommodate a television personality may seem incongruous, but Wilson revered success, whether in the field of business or entertainment, and few successes were, in their way, more resounding than that of David Frost.

He was touchingly keen to honour Laurence Olivier. When offering him a peerage he stressed, as was his wont, that he was doing so because he felt the actor could do a useful job in the House of Lords. To his dismay Olivier refused. At once Wilson back-pedalled. The suggestion that the actor could do a useful job did not mean that any serious labours were expected. A very occasional speech on some suitably theatrical occasion would be more than enough.

Anniversaries and family celebrations meant much to him. He marked his fifty-sixth birthday by taking Mary to a matinee of *Hello Dolly*: "He spent the rest of his birthday whistling and singing tunes from it."[1] When he went to Oxford to see his son Robin get his degree, Crossman thought him "looking ten years younger ... all that pontifical statesmanship off him, nice and fresh just as I knew him before".[2] The fact that Robin had got a First gave his father great pleasure, as did Robin's marriage in Dawlish. Michael Stewart was present and noted that the crowds were thick and enthusiastic in spite of the heavy rain. This, he concluded hopefully, showed "the personal esteem in which Harold was held, despite the Government's difficulties".[3]

The Isles of Scilly continued to be a cherished centre of family life. In November 1967 Wilson was invited to become an Honorary Elder Brother of Trinity House. He accepted with alacrity and requested a flag, which he flew from a pole outside his bungalow in St John's. The captain of the ferry, the *Scillonian*, also flew the flag whenever Wilson made the journey from Penzance to his island home. At Chequers it was more difficult to keep work at bay, though Wilson usually managed to spend two or three hours each weekend playing golf with Marcia Williams's brother, Tony Field. In spite of his love of the house, he seemed to Crossman to perch as an uneasy guest whenever he was there, anxious in no way to transgress the limits of what he could properly do. When Mrs Castle had to be got home late at night after a long meeting, Wilson did not send for an official car but routed his son out of bed to drive her.[4]

Paddy, his golden labrador, had no such inhibitions. He had not merely chewed up two leather leads and various shoes, blankets and rugs but, wrote a dismayed housekeeper, "completely destroyed some new kitchen corridor matting, after only a fortnight's use. I hope that the Prime Minister will be willing to pay the cost of renewal." Marcia Williams was sceptical: "Am I to take it, since you ask for £27.4s, that Paddy destroyed 23 yds of vinyl floor covering 27" wide and 3 vinyl mats? It does seem rather a lot for one dog."[5] But Paddy had done just that, and incurred other expenses too, by roaming the countryside and having to be rescued and returned by the local Dog Rescue Society. Nothing shook the Prime Minister's affection for his dog but Paddy caused much irritation to those who had to tidy up after his various outrages.

The entourage at Number 10 remained broadly constant: Marcia Williams and Tommy Balogh; Shore and Kaufman; Michael Halls, the private secretary, and Michael Palliser, the supremely competent and professional man from the Foreign Office. Balogh was the most at risk. The civil servants loathed and resented him, and though Wilson appreciated his effervescence and endless fecundity, he was frequently irritated by his importunities. Balogh railed against the "iniquitous" decision of Brown and Callaghan not to offer export subsidies and demanded that Wilson reopen the question. "I really have done all that is justified," replied Wilson in mild exasperation. "I stopped it twice and left it to arbitration ... If I were to refuse to accept it now I might as well sack all the Ministers and run everything myself."[1] It was Burke Trend who finally brought the full weight of the establishment to bear on the problem of Balogh's future, convincing Wilson that the economist was so disruptive of good order as to be a serious liability. Wilson spent two hours trying to persuade Balogh that it was his own idea that he should return to Oxford – "The fact is Harold can't stand people being hurt," wrote Crossman resignedly – but signally failed.[2] In fact Balogh remained for another fourteen months and then it was the demands of the university rather than the civil service which took him from Whitehall. Wilson continued to see him and to ask his advice; as likely as ever to ignore it but feeling deprived without access to the unpredictable brilliance of this awkward, blundering yet strikingly talented man.

Marcia Williams was Balogh's most ardent champion. Bowden and Short felt that, after the 1966 election and the departure of Derek Mitchell, her power was in the ascendant and she made it ever more apparent.[3] Conciliating her was Wilson's usual practice and he would often give way to her on matters which he felt to be of minor importance, not necessarily because he thought she was right but for the sake of a quiet life. Crossman found himself endowed with a junior minister whom he felt unsuitable and, knowing he would never be able to alter Wilson's decision himself, deputed Marcia to do it. The appointment was annulled.[4] The Prime Minister was as ready to spring to his political secretary's defence as to bow to her opinions. He wrote indignantly to Willie Hamilton about a *Private Eye* article which alleged she had refused to undergo positive vetting by the security service: "Marcia was so vetted in 1964, reviewed in 1969 and is now being re-reviewed."[1] But though her influence showed no signs of waning, in Benn's view her judgment was less sure. "She is now almost a courtier in a fading court," he wrote early in 1969; and the fact that the court was fading, he believed, was in part her doing.[2]

Wilson had started his new government very much in control of his public image. Two disparate incidents demonstrate his mastery of the techniques by which his reputation for energy and forcefulness was projected through the media. To refer to the Aberfan disaster in such a context is perhaps unjust to him. There can be no doubting the sincerity of the appalled horror with which he heard the news of the collapse of a pit mound and the burying of the village school with 116 children inside, nor the dismay he experienced as he walked around the shattered village and talked to the bereaved. Everyone who saw him at the time attested to his grief.[3] But he also relished the dramatic role of the Prime Minister who arrives from the skies, sweeping away every bureaucratic barrier that might be put in the way of those charged with the rescue, pledging full support to the survivors and an immediate enquiry. He had the same satisfaction at less cost in human suffering when the supertanker *Torrey Canyon* ran aground off the Isles of Scilly and threatened to shed enough oil to cause one of the world's most fearsome ecological disasters. Wilson was soon on the spot, taking personal command, authorising the RAF bombers to go in, watching the onslaught from the coastguard tower. In fact he played a perfectly sensible and constructive role, but contrived to appear faintly absurd in the eyes of the more cynical among his colleagues. Wilson "adores being in action – acting as the great commander organising his forces", wrote Crossman.[4]

But the excellent relationship he had established with the media did not survive far into 1966. He believed himself to be the victim of a deliberate campaign to bring down his government, planned and executed by the Tory press magnates who were resolved that the election of 1966 must not be followed by another Labour victory. This was not wholly unjust, but Wilson contributed vigorously to the process and in part initiated it. He could not accept that the press had no obligation to support a government which was doing unpopular things or seemed to be making a mess of its policies. He had gone out of his way to oblige them; when things went wrong, surely they should do the same for him? Arnold Goodman tried to persuade him that it was impossible to bank credit with the press, every day began with a clean slate; Wilson persisted in believing that, if successfully wooed, they would stay won. When journalists criticised him severely over Rhodesia or, later and more forcibly, devaluation, Wilson began to grumble about the treachery of Lobby correspondents and to question their honesty and professional capacity. The political correspondent of *The Times*, David Wood, incurred his particular displeasure and he told the new proprietor, Lord Thomson, that he ought to sack him. The editor's very proper response was to promote Wood to political editor, but this merely encouraged the Prime Minister to renew the assault.[1] In May 1967 he indulged in what Barbara Castle described as an "astonishing outburst" against *The Times* for its reporting of the PLP's attitude towards Europe: "Frankly, I was appalled. I think Harold is getting quite pathological about the press."[2] Even worse than Wood, however, was Nora Beloff of the *Observer*, who outraged the Prime Minister by speculating in her column about the political role of the kitchen cabinet and in particular of Marcia Williams. David Astor, the editor, was summoned to the House of Commons (though Goodman persuaded him to announce that it was *he* who had sought the interview). Wilson brought out a file of Nora Beloff's articles, with the offending paragraphs marked in red, and complained that it was scurrilous to treat his political secretary in such a way. Astor retorted that Beloff was only reporting a matter of political importance that was already being discussed by backbenchers. As it happened Beloff was anyway due for a posting to Washington. So that the Prime Minister should not imagine that she was being taken off her London job because of his criticisms, Astor followed up his visit with a letter making it plain that he fully supported Beloff and that she would be returning to the London job before long.[3]

It was the D-Notice affair that did almost irreparable damage to Wilson's relationship with the press. The D-Notice was a device for preventing the publication in the press of material judged to be damaging to national security. When the *Daily Express* carried a story about official interception of international cables, Wilson at once denounced this in the House of Commons as being "sensationalised and inaccurate" and published in open defiance of the D-Notice system.[4] Too late, he discovered that the matter was not as clear cut as he had supposed; at lunch with the journalist Chapman

Pincher, the D-Notice secretary, Colonel Sammy Lohan, had indicated
that, though he would prefer the piece not to be published, to do so
would not necessarily be in breach of an order. Under pressure from
Heath, the Prime Minister agreed to the setting up of a committee of
Privy Councillors under Lord Radcliffe to enquire into the matter.
Some four months later the committee reported in terms which acquit-
ted the *Daily Express* of anything more than mild indiscretion. Wilson
had so far only been guilty of precipitancy and a failure properly to
consult the government's law officers; now he compounded his original rashness by an uncharacteristic display of truculence. He insisted
on issuing a White Paper[1] which challenged the committee's findings
and maintained that there had been a witting breach of the D-Notice
system; Lohan's incompetence, it was suggested, had mitigated but
by no means excused the newspaper's delinquency. His report could
not be "rejected" in this way, Radcliffe protested: "You might say
you did not agree with the result of the Cup Final and that the referee
had given the wrong decision. But it would not be much use saying
you rejected it – even if you had a loyal vote to support you."[2]

Some of Wilson's supporters were far from loyal. Most of his
Cabinet were disquieted, some were appalled. Castle and Crossman
grumbled together: "The evil genius had once again been George
Wigg – 'Harold's Rasputin'. George Brown had pleaded with Harold
not to take this line – so had Burke Trend – but he was adamant ...
'He is going off his rocker,' I said, and Dick agreed."[3] A combination
of obstinacy, genuine concern for national security and fury against
Pincher and Lohan seem to have been the principal factors. Together
they betrayed him into behaviour which he himself later described as
"heavy-handed and over-hurried" and as being "one of my costliest
mistakes".[4] The cost was the resentment of almost the entire national
press. Wilson realised only too well the damage he had done. "I think
we should play things very slowly for the next three months to see
how the Press react," he told his press secretary, Trevor Lloyd-Hughes,
in July 1967. "At the present, still infected by D-Notices, they are
warmly hostile: they may get over it. But we must in no circs run
after them. 3 months of cold but correct relations will stimulate those
on the Press ... who will realise cold war can't continue. Certainly
we need to rethink lobby questions."[5]

Of course, as all Prime Ministers must, Wilson did run after the
press. The "White Commonwealth" system, by which a little group
of favoured Lobby correspondents was cosseted with particular atten-

tion, was a direct response to the furore caused by the D-Notice affair. It worked to a limited extent, but after 1967 it was never to be glad, confident morning again. Ten years later, according to Chapman Pincher, he and Wilson met in George Weidenfeld's house. "What a pity we fell out over the D-Notice business," said Wilson. "It was all my fault, and I'm very sorry about it."[1]

His relationship with the BBC was not much happier. His obsession with the BBC and with leaks from the Cabinet were "his most outstanding weaknesses as a leader", judged Crossman; "He is obsessed with the mass media," complained Benn, when he had ranted in Cabinet about the way he had been treated on radio.[2] He did not go so far as Benn in believing that state control was desirable – "Gurus should remain on the Wolverhampton circuit," he minuted, thus comparing the extremism of Enoch Powell with Benn's intemperate views on government intervention[3] – but he was certainly not beyond bringing pressure to bear to ensure that the BBC behaved as he felt was proper. A fence-building visit by Hugh Greene and the chairman, Lord Normanbrook, to Number 10 shortly after the 1966 election did little except highlight the points of difference,[4] and when Normanbrook retired Wilson decided to put in, if not his own man, then at least one whom he thought would share his views. His first idea was to appoint the former Herbert Bowden, now Lord Aylestone; when Aylestone refused, he turned to the chairman of Independent Television, Charles Hill, the former Radio Doctor. Such an appointment, remarked Normanbrook's deputy, Robert Lusty, was like Churchill inviting Rommel to command the Eighth Army at El Alamein.[5] Almost everyone in the BBC was apprehensive; but Rommel donned his new uniform with disconcerting enthusiasm and Wilson soon found that his nominee was as determined to protect the corporation's independence as ever Normanbrook had been.

The Prime Minister's reaction was to crack the financial whip. In March 1968 he declared that he was "allergic to any increase in BBC revenue". What the corporation should do was make itself more efficient. Could not the *Radio Times* and the *TV Times* be amalgamated, with all the profits going to the BBC? "One should also examine whether the public ought to go on subsidising the issue of *The Listener*, which I understand is losing heavily. We do not subsidise other newspapers or periodicals."[6] His objurgations had little effect. Early in 1969 he protested furiously about a biased report of his meeting with President Nixon in which he was accused of "overt importuning". Would any BBC employee, he asked "have been allowed to mount such a programme ... on Harold Macmillan or any of my other predecessors?"[1] From time to time he certainly was treated with unprecedented roughness. A comedy programme posed the question of how one could tell whether Wilson was lying. The answer was: "If one can see his lips move." Wilson protested, an apology was made, but the joke was repeated on another programme. A libel action was threatened and Hill called at Number 10 to try to make peace. He found Wilson "intensely suspicious of the BBC, even regarding it as a conspiracy against him and his government", but at least the Prime Minister dropped the idea of the libel action.[2]

And so the quarrel grumbled on, with periodic eruptions when the Prime Minister felt himself particularly misused. In December 1969 Wilson berated Hill for not allowing him to broadcast on the evening of a day in which he had spoken in the House of Commons: "He was utterly disheartened by his present relationship with the BBC and saw no way out of it." Hill said that Wilson's remarks filled him with despair. There was no conspiracy against the Prime Minister; he was describing a corporation Hill did not recognise. "I am describing the facts," Wilson retorted.[3] The electoral campaign of 1970 was poisoned for Wilson by the conviction that he was being misrepresented or ignored by the BBC. The corporation employee in charge of the arrangements to broadcast the Prime Minister's speech at Swindon reported to Number 10 that a scaffold was being erected for his convenience. The use of this slightly ambiguous phrase confirmed Marcia Williams's worst suspicions. Since the Prime Minister preferred to speak from a window, she retorted, a gallows would not be called for. The BBC had the last laugh when the sash of the window broke and Wilson had to speak with it resting heavily on his shoulders.[4]

Wilson's other obsession, with leaks from the Cabinet, was little less destructive. Certainly both issues took up an altogether disproportionate amount of his time and energies. He told the Lord Chancellor that leaks constantly preoccupied him: "We gave the subject a good airing this morning but it is one on which frequent reminders to our colleagues seem necessary."[5] The trouble was that his colleagues were convinced – with considerable justification – that many of the worst leaks came from Number 10. Jay complained that even when he slipped in through the Cabinet Office so as to have a private word with the Prime Minister, the fact was reported in the newspapers next day: "By 1967 a belief had spread ... that information, however confidential, given to No. 10 might find its way somehow to the press staff, who seemed to be a law unto themselves."[1] In view of this, members of the Cabinet were indignant when Wilson instructed the Lord Chancellor to interrogate them so as to establish who was responsible for a leak. On another occasion Roy Jenkins flatly refused to fill in a questionnaire probing into every contact he had made over the relevant period.[2]

Wilson strayed into another minefield when he tried to impose on the Cabinet the recommendations of the Committee on Ministerial Publications. Barbara Castle found the proposal "that the Secretary of the Cabinet should have the right to dictate deletions or amendments quite intolerable. Advice and a sense of responsibility are one thing: censorship another." Crossman was equally disgusted. At a time when, with Wilson's blessing, Crossman was trying to liberalise the PLP it appalled him "that members of a Socialist Cabinet should be wasting their time on trying to compel each other to be honourable men ... I cannot possibly either give a written undertaking or accept the censorship of any civil servant."[3]

Such strident sensibilities did not make for harmony in Cabinet. Marsh, who joined the Cabinet after the 1966 election, wrote that he had "never worked among a group of people who disliked and distrusted each other quite as much as that band of brothers".[4] Any group of powerful personalities, frequently in competition with each other, is likely to breed discord, but Wilson's Cabinet did seem peculiarly prone both to individual vendettas and to factional battles – between university intellectuals and proletarian union-members; devaluers and the champions of sterling; Europeans and anti-Europeans. So quick were the press to assume dissension that Wilson would hurry up discussion so that the Cabinet would finish by 1.00 p.m. and avoid giving any impression of prolonged and therefore acrimonious debate.[5] Nor was the atmosphere in political circles around the Cabinet any more healthy. Wigg was accused by Crossman of having "reviled and slandered" him when talking to Tom Driberg. The conversation, retorted Wigg, "was no different in character to the hundreds of courteous, well-intentioned exchanges which took place between Members of all parties every day".[1] Give or take an adjective or two, he was probably right. Wilson himself, though one of the most adept of conciliators when he wanted to be, did little to ease the tension. Paul Johnson once asked him why he never had other ministers – except for a few cronies – round after work for a drink and to talk things over. "I have to spend all day with those horrible people," exclaimed Wilson. "Do you think I want to spend the evenings too?"[2]

When Wilson was on a visit to Ottawa and George Brown left in charge it was remarked that business was settled far more quickly. Everyone agreed, recorded Castle, "that Harold spins things out something terrible, interjecting a commentary of his own between every speech". Douglas Houghton pleaded that Wilson enjoyed listening too. "I said he conducted Cabinet like a don at an interesting tutorial."[3] Such criticism was fair as far as it went. Wilson often seemed a weak or prolix chairman. But what Castle was ignoring was the uncommon skill with which he used apparent verbosity or irresolution as tools to achieve his ends. No one was a better judge of how long a discussion should be allowed to ramble on before inertia and exhaustion supervened; no one could terminate it more effectively at the first moment when it was possible to sum up in the way which had been intended all along. Time and again his colleagues belittled his arguments and condemned his feebleness; yet at the end of the day it emerged that his view had prevailed. The business might have been transacted more rapidly under Brown but the meeting would also have been more likely to end in irreconcilable deadlock. A more valid criticism of Wilson's chairmanship was that he was so preoccupied by immediate issues that he allowed no time for strategic planning; he "doesn't believe in that," wrote Benn, "neither do the Civil Service; if they can keep Ministers busy, so much the better".[4] When Roy Jenkins complained that there was no long-term plan for any part of the government's policies, Crossman maintained that Wilson did have certain long-term objectives – on housing, or the special relationship – but agreed that he was an "opportunist, always moving in zig-zags, darting with no sense of direction but making the best of each position he adopts".[5]

Both Healey and Crossman accused Wilson of packing his Cabinet with toadies and yes-men, so as to ensure that the majority would be on his side.[6] The presence of both these turbulent spirits in his Cabinet, not to mention Jenkins, Benn, Castle, Brown, Callaghan, Jay, Cousins and others, suggests that if he really tried to have a Cabinet of yes-men he was remarkably unsuccessful. Indeed, it was largely because the more prominent members of his team were so far from being toadies that he tried to avoid having any sort of inner Cabinet where he could be more easily overborne by their pressure. The subject was discussed at a particularly lively meeting with Brown and Callaghan in November 1967. Wilson recorded their conversation. He said that he had been thinking of forming an inner Cabinet, whereupon Brown said that this was what he had constantly asked for, but had never been able to get the Prime Minister to consider. Then they turned to its ideal membership. Stewart was dismissed as being over the hill. Healey was accepted. The name of Jenkins provoked an explosion from Callaghan who maintained that he was the arch plotter who had tried to destroy each member of the leading triumvirate in turn. Jenkins, he claimed, was as far over the hill as Stewart. He put forward Crosland as an alternative. Crossman was accepted as being needed to corral the left but Castle talked too much. Fred Peart could be included as a counter-weight to Healey but Ray Gunter was dismissed as a leaker (a striking accusation given the characteristics of the three protagonists).

To Wilson's mild consternation, the conversation then turned to the subject of the succession at Number 10. Brown, who was by this time

pretty high ... repeated that he was not a candidate for the succession. I said that there was no vacancy. Jim said, quite, and that he had reached the limit of his ambitions – an elementary schoolboy who had become Chancellor ... They then started talking about what would happen if I got under a bus. I said that I had no intention of so going and that I thought this was very morbid. George was too excited to be put off (I had received a message from Palliser to say that Thomas [Balogh] was in the Private Office outside and would we keep our voices down. Later I heard that Thomas had asked who was that woman in there. The woman was in fact George screaming). George asked Jim if he would stand if I did get under a bus. Jim said yes. And George said who did he think would stand against him, because George would not. Jim said, Roy. George was anxious to know whether Jim thought he could beat Roy and sharply reminded Jim that if he didn't this would be Jim's second defeat, and like Adlai he could not then run again. I called them to order, wanting to sum up the meeting, and protesting my health and virility ... As Jim was going George asked if he could stay behind and speak to me. He said, do not trust Jim, he is after your job. I had learnt a great deal about human nature.[1]

After this somewhat unpropitious airing it was unsurprising that the idea of an inner Cabinet languished for a time. Brown continued to press for it, however, and in April 1968 Wilson succumbed to the extent of creating a "Parliamentary Committee" of ten members which would not take decisions but would, it was hoped, give a more coherent political direction to the work of the government. In Crossman's view, the Prime Minister never thought it particularly useful or tried to make it work and many years later Wilson told the Commons Expenditure Committee that he did not think it had been a good idea.[2] It lingered on doing nothing very much until April 1969, when the circumstances of the moment forced him to accept the *de facto* existence of a smaller and more powerful group;[3] this initiative in its turn foundered on the rivalries and jealousies of those concerned and the reluctance of Wilson to expose himself to the pressure of his nearest rivals.

His relationship with the PLP was often quite as turbulent. Crossman saw Wilson as being torn between the traditional, disciplinarian approach of Wigg and Callaghan and the more libertarian attitude of Crossman himself and Silkin.[4] Wilson's personal predilections were strongly towards the latter; his tendency was to leave the private member as nearly as possible in freedom while demanding loyalty from ministers. When promoted in 1968 David Owen said to Wilson: "But I've been one of your harshest critics." "Well, you won't be able to be one any more," said Wilson with some satisfaction.[5] But certain subjects – notably defence, Vietnam and the prices and incomes policy – so divided the party that Wilson found his liberal instincts at variance with the needs of a Prime Minister who had to maintain a united front in the House of Commons. It was the last of those issues, on which Callaghan's support was not to be counted, that caused the Prime Minister most concern. Wilson was "wild", Crossman noted as early as February 1967, because Callaghan was trimming on prices and incomes so as to win trade union votes at the party conference.[6] "Relations between the two men do not appear to be close," reported the American Embassy at the same period, though Wilson seemed to be comfortably in the ascendant. "To many, he *is* the Labor Party and its fortunes are dependent on his own success."[7]

His ascendancy seemed less marked as the TUC and NEC united

in opposition to any sort of incomes control. Crossman described him "pacing up and down in what was for him real dismay".[1] The union leaders went to Number 10 at the end of February to discuss incomes policy. Wilson and Stewart poured cold water on their ideas for a voluntary policy; the unionists were no less emphatic in denouncing any sort of statutory control. A clash between party and unions seemed a real possibility; the question was whether the party would remain united in such a confrontation. Before the test could come, however, a dangerous public split became evident in the field of defence. Dissatisfied by what they felt to be inadequate spending cuts, particularly east of Suez, sixty-two left-wing MPS abstained on the government's defence White Paper. Wilson decided to face the rebels down at a meeting of the PLP. Crossman found him putting the finishing touches to his speech: "He was infatuated with its toughness – nobody had ever talked like this to the Party before, he said."[2] It contained one remark that remained to haunt him for years thereafter: every dog, he said, was allowed one bite, but if it became a habit then its owner might have doubts about renewing its licence. It was an impromptu remark that surprised his staff as much as the PLP; Wilson claimed when he got back to Downing Street that he had slipped it in as a piece of light relief. It was not seen as such by the libertarians: offensive, complained Benn, "it was very insulting to imply that we were all dogs and he was our trainer"; "so crude it is difficult to understand how Harold could have so lost his touch", was Barbara Castle's verdict; while Michael Foot found it "deplorable".[3]

Crossman was dismayed because he feared the speech might herald a return to draconian party discipline. Wilson had promised that he would back him against the reactionary party chairman, Emanuel Shinwell, but he had delayed in acting, with the result that the confidence the new regime had built up had been shattered. Shinwell was boasting openly of "the breakdown of the new liberal regime", moaned Crossman. Wigg and the party chairman had triumphed. Even if Wilson felt "disinclined to throw a colleague to the wolves, I am now resolved to throw myself ... unless of course Manny goes". "Tell Dick not to be so bloody daft," was the Prime Minister's terse instruction to Marcia Williams when these complaints reached his desk.[4] She did so, more or less in those terms, and sure enough it was Shinwell who resigned a few weeks later. It was not the only occasion that Wilson found himself coping with the fall-out from Crossman's susceptibilities. In October 1967 the Duke of Norfolk wrote in dismay to report that Crossman proposed to absent himself from the State Opening of Parliament because of "his anti-monarchical views". It was not so at all, replied Wilson. "Mr Crossman has told me that he has a certain phobia about participating in processions," but he still expected to be there. The phobia was overcome and the procession did not have to take place without the Lord President's participation.[1]

Not all the left were so easy to cajole back into line. Sydney Silverman wrote to the Chief Whip, copying his letter to the press, to denounce Wilson's speech to the PLP as "the most dangerous attack on social democracy ever made in this country in my time" (which, coming from a Jew who had lived through the Battle of Britain, was quite something). He did not write to Wilson himself, he said, because the Prime Minister was "too sure he is right, too contemptuous of other people's opinions". He disagreed with Wilson on a wide range of topics, but above all on the proposed statutory incomes policy where the government proposed "the abandonment of a clear socialist principle in favour of something very like a Fascist principle".[2] Few were as extreme in their condemnation as Silverman, but even staunch friends like Barbara Castle were ill at ease. When she, Benn, Balogh and Shore met at Crossman's house, the latter suggested that Marcia Williams should also be invited in case Wilson became suspicious. "Barbara blew up. 'He pushes his friends to one side,' she said. 'He takes us for granted and appeases our enemies. The only way to impress Harold is to make him fearful. We ought to let him know we are sitting together and discussing what to do.'"[3] When the by-elections and county council elections in April 1967 proved calamitous for Labour, Foot remarked sourly that Wilson's achievement was supposed to have been that he had captured the middle ground: "Well, maybe Labour did capture the middle ground, and lost the rest ... You can't run the Labour party without a militant rank and file. It is not more machinery we want, it is light and heat."[4]

While 1967 was marked by the increasing disaffection of the left, it saw too the emergence of Roy Jenkins as a threat from the right. In May Jenkins began to demand a clearer statement of Labour's aims and an unequivocal commitment to economic growth.[5] In July Crossman had described Jenkins as the man "Harold ... detests and whose influence he really hates in the Cabinet".[6] Hatred and detestation are strong words – more Crossmanlike than Wilsonian – and though Wilson undoubtedly looked askance at Jenkins's ambitions, for most of the time he admired and quite liked him. But liking is not a powerful consideration in politics and his feelings would certainly not have prevented Wilson pushing his rival to the wolves if the chance had occurred. With Jenkins taking his own line, Callaghan making a pitch for the union vote and Brown resigning at monthly intervals, it must have seemed to Wilson that he was cruelly beleaguered.

In such circumstances he could not afford to put a foot wrong, nor did he often take even the most unimportant step without considering all the political implications. Ken Dodd asked him to send a suitable message for National Laughter Week. He said that he had also approached Ted Heath. How unfortunate it would be, said Marcia Williams, if Heath replied and Wilson did not. "Better not," Wilson minuted. "Suppose I answer and he doesn't?"[1]

Not every issue could be so easily disposed of. In 1967 the former Tory minister Anthony Nutting wrote a book about the Suez crisis in which he was fiercely critical of the government's handling of the matter. He had been a junior minister in the Foreign Office at the time and made use of some privileged information to expose the double-dealing with the Israelis and the French. There was obvious advantage to the Labour Party in the book's publication, Wilson told Trend, "but this is not and should not be the test, and any gains of that kind would be bought at a heavy price in terms of the general conduct of public life". He felt he should discuss the matter with Macmillan and perhaps Heath, with a view to making a joint approach to the author or the publisher. "Intervention will be known, whether we succeed or not. The publishers would hardly keep it secret, and if they did the fact that *The Times* have the serial rights would be certain to lead to a big news story. Since Rees-Mogg would probably like to characterise me in a '1984' capacity (even though this is about Suez!) I should be much reinforced if the decision were made jointly with, or after consultation with, Macmillan or Heath." There were few sanctions to be invoked, whether the Tory leaders cooperated or not. The Queen could be asked to remove Nutting from the Privy Council. Legislation was another possibility "but this would be extremely difficult and might have the effect of ruling out memoirs such as those of Churchill, Attlee and others ... On the present case I am not hopeful that Nutting will prove to be a gentleman. He has gone too far ... Being realistic, my guess is he will go ahead whatever we do or threaten to do. It may be also that our attempt to suppress it will lead to the whole affair being more sensationalised and will draw far more attention to the book. But the real problem here is precedence and all this may be worth it if we are able to get some sort of solution for the future."[1]

Wilson's attitude to this problem, with its keen perception both of the public good and of private or political advantage, and the whole issue permeated with a fusty but none the less authentic sense of basic decency, is typical of the man. The same spirit coloured his reply to Michael Stewart when the latter raised that recurrent Labour hobby-horse, the national minimum wage. "This could be a very useful ingredient in any settlement," reflected Wilson – and so was politically desirable. "It would be of the utmost value in dealing with the social ... problems of the lower-paid worker" – it was a good thing to do. But the cost would be some £300 million; "it would therefore have to be part of the settlement that the total increase in incomes over the year for all those not on the minimum wage would have to be correspondingly reduced" – the national interest demanded that benevolence be tempered with discretion.[2] Barbara Castle observed him with mingled affection and dismay as he argued the pros and cons of devaluation at Chequers in July 1967. "He is *not* just a cynical schemer," she concluded. "He has his own clear views and principles: he is not afraid to defy orthodox opinions or the Establishment. At the same time he is very pragmatic, not stirred by great ideals. And he is terribly tempted to find *ad hoc* solutions, at which he is very good."[3]

Certainly no great ideals were involved in the Cabinet reshuffle of August 1967. At the back of Wilson's mind was the conviction that Brown would soon resign for good and that he would then need Stewart back at the Foreign Office. He played with the idea of expediting this process by appointing Brown Ambassador to the European Community with his residence safely in Brussels.[4] In the meantime he moved Stewart to a coordinating role and himself took charge of the DEA, with Peter Shore promoted to Secretary of State to assist him. Houghton and Jay were the two leading casualties; both, ostensibly at least, on grounds of age. Houghton was sixty-nine but felt that he still had a useful role to play and was to prove a dangerous enemy to Wilson as chairman of the Parliamentary Labour Party. Jay, who was only sixty, was convinced that he was being dismissed because of his outspoken opposition to the Common Market. This consideration may have been an element in Wilson's thinking, but if it had been the principal factor he would surely not simultaneously have promoted Shore, whose opposition to British entry was quite as heartfelt and little if at all less vociferous than that of Jay. Wilson broke the news to Jay in the first-class waiting room at Plymouth railway station. His detective remarked that the Prime Minister seemed more upset after the interview than he had ever seen him. Knowing how Wilson hated to sack people, his staff had brought along a bottle of brandy, and the Prime Minister consoled himself with a couple of glasses as he moved on from Plymouth to London.[1]

Wilson was convinced that the reshuffle was a masterpiece of party management. There were now seven potential Chancellors, he told Crossman; Jenkins was no longer the only alternative to Callaghan. It was "one of the most successful political operations that's ever been conducted ... I've completely foxed them all." His taking over of the DEA was "the greatest coup ever".[2] He told Castle that getting any reaction out of Stewart during his tenure of the DEA had been "like throwing darts into cotton wool"; he had no intention of changing policies, but wanted to make sure that the policies were energetically carried out.[3] He took his new role seriously, cancelling a long-arranged visit to Canada because "the additional direct responsibilities in the economic field which I have now shouldered ... are likely to affect my programme during the next few months."[4] But it was a high-risk policy. There could be no one else to blame if the economy failed to expand. Hugh Cudlipp thought the move arose from a mixture of defiance and vanity, "but now he has taken the hot seat he will be made to sit on it".[5] Samuel Brittan remarked that in retrospect the change seemed to have been mainly a device for promoting the inexperienced Peter Shore.[6] Bringing Shore forward was certainly part of Wilson's plan, but the real enthusiasm he felt for the DEA and the philosophy of state intervention in the industrial sphere was in itself enough to explain a last, half-despairing effort to get the show on the road again.

Some evidence of progress was urgently needed. The disastrous string of by-election losses continued into the autumn. The replacement of Lord Carron by the hard-left Hugh Scanlon as leader of the Amalgamated Engineering Union (AEU) meant that the balance of power in the TUC swung strongly away from its traditionally moderate position. The party conference at Scarborough in October 1967 was a personal success for Wilson, but one in which he gave many hostages to fortune in the form of proud words about what had been done and was being done under Labour to help the sick, the old, the children and the socially deprived. "Sooner or later, probably sooner," noted Cousins, "delegates will realise that Harold promised the jam before the fruit harvest has set."[1] Even before Cousins aired this opinion an economic storm had blown up which threatened not merely to destroy the harvest but to uproot half the trees as well.

Since the crisis of September 1966, comparative stability had returned to the British economic scene. In the spring of 1967 sterling was strong, trade in surplus, bank rate down to 6 per cent. Callaghan's cautious budget did nothing to destroy the belief that recovery had arrived. It was the Middle East war of June, with the closure of the Suez Canal, and the Nigerian civil war, which simultaneously cut off oil supplies from Britain's only other short-haul source, that sent oil prices soaring. Sterling was soon in trouble again, and when Wilson's takeover of the DEA was followed by a string of reflationary measures – relaxation of hire-purchase restrictions, a halt in the closure of uneconomic coal mines, new subsidies for firms in areas of unemployment – the pessimists took it for granted that a crisis was imminent. Wilson was an optimist, but his opinion was not very different. He even told Crosland in October that he had an absolutely open mind on devaluation: "The trouble with Harold is that one hasn't the faintest idea whether the bastard means what he says even at the moment he says it."[2] Strikes in the docks and on the railways, which defied the Prime Minister's personal intervention, put yet more pressure on a tottering pound. At a meeting of the Economic Strategy Committee of the Cabinet on 8 November Callaghan claimed that he was still opposed to devaluation, which would be an "economic and political catastrophe". There was no question of his reconsidering the issue for several months.[3] For those versed in the ways of Chancellors, there could be no firmer indication that devaluation was inevitable and would swiftly follow.

In fact Callaghan was in two – or on a bad day three or four – minds about the issue. On 4 November he was in despair at the panic selling of sterling and convinced that devaluation would be necessary in a few days. Wilson noticed that, while the Chancellor was depressed about the fate of the currency, he "seemed singularly bullish in a personal sense". He remarked with some relish that many people were discussing the Prime Minister's position in the light of the latest by-election results. It was clearly his view, thought Wilson, that a change in the leadership might soon be needed. When the Prime Minister heard "whether truly or not, that Jim was going around with colleagues saying that he wanted to devalue but that I was interposing a political veto", he had no doubt whom Callaghan considered should be the beneficiary of such a change. A coup was imminent. It seems most unlikely that any precise threat in fact existed, except in Wilson's imagination; in any case, on 7 November, the Chancellor in the House of Commons allowed himself to be goaded by the left into expressing some distinctly unsocialist views about the need for a "pool of unemployment". "This at any rate put paid to any challenge from Jim on the leadership issue," observed Wilson with satisfaction.[1]

Wilson contemplated visiting Washington in a last-minute attempt to persuade Johnson to back sterling. Vietnam might have served as an excuse – though Johnson would not have been likely to respond enthusiastically to any *démarche* flying under those particular colours. Michael Halls suggested the ostensible reason for the Prime Minister's visit might be to see his son, Robin, who was at university in Boston. A courtesy call to Washington could then be tacked on as an after-thought. Whatever the gift-wrapping, the journey would have achieved nothing. Though the US Treasury still contemplated a rescue operation, the State Department and the President had given up the battle to save sterling and now were concerned only to limit the damage done by devaluation. When the news finally came, as Johnson put it: "We had been forewarned, of course, but it was still like hearing that an old friend who has been ill has to undergo a serious operation."[2] At least the old friend was not expected to die under the anaesthetic, and by 12 November Callaghan had changed tack and decided that he did not even need to go under the knife. At an emotional meeting with Brown and Wilson he declared that devaluation would do more harm than good. A brandy-sodden Brown, whose performance was marked mainly by his unavailing efforts to enunciate the words "fundamental disequilibrium", pledged eternal allegiance to Wilson but regretted the fact that the press did not believe a word the Prime Minister said. "I said that I interpreted George as saying that we three must stand firmly together. Yes, said George, the rest of the Cabinet does not matter, but we must be firm with the Party." Brown's personal solution for the crisis was for Wilson to emulate de Gaulle's recent action and declare a state of national emergency. Wilson pointed out that France was at war in Algeria.

In spite of the Chancellor's protestations, by 15 November it was no longer a question of whether to devalue but when and by how much. Some reports suggested that Callaghan wanted to devalue by more than the 14.3 per cent which was the final figure but was overruled by Wilson and other members of the Cabinet.[1] There does not seem to be any real basis for the story. The figure was recommended by the Treasury and accepted without much debate; the Cabinet occupied itself almost entirely with wrangling over the round of cuts that would have to accompany devaluation if it were to achieve its object. Callaghan was in the deepest gloom, telling the Cabinet when on 16 November he announced the decision to devalue, that it was "the unhappiest day of my life",[2] and pledging that he would resign as soon as the dust had begun to settle. Wilson, on the other hand, was conspicuously cheerful, even euphoric. Hugh Cudlipp called on him on the day of the public announcement, to find him neither crestfallen nor jittery: "The balance of payments had become an aching tooth, he said, and he and Callaghan, three weeks ago, had decided to have it out."[3]

It was this resolute determination to make the best of it that led Wilson into one of his greatest indiscretions. The brief which the Treasury had prepared for the broadcast in which the Prime Minister explained the situation to the nation contained the sentences: "Devaluation does not mean that the value of the pound in the hands of the British consumer ... is cut correspondingly. It does not mean that the money in our pockets is worth 14 per cent less." Wilson liked the phrase, and when Gerald Kaufman said that a relation of his was worried by the fact that her savings would now buy 14 per cent less, he decided to appease the fears of her and many like her by making the Treasury draft a little punchier and reassuring her that "the pound in her pocket" was not now worth 14 per cent less than the day before. Anyone who listened to the whole of his speech would have realised what he meant, but as a politician of his experience should have known, a telling phrase will always be taken out of context and used in evidence against the speaker. Wilson became stamped as the man who pretended that devaluation would not affect the buying power of the pound; worse still, the man who tried to pass off devaluation as a triumph instead of the economic defeat that it was. Tony Benn referred to his "absurd broadcast saying 'The pound in your pocket won't be devalued' ", and if Benn could represent it in such a way, how certain it was that the Tories would have a field day.[1]

Callaghan made no such attempt to put devaluation in a better light. His initial reaction was that it was a bitter personal humiliation and that he must at once retire from the government, perhaps even to private life. Wilson was disturbed; partly because he felt the Chancellor had no reason to reproach himself; still more because the thought of the man he felt to be his principal rival loose to make mischief on the back benches was one that he found alarming. Without too much difficulty he persuaded Callaghan to do an exchange with Jenkins and take over the Home Office. With remarkable resilience the new Home Secretary bounced back and his son-in-law, Peter Jay, was soon reporting in *The Times* that it was Wilson who had opposed devaluation and Callaghan who had in the end insisted on it. "There is no doubt that Jim sees himself at the very least as the Crown Prince again," wrote Barbara Castle.[2] But his final judgment on the episode was generous beyond the needs of mere politeness. "I cannot write too highly of Harold Wilson's personal consideration and kindness during this period," he said in his memoirs. "He was as tired as I was and was beset by many concerns other than devaluation but he never showed impatience or irritation."[3]

If Crossman had had his way the new Chancellor would have been Anthony Crosland. Crosland was cleverer and a better economist than he was, said Roy Jenkins, but Wilson had greater confidence in Jenkins's ability to control the House of Commons.[4] Marcia Williams lobbied on Jenkins's behalf, but little pressure was needed: Wilson was never comfortable with Crosland, who he felt was Gaitskell's chosen heir and as such despised and resented him, while Jenkins he found it easy to work with.[5] He was also anxious that he and the new Chancellor should be, in Jenkins's words, "bound together, if not by hoops of steel, at least by bonds of mutual self-interest".[6] "Harold has now finally nobbled his one serious rival," was how Barbara Castle saw it.[7] But he paid a price. In his biography of Jenkins John Campbell has claimed that, when he became Chancellor, "the Prime Minister was effectively in his power".[8] Certainly Jenkins was in an immensely strong position – the "dominant force in Cabinet", Crossman called him[9] – and it would have been almost impossible for Wilson to shed him. The new Chancellor in effect vetoed Barbara

Castle's transfer to the DEA when Wilson wanted to move her there in recognition of her good work at Transport.[1] But Jenkins was equally bound to Wilson; he knew that a large section of the party would never willingly accept him as Prime Minister and that the best way for him to reach Number 10 would be as Wilson's designated heir. The two men stood or fell together. Most of the time they also worked together in fair harmony. While Callaghan was at the Treasury the door between Number 10 and the Chancellor's house at Number 11 was usually closed, with Jenkins there it was very often open.[2] Things did not always run smoothly. In mid 1968 Wilson, in an obvious reference to Jenkins, said that certain leaks arose "from the ambitions of one member of the Cabinet to sit in my place". When Jenkins subsequently reproached him Wilson replied "bitterly but honestly and therefore impressively: 'Well, you may find this an intolerable Cabinet to sit in; but I can tell you that you cannot be any more miserable about it, or find it any more intolerable, than I do to preside over it.'" In fact it was Crossman who had leaked; once convinced of this Wilson apologised handsomely and said that the succession to Number 10 was obviously Jenkins's.[3]

When he wrote to Lyndon Johnson to explain the decision to devalue, Wilson evoked his favourite analogy when he concluded: "Each of us, I suppose, must at times have suffered the misery of an abscess which breaks out, is temporarily healed, then breaks out again. Each of us has shrunk from having the tooth pulled out. But when we finally decide to do so, the feeling of relief is not simply an illusion. The removal of a certain poison from the system purges the whole system itself." That was the case, he argued, with Britain today. But everyone realised that, if the world's confidence was to be held and resources switched to the export drive, "an exceptionally ghoulish package of further measures" would be needed.[4] The "ghoulish package" was indeed calculated to strike dismay into the heart of any reforming element in the party. The raising of the school-leaving age to sixteen was deferred for two years, prescription charges were reintroduced, the public sector housing programme cut back. "The only genuine support left in the Labour Party came from careerists, sycophants and paid Party officials," stormed Paul Foot.[5] But it was the defence cuts that caused most grief in Washington. A decision in principle was taken to speed up the withdrawal from east of Suez – a conclusion that was to involve Wilson in much painful personal diplomacy over the following few months – but more immediate was the cancellation of the F111A.

The F111 was the aircraft that had been ordered from the United States when the Labour government stopped work on the TSR2 in 1964. Its cancellation was a fearful blow to Denis Healey, who felt that he had let down the Royal Air Force. He contemplated resignation, but was deterred by the fact that, if he went, Crossman would probably succeed him.[1] At the Cabinet that took the fatal decision, he "behaved with enormous courage and dignity", recorded Tony Benn, while Brown, arguing the same case, was "emotional, sensational, but immensely powerful in personality". Only Wilson was "never quite equal to the occasion".[2] But Wilson had his way. The opposition that most disturbed him came from the American President, who wrote to say that the cancellation of the F111 would be regarded as "a total disengagement from any commitment whatsoever to the security of areas outside Europe and, indeed, to a considerable extent in Europe as well. Moreover, it will be viewed here as a strong indication of British isolation which would be fatal to the chances of cooperation between our countries in the field of defence procurement." For good measure, Johnson threatened financial penalties, the scrapping of present offset arrangements and the cancellation of existing orders for British weapons.[3]

Wilson's reply was distressed, but he gave not an inch on the main issue. "Some of the decisions we have taken on the home front strike at the very root of principles to which many of us have been dedicated since we first went into politics," he told the President. The British people were "sick and tired of being thought willing to eke out a comfortable existence on borrowed money". They were ready to accept sacrifices at home but demanded that "we must no longer continue to overstrain our real resources and capabilities in the military field abroad". The decisions had not been taken in the spirit of "Little England" but in a determination to find a role commensurate with the nation's means. "Believe me, Lyndon, the decisions we are having to take now have been the most difficult and the heaviest of any that I, and I think all my colleagues, can remember in our public life ... We are taking them because we are convinced that, in the longer term, only thus can Britain find the new place on the world stage that, I firmly believe, the British people ardently desire. And when I say 'the world stage', I mean just that."[4]

Wilson had a few carefully selected journalists to lunch the Sunday after devaluation. He claimed, according to the usually reliable James Margach of the *Sunday Times*, that he had become the most powerful Prime Minister since Walpole. "I can do whatever I like now ... in economic and financial policies ... My announcement this morning is very, very bad news for Ted." To Margach it seemed he was boasting that devaluation was the final step in a long and skilfully executed campaign.[1] He failed signally to convince his audience. The press reports ranged from the lukewarm to the offensive; in particular his "pound in your pocket" remark was denounced as complacent at the best and more probably dishonest. In the House of Lords he was attacked by the former Governor of the Bank of England, Lord Cromer. Some said that Cromer had no business to speak publicly in such a way, but he had unique authority and his indignant condemnation of the government and call on Wilson personally to resign as unworthy to lead the nation did real harm to the Prime Minister's reputation. The whole devaluation episode "was terribly damaging to him personally", said Peter Shore. "He felt it, and it was damaging to him politically as well."[2] However he might bluster to the press, he knew that his reputation was in shreds and that it would take much time and hard work to restore it. But his incredible resilience and optimism bore him up. "It has been a very bad week for the P.M.," Marcia Williams told his father on 23 November. "It is bad enough to fight the enemy in front, but when you have to look over your shoulder the whole time as well, as you can guess, this is very tiring and bad for the nerves ... However, I think everything is now under control, though it is going to be hard going for some time."[3]

XIV

Strains Within the Cabinet

1968

L ong before the reverberations started by devaluation had died away the Cabinet became embroiled in another crisis of lesser significance but considerably greater bitterness. The South African arms affair is often cited as an illustration of Wilson's malign deviousness. At the very least, he did not emerge from it with enhanced credit.

South Africa was one of the few issues on which Wilson felt passionately. When he came to power in 1964 almost his first action was to instruct the civil servants to review any contract with South Africa that could involve the strengthening of their military potential and to ensure that no similar contract was entered into in the future without his specific authority. His feelings on the subject were well known. When lunching at *The Times*, Barbara Castle conceded that Wilson was often calculating and even unprincipled: "If he didn't feel something – such as Honours, about which he had never been Radical – you couldn't interest him. But he *had* cared genuinely about arms for South Africa."[1] When in September 1967 he found himself confronted by a united front of Brown, Healey as Defence Secretary and George Thomson as Commonwealth Secretary, demanding a resumption of the sales of strategic arms that could not be used to put down a civil insurrection, he was, wrote Crossman, "miserable and unhappy and divided in his mind".[2] But, as Brown was later to make embarrassingly clear, he was not as free from involvement in the decision-making process as he would have liked people to believe.

Three months later, with the economic arguments for arms sales now at least as important as the political, it was Callaghan who reopened the subject. Wilson eventually conceded that, in principle, the sale of naval weapons to South Africa should be resumed but that there should be no final decision or public announcement except as part of the deflationary package which was to follow devaluation. The news of this decision soon leaked out and two Labour backbenchers, Kevin McNamara and John Ellis, called on the Chief Whip, John Silkin, and said that they wished to put down an Early Day Motion condemning the sale of *any* arms to South Africa. In Silkin's view this move was not inspired by Wilson; nevertheless, when he told him what was being proposed, the Prime Minister "not only agreed, he was enthusiastic".[1] "Let the Party be mobilised," Wilson said to Castle. A letter from junior ministers saying that they would accept no change, would be a help. "But remember, none of this must be traced back to me."[2] A strong swell of opinion built up in the PLP, spreading far beyond the hard left to some of the most traditionally loyal and moderate of party members. George Brown was in Brussels and Wilson telegraphed him on 13 December to report that the affair had "gone through the roof" and that feeling in the party was at "explosion point". It was no longer possible to defer a final decision till the New Year and the question would be considered at the next Cabinet. Healey would put the case for selling arms "but, in fairness to yourself, I feel bound to advise that you should seriously consider returning also in time for the meeting." Brown, in his reply, was sceptical about the strength of the feeling against arms sales in the party, and explained the obstacles in the way of his return. "It is impossible to judge at your distance the feeling in the Party, which I think you will agree I fairly predicted," Wilson cabled back. "With all the emphasis at my command I would adjure you not to sacrifice the possibilities of a satisfactory European solution in order to return to London to fight a South African battle. First things first and they are European." But opinion in the party was now such that "we cannot maintain our stability or credibility without an immediate decision. This must be settled tomorrow. You know where I stand and the party reaction has confirmed that position."[3]

Brown did not accept this beguiling invitation to stay away but stormed back to London in the conviction that the party reaction was spurious and had anyway been fomented by Wilson. On the first point he was clearly wrong; Denis Healey, who felt much the same at the time, subsequently admitted generously that he had "showed gross insensitivity to the hatred of Apartheid both in my party and the Commonwealth".[4] On the second the evidence is more equivocal. The most likely answer is that while Wilson did not personally whip up opposition to the arms sales except when talking to a few intimates, he made no secret of his feelings and thus encouraged the growth of protest. Brown had reason to feel aggrieved but not betrayed. At the Cabinet on 15 December, however, the talk was all of treason. It "was the most unpleasant meeting I have ever attended," wrote Healey. "George Brown was thunderous in denouncing Wilson's campaign of character assassination and his manipulation of the press." Both Brown and Healey insisted that the Prime Minister had condoned if not actively encouraged negotiations with the South Africans.[1] Gordon Walker called the atmosphere "sulphurous" and shared Brown's conviction that Wilson had been responsible for the feeling in the party.[2] Though estimates of the rival factions differ, a clear majority of the Cabinet was in favour of defying party opinion and continuing with the sales. Only Crossman, with a proposal to defer the final decision, saved Wilson from a humiliating defeat.

Brown as so often then proceeded to overplay his hand. His weekend was devoted to vigorous and tendentious leaking of the case for arms sales to the press, with the result that when the Cabinet reconsidered the matter on 18 December Wilson was able to take the high moral ground and claim that the credit of the government was at stake. Gordon Walker, for one, stuck to his view that the case for resuming sales was unanswerable but insisted "all that mattered now was to reassert the authority of the Prime Minister and Cabinet".[3] Wilson must announce a decision against the sale of arms. Brown was isolated and that evening wrote furiously to Wilson. He denied that he had conducted any briefing of the press except through his press officer, to "clear up the mess which the Friday morning papers ... had appeared to do to my position in the party". As to the main issue:

You challenged me when I said that all my contacts with Muller [the South African Foreign Minister] have been in terms which you yourself had approved ... At every stage since we first discussed this you have taken the line along with me that this might well be the right thing to do but that timing was of the greatest importance. In June ... you selected the words in which I was, again in your words, "to tip the wink" to Muller. You changed my words, which were going to be that we "probably" could supply these arms, and you said "we might well be able" or "possibly could" supply these arms. I chose the words "we might possibly". May I repeat they were your words and at no time since have we exceeded them ... At no time until now have you ever raised the issue of a moral objection. You have always raised the question of timing and the Party reaction. When you saw Muller with me, the South Africans thought you said there was no issue of principle but only one of timing ... We shall pay heavily for today's statement and decision ... If I may say so, you seemed more concerned to get me hooked on a Cabinet repudiation in the press which I had nothing to do with than to face the consequences of your own position over the last six months.[1]

In his reply Wilson merely said that he had been referring to Brown's latest personal letter to Muller, which he had not seen in advance, and not to the earlier correspondence.[2] The two accounts are not incompatible, but it is clear from Brown's letter that Wilson went far further in condoning, or even supporting, the approach to the South Africans than he would have liked to be generally known or could easily have reconciled with his conscience. The row did nothing to lighten his mood as he retreated to the Isles of Scilly to prepare for 1968. "This Government has failed more abysmally than any Government since 1931," mused Crossman on New Year's Day. "In Harold's case the failure consists in tearing away the magic and revealing that he's really been failing ever since he entered No. 10."[3] On 18 January, twenty-six left-wingers abstained over the public expenditure cuts. A "Wilson-must-go" campaign was waged in sections of the press. Wilson dismissed the leading malcontents as being composed only of such maverick figures as Lords Robens and Shaw-cross and Cecil King but Joe Haines told Ted Castle that at least a dozen members of the Cabinet were convinced that the Prime Minister was finished and were just waiting for the moment to strike.[4] Cecil King broached with Benn the possibility of a coalition, perhaps under Healey. "I think Harold is in serious danger," noted Benn.[5]

The alienation of the left became still more marked when an influx of Kenyan Asians led to the hurried application of a quota system to keep the entries down to 1,500 a year. Wilson's bacon was to some extent saved by Enoch Powell, whose celebrated "rivers of blood" speech in April 1968 gave the Prime Minister a chance to make a comprehensive and uncommonly effective attack on racialism. Whether the speech did Labour any good in the imminent borough elections may be doubted, but it restored the morale both of the Prime Minister and of all but the most illiberal sections of the Labour Party.[6] To Cyril Osborne, a Tory member of notably traditional views, he refused even to contemplate a total ban on immigration; no figures he had seen, he insisted, "remotely support your suggestion that we can foresee a time when coloured people in this country will out-number the white".[1]

After the furore over South African arms – a crisis notable in particular for the fact that George Brown did *not* resign – it seemed certain that the final instalment of that long-running adventure serial could not long be delayed. It came in March, when there was a sudden squall over the price of gold. Unusually for a financial crisis, Britain was neither responsible nor the most directly concerned, but its involvement was still potentially calamitous. "I understand there may be a special immediate jeopardy to sterling," cabled Johnson. "That is a matter of concern not only for you and me but also for the countries associated with us in the Gold Pool ... You are right to say that we must act in a way which holds our two nations together. If we act on this basis, I believe we can find that way this weekend."[2] "That way" was to be a two-tier arrangement under which the central bankers of the Gold Pool would undertake to sell gold to one another only in settlement of monetary deficits. To implement this system would involve temporarily closing the Gold Pool, which in its turn required the closing of the London foreign exchange and the dec-laration of a bank holiday. By 8.00 p.m. on 14 March the urgency had become desperate. The key ministers gathered in Downing Street. Only the Foreign Secretary was absent. According to Wilson, search parties combed the House of Commons, the Foreign Office and other likely places and reports came back that Brown was either not to be found or in no condition to make an appearance. According to Brown, he was at his official house in Carlton Gardens until he returned to the House later that evening. He claimed that Wilson had told his secretary not to continue the hunt since "the Prime Minister didn't particularly want me after all".[3] Wilson probably didn't, but he must have known how much trouble would be caused if Brown were made to feel excluded and at the worst he was guilty of tact-lessness in not having him pursued more vigorously.

When Brown got to the House he discovered that high-level dis-cussions were under way at Number 10, and that he was not there. He was particularly affronted by the fact that Peter Shore was among those present. He gathered together a group of ministers who might also have reason to feel discriminated against and telephoned Wilson to summon him to explain his conduct. He was "very angry and noisy and said he was bloody angry and dictated my presence at the House", recorded Wilson.[1] The Prime Minister at first agreed to go over, then had second thoughts and invited the dissident ministers to Number 10. A grisly scene followed, with Brown abusing Wilson, accusing him of lying and deliberately seeking to humiliate him. Once again he overplayed his hand; the other ministers had been ready to deplore their exclusion from the earlier discussions but were so disgusted by Brown's conduct that they accepted the Prime Minister's handling of the situation with no demur. Richard Marsh, who was one of Brown's group but accepted that the need for quick action had been paramount, described how Brown "stood breathing flame and fury down Harold Wilson's neck. Harold looked as if he was about to hit him." Next day Marsh told Wilson that in his view Brown had not been drunk but that his behaviour had been unacceptable and that he must go.[2]

He went. Burke Trend suggested that Wilson put out a peace feeler. Wilson refused: "I had stood enough from George over a dozen or more similar incidents and if he were going to go this was the best possible issue since there could be no disagreement on policy, and since his behaviour had been condemned by a dozen Ministers as intolerable."[3] When he resigned, Brown widened his assault on Wilson to a condemnation of the "presidential" system the Prime Minister was seeking to introduce into British politics. Time and again he so managed things that "decisions were being taken over the heads and without the knowledge of Ministers, and far too often outsiders in his entourage seemed to be almost the only effective 'Cabinet'."[4] This was a bit hot, complained Wilson, given that Brown had repeatedly blamed him for allowing Cabinet discussion where none was necessary: "Again and again George had said I ought to decide more things outside the Cabinet, or, alternatively, tell the Cabinet what I wanted and insist on it."[5] But Brown was not the only minister to dislike Wilson's habit of transacting business in a little coven of personal cronies and presenting the results to ministers virtually as a *fait accompli*. Brown's phrase, "I don't like the way you run your Government," wrote Barbara Castle, "was one of the most telling he could have produced because everybody knows it is near the bone". Crossman agreed: "If I were ever to resign it would be precisely because I can't stand the way Cabinet is run."[6] Brown was allowed to go without a murmur because his instability and turbulence had finally been too much for his colleagues, but the fact that his resignation caused no revolt did not mean that Wilson could count on continued acquiescence in his leadership.

With Stewart back at the Foreign Office in place of Brown and Roy Jenkins establishing his reputation as Chancellor with a budget that was tough but almost universally well received, the government began to look as if it might settle down. Instead of rejoicing in the possibility, Wilson chose to indulge in another reshuffle. Castle wanted to go to the DEA. Wilson at first encouraged the idea, then told her that Jenkins would not accept it. Realising the effect this admission might have, he hurriedly sought to disabuse her of any idea that the Chancellor was all-powerful. He had just sent him away with a flea in his ear, he boasted. "He has tried to tell me how to run my own Cabinet. I told him he had better remember who was Prime Minister."[1] In fact he knew Jenkins was indispensable; Castle was instead moved to the Ministry of Labour, to prepare the ground for what was to be Wilson's most important battle in 1969. An indignant Marsh took her place at Transport. When he complained that he still had an important job to do at the Ministry of Power, Wilson replied that he needed a Minister of Transport who would be good on television. Marsh retorted crossly that he did not consider himself an entertainer and Wilson closed the discussion with the words: "I think, Dick, the captain of the team is entitled to place the field."[2] The captain proved less resolute when he tackled Denis Healey. The Secretary of State for Defence stated firmly that he proposed to stay where he was until after the July White Paper and anyway found Technology an insufficiently challenging prospect. He was more attracted by Wilson's other suggestion – that he might become First Secretary with responsibility over the whole field of social affairs, though only if he had "a control of at least the Ministry of Health and the Ministry of Social Security as direct as I have now of the Army, Navy and Air Force departments".[3] Callaghan was to stay at the Home Office: "I will break his heart," Wilson told Castle vengefully. He contemplated leaving Callaghan off the Parliamentary Committee – the inner Cabinet – but changed his mind. "He said he has decided it's better to have him under his eye. The old excuse, which merely means that when it came to it Harold ran away."[4]

Gordon Walker, who had been dismissed from Education, remarked balefully that "Harold Wilson is finished."[5] Others with less immediate reason to wish it true said much the same. Cecil King, the *Daily Mirror* chairman, had been waging an unrelenting campaign against Wilson for the best part of two years, inciting Callaghan, Jenkins and Healey in particular into a revolt against their leader. On 9 May he came fully into the open with a statement announcing that "the greatest financial crisis in history" was about to break and that it could not be averted by "lies about our reserves". Coming from a member of the Court of the Bank of England, this seemed to Wilson to be unacceptable: "I presume the Treasury will lose no time in discussing with the Governor of the Bank the action that is appropriate in such circumstances."[1] King forestalled him by resigning from the Bank and the following day linked the coming economic crisis with the bad election results in the borough elections as the basis for a resounding message in the *Daily Mirror*: "Enough is Enough ... It is up to the P.L.P. to give us a fresh Leader – and soon."

"Cecil is a fool," boomed Crossman at a party after King's article appeared. "We'll never get rid of the little man now ... He's given him security for life."[2] He was more reflective in his diary where he concluded that, though King's attack might have won Wilson a little time, it was inevitable that he would soon be replaced, probably by a Jenkins/Castle axis.[3] Even within Number 10 the mood was apprehensive if not wholly pessimistic. "Things really are black," Marcia Williams told the Prime Minister's sister, Marjorie, "and he needs this week to concentrate on trying to hold things in Parliament. I am afraid it is as bad as it sounds. Still, there we are, it has to be faced, and if he soldiers on despite all the unpleasantness I am sure he will be all right."[4] Soldiering on was made no easier when, a few weeks after King's onslaught, the Minister of Power, Ray Gunter, resigned on grounds very similar to those of Brown. He had been displeased when shifted sideways in April to make way for Barbara Castle, now he made his displeasure vocal in a fierce attack on Wilson's style of leadership. On the back benches he made common cause with Gordon Walker, Houghton, Mayhew and other disaffected ex-ministers who, for one reason or another, felt they had been ill-used. They had a rich vein of discontent to mine. The Wilson government "was in difficulty with all Britishers and confronts divisions within the Labour Party", Dean Rusk told the President; the London financial community has lost confidence in the Wilson government, added the Secretary of the Treasury; Wilson's blind refusal to admit that devaluation was a failure had "deepened distrust and sapped public support", contributed the American Ambassador.[5] "Wilson must go," was the common cry of all the dissidents, but who should take his place was as usual harder to decide. The two most obvious claimants were Jenkins and Callaghan. Jenkins had been discreetly lobbied by Mayhew in December 1967, had agreed that the "anti-Wilson, anti-Left" group must stick together, but saw no immediate prospect of getting rid of the Prime Minister.[1] Five months later, when Gordon Walker approached him, he was a little more forthcoming. He said that Gunter and Callaghan were both fiercely opposed to Wilson and that he had an excellent relationship with Crossman, who might play a decisive role in a crisis. By mid June, "The Conspiracy is now in full swing," wrote Gordon Walker in his diary – the addition of the capital C somehow adding a dreadful import to the statement. "A wholly secret inner core" – Gordon Walker, Mayhew, Dick Taverne, Ivor Richard, Bill Rodgers, Austen Albu – were busily compiling lists of supporters and had reached 120, though of varying degrees of trustworthiness. Douglas Houghton was "wholly for removal of Harold and ready to act".[2] The gang met in Roy Hattersley's room. Hattersley always maintained that he never played a leading role among the conspirators. He did not take their activities very seriously, being inclined to agree with Crosland who remarked angrily: "All you do is fucking talk!" But Wilson was convinced he meant mischief; once, when several newspapers tipped Hattersley for promotion, Wilson remarked to him darkly: "It's better to have one Prime Minister on your side than ten editors."[3]

It was Jenkins whose refusal to move at the beginning of July aborted the conspiracy. "He clearly did not want to be implicated in actually launching an action," noted a disillusioned Gordon Walker.[4] Jenkins could not believe that Callaghan would be prepared to bring down Wilson only to raise another, still younger rival in his stead. Callaghan was quite as hesitant. In June 1967, he told Mayhew, thirteen Labour MPs had at one time or another urged him to make a bid for Number 10. His reply always was that he was fifty-six years old, was much enjoying his farming, and had no wish to go further. But Mayhew felt that he believed he had a better claim than Jenkins.[5] Callaghan now admits frankly that his main reason for not standing was that he did not think he could unseat Wilson. He felt no loyalty to the Prime Minister. He resented the way in which the easy access he had enjoyed as Chancellor disappeared once he had become Home Secretary. A display of affection or trust might have retained his loyalty; as it was injured pride drove him away. But it was not potent enough to drive him into a revolt which he felt sure would fail.

Though no one of his Cabinet colleagues was able or willing to strike a lethal blow, many of them seemed happy to maul him whenever a chance arose. A prime occasion arose in July, which was all the more galling for Wilson in that the issue was one about which he was not particularly concerned. A new General Secretary was needed for the Labour Party. Wilson had originally favoured the inside man, Harry Nicholas, but was told he was felt to be too old. Various other names were canvassed before Wilson gave a rather tepid blessing to the candidature of Anthony Greenwood, the Minister of Housing. Brown now struck: "I took the view that it was bad constitutionally and would be bad in practice, for the Secretary to the Labour Party to be regarded in any way as the Prime Minister's nominee" – in other words, if Wilson wanted Greenwood, Brown was *ipso facto* against him.[1] When the appropriate subcommittee of the NEC met on 15 July, Brown, who, according to Wilson's account, "was three quarters tight", moved that Harry Nicholas be appointed. Callaghan seconded the nomination. "George then went into orbit and said everybody knew Greenwood was the Prime Minister's candidate and why didn't he say so?" Wilson said his original intention had been to play no part; it was Brown who had persuaded him to take a line. Brown insulted Gormley – the miners' leader – Gormley walked out, Brown walked out, Eirene White, then Minister of State at the Welsh Office, pursued them and brought them both back. Callaghan argued against Greenwood, saying he would not be a unanimous choice. Wilson said nobody now would be; "it was our duty to try and minimise the harm that had been done". Brown and Gormley then rowed again and Brown "for the first of several times, said that what was happening was why he had left the Government". Wilson moved that the question be put, "George argued that it should not and said that this was why he had left the Government". After the vote went four–two to Greenwood, Brown protested that Wilson had voted. It was pointed out that as a member of the committee he had a perfect right to. "George said that this proved that Greenwood was the Prime Minister's candidate. George then got up to walk out again."[2]

Even allowing for the fact that the account came from Wilson, the meeting was clearly nasty, brutish and not nearly short enough. Two names went forward to the full NEC and Nicholas was selected by fourteen votes to twelve. A result which would have seemed perfectly satisfactory to Wilson two months before was now presented by the press as a humiliating defeat. Wilson blamed Callaghan: "The time will come when I'll dig Jim's entrails out for what he did to me," Crossman quotes him as saying.[1] It led to another burst of speculation about Wilson's future, but in fact the chief conspirators had already abandoned the hunt. The Tory Party was itself in some disarray; the trade figures were improving, opinion in the PLP seemed to be shifting back towards cautious support for the Prime Minister. Though the unions moved strongly against the government's prices and incomes policy at their congress in September, Cousins reaffirmed his loyalty to Wilson as the party leader. At the Blackpool party conference in October he went still further. Cousins's motion calling for the repeal of all incomes legislation had been carried by almost five to one but Wilson's conference speech made little of this and instead painted a rosy picture of a Britain which, in spite of the evil machinations of the Tories, was at last breaking through to a bright socialist future. "Magnificent balderdash", David Watt described it,[2] but it was what the party wanted to hear and they applauded him rapturously. The ovation, declared Cousins, "was a demonstration of our satisfaction at his leadership, and the fact that we recognise him as leader of the Labour Government and that we certainly have no wish for him to be changed for anyone else either within the Party or from another Party ... If we have differences with him over legislation about incomes policy, then our differences are over that – and not over his continued leadership of the Movement."[3]

Though his position might have been temporarily restored, Wilson was given no time to relax. In November the extreme fragility of sterling was exposed yet again when the strength of the Deutschmark led to rumours that it was to be revalued. The inevitable result was increased pressure on the other Western currencies. German hesitation turned an embarrassment into a crisis, and when a summons to the world's monetary leaders to attend an emergency conference in Bonn was accompanied by a statement that the parity of the mark would be maintained, Wilson and Jenkins decided that the German government must be pressed to agree to immediate revaluation. The ambassador, Herr Blankenhorn, was summoned to a late-night meeting at Number 10. Wilson, tired, worried and irritated, was far from at his best. "We expressed ourselves strongly," he described it; the expressions included a description of the German attitude as "irresponsible" and "intolerable" and barely veiled hints that if the pound sank any further Britain would have to reconsider its defence commitments on the continent. A "ludicrous piece of misjudgment and of insular self-deception", Crossman described it.[1] Certainly Wilson's tirade achieved little. The currencies steadied but Jenkins was still forced to introduce another package of deflationary measures. The situation was so volatile that when Wilson, on 5 December, paid a brief visit to Cornwall to see his father in hospital, the more imaginative journalists announced that he had resigned, that Jenkins had resigned, that both had resigned and, for good measure, that the Queen had abdicated.[2] The discovery that none of these was true and that Britain's trade was satisfactorily in surplus stemmed the run on the pound and 1968 ended in comparative tranquillity. The crisis had underlined, however, the extreme vulnerability of the British economy. It was one of the factors that impelled Wilson into his boldest attempt to attack the problem at its roots and, with one stroke, to set industry at home on a sounder basis and to re-establish Britain's international credit.

XV

In Place of Strife

1969

The story of *In Place of Strife* is of peculiar importance in Wilson's life as being almost the only occasion in a career devoted to the pursuit of consensus in which he flung compromise and party unity to the winds and fought his battle to the verge of the last ditch. The starting point was the publication in June 1968 of the Donovan Report on trade unions and employers' associations. After three years of cogitation a Royal Commission under Lord Donovan had come up with conclusions which were reasonable, prudent, well argued and largely inadequate to solve what had become a problem of an alarmingly urgent nature. The report urged more wage bargaining within individual firms and less on a national scale, proposed the setting up of an independent Commission for Industrial Relations (CIR), envisaged that the leaders of unofficial strikes might not in future be immune from all penalties, but rejected the legal enforcement of collective agreements or the possibility of criminal proceedings. A few years before it would have seemed judicious, by the second half of 1968 it was already out of date.

The report was published amidst an explosion of militancy and unofficial strikes. In the previous five years there had never been as many as three million days lost in strikes; in the first eight months of 1968 alone the total rose to 3.5 million and the workers' frustration grew ever greater as they endured the rise in the cost of living that followed devaluation and continued limitations on their wage demands.[1] Popular support for curbs on the unions had been shown clearly in a series of opinion polls and dissatisfaction with the government's failure to act was felt to be the largest single factor in the collapse of Wilson's popularity rating from 69 per cent in 1966 to a mere 33 per cent by January 1969 (the fact that Heath's popularity had fallen too was taken to be evidence that the public had almost as little confidence in his capacity to take a strong line). Wilson was thus well aware that something dramatic was expected, or at least hoped for, from him. He had been convinced for several years that unofficial strikes were Labour's biggest electoral handicap and he believed that it was the seamen's strike in 1966 which had sabotaged national resurgence under his leadership. One of his pet maxims was that Canute would have got better results at high tide; so far as the unions were concerned he was convinced that the tide was fully in and that he could safely drive back the waters without risking more than slightly dampened feet.

Though Barbara Castle, his new Minister of Labour, knew that the Prime Minister would be generally sympathetic to her ideas, it was she who prepared the first draft of a White Paper which was to base itself on Donovan but go beyond it in certain vital respects. From the first moment she expounded her ideas to Wilson at the beginning of December 1968 it was clear that, while the union movement would accept the bulk of what was proposed with alacrity, they would take exception to three clauses: the discretionary power given to the Secretary of State to order a twenty-eight-day conciliation pause before a strike could begin; similar powers to order a ballot among potential strikers; and a provision that the findings of the CIR on certain disputes could be backed by fines on employers, unions or individual strikers. These were what the left-wing member, Eric Heffer, described as "the spoonful of tar in a barrel of honey"; they were, of course, the provisions that appealed most strongly to Wilson.[1] He was lyrical: "Barbara has not so much out-Heathed Heath as out-flanked him," he told Marcia Williams. The legislation, he was convinced, would be immensely popular and an election winner; it was also essential if the prosperity of the nation were to be restored. The industrial unrest of the last year had saddened and sickened him; he was convinced that the run-of-the-mill unionist would welcome new laws to curb wildcat strikes. There would be opposition, but the worst of it would come from communists and die-hard reactionaries. He believed that he would be able to overcome it. He had planned to set up a ministerial committee to discuss the White Paper but now decided to proceed in an informal group of colleagues – the law officers plus Castle, Fred Lee and the Leader of the House, Fred Peart – who he knew would be sympathetic and on whose discretion he could depend. "Of course I was pleased but a little nervous too," commented Barbara Castle.[1] She had reason to be the second at least.

It was a risky tactic. There were two particularly unfortunate features about this decidedly irregular procedure. The first was that Callaghan, who Wilson knew to be passionately concerned with the issue, was nevertheless – or, perhaps more accurately, for that reason – excluded from the discussions. Though he must have suspected what was in the wind, the first notification he received came when Richard Marsh warned him that Mrs Castle's paper was to be put as a late item on the agenda of a Cabinet meeting just before Christmas. Wilson's plan seems to have been that the paper would not be reached until shortly before lunch and would then more or less be nodded through. Marsh had been told by Burke Trend – correctly but disingenuously – that no Cabinet committee was considering the question and it was only his wary nature and obstinacy that procured him an early look at what was being proposed. As a result he was able to ensure that any serious discussion of the paper was deferred to the New Year.[2] Callaghan very reasonably felt aggrieved. In the long run this probably made little difference. He would have opposed the legislation whatever the circumstances. But the bitterness and obduracy of his opposition can in part be explained by the fact that he felt he had been wilfully shut out from discussions when his voice should have been heard.[3]

The second unfortunate feature was that some of the union leaders *had* been consulted. In mid December, after a meeting of the NEC at Chequers, Wilson had invited Cousins, Jack Cooper, General Secretary of the General and Municipal Workers Union, and one or two others to stay on for supper and took advantage of the relaxed atmosphere to mention one or two of the more contentious clauses in Barbara Castle's forthcoming paper.

After Christmas Castle went even further and took the Finance and General Purposes Committee of the TUC into her confidence, while the Cabinet had still not discussed the question. The result was that, by the time the paper had been tabled for a meeting on 3 January, most of the Cabinet felt that they had been bypassed and slighted. Crossman, Crosland, Judith Hart, Roy Mason and, of course, Callaghan insisted that they were not prepared to be confronted with a *fait accompli* and Wilson agreed that the whole question should be referred to a subcommittee for further, though urgent, examination.

It is conceivable that if Wilson had insisted on taking the whole affair at a gallop he might still have got it through with only a minor revolt in the Cabinet and PLP. As it was, the unions had time to concert their opposition and to impress upon the parliamentarians the dreadfulness of the split within the party that would ensue if the leadership persisted in this wild initiative. The General Secretary of the TUC, George Woodcock, who had expressed cautious approval of Castle's plan, collapsed with a heart attack shortly after *In Place of Strife* was published, and with his departure any inclination to compromise perished on the union side. Wilson, for his part, seemed equally little disposed to moderation. On *Panorama*, on 20 January, he said that any compromise was impossible: "We have got to do what is right and go on regardless of unpopularity." Privately his view of the union leaders became ever more bilious – when someone compared them with feudal barons he retorted angrily, "They're not barons, they're bloody dukes!"[1] A strike in the Ford Motor Company, in which the workforce rejected a settlement agreed to by their leaders, confirmed all his worst suspicions. In a speech in his constituency he asserted that the strikers were "making a mockery of all our efforts to build up employment on Merseyside". "I want it to be clearly understood that the Government means business." Apprehensively, Harold Lever commented that *In Place of Strife* would better be called *In Chase of Strife*.[2]

It is pointless to speculate whether the credit or blame for this determined attitude rests more with Wilson or with Castle. It was Wilson who gave Castle the job and indicated the direction in which he expected her to go. It was Castle who did the work and got the paper on the table. From then on each sustained and egged on the other. Wilson's affection and admiration for Barbara Castle made him more stalwart in defence of *In Place of Strife*; her determination not to retreat was inspired by her personal loyalty to him as well as to the policy. Paradoxically, if *In Place of Strife* had had a champion less colourful, less eloquent, less persuasive than Barbara Castle, it might have enjoyed greater success. The cautious and male-chauvinist union leaders resented the pressure of this redoubtable Amazon and reacted against it by a stubborn determination not to yield an inch. So, for that matter, did James Callaghan. If someone nearer to their own kind had been in charge of the negotiations they might have proved more amenable.

Probably, though, Callaghan's attitude would always have been enough to foment their resistance. In the NEC on 26 March the government's policy was rejected on a resolution proposed by the miners' leader, Joe Gormley, and supported by Callaghan. Callaghan's speech, wrote Eric Heffer, "brought out into the open that there were powerful voices at Cabinet level who were opposed to what Barbara and Harold were doing".[1] Castle insisted that Wilson ought to demand Callaghan's resignation; Wilson replied that he could take no immediate action as he was just about to leave for Nigeria but that he would be very tough when he got back. "I'll believe that when it happens," wrote Castle in her diary.[2] From Lagos Wilson cabled Fred Peart, to say that he was watching the Callaghan situation carefully and would take firm action on his return. "Meanwhile would welcome your assessment of developments. Essential that you watch what Houghton does. Essential that no party meeting on party situation takes place in my absence." Peart replied that there was considerable annoyance in the party, both at Callaghan's behaviour and the fact that he had so far been allowed to get away with it. "I think action must be taken on this point very soon if we are to stop total disintegration." (It is symptomatic of the scale of values which prevailed within Number 10 that this telegram was prefaced by another on the same subject – now missing – which Michael Halls described as "a personal message to you from Marcia and the more important of the two".)[3]

Wilson returned to find a plea from the Home Secretary awaiting him. "The Party situation is serious," wrote Callaghan, "both in terms of morale and policy – of course the two are closely linked – and confidence is at a low ebb. We haven't much time left. Can we make a fresh start and get the PLP, the Cabinet, the Party and the TUC to pull together? If we can't, we shall *all* fail. Maybe we shall anyway, but the first condition of success is to have the 4 different elements on the same side."[4] This *démarche*, however, did not herald a more restrained approach in Cabinet. The following day Callaghan was defiant, saying that he had no need to apologise and that, if the government persisted with the White Paper, he would have "to consider his position". Far from being tough, the Prime Minister, according to Castle, made "some very generalized and conciliatory noises indeed ... I've never seen him more weak-kneed."[5] If the press next day was to be believed, however, Callaghan had been most sternly taken to task and put on probation not to offend again.

When the White Paper had first been mooted in Cabinet Roy Jenkins had called for the immediate introduction of a short interim bill. Castle had argued against a measure which would inevitably emphasise the penal clauses. The intransigence of the unions and Callaghan's attitude, however, together changed her mind and by early April a short bill was being prepared to be put through as part of a budget package. Would Callaghan resign? asked Crossman. "I don't mind if he does," said Wilson.[1] The fact that the compulsory strike ballot had been omitted from the short bill might, it was hoped, make it more palatable to the unions. In the view of a senior civil servant, however, it was still a desperate throw. Wilson was "playing his last ace card. He had clearly given up hope of convincing the unions and taking them along with the Government's proposals. He had decided to risk all on taking public opinion with him."[2] His view of the unions' likely response was confirmed on 11 April when a TUC delegation confronted Wilson and Castle and told them bluntly that there had been no criminal law in industrial relations for a century and they did not propose to accept one now.[3] Wilson gave no grounds for them to think that the government would relent, but his reluctance to split finally with the unions was well demonstrated in a letter he wrote to Barbara Castle three days later. He was anxious to find a way to make the principle of financial sanctions more acceptable. Would it be a good idea to set up a National Lay-Off Fund, to be financed mainly by a levy on employers, which would be used to compensate workers who lost their jobs through other people striking? "What the TUC ... find repugnant is the imposition of criminal fines, with the money paid to some anonymous and grim authority. Suppose we therefore were to say that the Industrial Board could levy payments on unofficial strikers, these payments to go into the Lay-Off Fund for the benefit of other workers, indeed nationally, for the benefit of those put out of work by the strike ... Clearly what I am proposing is window dressing but should not be dismissed entirely on that account. Taken in conjunction with any ideas you may have about the strike ballot ... it might just do the trick with the General Council and with many of our back-benchers."[4]

Even as he wrote he must have known that he was grasping at a singularly frail straw. He was already making his dispositions for a long and embittered battle. When the Chief Whip, Silkin, told him that while he could get a bill based on *In Place of Strife* through the House, he believed that it would split the party in the country, he was dismissed.[5] Silkin was "the most gentle and probably the most successful whip in Labour's history", wrote Leo Abse.[1] His sacking and replacement by the more rigid and authoritarian Bob Mellish, the Minister of Works, was an indication that no deviation from the hard line would be tolerated. Wilson had in fact lost confidence in Silkin's liberal approach, which had conspicuously failed to produce a PLP as amenable as the Prime Minister thought necessary. He would probably soon have got rid of him in any case, but the timing was certainly dictated by his determination to force through the bill. The change in style was quickly apparent when Mellish clashed angrily with Michael Foot at the first meeting of the PLP which he attended as Chief Whip, and later at a meeting of the Tribune Group. In the discussion he said that the bill was sacrosanct to the Prime Minister. Ian Mikardo remarked sourly that the word "sacrosanct" could surely not be in Wilson's vocabulary.[2]

A little unfairly, in view of the fact that the change was intended to expedite the passage of her beloved bill, Barbara Castle was outraged by Silkin's dismissal, especially since Wilson had the same morning told her that it was still only a possibility. "When he does this he is a timid, awful little man who to avoid a scene lies and is evasive," she stormed to Crossman. She wrote Wilson "the sort of letter on which he ought to ask for my resignation"; characteristically Wilson's response was to ask Crossman anxiously whether he thought there was any risk she might resign.[3] Wilson had simultaneously tried to appease her by setting up an inner Cabinet, called for the sake of variety the Management Committee, to replace the moribund Parliamentary Committee. Even this was delayed, however; Castle wrote suspiciously in her diary that her husband believed "Marcia was once again acting as an evil genius. She is probably advising against an inner cabinet because she is against putting Harold's power in commission."[4]

With Castle denouncing his cowardice and spinelessness, Wilson must have been especially appreciative of the letter he received a few days later from the former Tory MP, Robert Boothby. "I can no longer resist the temptation to say how much I have admired your sustained and invincible courage during recent months, and particularly weeks," wrote Boothby. "I move around a good deal and can truthfully add that this opinion is coming to be ever more widely held, sometimes in the most unexpected quarters."[5] The most unexpected of all those quarters, Wilson might reasonably have felt, would have been the PLP. Rumours flew around that up to a hundred Labour backbenchers were about to demand his resignation. Crossman called at Number 10 and found him "frightened and unhappy, unsure of himself ... The great india-rubber, unbreakable, undepressable Prime Minister was crumpled in his chair."[1] Probably Crossman over-dramatised or ignored the fact that Wilson was recovering from a violently upset stomach, but the Prime Minister had reason to be apprehensive. The hundred rebel MPs, though they no doubt existed, were by no means a coherent body ready to show themselves in public, but the plotters were hard at work again. Once more, it was the hard core of unreconstructed Gaitskellites who made the pace. At a "1963" dinner – the Gaitskellite dining club – in May 1969 Crosland announced that Wilson must go and all sixteen members present agreed that the time had come.[2] It was a replay of 1968. High hopes quickly foundered; a list of 120 potential rebels withered to a mere forty-eight who were prepared to commit themselves publicly. Worse still, the two potential replacements were loath to act. Jenkins told Gordon Walker that the centre of the party would never be prepared to move against the Prime Minister while the issue of *In Place of Strife* was still open; Callaghan, when asked whether he would stand against Wilson, replied that "no solid body of the Party was in favour of a change of leadership."[3] What he objected to, he wrote in notes at the time, was not the main thrust of *In Place of Strife*, but the "shabby and squalid intellectual dishonesty which pretends that these clauses are going to solve unofficial strikes and, therefore, are vital for our balance of payments problems".[4]

A problem for the conspirators was that two issues had become confused. Some, notably Douglas Houghton, were intent above all to see *In Place of Strife* rejected and considered the eviction of Wilson to be a secondary objective; if indeed desirable at all. Others favoured or were anyway prepared to acquiesce in the proposed legislation and merely wanted a new Prime Minister. By his wooing of the unions, Mayhew told Longford, Callaghan had made impossible any close cohesion between the two factions and had thus wrecked the prospects of the plotters.[5] Wilson either did not know this or chose to ignore it. He took the threat very seriously, though he managed to joke about it in public. At a May Day rally he declared: "May I say for the benefit of those who have been carried away by the gossip of the last few days, that I know what's going on" – then, after a portentous pause – "*I'm* going on." The last words were a bright idea of Joe Haines, who had been recruited from the *Sun* as deputy and

9a. The 1964 Labour Cabinet.

9b. (*Right*) In earnest conference with Lord Goodman – "the original Pooh Bah", as Wilson described him.

10a and 10b. With Lyndon Johnson (above) and Richard and Pat Nixon (below). The bouquet should have been transferred to Mary Wilson before the photograph was taken, but this courtesy was overlooked.

11a, 11b and 11c. Wilson's affection for the world of "show-biz" was much manifested at Number 10. With the Beatles (above) in 1964. His decision to make them MBEs the following year was considered by Tony Benn to be an "appalling mistake". Right: he is interviewed by Gina Lollobrigida. Below: he sings along with Vera Lynn, a special favourite whom he made a Dame.

12. Wilson, with Paddy, his beloved labrador, when a puppy.

13. In the Isles of Scilly with Mary and Paddy in 1973.

14a. Wilson with Joe Haines at a Party Conference in Blackpool, looking more like a mafia boss and his henchman than a prime minister and his press officer.

14b. (*Below*) Wilson with Bernard Donoughue, with a somewhat breathless Marcia Williams trailing behind.

15a. Wilson with Barbara Castle at the Party Conference in November 1974.

15b. With the Australian Prime Minister, Gough Whitlam, and his publisher, George Weidenfeld.

16a. Wilson and Anthony Crosland are handed a pamphlet by a Ford shop steward at the entrance to Transport House.

16b. The 1974 Labour Cabinet.

later chief press secretary and thought the statement by itself was a little flat.

The left fumed ineffectively but could achieve nothing by themselves. Neil Kinnock and Terry Burns discussed "packing in Labour and forming a new party, to be founded on the trade unions". They even thought of a name for it – the Social Democratic Party – an idea which they might usefully have patented.[1] But it was the veteran moderate, Douglas Houghton, who struck the most effective blow at the government's policy. At a meeting of the PLP on 7 May he solemnly declared that no good that a contentious bill of this nature might do to the economy could possibly outweigh "the harm we can do to our Government by the disintegration or defeat of the Labour Party".[2] Coming from the respected and well-liked chairman of the PLP the impact of the statement was devastating to Wilson. It was quickly followed by a tumultuous Cabinet meeting in which Callaghan, in Benn's phrase, "more or less made an open challenge to Harold's leadership".[3] Crossman demanded that Callaghan should resign and Wilson angrily said that he had no intention of making way himself "since he was certain no one else could form a government".[4] According to Crossman, Callaghan crumpled in the face of this defiance but at lunch with Douglas Jay on the same day the Home Secretary was in a bellicose mood, using strong language about the way Wilson had tried to push *In Place of Strife* through the Cabinet and claiming Castle and Jenkins were the only other committed supporters of the bill.[5] Callaghan did not accept Crossman's invitation to resign, nor did Wilson suggest he should, but the Home Secretary was formally excluded from the newly formed Management Committee. The punishment caused him little grief; Wilson never pretended to like the Committee or to make much use of it. The first time it met he had just been having a private conclave with Crossman, Castle and Jenkins – who were in effect the real inner Cabinet. Wilson asked them to slip out and then reappear as if they had just arrived, so as not to give the Management Committee proper the feeling that decisions were being taken in their absence.[6] Whether or not this device was successful, meetings of the committee became increasingly erratic. So long as Callaghan remained in the Cabinet it clearly made little sense to exclude him from the inner Cabinet, and increasingly the latter became a rather pointless piece of extra machinery.

With *In Place of Strife* dominating the summer of 1969, its two architects, Wilson and Castle, were left to make the running. Their grasp on power seemed precarious, however. Wilson astonished Castle by remarking that he did not expect to get a deal with the unions but that "he and I were now too committed to back down. He therefore intended to make this a vote of confidence in *him* and, if we were defeated, he would stand down from the leadership." If Crossman, Jenkins and a few others threw in their lot with him, so much the better, but if necessary he and Castle should go alone. "I believe he is positively looking forward to being free to bid for the recapture of the Leadership in Opposition."[1] The unions duly performed their role in this scenario. They had been making conciliatory noises for some weeks but had failed to move on the vital question of unofficial strikes. On 1 June a group of union leaders dined at Chequers. Jack Jones was disconcerted when he found that Barbara Castle – "the queer one", as he called her – was present since he had been hoping for an easier run with Wilson by himself.[2] But Wilson was in no mood to compromise. Hugh Scanlon stated flatly that he would never accept any legislation that included penal powers. "If you say that, Hughie," replied Wilson, "then you are claiming to be the Government. I will never consent to preside over a Government that is not allowed to govern. And let us get one thing clear: that means we can't have a Labour Government, for I am the only person who can lead a Labour Government." Scanlon accused him of becoming a Ramsay MacDonald. "I have no intention of being a MacDonald," retorted Wilson. "Nor do I intend to be another Dubcek. Get your tanks off my lawn, Hughie!"*

But, though he might defy the unions, he could not ignore the fact that support in the party was seeping away. David Ennals, a moderate and junior minister, was typical of the solid centre on which the Prime Minister was accustomed to depend. "I believe that the TUC should now be given a chance to show whether their plans will work," he wrote in early June. For the government to continue to press for the penal clauses would sacrifice all the concessions that the unions had already made. "We might get the legislation through Parliament (though I think it is doubtful) but, if we got the Bill, there are enough determined men in the TU movement to ensure that industrial relations were worse, not better, as a result. The effect on the party would be catastrophic if we were to be plunged into a bitter conflict

---

* Several accounts of this dialogue exist, all similar in essence. This one corresponds with the recollection of Lady Falkender.

with the trade union movement. In my own constituency it would be very difficult to mount an effective electoral campaign, let alone win it. I fear we would be decimated."[1] Barbara Castle was apprehensive that the pressure was beginning to tell on Wilson and detected a dangerous readiness to compromise on his part as the negotiations dragged on into the middle of June. She exclaimed angrily that she believed they were heading for a sell-out and that she would never be a party to it. "He just can't resist drafting," said one of her officials indulgently.[2] He was right. Wilson thoroughly enjoyed exercising his skill in drafting weasel words which meant whatever one wanted them to and was busily producing formulae which might save the unions' face. But on this occasion at least he was still not prepared to hedge on the basic elements of his position.

At the Cabinet of 17 June he and Castle found themselves almost entirely isolated. Though the Chief Whip was not formally a member he insisted on making clear that in his view the party was not behind the legislation; the unions had gone far enough to meet the government to ensure that there would be little stomach left for a battle to the death over the remaining points of difference. Minister after minister doubted the need to force things further; the most effective intervention came from Peter Shore, who was so much considered to be Wilson's man that his rejection of direct confrontation with the unions was a destructive blow to the Prime Minister's position. When the Cabinet broke Wilson stormed out, snarling to Joe Haines who was waiting for him outside: "I don't mind running a green Cabinet but I'm buggered if I'm going to run a yellow one!" His fury faded as he savoured this phrase and he added cheerfully: "I'll use that."[3]

That evening things went even worse. Roy Jenkins, previously the most ardent supporter of the bill apart from Wilson and Castle, quietly dissociated himself from the initiative; Michael Stewart, who might have spoken up for the bill, was absent in the House of Commons; in the end only the Minister of Agriculture, Cledwyn Hughes, and George Thomas – hardly the most powerful of supporters – remained aligned with the Prime Minister. Wilson began to bluster, accused the Cabinet of being soft, cowardly, lily-livered, threatened to resign. His colleagues were disturbed but unshaken; in the end the most he could achieve was agreement that he should continue to negotiate as best he could but with no assurance that the Cabinet would support him if the deadlock with the unions continued.

"We've won," Wilson exclaimed exultantly to Castle. She, knowing only too well that the union leaders would be left in no doubt as to the weakness of the Prime Minister's bargaining position, was less optimistic.[1]

Fortunately for Wilson the union leaders were as reluctant to drive him to resignation as he was to resign. When the Prime Minister met the General Council of the TUC they still refused to contemplate accepting penal legislation or making any changes to their rules but undertook to enter into a "solemn and binding undertaking" to scrutinise the government's proposals on unofficial strikes. "Solomon Binding – sounds like a character out of George Eliot," an irreverent official remarked when the news became public; the assurance was almost as fictional as Mr Binding could ever have been, but it gave Wilson something he could take back to Cabinet and represent as a further concession by the unions. He and Castle resolutely put the best face on things. The unions' undertaking was "more binding than an exposition of the rules," Wilson told Healey. "This therefore gives us all we wanted. Cabinet and PLP very happy.'[2] Certainly the Cabinet and PLP were relieved. In June 1969 there was nobody who would have liked to see Wilson resign on such an issue. But though Castle assured the Cabinet that the settlement was all that could have been desired "due entirely to the superb way the Prime Minister handled the talks"; and though Wilson claimed that he had been accorded "an ovation unparalleled at Cabinet meetings",[3] nothing could conceal the fact that he had been defeated and had climbed down. Marsh's terse summary of the Cabinet's reaction sounds more convincing: "George Thomas said Wilson was marvellous, and Dick Crossman said he would now have to rewrite a chapter in his book on the power of the Prime Minister. No one else spoke!"[4]

In the short term the imbroglio over *In Place of Strife* was damaging to Wilson and his reputation. He emerged, said Benn, as "a small man with no sense of history and as somebody really without leadership qualities".[5] Crossman profited by the occasion to send the Prime Minister a weighty rebuke which he described to his wife as being in the tone of "a senior house master addressing an unsuccessful headmaster". He felt, he said, that the new sense of responsibility shown by the TUC was of real importance but it had been achieved at a painful cost in Cabinet solidarity. Wilson had accused his ministers of being soft and cowardly and ratting on Cabinet decisions. "I want you to understand what it is that makes honourable, decent colleagues behave in what you feel is such an unworthy way." The Cabinet felt that it had been bounced into accepting the White Paper and "the appalling risks it implied" as a result of private discussions between Wilson and a handful of favoured intimates. "I am not arguing that Prime Ministers are *never* entitled to take only a few colleagues into their confidence on making a big decision and then swing the Cabinet behind. But you can only afford to do so on rare occasions." With Wilson it had become the norm. Wilson's leadership in the past five years had "consisted of a series of sudden adventures and new initiatives, in launching each of which you have associated with you a different group of colleagues. Someone less energetic and bouncy would have kept a better continuous control of the Government's whole strategy and had more time to observe the morale of the Cabinet." Crossman's letter ended with a plea to Wilson to mend his ways, to become more detached and to give himself time for central oversight of Cabinet policy – advice which the Prime Minister was to follow when he returned to power in 1974. For the moment, Wilson claimed to have written a long reply to Crossman but to have decided not to send it but instead to reserve it for his memoirs.[1] No letter of that nature seems to survive. Crossman's reprimands were kind compared with those of the press, which were almost entirely abusive. Wilson was portrayed as a humiliated and defeated man – to Castle's indignation, who felt that the proper target was not "Harold personally" but "a cowardly Cabinet".[2] For Healey, *In Place of Strife* had done for Wilson what Clause IV had done for Gaitskell, led him into a hopeless battle which destroyed the unity of the party without any corresponding advantage or real hope of it.[3]

Yet in the longer term, or to those detached from the immediate struggle, things looked different. "I have had my fill of the sordid and morbid press campaign against you," wrote Lee Kuan Yew. The bill was both necessary and popular with the public yet "the press have deliberately worked up hysteria amongst the PLP, until they look like Gadarene swine plunging headlong to perdition."[4] The history of industrial relations in Britain over the following decade does not suggest that the unions' undertakings – however solemn and binding in their nature – were adequate to meet the needs of the time. If the reform of the unions was not undertaken by a friendly Labour government, Wilson always maintained, then it would fall to the hostile Tories. The defeat of Harold Wilson made inevitable the eventual triumph of Margaret Thatcher. Wilson was convinced that the policy he advocated was right for the party, for the unions and for the country, and he pursued it with striking determination and single-mindedness. He fought his battle to the last ditch and in the end, in Peter Jenkins's phrase, "he did not climb down, he was dragged down".[1]

The last word belongs to the man who was with him almost the whole way and only at the last minute deserted the foundering ship. Roy Jenkins summed up the dénouement of *In Place of Strife* with characteristic generosity. "Wilson," he wrote, "behaved with a touch of King Lear-like nobility. He sounded fairly unhinged at times and there was a wild outpouring of words. But he did not hedge and he did not whine ... It was a sad story from which he and Barbara Castle emerged with more credit than the rest of us."[2]

Samson had not brought down the pillars of the temple but he had given them a nasty shock. It remained to shore up what was left of the building. Wilson set himself to the task with his usual resilience. Crying over spilt milk had never been a habit of his. Within a few days of his defeat he was remarking to William Armstrong: "Poor Barbara. She hangs around like someone with a still-born child. She can't believe it's dead."[3] Wilson knew it was dead, gave it a decent burial and looked to the future. He contemplated calling back Brown and visited him in July after his former deputy had emerged from hospital. The approach backfired; Brown refused to return except in his former position and this Wilson would not contemplate. A newspaper story in September reported that Brown would not be coming back since he could work just as effectively for the party from outside. "Why he failed, as a matter of common courtesy, to tell me of his decision ... must remain a mystery to me," wrote Brown huffily.[4] Reconciliation with Callaghan was easier to achieve; in September he was admitted back to the Management Committee. "I think he is behaving now," Wilson confided in his colleagues;[5] which, since Callaghan had won his point and had nothing left to misbehave over, was hardly a matter for surprise. Yet Wilson was in no mood to recant himself; at the TUC meeting in Portsmouth in the autumn he made "a speech of unrepentant courage", making no apologies for his aborted legislation and urging the unions not to backslide on their undertakings.[6] His confidence was bolstered by the trade figures, which showed a comfortable surplus. The standing of Labour in the country was recovering; a crop of by-elections in October, which at one point had seemed likely to prove disastrous, turned out considerably better than expected. The swing to the Tories, which had been up to 20 per cent, now dropped back to 11 per cent. Hopes of a Labour victory at the general election which had to come some time in 1970 or early 1971, for long at low ebb, now began cautiously to revive.

The greatest danger to the government lay in the avalanche of pay claims, which showed no signs of moderating however good the intentions of the unions. At a press conference in January 1970 Wilson passed on a question on this subject to Barbara Castle. "It is only this incredible capacity of his to take occasions like this in an almost offhand way that keeps him going, I suppose," mused Castle. "He saves his real thinking and intriguing for the House of Commons and power relationships."[1] When the matter was discussed in Cabinet in February, Wilson suggested that all increases should be phased in three stages, thus ensuring that there would only be one increase before the election and that the Tories would have to carry the can for the remaining two-thirds if they won. "It was the crudest political statement I had yet heard," wrote Benn. His opinion of Wilson dropped to its lowest point.[2]

In such an atmosphere every happening was scanned for possible political advantage or disadvantage. A Czech defector, Joseph Frolik, fed MI5 with stories that various Labour members, including Will Owen, Tom Driberg and the Postmaster-General, John Stonehouse, were in the pay of Czech intelligence. Wilson was sceptical, the more so since MI5, in a moment of over-excitement, confused Will and David Owen and maintained that the latter was a spy. He had no intention of blocking an enquiry, however, and his prudence was justified when it was found that Will Owen had indeed been taking money from the Czechs in exchange for – largely worthless – information. No evidence was found to justify prosecution of either Driberg or Stonehouse, though the Prime Minister had no illusions about the probity of the former and the latter was to come to a spectacularly sticky end in Wilson's final administration. Though Wilson still had exaggerated respect for the intelligence services in fields where he had no specialised knowledge – as in the effect of sanctions on the Rhodesian economy – he reckoned that he knew more about his colleagues than they did and was prepared to make his opinion clear. But if the needs of the party demanded the sacrifice of a few individuals, then he would be ready to oblige.

Even with an election imminent he did not play party politics on every issue. In November 1969 the Duke of Edinburgh, while in the United States, made some remarks on television about the royal family going into the red because of the inadequacy of the civil list. Castle, Crossman and the republican wing of the Cabinet took exception to this and wanted to make some political capital by setting up a select committee to enquire into the whole question of the royal finances. Wilson had considerable and probably well-justified doubt as to whether there were many votes to be gained out of being unpleasant to the royal family, but rallied to their defence for quite different reasons and would have done so even if the balance of advantage had clearly been the other way. He refused to succumb to the pressure of his left wing and produced in the House of Commons what Crossman described as "the best parliamentary performance I have ever seen". As Crossman admitted, this was not a standard piece of Wilsonian party polemic. He was so good, "because Harold cares so passionately about the Queen and the monarchy". His object was to protect them and to prevent the problem of their finances being turned into a political football and kicked around between the parties. "It was astonishingly different from his normal performance and I thought, 'Oh God, Harold, if only you could behave like this on other issues and not always feel that everything is a matter of making party capital.' "[1]

The reform of the civil service was another issue which was close to Wilson's heart and not viewed by him primarily as a pawn in the game of party politics. Shortly before the 1966 election he had set up a Royal Commission under Lord Fulton which he had originally intended to enquire into the whole world of public administration, including the relationship of civil servants to ministers. Under pressure from the mandarins, the terms of reference had been whittled down and the final report, published in June 1968, concentrated on recruitment and training and eschewed any fundamental examination of the relevance of the civil service to the needs of the present day. Fulton "and Harold are tremendous buddies who live in the same world of uninspired commonsense", wrote Crossman. "The Report is perfectly sensible but, oh dear, it lacks distinction."[2] It recommended a new civil service department, a civil service college and the abolition of the system by which recruits were graded according to an arcane scale of values which dictated from the start the sort of work they could expect to do throughout their careers and the level to which they could hope to rise. Wilson found it hard to whip up much enthusiasm in Cabinet for these proposals, indeed the Chancellor led a strong opposition to their main thrust, but he persisted and at least acted quickly on the first recommendation, appointing Lord Shackleton as minister responsible for the new department, working directly to him. Shackleton set to work to establish the new system, but the civil service has always been adept at braking or emasculating reforms about which it has reservations, most of all when the reforms concern its own workings. The college was in the course of being set up by the time of the 1970 election but little progress had been made on other fronts and the Fulton Report, in itself only a shadow of what Wilson had once intended, was no more than the shadow of a shadow by the time it had worked its way through to implementation on the ground.

The Prime Minister's private secretary, Michael Halls, was, Wilson wrote, "the epitome of the new management type envisaged by the Fulton committee"[1] – a fact which perhaps explained some of the scepticism with which he was viewed in the higher reaches of Whitehall. He had been an energetic champion of the report and his sudden death in April 1970 helped take some of the impetus out of what was anyway a flagging enterprise. His death was a personal blow to Wilson: it had been a very great shock, he told a friend, "and a tremendous loss to us all, and I am afraid I shall take a long time to recover from it".[2] To sorrow at the loss of someone whom he had liked and trusted, Wilson added a sense of guilt; he knew that Halls had been promoted beyond his proper level and that the strain this had imposed on him had contributed to his fatal heart attack. It was an appalling blow for him, wrote Crossman; the two men were naturally attuned to each other, men of the same scale; "Halls was a small civil servant and even if Harold is a successful Prime Minister he is a small politician."[3] Small or not, Halls's death could hardly have come at a more unfortunate time, when a general election would shortly absorb all the energies of the political staff and make it essential to have someone who knew the ropes and could be fully trusted in charge at Number 10. Halls died on 3 April; within a fortnight Wilson was to make up his mind that the election should be in June. Already, at their conference at Selsdon, the Tory leaders had marked out the battle lines with their pledges to reduce taxation,

restrict immigration and reform trade union laws. The conference
had been a great propaganda success, Wilson grudgingly admitted.
The time had come for Labour to go on the offensive. Were ministers
prepared to go into action to destroy the other side? he asked the
Management Committee. "Harold always asks this when the critical
point comes and implies that only he does it," noted Crossman
resignedly.[1]

After nearly six years of government, what sort of record did Wilson
have to defend? Those disposed to do so could compile a formidable
dossier of accusations. They could point to a series of financial crises
and a forced devaluation; to a military retreat from east of Suez
undertaken not on grounds of principle but under the pressure of
force majeure; to a party riven by differences over Vietnam with
an unprecedented series of by-election losses to account for and
membership fallen from 830,000 to 680,000; to an unsolved Rhodesian problem and a Europe as reluctant as ever to accept Britain as
a member; to unregenerate unions defying all efforts to reform them
and an ever more grossly inflated bureaucracy in the public sector.
Most cogently of all, he was attacked for running an unhappy ship,
still worse, an unhealthy ship. John Freeman spoke for many of the
junior and some of the senior ministers when he bemoaned the
seamier side of the Wilson administration. All decisions, it seemed to
him, were taken on the grounds of personal or party advantage rather
than the national interest.[2]

And yet this was not the whole story. The Labour government had
inherited a balance of payments deficit of £800 million a year; it went
to the polls in 1970 with a surplus of £600 million which showed
every sign of growing still larger. The vast majority of the population
was better off, wages had risen faster than the cost of living in five
out of the six years Wilson had been Prime Minister. Britain was a
fairer place; pensions, children's allowances, redundancy payments
had been introduced; more houses had been built in the public sector
and a start had been made in tackling the problems of race relations.
Universities and polytechnics throve, the Open University was on
the march. Capital punishment had been abolished, penal reform
advanced, the rights of women and homosexuals strengthened.
Regional development had been encouraged – in south Wales, the

north-east and Clydeside in particular.[1] Not all this was directly to Wilson's credit, any more than the catalogue of disasters could be held entirely against him, but if he is to be damned for the first it seems only fair that he should be praised for the second.

Shortly before the election Harold Wilson told Roy Jenkins that, if he won, he was determined to hand over the premiership in the course of the next government. Jenkins had heard this before and had never paid much attention; Wilson was only just fifty-four and it seemed inconceivable that he was seriously thinking of retiring. This time however Wilson specified a date: by 14 June 1973 he would have been in office longer than Asquith. That would be the time for him to go. For the first time Jenkins believed that he might really mean it.[2]

XVI

Foreign Affairs

1967–1970

Nothing would have pleased Wilson more than to exhibit on the hustings in 1970 a settlement of the Rhodesian problem. Nothing could have seemed less likely. Wilson had finally accepted that the only way he could bring effective pressure on Smith's government was through South Africa. He loathed the South African regime and yet felt bound to conciliate it. One of the factors that had lent an equivocal air to his attitude over the supply of arms to South Africa was his fear lest, if he were too intransigent, the South Africans might get their own back by egging on the Rhodesians to reject a settlement. He was extremely sensitive to criticism of his posture. Late in 1969 Roy Hattersley in an interview on television remarked that a man's attitude towards South African trade had to be a personal one. The Prime Minister, he thought, had said in the House of Commons that he and Mrs Wilson bought very few South African goods. "The Hattersley household buys none. But that is a matter of private conscience." Wilson, not surprisingly, took exception to this piece of holier-than-thouness. It suggested, he wrote crossly, that he was half-hearted in his dislike of apartheid. Would Hattersley in future please confine himself to discussing the Prime Minister's well-known views on the sale of arms?[1] But his reluctance to offend Pretoria caused dismay abroad as well. "If we dilute our policy towards South Africa to harmonize with the United Kingdom, we risk becoming identified as a protector of the white redoubt," the State Department warned the President.[2]

By the middle of 1967 Wilson was talking of a resumption of negotiations with Ian Smith and writing indignantly to Duncan Sandys to deny that he was insisting on immediate African rule in Rhodesia: "I have made it clear that immediate or even early majority rule is out of the question."[1] The conscience of the left began to stir. "I am not going to hand the Africans over to those white fascists," reflected Barbara Castle. But then, she was honest enough to admit, she had no wish to "hand the Europeans over to the Nkomos and Sitholes, who can't even agree". She argued against further talks, but did not see how they could be avoided.[2] In October 1967 the South African Prime Minister wrote to report that Smith was now prepared to settle on the basis of the 1961 constitution with provisions included to satisfy the "Six Principles", the conditions safeguarding the rights of the black majority on which any negotiated settlement would have to be based. It seemed that progress really might be possible.[3] To step up sanctions would merely make a settlement more difficult, said Vorster. They were certainly not being successful in bringing the Rhodesian government to heel. The crucial import to deny the Rhodesians was oil. In spite of an embargo which in theory was powerfully enforced, Rhodesia continued to get most if not all the oil it needed, apparently through the Portuguese colony of Mozambique. British ministers at first believed that the main offender was the French oil company, Total, but compelling evidence was later assembled to show that Shell and BP were also heavily involved. How much Wilson knew personally about the traffic is obscure. Enough information was available to Number 10 to make it evident that either his officials were deliberately keeping him in the dark – which seemed highly unlikely – or that he preferred not to enquire too deeply. It is a curious episode, since both his pride and his personal convictions might have been expected to lead him to insist that sanctions should be applied with the utmost vigour, but an element of self-deception, wilful or not, was involved. He himself used later to maintain that, though he believed that there had been breaches of sanctions by the British oil companies, he had been misled by the intelligence services into thinking they were trivial in scale. The defence is inadequate; at the very least he must have been told enough to satisfy him that there was more to know and that it was his duty to find out.[4]

The financial crisis at the end of 1967 so far absorbed Wilson's energies that he did not contemplate any serious initiative until the New Year. Then, in March, in what seemed calculated defiance of international opinion, the Rhodesian authorities executed a group of African prisoners who were under sentence of death, some for offences committed after the UDI. Though in Cabinet Wilson announced that this had "effectively slammed the door" on further negotiations, he almost simultaneously told the Governor of Rhodesia, Humphrey Gibbs, that this was not the case but that the Cabinet now had "to reckon with the sense of outrage which is rightly felt throughout the world at the recent illegal hangings ... In this situation it is proving extremely difficult to keep the whole Commonwealth – not only its African members – together." He called for patience and prudence; "we shall be prepared to pick up the threads again as soon as we are satisfied that we are dealing with people who can be trusted to give effect to the spirit as well as the letter of the six principles."[1] He was still reluctant to contemplate any step which might lead to a breakdown of law and order in Rhodesia. "His paralysis of will when the chips are down is his great liability," fulminated Castle. "He would rather drift into disaster than meet it half way."[2] Instead he confined his efforts to calling for mandatory sanctions on Rhodesia at the United Nations. Even this seemed excessive to the Australian Prime Minister, John Gorton, who complained that the black Rhodesians would be the first to suffer. Most members of the UN would think that the British proposals did not go far enough, replied Wilson. His measures were the minimum needed if "we were to head off quite unacceptable proposals for the use of force or for sanctions against South Africa and Portugal".[3]

Within three months another exploratory and informal mission was on its way to Salisbury, this time consisting of the proprietor of the *Sunday* and *Daily Express*, Max Aitken, with Arnold Goodman as legal adviser and minder. They got sufficient encouragement from Smith to convince a very easily convincible Wilson that it was worth holding another round of talks. There was "a widespread feeling in the country in favour of a settlement of the Rhodesian issue," he told Michael Stewart, "and this would therefore be of great political value". Rhodesia was "a millstone round our necks", and he did not feel justified in rejecting any negotiations if there seemed a real possibility that they might lead to the installation of a broad-based government and the acceptance of the Six Principles. If the white Rhodesians would accept this position, he could return to the Commonwealth and ask to be released from the commitment to insist on NIBMAR. Smith at the moment still seemed intransigent on certain vital issues but, "I believe that we should put ourselves into an impossible position in national politics – and possibly internationally – if his refusal to give away all his negotiating points in advance were used by us to justify a refusal of negotiations."[1]

These were the words of a man resolved to engage in talks however dire the auguries. He was not optimistic, he told President Johnson, but he had been given just enough encouragement to justify the effort.[2] He presented his decision to the Cabinet as a *fait accompli*, then made a great show of asking everyone for their opinion. "I get a bit sick of being asked for my view when the TV cameras are outside and everyone knows you are going," complained Callaghan. "I will wish you good luck and say no more."[3] Callaghan, at least, was generally in favour of the initiative. From New York the UK permanent representative at the United Nations, Lord Caradon, said bluntly that he would resign rather than defend a settlement based on the 1961 proposals.[4] Kaunda threatened that he would consider any withdrawal from the pledge to insist on NIBMAR as "a capitulation to the forces of racialism".[5] Wilson's trump card was his plan to offer substantial sums of money to help the higher education of the African population. This was something to which Smith could hardly take exception, yet by speeding up the timescale in which Africans would become qualified to vote, it would appease Wilson's critics from the black Commonwealth. Wilson estimated that Britain might have to provide £5 million a year for ten years. "I am sure," he wrote to Jenkins, "that in considering this proposal you will bear in mind not only that a settlement should be of early assistance to our general balance of payments, but also that the Rhodesians owe us considerable sums of money, of which we shall be in a position to secure the repayment as part of a settlement."[6]

For the talks the two leaders returned to Gibraltar, this time holding their meetings not at sea but aboard HMS *Fearless* alongside the quay. It soon became clear that the main stumbling block lay in the difficulty of guaranteeing that the African population would in fact be allowed to advance unimpeded towards majority rule once independence had been granted. Wilson proved to be "very naive on some issues", a senior official, Maurice James, remembered[7] – a charge which could certainly not be levelled at his opposite number, Ian Smith. Smith made concessions, but Wilson made more, and the terms that were taken back for consideration in Salisbury and London went to the limit of what could be offered if the Six Principles were to be preserved. Some said they went too far. That Wilson himself was alive to the risks was shown by the telegram he sent to Stewart in New York just before the talks ended: "I do not think a settlement is likely with Smith but it remains a possibility." If it comes off "I want to speak to Caradon personally before he makes any public pronouncement."[1] Resignations from within his own ranks were the last things Wilson wanted if a settlement were reached. Nor was Caradon the only doubter: Shirley Williams deplored a situation where Britain might find itself "aligned *against* the developing world, against the developing members of the Commonwealth and Canada, and on the same side as South Africa"; while Reg Prentice, Minister of Overseas Development and one of the most right-wing members of the government, found the *Fearless* proposals unacceptable: "I should be likely to resign if a settlement were reached on terms which I could not regard as fulfilling our basic obligations."[2] Perhaps unsurprisingly, the talks on *Fearless* had been markedly harmonious. The only serious problem a Foreign Office official could remember related to the question whether Wilson could read the first lesson on Sunday morning without Smith reading the other. Wilson was quite happy for both of them to perform but his PPS, Harold Davies, exclaimed in dismay that it would be political dynamite and go down badly with Labour voters. In the end the captain read both.[3] Smith was "urbane and charming", wrote Marcia Williams; she felt that he and Wilson "had rather more in common with each other than they would probably have liked to admit".[4]

Wilson could hardly have expected to escape unsavaged by the black Commonwealth leaders. Milton Obote hinted broadly that Uganda would leave the Commonwealth if the *Fearless* terms were ratified, an attitude which George Thomson, the Commonwealth Secretary, feared might well be shared by the President of Kenya, Jomo Kenyatta;[5] while Kaunda wrote to Wilson in terms so blistering that the Prime Minister's reply rang with genuine distress. Why are you "so ready to give more credence to evidence planted with malicious intent than to the assurances I have given you direct?" asked Wilson. There was no sell-out, no abandonment of the Six Principles, in particular the fifth, "which transcends all the others in that it lays down that any settlement must be shown to be acceptable to the people of Rhodesia as a whole ... While you might question our judgment, you have no cause and equally no right to question our good faith."[6]

If at times he wondered what he had got himself into, Wilson showed no signs of disquiet and continued doggedly down his chosen path. The next step was to send George Thomson to Salisbury to establish whether the tentative accords established on *Fearless* could be developed into a full settlement. Thomson had, indeed, authority to trade off certain points in the British position if to do so would lead to a quick return of the Rhodesians to legality and was "deeply disappointed and perplexed" when forbidden to offer the alternative propositions until it was known whether Smith would concede on the other outstanding points. "We must ask you to remember our difficulties here," replied Wilson, "which would become very grave indeed if we departed too far or too fast from the tactics which Cabinet agreed before you left."[1] To the relief of most of the Cabinet the initiative foundered like its predecessors; even Wilson felt some satisfaction that he did not need to defend a highly unpopular settlement to his party. He had no illusions about the reception he would have received: "Comparison with Munich is so misleading," he wrote to the MP for Portsmouth, Frank Judd, "that I am frankly astonished that it should be used by members of the Parliamentary Labour Party to their own Government. There would be nothing racialist in an honourable settlement specifically designed to safeguard the position of the Rhodesian African. I do not accept that it would lower our standing in the world."[2]

He would also have had the still more dismal task of defending the settlement at the Commonwealth conference of January 1969. Some months before Wilson had written to the Prime Ministers in Ottawa, Canberra and Wellington to say that this could be the most important conference yet:

It seems to me that if we are to regain full support for and confidence in the Commonwealth among its members, at a time when many critics question its relevance and value in the modern world, the meeting must be a constructive success, and be seen to be a success. I think we should all be diminished if the Commonwealth broke up in anger or died of inanition. And if we cannot between us develop this system of international cooperation, with the advantage the Commonwealth enjoys of a common language and shared traditions in almost every field of human activity, we face a poor prospect in the search for peace and a more general detente in the world at large.[3]

It was vital, he thought, that the conference should not be dominated by a single issue, as it had been in 1966. If the *Fearless* terms had been agreed by Smith, this hope would have been faint indeed. As it was, the debate on Rhodesia occupied two days, with much vigorous discussion and some acrimony. Wilson's speech was received, if not with approbation, then at least with some sympathy. The majority of those present seemed to feel that British policy was misguided but not intolerably so, and that Wilson should be left to handle matters in his own way. Wilson managed the meeting with great skill and to good effect: he was at his best, remarked Crossman sourly, chairing a Commonwealth conference "where nothing much is happening, and all that is required is skill, tenacity, agility, subtlety at keeping the thing going and no great imagination or strategy".[1]

Matters dragged on for another year, when Rhodesia declared itself a republic. It made no real difference, but this further breach underlined disagreeably, just before the election, how little had been achieved by the British government since the UDI.

Hard though he tried, he had no more to show for his efforts over Vietnam. He was still convinced that he had a role to play as honest broker between the Americans and the Russians. His reward was to cause some irritation in almost every quarter. Johnson was on the whole well disposed towards him and sympathetic to his domestic problems, but his exasperation at Britain's failure fully to support the American position from time to time boiled over: "I suppose I'll have that little creep camping on my doorstep again!" he is said to have remarked when he heard that Wilson had called the 1966 election.[2] Bertrand Russell, on the other wing, was still more condemnatory; when visas were refused for Vietnamese witnesses who were to testify at the "International War Crimes Tribunal" which he proposed to hold in London, Russell wrote angrily to the Prime Minister, claiming that "such an illiberal action is in keeping with the record of your Administration".[3] Undeterred, Wilson ploughed on. Early in February 1967 Kosygin visited London. Wilson telegraphed enthusiastically to Johnson to report that there had been a significant change in the Russian attitude. Kosygin was now "obsessed with Chinese behaviour and anxious to see an end to the Vietnam war because ... the continuance of the war strengthens the hands of the Chinese". He had suggested that Hanoi was now ready to settle by negotiation: "Exactly what would you be prepared to accept in the forms of a sign from North Vietnam sufficient to bring about a cessation of the bombing?"[4] On the basis of what he thought to be firm assurances from Washington Wilson then told Kosygin that the Americans would stop bombing North Vietnam "as soon as they are sure that infiltration from North Vietnam to South Vietnam will stop". Rather to his surprise, Kosygin seemed genuinely interested in this formula. What he did not know but Kosygin did, was that there had been a hardening of the line in Washington and a message had almost simultaneously been conveyed to Hanoi saying that the Americans would stop their bombing as soon as they were sure that infiltration "had stopped". Either through "sheer carelessness or bureaucratic confusion" – to quote from the American publication of the official documents[1] – London was not informed of the change in line. When Chet Cooper, who had been sent to London by Johnson to be in attendance during the negotiations with Kosygin, protested to the President's adviser, Walt Rostow, the latter retorted with some brutality: "Well, we don't give a goddam about you and we don't give a goddam about Wilson."[2]

"You will realise what a hell of a situation I am in for the last day of talks," wailed Wilson. ". . . I can only now get out of this position if I say to him either that I am not in your confidence or that there was a sudden and completely unforeseeable change in Washington which, as a loyal satellite, I must follow. I cannot say either . . . I am standing by, as I must, the document which I handed to Kosygin . . . before I received Rostow's message. Both Kosygin and I know that, as of today, you cannot accept this. The only thing I can do is to say to Kosygin: if he will go along with this one and press it on Hanoi, I will similarly press it on you. If I do get Kosygin to agree, then I must press our line on you, and if it is impossible for you to accept we shall have to reason together about the situation which will then arise."[3]

Johnson was not quite so harsh in his response as Rostow had been but he gave Wilson little encouragement. He did not believe that the matter could turn on a matter of verbs or tenses. They wanted and had always wanted "an assured stoppage of infiltration" – a promise that infiltration would stop in the future was not enough and the North Vietnamese knew this as well as anyone. In an earlier telegram Wilson had said that he and Kosygin were like two lawyers trying to get a settlement out of court. "I am always glad to know that you are in my corner," Johnson concluded drily, "but I would have some difficulty, in view of my responsibilities and problems here, in giving anyone a power of attorney."[4]

Cooper had no doubt that the main blame for the imbroglio rested with Washington, but equally considered that Wilson had acted with impetuosity and overestimated the value of his enterprise. "He didn't have peace within his grasp, he was always overly optimistic about it ... The U.S. administration regarded Wilson at best as marginal, at worst as a nuisance; and did not bother to keep him informed of their own thinking, even when he thought he was negotiating on their behalf."[1] Wilson was untroubled by such reflections; he assured Crossman that he possessed the "absolute confidence" of both Kosygin and Johnson.[2] But he was uncertain enough about Johnson's second thoughts to send the President a long memorandum summarising what had happened in London. He doubted whether Rostow, whom he deeply distrusted and described as Johnson's Rasputin,[3] had reported the matter fully or fairly. "Moreover," he told Brown, "while it could be argued that at a time when we need support from [the President] over the German offset problem, we should not press him over Vietnam, I think that on balance it is just as likely that he may feel some concern at the way things were handled in London while Kosygin was here, and that a message reminding him of this could dispose him sympathetically over offset."[4]

Whether or not Wilson's message affected Johnson's attitude, the President did seem to take greater pains to retain Wilson's support during the rest of 1967. His view of the special relationship was probably close to that delicately set out by Kissinger: "We do not suffer in the world from such an excess of friends that we should discourage those who feel that they have a special friendship for us."[5] When Wilson went to Washington in June he was received, as Tony Benn sourly expressed it, "with all the trumpets appropriate for a weak foreign head of state who has to be buttered up so that he can carry the can for American foreign policy".[6] In October, when Wilson stoutly defended the American position at the party conference, Johnson was still more glowing in his tributes. "With what I confront every day," he wrote, "it was not hard for me to reconstruct what you faced. I think you understand how much it matters that the government of the country which means most to me, aside from my own, is lending its support for what we all know is right, despite the storms around us."[7] But the price of Johnson's adulation was trouble at home. The Chief Whip warned Wilson that "unease and opposition on Vietnam was no longer the prerogative of the Left, but now spread across the centre and the right." Most alarming of all, Roy Jenkins was said to have been brainwashed by J.K. Galbraith while in Washington and persuaded into a strongly anti-government position. "I told the Chief Whip to treat this with the greatest seriousness," recorded an alarmed Wilson.[1]

Some gesture was essential if he were to keep the party united. He planned to make it in Washington in February 1968 when at a White House dinner Wilson responded to Johnson's bland and platitudinous speech of welcome with a brisk attack on American policy in Vietnam. The young Winston Churchill – grandson of the former Prime Minister – who happened to be present, was sickened by what he felt to be patent playing to the London gallery; on the left wing of that gallery Barbara Castle was notably unappeased, surmising that Wilson had cleared his text with Johnson in advance; but with most moderates, Tory as well as Labour, the speech was a success.[2] The text had *not* been cleared with Johnson in advance but the President knew pretty well what was coming and was not unduly discomposed. Wilson confirmed that his heart was still in the right place when he reported to Johnson from New York on the "pretty disheartening" two and a half hours he had just spent with U Thant at the United Nations. Brown had described U Thant as "wet, repeat, wet" and Wilson concurred. He had been dismayed by the Secretary-General's "weak-kneed and biased posture ... The Russians have clearly put him through the wringer in Moscow." U Thant's main themes were condemnation of the American bombing in North Vietnam and criticism of the conduct of the recent elections in the South. Wilson responded with what he described as "a reasonably controlled burst of temper" and said that U Thant ought to stop making contentious and one-sided statements and concentrate on getting people round a conference table.[3] It would be surprising if Wilson's haranguing of the Secretary-General was anything like as forthright as he represented it to Johnson, but he achieved the object of the exercise – to emphasise that though he had to make occasional public gestures, privately he was still sound in his defence of American policy.

In the expectation that Senator Hubert Humphrey would succeed Johnson in the election at the end of 1968 Wilson had chosen John Freeman to be British Ambassador in Washington. The strategy came disastrously unstuck when the Republican, Richard Nixon, was elected. Freeman had insulted Nixon in the *New Statesman* when he described him as "a man of no principle whatever except a willingness to sacrifice everything in the cause of Dick Nixon", and the new President's first reaction was to refuse to have anything to do with him. Freeman offered to resign but Wilson stuck by his guns and, against the advice of the American Embassy, included the British Ambassador in the first dinner he gave for Nixon in Britain. He was proved right when Nixon greeted Freeman with striking generosity. Wilson gratefully wrote on the President's menu: "You can't guarantee being born a lord. It is possible – you've shown it – to be born a gentleman."[1]

In spite of this propitious start, Kissinger claims that Nixon never liked Wilson. He distrusted his views and resented the way in which he greeted the President "with the avuncular good will of the head of an ancient family that had seen better times but is still able to evoke memories of the wisdom, dignity and power that had established the family name in the first place". When Wilson suggested that they call each other by their Christian names, "A fish-eyed stare from Nixon squelched this idea."[2] Fish-eyed or not, by March 1969 the President was starting his letters "Dear Harold" and signing them off "Dick Nixon".[3] Freeman felt that the two men got on well together; a pair of tough, professional politicians who turned out to have far more in common with each other than the theoretically more compatible Nixon and Heath.[4] Certainly Nixon's first overture as President was notably flattering. He was intent, he assured Wilson, "upon upholding the close relationship between British Prime Ministers and American Presidents". He therefore wanted to visit London first in a round of the European capitals he was to make early in 1969. "I am most anxious to get your views on a wide range of problems."[5] Wilson foresaw the possibility of hostile demonstrations and was anyway unsure whether a close relationship with the American President would be something to boast about with a general election in the offing.[6] Nixon was therefore received at Chequers, but was greeted with such enthusiasm that he had no reason to feel slighted.

Wilson was soon convinced – as anyone who knew him well would have predicted – that he had achieved as intimate a rapport with the new President as he had ever enjoyed with his predecessor. Nixon's real view of Wilson was probably much as Kissinger represented it, but he would also have endorsed his Secretary of State's more positive opinions: "In my experience Wilson was a sincere friend of the United States. His emotional ties, like those of most Britons, were across the oceans and not across the Channel ... He had spent much time in the United States; he sincerely believed in the Anglo-American partnership ... As to his reliability ... With the United States I always found him a man of his word."[1] But though Nixon may have valued his support, he did not take Wilson seriously enough to change policy to suit his views. He was genuinely anxious to disengage in Vietnam, but not at a rate that would give his ally any electoral advantage. "Vietnam must be counted as one of Harold's greater failures," commented Barbara Castle, after hearing of Nixon's supposed schedule for a phased evacuation.[2] It was the My Lai massacres and the extension of the war to Cambodia, not any move towards peace, which were in the minds of the British public when they went to the polls in June 1970.

Much though the Americans hoped for some gesture of support for their policy in Vietnam, they were at least as anxious that Britain should not renege on its international responsibilities, whether east of Suez or in Europe. Emotionally, Wilson was as committed to the global role as his allies could have wished; the cruel facts of economics inexorably forced him to accept a more restricted field for British policy. The financial crisis of July 1966 led to British insistence that the German government should meet the full cost in foreign currency of maintaining the Army of the Rhine. Withdrawal was the only alternative. Johnson at once expressed alarm about "the dangers of an unravelling in NATO which could easily get out of hand".[3] Some hard bargaining followed, at the end of which the Americans offered to buy $35 million worth of military equipment in Britain to help offset the costs of keeping troops in Germany. Such a package, Rostow assured Johnson, would "further nail Wilson East of Suez".[4] Wilson, who was more than happy to be nailed there if the cross were made sufficiently comfortable, promised that there would be no substantial withdrawals before, at least, June 1967.

But by early 1967 the demands in the PLP to withdraw, or at least cut down British forces east of Suez were becoming too clamorous to ignore. At a party meeting Woodrow Wyatt remarked that the only explanation for present policy must be the need to satisfy the American paymaster. Wilson indignantly, if somewhat disingenuously, denied that there was any link between American aid and a British presence east of Suez. In that case, retorted Wyatt, British policy was even sillier than he had supposed.[5] The line could not be held indefinitely. By the middle of the year a compromise had evolved under which British forces in South-East Asia would be substantially reduced, and phased out altogether in the course of the next decade. Wilson wrote to the Prime Minister of Australia, Harold Holt, to warn him that the best basis for planning would be an assumption that British forces would be withdrawn "by sometime in the mid 1970s". It might be possible to develop facilities in Australia to rehouse some of the departing forces. "None of this as you will understand affects our firm intentions to stand by Australia as Australia has stood by us in two World Wars."[1] Not surprisingly uncomforted by this pious assurance, Holt replied that he was "gravely troubled" by Wilson's news: "You have not fully realised the moral influence ... that British wisdom and experience – which must be desirably backed by a continuing British presence – can bring to ... this area of the world."[2] Wilson would willingly have lavished all the wisdom and experience in the world on the Asian and Australasian Commonwealth, but a continuing British military presence was more than he dared promise.

When Wilson had visited Washington earlier that year, Johnson had been warned that Britain's intentions east of Suez looked like being "inimical to U.S. interests". He should "maintain the hard line that the British plan is unacceptable ... We have assisted the British in Europe and elsewhere and are in no position to assume added responsibilities."[3] Now the American Ambassador, David Bruce urged that the President should be more flexible. Wilson was "under heavy pressure and wants to have something to satisfy party". An announcement that he proposed to withdraw from east of Suez would be "probably the juiciest bone he could throw his critics". The vital thing was that he should not weaken in his long-term strategy on the domestic economy and entry into Europe. "The Prime Minister shows every sign of keeping his nerve. He is visibly self-confident, retains all his skill and aplomb in public performance, and apparently continues his mastery over his Cabinet and his Party." But his difficulties were real and considerable; he needed and deserved support.[4] Johnson was not prepared to go as far as Bruce would have liked, but when he confronted Wilson on British plans east of Suez he contented himself with hoping that the British would find some way of putting off the decision "and not take any step which would be contrary to your and our interests and to the interests of the free nations of Asia".[5] Even if Wilson had wanted to oblige his friend he would not have been allowed to do so by the party. The Defence White Paper of July 1967 confirmed the British intention to reduce their forces in South-East Asia by 50 per cent by 1970/1 and to withdraw completely by the mid 1970s. Its publication provoked fresh reproaches from the Commonwealth leaders. It was not just a question of economics, claimed Holt. "We see the UK Government as having taken historic decisions to reduce its world rôle and contract, to a significant degree, from the kind of international responsibility Britain has carried for many, many years." Australians must now "re-think our whole situation".[1]

Pained reproaches became furious abuse when, after devaluation at the end of 1967, Wilson announced that the withdrawal from South-East Asia would be accelerated. Thomson and Brown were sent abroad to sweeten this bitter pill as best they could and found the task an unpleasant one. In Singapore Thomson was assailed by a "fighting mad" Lee Kuan Yew, who threatened to withdraw his sterling balances from London and take revenge on British commercial interests: "My officials reported to me that they had never in their experience been subjected to such a systematic campaign of pressurisation." He fared no better in Canberra, where he found the new Prime Minister "appalled and dismayed". John Gorton claimed that this policy would reduce Britain "to a status a little less than Italy and a little more than Sweden".[2] In Washington, Brown said that he would defend the policy as well as he could, "but I fear I must tell you plainly that I think that we have taken wrong decisions. Much worse than that, we have taken them for the wrong reasons."[3] His best proved not to be good enough. Johnson wrote to Wilson of his deep dismay "upon learning this profoundly discouraging news ... tantamount to British withdrawal from world affairs ... The structure of peace-keeping will be shaken to its foundations."[4] It all made depressing reading for a Prime Minister who had believed so fervently in Britain's imperial role and the sanctity of Commonwealth ties.

Barbara Castle for one believed that the pangs caused Wilson by the retreat from empire were compensated for by the conviction that it would ease Britain's passage into Europe.[5] There was some truth in this. Wilson had satisfied himself that one of the main reasons behind de Gaulle's opposition to British entry was the general's conviction that Britain was more concerned to play junior partner in a global alliance with the United States than to join whole-heartedly in Europe. It took some time, however, before he accepted the inevitable conclusion: that, so long as de Gaulle was there, the price of entry would be the abandonment of Britain's role outside Europe – indeed, he never wholly gave up the hope that the two could somehow be reconciled. By the autumn of 1966, however, he had become a decided, if sometimes covert, supporter of British entry. It took "tremendous pressure", said Brown, to persuade him to adopt a more positive attitude towards the Common Market, and to induce enough of his followers to follow his lead.[1] The pressure did not come only from the Marketeers in his own Cabinet. "Your entry would certainly help to strengthen and unify the West," Lyndon Johnson told him. "If you find on your way that there is anything we might do to smooth the path, I hope you will let me know."[2] But in fact neither the eloquence and determination of Brown nor the blandishments of the American President were necessary. The door was already open. When Michael Palliser was seconded to Number 10 from the Foreign Office earlier that year, he warned Wilson that he was a passionate European and might therefore be unsuitable. "We shan't have any problems over Europe," Wilson assured him, and they never did.[3]

His change of heart was not made generally public until a weekend meeting at Chequers on 22 October 1966. It was on this occasion that he first aired his plan for a series of exploratory visits to the European capitals to be conducted in harness by George Brown and himself. The two-man team, he explained, was to ensure impartiality; Brown was known to be a champion of the Common Market; he himself had hitherto been an opponent of British entry. "He tried to convey the impression to the anti-Marketeers that he was still sceptical," wrote Douglas Jay, but Jay for one was certain that the Prime Minister had already sold out to the supporters of British entry.[4] Richard Marsh thought the same. Of those present, Marsh and Willie Ross, the Secretary of State for Scotland, were the only two who unequivocally opposed the suggested mission. When Crossman later told him that he had been a fool for speaking out, Marsh replied, "It's quite clear that Harold wants to get us in." "Of course he does," retorted Crossman, "but the General will save us from our own folly and that's why I supported him."[5]

The next step was to convince the EFTA countries that Britain was not betraying them. The relevant Prime Ministers were summoned to

Lancaster House and assured that their interests would be at the forefront of British minds during the negotiations. With some doubts, they acquiesced. "A thoroughly discreditable proceeding," Jay called it. Brown was at his most persuasive and ebullient. At the end of the meeting, he called for a typist and retired to draft a communiqué. After a pause Wilson followed him. "I ask for a typist, and all I get is a prime minister," complained Brown loudly. Wilson retreated and walked in the garden for twenty minutes.[1] The partnership between the two was never notably harmonious. Desmond Donnelly, who followed them from capital to capital, was dismayed by the way each overtly criticised the other.[2] Brown complained to Crossman that Wilson's presence on the tour did not help at all. So far as the actual negotiations were concerned this might have been true, but at the very least the fact that the Prime Minister was engaged on such a mission must have made it clear to the Europeans how seriously the enterprise was being taken. Crossman retorted to Brown that Wilson's presence might not have helped in the talks but it certainly did help convert Wilson.[3] Not much conversion was needed by 1967 but there can be no doubt that Wilson returned from the tours a more overt and committed advocate of British entry.

Rome, the first stop, was an easy one since the Prime Minister, Aldo Moro, was strongly in favour of British membership and ready to take account of its problems as a member of EFTA and the Commonwealth. Bonn was scarcely more of a problem; Dr Kiesinger proved equally well disposed, though Wilson doubted whether he would do much to press Britain's case with de Gaulle.[4] It was in Paris that the mission would succeed or founder. Donnelly was convinced de Gaulle had been put off by Wilson's long exposition of Britain's problems in joining Europe, though responding a little better to Brown's more unequivocal enthusiasm.[5] Wilson was equally sure that he had made an excellent impression. He told the Cabinet that the General had been much struck by the statistics of British grain production. When he was asked by Healey how de Gaulle had expressed his interest in this, Wilson answered that he had said little. "Perhaps he was bored," suggested Healey.[6] In retrospect it seems obvious that no amount of eloquent exposition would have affected the General's thinking: his mind was already made up. At the time, though, he was sufficiently non-committal to leave a ray of hope.

At the beginning of March Wilson set out his views on the subject for Burke Trend (it is a curious commentary on his relationship with

Brown that he urged Trend not to show his memorandum to anyone in the Foreign Office since he had not yet discussed it with the Foreign Secretary). After all that had been achieved in the tour of the European capitals, Wilson said that he was convinced Britain should immediately apply for admission. The right course would be for him to announce in mid April that a formal application would now be made. He would identify the three or four difficult problems but emphasise that, given goodwill, all were soluble. "This solution means that we are not making an unconditional application, and the French may take advantage of this. But I believe an application which took no account of these issues would not be acceptable to the Cabinet, still less outside."[1] Hugh Cudlipp urged Wilson to present his conversion to Europe as an admission that he had been wrong before. "Yes, I see that," responded Wilson. "I will establish that at least one politician, and a Prime Minister at that, is honest with the public."[2] The urge to be honest was, however, curbed by the fact that he was not yet ready to admit, either to the Cabinet or to the world at large, that he had come off the fence. Barbara Castle thought that he was manoeuvring brilliantly: "I remain convinced he is anxious to get in ... and he has succeeded in guiding us into a discussion of the details which is more effective than anything else in making principles look less important."[3] But dexterity in the Cabinet did not cut much ice in the capitals of Europe. Donnelly compared Wilson's position to that of a man trying to seduce a girl when two gins behind: "The suitor then gulps four gins to catch up, and she is usually insulted by the former and repelled by the latter!"[4]

Wilson's problem, a precursor of what he would face in 1975, was to get Cabinet agreement to the European policy he believed to be correct without losing those members who disagreed passionately with it. He was convinced that delay would merely exacerbate the existing differences and told ministers that they must make up their minds quickly so that, if the application *were* made, it could come directly after the latest "Kennedy Round" of negotiations for the liberalisation of world trade.[5] That he privately regarded the question as settled became embarrassingly clear at Cabinet on 20 April, when Healey remarked on "the importance of not coming up to the jump unless ..." Wilson broke in, "We *are* at the jump!" Healey angrily retorted: "Pardon me, Prime Minister, but some of us were always opposed to making these approaches at all and only agreed last year to what we thought was an unwise decision because we were assured that we would not be committed in any way. We simply cannot accept that we are compelled to make a decision now."[1] Wilson hurriedly withdrew, but his real views were set out in the telegram he sent to Brown in Washington that evening. The Cabinet had been "a real turn-up for the book," he reported. "The fence-sitters moved over." Only Jay and Healey were still inflexible; everyone else agreed "we should 'have a bash' and, if excluded, not whine but create a Dunkirk-type robust British dynamic". At the best, he believed, the Cabinet might decide 19–2 in favour of an application, though four or five against was more probable.[2] The success of his tactics was shown on 1 May when he read out a draft statement on the British application. Marsh, Jay, Peart and Castle expressed various degrees of dissent. Greenwood then said: "No, let us all agree." The Prime Minister asked hopefully: "Are we all agreed?" "Many said Yes – no one said No."[3]

The key to British acceptance still lay in Paris and Wilson returned there in June. There was much affable small talk, including a discussion of the ethics of cheating at patience. (When he got back to London Wilson commissioned from de la Rue a set of patience cards with the Cross of Lorraine printed on the back to present to the General on his next visit. There was no next visit. After de Gaulle retired there was some discussion of what should be done with the cards. It was decided to send them to him on his eightieth birthday.) He died, over the patience table, two weeks before he reached that age.[4] But little if any real progress was made. Wilson found de Gaulle in "gloomy, apocalyptic mood", preoccupied by British subservience to American interests and convinced that an enlarged Common Market would rapidly follow the same course. "I found myself watching this lonely old man play an almost regal 'mine host' at Trianon," Wilson told Brown, "slightly saddened by the obvious sense of failure and, to use his own word, impotence that I believe he now feels ... Against this background I feel paradoxically encouraged. He does not want us in and he will use all the delaying tactics he can ... but if we keep firmly beating at the door ... I am not sure that he any longer has the strength to keep us out – a dangerous prophecy, as prophecy always is with the General, but I thought you should have my personal impression for what it is worth."[5] To the French journalist, Dominique Bromberger, he went still further and told him that he had been left with the impression de Gaulle would probably support Britain's entry.[1] He assured Cabinet that his visit to Paris had made British entry more likely. Healey and Crossman at least did not find his arguments particularly convincing.[2]

That they were justified in their scepticism was shown in November 1967, when de Gaulle vetoed the British application with brutal directness. Wilson maintained that this was the result of a change of heart on the General's part, brought about largely by Pompidou's qualms on economic grounds. He told Wayland Young that he would have been right to press Britain's application even though he had known what line the French would take. He was equally right to persist in it after the rejection. But nothing was immutable, he went on, and it would be wrong to try to lay down a rigid strategy which would dictate British policy over the next few years or decades. "It is perfectly arguable that one of the reasons we have got ourselves into some of our foreign policy difficulties has been because we set ourselves planned objectives on the basis of a reasonable appraisal both of our interests and of our resources, but were then obliged to abandon those objectives through circumstances that were often at least partly unforeseeable. I wish one could have a foreign policy with every option foreseen and protected ... But I do not think it is possible."[3] There spoke the dedicated opportunist and pragmatist. Though Wilson had chosen temporarily to espouse the Common Market, he did not feel himself committed to any such liaison if the balance of advantage seemed to switch the other way.

De Gaulle's veto ensured that nothing much happened on the European front until 1969; any hope of a French change of heart was then dashed by the absurd "*Affaire Soames*". Christopher Soames, the British Ambassador in Paris, had been treated by de Gaulle to a somewhat rambling lecture on the future of Europe, in which he seemed to be proposing secret bilateral talks with Britain on the restructuring of the Common Market. A deeply suspicious Michael Stewart urged Wilson to be cautious. De Gaulle was trying to trap the British: if they accepted his offer, he would "be able to represent to Kiesinger, and others, our readiness to try to do a deal with the French"; if they refused, he would claim that he had "offered to try to settle out-standing differences with us, but we have turned him down". Wilson should take advantage of a visit he was on the point of paying to Bonn to tell Kiesinger of de Gaulle's approach and thus expose French perfidy to her continental allies. Wilson agreed, undertaking to describe the French initiative "in such a way as to point up the essentially anti-Atlantic nature of the de Gaulle approach".[1] Wilson subsequently claimed to have been annoyed by the Foreign Office's handling of the matter and himself to have spoken to Kiesinger only in the most neutral and guarded terms.[2] His response to Stewart does not suggest that there was any marked difference between the two sides of Downing Street. De Gaulle was outraged when the gist of his message to Soames was passed to all the Chanceries in Europe and any possibility of a fresh approach to the Common Market disappeared. The real trouble, concluded Crossman, was "the infantilism of Harold and Michael Stewart, priggish children who showed moral disapproval of the de Gaulle overture".[3] The comment seems unfair; the British reaction was justifiable both on grounds of morality and *Realpolitik*. What is less easy to condone is Wilson's attempt to disassociate himself from that response when it did not produce the hoped-for results.

In April 1969 de Gaulle resigned. The way seemed to be opening for a renewed application. Wilson left a few months for the dust to settle and then wrote to all ministers to urge them to stress that "we are ready to open negotiations with the Community as soon as possible and join if the right terms are available ... There is no need to be obsessed by safeguards and the negative aspects of our application, though the Government has these fully in mind. There are plenty of positive points to put across about the opportunities that membership of the Community would offer for our influence abroad and economic well-being at home."[4] Crossman in Cabinet complained that the official line was that Britain would only go in if the terms were right. "The PM looked a bit peeved and his face puckered." He and Stewart were "still hell-bent on getting the negotiations going as fast as they possibly can".[5] Jenkins told Thomson that he was going to be Foreign Secretary in the administration that would be formed after the 1970 election. Thomson would be offered the choice of going to his own department, probably Defence, or staying in the Cabinet in charge of the negotiations for entry into Europe. Thomson said that he would choose the latter, but only after Jenkins had assured him that Wilson intended to see the negotiations through to a successful end.[6]

Yet for students of Wilsonian tactics, there were signs that he was preparing to hedge his bets. The White Paper which the government published in February 1970 on the likely economic consequences of British entry was a cautiously balanced document, and Wilson's speech in the debate that followed was no less cautious and balanced in its nature. Indeed, when he berated the Tories for being ready to sacrifice cheap food from the Commonwealth without any corresponding advantage, he seemed to be distancing himself from his more partisan European supporters.[1] It was a question of nuance and tone rather than outright declaration; nothing was inconsistent with what had gone before. The final position was that he still favoured entry on the right terms, but the emphasis seemed almost imperceptibly to have switched from the favour to the rightness. He was not yet retreating from his support for British entry, but he was placing on record the fact that a line of retreat existed.

Yet another issue in foreign affairs split the PLP. In Nigeria in 1967 the Ibos, under Colonel Ojukwu, attempted to secede. Civil war followed. The position was complicated by the fact that all Nigeria's oil, on which Britain in part depended, was to be found in the Ibo areas. The Nigerian Prime Minister, General Gowon, at once wrote to urge Wilson to do nothing which would impair the corporate existence of the republic: "I need hardly add that any attempt at recognition of the so-called Republic of Biafra as a sovereign state will amount to interference in the internal affairs of my country and will be regarded as an unfriendly act."[2] Wilson needed no such warning; his sympathies were with the central government and he was anxious not merely to say so publicly but to supply it with all the arms it needed to end the war successfully. The Biafrans, however, had genuine grievances as well as a potent propaganda machine which stirred up much popular feeling in their favour. Wilson found that many members of his own party, including some of his most loyal followers, were convinced that the Nigerian government was practising every kind of atrocity and that the Ibos were innocent victims of ruthless militarism. For Wilson it meant "bitter and indescribably unhappy sessions" in the House of Commons, and outrage in the country among those whom he considered his natural supporters.[3] His policy was to continue to encourage and supply the Nigerian government while urging it to practise moderation and to be ready to negotiate a peace. "I should let you know frankly", he wrote to Gowon in April 1968, "that the friends of Nigeria feel that an effort should now be made to test the sincerity of 'Biafran' readiness to negotiate." Gowon replied that the rebel readiness to treat was no more than propaganda; he had himself been busily making overtures, but to no purpose.[1]

In the face of swelling resentment Wilson clung to a few basic tenets which he deemed indisputable: the regime in Lagos was the legitimate government of Nigeria; Britain was traditionally the country that had supplied Nigeria with arms; if denied arms from Britain Nigeria would turn to Russia; to refuse arms would therefore be to protract the war unnecessarily and to no advantage. But by the end of 1968 he had a serious revolt on his hands. He told Michael Stewart, then in Madras, that at Cabinet no senior minister had supported the policy and the Lord Chancellor, First Secretary and Home Secretary had all spoken against it. "There is a real danger that the policy might go down at Cabinet. You and I would then face an intolerable situation. The effect would be to put foreign policy much more into commission in the Cabinet than we could ever accept; and we might find that, having once tasted blood, they would subject other issues, from Greece to Germany and through Vietnam, to the same treatment."[2] Remembering that "they" were not ravening left-wingers but Wilson's closest Cabinet colleagues, it is easy to under-stand that he felt beleaguered. When the Chief Whip told him that, in a vote on Nigeria, the government would probably go down unless the Conservatives forbore from taking advantage of the Labour split, he felt something close to despair.[3]

His response would have surprised nobody who remembered his performance when in a tight corner over Vietnam. In March 1969 he announced that he was to visit Nigeria. His colleagues were doubtful about the value of the enterprise, the opposition were derisive, but to the average party member it seemed that he was at least *trying* to do something and could not be accused of fiddling while Nigeria burned. In fact the visit turned out well: Gowon agreed to negotiate uncon-ditionally and to stop indiscriminate bombing; what was more, he was quite happy for Wilson to meet Ojukwu; it was the Biafran leader who refused to avail himself of the opportunity. Barbara Castle grumbled about "endless pictures on television of Harold and Gowon swearing eternal friendship to each other and I believe Harold will come back more committed to the Nigerian cause than ever ... I do wish Harold would curb his passion for playing parts on the international stage, particularly as they never come to anything."[4] But though this visit might not have come to anything very concrete, at least it bought him time. The hardcore Biafra lobby was unappeased but the mass of moderate opinion which had rallied to their cause decided that, after all, there might be something to be said for the Nigerian case. How long this change in opinion would have lasted was, fortunately for Wilson, not put to the test; before it could swing back again Biafran resistance had collapsed. "I believe Gowon has come well out of this so far," Wilson told Nixon, "and I continue to remain in no doubt that he is determined to act generously and to bring about reconciliation in Nigeria so far as lies in his power."[1] With relief Wilson's colleagues recognised that they had backed the winning side and that the best had probably been made of what was a thoroughly bad job. Crossman, who had criticised the Prime Minister as sharply as anyone, now generously admitted that the outcome proved "the wisdom and foresight of Harold Wilson and Michael Stewart".[2]

For the British economy the civil war in Nigeria, with the consequent disruption of the flow of oil, was doubly embarrassing because it coincided with war in the Middle East. In May 1967 the Egyptian president, Gamal Abdel Nasser, announced the closure of the Straits of Tiran to Israeli shipping. In any circumstances Wilson would have been predisposed to see the merits of the Israeli case. He was sympathetic to the Jewish community, enjoyed their company, admired their intelligence and financial acumen; he knew few Arabs and none particularly well. In the 1950s and 1960s he, Crossman, Bevan, Castle and a few others had seen a lot of Yigal Allon and other young Jewish socialists then in London and became committed to their cause. Wilson saw them as: "social democrats who made the desert flower" and Israel as "a wonderful experiment in socialist politics".[3] He disliked being called a Zionist, but in so far as that title meant the championship of the right of the Jews to maintain their own nation state, he most emphatically was one.

The Arabists in the government were dismayed by what they saw as their leader's prejudice. On a visit to Israel as deputy opposition spokesman on foreign affairs, Christopher Mayhew had been sickened by the arrogance shown by the Israelis towards the Arab refugees. He argued angrily with them and they complained to "their friend and supporter Harold Wilson". Mayhew was convinced that

Wilson's recollection of this fracas explained why he was not offered a job in the Foreign Office when the Labour government was formed in 1964.[1] Probably he was right. But Wilson tempered his partisan support of Israel with a certain amount of prudence and common sense. He had no wish unnecessarily to offend his Arabist supporters. Shortly before Nasser's action in the Straits of Tiran Richard Crossman had been invited to attend the Balfour Declaration celebrations in Israel. Uneasy at the thought of the publicity which this articulate and turbulent Zionist might stir up in such a forum, the Foreign Secretary vetoed his acceptance. Indignantly Crossman protested to the Prime Minister. Presumably, he wrote, Brown would object still more strongly if he were to address "an organisation as blatantly biased in favour of the Jews as the Anglo-Israel Association". Marcia Williams added the comment: "I quite agree." Wilson wrote: "OK Tony Greenwood." "I was trying to indicate that I thought Dick should be allowed to do both," protested Marcia. "Where did Tony Greenwood come in?" She asked for a reply to Crossman's minute. "No, I'd leave it," replied Wilson. "Dick can raise with me if he likes – but our last six meetings he has appeared content." "Dick is not at all content," rejoined Marcia, "particularly since Ted Short has been chosen to go to Israel." "Leave it with Dick," was Wilson's last word, to which Marcia responded by urging Crossman "to raise with the Prime Minister once again the question of Israel and the Balfour Declaration Celebrations". Her persistence was striking, but it was still Short who went.[2]

Wilson saw no such reason for reticence in this new crisis. He had assured Levi Eshkol, the Israeli Prime Minister, that the Straits of Tiran should stay open and that, if the Egyptians sought to block them, "we would promote and secure free passage."[3] On 22 May Nasser made his declaration about the closure of the Straits. A stormy Cabinet followed. Brown demanded an "immediate and unequivocal statement by the maritime powers" that the right of free passage would be maintained, by force if necessary. Healey argued that this was militarily impracticable. Wilson "jumped in angrily. Of course there were dangers. But there would be danger if we did nothing." Callaghan began to argue about the cost and the effect on sterling. "PM in an angry aside: 'I am sick and tired of your constant veto!' PM was most belligerent."[4] As usual, nothing was decided; Thomson was dispatched to Washington to find out what the Americans planned to do. Abba Eban, the Israeli Foreign Minister, called on de

Gaulle, who told him that he should not fire first. He continued to London, where "my best hope ... seemed to be in the heavy influence of public opinion on official policy and on Harold Wilson's personal understanding of Israel's predicament". Wilson, claimed Eban, was forthright in his undertaking that Britain would join with others in an effort to open the Straits.[1] Wilson told Lester Pearson that he had urged restraint but, if the United Nations could not guarantee freedom of passage, "I am afraid Israel may feel obliged to strike first."[2]

The Prime Minister now indulged in a flurry of personal diplomacy. He urged Kosygin "with all the emphasis at my command" to attend a four-power conference as proposed by de Gaulle: "I do not often address you personally in this way, but I believe that we are all at a grave turning point in world affairs."[3] Johnson he spoke to while he was in New York; he found him "still very unclear what to do" but ready to contemplate some form of joint action by the maritime powers.[4] "Joint" was the key word as far as Johnson was concerned; he told his advisers that, if it came to a show of force, "I want to see Wilson and de Gaulle out there with their ships lined up too."[5] But before the cumbersome machinery of international action had been given a proper chance to operate, the Israelis had lost patience and struck. The Six Day War ended in a devastating defeat for the Arabs and almost equally disastrous economic consequences for the West, Britain in particular. The closure of the Suez Canal and the interruption to oil supplies from the Middle East played havoc with the balance of payments and prepared the way for devaluation.

The episode caused a furore some years later, when a chapter in Patrick Gordon Walker's book on Cabinet government which described a hypothetical crisis and its handling by ministers[6] provided the basis for a somewhat sensational story in the *Daily Mail* under the headline "The Day Wilson Almost Went to War".[7] The newspaper's account went considerably further in attributing precise plans for military intervention to Brown and Wilson than was justified by the evidence, but the tone of the Cabinet discussion was captured in a way which most of those who were present would have felt was faithful. Certainly it was going too far to claim, as Wilson did in his record of the Labour government, that "Not one sentence, or thought, contained in the article had the remotest connection with fact."[8] He seems to have been concerned lest the *Daily Mail* story would embitter Britain's relations with the Arab world, which were just beginning to get back on an even keel after the upsets of 1967. His denial would have been unconvincing even if so much evidence to the contrary did not exist. As Brown characteristically put it: "It would have been bloody stupid ... if at that stage the Foreign Office hadn't been thinking of every bloody possibility";[1] and what the Foreign Office thought, Brown would be certain to divulge in Cabinet.

Wilson's eager involvement in foreign affairs meant that he devoted far more time to the periodic crises that erupted around the world than his closest advisers thought was proper. When the minuscule Caribbean island of Anguilla in 1969 decided to secede from the federation with St Kitts and Nevis into which it had been welded Wilson was intimately involved with the decision to send a few policemen, backed up by a contingent of Royal Engineers, to restore order and central government. The action was perfectly sensible but the Prime Minister could not resist the temptation to dramatise the situation. Arriving in Cabinet he announced portentously: "You will wish to know that another wave went in last night." The "wave" comprised six police constables.[2] Crossman described the intervention as an "idiotic fiasco" arising from the Prime Minister's "failure of central direction".[3] It would seem fairer to describe it as a failure in public relations arising from the Prime Minister's over-enthusiastic determination to be seen to direct everything himself.

Another teacup in which Wilson did not wish to see a storm was the Falkland Islands. He had high hopes that the problem could be disposed of by transferring sovereignty to the Argentinians on terms acceptable to the inhabitants. Lord Chalfont was sent out at the end of 1968 to investigate and returned with the news that the Falklanders would not contemplate such a solution. Wilson considered persisting with his policy but was soon writing to Stewart to report, "Opposition to anything that looks like yielding to Argentinian pressure has now built up to such an extent that we are bound to have very real difficulty in holding to our present course ... There is mounting opposition in the Cabinet to what was agreed before: feeling in the House is very strong and cuts right across the parties: and Heath is already beginning to make a big public issue of it."[4] The problem was brushed back under the carpet, to reappear periodically over the next quarter century.

The coup in Greece, by which a group of colonels took over the government, caused particularly embarrassing complications for a Labour government. The Foreign Office took the line that, since they were obviously in charge, the colonels should be recognised as the Greek government. Wilson saw the force of this but feared the reactions of the party. The colonels would probably govern badly, have little popular support, and would only be able to retain power by "open fascism; in which case the only gainers can be the Communists". Ought not the policy to be to stiffen the resolve of the King and encourage Greek conservatives to join the opposition? "Difficult, I know. But we already have one dictatorship in N.A.T.O. * I doubt whether the Alliance can survive many more and still retain the kind of support it needs within this country."[1] The King was soon in exile and the colonels' regime obstinately survived. Wilson continued to maintain that it was British policy to restore democratic rule to Greece but accepted the need to deal with the military regime and even to supply them with certain arms. The left wing in the Cabinet complained that this was rank hypocrisy. Wilson "sat wriggling with anger and discomfort", wrote Crossman. He and Stewart were "smug people", who combined "high moral principle with highly expedient practice".[2] The charge is one habitually brought against those in supreme power by those who wish they were. It was certainly not without foundation, but Wilson had to blend in his policy an alarming variety of more or less incompatible ingredients, and in the case of Greece it is hard to see how he could have ended up with a more palatable mixture.

Until the end of 1968 it seemed as if Ireland would not add markedly to the Prime Minister's list of troubles. Terence O'Neill pressed on with his programme of liberal reforms, but his right wing became ever more restive and put a brake on his more generous initiatives. When he called on Wilson at Number 10 in November 1968 he was urged to defy the hardliners and push boldly ahead with his reforms. He failed to do as much as Wilson felt was called for. "We should like to see a public pledge by the Government of Northern Ireland to take action to bring the Northern Ireland local government franchise into line with that operating in Great Britain ... We would also like to see a firm undertaking that the Northern Ireland Government will

* Presumably he had Portugal in mind.

by means of legislative or financial control exercise vigilance to ensure proper standards of housing allocation ... It is impossible for us to continue to defend a situation in which Parliament in Westminster retains supreme authority, but that authority is not brought to bear to ensure that all parts of the United Kingdom enjoy the same high standards in this respect." O'Neill responded that any review of the franchise would follow the reshaping of local government and would require an electoral mandate.[1] With a view to securing this he shed his right wing and held a general election. The results were disastrous: the Unionist Party split, Ian Paisley loomed horrible on the scene. O'Neill battled on but was soon forced to retire; his successor James Chichester-Clarke continued along the same path but with diminished enthusiasm. In August 1969 ferocious violence broke out in Northern Ireland.

Wilson knew that the government in Westminster would be asked to send in troops; he knew that he would not be able to refuse such a request; he knew that if the troops did their job properly they would be treated as enemies by the extremists on both sides. He cast around for any alternative, however far-fetched. At one moment it is said he even invited Denis Hamilton, then Editor-in-Chief of Times Newspapers, to Chequers so as to ask him whether the *Sunday Times* would support a proposal to evacuate the Protestants from Northern Ireland.[2] But there could be no escape. When the moment came, the introduction of the troops passed off well, thanks largely to the dexterity and obvious fairness which Callaghan had shown when he visited Northern Ireland. A few months earlier Healey had told Cecil King that he thought Ulster was more likely to bring Wilson down than any other issue.[3] In the event it turned out to be, if anything, an electoral asset. Wilson told Callaghan that he considered the strong action that they had taken and its apparent success to be "a turning point in the standing of the Labour Government, for we appeared to be handling an unprecedented situation with firmness and authority".[4] But though he took some comfort from this reflection, he knew he was locked into a situation from which it would be exceedingly difficult to disengage. It was a liability which would linger on to plague him when he was next in office.

XVII

Electoral Defeat

1970

The most surprising thing about the 1970 election is not that the Conservatives won but that Labour started the campaign as clear favourites. Only a few months before, the opposition had enjoyed a formidable advantage in the opinion polls. In the wake of the fiasco over *In Place of Strife* the only question seemed to be, how great would be the margin of the Tory victory? Since then the economic climate had improved, Britain's balance of trade was once more in the black, but the improvement, though dramatic, had few of the marks of permanence and had been offset by reverses on other fronts. The county elections at the beginning of April had produced poor results for Labour; few counties were regained which had been lost in the disastrous elections of 1967 and Lancashire, traditionally the bell-wether for the country as a whole, remained strongly Conservative. Roy Jenkins's budget, though few were worse off as a result of it, was far indeed from being a give-away bonanza. Wilson would have liked it to have been more generous but Jenkins insisted on prudence and had his way. The result certainly attested to the government's probity and to the overall success of its economic policies, but it did not win many hearts among the uncommitted. Wilson professed to consider the new image of the Tory Party as fostered at the Selsdon Park conference – tax cuts, and hard-headed business solutions to every problem – as playing into Labour's hands, and told the Cabinet that the Labour government in Sweden had just triumphed in almost identical circumstances.[1] At the time it took place, however, he had admitted Selsdon Park to be a striking propaganda success, and it was obvious that the Tory Party under Heath would fight a coherent and dangerous campaign. The main consolation was to be found in the opinion polls which, though they still showed a Conservative lead, were moving steadily in Labour's favour.

For Wilson this was the decisive factor. He convinced himself that there was a tide flowing for Labour and that it would be folly not to take advantage of it. He "consulted fully", he wrote later, and refused to commit himself until he had secured the unanimous support of the Cabinet.[1] Literally, that is correct; but the underlying reality was of a Prime Minister convinced of the merits of an early election, cajoling and browbeating a less confident Cabinet into accepting his decision. He "professed to be open-minded", said Joe Haines, the press secretary at Number 10, but in fact he was resolutely committed.[2] There was no need to have an election in 1970 but if it had been postponed till 1971 it could not have been delayed beyond April, which left little room for manoeuvre. Decimalisation was also due to be introduced in February 1971, and Wilson believed this would provoke so much short-term resentment that it could well be an election loser by itself.[3] The choice was therefore between the late spring or autumn of 1970 – in effect June or October by the time the Prime Minister put the matter to the inner Cabinet on 8 March. Almost the only person to have a decided view was Wilson, who said bluntly that he was afraid of delay: "I remember how the City has invoked a run on sterling before and it could do it again." Castle says opinion was fairly evenly divided, Benn that there was "a sort of consensus" in favour of June; certainly the unanimity which Wilson craved was not yet evident.[4]

Wilson claims that he finally made up his mind that 18 June should be the day at a meeting the evening before Jenkins presented his budget. In discussion with his inner circle – Shore, Kaufman, Haines and Marcia Williams – he argued that an early election would dislocate Tory plans, which assumed nothing would happen before the autumn. "All agreed an early election was desirable," remembers Haines,[5] but Kaufman and Williams in fact remained sceptical and urged delay up to the very moment Wilson set off for the palace to report the possibility of a dissolution. They failed to shake Wilson, who was equally unabashed when the inner Cabinet a week later continued to have doubts. Indeed, the Chief Whip argued strongly that the average member did not feel he would be ready to fight an election before 1 October. "We realised today that autumn is the only time," concluded Crossman.[6] Wilson realised only that more persuasion was needed. By 5 May Peart, Mellish and, more hesitantly, Callaghan had rallied to his view; Crossman and Castle were still resolutely opposed. It was the opinion polls over the next few days, showing a Labour lead of 3 per cent, which brought the doubters into line. "We were all in favour of going through what looked like a window of opportunity," said Jenkins.[1] "In favour" was a little strong for Crossman, who did no more than grudgingly acquiesce: Wilson, he wrote, "made up his mind a month ago he wanted June and waited for the facts to come his way. Perhaps we could have dragged him back but events have been on his side."[2] When two polls published the same evening showed Labour 3.5 and 6 points ahead, even Crossman conceded that the right decision had been made.

The Tories, declared the *Economist* on 16 May, faced "the apparent certainty of humiliating defeat". Wilson fully shared that view. "As politician to politician and expecting no comment," he wrote to Nixon, "I thought I should mention to you that I have always hoped to be able to time the election during the summer. The recent trend in public opinion polls showing all five national polls portending a government victory ... has led to widespread expectation of a June election." Nixon need not fear, he added, that anti-Americanism or the Common Market would figure largely in the campaign. "In Britain it is very rare for foreign affairs to play a leading part in a general election. In the last two elections, for example, out of fifty or sixty speeches each time I have made only one relating to foreign affairs."[3] If he expected Nixon to rejoice at or even accept the apparently certain Labour victory, he was sadly wrong. Kissinger records that Nixon was "an unabashed partisan of the Tories" and convinced Heath would win: "When his prediction came true, he was so elated that he called me four times one night in Mexico City, to express his joy and receive my confirmation of his prescience."[4]

Without subscribing to theories about the "presidentialisation of British politics", wrote the historians of the campaign, they were convinced "that Mr Wilson and Mr Heath each exercised ... a quite exceptional pre-eminence in shaping the situation".[5] Crossman, by no means a consistent admirer of the Prime Minister's performance, went still further: "Harold, whom a few months ago I described as just one among his colleagues, is now right ahead, far ahead of anybody else, dominating the television every day. What a remarkable man."[6] Wilson would have accepted and revelled in the praise. At Cabinet he grumbled about the lack of support he had been receiving. Some ministers were "just not behaving as if there were an election" and were leaving it all to him. "Well, Harold," put in Barbara Castle sweetly, "it is a presidential campaign." " 'Yes, it is,' he retorted, perfectly seriously."[1] He went through the motions of praising his "winning team", notably Jenkins and Callaghan, and he sometimes left the handling of press conferences to senior colleagues, but his efforts hardly carried conviction.[2] Marcia Williams could always be relied on to remind him of his pre-eminence. "Remember, fellers, that our loyalty is to Harold Wilson," Haines remembers her saying in a later campaign. "No-one else. Never forget that."[3]

It was Mrs Williams who was largely responsible for the most conspicuous innovation of the Labour campaign – the walkabout. Wilson had been much impressed by the success which the Queen had enjoyed in New Zealand when she broke away from the official cortège and mingled with the crowd. The technique contrasted dramatically with the stage-managed, ticket-only mass meeting favoured by the Tories – here was a politician who was not afraid to meet the people face to face. Up to a point it worked; Wilson enjoyed the walkabouts and so did the people whose hands he shook. But nothing was said. Night after night Heath was to be seen on the screen pontificating about major issues, while Wilson bobbed around affably among the crowds. The latter made for the jollier photographs but the impression was left that Heath was the more serious politician. Wilson underestimated the leader of the opposition, derided his lack of charm, and featured Mary prominently in the campaign so as to underline Heath's bachelor status. One of his more malicious jokes was that his campaign slogan ought to be: "Heath for Queen, Wilson for Prime Minister".[4] His very quickness and mastery of the media sometimes worked to his disadvantage. "Mr Wilson insisted on being filmed in the garden of Number 10," Heath remembered, "and he sat down in a very comfortable chair with the sun shining and artificial geraniums all the way round him – put there for the event – and it was the old stuff all over again. But I was against gimmicks."[5] If you have to compete with a quicksilver debater, full of tricks and master of repartee, then a dogged, no-nonsense approach is as good as any.

Wilson's over-confidence prevented him realising this until it was too late. The most frequent criticism of his electioneering style in 1970 was that he was complacent. He cockily assumed that the day was won and kept asking people to tea at Number 10 after the election, complained Woodrow Wyatt: "The electorate enjoys punishing hubris and those who take them for granted."[6] Leo Abse denounced the "public display of unjustified vanity" shown by Wilson in his "vulgar presidential campaign".[1] These were both enemies of Wilson, but even among those less fiercely hostile his style of campaigning caused disquiet. Michael Foot felt that his talk of Labour being the natural party of government damaged the cause – "he was very complacent"; while Hattersley was disturbed by the discussions between senior ministers as to which portfolios they should take.[2] When Wilson's words did get across to the public, his manner sometimes seemed tired and lacklustre. Wendy Hiller, the actress, wrote after the election to offer to make his television appearances "more attractive and spontaneous. I don't mean you sound plastic, but you start in the wrong key and you need to be given the right one."[3] When Jack Jones invited him to address 600 officials from the Transport and General Workers Union (TGWU) assembled from all over the country, Wilson "said little or nothing about the future and displayed as much fervour as a cold fish".[4]

Such criticism, it is important to remember, came after the event. At the time few felt that there was anything seriously wrong with his performance. But he deliberately elected to fight the campaign in a low key which left little scope for passion or pyrotechnics. In the Transport House handouts of his speeches the words "responsibility" or "Tory irresponsibility" occurred twenty-one times, the word "socialism" only once.[5] "We're really asking for a doctor's mandate," Wilson told the inner Cabinet. "We're the best doctors the country's got";[6] and it was as Dr Wilson, the trusted, experienced family physician, that he fought the election. This caused some concern to William Camp, a public relations expert imported on Balogh's recommendation when Kaufman went off to nurse his constituency. He told Wilson that he saw dangers in doing a Baldwin – fighting an election under the banner of Safety First. Wilson replied that he did not fancy himself scratching pigs; but that in effect is what he did. Camp found his main problem was to overcome Wilson's paranoia about the press. He tried to organise a party at the Belfry Club where Wilson could chat informally with journalists who would be on the campaign tour, but was told to cancel it as too many enemies were on the list and it would anyway be too late to achieve anything. The Prime Minister's relationship with Transport House was hardly more harmonious and there was little coordination of the efforts of individual ministers and officials.[7] Organisation was rarely a strong feature of Labour electoral campaigns, and 1970 was worse than most. The situation was made still more difficult by the fact that

Transport House had made its plans on the basis of an autumn election. One of the reasons for going to the country in June was so as to catch the Tories unawares; in fact it was the Tories who reacted more rapidly and positively. A campaign which was supposed to build up slowly, with a long period of concentration on Tory misdeeds switching in due course to a triumphant affirmation of Labour competence, got out of kilter and had hardly progressed to the second stage before it was too late. Another approach had quickly to be devised, and pretty uninspiring it turned out to be.[1]

The only person who effectively shared the limelight with Wilson and Heath was Enoch Powell, and he probably caused as much embarrassment to his own party as to Labour. Race was one of the many emotive issues which Wilson would have preferred not to discuss. Incensed by a particularly provocative speech of Powell's, however, Tony Benn took up the issue in abrasive terms. His speech cost the party five seats, Wilson later grumbled;[2] a statistic difficult to prove or disprove, but improbably large given that Heath was as concerned not to support Powell as Wilson not to denounce him. But this was one of the few moments in the campaign when passions flared. Rather more eggs or bags of flour were thrown than in previous elections but the violence was not as bad as the police had feared; the worst moment came when Wilson's temple was bruised by a well-aimed hard-boiled egg, a missile which could have done serious damage if it had landed a couple of inches away on a spot where the Prime Minister had recently had a cyst removed.

Superficially, all seemed to be thriving in the Labour camp. There were occasional setbacks. A sharp rise in the retail price index gave the Tories something to complain about. The former Governor of the Bank of England, Lord Cromer, rose like the ghost of Hamlet's father to exact revenge. The economy, he claimed, would be in a worse condition for the incoming government than had been the case in 1964. Wilson complained that an attack of such a nature was unethical coming from a man who had been in Cromer's position. Whether or not the point was justified, the opinion polls did not suggest that Cromer's objurgations were taken very seriously by the electorate. By early June the odds were twenty to one on Labour and some bookmakers were announcing that their books were closed. A threatened newspaper strike could have proved damaging but some hectic personal diplomacy by the Prime Minister helped ensure that only three days' production was lost. The strike cost him some valuable campaigning time and distracted public attention from the Treasury announcement of a £606 million surplus in 1969/70, but the success of his intervention probably did more to boost his reputation. A week before the election the polls showed Labour with a twelve-point lead. "Well, it's all sewn up," said his detective. "No, it's too much," replied Wilson. "I know our voters. They won't bother to turn out."[1] His remark may have been no more than a routine crossing of fingers to avert the evil eye, but it proved to be uncommonly prescient.

An article which appeared in the *Spectator* on 13 June, written by one of the shrewder political commentators, George Gale, showed how completely the chances of a Tory victory were being dismissed. Wilson, wrote Gale,

has bestrode this election like a cosy pet and cuddly toy Goliath. I cannot contemplate his performance without wanting to break into hoots of laughter; and laughter chiefly with him, what's more: not against. It has been a very funny performance ... As Ted Heath has nightly said (missing the point, alas, in saying it) nothing has been too trivial for him ...

His cool, his calm, his confidence is like nothing I have ever seen from a Prime Minister (or Opposition Leader) fighting an election. Until around February he thought he might lose; but then he suddenly knew ... that he had made it ... Each day's campaigning finds him more relaxed and more at ease with his own political future. He looks ahead with pleasure, secretly telling himself, I think, that now, now will come the time, now that the economic problem of the balance of payments is manageable, now, now when he has won thrice over, will be the chance to change the place, to make the country different, to show himself to be a great Prime Minister.

And then it all went wrong. It is hard to be sure why support for Labour slipped so dramatically. Probably the polls always exaggerated the solidity of their advantage. Unexpectedly bad trade figures for May suggested that the balance of payments was not so easily manageable as Gale had supposed. England was knocked out of the soccer World Cup quarter finals after leading 2–0 at half time. Heath was exceptionally effective in his final television appearance. But there were other long-term factors which had worked throughout the campaign.

Wilson always blamed the BBC and the female vote. His perpetual guerrilla war with the BBC erupted in fierce exchanges. Charles Curran, the new Director-General, suggested a *Panorama* programme which would deal with foreign affairs and feature Michael Stewart. Wilson countered with Healey and defence, forcing the reluctant Stewart to withdraw his acceptance. Curran protested, but eventually agreed to Healey, though allowing Alec Douglas-Home – who refused to appear on the same screen as Healey – to be interviewed separately. At a press conference Wilson angrily maintained that it was for the party leaders, not the BBC, to nominate speakers and subjects.[1] The campaign was punctuated by indignant telephone calls, usually relating to the alleged iniquities of John Grist, then in charge of Current Affairs. After the election Wilson drew up a dossier listing what he maintained to be instances of BBC bias. On *Election Forum* he had been put into a studio so hot that he sweated heavily, causing the *Daily Telegraph* to suggest that he had been embarrassed by the questions. The previous evening Heath had been deliciously cool. His big speech at Birmingham had not been carried, even though he had altered the time to suit the BBC. When he *was* featured, the BBC concentrated on episodes of heckling and egg-throwing. And so the litany went on: some of it justified; some fantasy; much of it relating to incidents that could have been avoided if he and his advisers had shown more tact and forbearance.[2]

His other factor, the female vote, is harder to pin down. Wilson told his detective that the election was all about prices: "The wives will tell their husbands they're voting Labour, but they won't."[3] He was convinced that, for the first time, wives were not waiting to vote with their husbands on their return from work, but had turned out during the day and voted for themselves. The male vote stayed solid; the female switched.[4] If prices were indeed the decisive factor, then the most damaging event of the whole campaign must have been the publication of worse than expected inflation figures on 19 May.

Forty-eight hours before the election a private poll commissioned by the Labour Party showed that a Tory win was a probability. Ron Hayward was so disturbed by the figures that he at once went round to Number 10 to discuss them with Wilson. The Prime Minister was unperturbed; he pointed out that all the other polls showed Labour ahead and, said Silkin, "went happily to defeat".[5] Others insist that he was well aware of what was likely to happen.[6] Certainly, by the end, he was not so confident as he professed himself to the party faithful. But it still caused him almost physical pain when the first result from Guildford was flashed on the screen showing a 5.3 per cent swing to the Tories. Wilson caught Marcia Williams's eye "and made a slight grimace". After the third result Marcia telephoned the girls in the political office at Number 10 and told them to start packing up their papers. As the night wore on, Wilson "impassive, though obviously downcast" sat alone on an enormous sofa at the Adelphi Hotel in Liverpool, looking "isolated and enigmatic".[1] In his own constituency the swing was 2.4 per cent against him. It was better than the national average but that was small consolation for the loss of a general election.

His extraordinary resilience was never more apparent than in the aftermath of defeat. After only two or three hours' sleep he was on the road to London. He arrived and at once told Haines that he had decided to write a book which would provide a bible for the next election. He had already roughed out the chapter headings.[2] When he had found time to do this is mysterious but the evidence was there for Haines to see. Roy Jenkins was in Downing Street when he arrived at 11.30 a.m. "He was looking appallingly battered, but he was wholly calm and unrecriminating, said, 'Well, there it is,' and displayed his great resilience almost ludicrously by rehearsing to me the speech he proposed to make in the debate on the Address ... He was altogether rather impressive, and the occasion moving."[3] He moved on to Transport House where members of the former Cabinet and the NEC stood on the platform to welcome him. Tom Driberg alone refused to join in. "That man misled us all and picked the wrong date," he said vengefully to Benn. "Why should I cheer for him?"[4]

Traditionally the incoming Prime Minister offers his predecessor the use of Chequers for the first few days after the election. Wilson duly retreated there for the weekend. Balogh, Shore, Kaufman and Marcia Williams – the most faithful of the faithful – assembled for a post-mortem. They were too exhausted and depressed to come up with anything very constructive. Away from the limelight Wilson let his real feelings show: his disappointment, his irritation with those whom he felt had let him down, his determination to get his own back on the usurper Heath. Some had expected that he might give up the leadership after a decent interval in which a natural successor could come forward. Instead he spoke of the probable date of the next election and by what margin he would win it. No one could hear him and doubt that he meant to stay in charge of the Labour Party and, in due course, return to Number 10.

XVIII

Adjusting to Opposition

1970–1971

Though at one level Wilson contrived to appear resilient, active, busily planning for the future rather than repining over what was past, those who were close to him attested to the deep shock and gloom into which he had been thrown. It was the first time in his life that he had suffered unequivocal and calamitous defeat. There had been setbacks, tactical reverses, periods in which he appeared to have over-played his hand or been exiled to the wilderness, but there had never before been a moment at which everything seemed lost. He had engaged in a public battle and emerged a clear second-best; and what was worse, he had emerged second-best to a man whom he disliked and despised; who, he had convinced himself, was palpably his inferior. To have been outmanoeuvred by Macmillan in his prime would have been galling, to be driven from Number 10 by the loathed Heath was almost insupportable. Wilson was angry, he was hideously disappointed, he was humiliated, perhaps most noticeably of all, he was physically exhausted. "He was dead-tired," wrote Crossman of him during an earlier crisis. "His face was parchmenty and flattened out like that of an old tortoise, and his eyes so tired they were scarcely moving."[1] In 1970 it was far worse. After previous elections he had been sustained by the need to carry on, to shape his new ministry, to plan the future. Now there was nothing.

It was not nothing, of course. Wilson was still leader of the Labour Party, a considerable figure in the politics of the country, a man who commanded the constant attention of journalists and photographers, a figure of power to be deferred to and courted. But it was not the same. When Othello, that most human of great men, bemoaned the loss of his occupation, it was the perquisites of office which he above all lamented: "the neighing steed and the shrill trump, the spirit-stirring drum, the ear-piercing fife, the royal banner and all quality ..." For Wilson it was the car waiting for him night and day, the phalanx of deferential secretaries, the incomparable telephone exchange of the Prime Minister's office, the visits to the palace. A photograph of the period shows the Wilsons' harmonium being manhandled out of the back door of Number 10. At the same moment Heath's piano was approaching by the front. It symbolised not just a change in style, but a change in physical possession.

When Wilson first ventured to the House of Commons after the election, wrote George Caunt in his diary, he "still looked rather stunned, but ... after doing some work and meeting a few people, was his old self again". It did not take Caunt long to realise that this was no more than window-dressing; by early August he had gone to the other, equally erroneous extreme of dismissing Wilson as a "burned out case who will get drunk on his memories".[1] In fact Wilson was far from being burned out, but he found it hard to adjust to the realities of the present day. He veered between luxuriating in the glories of the past and counting the months before he could expect to regain his rightful heritage. A few months after the election he was telling Richard Marsh that "this Government would not last eighteen months. He [Wilson] takes little part in the business of the House, but embarrasses new members by recounting the brilliant speeches he made years ago."[2] He seemed to be more preoccupied by the battles of the past than planning a strategy for the future. His grudges against those whom he blamed for his downfall remained as virulent as ever. When he was invited to a dinner in honour of the Beaverbrook journalist John Gordon, Marcia Williams minuted: "I have declined this ... I really don't think you can honour John Gordon in view of his persistent outright hostility to the point of telling lies." "Quite right," wrote Wilson approvingly. But he did not push his antipathy to the Beaverbrook press to the extent of inconveniencing himself. When Max Aitken wrote to invite him to be the Convocation Speaker at the University of New Brunswick, with all expenses paid and an honorary degree thrown in, Wilson commented: "He's a sod, of course. But it's out of term and I *cd* go to Ottawa – Trudeau being a goodie."[3]

He found some comfort in the obvious satisfaction his wife and children took in being quit of Number 10 and having a chance of seeing him from time to time without a bevy of officials and politicians buzzing around like wasps zeroing in on a succulent plum. Harold

Wilson's father, now aged eighty-seven, had been staying in the flat in Downing Street so as to be on hand to celebrate his son's victory. Looking "sad and tired", he had to be packed back to Cornwall.[1] But though Mary Wilson was genuinely distressed at the pain that had been inflicted on her husband, she could not pretend to share her father-in-law's disappointment. The pomp and circumstance which had meant so much to the Prime Minister had to her been actively distasteful and she accepted with equanimity the fact that they would thenceforth be living in less grand a manner. So far as creature comforts were concerned, the loss meant little to Harold Wilson either. Almost the only luxurious trapping which he missed for itself, rather than as a symbol of supreme power, was the ever available car. He told the publisher Paul Hamlyn that he was "not very flush", and, according to Cecil King, was therefore going to give up a chauffeur and was learning to drive.[2] Unfortunately – in the opinion of his family at any rate – King got it slightly wrong: he already knew how to drive, or thought he did. Even when in regular practice, however, he had been an appalling driver and the years of office had neither sharpened his reactions nor improved his judgment. Marcia Williams remembered turning out of the House of Commons car park into Parliament Square with Wilson at the wheel and Aneurin Bevan seated beside him. He emerged with the car in third gear, promptly changed up into top, and crawled juddering around the square with furious buses on his tail and an agitated Bevan beside him, muttering: "Go on, boyo, give the car a break – change down!"[3] Since then, things had got worse. He tried a little to relearn the techniques, but soon despaired.

The most immediate problem was to find somewhere to live. He was out of Number 10 within twenty-four hours, and to see Heath keeping the courts where he had gloried and drunk deep was almost the most painful part of the transition. Heath complained bitterly about the dry rot – which he claimed that Wilson had deliberately ignored so that it would not be repaired at a time inconvenient to him – and at once banished the inadequate copies of portraits of British worthies that had hung since time immemorial on the walls, to replace them by original Gainsboroughs and Reynoldses which, though better painted, had no particular association with the house. He had a party to celebrate the refurbishment of the state rooms and invited the Wilsons. "I hope you like it," he said to Mary Wilson. "If we get back, we'll restore the old paintings," said Mary firmly. They did so, too. Heath, perhaps, had the better taste, but the Wilsons a surer grasp on history and what Number 10 was all about.

For the first fortnight after his eviction from Downing Street Wilson, who had sold the house in Hampstead some years before, camped in a flat in Arlington Court belonging to Desmond Brayley, a rich friend of Mellish and George Wigg who was to figure briefly and embarrassingly in the next Labour government. Then, in July, he moved into 14 Vincent Square, where he expected to stay several months. The house belonged to the film producer Jerry Epstein, who let it to the Wilsons at eighty guineas a week, with the services of a chauffeur thrown in. It was a useful transit camp but far more expensive than Wilson could afford. Not that the alternative was cheap. At the end of 1970 they moved into a Georgian house, built in the 1720s, in Lord North Street, one of a cluster of elegant and extremely expensive eighteenth-century streets within easy distance of the House of Commons. Except for the first-floor drawing-room the rooms were small and the house was on five storeys, but it was unequivocally grand. Since the lease was for twenty years the price was only £20,000, but the upkeep, and the expenses of Mrs Pollard, the housekeeper who lived in the basement, took up a great part of Wilson's available income.

Life at Chequers had also given the Wilsons a taste for country living. In October 1970, for £21,500, they bought Grange Farm, a pleasant house near Great Missenden and only six miles from Chequers, with a handsome Elizabethan barn that was turned into an area where Wilson could work and store his papers. It had little land but was conveniently close to Ellesmere Golf Club, which he patronised as often as he could. The other members were predominantly Tory but were more pleased than otherwise to have the former Prime Minister among them. One exception wrote to accuse Wilson of "self-righteous prating" and said that he would be happy to discuss with him what was wrong with the Labour Party when next they met in the club. Personally, replied Wilson, "I have always regarded golf as a sport and this and other golf clubs as essentially non-political. I have never engaged in political arguments in Ellesmere Golf Club and do not intend to do so."[1]

A rented house in Lord North Street, a country house in Buckinghamshire, a cottage in the Isles of Scilly, these were the appurtenances of a rich man. Yet Wilson was not rich. There was plenty of gossip about this apparent discrepancy. In September 1971 *Private*

Eye printed a story stating that Wilson had just paid his eighteenth visit to Russia, that only four of these had been at the expense of the taxpayer and that some had been paid for "by Wilson's good friend Sir Joseph Kagan, the manufacturer of waterproof garments who has employed Wilson as commercial traveller and male model for the last seven years at an annual salary of £5,000 to £10,000". Wilson did not seek to deny that while in opposition he had worked irregularly but not infrequently for Kagan (though hardly, if at all, in Russia) and had been paid generously for what he did. Nor did he conceal the fact that Kagan had contributed in kind if not in money towards the running of his political office in Downing Street. He found extremely damaging, however, the allegation that he had been on the payroll of a businessman during all the years that he had been Prime Minister. He told his lawyers to sue for libel: he was not interested in damages, he told them, he wanted "an apology, a clear retraction, costs and an undertaking about the future". He was tempted to insist that the journal should never mention him again, as other victims of *Private Eye* had done, but realised that for a man in his position such a provision would be impossible. He did feel, however, that "they should respect his privacy on other than public matters."[1] In the end he got almost all he asked for.

Wilson's main source of income came from his writing and lecturing. Almost before he had moved into Vincent Square he was at work on a record of his years as Prime Minister. His aim was twofold: to earn enough money to set himself up in opposition and to get down on paper his account of what happened during these years before anyone else could do the same with a less sympathetic version. Both these he achieved; though the product of his labours was hardly a monument to English historiography or prose writing. The original plan, according to Joe Haines, had been that Wilson would dictate the raw material into a tape-recorder and Haines then transform it into a book. This arrangement, if it had ever been seriously envisaged, broke down before it had begun to work (on this, as on many other points, the accounts of Joe Haines and Marcia Williams are at variance; and since, in this case at least, the argument has scant relevance to Wilson's personality or politics there seems no point in setting it out in detail). The plan would not have worked out well, in any case. Wilson preferred drafting for himself and was a compulsive rewriter of other people's texts. In the end it saved time and effort for him to tackle the job himself. Martin Gilbert, the biographer of

Churchill, provided excellent unpaid and often unlistened-to editorial advice.

But much time and effort was called for. *The Labour Government 1964–1970* was a book of 850 pages including foreword, index and other trimmings – a text of getting on for half a million words. Wilson began work on it in July 1970 and it was published in July 1971. The achievement was prodigious, whatever the literary merits of the final product. "Marcia is driving Harold on and on," wrote George Caunt sourly in October. "He is working 4/5 hours a day and after lunch he has nothing further to eat and lives on whisky. Yesterday he was in a state of near collapse about 10 p.m. and had to be taken home."[1] The picture is over-dramatised. Marcia Williams certainly was anxious to see the book finished quickly, so as to get it out of the way and Wilson fully back into the political fray, but no pressure from her was needed. Partly as therapy for his recent defeat, partly because he could not bear to leave a job half done, Wilson immersed himself in his writing with terrifying single-mindedness. Some days he would write, mainly in longhand, 15,000 words – a quarter of a short but not unusually short novel. It was a feat that even a Stakhanovite or a Barbara Cartland would have found extraordinary. He paid a price: according to Haines, "the physical and mental toll was such that he did not recover fully from the effort for more than a year."[2]

He earned a price, too. The rights in the book were sold to the *Sunday Times* for £260,000. The sum was a remarkable one, even though it included an element for expenses and various subsidiary undertakings on Wilson's part. So as to minimise the liability for tax, the deal was presented to the Inland Revenue as being partly for the sale of documents. Since the book rights went for only £30,000 and there was not much else to be hoped for, the *Sunday Times* must have been counting on some pretty sensational material for their serialisation. This was as evident to Wilson's colleagues as to anyone else. On the way to de Gaulle's funeral in November 1970 Wilson was hard at work correcting what must have been proofs of the first part of the book. According to Heath, Wilson told him "quite three times" that he proposed to hold nothing back.[3] Similar stories spread throughout the PLP and caused some consternation. Douglas Houghton claimed to have warned Wilson that if he indulged in any "rough stuff" in his memoirs he would be answered in kind. He told Cecil King, however, that he did not think the warning had been necessary; Wilson was not the sort of man who would be guilty of such indiscretion.[1] Houghton was right. Wilson wrote a sentence about Crossman "exulting in set-back and defeat", then thought better of it and cut it out. Crossman was now editing the *New Statesman*, he explained to Martin Gilbert. "He can always hit back."[2] Almost the only colleague whom Wilson treated with ferocity was George Brown. Any doubts he might have had about these passages must have been removed when Burke Trend showed him the section in Brown's own forthcoming memoirs which related to the period when Wilson was Prime Minister. Certain parts of this, wrote Trend, went "a good deal further than the convention would normally permit in revealing the discussions between Ministers on sensitive issues of public policy and in discussing the personal relationships between members of a Government". This was particularly true of the passage on arms to South Africa.[3] Wilson raised no objection to Brown's handling of this issue; but if Brown was going to discuss personal relationships between ministers then he was damned if he would not do the same. Other ministers or any member of the party with whom he might expect to have dealings in the future were treated circumspectly. The book is fascinating to a student of the period as presenting an almost unedited stream of consciousness, relating what went on from day to day, crisis interspersed with crisis, trivial and great issues jostling side by side, one problem no sooner embarked on than put aside to make way for another yet more urgent. No other book has conveyed so vividly the hectic incoherence of a Prime Minister's life. It is, for that reason, difficult to read, a shapeless and generally insipid record which provides priceless material for the biographer but precious little joy for the general reader. "You say I must have had a detailed diary," Wilson wrote to a reader after publication. "In fact, I did not keep a diary at No. 10, but on a number of occasions of considerable historical importance I dictated a 'Note for the Record' so that all the relevant facts could be set down while still fresh in my mind. In some cases, I have quoted direct from these Notes."[4] The passages based on such notes are among the few which contain any vivid personal details or telling phrases; they are, alas, few and far between.

Choosing the title proved as difficult as anything. The publishers hoped for something dramatic and provocative. "I don't like a gimmick title," Wilson protested. "They don't live. Duff Cooper's *Old Men Forget* was the best one – but I can't use that. This book is meant to be serious history. On the whole I'd prefer a flat title – if anyone can think of one." Martin Gilbert suggested the eventual title,

The Labour Government 1964–1970, with the subtitle *A Personal Record*. "It's how I saw it from Downing Street," said Wilson. "I was on top of the elephant." Someone from the publishers – a consortium of Weidenfeld and Nicolson and Michael Joseph – wanted *Memoirs*. "It isn't memoirs," complained Wilson. George Weidenfeld suggested *Six Years*. "I don't mind that," said Wilson, but Gilbert pointed out that it was only five and two-thirds years. The promotion of the book was discussed at the same meeting. Wilson wanted a party for the political Lobby: "They are very important. They are the ones I am worried about." Weidenfeld proposed a joint party for Lobby, editors, other potential reviewers and personal friends. "No, the Lobby must have a special meeting," ruled Wilson. Gilbert put in a plea for the provision of galley proofs. "I don't care about misprints," said Wilson robustly. "I've been reading the *Guardian* for years."[1]

The critics gave the author little reason for satisfaction. "The reviews are all unfavourable," recorded Cecil King exultantly, "and the general feeling is that this orgy of self-justification has done him a lot of harm."[2] It was the lack of evidence of any coherent policy, whether in the shaping of the book or of the events that it described, which struck most readers. Peter Jenkins was reminded of a *New Yorker* cartoon of a king sitting on his throne, saying irritably to a small boy: "What do you mean, what do I do all day? I reign, that's what I do."[3] Jo Grimond wrote that the book was "like a dream, shapeless and leading nowhere ... nowhere does Mr Wilson indicate what were the aims of his government."[4] From Chicago Henry Winkler complained that the memoirs were not as well written as Macmillan's: "trudging from year to year in a dutiful but uninspired progression of meetings, manifestos, trips, votes and parliamentary bills".[5] David Watt was more generous when he described the book as "a surprisingly good read ... a lot of very crisp and humorous narrative to devour and at least two or three superb set-pieces to enjoy". But he still felt that it did not do Wilson justice: "The Labour Government and its Prime Minister were not exactly the greatest of the century but neither were they quite as bad as Mr Wilson manages to make out. It is ironic that a work which was obviously conceived as an exercise in self-vindication should be so self-incriminating."[6] The public voted with the majority of the critics: the *Sunday Times* did not gain significantly in circulation during the period of serialisation, while the book had sold a respectable but far from dramatic 22,000 by Christmas 1971 and heavy returns were expected in the New Year.

What, if anything, was to come next was the question that pre-occupied Wilson towards the end of 1971. Wilson, wrote King, was "now said to be writing a full-scale autobiography and has a girl collecting cuttings. After the fiasco of his first book, he will find the terms very different!"[1] Cuttings were in fact being collected, but only to help in the running of the office. It is most unlikely that Wilson had any such intention at this stage. Apart from anything else, he considered his career to be far from over. He played with various ideas but was reluctant to embark on anything that would take up too much of his time and energy. His writing career had already earned him some adverse comments. When the first draft of his book was nearing completion his literary agent, David Higham, asked leave to issue a statement making it clear that he would be responsible for all future writings. Wilson wanted nothing which would draw attention to his continuing role as author. "I would prefer no statements," he replied. "The Press attacks on me have reached levels that never occurred even when we were in Government, and a great part of this is centred on my writing habits, to say nothing of earning money thereby ... I am afraid in any case that since we met the Common Market question has kept me more than fully stretched seven days a week ... This may last for some months yet."[2] It was not till January 1973 that a contract was signed for a book to deal with the machinery of government – eventually to appear as *The Governance of Britain*. The advance was for a meagre £5,000, payable half on delivery and half on publication. This somewhat cautious assessment of his value as an author can have done little to encourage him to greater efforts and probably explained his reiterated regrets that pressure of work was preventing him getting on with the writing as fast as he would have wished.

Meanwhile there was the problem of establishing a base from which he could be an effective leader of the opposition. Even if he had wanted to work from home, as Heath had done, he would have met with considerable resistance from his family to the influx of papers and political aides that would have followed. For better or worse, he had to operate his office from the poky accommodation assigned for it in the House of Commons. Roy Jenkins was dismayed to find that Wilson had commandeered nearly all the available space for himself "and was sitting in it surrounded by vast piles of packing cases full of papers which he had taken from 10 Downing Street". Wilson must have been there on one of his relatively infrequent visits;

usually he worked from the leader of the opposition's more spacious room below. Jenkins was fobbed off with one small boxroom, later grudgingly increased to two.[1] To be fair to Wilson, it is hard to see what else he could have done: the papers had to go somewhere; so did Marcia Williams, Joe Haines and five secretaries; there simply was not enough room to go round. The offices were cramped, noisy and in every way uncomfortable; they hardly provided an environment in which calm deliberation could take place and morale gradually be restored. It was a "very difficult, unpleasant period" said Marcia Williams;[2] it cannot be said that the acrimonious atmosphere in the office made it any easier.

There was a brief and vicious power struggle. According to Joe Haines, Marcia Williams announced that she would consent only to serve as political secretary and that Haines must be in charge of the office.[3] She then reappeared, countermanded anything that he had done and reasserted her control. According to Mrs Williams, Haines had no experience of running an office and there had never been any question of him doing so. Her absence had occurred because she had been helping Mary look for a home in London.[4] George Caunt recorded: "Marcia returned today after 8 days absence ... and Harold Wilson looked overjoyed to see her back. It was fairly obvious that she had won again and Joe Haines, who had assumed command, went back into his shell frustrated and defeated."[5] The matter is only of importance in that it imposed additional strain on Wilson at a time when he was already under great pressure and in no state to cope with the misfortunes of others. He met the difficulty, as was his wont, by pretending that it did not exist and continuing on his way, leaving it to the others in the office to sort out their problems as best they might. Equally as usual, they did so in the end. Marcia continued as the dominant force. "She is determined that Harold Wilson should make a comeback and she will drive him back to No. 10," wrote Caunt.[6] Without her indomitable resolution and fighting spirit, it is at least possible that Wilson would have sickened of the whole business and handed on the torch to the nearest pair of hands. Ron Hayward told Benn that Marcia Williams was "running Harold", that she and her brother and sister were omnipresent, that Haines was the only other person fully in Wilson's confidence, that Alf Richman was "the baggage master", and that Gerald Kaufman was "round and about". "This is the kitchen cabinet – Harold's court," wrote Benn. "It has always been like that but it still annoys Ron, who has not got a lot of time for Harold. But Harold is a very shrewd operator."[1]

No operator, however shrewd, can manage without a regular income to make it possible. When Callaghan had to pay for his office in opposition he turned to the unions and Transport House; the scars left by the battle over *In Place of Strife* were still too raw for Wilson to wish to look in that direction or to expect great generosity if he had chosen to do so. Transport House put up enough to pay for a couple of secretaries or research assistants, but nothing on the scale Wilson felt he needed. Marcia Williams herself had to be paid from Wilson's personal funds. So did Joe Haines or someone similar, for Wilson was determined to have a press secretary independent of the Publicity Officer at Transport House. A group of management consultants was called in to advise on the best way of achieving what Wilson had in mind, and the probable cost. Their recommendations reflect the balance of power within the office: "Mrs Marcia Williams will be in complete control of all staff other than Mr Haines and she will be answerable for her actions only to Mr Wilson. Mr Haines will report directly to the Leader on subjects concerned with the Press or Press Statements and will have no other responsibility." Leaving to one side the salaries of Williams and Haines, they concluded that the total cost would be some £13,000 a year. In fact they underestimated, since they conducted their study at a time of year when work in the opposition office was at a low ebb. The true figure proved to be nearer £30,000, but even the original estimate would have been too much for Wilson, who was prepared to find some of the money from his earnings as author and lecturer but could not pay all the expenses for an indefinite period.[2] In Arnold Goodman's view the expenses were unnecessary anyway; the scale of Wilson's private office was a piece of vanity, demanded only by his exalted sense of the dignity of his office and his wish to provide for loyal supporters who would otherwise be out of a job.[3] Whatever his private opinion, however, it was to Goodman among others that fell the task of organising the financial backing and putting it on a stable basis.

The solution was found in a group of businessmen who were Labour sympathisers, or at least were prepared to make a modest investment in the hope that it would pay dividends if or when Wilson returned to power. The leading spirit and eventual chairman of the trustees was Wilfred Brown, a prominent industrialist who had been ennobled and brought into Labour's last government to take charge of the export drive. Rudy Sternberg, future Lord Plurenden, was another trustee; he and Samuel Fisher (also to become a peer) provided the main driving force, while Jarvis Astaire, Donald Gosling, Arieh Handler and Cyril Stein were among the other contributors. Though their names were often mentioned in this context, neither George Weidenfeld nor Joseph Kagan figure on the list; Kagan, however, had made erratic contributions to the running of Wilson's political office during the time that he was Prime Minister. The trust made its first contribution in November 1971 when donations to date were declared to be £10,000, of which £8,000 was at once paid over to meet expenses and £2,000 carried over to the following year.[1] By the end of 1972 the trust was in full swing and was meeting the major part of the cost of the political office. By that time Wilson had put in some £40,000 of his own money to maintain the office of leader of the opposition in the style which he thought proper.

Most of the contributors to the trust, and those other people who sustained Wilson when he was Prime Minister or leader of the opposition, were respectable businessmen; some of them idealistic; some self-interested; most, probably, a bit of both. A few were raffish figures who flirted on the fringes of illegality and, in one or two cases, were later decisively to overstep the mark. Wilson can fairly be accused of naïvety in accepting aid from such sources. But he liked them. He enjoyed the society of flamboyant, self-made men; and where he would have been ill at ease in the company of a traditional backwoods Tory peer, a swashbuckling adventurer, especially if Jewish, appealed to his romantic instincts. Yet both were equally unlike him. Wilson, provincial to the backbone, committedly *petit bourgeois*, had not the slightest wish to share the perquisites of the jet-set businessmen whom he had been delighted to entertain at Chequers or Number 10 and to whom he felt sincerely grateful. He expressed that gratitude in ways that many thought indiscreet, as the furore over his resignation Honours List made painfully clear, but that was the end of it. There were those who believed or professed to believe that Wilson traded political advantage or confidential information for financial support. No evidence supports this contention and everything that one knows about Wilson's character contradicts it. Personally he was strait-laced almost to a fault. Even if he had hankered after the fruits of corruption – which in fact left him singularly unmoved – or had been prepared to risk his career to obtain them, he could not have brought himself to accept a bribe.

His allies in the world of business or finance may have gained renown and even some more practical advantage from being known to hobnob with the Prime Minister but no decision that he made was ever taken against his better judgment and out of a wish to benefit them.

One helper who was far from raffish was Rudy Sternberg's namesake but not relation, Sigmund Sternberg. In collaboration with Wilfred Brown, Sternberg set up an independent economic consultancy organisation which would collate and disseminate up-to-date information to shadow ministers. The Rowntree Trust weighed in with a substantial grant – hence the fact that the researchers were nicknamed "The Chocolate Soldiers". Norman Hunt, future Lord Crowther-Hunt, was put in charge and interpreted the group's mandate as being, *inter alia*, to turn the vague policies of the NEC into potential legislation. The report he sent Wilson on this in November 1973 was intercepted by Marcia Williams, who took alarm and warned Wilson that it was unnecessary and dangerous and could cause "very great difficulty indeed if it got into the wrong hands".[1] Wilson concurred, and after some discussion with Sigmund Sternberg the group was encouraged to follow a less controversial course.

Though Wilson never rendered political favours to those who had assisted him, the situation was different when it came to honours. The Honours List seemed to him an admirable device by which friends could be pleased and helpers rewarded at no cost to anyone except perhaps a system which he regarded as more than slightly ridiculous. It is curious that Wilson, in most things so traditional, reverent of the monarchy, transported with delight himself when the Queen made him a Knight of the Garter, should have treated common or garden honours with such disdain. He did so, however, distributing them with the indifference that a multi-millionaire might have felt when he handed out small change to beggars. He could no more see the point of knighthoods than of a Cheval Blanc 1955 or a Rembrandt etching, but if it would please Desmond Brayley or Joseph Kagan to have one then why should they not be gratified? They were, in his resignation honours. George Weidenfeld and Sigmund Sternberg were also knighted, as was Joseph Stone, his doctor. If any eyebrows were raised at the time, Wilson ignored them. As Barbara Castle had remarked a few years earlier: "He was prepared to sweep aside nonsense like that to help his friends. His reformism consists not of altering the conventions like Honours, but in using them in unorthodox ways."[1] To those who took the system more seriously, "unorthodox" would have seemed too weak a word.

His main problem lay not in justifying the awards to personal friends – a practice he could legitimately claim defeated Prime Ministers had indulged in before, if rarely on so lavish a scale – but in finding space for party worthies who were unexpectedly out of a job. Anthony Greenwood was a particularly hard case. Wilson had proposed to make him chairman of the Commonwealth Development Corporation but, when Heath became Prime Minister, the appointment was rescinded. Wilson promised him a peerage as a consolation prize, but when Greenwood called on him on 9 July, the leader of the opposition "breathed fire and slaughter but spent most of the time telling me how badly Ted Heath had treated Harold's appointee, Joe Haines.* It is a great pity that over the last seven years Harold has become a worse and worse listener, but talks incessantly and consequently is grievously ill-informed about the situation – relying only on a small inner group of assistants who feed his phobia about plots. When I saw him ... he referred to the difficulty he was having with a Resignation Honours List as so many Members unexpectedly defeated would have to be accommodated. I told him very frankly and very firmly that I should expect him to honour his promise to me ... He looked a little shifty and said that it was virtually a certainty."[2] The certainty came home and Greenwood got his peerage, but there were many others who felt they had been ill-used.

Wilson was sensitive to any question about how his operations, political or personal, were financed, and in particular to any suggestion that his rewards for his writing were improperly high. This touchiness, coupled with his continuing suspicions of the BBC, led to the most spectacular explosion in mid 1971 – "the biggest and most furious row that a television programme in the English language has ever provoked", judged Anthony Smith, the editor of 24 Hours.[3] The original idea belonged to David Dimbleby, who felt it might be interesting to make a programme showing how the former leaders of Britain were adjusting to their lives in opposition. The title of the programme, Yesterday's Men, was not divulged to the participants, nor was the fact that it was to be accompanied by specially commissioned pop music; the result of which, the governors of the BBC

---

* Joe Haines has no idea to what this refers and can only suppose it must in some way have related to accommodation in the House of Commons.

eventually admitted, was to trivialise what appeared on the screen. All went swimmingly in the preparations for the programme until, in the course of a final filming session in Wilson's room at the House of Commons on 11 May, Dimbleby remarked that many ex-ministers were suffering financially but that Wilson was said to have earned between £100,000 and £250,000 from his book. "Has that been a consolation to you over this time?" Wilson angrily retorted that this was no business of the BBC's. Ted Heath had recently acquired a yacht which seemed as far beyond a politician's purse as Wilson's houses. Wilson threw this in his interviewer's face: "If you are interested in these kinds of things you had better find out how people buy yachts. Have you asked him that question?" He accused Dimbleby of snooping and listening to press gossip. "I think it is disgraceful ... If this film is used or this is leaked then there is going to be the hell of a row!"

An embittered dispute followed. The governors eventually agreed that this exchange should be excised from the broadcast programme, though not till after Jenkins and Callaghan had both threatened to withdraw their contributions unless the offending questions and answers were cut out.[1] News of the imbroglio was leaked to the press and received wide coverage. Worst of all, when the programme eventually appeared, Dimbleby's commentary included the words:

Only Harold Wilson became richer in opposition; using his privileged access to government papers he wrote 300,000 words in six months about Labour's time in office. The extracts from the book have been criticised, both for their excessive self-justification and because of doubts about whether Prime Ministers should profit so from the secrets of their governments. The serial rights of the book have certainly made him rich. During the year he bought Grange Farm in Buckinghamshire. And in Lord North Street, Westminster, a distinguished house within reach of the House of Commons. With the bungalow in the Scillies, it makes his properties alone worth over £60,000. Mr Wilson earned six figures for the book, but what those figures are remains a closely guarded secret.

The references to "privileged access" and his profiting from official secrets struck Wilson as being particularly damaging. On 16 July 1971 Arnold Goodman issued a writ for libel.[2] Wilson demanded an apology, his costs and a contribution to charity. In the end he got the apology, not in terms as abject as he would have wished but sufficiently contrite for him to be able to claim that honour had been satisfied. It was an unsatisfactory end to an unsavoury affair. Lord Hill considered that Wilson had mishandled the matter from the start: "He could, with his customary skill, have told Dimbleby to mind his own business. For once, he was caught napping."[1] Looking back on the incident, Wilson would probably have agreed. He could have contrived things so that Dimbleby was made to look impertinently inquisitive and would have been given no chance to append his somewhat tendentious commentary. That he made such a mess of it shows that he had by no means recovered from the wounds of his electoral defeat. He was tired, depressed and overwrought. Though he could still rise to the big occasion he found it harder to cope with the vicissitudes of daily life. His reactions were slower and his tactical judgment less sound than had been true in the past. The slowness of his recovery made more difficult what was to be his paramount task in the next years: the reassertion of his authority over his party and its preparation for the next election.

XIX

Opposition

1970–1974

Wilson had hardly settled back into London in June 1970 before a challenge came to his continued leadership. At the first meeting of the PLP after an election it was the practice that a leader of the party was appointed. Most people took it for granted that Wilson would be re-elected by acclamation. However a dissident back-bencher, Leo Abse, chose to oppose the nomination. The government had elected to fight on the personality of the leader, he maintained; it had lost and the question must now be asked whether it had the right leader. The scene at the PLP meeting resembled a Bateman cartoon: "The Wedding Guest who said there *was* Just Cause and Impediment ..." Abse's attack on the leadership caused consternation. The Labour MPs, he complained, "huddled together like a pack of hypnotized rabbits, silent, utterly immobilized and submissive ... unable to adjust to the fact that the listening opposition leader no longer could bind them by patronage or magic".[1] Quite what Abse expected to happen is hard to imagine. Even if there had been a sizeable number of members at that moment with a clear idea of whom they would like to see in Wilson's place, they would have felt it indecent to press their views on an occasion which was supposed to provide a rousing reaffirmation of Labour unity. "Everything went off pretty well in the circumstances," wrote a relieved Houghton. "I wondered at first if I had made a mistake in letting Abse ... come in early, but at the end we did get clear and emphatic approval to the programme and were able to make a clean job of the election of Leader." Nobody except Abse seemed particularly interested in conducting an inquest on the recent defeat "and in any case the Government will presumably soon show their hand and give us plenty to discuss."[2] When the following week Wilson showed himself in ebullient form in the debate on the

Address – "just like an India-rubberman, bouncing up again after his defeat", said Benn[1] – it must have seemed to the PLP that it was business as usual on the opposition front bench.

But for Wilson at least it was far from being business as usual. He would do his bit on the big occasions, usually be present for the Prime Minister's questions, but his appearances in the House of Commons were less frequent than when he had last been leader of the opposition. Partly this was because he was so heavily involved in writing his book, partly because he believed that there was nothing to be achieved by harrying the government until it had lived through its honeymoon period and given its opponents something to attack. He told Marcia Williams that he only intended to make two major speeches in the next three or four months and would otherwise say little in the House or outside it; "We can't do anything this year," he told Haines. "Politics won't mean anything for the rest of this year."[2] Haines felt that Wilson's attitude was so apathetic and defeatist that it must herald a determination to retire. His misjudgment endured. "This horse won't run!" he announced gloomily to his colleagues after a meeting shortly before the 1974 election.[3] Cecil King asked Heath how the leader of the opposition was faring and was told that he was lying very low. When he did appear his heart seemed not to be in it, "his big speech in the next debate was frivolous and ineffective." The Minister of Transport, John Peyton, remarked that Wilson was "boring and long-winded and showed no signs of his former skill".[4] Tory ministers are not necessarily the most objective witnesses but, except for the debate on the Address, there were few compliments from any quarter for his performance in the House of Commons. His handling of affairs within the party also seemed to show that his grip on power was weakening: "There is nothing presidential now about Wilson," said Houghton. "He consults his Shadow Cabinet on every-thing."[5]

There were those who thought that, even if the leader did not retire entirely under his own volition, he was in a frame of mind where he could readily be pushed. Shirley Williams believed he would be replaced before the end of the present parliament; Stonehouse told King that it was widely believed in the PLP that Wilson could not win another election: "He is tired and may drop out."[6] The knowledge that he was in the process of writing a book which, unless it was bland to the point of oblivion, would cause fresh dissension in the party, seemed an extra reason for anticipating his early retirement.

Such speculation was reasonable enough but assumed that, because Wilson was tired and preoccupied by other matters, he was therefore in a mood to hand over power. The contrary was true. He had every intention of remaining leader and in due course returning as Prime Minister, he told Benn.[1] When Humphry Berkeley, the former Tory MP who had recently switched camps to Labour, wrote to say that he hoped the speculation in the press about Wilson's imminent retirement had no foundation, he was firmly reassured "that there is absolutely no truth at all in the stories you have been reading".[2] Defeat by Heath had been insupportable, and the recollection could only be expunged by his triumphant return with his harmonium through the front door of Number 10 while the defeated Tory leader and his piano retreated through the back. To achieve that he would endure any degree of criticism, combat any quantity of intrigue. Houghton expressed it disagreeably but by no means incorrectly when he said that Wilson would "put up with any amount of humiliation if he still has some chance of returning to Number 10".[3]

As had always been the case, his enemies could never agree on a successor. For the left Benn was too junior and had not yet asserted himself as a national figure. Wilson initially encouraged him and believed that he would one day lead the party. According to Benn he even told him at one point that he would support him against Roy Jenkins in the election for deputy leader in 1971.[4] The promise was probably equivocal; when the time came, anyway, Benn had moved far to the left and had lost Wilson's favour. Michael Foot had greater stature, but was widely considered something of a maverick and had more or less voluntarily stood aside from the power structure of the party. Some people were so desperate that they even played with the idea of bringing back Cousins, but after the débâcle of his time in office he neither aspired to power nor would have received much backing. From the right the opposite was true; there was a plethora of candidates, each one resolved not to give way to the other. In so far as there was an heir apparent it was Roy Jenkins, firmly installed as deputy leader and treated by Wilson with the consequence due to the second person in the party. But if Jenkins had a chance, it diminished rapidly from 1970 onwards as he became more and more identified with the European cause and a minority group within the party. He was "boxed in totally on Europe", Shirley Williams judged by January 1971 – a box in which Wilson was resolved not to join him. Williams's own candidate was Denis Healey, a long shot who would have alienated the left of the party almost as effectively as Benn would have alienated the right. Benn thought Healey a "contemptible figure" and lumped Crosland under the same heading.[1] Callaghan was a safer bet, though Shirley Williams thought him "too old, discredited and right wing". Wilson usually saw him as the main threat, though by the middle of 1971 he was able to tell Benn triumphantly that he had successfully "warded off Jim Callaghan's assault on the Leadership".[2] It was the threat of being outflanked by Callaghan on the European issue that more than anything else dictated Wilson's own ambiguous and wavering attitude on the subject. Barbara Castle could have been a strong contender but her championship of *In Place of Strife* had cost her the support of the unions and her left-wing roots made her perpetually suspect to the right. In 1970 she announced that she was going to stand against Jenkins as deputy leader. Wilson saw that this would not merely split the party on left–right lines but, still more dangerous, would bring the problem of the party's attitude towards Europe to the fore at a time when he was determined to play it down. When he tried to persuade her to leave the field free for Jenkins she complained that she had a perfect right to stand. Wilson agreed, but retorted that he had a perfect right to resign rather than preside over a disintegrating rabble. Besides, he added with some brutality: "You won't get fourteen votes."[3] Either the threat of resignation or the disobliging prophecy proved effective: Castle did not stand.

The fact that there was no united opposition to his leadership did as little to allay Wilson's fears as had been the case when he was at Number 10. He was "totally obsessed with the leadership question", wrote Benn in the summer of 1971,[4] suspecting everyone, imagining conspiracies on every side. Crossman wrote to him reproachfully when Anthony Howard reported that Wilson had been asking whether the editor of the *New Statesman* – as Crossman had become after the election – was backing Callaghan to take over. "Oh dear! When will you understand that you have a few friends *who are friends for life*? I am one and that is why I shall support you as Leader as long as you want to stay Leader. It is only when you tell me you have had enough I shall start worrying about your successor. At present, even if you feel tempted I shall try to dissuade you."[5] The message was touching and Crossman probably meant it when he wrote it. His lifelong friendship, however, was not allowed to stand in the way of discussion with all and sundry about the need for a change at the top.

The party was in disarray, and many of those who themselves were not averse to stirring up disorder were ready to blame the leader for the trouble. Labour was disintegrating, Ray Gunter told Wigg, and it was not being helped by "that so-and-so Wilson".[1] Benn too believed that the party was in a bad way and that it was unlikely it could recover sufficiently to win an election if Wilson remained as leader. The British voter felt that Wilson was a trickster and quite enjoyed "the feeling of Heath as strong man who allows them to hold up their heads again".[2] Even the little band of the faithful grew alarmed at their leader's growing alienation from the rank and file of the party. Frank Judd, who had been appointed Wilson's parliamentary private secretary after the election, wrote in April 1971: "Candidly, I believe sessions with back-benchers – new *and* old – are urgently needed. It is being said that you have become too remote. This is not just indirect reporting. Critics have said it to my face and one or two loyalists have mentioned it to me in worried terms."[3]

Throughout what was left of 1970 and 1971 Wilson's closest advisers urged him to action – almost any action would do provided it was conspicuous. Marcia Williams nagged him to get together with the actor Stanley Baker to discuss party political broadcasts, "so that the momentum can be kept up and not lost, as usually happens with everything you do; namely, that you are enthusiastic at the beginning and when you are getting something out of it for yourself, but there is never any 'follow through' ". Three months later she tried again. She expected to be told there was no time, she said: "However, the most extraordinary things are fitted in and this is one of those things which I feel is something that is criminal to neglect."[4] Frank Judd, for his part, urged Wilson to travel the country so as to popularise himself and "establish direct personal contact . . . with ordinary folk". This was most important, agreed Marcia; careful planning should start now. "Yes, but I've got country (mainly party) engagements every week from now to Xmas," commented Wilson plaintively.[5] He had no wish to stir things up unnecessarily. In January 1971 he did his best to persuade the striking electricians to go back to work. "He is afraid, as I supposed," wrote Cecil King, "that too direct a challenge to the Parliamentary majority would lead to an election and a majority of 200 for the Tories . . . Wilson thinks the Tories will be in a horrible mess sometime next year and that is when there will be an election and his own return to office."[6]

He was as anxious to avoid turmoil within the party as

confrontations with the government. A recent convert to socialism suggested that the "antiquated and misleading" name of "Labour Party" should be dropped in favour of something more relevant like "Democratic" or "People's" Party. Wilson must have recalled the reaction of the traditionalists when similar ideas had been floated under Gaitskell. "Whereas, as you say, the word may conjure up Victorian conceptions of hard and exploited manual labour," he replied, "nevertheless, as a political name it has now become respectable and honoured ... Perhaps the best answer is to be found in the constitution of the Labour Party, which directs its appeal to 'all workers by hand and by brain'. That pretty well includes all of us in this country, give or take a few thousand spivs, speculators and those who seek to earn a living – and more – by gambling."[1]

But the opposition still had to oppose; a task which proved embarrassing for Wilson and Barbara Castle when Heath introduced legislation for trade union reform which in many ways was disquietingly close to what the Labour leaders had fought for under the banner of *In Place of Strife*. When the Labour government fell, the most immediate points of friction between it and the unions ceased to exist and their common cause against the Tory enemy became all that mattered. The last thing Wilson wanted was to disturb this harmony; equally, there was a limit to the number of words he could decently eat in public. The Chief Whip was well aware how popular the Tory legislation was likely to be in the country and saw the dangers of unconstructive opposition. Under the proposed new law unions would be required to register. Some at least were likely to refuse to do so. In such a direct confrontation the unions would expect the support of the opposition leaders. "In that climate I have a feeling that we would come off very badly on a political front," wrote Mellish. He urged Wilson to have private discussions with the General Secretary, Vic Feather, so as to try to work out some plausible alternative strategy which could be offered. "I have been having confidential talks with Vic – and the leading trade unionists – but the essence is that they must be kept absolutely confidential," replied Wilson.[2] Those talks were eventually to lead to the "Social Contract" of 1973. For the moment Wilson concentrated on those parts of the Tory legislation which were unequivocally harsher than anything he or Castle had proposed, and left it to Callaghan to take the lead in Labour's opposition.

In so far as Wilson played a leading role, it was to urge restraint on those hotheads who wanted to have a pitched battle over every clause. When the Tories introduced a Timetable Motion in January 1971 intended to force the bill through quickly, the Tribune Group decided to stage a demonstration by standing in front of the Mace and refusing to sit down when ordered to do so by the Speaker. Warned what was to happen, Barbara Castle telephoned Wilson and together they tried to persuade the would-be demonstrators to drop their action. They failed, but the Speaker – similarly forewarned – confounded the rebels' tactic by affecting not to notice that they were standing in front of him and allowing the debate to go on. Wilson later summoned those front bench members who had taken part in the exercise and remonstrated with them. He was almost as emollient as the Speaker, however, and stopped well short of a formal reprimand or an order not to offend again.[1]

When unemployment rose rapidly he was provided with an issue on which he could unite the party and attack the Tories without embarrassment. When Heath visited Brussels shortly after the number out of work had risen to a million, Wilson gleefully referred to him as "the first dole queue millionaire to cross the Channel since Neville Chamberlain".[2] The left relished his invective and the divisions over the union legislation were glossed over. At a joint meeting of the PLP, NEC and TUC a little later, Wilson pledged that, when the party returned to power, its first act would be to repeal the Tory legislation. That his private views of the union leaders had changed little since 1969 was, however, shown clearly later the same night at a dinner given by the CBI when Wilson shocked Benn by denouncing Jack Jones and Scanlon and implying strongly that he knew them to be communists.[3] Publicly he was able to win a little more favour with the unions when the Upper Clyde Shipbuilders collapsed in the middle of 1971. Wilson visited the Clyde early in August and visited the yards, taking some pleasure from doing so while Heath was sailing his yacht in the Admiral's Cup. He even told Benn that he was thinking of paying the visit arrayed in the uniform of an Elder Brother of Trinity House – a bizarre proposition which, since he never invested in the uniform, it seems unlikely was meant seriously. He stopped short of endorsing the action of the shipyard workers, who were conducting an illegal work-in, but urged the government to place orders with the firm and save it from the otherwise inevitable closure.[4]

* * *

One issue which drew him from his semi-retirement was Northern
Ireland. He and Callaghan were much criticised on the left in the
course of 1971 for not denouncing the Tory policy of internment.
Brian Faulkner, the new Prime Minister, called on them when in
London, and expressed his fears that the bipartisan approach in
Westminster on Irish problems might be breaking down. Wilson had
no wish for this to happen but realised that he must do something to
satisfy his militants. A show of activity was called for. In November
1971, with Heath's approval, he visited Northern Ireland. Among
others he met Ian Paisley, whom he found courteous and reasonable.
Paisley asked him to sign his copy of *The Labour Government 1964–
1970*: "I bought it wholesale," he explained. Wilson then moved on
to Dublin where he saw the Taoiseach and expounded his fifteen-
point programme for reunification after a long transition period with
the rights of minorities fully guaranteed. An element of the plan was
that Ireland should rejoin the Commonwealth: "a nonsense from
which I was unable to budge him", commented Haines.[1]

As ready as ever to read acquiescence into mere politeness, Wilson
returned to London convinced that he had achieved a real breakthrough. On 25 November 1971 he expounded his ideas in the House
of Commons, calling for reunification based on a constitution which
would be worked out by a commission including representatives of
the British parliament, Stormont and the parliament of the Republic.
Such a constitution would not come into operation until fifteen years
after an agreement had been concluded.[2] "It was an imaginative
speech," commented Callaghan, "but it was intended for long-range
consumption and was not designed for immediate effect."[3] In so
far as Wilson's prime object was to satisfy his own supporters the
exercise was almost entirely successful. There were some grumbles
from the left about the way he had handled the issue of internment,
but the main thrust was applauded from every quarter; it "completely defused Ireland as far as the Party was concerned", wrote
Benn.[4]

The success of his speech gave Wilson a taste for intervention in
Irish questions. In March 1972 he was back in Dublin, he claimed
with the knowledge if not overt approval of Heath, though the Prime
Minister later denied this. There he met three leaders of Sinn Fein:
David O'Connell, Joe Cahill and John Kelly. He spoke about the
massive backlash that would be provoked if the present violence were
to continue. During the recent truce, he said, he had been terrified

lest there might be atrocities for which the IRA would be held responsible even though it was the Loyalists who had perpetrated them. The backlash was no threat at all, said Cahill; the reason there had been no Loyalist atrocities was that they had been taken by surprise. Wilson said he had hoped that Gerry Fitt of the Social Democratic and Labour Party (SDLP) would attend the talks but "he had difficulties with your friends. He thinks that one day one of your friends will shoot him in the back." "Hardly in the back," retorted O'Connell, adding that Fitt was under no threat. "He is isolated ... the SDLP have completely lost touch with the situation."[1] Wilson told Conor Cruse O'Brien that he had seen the Sinn Fein leaders in the hope that he could persuade them to renew their truce for a longer period and that he could get the SDLP into the negotiations.[2] He did not flatter himself that he had achieved much: "We were planets apart," said Haines. "Words had different meanings."[3]

O'Brien left an account of their conversation. Wilson "told me, as he usually does when he meets any elected Irish representative, that he, in Huyton, represents more Irish voters than I do, which I am sure is true. For the rest, he patiently performed a pipe-filling ritual, so exquisitely long drawn out and so charged with implications of wise negotiations, that I am sure, at any Red Indian pow-wow, it would bring down the wig-wam. We, having heard some disquieting rumours, said how unwise it would be to negotiate with the IRA under present conditions ... Mr Wilson did not dissent. He continued to play with, or on, his pipe."[4] O'Brien's warnings did not deter Wilson from inviting the Sinn Fein leaders to Grange Farm to continue the discussions. The planets grew no closer together; if anything, at the second meeting they seemed still further apart.

After the Dublin visit Brian Faulkner issued a statement accusing Wilson of meddling in matters which he did not understand and planning the betrayal of British subjects in Northern Ireland: "I must conclude that Mr Wilson is, for some political motive, irresponsibly exploiting this most tragic situation." He obligingly sent Wilson a copy of the statement, adding in a covering letter: "I am bound to say that having examined what you said in Dublin with the greatest of care, I am unable to detect in it very much sympathy for that vast majority of people here who wish to remain in the United Kingdom and who are being subjected to these appalling outrages." Wilson was hurt by this attack. Faulkner had "totally misunderstood, and therefore misrepresented what I had said", he retorted. He had always condemned violence and had great sympathy for the plight of the Ulsterman.[1]

As is the usual fate of those who seek to regulate the affairs of Ireland, Wilson gained little credit for his efforts. The strictures of Faulkner were as nothing to the abuse of the anonymous author of a pamphlet called "The Evil that is Wilson", issued by the "Ulster-linked Association", which reminded its readers that nothing but treachery could be expected from the man who had returned the bones of Casement to Dublin; "And to show that there were no depths to the evil raging in his heart, the Evil that is Wilson returned to Dublin for heroes' funerals the bodies of Barnes and McCormack, two IRA fiends executed in 1940 for murdering 5 innocent people in the Coventry bomb outrage."[2] His own supporters in Northern Ireland were hardly better satisfied. "I feel that you should know," wrote Douglas McIldoon of the Northern Ireland Labour Party, "that every time you mention a united Ireland we lose more party members, more trade unionists contract out of paying the political levy, and no doubt these losses are only the tip of the iceberg as far as electoral support is concerned."[3]

Wilson's speech in the House of Commons may temporarily have defused Northern Ireland as far as the Labour Party was concerned, but a Hansard-full of speeches could not have done as much for the European issue. The more said, Wilson thought, the sooner broken; but silence became increasingly more difficult. When Labour left office Wilson was committed to reopen the negotiations for British entry into the Common Market. The terms, it had been stressed, must be acceptable, but no precise definition of acceptability had been framed. None of those closest to him thought it likely that he would prove exigent or would scrutinise the small print with particular care; indeed George Thomson, who would have been in charge of the bargaining, stated categorically that the terms eventually secured by Edward Heath corresponded closely to those which the Labour government expected to secure.[4] If Wilson had been Prime Minister in 1971 he would almost certainly have urged the party to accept the terms and, with the momentum that would have been behind him, would probably have won the day without too damaging a revolt from the anti-Europeans. But he was not Prime Minister in 1971 and the triumph, if triumph it was, belonged to Heath – an infinitely less alluring proposition. Wilson still wanted Britain to be in Europe, but he wanted Heath's contribution to be discredited and he was not prepared to risk the unity of his party to secure a vote for entry.

Unlike Jay or Shore on one side, or Jenkins and Thomson on the other, the issue for Wilson was still not one of principle. In this he was not uniquely cynical. Callaghan, Healey, Crossman, even Benn, were all agnostics; some inclined more one way, some the other, but all ready to agree that the balance of advantage was a fine one and that it was not a matter of life or death whether Britain went in or stayed out. Wilson's long-term objective, to which he adhered tenaciously whatever his apparent divagations, was to take Britain into or keep Britain in Europe with a united Labour Party accepting the decision. If that failed then he wanted Britain out but the party still united. Britain in Europe with a shattered Labour Party was unacceptable. The policy was not a particularly noble one, but given his difficulties and the final result it can hardly be denied that he pursued it with considerable skill and pertinacity.

The difficulty for Wilson in the spring of 1971 was that it seemed increasingly likely that Heath was going to be offered terms which the Tories would find acceptable, that a substantial section of the Labour Party would agree with them and insist that Britain should take advantage of the offer, but that another section, of roughly similar size and weight, would be passionately committed to its rejection. How should the shadow Cabinet resolve this dilemma? Benn had his own solution. As early as November 1970 he had suggested that, whatever terms the Tories might secure, Labour should insist that they be put to the nation in a referendum. If the Tories refused to do this, then Labour should pledge themselves to repair the omission when they returned to power. He found no support though Callaghan, more prescient than his colleagues, is reported to have said: "Tony has launched a rubber dinghy into which we may all one day have to climb."[1] Wilson was categoric in his opposition. In the course of the last electoral campaign he had been asked by Robin Day why it was all right for Gibraltar to have a referendum yet not for the United Kingdom to do the same. "We have a Parliament in the sense Gibraltar hasn't," Wilson replied, "and I think it is right that it is the Parliament which should take that position with a sense of full responsibility."[1] Attlee had claimed twenty-five years before that a referendum was "a splendid weapon for demagogues and dictators", and Wilson fully concurred;[2] it was a nasty gimmick, the sort of thing that might be acceptable on the continent but would not do in Britain. Against such opposition Benn's proposal had no chance; he could not even find a seconder when he raised it in the NEC. But it was not forgotten.

A gradual shift in Wilson's public posture became apparent in 1971. Jenkins thought he detected signs of wavering at the beginning of the year. He sought an interview with his leader. Wilson proved evasive but when he was finally cornered Jenkins urged that there should be a free vote among Labour members when and if the time came to vote on the terms secured by Heath. Wilson replied that he thought the party could be got to vote for entry but that "at the worst, the very worst, we can fall back on a free vote".[3] That was in February. In the shadow Cabinet on 1 March he was still insisting that all ministers were committed in principle to the idea that Britain should join the EEC.[4] So far so good for the Marketeers, but he was anxious not to appear to support entry at any price. When Heath sent out a stock letter to anyone who urged the Queen to refuse the Royal Assent to any bill admitting Britain to Europe, pointing out that the principle of entry was supported by all three parties and that the leader of the opposition had said in June 1970 that the government and parliament should decide, Wilson angrily scrawled on his copy of the letter: "This is bloody cheek!"[5] By April he was making a mildly anti-European speech at a luncheon in Birmingham, including one phrase about an invasion of Italian black-leg labour which made Jenkins wince.[6] At shadow Cabinet three weeks later Benn noticed that he was "still pretty pro-European but kept his position open". On television that night he was "awfully shifty".[7]

The principal explanation for Wilson's change of line seems to have been the emergence of Callaghan as an anti-Marketeer. In a speech at Southampton in May Callaghan seized the patriotic high ground and denounced all entanglements that might destroy the nation as its inhabitants now knew it and lead to the replacement of Chaucer's English by bureaucratic French. It was largely nonsense, as Callaghan was well aware, but it filled Wilson with alarm. He frankly admitted to David Owen, when the latter eventually resigned, that he would never have come out firmly against the Market if he had not feared being outflanked by Callaghan rampant on a little Britain and Commonwealth platform.[1] Healey told Cecil King that Wilson was afraid of Callaghan as an anti-Market candidate and so would come down against the Market himself. "It all sounds like Wilson being too clever by half," commented King disdainfully.[2]

Early in June Jenkins returned to the charge. Wilson expounded the difficulty in which he found himself: Jenkins was lucky, he suggested; *his* mind was made up; Wilson had to make a choice and every choice was wrong. Privately, he was well aware of the risk that if he committed himself overtly to Europe he would become the prisoner of the right and eventually, no doubt, its victim. Jenkins urged him, in his own interest as well as the interest of the country, to take a strongly pro-European line and risk defeat at the party conference. Wilson listened politely and professed still to have an open mind; but Jenkins was convinced that he was already lost. Against the wishes both of Jenkins and of Wilson a special Labour conference on the issue was convened for 17 July. It was no longer possible for the leader to sit on the fence. Reluctantly he descended on the anti-Market side. To Willy Brandt he explained that this change of heart had been actuated by the bad deal which Heath had secured: "I could not, in honesty, recommend these terms to my colleagues. They are quite different from those which the Cabinet had in mind in 1967." What was being proposed was an agreement "of more benefit to French agriculture than the general interests of Britain".[3] The argument was not entirely hypocritical, there were indeed elements in the terms which could cause disquiet to the shadow Cabinet. But it was far from being the whole story; Wilson's worries were primarily domestic and political and he was carried away by them almost against his will. "It was like watching someone being sold down the river into slavery," wrote Jenkins, "drifting away, depressed but unprotesting."[4]

Drifting away, but never so far as to be out of touch. "He spoke and came out clearly against the Market," considered Benn, but his speech struck Barbara Castle as being so low-key "that both pros and antis complained of his lack of leadership".[5] It took an aggressive speech by Jenkins at a party meeting two days later, in which he inveighed against those who ratted on their true convictions, to induce Wilson to complain about people who tried to organise "a party within a party" and to speculate how the more dedicated Europeans could reconcile their convictions with their holding of shadow offices. Even then, when William Rodgers asked him directly whether, in his view, being pro-Market was a bar to remaining on the Labour front bench, Wilson assured him that it was not.[1]

He was still uncertain how best to handle the issue within the party. When Gordon Walker said that he felt a free vote on the issue was essential, Wilson merely replied that he thought the party conference in October would vote by three to one against entry and that the PLP would go narrowly the same way.[2] He was wrong, in that the conference rejected British entry by five to one and the PLP by nearly two to one, but his sense that the weight of Labour opinion was emphatically against entry and that, if anything, that sentiment was growing in force, was proved to be entirely correct. This satisfied him that the most he could do was carry out an exercise in damage-limitation; when Labour returned to power would be time enough to consider how its present attitude was to be changed. In a letter which he wrote to Mellish directly after the conference but before the PLP vote he set out what he felt to be the overriding considerations. So far, he said, everything had been played "strictly according to rule", moving one step at a time and never considering what would be done in certain hypothetical circumstances. He congratulated himself that by these tactics he had got rid of "most of the poison, especially Press poison". No discussion about the form of whip to be applied when the matter was eventually debated in the House of Commons should be allowed until after the PLP had debated the issue. Then the Chief Whip and the leader must confer. "I think we are both in agreement about what it should be." If an instruction was issued as to how to vote, "it cannot be associated in any way with any intimation, written or oral, nod or wink, to the effect that the Whip is anything but what it says". On the other hand, the question of what would happen to anyone who defied the whip was "not a matter for prior discussion or consultation". By thus progressing step by step, Wilson believed, "we shall get through this very difficult problem with a united Party. In fact, we haven't done all that badly already."[3]

At this point Wilson had resigned himself to the fact that the party would have to be instructed to vote against entry and that Jenkins and other dissidents would probably defy the whip. As his letter to Mellish hinted, he hoped that the matter would then be allowed to rest, without too much talk of disciplinary measures. When Heath, however, announced that the Tories would enjoy a free vote on the matter, Wilson saw a chance to avoid a confrontation and declared that, in that case, Labour would have to do the same. Benn at once struck back: "I don't know what game you are playing," he told Wilson, "but we cannot have a free vote when the party had decided its view."[1] His argument prevailed, the whip was duly put on, and when the question was debated in the House of Commons, Jenkins and sixty-eight other Labour MPs voted with the government. In the debate Wilson, in Benn's view, "hedged so cleverly that it was clear that if a Labour Government was elected when he was Prime Minister, he would simply accept the Common Market".[2] Wilson would have denied this with some indignation and a reading of his speech suggests that he was more emphatic in his rejection of the present terms than Benn considered.[3] Certainly he was not prepared to accept an invitation to the signature of the Treaty of Accession in Brussels early in 1972; in the circumstances, he told Heath politely, Labour representation would be inappropriate.[4]

Benn was probably right when he predicted that, left to himself, Wilson would quietly acquiesce in British membership and do nothing to disturb it when he returned to power. But he knew that he would not be left to himself. His objective was to keep the situation fluid. There was strong pressure within the Labour Party for a commitment to withdrawal from the EEC as soon as they returned to office. This Wilson was determined to prevent. Equally, he could not hope to get away with doing nothing. The rubber dinghy which Benn had tried to float a year before now began to seem more appealing. Wilson was so categorically committed against the principle of a referendum that even he found it hard to see how he could now scramble aboard, but the temptation was a real one. With the majority of the shadow Cabinet he decided not to support an amendment put forward by an anti-European Tory to put the matter to a referendum, but when, the following day, Pompidou announced that there would be a referendum in France on the extension of the Community, it seemed that he was being given a chance to change his mind. On 22 March, with Wilson tactfully absent, the NEC pronounced in favour of the idea, and at the shadow Cabinet the following week Wilson changed sides. A dismayed Roy Jenkins asked to be allowed to speak against the shadow Cabinet's new decision at a meeting of the PLP. Wilson ruled that this was out of the question. "In retrospect," wrote Jenkins, "this made me think that he must have fixed upon a strategy of forcing us into submission or resignation, probably the latter."[5]

This conclusion oversimplifies Wilson's attitude. When Jenkins told his leader that he proposed to resign from the shadow Cabinet he was met with a "calm dismay" and "a somewhat more than nominal attempt to dissuade me". When Jenkins tried to discuss the details of his departure, Wilson said: "I find it difficult to start making the funeral arrangements before I am absolutely convinced of the death."[1] He would have been gratified if Jenkins had changed his mind, especially since Harold Lever and George Thomson, for both of whom Wilson had great respect, were sure to resign at the same time. But he was not prepared to make any serious sacrifice so as to retain him. Jenkins's letter of resignation can have done little to soften Wilson's heart. One phrase in particular must have offended him: "I did not envisage that, in a relentless and short-sighted search for tactical advantage, issues on which I thought the party had a settled mind would be reopened, and that I would be required to vote for Conservative amendments directly contrary to positions which we have all long since taken up." He was probably equally disturbed by a letter of the same date from Shirley Williams, who wrote that she was not resigning since on the whole she favoured the idea of a referendum. "I am, however, deeply disturbed by the increasing commitment of the Shadow Cabinet towards opposing not only the terms but the principle of entry into the European Community. It has saddened me to see, week after week, the Parliamentary Party being asked to vote with right wing Tory MPs whose principles we reject. I continue to believe that the best opportunity we have to advance our socialist objectives lies in forging the closest possible links with our fellow socialists and trade unions across the Channel."[2]

The advancement of socialist objectives was not a matter to which Wilson habitually devoted a great deal of thought. Early in 1972 Walter Behrendt, the President of the European Parliament, asked to see him to discuss "the development and strengthening of parliamentary democracy in the Community", and the prospects for the participation of Labour MPs in the "Socialist Group of the European Parliament". For some reason Wilson did not see Behrendt's letter till too late. "It's as well I didn't," he minuted, "as I have no views on the matters he wants to discuss."[3] But on purely practical grounds he did think Britain would be better off in Europe, and he agreed with Shirley Williams that the party was moving dangerously far towards blanket opposition to such a policy. He made it his business to check and, if possible, even reverse the trend. In May 1972 he told Benn that he would resign if the party committed itself to coming out. He was convinced that the next party conference would see a strong demand to commit Britain to withdrawal, a campaign which he suspected might be linked to a move to replace him by Callaghan.[1] It would have been easy for him to accept the views of a majority of the party and thus head off any revolt by Callaghan's supporters. He resisted the temptation, however, and argued that it should be the object of any future Labour government to renegotiate the terms secured by the Conservatives and, if they felt that the result they thus achieved was acceptable, to recommend it to the electorate at a referendum. "He showed great courage in refusing absolutely to reject British entry in principle," wrote Healey, whose admiration for Wilson was in general something short of ecstatic.[2] Willy Brandt was one of Wilson's many friends on the continent who was disconcerted by what appeared to be his *volte-face* over Europe. "It was only with the utmost difficulty, including my throwing the leadership itself into the stakes and threatening to resign," Wilson told him in December 1972, "that enabled me to carry Conference in October on a policy statement which rejected the very potent attempt to commit a Labour Government to pulling out of the Community."[3]

The "very potent attempt" was frustrated and Wilson was left with a freedom of manoeuvre which gave him an excellent chance of keeping Britain in Europe when the opportunity arose. He knew he had won; Jenkins knew he had won, and showed it when he rejoined the shadow Cabinet at the end of 1973; even the anti-Marketeers suspected that he had won, though they still hoped that he would play at least a neutral role when the time came for the referendum. The price that he paid was to be damned as a time-server and a turncoat – a "tethered, sacrificial goat" to party unity, as the *Daily Mirror* once described him. He knew that he was playing an ignoble part, resented it, but endured it stoically in the interests of achieving the end he wanted. It frayed his nerves. Once, in shadow Cabinet, he turned furiously on Roy Jenkins, who had said that he could not in conscience follow a certain course, and exploded: "I've been wading in shit for three months to allow others to indulge their conscience."[4] Wading in shit is neither decorous nor congenial but from time to time it may be necessary for someone to do it. The referendum campaign of 1975 was to show whether this had been one of those occasions.

Emotionally Wilson lost little sleep over Europe; Israel was another matter. When Callaghan became Foreign Secretary Wilson told him that he would leave him a free hand to execute the policy he thought best "with the exception of two areas – Israel and South Africa; the latter because of his honourable detestation of apartheid".[1] He was prepared to endanger even his precious relationship with the Russian leaders so as to secure a better deal for Russian Jewry. He told Martin Gilbert that since 1964 he had been active in trying to get Jews out of Russia. He once refused to visit the Bolshoi on the grounds that he could not watch ballet in Moscow while the leading dancers, the Panovs, were denied exit visas. Cyril Stein gave him details of the ill-treatment meted out to Jews in Russia; he deliberately left his papers lying around on the table of the *dacha* which had been put at his disposal by the Russian government so as to ensure that the fact of his knowledge and concern got back to the authorities. This oblique approach seemed to work best. When he raised certain cases directly with Kosygin, the latter affected to fly into a rage. He later told Wilson privately that it was unwise to refer to such questions in front of subordinates; he would do what he could, he promised.[2]

When Israel was attacked in October 1973, during the feast of Yom Kippur, Wilson at once went into action. He telephoned the Israeli Ambassador every day and asked to be kept closely in touch with developments. "It is extremely encouraging for Israel to have such a staunch friend as you in its hour of need – and this is appreciated by all who love Israel," Sigmund Sternberg told him.[3] The Israelis said that the most useful thing he could do would be to persuade the government to relax the embargo on arms exports to countries involved in the war. Wilson at once wrote to Heath to ask whether, since Arab countries not involved in the war were actively and publicly supplying the Arab belligerents with arms, the British government would not at least release a cargo of 4,000 shells for the Centurion tanks which Britain had in the past supplied to Israel. This "would make a very big difference, and probably contribute over the days ahead to a reduction of casualties". Heath might reasonably have wondered *whose* casualties Wilson expected to be reduced if the shells were supplied; all he said, however, was that such behaviour would be "inconsistent with our call for an immediate cessation of hostilities ... We really cannot make any exceptions to this decision."[4]

When the matter was to be debated in the Commons, Wilson insisted that there should be a three-line whip imposed on the PLP. Jenkins objected strongly. "Look, Roy," snarled Wilson, "I've accommodated your —— conscience for years. Now you're going to have to take account of mine. I feel as strongly about the Middle East as you do about the Common Market."[1] The shadow Cabinet accepted his line but he soon found that he had a party revolt on his hands. Russell Kerr, a prominent member of the Tribune Group, wrote to urge that the whip should be withdrawn. To keep it on would "reopen some old and very deep scars within our Party, and to no very good purpose". Three-quarters of the Tribune Group shared this "marginally pro-Arab line", and Kerr felt there was little doubt that, if the whip was enforced, "our Party would, much more than the Tories, reveal itself as bitterly and irreconcilably divided".[2] In fact the rebels proved to be more or less evenly distributed: seventeen Tories voted with Labour, fifteen socialists with the Conservatives. In the debate Wilson pleaded fervently that help should be given to this "democratic socialist country" with "a remarkable record in the social services ... Therefore I believe that something is owed by some of us to the only democratic social state in that vast region. Indeed, by any test that would apply it is the only democracy in that region."[3]

No disciplinary action was taken against those MPs who had voted against the whip but some months later Andrew Faulds was dropped from the front bench. He complained that this must be because of the "unacceptability" of his views on the Middle East. Not at all, replied Wilson; there were others on the front bench who held similar views and who had never been criticised for it. It was because of his "uncomradely behaviour" in impugning the patriotism of Jewish MPs by implying that they had dual loyalties.[4] No doubt Faulds had been particularly provocative, but he was one of the most vociferous of Labour's Arabists and it must have given Wilson some satisfaction to reduce him to the ranks. Though fiercely pro-Israeli, however, he could be statesmanlike on occasion. In March 1974 he wrote to Anwar Sadat, the Egyptian Prime Minister, to reaffirm that Labour's objective was "the earliest possible just and lasting settlement in the Middle East ... We recognise that this will have to satisfy the Arabs' determination to have their territory restored and of the Israeli need to live within secure and recognised boundaries. It would also have to offer the Palestinians a stake in the future."[5]

It was the need to hold Labour together over the Common Market which brought Wilson back into the mainstream of party politics.

Before that was achieved, however, he had been given a stormy passage, and what was seen as his trimming and indecision over Europe did nothing to make it easier. More and more members felt that he was a passenger not in control of the party and that, if he were to remain as leader, he must mend his ways. James Dunn, from the Whips' office, wrote in April 1972 to point out that in the 120 divisions in the last six months the leader's record had been: votes 70, absent paired 38, absent without permission 12. "Harold, the figure in that last column should read nil. Your example is carefully watched and from time to time unnecessary comments are made."[1] When he did appear in public he seemed sometimes to have lost his touch. A BBC Audience Research report on one of his party political broadcasts at the beginning of 1973 showed that twice as many people thought it "not at all informative" as "highly informative"; four times as many thought it "very biased" as found it "very well balanced"; four times as many said it "didn't hold my attention" as found it "completely gripping". Not surprisingly a majority of the listeners did not share these extreme views and found him "competent" and "incisive", but those who were unfavourably impressed were significantly greater than in earlier surveys.[2]

The last eight months of 1972 saw an extraordinary wave of recrimination break over the unfortunate Wilson: mainly it came from the left. In May, reported Benn, the Tribune Group called on Wilson to tell him how much they disliked his leadership: "Stan Orme said it was like punching cotton wool."[3] The following month the *New Statesman* weighed in with a diatribe all the more extraordinary for being addressed to a man who had for long been considered its favourite son. A visit he had paid in 1971 to ex-President Johnson provided the main *casus belli*: "Even today it is doubtful if he has begun to understand the enormity of the affront that he delivered to the British Left. Certainly only a political leader with either a casual indifference to, or a callous disregard for, the feelings of his followers could have done what Mr Wilson did last year." But then the attack swelled into an exultant denunciation of the man and all his works. To the electorate, particularly the young, announced the *Statesman*, Wilson "stands today as the principal apostle of cynicism, the unwitting evangelist of disillusion. There have been just too great a number of tawdry compromises, too regular a series of clumsy attempts at vindication, too relentless a succession of political *pas de deux* danced solo. We say it with reluctance but we believe it to be true. Mr Wilson has now sunk to a position where his very presence in Labour's Leadership pollutes the atmosphere of politics."[1]

If Wilson had chosen to champion the cause of British withdrawal from Europe he might have won back some of the left's esteem; as it was his attitude was added to the list of "tawdry compromises" of which he stood accused. Just before the party conference in October Eric Heffer remarked that one only had to cast a quick eye over the resolutions to see how distrustful the party had become at the grass-roots. "They feel that too often they are ignored. They were so ignored during the lifetime of the last Labour Government. Conference decisions were flouted . . . Today, and rightly so, pragmatism is a dirty word."[2] Wilson made occasional efforts to propitiate the angry young men of the left, but to little avail. In July 1972 he wrote to the Soviet Ambassador nominating four young men "with a big future" for a visit to Russia.[3] All were inclined to the left; one was a particularly strident critic, Neil Kinnock. Wilson took particular pains to court this up-and-coming young socialist. He told him he would ask him to second the Queen's Speech as soon as he had a chance to draft one. Kinnock felt there might after all be hope for the future in the present leadership and began to talk excitedly about all that Labour would do after the next election. "Don't be stupid, Neil," said his wife tartly. "These are the people who sold us out last time, and they'll do just the same next."[4]

To win the affections of the Tribune Group might be beyond Wilson's powers; to stage-manage some sort of a rapprochement with the unions promised to be easier. A Labour shadow Cabinet would always find it less troublesome to get on with the trade unions when it was safely removed from power and had no responsibility for wage restraint or keeping Britain at work. In 1971 and 1972 the relationship was still cosier, since both sides were united in resisting the Conservative industrial legislation. The TUC leaders knew perfectly well that Wilson, in power, would have endorsed 80 per cent or more of the Tory bill, but they preferred to forget the fact and Wilson had no intention of reminding them. Hugh Scanlon's election to the leadership of the engineers' union in 1969 meant that the two largest unions, controlling by themselves 30 per cent of the conference vote, were securely in left-wing hands. The NEC was moving the same way. Wilson's recollection of the battle over *In Place of Strife* left him in no doubt that he could anticipate trouble when back in office. For the moment, however, all were agreed in wishing to see Labour win the next election. To achieve that result Wilson was prepared to be conciliatory, and the unions to utter the most dulcet noises about the cooperation that could be expected by a government with which they felt ideologically akin.

The Social Compact of February 1973 – or Social Contract as it was later called – was the fruit of this wooing. Together with Wilson, Jack Jones was the principal architect of the accord, more formally known as *Economic Policy and the Cost of Living*. This document set out a strategy by which labour relations might cease to be the bugbear which had bedevilled British economic life for so many years. It comprised food subsidies, price controls, control of housing and rents, increased investment in industry, and a redistribution of incomes and capital, as well, of course, as the repeal of the Tory Industrial Relations Act. It constituted an agreement by which the unions would voluntarily impose restraint in pay demands as part of a wider settlement on economic and social policy; or at least Wilson thought it did: the unions' *quid* offered in exchange for the shadow Cabinet's *quo* was not set out with any precision. The trouble was that there was not the slightest reason to believe that a new Labour government would be any more successful in performing its side of the bargain than it had been in the past or that, even if it seemed on the way to fulfilling its promises, the TUC would be able to persuade its members to show enough restraint to make the process work. The Social Compact was a programme of pious hopes with precious little evidence offered that either side to the bargain would be willing or able to perform its part. It was "a load of codswallop", the chairman of the Public Accounts Committee, Edmund Dell, told Healey.[1] Healey disagreed. So did Barbara Castle, who wrote in her diary that this new concordat with the unions was "far more hopeful than the arm's-length relationship we had last time".[2] On reflection, however, Dell was unconvinced. Indeed he became increasingly certain that "codswallop" was an understatement and that the Social Compact was actively mischievous. He felt that it committed Labour to accepting an automatic correlation between prices and wages which, in a period when the rocketing cost of oil made substantial inflation inevitable, threatened to transform an already dangerous process into out-and-out disaster. It was a prescription for hyperinflation. Almost as bad, the Social Compact tacitly conceded that the TUC was a power equal in status to the government, to be consulted if not deferred to on every major issue of domestic policy. In Middlemas's words: "The balance of power in industry shifted further – to the detriment of employer and management."[1]

As ever, Wilson tried to convince himself that he had established a special relationship with his interlocutors which meant he could place confidence in their assurances. In November 1973 he told Sigmund Sternberg that his "personal relations with the leaders of most of the individual unions are very good and I have had a number of discussions with them on a man-to-man basis in recent weeks, union by union and problem by problem".[2] But even he did not delude himself that any sort of rigid commitment to an incomes policy could be read into the unions' endorsement of the Social Compact. "What we want is more the creation of a mood than a compact," he declared revealingly at a meeting of the TUC Liaison Committee early in 1974.[3] Nor did his transitory love-feast with the union leaders reconcile him to the NEC. On the contrary, 1973 saw him regarding that body with ever more marked distaste and grasping at almost any excuse to avoid attendance at its meetings.

More than any other factor, it was Tony Benn's predominance in the NEC which made it so suspect an organisation in Wilson's eyes. When he appointed him Minister of Technology Benn had been one of Wilson's best hopes for the future; the next leader but one and possibly even his successor in 10 Downing Street. As Benn had moved left, however, disenchantment had set in: "He immatures with age," had been one of Wilson's less offensive comments. As the left became more and more hostile to the leader's policies, and Benn more and more identified with the left, so Wilson elevated this on the whole guileless man to a leading place in the pantheon of plotters. Such suspicions were unjust, but Wilson was right to believe that while he himself had been preoccupied with Europe or other matters remote from domestic politics, Benn had been building up a position of considerable strength on the left and evolving radical solutions for the country's economic future which were far from anything that the Labour leader felt he could espouse. In particular he was dismayed by Benn's ideas for an industry bill which would include a vast extension of nationalisation in the fields of banking, insurance, building societies, building, road-haulage and shipbuilding and the setting up of a National Enterprise Board (NEB) to take over the twenty-five biggest companies in the country.

Battle was joined on 23 March 1973 at the Home Policy

Committee, when Wilson and Healey made it clear that they thought Benn's proposals were without merit, either economic or electoral, and would, indeed, doom the Labour Party to permanent opposition. Benn was unrepentant; if Britain was ever to become truly socialist then the great redoubts of capitalism must first be stormed. He persisted with his ideas and in mid May aired them at a joint meeting of the shadow Cabinet and NEC at the Churchill Hotel in London. Wilson was particularly vituperative about the proposal to nationalise the twenty-five leading companies. "Who's going to tell me that we should nationalise Marks and Spencer in the hope that it will be as efficient as the Co-op?" he asked, a jibe which caused considerable offence to the Co-op-sponsored MPs when it got back to them. When Benn referred to conference resolutions approving the nationalisation of banking and insurance, Wilson retorted, with more honesty than tact: "We only take notice of Conference resolutions when it suits us, everyone knows that."[1] A fortnight later the NEC voted to retain the commitment to nationalise the leading companies. Wilson argued for several hours for the deletion of the undertaking, claiming that the party could never hope to win an election with such an albatross slung around its neck. When he was finally defeated, he grimly reserved the position of the shadow Cabinet.[2] "The party is now firmly launched on a left-wing policy," wrote Benn exultantly, "... it is a remarkable development of views that we have achieved in three years of hard work."[3] Wilson reproached himself that he had allowed the hard work to go on without taking steps to divert its course; if the left-wing policy could not be reversed, then at least it must be stopped in its tracks.

Wilson attacked Benn's proposals on the grounds that the twenty-five companies would be far less efficient if nationalised; he also argued that the NEB should not acquire assets in its own right but should merely act as a holding company for assets already in public ownership. This, he said, was what was envisaged in Benn's paper. In fact the opposite was the case, Mikardo complained: the document assumed the NEB would acquire "a substantial addition of companies from the present private sector".[4] Benn was further outraged when he learned that Wilson, not he, was to introduce the industrial debate at the party conference: "Here was the man who had been trying to stop the industrial policy all summer, who threatened to veto it and now wants to present it."[5] Wilson eventually agreed that Benn should wind up the debate, though he gave no indication that any conclusions the conference might arrive at on the subject would find a place when the time came to draft the manifesto for the next election.

Wilson's plan was, in fact, for the shadow Cabinet and the NEC to meet before the conference and decide what should go into the manifesto – presenting this to the conference as a *fait accompli*. The NEC found the proposal unappealing and refused to attend the meeting. Wilson did not take the news too tragically: "We all know what the National Executive is like on the eve of the re-elections," he remarked. "It goes though a menstrual period." He was sure that Benn was at the bottom of the executive's attitude, however; just as it was Benn who had been leaking stories to the press about the row over public ownership. He turned on his colleague and said angrily: "You talk about your works in Bristol. Well, I was in Derby the other day and all they asked me was, why did Tony Benn make those silly statements?"[1] In fact the conference passed off without the rifts in the leadership becoming too apparent. Wilson, in his opening speech, contrived to sound more enthusiastic about further nationalisation than in fact he was; Benn, in his conclusion, confined himself for the most part to generalities which went down well on the floor but did not commit his colleagues to anything too uncomfortably precise.

A related row between Wilson and Benn concerned the compensation that would be given to investors in companies that were taken over. In May Benn hinted broadly that people buying shares in Rolls-Royce – a manufacturer that had recently been rescued from bankruptcy by the government – might find their assets taken over by a future Labour government without compensation. Several shadow ministers condemned Benn's remarks. Wilson had in fact authorised them in a telephone conversation though it seems unlikely he had expected them to be quite so explicit and challenging. Now he recanted, disowned Benn and issued a categoric statement: "It is *not* the policy of the next Labour government to nationalise Rolls-Royce Motors without compensation." He could have handled the matter a lot better, but with the memory of the fracas still in everyone's minds he had some grounds to complain when, with Benn's approval if not at his instigation, the NEC in October passed a motion that no compensation should be paid for shares acquired in companies that had been nationalised and then denationalised. It was "legalised robbery", complained Callaghan;[2] and Wilson made sure that it found no place in the party manifesto.

The indignation of the far left at this attempt to thwart their initiatives became ever more strident. Ian Mikardo accused Wilson of imposing dictatorial rule on the Labour Party. Even before 1970 he had "started changing the operations of both the Government and the Party from democratic management to presidential rule". Now, in opposition, he was accelerating the process.[1] The Tribune Group strongly disputed his right to exclude anything he disliked from the manifesto. Nor was this "the only method by which he sought to rule over the Party like a Roman emperor of old". He told ministers who were members of the NEC that they must follow the official line, even if this was at variance with party policy: "a gross violation of basic democratic principles", stormed Mikardo. A particularly intransigent section of the Tribune Group was the Campaign for Labour Party Democracy (CLPD), twelve or so left-wing activists, among them Neil Kinnock, who banded together in opposition to Wilson's refusal to put the NEC proposals on nationalisation into the manifesto. Like Mikardo, the CLPD envisaged Wilson not just as a reactionary but as a ruthless and authoritarian figure. If Wilson was in fact bent on behaving as a dictator, he proved remarkably ineffective. The manifesto excluded some of the NEC's more categoric recommendations but was far nearer in tone to Benn's paper than Wilson would have liked, while he was unable, indeed made little effort, to curb the public utterances of his more radical colleagues.

But it was not only the left who were out for Wilson's blood. In July Bill Rodgers told Benn that Wilson was now "a liability. He was meaner than he used to be, he hadn't matured as a statesman ... the middle of the Party was getting disillusioned. The new M.P.s had come into Parliament in 1970 thinking he was wonderful, and the more they saw of him, the less they liked him."[2] The *Guardian*, not to be outdone by the *New Statesman*, printed an interview in which it was suggested that many people who used to work for Labour would not do so now "because they didn't believe a word Mr Wilson said". Wilson wrote an injured letter to the editor, Alaistair Hetherington, challenging him to cite a single case where something he had said could not be believed – a challenge which Hetherington sensibly did not accept.[3] The word spread. Greenwood, in Singapore, lunched with Lee Kuan Yew in November 1973. "He has little confidence in H.W. but sees no likely alternative. He says that Harold, viewed from a distance, seems completely to have lost his touch and to be living in a quite irrelevant, dream world."[1] About the same time, John Silkin considered it likely that there would soon be a coalition. Wilson and Heath would both be dumped and Whitelaw would invite Callaghan to become Prime Minister.[2]

This is not the whole story. It is easy to forget that the majority of Labour voters in the country and a large proportion of the PLP were perfectly well satisfied with Wilson's performance and had no doubt that he was the man best qualified to lead the party back to power. People are more likely to commit hostile comments to paper than to record the fact that they think Smith or Jones is doing well, and many of the most disobliging comments about Wilson came from people who, for one reason or another, felt themselves his enemies. Silkin, Rodgers, Greenwood, Benn, were all men who had a grievance against their leader, and were happy to hear and pass on anything to his discredit. Nevertheless, Wilson was unpopular with a wide range of his so-called supporters at the end of 1973. He was probably no more vulnerable than he had been in 1968 or 1972 but the erosion of support can be an inexorable process and in every way he was less resilient than he had been in the past. It would have taken a political hurricane to displace him before the next election, but if he had lost that he would not have survived for long as leader of the party. Fortunately for him, Heath now intervened to save him from this dismal fate.

In November 1973 the National Union of Miners (NUM) began an overtime ban in support of their pay claim, which exceeded the limits laid down by the government's counter-inflation laws. With the Yom Kippur war simultaneously threatening Britain's oil supplies, it was clear that a serious energy crisis was at hand. Joe Gormley, the miners' leader, told Wilson that a compromise could be reached if the government would agree to pay miners for the time they had to spend at the pithead preparing to go down to the coal-face or washing when they came up again. "Oh!" Gormley remembers Wilson saying. "Well, of course, Joe, you do realise you're pulling the Tory government's irons out of the fire for them?"[3] He effectively put them back in again by writing to Heath on 23 November, suggesting this solution to the problem. Heath replied briefly that it would cost too much, and Wilson made it impossible for the Tory leader to reconsider his position by publishing the exchange of letters. "I will never forgive Harold Wilson for it," wrote Gormley, who was as anxious as any member of the government to reach a negotiated settlement.[1] Wilson did, however, at the same time send Heath a separate, confidential letter in which he said that his "soundings about coalfield opinion leave me with a strong and disturbing impression". The traditionally moderate miners' leaders were as militant as any of the usual activists. "I believe this is a serious matter." The Durham miners were particularly aggressive, though in the past they had always been immune to pressure from communists or other extremists. Heath, politely but coolly, thanked him for "letting me have your confidential impression of opinion in the coalfields to add to the other information available to me".[2] Probably Wilson expected no more. It is hard to be sure what he intended by this *démarche* but the fact was that he took pains to warn Heath of the risks he was running in a way that could be of no possible gain to himself. He was out to exploit the disaster in the interests of his party but he was not quite such an arrant mischief-maker as Gormley supposed.

By mid December the energy crisis had become reality. Heath imposed a three-day working week. In discussions of tactics, Wilson was insistent that Labour should present itself as the future "national government" and should play the card of national unity as often and as vigorously as possible.[3] Heath declared a State of Emergency and the likelihood that he would call a general election on the issue of "Who governs Britain?" seemed greater every day. A possible escape from the impasse was offered by the Relativities Report, which the Pay Board had been preparing. This compared the rewards which were offered in the various industries and identified special cases in which a breach of the normal pay restrictions could be justified. It seemed that it would not call for too much ingenuity to use this mechanism to sanction concessions to the miners. The report was published in mid January and Wilson wrote to Heath urging him to apply it to the miners' case. "I am alarmed at the unguarded way he has gone overboard for the whole report, with none of the reservations I had urged on him," wrote Barbara Castle. "He really is the most reckless tactician, always getting himself into corners."[4] Heath blocked the approach by retorting that he would be happy to apply the report to the miners if the unions would accept the principle and the proposed machinery. When a miners' ballot showed 81 per cent of the members in favour of turning the go-slow into an all-out strike, the pressure on Heath to call an election became irresistible. He did so on 7 February. After three and a half years in opposition Wilson had the possibility of a return to Number 10. He had no doubt that it would be his last chance.

At the end of 1970 Wilson told Benn that even if he had won the last election he would only have remained in office for three years. If he won the next election he would not serve the full term. "He is determined that he will never be defeated again."[1] Benn, not unreasonably, was sceptical.

XX

The Two Elections

1974

W ilson had gone into the 1970 electoral campaign convinced that he was going to win, had remained confident until almost the very end, only to suffer shattering disappointment. In February 1974 he began the campaign resigned to defeat, remained despondent until almost the very end, and then found he had achieved, if not a triumphant victory, then at least a result good enough to put him back into Downing Street. There had been good cause for his despondency. After three years of poor showing at the opinion polls the tide seemed to have turned in favour of the Tories. An NOP poll on 10 January showed them 4 per cent ahead and, even if there had not been a miners' strike, Heath might have been considering whether he would be justified in calling an election. Wiseacres warned him that the British voter did not like an election centred around a single issue; but how well chosen the issue seemed to be. If Labour backed the miners they would be seen as the party of disorder and industrial unrest, supporting a selfish and irresponsible minority against the interests of the state. If they denounced the miners' tactics they would be betraying the working man, enraging the unions, splitting the party. Wilson was impaled by a dilemma whose horns the Tories had lovingly sharpened and tipped with poison.

What they did not sufficiently take into account was that it was a situation tailor-made for a display not merely of Wilson's talents, but also of the principles in which he genuinely believed: consensus, compromise, moderation. On the actual issue in debate he felt less than passionate; he thought the miners had a reasonable case and that they had been ineptly treated, but he would certainly not have gone to the stake to secure them all that they were demanding. The role in which he chose to portray himself, and which he projected with marked success, was that of conciliator. Heath had chosen to identify himself with one side in the war between capital and labour; Wilson would be above the struggle. It was not a part which lent itself to drama or pyrotechnics; indeed, it was low-key and sometimes dull. "Watched Harold on television," wrote a disgruntled Benn. "All this 'national interest', 'working together', 'keep calm and keep cool', and 'a Labour Government will knit the nation', seems absolute rubbish to me now."[1] But the nation did not agree. There was a lot of luck about the Labour victory of February 1974; it could easily have swung the other way; but Wilson's appeal to the electorate was far more potent than either his colleagues or his opponents, or indeed he himself, realised at the time.

According to Haines the strategy as evolved by Wilson and Marcia Williams was to make little use of Transport House and concentrate the appeal to the electorate on "the polling power of the Leader".[2] If that was ever the intention it must have been quickly abandoned. There was nothing presidential about Wilson's conduct of the campaign. His cooperation with Transport House was closer than it had been in earlier elections, and he seemed more ready to consult advisers outside his intimate circle and even to listen to what was said. He largely forswore the walkabouts which had been so prominent in 1970, claiming that he already understood the ordinary people: "Mary and I *are* ordinary people." On one of the few occasions on which he did indulge in one he was embarrassed by his success. In Huddersfield, he recalled some years later, he was "nearly trampled to death by over 7,000 people in the new shopping area, nearly all on my side. I am sorry to say some shop windows got broken by sheer enthusiasm."[3] Far more than previously he emphasised the team, made a point of not taking the chair at press conferences and encouraging long answers from Callaghan, Healey, Jenkins or whoever was beside him. The Labour candidates seemed embarrassingly ready to take the same view about his importance in the campaign – only 2 per cent referred to him in their addresses, as opposed to ten times as many Tories (still not an impressive figure) who invoked the name of Heath.[4]

It does not follow from this that Wilson played an inconsiderable role in the election. In an early meeting with his team, Wilson announced that the campaign was going to be like the Civil War. He described "in impressive detail" the battle of Marston Moor and said he was going to follow Cromwell's strategy: in the first week, contain the Tory attack; second week, counter-attack on the basis of better economic policy, the Social Contract and plans to reduce prices; third week, skirmishes on the flanks, exploiting such issues as Enoch Powell or the EEC.[1] The surprising thing is that things did more or less turn out as this master plan dictated. Wilson throughout took the line that, though the miners' strike had provoked the election, it was not the main, still less the only issue. Callaghan was left to take the lead on the dispute and more general questions of industrial legislation, Wilson concentrated on prices, houses, mortgages, unemployment. He discussed such issues in characteristically undogmatic terms. He was saddled with a party manifesto couched in terms more radical and doctrinaire than he would himself have favoured and a new General Secretary at Transport House who believed in a massive redistribution of wealth and more extensive nationalisation. He over-came this handicap by ignoring them both, or at least paying no more than lip-service to their ideology. He believed that the 1970 election had been lost, not because committed socialists were dissatisfied with the political posture of their government but because housewives were fed up with inadequate services and high prices. Benn said repeatedly that the 1974 election was all-important because, if Labour won, it would be the first time that they had done so with a genuinely left-wing programme.[2] Wilson would cross that bridge when he came to it; for the moment he intended to win the election in spite of rather than because of the left-wing programme.

His trump card, which he played gingerly and with some doubts about its credibility, was the Social Contract. His doubts were reinforced when, the day after he referred to it in a speech at Not-tingham, Hugh Scanlon denied that any specific agreement had been entered into by the unions. Heath poured derision on his speech: where is this famous contract? he enquired; produce the piece of paper.[3] Fortunately for Wilson the majority of the union leaders rallied to confirm that the contract *did* exist and that the unions were pledged to practise moderation and to make it work. But Scanlon was not the only union leader who posed Wilson problems. Though he might treat the miners' strike as a subsidiary issue, he knew that it could at any moment explode in a way that would be damaging to Labour's prospects. When Heath invited him and the Liberal leader, Jeremy Thorpe, to join in a call to the miners to stop the strike, he retorted by urging that the three party chiefs should sit down with the miners and representatives of the TUC and the CBI to thrash out an agreement. But he was constantly alert to any risk that he might be branded as an extremist or one who allowed extremists to flourish. When Mick McGahey, the leader of the Scottish miners, referred to the possibility that troops might be called in to break the strike and urged them in that case to remember their working-class origins and be prepared to defy their orders, Wilson at once saw the risk that the Labour Party might be tarred with the brush of sedition. A hundred MPs were rustled up to sign an order paper deploring the politicisation of the strike and he and Callaghan issued a statement in which they "utterly repudiated" McGahey's speech. In the shadow Cabinet Benn and Foot complained that this was over-reaction; Wilson retorted that most of the miners' MPs had supported his action and that if he, as leader, had failed to speak promptly and firmly it would have cost Labour the election.[1]

The inner entourage had been reinforced by the time of the election by Bernard Donoughue, senior lecturer at the London School of Economics. Donoughue was a protégé of Harry Kissin, who felt that, from every point of view, it would be useful if he were to find a niche at Number 10. When Kissin offered to organise a private opinion poll for the 1974 election, he threw in Donoughue as part of the package. Initially it was envisaged that he would serve only during the campaign, but by the time the election was over he had become part of the team and had been invited to serve at Number 10 for the two years that Wilson expected to be there. Eventually he was asked to continue under Callaghan. To the ever-suspicious Balogh it seemed that Donoughue had been "imposed" on Wilson by big business: "So to some extent Harold is really a slave to a clique of British industrialists, which explains a lot of his attitudes on industry."[2] This seems a somewhat tendentious presentation of the facts. Donoughue's function at Number 10 was to be adviser, in particular on economic but increasingly on a far wider spectrum of general issues. The advice that he gave, whether it was good or bad, was usually remote from anything that a "clique of British industrialists" would have approved and he saw his role more as keeper of the Prime Minister's conscience than subverter of his principles. In the electoral campaign his foremost function was to draft the economic sections of Wilson's major speeches – unsurprisingly the style had to be full-bloodedly "Wilsonised" by Joe Haines before it had any chance of acceptance. The practice was not conspicuously successful. It was remarked that Wilson's speeches were less effective in this than in earlier campaigns because "he relied more on other people's words which didn't suit his rhythm".[1]

Whether it was the nature of the campaign he had decided to fight, a deliberate attempt to conserve his resources, or the exhaustion and depression which grow in those who think they are engaged in a losing battle, the first weeks of the election exhibited a disconcertingly uncertain Wilson. Benn, for one, was convinced that the Labour leader was being catastrophically out-performed by Heath. Wilson was "really fooling about on the fringes, seen at press conferences and ticket-only meetings; whereas Heath is on the streets in walkabouts, giving a sort of de Gaulle impression" (a curious mirror-image of the rival approaches to the 1970 election). While Heath was doing "a brilliant party political broadcast", Wilson was "floundering away about the price of petrol". He looked nervous, thought Benn; "I think he does realise that he is perhaps within a week of the end of his political career."[2] Cecil King agreed: "Ted has been better – much better than in 1970; Wilson has been worse."[3] Praise from such a quarter was hardly to be expected, but it was Joe Haines who described Wilson's performance at the beginning of the campaign as "abysmal ... I watched his speeches fall from tired lips on to a leaden audience."[4]

It was not from want of trying on the part of those who stage-managed his appearances. Stanley Baker and others from the film world were called in to lend a professional touch to his appearances. His speeches were presented with far greater care than ever before, a huge set displayed behind him, lectern in the ideal position, microphone with cut-off switch. A make-up man was employed to eliminate dark shadows and shiny skin, his hair was freshly washed and elegantly cut. New suits were bought for the campaign, blue and grey – Wilson would never be smart but he looked like a rather higher level of bank manager than was habitually the case. He drank Lucozade to give himself energy and a mixture of lemon and honey for hoarseness; since the latter might have looked like whisky, green glasses and carafes were used.[5]

In the latter part of the campaign at least part of Wilson's malaise may have been induced by worry over an incipient scandal which threatened seriously to damage Marcia Williams and peripherally make trouble for him as well. In the 1960s Marcia's brother, Tony Field, a trained geologist, had acquired some slag-heaps and a quarry near Wigan with a view to selling the stone and slag as hard core for motorways. By the time these were exhausted a property boom was in progress. Field made an arrangement to exploit the site with a businessman named Ronald Milhench, who subsequently proved to be a not very efficient confidence trickster. Marcia had been a sleeping partner in the original enterprise and thus would benefit from any development of the site. Milhench sought to further his efforts by brandishing a supporting letter on House of Commons writing paper, which purported to be signed by Harold Wilson. The signature was eventually shown to be a clumsy forgery, but not till after the press had been whipped into a frenzy of excitement. Nothing remotely illegal had been done by anyone except Milhench, but it was unfortunate that Wilson's former office manager should be so publicly involved in an enterprise which Wilson defended as "land reclamation" but which was portrayed by his opponents as being the sort of land speculation which the Labour Party traditionally condemned. The story in the *Daily Mail*, which hinted at the more lurid details, did not appear until the campaign was over, but a telephone call from the *Guardian* caused some alarm, and the possibility of disagreeable publicity was a nagging source of disquiet for Wilson, not to mention Marcia Williams.

Even without this distraction, however, it would have been a difficult time. Donoughue describes Wilson as being "clearly worried, puzzled and even bewildered about what would be the result".[1] He did not expect to win, believed Benn, nor was he really sure he wanted to, since if he was carried into power on the back of a successful miners' strike he might find himself the prisoner of his left wing.[2] The second part of this was fanciful – Wilson very much wanted to win – but the best he dared hope for was that he might emerge as leader of the largest party and even this prospect seemed remote. On the last Sunday before polling day Jenkins described him as "tired, depressed and expecting defeat, keeping going with some difficulty and gallantry".[3] When next day the Labour Party's private poll showed figures even worse than those that had gone before, it seemed that all was over save the gracious acceptance of defeat. And yet, though nobody suspected it, the tide had already turned and the Conservative lead was rapidly being swept away.

A variety of factors accounted for this belated swing. A week before polling day came the announcement of what seemed to be a schoolboy error in the Coal Board's arithmetic: the miners' pay was not 8 per cent above the average for industry but 8 per cent below it; their claim was clearly justified; the agonies of the three-day week had been unnecessary. In fact the new calculations were over-simplified and anyway based on a false assumption; there had been no blunder. The damage was done however; the correction of the error had nothing like the impact of the error itself and the government seemed guilty of dithering and incompetence. An announcement that retail food prices had risen by 20 per cent in the previous year did even less to help the Tory cause. Disastrous trade figures, showing a deficit of £383 million, the largest ever recorded and twelve times greater than the corresponding figures for June 1970, added fuel to the fire. Campbell Adamson of the CBI rashly remarked – as he thought, off the record – that he would like to see the Industrial Relations Act repealed, and found his indiscretion headlined in every newspaper.

But it was Enoch Powell who probably did more than anyone to destroy the Tory cause. In early February he had decided not to stand because he could not in conscience support a party which had taken Britain into Europe. This would do Heath "an immense amount of damage", thought Benn. "If only Harold would look and sound a bit more convincing, we might have a good chance."[1] Meeting Wilson in a lavatory at the House of Commons, Powell told him that he planned only to make two or three big speeches and that these would be confined mainly to Europe. Wilson established when these speeches were going to take place and timed his own comments on Europe so that he did not seem to be following Powell's lead.[2] But though he had expected these interventions to be helpful Wilson had not dared hope for Powell's speech at Birmingham a few days before polling day, in which the former Tory minister denounced the election as fraudulent and advised people to vote for Labour since they were the only party which was committed to giving the country the chance to make up its own mind about Europe. It seems improbable that many voters actually changed their minds as a result of Powell's speech, but it may have affected the undecided and psychologically it was a blow to Tory morale at a moment when, for the first time, they were beginning to feel vulnerable.

Though Powell urged people to vote Labour, it was only because he so disliked the Conservatives, and most of what happened in the closing stages of the campaign did more to disenchant voters with the Tories than to impel them to the other end of the spectrum. The beneficiaries were above all the Liberals. In elections from 1945 to

1970 the Liberals and the other smaller parties had won on average only 7 per cent of the total vote; in 1974 they won 25 per cent. It is a curious phenomenon that, up to a level of 17 or 18 per cent or so of the total vote, a swing to the fringe parties seems to damage the opposition, but if it gets substantially beyond that the fringe's gains are at the expense of the party in power. Wilson was largely unaware of this movement, but in the last few days before the poll he seemed to detect a mood of hostility towards Heath which could only be encouraging. He was still far from optimistic when he moved to his constituency for the final stages of the campaign. He settled as usual in the Adelphi Hotel in Liverpool, then, for the last night, switched to the Golden Eagle at Kirby. He reckoned that, if he was going to go down to defeat, he would rather do so amid his own constituents and thought too that, if he chose a smaller and more remote hotel, it would make it more difficult for the press to persecute him. In fact they followed him to Kirby and, as their night wore on, it became increasingly likely that they were seeking not the first photographs of a broken man but an interview with the new Prime Minister.

It was not until late the following day, 1 March, that the picture became clear. Labour was the largest party with 301 seats. The Conservatives had 297, the Liberals 14 and others, mainly nationalists of various persuasions, 23. The Liberals, if they wished, could keep either of the larger parties in power. Wilson's assumption was that, as leader of the largest party, he would at once be invited to form a government, but Heath insisted that, as incumbent Prime Minister, he must be given the first chance to see whether he could put together the support necessary to remain in office. It was "rather as if the referee had blown the whistle and one side had refused to leave the field", commented Wilson mildly.[1] Opinions vary as to how he supported this check to his hopes. According to Jenkins he "got agitated and talked about issuing a denunciation of constitutional impropriety", and had to be persuaded that a policy of dignified impassivity would be more effective.[2] Barbara Castle, however, found him confident that he would eventually get in and "chuckling over the situation". He was already planning his attack on the Queen's Speech if Heath did succeed in doing a deal with the Liberals. " 'Footwork is my strong point,' he murmured modestly." He told Castle that his next government would work much more as a committee, with no more off-the-record conversations or Lobby briefings. " 'That sounds okay,' I replied, relieved. So long as he doesn't renew that vendetta with the press. Certainly Harold is the only man for this tricky hour. It could be that he has really learned the lessons of last time."[1] Probably both reports were correct; in the tension of those days it would have been surprising if Wilson had not veered from mood to mood. He did not have long to wait. Heath's negotiations with the Liberals quickly foundered. On Monday 4 March at 7.00 p.m. Wilson was summoned to the palace. Within an hour of his appointment he was back at Downing Street.

Any Prime Minister who finds himself in charge of a minority government is obsessed above all by one question: how soon he can safely ask for a dissolution and try to put his rule on a more stable footing. Until this has been resolved, indeed, he can hardly address himself to the business of running the country. Life must go on, however, and there are many decisions to be made, however temporary their application may turn out to be. The first for Wilson was where he was going to live. It was a question on which his wife had decided views. Barbara Castle talked to her about her life when they met at a Labour women's conference in June 1974. " 'Of course I hate it,' she told me. 'But then I always have. But I do my job.' Then she added, almost as an afterthought, 'But I'm glad for Harold. He needed this. He went through such a rotten time.' Nonetheless, I feel Harold has an incipient revolt on his hands in that quarter."[2] There was no revolt, but there might have been if Mary had not had her way on two points. The first was Wilson's often stated determination not to remain in office more than the two years needed to break Asquith's record. How far Mary contributed to this decision is hard to assess; probably a great deal. Wilson knew that his wife loathed the business of being wife of the Labour leader; he had made her put up with it for eleven years already; there was a limit to what he could ask her to endure. But she might have found even an additional two years unbearable if she had been asked to move back to the flat in Downing Street. Fortunately Wilson did not need much persuading. He knew he would only have two years at Number 10; if the next election went wrong it might be a great deal less than that; to give up the house in Lord North Street for so short a period made little sense. He did not see much less of his wife as a result; as often as not she came over to Number 10 for lunch while even when she lived above the shop at Downing Street he had usually worked until late at night in his office.

He could be back home in three or four minutes, and at least Mary could be reasonably sure that when he did come he would not have a platoon of secretaries, colleagues and advisers at his heels, clamouring for his attention.

Marcia Williams was also much away from Downing Street in the first few months after the election. The slag-heap scandal gave the press a bonanza: even if they had regretfully decided that the Prime Minister could not be involved, they still had high hopes that they could drag down his political secretary. On 18 March the *Daily Mail* ran a long story on the nefarious Mr Milhench and his land deals; two weeks later the forged letter was published. With unattractive enthusiasm the press laid siege to Marcia's house in Wyndham Mews. Wilson defiantly rose to the family's defence in a *World in Action* programme. Tony Field had performed a public service in removing the slag-heaps, he said, and had nearly bankrupted himself in the process. "I have the fullest confidence in everyone concerned in this story. The whole thing is a pretty seamy, squalid press story. This doesn't happen to Conservative prime ministers: the aim is to destroy the Labour Government."[1] He had been strongly urged not to mix himself in the affair more than was strictly necessary, but he had no intention of letting his friends suffer without coming to the rescue. It was not the last chivalrous indiscretion of which he was guilty.

When the furore was beginning to die down for lack of fresh fuel, Noyes Thomas of the *News of the World* predicted that Marcia Williams would shortly be offered a life peerage and made a minister. According to James Margach, Wilson instructed Haines to deny the story and to refuse to admit Thomas as a Lobby correspondent. The Lobby rightly refused to accept this boycott of one of its members and the matter was dropped.[2] Wilson's indignation was the greater because Thomas had got it partly right. Wilson had always intended eventually to reward Marcia with a peerage and the treatment to which she had been subjected determined him to do so at once instead of waiting for the resignation honours. He told the Queen that his intention was to "do a Harvey Smith" at the press, Smith being a celebrated show-jumper who had caused a stir when he stuck two fingers up derisively to show his disapproval of some standers-by.[3] He felt sure that she would understand the terminology, he told Martin Gilbert.[4] He returned from Easter in the Isles of Scilly resolved to act at once. In a letter which he sent Mrs Williams on 18 May –

one suspects for the record – he wrote: "I know you don't really want to be on the list but I want you on it."[1] Five days later it was made public. "The amusing news tonight is that Harold has made Marcia Williams a peer," wrote Benn in his diary.[2]

Not everyone was amused. Haines and Donoughue argued earnestly against the proposed honour, claiming that it would damage the party and revive press interest in the land deals. Wigg went still further and announced that so many party workers would be alienated that it would lose Labour the next election.[3] Wilson was unmoved. The only thing that was at all surprising about the proposal, he maintained, was the timing. Macmillan had created his political secretary Lord Egremont, Roy Jenkins's special assistant had renewed life as Lord Harris of Greenwich, why should he not do the same thing for his equivalent of these worthies? Fourteen other creations were announced simultaneously. Marcia Williams was duly installed as Baroness Falkender on 23 July 1974, with Wilson watching from the steps to the throne. "It is astonishing how many people are outraged at Harold's gesture – including Mik[ardo]," wrote Barbara Castle. "It is typical of Harold that he should have gone to watch his own handiwork. The cheeky chappy is also a stubborn one."[4]

Heath had criticised Wilson's handling of the land-deals affair, arguing that while members of the staff at Downing Street were under suspicion they should be suspended from their duties. Marcia Williams's ennoblement was at least in part Wilson's riposte to this attack. "Any implicit criticism of members of my staff has now been totally discredited," he told Heath in May. "The answer to the 'suspension' theory was that none of my staff was at any point under suspicion. Despite my offer, the police never bothered to visit my old offices, examine the notepaper disappearances or typewriters, or interview any staff. Suspension would have made them suspect and given scalps to the Tory press."[5] Wilson was convinced that the whole affair was only the tip of an iceberg of misinformation and half-truth which the press had amassed for the destruction of the Labour Party. He told the Cabinet in April that two of its members were being pursued and were liable to attack at any moment. This showed Wilson "in his cheapest light", thought Benn. "If he really had any information about two people in the Cabinet who were being tailed, the decent thing would be to tell them."[6]

The second part of Thomas's prediction, that Marcia Williams would be made a minister, proved less reliable; if Wilson had ever had such an intention he must have dropped it when he saw how much trouble it would stir up. He had no need of reinforcements; a powerful group of experienced and extremely able ministers was available from his last administration. Fourteen members of the new Cabinet had sat in its predecessor; almost the only serious loss was Crossman, who was in the final stages of cancer and who died shortly after being offered a life peerage by Wilson and accepting it.[1] Wilson called his Cabinet "the most experienced and talented this century"[2] and, though some hyperbole may be expected from anybody in his position, Callaghan, Jenkins, Healey, Crosland, Foot, Williams, Castle, Benn, Shore and Lever were a formidable nucleus for any team. Such an array of powerful and ambitious candidates for the leading jobs presented its own problems, but this was the sort of problem that Wilson relished, balancing one bloc against another, neutralising a minister here, bringing on another there. Cabinet-making was always a delight for Wilson; all the more, on this occasion, because he had not expected to be able to exercise his skills.

Roy Jenkins was the trickiest problem. He wanted to return to the Treasury, but Healey was firmly installed there. Healey would have been ready to move to the Foreign Office, but this was a post Callaghan had no intention of surrendering. Marcia Williams, as she still was, fought Jenkins's corner with characteristic vigour, but not even her efforts were enough to overcome the obstacles in Jenkins's path. Wilson hinted broadly that Jenkins was once more his designated successor and that the Home Office was an excellent place in which he could sit out the time until a new Prime Minister had to be appointed.[3] Jenkins was not wholly convinced and showed his disappointment by delaying his agreement for twenty-four hours and trying to exact a price for it in the shape of good jobs for those who had resigned with him in 1972. Donoughue for one considered that Jenkins was being punished for his resignation from the shadow Cabinet.[4] In a sense he was since, if he had not resigned his claim to the Exchequer would have been unassailable. Wilson, however, was acting in no vengeful spirit. He was no longer preoccupied by the fear that Jenkins might oust him from Number 10 and if circumstances had permitted would have been perfectly happy to see him once more installed as his neighbour at Number 11.

The appointment of Michael Foot as Secretary of State for Employment was more surprising, though not to Jack Jones, who had told Wilson bluntly that the unions would not accept the right-wing

Prentice and had put forward Foot as the ideal choice.[1] It was "an inspired move", thought Castle; turning a potential poacher into a gamekeeper.[2] This assumed that the poacher would change his state of mind as readily as he changed his uniform, something which not all those who knew Foot were ready to take for granted. Shirley Williams was in the Cabinet for the first time in charge of Prices and Consumer Protection, a key role from the point of view of the government's public relations even if short of effective power. Other ministers observed that Wilson seemed anxious to single out Williams for special praise and attention. A few months later Castle noted that the *Daily Mirror* had a long piece "building up Shirley as Harold's darling, the centre piece of the next Election and potentially the next P.M. What on earth is Harold up to? I haven't had a word of recognition from him about my efforts in the last few weeks."[3] Barbara Castle did, indeed, seem to be, if not out of favour, then at least no longer as close to the Prime Minister as she had been over so many years. Wilson, thought Donoughue, "seemed a little frightened of her, even bored by her increasing shrillness".[4] Joel Barnett, who had been opposition spokesman on Treasury matters since 1970, was moved into the most powerful job outside the Cabinet, as Chief Secretary to the Treasury. "You will have to make yourself very unpopular with your colleagues," Wilson told him, adding with delicate ambiguity, "I am sure you will do a grand job."[5] The Prime Minister's skills at man management were admirably displayed when he had to fob off David Owen with a parliamentary under-secretary's job instead of the rank of Minister of State which Owen felt he needed. Owen refused, but as he was leaving the room Wilson added as an apparently casual afterthought: "Of course, you'd be responsible for the Children's Bill." He knew that this was something close to Owen's heart and cunningly tossed it in as a last, as it turned out irresistible, bribe.[6]

From the beginning, Denis Healey noted, Wilson took "a much more relaxed view of his responsibilities" than in previous Cabinets. He interfered less and seemed no longer to be "plagued by the demons of jealousy and suspicion".[7] "I hold it self-evident," he told the PLP, "that this Party cannot be led by anyone except on the basis of a collective leadership which includes every strand of thought and idealism."[8] It was symptomatic of his new approach that at the first meeting of the Cabinet after the election he ruled that Christian names would in future be used instead of the formal ministerial titles which had prevailed before. "I should make it clear that it is not compulsory to smoke in Cabinet," he added obligingly.[1] He told the NEC that he was going to run his new government very differently. He had got the most experienced team in living memory and, "They are going to do the bloody work while I have an easy time." He would be, he said, using a soccer analogy which so appealed to him that he returned to it again and again, "the deep-lying centre half, not scoring all the goals".[2] But the change of heart was not complete. Within a few months Barbara Castle was complaining about Wilson's preference for settling everything in committee, "so Cabinets get shorter and shorter and the discussions on major policy items more perfunctory".[3] Michael Foot was one minister who deplored this tendency and insisted on discussing contentious issues in the Cabinet. Usually he would coordinate this with Healey in advance and together they would conduct a spoiling operation until they got their way.

One decision which Wilson had to take for himself, however much he might consult others first, was the date of the next election. This was discussed in Cabinet soon after the February election. Everyone agreed that the present position could not drag on beyond the autumn; Michael Foot and a few others believed that it would be right to seek an almost immediate dissolution so as to give the electorate another chance to elect a proper government.[4] Wilson strongly disagreed. If they were immediately thrown back into the turmoil of electioneering, the British public would be resentful and would be likely to take out their resentment on whoever they deemed responsible. The situation would be quite different if it could be demonstrated that the decision had been forced on the government by the opposition. At High Wycombe on 15 March Wilson gave warning that, if the opposition made it impossible for Labour to rule and showed that they intended to "play around with the future of the nation", then he would at once call an election.[5] A few days later it seemed possible that the government would be defeated in the House of Commons on a vote of no-confidence. "If that happens, then Harold would try for a Dissolution," wrote Benn, "and the question is, would the Palace give him one?"[6] Except in Benn's mind there was no doubt that the palace would have granted a dissolution in such circumstances. The situation could have been different if the Prime Minister had asked for a dissolution without being able to show that it had been made imposs-ible for him to govern. The Queen might then have shown her disquiet and tried to make him change his mind. If he had insisted, however, she would almost certainly have given way.[1] But Wilson had no wish to place her in such a position, and as it turned out the Tories were no more anxious to force an immediate election. The motion of no-confidence was withdrawn.

Since it was likely that his government would last for a few months at least, Wilson addressed himself to a limited overhaul of the machinery of Number 10. The civil servants, remembering the rows between Marcia Williams and Derek Mitchell and the introduction of Halls, had expected a purge to follow Wilson's return to Downing Street. Nothing of the sort occurred. Robert Armstrong, who had been principal private secretary to Heath, stayed on in the same role and the rest of the team were replaced only as their term expired. Lee Kuan Yew, arriving at Chequers for the Socialist International, was greeted by the Foreign Office secretary on the Number 10 staff, Tom Bridges, whom he had last seen working for a Tory master. "What, you still here?" he said, in real or feigned surprise. It seemed that there was to be no reversion to the bickering of 1964–70. Certainly all went smoothly between the political staff and the civil servants.[2]

Haines's role was expanded since the last administration; the distinction between the political and civil service press office was abolished and a unified team was established. Donoughue, as Senior Policy Adviser in charge of a newly established Policy Unit, took on a role comparable with that which had been played by Balogh, but both at Wilson's wish and because of the temperament of the new incumbent, the economic adviser was less concerned than in the past with theoretical speculation and more with practical responses to day-to-day problems. Frances Morrell, Benn's political adviser, lunched with Donoughue and reported that he "really saw his main role as spying on Ministers".[3] Probably Donoughue was no more keen to spy on Benn than Morrell on the Prime Minister, but antennae stretching out into Whitehall and beyond were necessary tools for him and Haines, and Wilson depended on them for information on what was going on quite as much as on his parliamentary private secretaries. Wilson was still anxious to preserve a barrier between his private and his official advisers, often to the disadvantage of the former. A list of the categories of document to which Donoughue might have access was worked out and presented to Wilson by the civil servant responsible. "You must be mad," said Wilson. "You can't show him all those papers." The Policy Unit was debarred from discussing defence or foreign affairs and Donoughue was excluded from many of the meetings with officials to which he might have contributed and where the civil servants responsible had expected him to be present. Wilson was equally determined not to allow the friction which had existed between Number 10, Transport House and the Labour backbenchers to persist in his new administration and the watchdog liaison committee which had first been set up in 1965 was now reinstated. The *Daily Mail* referred to the Prime Minister as having been "coerced" into agreeing to this. Indignantly, the General Secretary wrote to point out that the initiative had been entirely Wilson's.[1]

An institution which most people had expected to see abolished was the Central Policy Review Staff, the "Think Tank", which had been set up by Heath under the chairmanship of Lord Rothschild. Many of Wilson's colleagues believed this body to be contaminated by right-wing intellectuals and anyway redundant now Donoughue had established a reinforced Policy Unit in Number 10.[2] Wilson, however, admired Rothschild's questing and heretical intelligence and saw no harm in an independent unit which was quite as likely to challenge the received wisdom of the right as of the left. On 1 April 1974 he celebrated April Fool's Day by sending Rothschild a solemn memorandum:

In view of the current economic crisis, I would be grateful if you would give consideration to the following figures:

Population of the United Kingdom	54,000,000
People aged 65 and over	14,000,000
People aged 18 and under	18,000,000
People working for the Government	9,000,000
The Armed Forces	2,300,000
Local Government employees	9,800,000
People who won't work	888,000
People detained at Her Majesty's pleasure	11,998
Total	53,999,998
Balance left to do the work	2

You and I, therefore, must work harder, especially you, as I have felt no evidence of your considerable weight since I took office.[3]

The "current economic crisis" was quite as dire as anything Wilson had encountered between 1964 and 1970, mainly because of the

quadrupling of oil prices at the end of 1973 which had dealt a
fearsome blow not only to the economy of the United Kingdom but
to the whole industrial West. The Labour government inherited a
record trade deficit, an inflation rate of 15 per cent and rising,
declining production and slumping living standards, without even the
satisfaction of being able convincingly to blame all the nation's woes
on the previous government. When Peter Hennessy asked Shore why
Wilson's Cabinet, which was composed of seasoned veterans, seemed
to have been in a state of perpetual panic, Shore blamed it on the
increase in the cost of oil: "the whole post-war world, in a sense,
came to an end on that day. In his first year he had a trade deficit of
£3,500 to £4,000 million."[1]

Faced with problems on this scale it seemed to ministers as if they
were trying to check the lava flow from Mount Etna with a dustpan
and brush. One thing they could and did do quickly was to get the
miners back to work. Within three days a settlement had been
reached – "by simple if ominous surrender", as Donoughue described
it[2] – for an amount twice as great as the Tory government had offered,
though still £25 million short of the original claim. Healey's budget
at the end of March did little more than confirm that Britain was in
a desperate plight and that no improvement in living standards could
be hoped for during the current year. Increased pensions and food
subsidies softened the blow to the poorest but for everyone it was a
black picture, with taxation up to 83 per cent on earned and 98 per
cent on unearned income. Plans were prepared for a wealth tax but
these found little favour with the Liberals, ran into trouble in the
select committee and got nowhere. Wilson sought to make a small
personal contribution by urging the Chancellor to cut money on
official advertising. Much of it seemed to him "exceptionally tactless",
while still more had a party political motive. He doubted whether it
was cost-effective and thought that £2 or £3 million might easily be
saved by an economy drive. "I may be a rarity but I always turn over
the page when I see an advertisement."[3]

The fate of the wealth tax was only one of the frustrations which
confirmed the Cabinet in its determination to hold another election as
soon as it decently could. The budget as a whole was allowed through
but in June a motion condemning Labour's policy on industry was
carried by the opposition. By this time the summer holidays made an
immediate election impossible but Wilson in his statement made it clear
that he would be asking for a dissolution in the early autumn. The

transcript of a telephone conversation he held with the Australian Labour Prime Minister, Gough Whitlam, shows how his mind was turning. Whitlam complained that he was having difficulties with what he described as "our House of Lords". "*Our* House of Lords has been a bit contumacious recently," replied Wilson, "*and* our House of Commons – we haven't got the sort of majority we would like, yet anyway." "You'll be able to do things in your own time?" asked Whitlam. "Yes, absolutely, decide it ourselves," concluded Wilson.[1]

While waiting for that decision it was largely a question of marking time. Some things could still be done, however. The exercise of patronage need not depend on a majority in the House of Commons. The appointment of a new Archbishop of Canterbury was an issue that caused Wilson untold concern. Wilson favoured Dr Coggan, the Archbishop of York. He wrote on the subject to Sir Malcolm Knox, the philosopher and theologian:

As you say, we are both non-conformists, but the duties I have in respect of the established church are not just your or my business, but the business of everyone, and these are duties I take most seriously ...

I doubt if any ecclesiastical appointment has ever been the subject of more thorough consultations. There were many possibilities. I took the view of a very wide range of people both inside and outside the established church ... For the first time there was very full consultation with Bishops, clergy and laity within the established church. The name you mention to me was very much in the picture as were a number of others, including his brother. Both brothers were recommended by me to their present appointments.*

I was not concerned with outcries, as you called them. Since you mention Stockwood, I doubt if there would have been an outcry but I know him very well indeed, and I did not feel he was the right man.

The decision was not in any sense political ... there is a case for an appointment which will be of some short duration while the young lions fight it out. As for his age, and the relatively short expectancy of his position, it is not unfair to comment that Pope John was older but less was expected of him, and that his papacy will not be regarded by history as that of a pure caretaker.[2]

To the incumbent Cantuar, Dr Ramsey, Wilson wrote apologetically that he was sorry he had gone against the archbishop's advice: "I can

---

* Owen and Henry Chadwick, respectively Dean of Christ Church, Oxford and Regius Professor of Modern History at Cambridge.

assure you that I have only differed from you after long and careful thought."[1] But the choice of Coggan posed fresh problems. Three bishops in a row refused the offer of promotion to York to replace him. "I am puzzled and concerned by the difficulties which have arisen," Wilson told Coggan. "I fear that some at least of the story must be known to some of the Bishops and others. I think therefore that the person next approached will have to be told quite frankly that there have been these difficulties. I hope that you and the Archbishop of Canterbury will then be prepared to apply all decent pressure on that person to see a call to York as, among other things, a duty to be undertaken for the good of the church. Our next attempt must succeed."[2] It did, Stuart Blanch became Archbishop of York early in 1975.

Some of Wilson's other activities had greater relevance to the imminent election. In July he sent to all his Cabinet colleagues a list of "Little things which mean a lot", which would cost a comparatively small amount but which would mean a great deal to the average voter. The letter provides a fascinating insight into his favourite hobby-horses. The Open University, unsurprisingly, led the list. Others were: the preservation of small local breweries; the filling of empty office blocks; the abolition of hare-coursing (an old favourite. In September of the same year he wrote to J. B. Priestley refusing to set up a department specifically dealing with animal welfare but adding, "I have been an active campaigner against hare-coursing for the best part of thirty years");[3] the banning of juggernaut lorries; free television licences and telephones for the elderly; a bank holiday on May Day; fuller information for tax-payers on the way their money was being spent; and greater access to salmon and trout fishing; "our ultimate aim is to take all salmon and trout fishing rights fully into public ownership." Characteristically, he was concerned to save the pint as a measure for beer, even after Britain went metric.[4] This last preoccupation was symptomatic of a wider concern for the preservation of the Englishness of English life. However far he had convinced himself that Britain should join Europe, he remained a little Englander at heart. He minuted that he had no strong views about a proposed link road at Huyton. "Where my objection begins is to the construction in my constituency of a link road of one kilometre. I should prefer to think it is five-eighths of a mile or 1100 yards or thereabouts. *Huyton is in England.*"[5]

One of the things that concerned him most, particularly in view of the forthcoming election, was that the public perceived the Labour Party as having moved dangerously far to the left. Indeed, his private view was that the Labour Party *had* moved dangerously far to the left and that he had found no way to stop it. With Ian Mikardo installed as chairman of the PLP and Benn rampant among the industrialists, a new and strident radicalism seemed to be the order of the day. Only three weeks before the second election Lord Chalfont resigned from the Labour Party. He had not returned to government in February and his gesture did little more than formalise the end of what had never been a particularly convincing conversion to socialism, but it worried Wilson because Chalfont's doubts were to some extent his own. He was, wrote Chalfont in his explanatory letter, "concerned about the growing influence of the left wing of the Party and the virtual dominance, in more recent times, of the larger trade unions".[1] So was Wilson; and so, he feared, might be a damagingly large section of the electorate. He had no doubt that if Labour were safely returned he would soon find himself in confrontation with his left wing.

First, however, he had to get back. Early in May there had still been a strong feeling in the Cabinet in favour of a June election. Barbara Castle thought that Wilson himself had veered that way, but she, Callaghan and Foot all argued for postponement.[2] They won the day: it was concluded that 10 October was the earliest date on which an election could take place. The decision to go to the country had been forced on him, Wilson told President Ford, because "the twin problems of a high rate of inflation and the prospect of rising unemployment present us with an economic situation in which it is desirable that there should be a government with a clear majority ... Any election campaign is full of uncertainties. We do not have to defend a fixed rate [of sterling] (as we did in 1966 and 1970), and of course we shall do what we can to keep things steady, but I know that I can count on your good will, and indeed cooperation, if anything like a major run should develop."[3]

It was an uninspiring campaign. There was little to say that had not already been said at length in February. "What the people want, what every family needs, is a bit of peace and quiet so that they can plan for the future on a basis of real security for the whole family," declared Wilson in Bolton.[4] It was more than anything else the desire for peace and quiet which led the voters to give Labour an overall majority but in the meantime three weeks had to be filled with talking. Wilson behaved with his usual frenetic energy. After an enthusiastic walkabout at Milnsbridge, he dashed with police escort at 115 m.p.h. to Leeds for regional television, then back to London for a late meeting.[1] The emphasis on the team was even more marked than in the previous election, as also on the Social Contract and on the role of Labour as the only force that could bind Britain in unity and social harmony. The Common Market was deliberately played down as an issue; though it provided one moment of drama when, at a press conference with Wilson in the chair, Shirley Williams was asked whether she would resign if the referendum led to Britain's withdrawal from Europe. Wilson tried to brush the question aside with talk of Cabinet solidarity but Williams insisted on answering and said that, in such circumstances, she would not remain in politics. Next day Jenkins said that he too would resign. Shore, for the anti-Marketeers, said that if his side lost he would do nothing of the sort; having called for a referendum he would accept the verdict, whatever it might be.

However much Wilson tried to play down his individual role as leader, the press inevitably presented the election as being a battle between him and Heath. They had already met twice on the hustings; each had won once; this was likely to be the decider since it seemed most improbable that the loser would survive to lead his party at the next election. The contrast in style between the two men, and the fact that they were popularly believed to dislike each other – a belief fully borne out by the facts – lent particular piquancy to their confrontation. In their study of the election, David Butler and Dennis Kavanagh invoked the wraiths of Gladstone and Disraeli.[2] Some of the grandeur of that rivalry was lacking, but so protracted and personal a confrontation had rarely been seen in British politics.

The fact that there were few serious issues to be discussed meant that unsavoury trivia got disproportionate attention. Chapman Pincher in the Daily Express carried a story about Michael Halls's widow suing for £50,000 as compensation for her husband's death which, she claimed, had been brought about largely by the strain of working with Marcia Williams. Wilson, overreacting, referred to "cohorts of distinguished journalists", raking muck with which to daub the Labour cause.[3] Historically, the strength of a cohort ranged between 300 and 600, but even if such pedantry were set aside Wilson was hard put to identify even a platoon of journalists – distinguished or not – who were engaged in this activity. He himself got into trouble when his parliamentary private secretary, William Hamlin, attacked the former Labour minister and current Liberal candidate for Bath, Christopher Mayhew: "Does Bath want a part-time member? You might note, too, that he never sits on standing committees or anything else." The accusations were unfair, the Conservative candidate, Ernest Brown, complained to Transport House, and Hamlin was censured. Wilson was not directly involved but it was close enough to home to cause embarrassment.[1] However, the talk was mainly of scandals that never arose but, it seemed, might suddenly come to the fore. Barbara Castle heard that the *Sunday Times* was going to reveal that Short owned six houses; Wilson said that there was a rumour that his income tax returns had been photocopied; Benn was asked whether he had been lured to a flat in Bickenhall Mansions to smoke cannabis.[2] There was nothing of consequence in such trumpery, but two at least of these scraps of gossip were to recur in heightened form before too long.

The electorate duly opted for peace and quiet. Liberal support slumped and Labour's share of the popular vote rose to 39.2 per cent, against 35.8 per cent at the previous election. Translated into seats and even without allowing for the non-voting Speaker, that gave Labour 319, an overall majority of three. Since the total ranged against them included thirteen Liberals, eleven Scottish Nationalists (SNP), three Welsh Nationalists and one SDLP member from Northern Ireland – all of whom were at least as likely to vote with Labour as against it – the situation was not so precarious as the figure for the overall majority might have suggested. "I am pretty sure that the majority of three will prove to be more numerous in practice," Wilson told Lee Kuan Yew. "As you say, the Opposition are a mixed bunch, and I do not rate the chances of their combining on a single issue very highly. The main point is that we do now have a firm Parliamentary base from which to deal with the serious problems, and this was not possible in the last Parliament."[3]

XXI

Britain and Europe

1974–1975

The first "serious problem" which dominated Wilson's thinking and which had to be resolved before the government could address itself properly to any of the others, was Britain's place in Europe. The Conservatives had put Britain into the EEC; should Labour now take it out again? Formally, Wilson still had an open mind. As late as July 1974 he remarked in Cabinet that he "thought the odds were against staying in the Market" and that he was still undecided whether the issue should be put to the nation in a referendum or an election.[1] Nobody took him seriously, and with good reason. Long before the autumn general election Wilson was clear that he wished Britain to remain in the Common Market; that the only way this would be acceptable to the Labour Party would be if a clear majority of the British people had shown that such was their wish; that since both parties were split on the issue an election would achieve nothing and a referendum was essential; that he proposed to recommend British membership when the time came for a vote to be taken; and that the only way he could reconcile this attitude with the line he had taken while in opposition would be by ensuring that the terms for British membership were in some way varied so that he could plausibly maintain that the balance of advantage had changed. Patiently, and with considerable skill, he now settled down to devise a scenario that would incorporate all these points.

Agreement on an eventual referendum was an essential first step. If the principle had not been accepted by Wilson in 1973 he could never have prevented the Labour Party committing itself irrevocably to withdrawal from the Market. Labour's commitment to a referendum, wrote Vernon Bogdanor, "may have contributed to their two election victories in 1974: certainly it defused what could have

422

been a deep populist resentment against politicians who were denying to the electorate the right to decide so central an issue".[1] By the time the October election was over it was taken for granted that a referendum would follow once the process of renegotiation was complete. Indeed the decision had to all intents and purposes been taken at the Cabinet before the Queen's Speech in March when it was decided that the government should commit itself to seek changes in the policies of the EEC and then put the result to the electorate.[2]

Directly after the February election a Cabinet committee had been set up to handle the process of renegotiation, with the Prime Minister in the chair and a few anti-Marketeers added to give an air of impartiality. The real work, however, was to be done by a sub-committee under Callaghan, with Wilson lending a hand at EEC summit meetings or similar occasions. In his memoirs Wilson stresses that he was anxious to make sure that the work was not monopolised by officials from the Foreign Office since they were believed to be so totally committed to British membership that they might surrender vital national interests.[3] Officials from other ministries were indeed drafted in, but for the most part they shared, or soon adopted, the Foreign Office point of view. The decision to put Callaghan in charge was, in John Silkin's view, an enormous blunder; it meant that all negotiations were in the hands of officials "whose motto is, 'If at first you can't concede; try, try, try again' ".[4] One man's blunder is another man's master stroke; neither Wilson nor Callaghan saw anything wrong with the way the bargaining was conducted. Wilson ostentatiously avoided involvement in the minutiae. When Jean Monnet, architect of European unity, called on him in London, he said that he intended to give the Foreign Secretary a free hand; and it was true, wrote Callaghan, "in the months ahead he gave me the fullest support at all times and our relationship was never closer".[5]

The first public admission of the way Wilson's mind was moving came in April when he returned from Pompidou's funeral, where he had had a long conversation with Willy Brandt. He was now beginning to think, Wilson told the Cabinet, that he could get what he wanted for Britain without the Treaty of Rome or the Treaty of Accession being amended. "This was the first clear line I had of Harold's attitude to the Market," wrote an apprehensive Benn, "acting the pro-Marketeer again as he had when he was last Prime Minister."[6] The anti-Marketeers watched helplessly as Callaghan and Wilson gradually established the base from which they could launch their campaign for the conversion of the British to the European idea. In the House of Commons in June, Callaghan presented a progress report with such apparent balance that "it is difficult to fault him," wrote Castle. "Nonetheless, the scenario is being built up, with Harold's help, to enable us to stay in."[1] Wilson continued to profess neutrality. A fortnight after Callaghan's speech, Jack Jones told Benn that the Prime Minister had just assured him that the Common Market would never accept the proposals and that Britain would be out within six months. "You must be joking," said Benn bitterly.[2]

During this interim period Wilson saw his main function as being that of holding the line in London while Callaghan worked on the detailed renegotiation. To keep his team in outward harmony was not easy. The Marketeers were by no means reconciled to the principle of a referendum. Wilson several times assured Harold Lever that there was no need to worry, when the time came he would ensure that the result was the right one; Lever believed what he said but Jenkins and the other partisan supporters of British membership were not confident that the Prime Minister could deliver what he promised, or even that he really meant to try.[3] At Cabinet in July Jenkins reiterated his dislike of the referendum and refused to be tied down to any rigid timetable for its use.[4] Meanwhile Benn was stirring up the NEC in opposition to the negotiations. "I told him that he should not be proposing resolutions for the NEC without the agreement of the responsible Minister," Wilson cabled to Callaghan in Ottawa. "He accused me of wanting the Party to die when we were in government. I pointed out that there was no conceivable hurry about his proposal. There was little chance of completing renegotiation until after the election."[5] In spite of the Prime Minister's admonition Benn persisted with his motion. "I do not regard this as acting as a member of a team," Wilson told him crossly. He was still crosser when told that Benn had been appointed chairman of a party committee set up to monitor the progress of renegotiation. Wilson supported the idea of such a committee, he told Benn ("tolerated" would have been more accurate), but it could not include ministers. "We simply cannot have one Minister, by virtue of his membership of the NEC, acting in a monitoring, invigilating role on the work of another Minister, who is himself acting on the instructions of the Cabinet."[6] "It was a real shot over my bows," wrote Benn ruefully in his diary.[7]

After the October election the pace quickened. A crucial role was played by the German Federal Chancellor, Helmut Schmidt. At the

Labour conference in November he addressed a party still predominantly hostile to the idea of Europe and argued the case for continued British membership with wit and moderation, leavened with a nicely calculated modicum of passion. He laid the greatest stress on the economic advantages. "I see it all absolutely clearly now," wrote Benn gloomily. "The argument that will be used for contributing to the Community Budget is that it saves jobs. Next it will be, we have got to *stay* in Europe to save jobs."[1] Schmidt moved on to spend the night at Chequers, where he persuaded Wilson that Giscard d'Estaing, the French President, still needed convincing that Britain was serious in its intentions. A visit to Paris for a personal talk would pay dividends. Wilson allowed him to fix up a dinner at the Elysée for a few days later. It went well. The two leaders did not attempt to resolve the contentious points which were still being negotiated, but Wilson assured his French colleague that Britain accepted the principles of the Common Market and that he personally was well disposed towards it.

On his return to London he wrote to Schmidt to express his feelings about how things now stood. "The issue of the sovereignty of Parliament, particularly in relation to regional aids, and to industrial and fiscal policies, is one of special and emotive importance to many people in the Labour Party and outside it." On the more mundane issues considerable progress had been made. The EEC had agreed to allow the developing countries of the Commonwealth to send 1.4 million tons of sugar to Britain. Giscard had also accepted that the British liked New Zealand butter and that the eating habits of a nation could not lightly be changed. Britain would be applying for the entry of 140,000 tons of New Zealand butter up to 1982 and perhaps beyond; "this is again one of the most emotive issues in Britain." The points that were going to be of the greatest importance, "in terms of presenting the results to our supporters in Parliament and to the country", were the Common Agricultural Policy, the community budget and the sovereignty of parliament. He assured Schmidt, as he had assured Giscard, "of my own readiness to commend continuing membership of the Community to the British people, if we can agree upon acceptable revision of the terms, and of my belief that revision that would be acceptable to our community partners and to us is attainable."[2]

The German and French leaders had convinced Wilson that the process of renegotiation would be eased if he now came off the fence and said publicly something on the lines of the final sentence in his letter to Schmidt. On 7 December, in a speech to the London Labour Mayors' Association, he made it clear that the negotiations still had a long way to go, and that they would have to end successfully before he would feel able to commend continued membership to the people, but that real progress had been made and was being made. He said nothing new, but he said it in a positive way and left the impression that he was optimistic about the outcome.[1] It was a far cry from his gloomy prediction to Jack Jones of a few months before.

The EEC summit in Paris a few days later marked a further advance. When he returned to report progress it was a grim day for the anti-Marketeers. He was at his worst, recorded Barbara Castle, "wordy, defensive and repetitive ... I had to strain to catch his rambling resumées. It was a familiar technique: when Harold reduces everything to a boring, and almost bored, low key, I reach for my critical faculties." He insisted that there had been no pressure for greater surrender of sovereignty, and that economic and monetary union were "dead as mutton"; the only reason he had tolerated words in the communiqué about these being the final goal was because they so obviously meant nothing.[2] Wilson had agreed to abandon the unanimity rule and to have a directly elected parliament, said Benn. When he and Shore denounced these decisions Wilson turned on them and said indignantly: "I strongly resent the idea that I was an innocent abroad, that I went there and was just swept along. I've been negotiating since some members of this Cabinet were at school. I've been standing absolutely firm on the Manifesto, more than other people." "He was really het up," concluded Benn.[3]

Het up or not, he was still determined to avoid a situation where the anti-Marketeers revolted against what it was becoming more and more clear would be the official line and resigned en bloc from the Cabinet. A way of avoiding this had been suggested towards the end of 1974 by Foot, Benn and Shore, who pleaded that ministers should be allowed to state publicly their personal convictions on the issue, whatever the official line: "We think that in this way the Cabinet can best retain its basic unity." On Christmas Eve Wilson replied that he felt collective responsibility must be maintained until the negotiations had been completed and the majority line decided: "Then let us talk about how to put the issue to the people."[4] Foot pursued the question in a meeting with the Prime Minister early in 1975. An agreement to differ was not unprecedented, he said; his own father, Isaac Foot, had been a member of the National Government of 1932 which had accepted that ministers could follow their own line over import duties. A failure to agree to similar flexibility in 1975 would inevitably lead to one or other group of ministers resigning in dudgeon.[1] Wilson saw the advantages of the proposal. Before he could put it to the Cabinet, however, Benn wrote to his constituents to declare that this was the policy he personally would advocate. An "agreement to differ" *might* be the way out, Wilson wrote to him sternly, but "none of us is entitled to take that for granted until we have discussed the whole question and taken our decisions in Cabinet. An agreement to differ would itself have to be a collective decision, not a decision any of us could take for ourselves. In the meantime it creates an impression of disarray and adds needlessly to the difficulties of the Government as a whole if individual members of the Cabinet jump the gun as you have."[2]

Wilson put the proposal to the Cabinet on 21 January. It was unprecedented, he said (Isaac Foot or no Isaac Foot), and would only take effect from the time the referendum campaign proper started; even then it was essential that everyone should behave in a comradely way and avoid personal attacks on each other. "Once again I was struck by our astonishing harmony," mused Barbara Castle. "It really does look as though Harold's long period of humiliation has not been in vain and that the Party's unity is emerging as an exercise in genuine party democracy." Her enthusiasm did not prevent her predicting that the renegotiated terms would not match up to the requirements of the manifesto and the result would be a messy middle-of-the-road muddle. "I'm at my best in a messy, middle-of-the-road muddle," retorted Wilson. "Everybody hooted with laughter," Benn recorded in his diary. "It was a very revealing comment, but Harold is at his best in these circumstances, laughing at himself." Mellish passed Benn a note which read: "He's like a great hippopotamus who likes flopping about in the mud."[3]

So far the debate had been hypothetical; until the negotiations were complete Wilson – in theory at any rate – did not know whether or not he would wish to recommend the terms to the British people. The last round took place at the EEC summit conference in Dublin in March 1975. It was in effect stage-managed: everyone present knew the points which needed to be settled; everyone knew more or less the extent to which they were prepared to make concessions to the British point of view; everyone was certain that this would be acceptable to the British Prime Minister. The final discussions took place on Wilson's birthday, proceedings were interrupted while a vast cake was wheeled in and the ritual singing of "Happy Birthday to You" took place. One at least of Wilson's civil servants was resentful of the Prime Minister's reluctance to concentrate on the detail of the negotiations. At Dublin, he complained, Wilson was so preoccupied by the celebration of his birthday and his wish not to disturb the harmony of the occasion that he failed to make any proper analysis of a proposal by Schmidt which could have been considerably improved – an omission which cost the Treasury many millions of pounds.[1]

On 17 and 18 March the Cabinet met to decide what recommendation they should make on the terms that had been secured. With Wilson and Callaghan strongly urging acceptance the result was a foregone conclusion. Sixteen ministers were in favour; only seven were against and resolved to disassociate themselves from their colleagues and fight for rejection in the referendum. Even six months before there would have been a clear majority against membership. It is impossible to say conclusively whether the improvement in the terms obtained by Callaghan was responsible for changing people's minds or whether it merely provided a plausible justification for an evolution which had taken place for quite different reasons. Roy Jenkins for one had no doubts on the subject. Renegotiation, he wrote, "was a largely cosmetic enterprise, producing the maximum of ill-will in Europe and the minimum of result (except for a smoke screen under which both Wilson and Callaghan could make their second switch of position on Europe within five years)".[2] That is a somewhat harsh presentation of a judgment which nevertheless contains a great deal of truth. Some at least of the "gains" which Wilson chalked up to the credit of the renegotiations would have been achieved in any case, notably through the Lomé Convention, which made better provision for the poorer Commonwealth countries than could have been secured in a purely European context. But there were real gains too, notably in the discount for any country whose proportion of the EEC's total wealth was smaller than its share of the budget. This was a principle which France and Germany accepted only with reluctance and which seemed likely to be worth £100 million a year or so to the United Kingdom. On butter, too, real progress had been made, enough to help New Zealand through the transition years while it was adapting to a world in which Britain was a part of the EEC. It was not a triumph but it was a bit more than the purely cosmetic enterprise which Jenkins derided. Whether the gains were worth the trouble and irritation is another question, but there *were* gains and Wilson and Callaghan were justified in taking modest pride in them.

Now that we have announced our support for continued membership, Wilson told Schmidt, I would like

to thank you for all that you have done personally to make it possible for me and the majority of my Cabinet colleagues to reach this conclusion. You know enough about the political background here to understand the importance for me of being able to report substantial progress on the points which were covered in the manifestos on which the Labour party fought the two elections last year. We knew that we were asking a great deal of our Community partners in this. For our part, I hope that the outcome is a sufficient demonstration that we have all along wanted and intended this to be a genuine negotiation for a favourable outcome ... We shall now work for a favourable result in the referendum ... It would be rash of me to claim that the result is a foregone conclusion: but the Foreign Secretary and I will certainly be using such influence as we have to convince the voters that on the terms now available to us, continuing British membership of the Community is good for Britain, good (if I may say so) for the Community, good for the Commonwealth (almost all of which has expressed the hope that we shall stay in), and good for the world. That is certainly my view, as I believe it to be yours: and I am very much hoping that it will commend itself to the good sense of the British people.[1]

Wilson had now two concerns: that the British should vote to stay in, and that as little damage as possible should be done to the Labour Party in the process. His object was to keep the campaign in as low a key as possible and to stop the more full-bloodedly committed of his colleagues tearing each other to shreds in the course of the debate. When he first told the House of Commons that the government proposed to recommend the renegotiated terms to the nation he was met with a certain amount of derision. There were cries of "What a charade!", and when he reported that he and Callaghan had found the EEC "much more flexible than I think either of us expected", Jeremy Thorpe called out, "It was mutual."[2] But he remained resolutely emollient and maintained the same note of quiet, almost resigned approval for British membership when the matter was debated in the House on 7 April.[3] "He did not predict disaster if we left the Community nor great things if we remained in," reported the *Daily Telegraph*. "To his vast repertoire of roles, which includes that of the kindly family doctor, it looks as if he will add, during the referendum campaign, that of anaesthetist."[1]

Unfortunately feelings ran so high on both wings that Wilson's anaesthetic arts proved inadequate. "I think we managed to keep our personal relations reasonably good," Shore told Peter Hennessy.[2] It depends on one's definition of "reasonably". Wilson told his Cabinet menacingly that, in the reshuffle after the referendum, he would "judge people on the basis of whether they behaved in a spirit of comradeship".[3] There was nothing very comradely about Roy Jenkins when he said, or was quoted in the *Daily Express* as saying, that those who backed the losing side in the referendum should at once resign. Wilson wrote reproachfully to his errant colleague. If Jenkins had in fact said that, would he please now disavow it? Shore, Foot and Benn had already pledged themselves to accept the result of the referendum. "In the, one hopes, likely event that the vote will be positive, it will be my task to try and get the Party united together, the wounds healed, etc, as quickly as possible. This would not be possible on the basis of a one-sided or unrepresentative Cabinet."[4] Nor was Wilson gratified when Jenkins denounced Benn at a press conference, saying that he found it impossible to take him seriously as an economics minister. The same afternoon Jenkins accused Hugh Scanlon, the leader of the Engineers' Union, of rigging ballots – a charge which quickly provoked a writ for libel.[5] The attack on Benn, complained Wilson, "cannot be regarded as other than a breach of the guidelines". It was being interpreted in the press as meaning either that "you are putting irresistible pressure on me and limiting the options in a reshuffle, or that you are already privy to my intentions about Tony Benn, which of course is not the case." Worse still, it had upstaged Wilson's forthcoming speech and switched the argument from principles to personalities. In Wilson's most recent radio interview on the BBC with John Timpson, the interviewer had gone "straight in with it and wanted to pursue it – until I somewhat rudely interrupted him and told him to go on with the programme, which was about real issues ... What I fear is that, when Tony Benn was clearly alienating votes, including Labour votes, there is bound to be some sympathy now and the temperature has been raised in the wrong way."[6] Whether or not Jenkins accepted the force of this argument, things settled down and the all-important television debate between Benn and Jenkins was good-tempered; or at least did not degenerate into an exchange of insults.

But it was Benn who provoked Wilson's fiercest indignation and drove him – or so the Prime Minister alleged – to the verge of resignation. Viewed objectively there seems little to choose between the campaigns waged by the two wings but Benn, because he was the one who opposed the government's majority view, seemed to Wilson to be the worse offender. At one point the Prime Minister summoned Michael Foot and Barbara Castle to a late-night meeting in his office in the House of Commons and said that he could not carry on. It was undignified and sordid. He was being made to look like a crook.[1] He particularly objected to Benn's efforts to whip up the NEC into fresh demonstrations of their hostility to the Market. "Am I in a credible position if hostile NEC action is taken by Ministers?" he asked in Cabinet. After he had left the meeting the Lord Chancellor declared in awe-struck tones that the Prime Minister was "near to resignation. It could be a disaster for social democracy if he went."[2] It is improbable that he in fact seriously contemplated anything so extreme but it was a frustrating period – defending a position which he had previously attacked and confronting all those whom traditionally he had thought of as his allies. If the NEC had done as Benn wanted and engaged in all-out war against the leadership, then the pressure might really have become unbearable. As it was it concluded that neither the will nor the funds existed to launch a national campaign against the Market and that members would be as free to oppose or defend British participation as members of the Cabinet. The anti-Marketeers were incensed at this decision, which in effect meant that Transport House as such remained aloof from the debate. "No clear explanation was ever offered why or how the NEC reached this odd conclusion," wrote Jay, "which was contrary to what its members assured me they expected."[3]

Wilson paced himself carefully in the campaign. At the special Labour Party conference at Islington on 26 April he "made a down-beat speech, contrary to the exhortations of the pro-Market press". In Castle's opinion, "He was obviously unhappy before he began and even more unhappy at the lukewarm reception he received at the end." Lukewarm speeches receive lukewarm responses and Wilson's speech was deliberately contrived not to excite anybody who felt strongly about the issue. He would have been still more unhappy if the Marketeers had applauded lustily his cautious support for their cause. But it is still disagreeable to be received in depressed silence by an audience one is accustomed to enthuse. "My heart went out to him, because I am very fond of him," wrote Castle. To cheer him up she told him how successful he had been in lowering the temperature. "Harold came to life. 'I intend to play it low key throughout. The decision is purely a marginal one. I have always said so. I have never been a fanatic for Europe. I believe the judgment is a finely balanced one.' "[1]

But he proposed to raise the key of his performance as the campaign wore on. An extra weapon was given him at the Commonwealth conference in Jamaica when Michael Manley, the Jamaican Prime Minister and chairman of the conference, without overmuch prompting, made a statement to the effect that continued British membership of the Common Market would be in the best interests of the Commonwealth as a whole. This declaration both weakened one of the central planks of the anti-Marketeers' platform and immeasurably eased Wilson's conscience. The Prime Minister had never previously been able wholly to reconcile his almost atavistic respect for the Commonwealth with his new-found faith in Europe. Now the two could be happily harmonised. He returned to join the battle with renewed heart and vigour; even Jenkins, who had been less than enthusiastic about Wilson's conduct of matters in the early stages of the campaign, admitted that he was "effective" towards the end.

To Wilson's mind, a close finish in the referendum, or a result in which England voted one way, Scotland and Wales another, would have been almost as unsatisfactory as defeat. He had little doubt that the Marketeers would win, but until the results were in he was uncertain about the scale of the victory. He had no cause to worry. On 5 June 1975 67 per cent of those who voted opted for British membership, every region except the Western Isles and Orkney and Shetland showing a clear majority for staying in. "Confirming all I said over a glass (or more) together on Friday night," Wilson wrote to Callaghan, "I should like to offer you my personal congratulations on all you did to achieve this great nation-wide result. As you have pointed out, the polls were against us as recently as last December. With you, I agree that two successful Summits made a great impact. But basically it was the success of your renegotiations and the way in which you master-minded them that brought about this result."[2]

It was his own victory, too, and he knew it. Wilson had found the only way of getting Labour consent to Britain staying in Europe, judged *The Times*. "He has shown great political skill and insight." The result of the referendum was "quite frankly a triumph for Wilson", said the *Daily Telegraph*.[1] With the possible exception of Callaghan, there was no other Labour leader who had "the dexterity, the patience, the detachment, the good judgment" to achieve the same result. But it was a curiously joyless triumph. Benn put his finger on Wilson's malaise when he said that the referendum was the third general election since the beginning of 1974, that it was Wilson's third victory, but that Labour had lost.[2] Wilson knew that he had gained the acquiescence of the Labour Party in Britain's membership of Europe, but he did not flatter himself that he had won their hearts. He was not even sure that he had won his own. Jenkins too was struck by the fact that, though Wilson had performed effectively and had undoubtedly got the result that he wanted, he seemed to take no pleasure in the victory.[3] Marcia Falkender believes that it was in part a sense of unease at his own behaviour which led him to view Benn's fervent preaching of the anti-Market doctrine with such bitter irritation. Wilson was well aware that she herself was at the time a convinced opponent of British membership.* Nevertheless, she went to Chequers to help him draft his last speech on the subject. As she was about to drive away he walked over to the car window. "Thanks," he said. "I know how much it hurts."[4] He knew because it hurt him too. He was sure he had on balance done the right thing, but it hurt to take a different line from all his closest political allies; it hurt to appear as the champion of Europe at a possible cost in national sovereignty and the cohesion of the Commonwealth; it hurt to be dubbed a time-server and a trimmer.

The limits to Wilson's conversion were shown clearly at the Rome summit in December 1975. Britain refused to agree to the fixing of a firm date for community-wide elections to the European parliament and was still more conspicuously odd man out when Callaghan and Wilson would not accept that France, as host country, should alone represent the Community at a "North–South" economic conference to be held in Paris. Issues would be debated on which Britain, as a member of the Commonwealth and as an oil-producer, would have points to make which might be different from those put forward on behalf of the Community as a whole. Schmidt and Giscard argued

---

* Both she and Mary Wilson voted for British withdrawal from Europe.

that this attitude was a challenge to the credibility of the EEC; Europe *must* speak with one voice. The British insisted that it shouldn't, wouldn't and couldn't. In the end an absurd compromise was reached by which Callaghan would also represent the EEC but would only be allowed to talk for two minutes. When Wilson reported on the conference to the House of Commons he found himself attacked by his own pro-Market supporters and denounced by the Tories as the saboteur of the system he had so recently been championing.[1]

Where Wilson's heart still really lay was shown clearly in a letter – joking, but not unserious – which he wrote to Lord Beaverbrook's son, Max Aitken, in March 1976, to thank him for a visit he had organised to the Express Newspapers:

I am sorry to have to spoil this letter by a very serious criticism. On returning to Downing Street and studying more closely the copy I took off the production line – and paid for – I was shattered to see the full text of the main story which I had seen first on metal and then on paper. It was a story from Australia, clearly, since Sydney was mentioned, but the dateline referred to the *Standard* Foreign News Desk. Foreign! Having repeated, which you confirmed, my long-standing commitment as a Commonwealth man – and I have even used your house-flag phrase "Empire" on many occasions – it was a shock to me to find Australia regarded as part of the foreign world. The fact that the Conservative interlopers in the early '70s expelled Australia from the sterling area is not enough to justify this outrage.

When, rightly or wrongly, I amalgamated the Foreign and Commonwealth Office, I insisted then that the Secretary of State should be known as the Foreign and Commonwealth Secretary. Not once in the last two years have I ever called on Jim Callaghan to make a point in Cabinet, except with that full title.

And now, today's *Standard. Et tu Brute!*

Do not forget that in the afterworld you will have to render account to the great founder of Beaverbrook Newspapers. There is still time.[2]

XXII

The Last Administration

1975–1976

Only when the referendum was safely out of the way could Wilson fully concentrate on what was the most important challenge of his last government, the battle for the soul of the Labour Party, a battle which for him resolved itself above all into a personal duel with Tony Benn. It was a battle which superficially he won, but the party which he handed over to Callaghan had moved far further to the left than was apparent from his style of government.

"No Cabinet," wrote Barbara Castle despairingly in March 1975. "Cabinet government barely exists any more and is certainly going to be broadly in abeyance until the referendum is over."[1] Before the referendum period the lack of a parliamentary majority had been adduced as the reason for inactivity. When Benn complained that in the speech on the Address the previous year Wilson had retreated from the manifesto commitment on public ownership, Wilson pleaded that the position in the House of Commons made a cautious Queen's Speech inevitable.[2] Up to a point he welcomed the chance to evade the pressing but probably insoluble questions of the Labour Party's attitude to nationalisation or the need for wage restraint. A problem shelved is a problem solved was his private though not often articulated belief. Sometimes it worked. In 1974 and 1975 it did not: the economy stagnated, inflation built up, wage demands soared and the country slithered into crisis.

While the party moved towards the left, Wilson found himself, or at least seemed to his colleagues to be, edging steadily towards the right. It is always a danger signal to the party faithful when a Labour minister is fêted in the City. Luke Meinertzhagen, a senior partner in Cazenove's, wrote in March 1974: "I never thought that I could be so impressed by a Socialist P.M. He was most impressive and provided his Government are restrained I am sure he is the man to lead the country at the present time."[1] When Benn lunched in the City he found: "They thought how wonderful Wilson was, and how realistic the Government was ... The truth is, like most City gents, they want Wilson to go on."[2] The Prime Minister was beginning to emerge more strongly as an "anti-union man", complained Benn. When a discussion of miners' pay took place in Cabinet at the end of 1974, Wilson saw it all "in terms of politically motivated men".[3] Nor was it only among the miners that he found politically motivated men. Winston Churchill went to Portugal early in 1976 and was told by the socialist leader, Mario Suarez, that the BBC Portuguese Service broadcast communist propaganda. Churchill took the story to Wilson and within two weeks three officials on the service had been dismissed. (They appealed against their dismissal and, on investigation, were found to be card-carrying communists.)[4] Wilson was not prepared to join the ranks of "indignant ex-Colonels from Cheltenham", but he had a sneaking sympathy for some of their views. He wrote to Barbara Castle, now Secretary of State for Social Services, about the widespread criticism of "scroungers ... The Press can be relied upon to sensationalise lazy but fecund Irishmen coming to this country, drawing Social Security benefits for months if not years on end, while at the same time fathering numerous children. We must not underestimate the effect of even a few of these press stories. Could you tell me what is being done to investigate cases of this kind?" He had no wish to hound the under-privileged; none the less, "I get complaints about long-term unemployed, who do not appear to have any justification for long-term unemployment, getting away with it."[5] To Frank Kearton, the chairman of the newly formed British National Oil Corporation, Wilson congratulated himself on his mastery of political timing and compared himself with Stanley Baldwin. "That just about sums him up," concluded Benn bitterly.[6]

The underlying dispute between Benn and Wilson over economic policy had grumbled on through 1974. In April Benn launched a challenge when he set up a working party under Eric Heffer to prepare a Green Paper which would give the NEB power to acquire companies and impose planning agreements. The CBI protested, and Wilson made it clear that he shared their disapproval, but Benn persisted. The paper eventually proposed a vastly strengthened NEB with an income of £1,000 million a year to spend on the acquisition of British companies. Wilson's criticism now widened into a general attack on

Benn's use of the NEC to further his political ends. Ministers were not free, protested Wilson, "to disassociate themselves from certain of the Government's policies and to allow this to be known to outside bodies". His eventual aim was that no member of the Cabinet "might offer himself for election to the N.E.C.".[1] Benn dutifully circulated this minute to his junior ministers for their edification, but Wilson would not have been pleased by the covering note in which the Secretary of State adjured his colleagues to remember: "Labour leaders must think, and act, and speak politically over the whole range of political issues that touch our people, or stir our convictions ... In the end it is our loyalty to what we believe that offers the only ultimate safeguard in our conduct."[2] In his diary Benn wrote that his "relations with Harold are absolutely rock-bottom ... He really does think that my public statements about 'open government' and so on are destroying the Labour Party, whereas I think it is the only hope."[3]

It was Benn's industrial policy rather than his advocacy of open government that most nearly provoked an open rupture. His continued emphasis on nationalisation and a strengthened NEB spread panic among Britain's business managers and convinced Wilson that his turbulent minister might cost Labour the next election. In mid June the Prime Minister instructed Benn to make no further speeches on the subject, "until he has had the chance of a word with me, with no date fixed for that ... I shall take no notice of that whatsoever. You can't tell a Secretary of State not to make speeches."[4] In fact Wilson had his word only three days later. "He was red and angry and sounded bitter." He accused Benn of being lazy, indecisive and disloyal: "The truth is that he is furious that I have turned Industry, which was intended to be a non-Department, into one of the most exciting departments in Whitehall."[5] But though Wilson strongly disapproved he was not prepared to commit himself to an outright and public assault. When Edmund Dell, the Paymaster-General, wanted to attack Benn's views in a speech to the Luton Chamber of Commerce, Wilson restrained him. He was going to deal with Benn himself in a speech the following night, the Prime Minister said: "If you do anything then Heffer will come in and there will be thirty speeches." In fact Wilson dealt with the matter so circumspectly that his speech was widely taken as supporting Benn's views. "Wilson had simply ratted on me," complained an indignant Dell. He concluded that the Prime Minister was "engaged in one of his complicated political calculations". The TUC and the left had to be persuaded that the government had lost none of its radicalism in industrial matters.[1] He was not entirely wrong. Wilson was determined to deal with Benn, but in his own time; and this was not when the debate over Europe still had to be resolved.

Something had to be done, however, before Benn got such a head of steam behind his proposals that it would be extremely difficult to oppose them. When, early in July, Benn expounded his vision of a super NEB in Cabinet, Wilson expostulated that one could not have a marauding body of this kind "going round the country grabbing firms". He dismissed out of hand Benn's plan for a hit list of private companies which merited nationalisation.[2] "Harold is driving me to desperation," wrote Benn, "and I am just hanging on, and being courteous and not even complaining."[3] Rumours of dissension began to spread and on 1 August Robin Day on television asked Wilson who spoke for the Labour Party on public ownership. "I'm in charge," said Wilson. "I'm in control."[4] That his control was not complete was shown the following day when the Cabinet went further in endorsing Benn's view of the NEB than the Prime Minister, left to himself, would have thought wise. But the next day the *Daily Mail* carried the headline: "Wilson goes cold on Benn" and the rest of the press followed the same lead. "It was a very, very dishonest briefing by Number 10, and Harold knows it," complained Benn.[5] Once the idea spread around Whitehall that Wilson viewed Benn's policies with little enthusiasm then "the civil servants took their cue." They had never liked the idea of an aggrandised NEB; now they devoted themselves to watering down the concept. "I'm sure that Tony Benn felt himself betrayed by his Prime Minister," Donoughue later said.[6]

That their differences were not confined to industrial questions became embarrassingly obvious in October when the Royal Navy paid a routine visit to the South African naval base at Simonstown. The NEC passed a resolution criticising the government for allowing this to happen and Benn, Judith Hart and Joan Lestor all voted in favour of it. Wilson's fury at this challenge was fanned by a story in *The Times*[7] on how he had been snubbed and humiliated. He stormed about the "open defiance of collective responsibility" shown by certain ministers and addressed a personal minute to the three offenders demanding a guarantee that they would never offend again. A failure to provide such an assurance would be treated as tantamount to resignation.[1] Benn consulted with Mellish, who advised him to give way graciously. Wilson did not dislike him, he said comfortingly, but "he is terribly conscious of his own status, so when he over-reacts it obviously explodes all over the place. I think at one time he thought you were trying to get his job . . . You see, Harold can't bear to appear to be responding to pressure."[2] Benn and the other ministers sent temporising replies, affirming their loyalty to the party but urging that even Cabinet ministers should have the right to express deeply held opinions. Not publicly, and certainly not in the NEC, Wilson in effect responded. Collective responsibility must be respected, he told Hart; he must at once have "an unqualified assurance that you will from now on comply with its requirements and the rules that flow from it".[3]

By this time Wilson's loathing of the NEC was becoming embarrassing in its intensity. He thought the union representatives were for the most part second- or third-rate hacks, the members of Parliament drawn from those who were not good enough for office; and the ministers almost invariably among the most dissident and troublesome in the government. He played with the idea of forbidding ministers to become members, but regretfully decided that such a step would cause more trouble than it would save. When Benn came top of the NEC election in November 1974 his worst suspicions were confirmed. He turned to Barbara Castle and drawled (or so Castle said; it is difficult to imagine a Wilsonian drawl): "He is becoming quite a young hero, and I think it is a pity."[4] For the first time in years Wilson did not get a standing ovation when he addressed the party at conference: his relative failure and Benn's triumph gave the latter immense satisfaction and dazzled his private secretaries: "All of a sudden they realised that this enormous centre of power, namely the Labour Conference . . . was dominating Parliament; it was much more important than Parliament."[5] This was wishful thinking, but the fact that Benn could think it and even seem to have some grounds for doing so, was a measure of the kind of battle Wilson had on his hands. Nobody doubted that he would fight the battle to the end. At the Labour Party Christmas entertainment at Transport House one skit showed Wilson as a mafia boss, with Haines as his henchman saying of the would-be rival *capo*, Tony the Wedge: "You made that guy, boss; with your little finger you could break him."[6] It was a light-hearted joke, but it concealed an unpleasant truth.

It was another six months before the breaking came, and even then the operation was conducted with restraint, designed to hobble rather than to maim. As the referendum approached, the anti-Marketeers became more and more apprehensive of the Prime Minister's likely conduct if he won the day. He would be the prisoner of the right, said Barbara Castle. There would be a purge of all his former allies. Foot, Shore and Benn would have none of it. Foot agreed that Wilson was "naturally to the right politically" but was certain that he would stick to his usual tactic of conciliating rather than confronting his critics. "I often marvel at the complacency of my left-wing col-leagues," wrote Castle impatiently.[1] Foot was unpersuadable, insisting even after the result of the referendum was known that Wilson would do nothing to disturb the balance of his Cabinet. Benn accepted that this might be so, but was still sure that he at least would be moved from his present job. "Why does he always work with his enemies, when we are his real friends?" asked Balogh sorrowfully. We are not his friends, retorted Benn: "He's the cleverest political leader we have had for a long time, but why should we believe all that nonsense?"[2]

In the event both Foot and Benn could claim to be right, and even Castle accepted that a wholesale purge was not planned. At the first Cabinet after the referendum, she wrote, Wilson was in his "best, 'I'm going to get tough now', prime-ministerial mood. I felt it didn't bode good to any of us Dissenting Ministers, though I doubt whether he will do a clean sweep immediately. That wouldn't be his style: he prefers picking people off one by one."[3] It was neither his style nor his intention; Wilson felt no grudge against any anti-Marketeer except Benn, and against him only because he was Benn and not because he was an anti-Marketeer. The referendum was something that had had to be got out of the way before Wilson could put his political house in order. He apparently told Crosland that he was going "to use Tony Benn to display my sense of humour". "I don't entirely blame him," commented Crosland. "He's put up with hell for the past fifteen years, and now he doesn't care and is going to enjoy himself."[4] Certainly Wilson took great pleasure in the ingenuity of some of his ministerial general posts and may well have derived special relish from this one. But he moved Benn from Industry because he believed that he was proving a liability in that spot, was losing votes and disturbing business confidence. He offered him another job because he respected his talents, and did not want to appear to surrender to a clamour for Benn's blood from the City and industrial magnates. He also knew that a sizeable group in his own party would view Benn's dismissal as an act of war and for that matter would not be best pleased by his demotion.

A formidable body of opinion did indeed rally to Benn as soon as it appeared that his position might be in jeopardy. "Any move of Mr Benn away from the Secretaryship of Industry ... would be a grave affront to the Trade Union movement," threatened Jack Jones.[1] Michael Foot and the new General Secretary of the TUC, Len Murray, were equally resolute in Benn's defence. "So I feel the support of the great strength of the Labour movement," wrote Benn in his diary.[2] Wilson felt it too, but he knew that, though the Labour movement might huff and puff, there was precious little they could do about it if he stuck to his decision. If he had ever thought of dropping Benn altogether he quickly abandoned the idea, but if Benn chose to reject the new job that he had in mind for him then Wilson would not feel much distress and Foot, Jones and Murray would have to lump it. On 30 April, while in Jamaica for the Commonwealth conference, he gave Harry Boyne of the *Daily Telegraph* a hint of what he had in mind. Boyne said he supposed he should byline the story as being merely from "a *Daily Telegraph* reporter". "No," said Wilson, who knew exactly what nuance of official corroboration he wished the story to bear, "you can make it 'By Our Political Staff'."[3] The following day Benn read it in the *Telegraph*. "In effect Wilson has destroyed my credibility as a Minister with my own officials," he wrote bitterly.[4]

The blow fell in early June. Wilson told Benn that he wanted him to move to Energy – "a very important Department, dealing with North Sea Oil". According to Benn he did little more than ask how long he had got to make up his mind, and then left the room to consult his wife and his closest allies.[5] Lady Falkender has him haranguing Wilson for half an hour and then leaving the Prime Minister in such confusion that he had to ask whether or not Benn had accepted the new job.[6] Possibly this latter account runs two meetings into one. The upshot, anyway, was that Benn did take the new job and was left in a decidedly vengeful frame of mind. "Actually, the Labour Government's days are numbered," he wrote when he first realised what was happening, "and certainly the days of Wilson as Leader – his style and his politics – are numbered ... I wouldn't be surprised to find a Callaghan Government formed within a couple of months."[7] Castle told Wilson that she had urged Benn to accept his new office. "You're a good girl," the Prime Minister replied. "I could never get you to be a bad girl even in the days when you and I were younger" (a riposte which amused Castle since, she claimed, he had never even tried to make a pass at her).[1]

Though Benn personally might have been side-tracked to a role where he could do less mischief, no amount of juggling could conceal the fact that there had been a fundamental shift to the left in the PLP. Mellish, the Chief Whip, reported at the end of 1974 that feeling in the party was running high. "What is most distressing has been the large number of new Members who came in in February and October who have joined the Tribune Group. This Group is more arrogant than ever before, there is even the suggestion that it has its own whipping and certainly its Monday meetings decide the tactics for the week." His position was being undermined. "We have, as you know, always been a Party that quarrels about almost everything, but my bonhomie, I think, is not sufficient today and I really do believe that you should get a replacement."[2] Benn himself had always refused actually to become a member of the Tribune Group, though he had made no secret of his sympathies with its objectives. Now he was told "there was no middle ground, and people wouldn't understand why I wasn't in the Group."[3] If the doctrine was to be generally accepted within the party, where would it leave Wilson, who had made occupation of the middle ground his prime preoccupation since he had first become leader? Castle for one was convinced that all was still basically well within the Labour movement. When the press exulted over what they saw as a split over Healey's new pay guidelines, she commented: "The media will never understand this baffling movement of ours and they certainly do not understand the deep-rooted new concordat between the Government and the trade unions."[4] Wilson did not understand it either, or rather, he had doubts about the deepness of the roots. It was the polarisation within the party which seemed to him more real.

An issue which threatened to accelerate the movement at this time was the report of the Top Salaries Review Body. This body had recommended handsome pay increases for those within the public sector – judges, generals, heads of nationalised industries – who were already among the better rewarded in society. At a time when rigid limits on pay increases were being urged on the unions, this seemed to several ministers, Foot and Castle in particular, to be unjust and socially divisive. They would have favoured rejecting the report out of hand, or at least postponing its application until the nation could afford it better. Wilson was convinced that it had to be accepted in principle, though he was ready to envisage ways by which it might be made less distasteful to the lower-paid. He suggested to the Lord Privy Seal that acceptance of the recommendations should be accompanied by an appeal for restraint. Perhaps the appeal should be reinforced by Cabinet ministers agreeing not to draw part of their salaries. "I have made it clear ... that I have generally regarded this sort of gesture by Ministers as a pretty pointless gimmick, but in our present situation, and in the context of the sort of package I have in mind, it might have more to commend it, as a sprat to catch a mackerel." The mackerel would have consisted of a voluntary agreement by top earners to stage their increases over the year, with the intervals between increases growing longer as the level of income rose.[1]

When the issue came to Cabinet, Wilson found the middle ground hard to maintain. On the one hand Lever was for accepting the report *in toto* and without qualification; he did not make the atmosphere in Cabinet any more harmonious by remarking provocatively that he paid his cook more than was earned by some of the senior civil servants. On the other, Foot threatened resignation if any part of the report was accepted, claiming it would disastrously undermine the Social Contract. In the end, and after much acrimony, Wilson slipped through his compromise of phased increases; anything else, he argued, would penalise unfairly the small section of the community which was subject to government control.

The level of salaries paid to senior officials was only a tiny part of the problem of wage restraint. Wilson would have liked to postpone the issue until after the European question had been resolved, but it could not be ignored. The scars left by the battle over *In Place of Strife* were hardly healed, and he was resolved not to re-open them. Again and again, in the course of 1974, he asserted that he would never support any sort of statutory incomes policy.[2] When Donoughue's Policy Unit told him that a formal incomes policy would be essential before the end of the year, he replied: "Analysis fine, except any mention of incomes policy is out."[3] He continued to pin his faith in the Social Contract. But with the cost of food, energy, transport and rents rising relentlessly, and with the government's social and industrial legislation, which had been a *quid pro quo* for the unions' acquiescence in wage restraint, largely paralysed by parliamentary opposition, the unions were in no mood to make the contract work effectively. By October 1974 the retail price index had risen by 8 per cent, wages by 18 per cent.[1] To the Treasury Minister, Edmund Dell, Wilson's inertia seemed deplorable, almost criminal: "For month after month, the Government had sat back watching inflation rise; frightened, apparently, of the political cost of confronting the unions with the inflationary consequences of their actions, listening uncomplainingly to the self-exculpatory nonsense emerging from the lips of one trade union leader after another ... It is difficult to imagine greater irresponsibility."[2]

With Stage Three of the Conservative prices and incomes policy due to run out in July 1975, and the unions clearly considering that they had been generous in letting it continue for so long, it was obvious to Wilson as well as Dell that something must be done. Wilson was still strongly of the view that whatever policy was arrived at must be in essence voluntary. When interviewed by Robin Day as late as 23 May, he still dismissed stoutly any suggestion that the government was planning a counter-inflationary package to be introduced before the referendum: "If there were a package that could counter inflation," he said, "we would have introduced it already." Statutory wage control was out of the question: "There are no circumstances short of war or something of that kind which would justify this."[3]

He must have had his doubts even as he spoke. Inflation generated by the increase in the price of oil and the worldwide economic chaos which followed were making nonsense of every prophecy. By June three proposals for curbing wage-related inflation were being mooted: the purely voluntary policy to which Wilson was still formally committed, the hardline Treasury approval of statutory restraints, and a compromise evolved by the Policy Unit in Downing Street. It was, of course, the compromise which Wilson privately, and more and more publicly, favoured. It was based on the principle of a flat increase of £5 or £6 a week, so that the richest would receive the same £250 or £300 per annum as the poorest. In theory the policy would be voluntary, but it would be backed by a battery of sanctions which would make life extremely difficult for the employer who overstepped the norm. It is a measure of the panic which was beginning to grip the nation that the unions did not reject this idea out of hand but countered with a variant which would have allowed an increase of £10 a week on any income under £7,000 a year.

When the Cabinet met at Chequers on 20 June only Foot and Benn argued with real passion for a fully voluntary policy. Benn pleaded for an attempt to win the support of the shop floor. "I am accused of looking forward to the promised land," he declaimed. "The Cabinet is in the desert, looking back to Egypt!" "If Moses had turned right instead of left, he would have struck oil," put in Wilson drily.[1] The centre right won the day, and a clear majority favoured a £10 limit with a tight timetable for the imposition of a statutory policy if the voluntary approach could be shown to have failed. For Benn the decision spelt disaster. As he left Chequers he nudged John Silkin who was beside him and pointed meaningfully at the portrait of Ramsay MacDonald.[2] But at least he had been spared the worst outcome, immediate acceptance of the Treasury's demand for a statutory policy.

On this point at least Wilson was still of the same mind as Benn. A week after the Chequers meeting he wrote to the Chancellor hoping that the Treasury would not "waste effort in analysis of the two options for immediate purposes we effectively discarded: namely, on the one hand, a purely voluntary policy resting solely upon what the TUC can offer and, on the other, deciding now upon a statutory policy which in the last resort would rest upon criminal sanctions. Our objective is for the Government to develop a policy of its own; which will be voluntary, which will command the maximum acceptance by the TUC and in the country, and which will embody acceptable targets for price and wage increases in the coming year." The Treasury should be concerning itself with such matters as the best way in which wage targets could be established – by percentage, flat rate or a combination of the two; the possibility of inflation linking for pay awards; price stabilisation; a total freeze on the highest incomes; and a link between wage settlements and productivity. One point that needed consideration was the compensation to be paid firms who suffered financial loss by standing up to extravagant pay demands.[3]

The Treasury had no intention of wasting its time analysing a purely voluntary policy, but considered that time devoted to thinking about a statutory policy would be well spent whether the Prime Minister had vetoed it or not. Another sterling crisis was on the way and when the hurricane was blowing any port was going to seem welcome. On 30 June Wilson opened the Royal Agricultural Show at

Stoneleigh and made a complacent speech dismissing the need for an incomes policy. Even before he got into the aeroplane to fly back to London he had been told that the foreign exchange markets were in turmoil and a catastrophic run on sterling was developing. That evening he told Healey that he might, after all, accept a statutory policy provided it was directed only against employers who offered too much.[1] With Kuwait and Saudi Arabia threatening to withdraw their deposits from London if sterling were not rapidly stabilised, it was obvious that something must be done and done rapidly. The Treasury was ready with its preferred solution. Opinions differ widely about the exact significance of its proposals. To Edmund Dell the draft statement prepared by the Treasury seemed a modest proposal which took due account of Wilson's susceptibilities and the government's commitments to the unions, and asked for no more than the minimum necessary to reassure foreign bankers.[2] To Haines it was an extravagantly reactionary demand which would have required the government to "abandon its manifesto commitments and commit suicide".[3] Even if Haines's view of the statement was the right one, the Treasury was behaving responsibly in putting forward what it believed to be essential. Where it could be criticised, and was criticised by the Secretary of the Cabinet, John Hunt, was for its failure to put forward any alternative approach: to judge by the draft the Chancellor sent over to Downing Street during the night of 30 June a failure to accept a statutory policy would inevitably be followed by the rapid collapse of sterling and national bankruptcy.[4]

To Haines and Donoughue it seemed dangerously likely that Wilson would succumb to this pressure; at a meeting of the Cabinet Committee after he got back from Stoneleigh he was noticeably less robust than he had been, "converted by the familiar tolling of the sterling bells".[5] They argued with him fretfully in Number 10 just before a dinner party in honour of Leo Tindemans, the Belgian Prime Minister; Wilson, said Donoughue, accused them of being unrealistic. When the draft Treasury statement arrived at midnight, Haines and Donoughue intercepted it and dictated a stern rebuttal, arguing that the doctrinaire approach which the mandarins advocated would split the Cabinet, alienate the unions and prove unenforceable. According to Donoughue again, Wilson said they were being neurotic and dismissed their arguments; then, during the night, reflected on what they had said and resolved to have one more try at securing an effective voluntary policy.[1] Wilson's own recollections, unsurprisingly, are rather different; it was the Treasury which he felt to be depressed and fetishist; he had never intended to give way to its demands.[2] His version of events sounds improbably bland; the weight of evidence strongly suggests that, if he had not been bolstered by his advisers from Number 10, he would have followed the Treasury line at least so far as to bring about the almost certain resignation of Michael Foot and probably other ministers of the left as well. As it was, Denis Healey next day announced that the TUC would be given another week to impose effective limits on wage increases. If they failed to do so within that period then the government would have to undertake the job itself.

Any prospect of the TUC delivering what was asked of it would have been at once destroyed if a wage claim by militant coal miners for £100 a week had been accepted or any important concessions made to them. The miners' union was meeting in Scarborough at the end of the week and Wilson flew there to bully or cajole them into moderation. "Never, in thirty years in Parliament," he said, "had I prepared a speech with such care – dictating, writing, amending, inserting, discarding and drafting again."[3] Once again Haines's recollection differs; he maintains the speech was drafted by him and the Prime Minister added only a few declamatory flourishes and some familiar references to the miners' leaders.[4] Whoever wrote the words, however, the spirit was Wilson's and the blend of hard economic realism with an emotional appeal to patriotism proved uncommonly effective. One sentence in it disturbed Marcia Falkender: "What the Government is asking for the year ahead, what the Government has the *right* to ask, the *duty* to ask, is not a year for self, but a *Year for Britain*." Since Wilson himself proposed to quit his job in eight or nine months, she asked, would it not look odd if he demanded that others give a year for Britain?[5] Wilson took the point but was too pleased with the phrase to abandon it; after all, no one at Scarborough knew he was going to go, so the effect of his appeal would be unimpaired. It worked: the leadership voted in favour of retaining the demand for £100 a week, but only as a long-term objective; a pithead ballot approved their decision, and the miners settled for a £6 a week increase in accordance with the guidelines. As to the issue of whether statutory powers would be introduced to enforce wage restraint, Wilson resolved it – or contrived to avoid resolving it – with one of those flights of verbal trickery of which he was such a master. There were to be no statutory powers – so Foot was satisfied. But there *would* be if it was shown that they were essential – so Healey too was placated. Back-up powers were passed to allow the rapid introduction of statutory sanctions if the voluntary policy failed. It could have been said that this was a case of neither having one's cake nor eating it, but for the short term at any rate it worked.

Wilson now did for the nation what he had already done for the miners. On 20 August he appealed on television for support for the counter-inflation policy. He "looked tough and piggy-eyed," noted Benn, "and although the message sounded reasonable, it was the Ramsay MacDonald line all over again". The suspicion that Wilson was plotting a sell-out to the capitalists and the formation of a coalition government obsessed the left. When Whitelaw on television the next day made a speech on lines not unlike Wilson's Benn noted balefully "so that is the National Government being formed under our very eyes".[1] In fact Wilson disliked the idea of a national government quite as much as did Benn. He told the Tory MP Victor Goodhew that: "except in war time, coalition governments have been characterised by drift, lack of determination, in-fighting and political faction far worse than anything in any Government of any Party, if it is a Government of a single Party. In my view this would be a prescription for national disaster. The present situation demands a strong Labour Government able to carry out its programme and policies, twice approved by the British people, and to work with both sides of industry to try to solve our problems on the basis of consent."[2]

Strong government was certainly needed as winter set in and Healey presented the bill for keeping sterling afloat without a statutory wages policy. He asked for cuts of £3.75 billion, and made it clear that he would resign if he did not get at least £3 billion. The critical Cabinet meeting was on 13 November: "You could tell it was big," wrote Joel Barnett, "for it included tea, which Tony Benn would drink from one of his famous mugs." The negotiations with the individual ministers had proved far more acrimonious than the Cabinet itself. At the end Barnett found himself still £140 million short of the minimum target, with several ministers threatening resignation if they were pushed any further. Normally Wilson would have pressed for the extra money to be found by additional cuts spread over a number of budgets. Instead, to Barnett's surprise, "he came up with a totally new proposition. He suggested that the balance be found by a straight percentage cut in the size of the civil service." It was agreed that the idea was worth looking at, and in the end it was the civil service which paid the price for keeping the Cabinet afloat with no further resignations.[1]

Sterling had been saved again, but for Wilson there was a dispiriting sense of *déjà vu*. Another crisis had been surmounted, but how long would it be before the next one? The left had been successfully faced down once more, but how many times could this be done without destroying the Labour movement? "I see no reason for the existence of a Labour Government," Barbara Castle scribbled angrily in a note she passed to Lever at a Cabinet meeting. "We have adopted the Tory *mores*. The only difference is that we carry out Tory policies more efficiently than they do."[2] Ebullient though he was habitually, Wilson felt something of the same despair. He kept a brave face on it but inwardly he must have winced when the young Labour firebrand, Neil Kinnock, declared in the House of Commons that, "The radical part of the Labour Party is bruised, and the bruise extends way beyond the Tribune Group to which I belong, to fellow members of the Parliamentary Labour Party and right out into the trade union movement." The unions, he claimed, were "going through torment"; he feared "that the Government are well on the way to changing their personality".[3]

The relationship between the Prime Minister and the NEC became ever more sour. On 9 July, when the sterling crisis was raging, Mikardo launched a fierce attack on Wilson, accusing him of neglecting his party and abandoning socialism.[4] Benn did his bit to exacerbate things still further. He enraged Wilson by encouraging the Home Policy Committee to embark on a study of the honours system. It is "my responsibility to advise the Queen on matters relating to honours", Wilson wrote to him indignantly. It was incompatible with the principle of collective responsibility for Benn "to initiate studies within the NEC machinery which fall within the responsibility of other Ministers".[5] This problem subsided, but within a few weeks Benn was stirring it up again, authorising chairmen of the NEC statutory committees to meet the press and disclose such matters as what policy recommendations had been put forward to the government. "Ministers cannot speak publicly in a non-Ministerial capacity," commented Wilson. Ministers must never "advocate support or vote for policies which fall within the responsibility of other Ministers".[6] It was yet another example of the clash between the free-thinker and the establishment, the believer in ever more open government and the champion of the traditional restraints and shibboleths. It would never be resolved but it was Wilson's misfortune that it was posed with such exceptional bitterness during his term of office.

Shortly after the financial crisis of the summer had quietened down the Newham North-East constituency Labour Party turned on its right-wing MP, Reg Prentice, now Minister for Overseas Development, and tried to reject him as being unrepresentative of their opinions. Twelve Cabinet ministers – including Jenkins, Callaghan and most other right-wingers – and 160 Labour MPs rallied to his defence. Neville Sandelson made himself responsible for whipping up support and asked Wilson for his blessing. Wilson replied that he had hitherto made a point of not interfering in purely party matters but that if Prentice were deselected, then: "not as Prime Minister, but as Leader ... I shall feel it my duty to raise the whole question of actions by small and certainly not necessarily representative groups who have secured a degree of power within a constituency." Ever since the days of the Wilson Report on Party Organisation he had been anxious about the "considerable number of constituency parties, mainly in safe Labour seats, where membership was small and often unrepresentative". The problem had not diminished and now needed to be addressed urgently. The action of the Newham constituency party was unacceptable: "Perverse action seeking to dismiss an MP can get very close indeed to constitutional interference in the rights and duty of an elected Member."[1] At the NEC in November he pleaded plaintively: "I have spent thirteen years so far trying to keep the Party together and I do not like what is going on."[2] Prentice was saved – to end up as a Conservative MP – but by the beginning of 1976 Wilson was asking himself whether it was in fact possible to keep the party together.

Meanwhile the business of government had to go on. It is curious how to Benn and others of the left Wilson seemed in his final eighteen months to be uniquely powerful, while to most of his ministers he appeared to be, if not abdicating, then at least loosening his grip on power. Crossman's theory of prime-ministerial power was turning out to be correct, mused Benn early in 1976. "The Prime Minister now has at his disposal his Private Office, the Cabinet Office, the Think Tank and Bernard Donoughue's own policy unit, and in this way power is moving further towards the centre." A few weeks later, Benn felt that Wilson now reigned supreme even in the NEC. "The Tory press support him, the City of London has made him Freeman, the General Council of the TUC supports him, the NEC supports him, the Cabinet supports him, the PLP supports him. He is unchallengeably powerful and I wonder what he will do next."[1] The view as seen from Number 10 was very different. Wilson believed that the TUC and NEC disliked him, the Cabinet plotted against him, the PLP slipped away from his control, the Tory press reviled him. Far from feeling that his power had become absolute, it appeared to him that it was draining away. He did not wholly deplore the process; indeed, it was to some extent voluntary. To Jenkins it seemed that he had no policies which he particularly wished to put forward and that he was coasting contentedly towards retirement. He never interfered in Home Office affairs, though when the Home Secretary sought emergency powers under the Prevention of Terrorism Bill, he found that Wilson, "as was frequently the case at a time of crisis, was at his best and most helpful".[2] Healey too found that he was transformed from the busybody who had interfered in every minister's affairs in the 1964–70 government; now he was content to let the Chancellor make his own economic policy and only to intervene if his help was called for in Cabinet or in the NEC.[3] The frenzied urge to seize the limelight on television was just as much a thing of the past: in the first five months after the election Wilson only appeared once on the screen, and that in a *World in Action* film where he was shown coming down the steps at Number 10 accompanied by his Cabinet, thus emphasising the concept of a team.[4]

On some issues, through choice or need, he still played a dominating role. One was devolution. As long ago as 1968 the Labour government had set up a Royal Commission under Lord Crowther to enquire into the constitutional framework of the British Isles and, in particular, the possibility of devolution for Scotland and Wales. In 1973, by now under Lord Kilbrandon, the commission reported. It was united in its rejection of federalism but divided on almost every other issue. When Wilson returned to power, he handed over responsibility for the question to the Lord President, Edward Short. A plethora of consultations now took place and a report was prepared for the Cabinet, while Shirley Williams with an ad hoc subcommittee of the NEC prepared a rival prospectus for Britain's future. Wilson initially stayed aloof, though he was urged on to action from an unexpected quarter, Al-Hajji General Idi Amin Dada VC, DSO, MC, President of Uganda. "I call upon you seriously," urged Idi Amin, "to consider granting freedom and full independence to Scotland, Wales and Northern Ireland, whose people have repeatedly demanded and have demonstrated in the elections . . . their respective eagerness and wishes to become independent of London . . . Each of these countries should be permitted not only autonomous self-government but full sovereign independence with their own flags and thus limiting the Union Jack to England only." In a covering note the British High Commissioner said that he had tried to persuade the Ugandans not to send the message but had found no official ready to take the matter up with the President. He added optimistically that he felt the letter showed "a continuing desire for better relations".[1]

Thus encouraged, Wilson received enthusiastically the proposals for directly elected legislative assemblies which eventually emerged from the long consultative process. To some it seemed that the enthusiasm was ill-judged and inspired by misguided motives. Some months before he had bullied a reluctant Secretary of State for Scotland into agreeing that some sort of legislative devolution was probably inevitable. Short, in arguing the case for such a move, said that it was electorally essential. Jenkins broke in angrily to protest that it would be insanity to break up the United Kingdom for the sake of a few extra seats at a general election. Dell fully concurred: "The frivolity with which the question of devolution in the United Kingdom was treated by the Wilson government reduced hardened civil servants to despair."[2] Certainly Wilson was no less aware than Short of the seats to be won in Scotland and Wales by showing some sympathy to nationalist sentiments. He had himself always been markedly aware of Scottish susceptibilities. When it was proposed to discharge the first tanker load of North Sea oil at the BP refinery in the Thames Estuary he urged that it should instead be sent to Grangemouth in the Firth of Forth; to stick to the original plan would ensure that the SNP used it as "an occasion for protesting that this demonstrates all that they have been complaining about: the diversion of Scotland's oil to England's pockets".[3]

For him, however, it was not just a question of window-dressing and a few extra seats. He believed both that the Scots had legitimate grievances and that to go some way to meet them would be the surest way of preserving the Union. "What we are attempting to do," he told the Labour MP Eric Moonman, "is to match what we believe to be the wishes of the broad band of Scottish moderate opinion, and to follow through in a practical way our long-held ideas about increasing democracy and bringing government nearer to the people." His object was "to satisfy this feeling of national identity without undermining the essential unity of the United Kingdom which the great majority of Scots wish to see preserved".[1] But though he believed devolution to be desirable in itself and championed it loyally until it finally foundered in the referendum of 1979, it was never a cause close to his heart. To Benn he complained that Short was always "chewing my ear off" on the subject; "I find it a bit of a bore."[2] The word "bore" recurs several times in the history of his 1974-6 government, usually related to devolution. "For Parliament devolution has been a bore," he wrote shortly before the referendum. "But it has helped to weaken the forces of separatism."[3] That, more than any fostering of democracy or winning of extra seats, was Wilson's overriding motive. Give a part to preserve the whole, make a concession to avoid having to make a bigger one: it was the philosophy that he practised all his life, and though the defeat of devolution in the referendum cast some doubt on his short-term judgment, in the longer term it is too early to say that he was wrong.

Another, less important issue on which Wilson played a central role but about which he felt more passionately was ministerial memoirs. It was the publication of Crossman's diaries, first as a newspaper serial, then as a book, which provoked the debate. Wilson was in a delicate position since at two points in his history of the 1964-70 administrations he had recorded details of Cabinet meetings. In each case, however, the Cabinet Office had passed his account. They had asked for about a dozen changes in the text which he had dutifully submitted for official approval. He had accepted all except one: "this concerned his account of the 'Soames affair' on which he felt that the comments reflected an attempt to protect an official who in his view ... had acted badly"[4] (in fact only a reader with considerable inside knowledge could deduce the identity of the official from Wilson's opaque text). His view of the innocence of his own indiscretions was endorsed by John Hunt, who said that Wilson's account of the two Cabinet meetings was unexceptionable since "in neither of them is there a blow-by-blow account, and there is no naming of individual Ministers".[5]

In Crossman's diary blows came thick and fast and the names of individual ministers abounded. In conversation Wilson was accustomed to say that he did not resent Crossman's diary but was amazed by it: "He didn't get a single fact right."[1] His entourage would claim that he would have preferred no legal effort to be made to prevent publication of either book or serial.[2] Probably that is true: Wilson had no wish to see the law officers of the Crown pitted against the widow of his closest political ally, not to mention Crossman's literary executor, Michael Foot, who happened also to be an important member of the Cabinet. The Cabinet Secretary stated that he did not consult the Prime Minister before initiating proceedings; it seems hardly possible that the Attorney-General was equally reticent, but at least it is clear that Wilson did not play a major part. Long before the Lord Chief Justice had pronounced on the matter, however, Wilson had concluded that something must be done to prevent the mischief recurring in the future. He was convinced that the publication of Crossman's diaries had done a grave disservice to Cabinet government. In particular he deplored the references to the Queen: "Any unauthorised disclosures of what had passed when Ministers had had audiences of The Queen or when she had entertained them at Windsor or Balmoral would serve to destroy the present relaxed and informal nature of her contacts with her Ministers." The same was true for a minister's relationship with public servants; the publication of details of Crossman's tiffs with Baroness Sharp was deplorable, and "particularly reprehensible" was the disclosure of what passed between a minister and his private secretary. Cabinet or shadow Cabinets should be inviolate, if only because those taking part would otherwise feel inhibited from speaking freely; "It was particularly important that a Minister who resigned with a bad grace did not feel free to make unauthorised disclosures about Ministerial discussions." Even if all these embargoes were observed, Wilson still felt that a gap of ten or twelve years should be left before publication would be in order.[3]

In April 1975, soon after the last newspaper extract from the Crossman diaries appeared, Wilson set up a committee of Privy Councillors under Lord Radcliffe to consider the whole question of ministerial memoirs. He made his own opinions very clear and the final Radcliffe report differed little from them. It was published early in 1976, with a prime-ministerial endorsement to the effect that he proposed to require ministers to sign a declaration that they would be bound by its conclusions. When it came to doing something to enforce this rule, however, Wilson was less forthright. He refused to take any action in the dying days of his administration, arguing that he had no weapons with which to secure acquiescence while his successor could make acceptance of a code of rules a condition of holding office. He did not believe, however, that Callaghan would have any more luck than he would: Michael Foot, for one, he felt sure would refuse to sign. The most he felt possible was that ministers should undertake to read and be guided by the Radcliffe doctrine. This provided that they should always show the Cabinet Secretary of the day anything they planned to write about their period in office and take his advice on points affecting national security, international relations and confidential relationships. The last of those three would cease to apply after fifteen years. To try to exact any undertaking more binding than this would, Wilson felt, be futile if not positively counter-productive.

Early in 1975 the Tory Party changed leaders. Heath's defeat at the hands of Margaret Thatcher provoked a generous tribute from Wilson in the House of Commons.[1] Heath's close friend Lord Aldington wrote to say that he had been much moved by the Prime Minister's encomium: "That you should decide to pay a tribute was fine in itself – the words you used and the thoughts behind them were – and will remain – splendid ... You know more than anyone about the feelings of political men – and woman. And you understand about friendship. So I think you know how I feel." Even Heath wrote to thank Wilson for his kindness in making the statement and the generosity of its contents – sentiments which did not endure long after the first flush of gratitude had died down.[2] Knowing that he would never have to fight an election against Heath's successor, Wilson could afford to view the advent of Mrs Thatcher with benevolent if mildly quizzical interest. Barbara Castle noticed that his first reaction to the election of the Tory leader was to make an amusing speech at New Zealand House and to show himself "more relaxed than I have seen him for a long time, making impromptu jokes, wandering around talking to everybody and conducting the Maori choir in the singing with the relish of a schoolboy on holiday. Nothing like a bit of sex challenge for bringing the best out in a man."[3] He told the Cabinet a few days later that he did not propose to indulge in confrontation with Thatcher in the same way as he had with Heath.[4] He was as good as his word. In the year in which he faced Thatcher as leader of the opposition their exchanges were often brisk and sometimes acerbic but they were not permeated by the palpable flavour of dislike which had existed while Heath led the Tory Party. Thatcher was probably more concerned about the risk of a poisoned dagger being thrust in from the benches behind her than of a mortal blow delivered across the floor of the House.

He could still be fierce, however, as in his assault on Nigel Lawson, to whom he took particular exception because he thought he had fought a racist campaign in the 1970 election. Lawson objected to some disobliging comments Wilson made on this subject in mid 1975. "The local press amply confirms the unsavoury impression about the nature of your campaign ..." retorted Wilson. "Whether it was your preference for crude personal attacks or for speeches which made headlines such as 'Lawson shatters colour truce', or your eve of poll speech which was, in the view of many people, a clear threat of intimidation designed to prevent one section of the community from exercising their right to vote, there is ample and well-documented evidence to support my statement in the House. Having refreshed my memory as to your activities in Slough, I now feel that, if anything, I was over-charitable."[1] In view of this uncompromising denunciation it is to Lawson's credit that he wrote to Wilson after the Prime Minister's resignation to confess that "in the thirteen years since we first met, although I have come to know you in some ways quite well, unlike many of my colleagues I have never (despite everything) found myself able to dislike you."[2] It was hardly a rousing affirmation of devotion but in the circumstances it did pretty well.

Wilson continued to deplore the activities of the press with as much vigour as he did the electoral tactics of Nigel Lawson. At a dinner in Number 10 in March 1975 he dragged up every instance of injustice that had been meted out to him during his years in office, whether by malign misinterpretation of his motives or a wilful failure to report his most important speeches. On the way to the House of Commons after the dinner he remarked approvingly to Dell that the Sergeant-at-Arms had ruled that MPs should have priority over journalists in the queue for taxis. "He evidently wished me to have no doubt regarding his detestation of the press."[3] But he combined this distaste with a very clear realisation of the importance newspapers had in the life of the country. Early in 1975 it seemed possible that a dispute involving the two leading printing unions might lead to the closure of several papers. His private secretary wrote to an official at the Department of Trade to say that the Prime Minister was disturbed by this prospect. He did not believe that the government could stand by and allow it to happen without taking action to save some at least of those which might be affected. "He would therefore like to be assured that urgent thought is being given to contingency plans for what might be done to save, say, *The Daily Telegraph* and *The Guardian*, if their collapse and disappearance from the scene appeared to be imminent. Clearly anything that was done could not be national-isation or public take-over, and would have to avoid all the risks of creeping Government control of, or influence over, editorial matter."[1] In the event no such action was called for but the impulse, from a man who felt he had suffered as much at the hands of the press as Wilson did, was a generous one.

Benn's Industry Bill was another cause which inevitably engaged Wilson's attention. Benn's vision had been severely watered down by the time it reached the statute book, with the capital available to the NEB drastically reduced, the power to make compulsory acquisitions removed and the planning agreements which it was originally sup-posed to be able to impose on industry rendered voluntary. "This wasn't just selling the pass," wrote Mikardo bitterly. "It was pre-senting it gift-wrapped to Labour's most implacable opponents."[2] Benn himself had been shifted from the battlefield by the time the bill became law in November 1975, replaced by the safer if less imagin-ative Eric Varley. Even before the NEB was established it was com-mitted up to, if not beyond, the hilt in the rescue of British Leyland. Leyland was Britain's only major nationally controlled motor manu-facturer and the prospect of its collapse was daunting, both from the point of view of jobs and of national pride. To give it the possibility of a fresh start meant that the NEB had to devote £450 million out of its original allocation of £700 million to this one venture. Little was left for the grandiose regeneration of British industry which had been Benn's ambition.

It was in part this shortage of funds which ensured that the NEB played no part when another motor manufacturer, Chrysler, ran into trouble towards the end of 1975. Warning flags had been hoisted in January when Wilson met the chairman of the American parent company and was told that their activities worldwide were in trouble and that the British subsidiary might well have to be closed. The Prime Minister expressed dismay and a cautious readiness to help; the matter then subsided to the back of his mind until November when it was brutally disinterred with the news that Chrysler worldwide had already lost $225 million in the course of the year to date and that the British company looked like being £40 million in deficit by the end of the year. Chrysler could no longer afford to carry it on; either it must close or the British government must take it over, lock, stock and barrel or at least in great part. Wilson's original reaction was that the firm was not worth saving. It would cost the government perhaps £200 million, with no certainty that they would end up with a company that would ever break even, let alone provide a reasonable return on capital. Chrysler was not a lame duck, he said in Cabinet, it was a dead duck.[1] The American management had behaved deplorably in allowing things to go so far without keeping the government in the picture and it would be wrong now to succumb to their blackmail. But then the counter-arguments began to be heard. If Chrysler closed, Britain's import bill for cars would rise still further and 27,000 people would be on the dole, at great cost to the nation both in unemployment benefits and the morale of those affected. The Secretary of State for Scotland, Willie Ross, argued with special passion that the huge new factory at Linwood near Glasgow must be kept open: it was the symbol of the government's determination to regenerate industry in Scotland; to let it go under would convince the unions that their needs were being ignored and thus undermine the shallow foundations of the Social Contract. Harold Lever believed that something could be saved from the wreck; an important contract with Iran was outstanding and this might lead to great things in future.

The Cabinet was divided. Benn's successor, Varley, and Edmund Dell from the Treasury were strongly against what they saw as an irresponsible misuse of badly needed funds. As it gradually became more evident that Wilson was succumbing to the arguments of the would-be rescue party, so the financial purists became more dismayed. "I've rarely seen Edmund so angry," wrote Joel Barnett.[2] If it had not been for Harold Lever, with his reputation for financial wizardry, assuring the Cabinet that there was a reasonable bargain to be had for the tax-payer, the fears of the sceptics would never have been overcome. Even as it was, five meetings were necessary before the recalcitrants could be brought into line. The government accepted a commitment for a sum not exceeding £162.5 million; within three years all but £7.5 million of this had been exhausted, and only a takeover by the French firm Peugeot saved the government from fresh humiliation. Memories of the affair were revived when Granada prepared a television representation of the relevant Cabinet meeting with all the roles taken by Lobby correspondents. Wilson was played by David Watt of the *Financial Times*: "It was an unrecognisable caricature of that or any other Cabinet meeting," wrote an offended Wilson.[1]

In the eyes of Roy Mason, Healey's successor as Secretary of State for Defence, the money lavished on Chrysler would have been far better spent on mitigating the cuts in defence which the financial problems of the country forced upon him. In October 1974 Wilson wrote to President Ford to tell him that the government had now completed "a review of our defence commitments and capabilities in the light of our economic position" and were ready to talk about their conclusions.[2] The Secretary of the Cabinet and the Chief of the Defence Staff duly set out for Washington. To the Americans it must have seemed a most unattractive package: accelerated withdrawal from east of Suez, a reduction of British forces in Germany, a cutback in naval forces assigned to NATO. The President took the news calmly but wrote to Wilson to say that, while he understood the economic problem, he would "regret it very much if the example of the United Kingdom could be cited by other governments as justifying a series of unilateral cuts". He hoped Britain would retain its capacity to act outside Europe; "for obvious reasons the United States should not be the only Western power which is capable of intervening on a worldwide scale."[3] Wilson's reply was a masterpiece of evasion. For a long time, he said, Britain had been carrying a disproportionately heavy load and there would be those who would argue, "not without reason I think", that even after the latest round of cuts this would still be the case. But Britain was determined to pull its full weight in the common defence of Europe. "We judge this to be the absolute priority ... We can no longer spread our forces round the world on the scale we have hitherto done, and we shall do better the things we must do if our own public opinion can be brought to recognise this."[4] To Gough Whitlam in Canberra he made it clear that the defence of Asia was not among "the things we must do"; "... we have been forced to the conclusion that our 1968 decision to withdraw our forces from South East Asia should now be carried out." They would be gone by April 1976.[1] It is a striking commentary on Britain's reduced role in the world and the diminished expectations of its allies since the defence cuts of 1968 that this dire news caused hardly a ripple in Australia or New Zealand.

They might have protested more vociferously if they had known the scale of the expenditure in which Britain was indulging in efforts to keep the nuclear deterrent more or less credible. Shortly before the Conservatives lost office they had embarked on the development of a system – code-named Chevaline – which would enable Polaris missiles fired from British submarines to penetrate the Russian defences and hit Moscow and other cities. The programme had only just been launched and was advancing in a series of six-month stages, so cancellation at the end of 1974 would still have been reasonably inexpensive.[2] Since Labour in its manifesto had renounced any intention of moving towards a new generation of nuclear weapons, it might have been expected that the Chevaline programme would cause some agonised debate in Cabinet. In fact it was scarcely discussed. Wilson produced the standard arguments for retaining the deterrent: that the French should not be the only country in Western Europe with nuclear weapons; that influence with the United States and Russia would be forfeited by its surrender; that if Britain pulled out of the deterrent race the Germans might be emboldened to come in. But he insisted that there was no question of developing a new system; the extra costs would be of the order of £24 million a year.[3] According to Benn, he blithely remarked that there was "a little bit of modernisation going on", and then left the Cabinet to unveil a plaque to the memory of Winston Churchill.[4] Benn was almost the only minister to argue with any force against the proposal, and even he was careful to say that, in decisions of this kind, "the Prime Minister had a special knowledge not open to others".[5]

Wilson must indeed have had special knowledge. The cost of weapons systems is notoriously liable to escalate and it is most unlikely that in November 1974 he could have known the full scale of the commitment which he was accepting, but unless he was both gullible and monstrously misinformed, he must have known that a great deal more than "a little bit of modernisation" was in question. With the support of Callaghan, and presumably the connivance of Mason, he obtained the Cabinet's agreement to a development of the deterrent system, the cost of which had risen from £24 million to £595 million a year even before he left office. By the time the Chief

Secretary, Joel Barnett, even heard of the project he was in opposition and chairman of the Public Accounts Committee. By then the cost was over £1,000 million. To slip it through was a piece of Wilsonian sleight of hand. The only justification could be that he believed it to be of paramount importance for the nation's security and did not trust to the good sense of the Cabinet to accept it if the real cost were known. In this latter assessment he was probably correct. The man who, as a former Secretary of State for Defence and current Chancellor, was best placed to prevent it was Denis Healey; in his memoirs he admits that he regards it as "one of my mistakes ... not to get Chevaline cancelled".[1]

More than anything else, it was Wilson's conviction that Britain's possession of nuclear weapons gave it a special status in Washington which induced him to authorise this massive additional expenditure. The resignation of Nixon after Watergate shocked and distressed Wilson. "There is a widespread understanding and appreciation in Britain of the courage which this decision required of you," he wrote to the ex-President in August 1974. "I would like you to know how greatly I have valued your contribution to the cause of world peace, to the Western alliance and to the relationship between our two countries."[2] It was a generous letter, more generous than might have been expected from the occasion on which Wilson avoided a potentially embarrassing meeting with the by-then-beleaguered President by hiding among the rose bushes in the garden of the British Embassy in Paris.[3] But he was quickly convinced that Ford thought as highly of him as Kennedy, Johnson or Nixon had also done. Relations with the United States were as good as they had ever been, he told the Cabinet after a visit to Washington in February 1975, adding in familiar vein, "the ceremonies of welcome went far beyond anything I have had before."[4] A fortnight later he was equally ecstatic over the welcome he received in Moscow: "They laid themselves out in an unparalleled way by all the standard tests."[5] He still saw himself as the only man who could communicate on equal terms and to equally good effect with Russia and the United States. He had been put out when the Foreign Office had deprecated his proposed use of the words "peaceful coexistence", claiming that the words enjoyed a special significance in Moscow and that if Wilson used them there it would seem that he was accepting the Russian interpretation. Wilson retorted that, if *he* used the words, his interpretation of them would be the one that counted, and stuck to his position. The visit went well; whether it was in fact "truly historic and ... a major factor in the history of Anglo-Soviet relations", as the Russian Prime Minister, Kosygin, asserted,[1] is more questionable, but it did a lot to refurbish a relationship which had grown a little ragged during the previous administration.

With Rhodesia more or less quiescent, the issues in foreign affairs which most concerned Wilson at the period were in the eastern Mediterranean. Cyprus was particularly troublesome. In July 1974 Archbishop Makarios, the President, was deposed in a coup d'état organised by fanatical Greek officers in the Cypriot National Guard. The archbishop was at first said to be dead but was extricated by a British helicopter from the monastery in which he had taken refuge and thus found his way to London. The Turks were not prepared to tolerate a situation likely to lead to union between Greece and Cyprus, or at least to make life uncomfortable for the Turkish majority in the island. The Turkish Prime Minister flew to London and asked for British cooperation in a Turkish invasion designed to protect his people. This was firmly refused, but within a few days a Turkish invasion was nevertheless taking place. Some officials had thought it obvious that this would be the next development and blamed Wilson for taking no steps to prevent it. Kissinger was known to be reluctant to put the US fleet between Cyprus and the Turkish menace, but if Wilson had appealed to Nixon there might have been a change of heart.[2] With his resignation now only a few weeks away it seems unlikely that the President would have responded enthusiastically to any such appeal, but Wilson should perhaps have tried. As it was the Turks were soon firmly installed at their end of the island and a brief and bloody conflict ended with a ceasefire on 22 July. It was a great pity that British attempts to avert the invasion had come to nothing, Wilson told Ford, "but it looks as though the Turks were determined on taking the law into their own hands, and now we are stuck with that situation. We don't see that there is anything that can be done in a military sense, either by ourselves or through the United Nations or anything else. It's got to be a long diplomatic haul now."[3]

One fragment of silver lining that emerged around this cloud was that the débâcle in Cyprus led to the fall of the military regime in Greece. Konstantinos Karamanlis became Prime Minister and held a plebiscite on the future of the monarchy. Wilson, who had been brainwashed by Mountbatten on the subject, believed that the return to his country of the exiled King Constantine would be in the interests of democracy and stability. When Constantine was rejected he wrote to him sympathetically: "Your deep devotion to your country, and your desire to serve it, have always impressed me strongly: and I think I can understand some of your feelings at the present time. May I say how much I admired your dignity and restraint during the campaign ... If you continue to make your home here, you will be very welcome among us."[1]

Further to the east, his well-known friendship for Israel caused concern among the Arabs when he returned to power. The Egyptian President, Sadat, wrote to explain that he and his fellow rulers "regard with some unease and apprehension the possibility of British policy deviating from the constructive line the United Kingdom has taken in the past few years, a line based on a positive and unbiased attitude as to what is right". He would wait and see, he said, but even if he did not expect the worst he was well aware of the risks.[2] His fears were exaggerated. Wilson's main preoccupation during this final period was to act as a middleman between the Israelis and President Ford, who was increasingly exasperated by their intransigence and the aggressive border raids which they launched into Lebanese territory. In the spring of 1975 Ford asked Wilson to intercede, dropping dark hints that if there was no improvement in Israeli behaviour the whole of American foreign policy towards the Middle East would have to be reassessed.[3] In July, during the Conference on Security and Cooperation in Europe which was held at Helsinki, Ford pressed the matter still further, telling Wilson that an "agonising reappraisal" of American policy was now under way. The Israelis had made sure that Eppi Evron, a former minister in the Israeli Embassy in London and a close friend of Wilson's, was "on holiday" in Helsinki during the time of the conference. He kept close to Wilson and Ford's threatening message was duly passed on through him.[4] How seriously the Israelis took it is another matter; they had been menaced in this way before without incurring any very calamitous penalties. Wilson, however, was concerned lest he might seem to associate himself too closely with the American threats. He assured a group of Israeli Young Socialists that Labour was no less friendly towards Israel in government than it had been in opposition: "his own friendship towards Israel was well known." He told them that one of the strongest arguments he saw against any attempt to reach a unified EEC foreign policy on the Middle East was that several members of the

Community did not share Britain's feelings on the Arab–Israeli situation.[1]

His predilection for constitutional monarchy as a form of government was shown in Spanish affairs as well as Greek. Juan Carlos had been another of Mountbatten's protégés before he succeeded to the throne and there had been several attempts to bring him and Wilson together. Though he had avoided any direct commitment, Wilson had been impressed by the young man's potential and was sympathetic to his problems after Franco's death. "I recognise, even if it cannot be put bluntly in public," he told Ford, "that King Juan Carlos has a very hard row to hoe. So we shall encourage him privately to move as fast as possible, but try to avoid public condemnation when we can, if the pace is slower than public expectation here may demand."[2]

He continued to believe that a middle ground was to be found in every potential confrontation. When the possibility that important oil deposits off the Falkland Islands might need to be exploited became suddenly more real, he insisted that a joint exploration of the area with the Argentinians was the proper way to proceed. "He was certainly not suggesting that we should aim now to hand over sovereignty to them," his private secretary told the Foreign Office. "If, on the other hand, we were to sit tight there was a real possibility of an officially backed invasion of the Islands which would be very popular within Argentina itself ... Any offer would show a willingness to talk and a recognition of long-term Argentinian rights within the area. Mr Callaghan said that we had to face the fact that the Argentines would keep coming back to the question of sovereignty. The Prime Minister accepted that this was a risk, but thought that we could play it slow, particularly if we were prepared to discuss not only joint exploration but to agree on the ultimate share in revenue, thereby giving the Argentine Government some of the *facts* of sovereignty without giving up the *legalities*." Callaghan acquiesced in the approach but gloomily predicted that news of it would be bound to leak out and would undoubtedly cause a row in the House of Commons. On the whole Wilson thought that this was more to be deplored than a confrontation with the Argentinians, even if the latter eventually led to war in the Falklands. Once again the initiative was curbed before it had properly begun.[3]

The fact that he was ready to do a deal over the Falklands did not imply any weakening in his instinctive loyalty towards the Commonwealth, which had survived Britain's entry into Europe and the referendum. In November 1975 the French proposed that a meeting of the economic Big Five at Rambouillet should be enlarged to include Italy. Wilson at once argued that, in that case, Canada too should be included. As "a distinctive combination of industrialised country and producer of raw materials", it would make a useful contribution. There was no need to fear that this would open the doors to all and sundry since nobody else had such a conclusive claim. "It would be a pity," he wrote somewhat menacingly to Giscard, "if differences over Canada were to mean that our discussions got off to a bad start or were to prejudice our chances of achieving a successful outcome."[1]

He was equally anxious to show himself a good Commonwealth man at the conference in Jamaica in May 1975. He caused some initial disturbance in the FCO by insisting that he represented Great Britain and not the United Kingdom, a whim explained by his fear lest Idi Amin should appear for Uganda and his determination not to find himself seated next to this grotesque monster.[2] That out of the way, however, he settled down to make sure that the discussion was constructive and fruitful, concerned with matters of vital interest to the participants such as world commodity agreements rather than the more enlivening but less significant political issues that were apt to monopolise such discussions. Manley, the Jamaican Prime Minister and thus in the chair for the conference, was especially appreciative of his efforts. The conference achieved "a real break through," he told Wilson. "Many others played a great part in arriving at the 'Concord of Kingston' but I believe it to be true to say that you and I were pivotal. There is a nice turn to the wheel of history in this, since you were so intimately associated with the great forerunner in the business of political management of international economies: the Commonwealth Sugar Agreement ... It would be a fine thing if a quarter of a century later, history should permit me to join you in the laying of wider foundations for the larger building which we now describe as The New International Economic Order."[3]

No New Order seemed a probability in Ireland. The Labour government's policy was initially to follow the line which had already been set by the Tories, and indeed by Wilson's earlier administrations: to encourage power sharing between Catholic and Protestant and to support the government of Brian Faulkner which was pursuing that end. The Taioseach, Liam Cosgrave, in March 1974 urged Wilson to call an immediate conference to give effect to the settlement which had been reached at the meeting at Sunningdale in December of the previous year. Wilson was cautious: he accepted that the settlement should be ratified as soon as possible but, "I am sure you will agree that the timing of a formal conference has to be carefully considered ... and I know that Brian Faulkner has reservations about holding a conference in the very near future. If we press ahead too soon we shall risk losing much of what has so far been achieved."[1] By not pressing ahead they lost it just as surely. In May a general strike, exacerbated by an angry and intemperate attack by the Prime Minister on loyalist "thugs and bullies" who sponged on the British tax-payer,[2] brought down Faulkner's government and effectively destroyed the power-sharing experiment. Some people believe that Wilson could have defied the strikers and fought harder to keep Faulkner in office; his capitulation was "suspiciously and unnecessarily quick", thought Donoughue, and dictated largely by his wish to avoid a major explosion in Northern Ireland with a general election imminent.[3] There is some truth in that, but divisions within the Cabinet probably preoccupied him at least as much. "Harold, being basically pro-Catholic as I am, will not want to have much truck with the Protestants," wrote Benn. "On the other hand he is a realist and he won't want ... to reach any decision at all until he is sure that he has the support of all the Cabinet," including the pro-Protestants, whom Benn considered to be Peart, Ross, Shore, Callaghan and Rees.[4]

Something had to be done, however. Lord Caradon volunteered to go to Northern Ireland as resident minister with full powers: "My qualifications are that I have already been a Minister, that I have experience of working with troops (in Cyprus and Palestine) and that no one, as far as I know, in Ireland has anything against me!" Wilson replied politely that he thought it better, for the moment, to keep power in the hands of the Secretary of State, Merlyn Rees.[5] He devised his own plan, which involved British withdrawal over a period of five years and the bestowal of dominion status on Ulster, but, according to Donoughue, was so alarmed by the implications of what he called his "Doomsday Scenario" that he discussed it only with a few senior officials.[6]

In the autumn of 1974 violence switched to the mainland. Bombs in Guildford public houses killed five off-duty soldiers while the second election campaign was in progress, but it was in November, when twenty-four civilians were killed and more than 200 injured in

17. Harold and Mary Wilson dressed for a gala occasion.

18a. With a crewcut Tony Benn at Number 10.

18b. In Hamburg with the German Foreign Minister, Hans-Dietrich Genscher, the Federal Chancellor, Helmut Schmidt, and the Foreign Secretary, James Callaghan.

19a. With the Queen at Balmoral – a photograph which Wilson carried with him in his wallet until it almost disintegrated.

19b. (*Right*) With Henry Kissinger outside Number 10 in March 1975.

20. Wilson's birthday celebrations during the EEC summit in Dublin in March 1975, the meeting at which the last details of Britain's "renegotiation" were worked out.

21a. With Neil and Glenys Kinnock at a meeting of the Labour Friends of Israel.

21b. With Margaret Thatcher. Judith Hart is on the left.

22a. With Hastings Banda, who was later incredulous that Wilson should propose to resign when he had "at least another twenty years to go".

22b. On the balcony of the flat in Ashley Gardens when the Pope visited London in Spring 1982.

23. (*Opposite page*) Wilson standing beside the statue of Benjamin Disraeli at Hughenden, a photograph taken during the filming of *A Prime Minister on Prime Ministers*.

24. Wilson dressed as a Knight of the Garter. The Duke of Grafton is at his side.

similar incidents in Birmingham, that the Home Secretary accepted drastic measures were essential. In Cabinet he asked for powers to deport certain Irish residents from the mainland back to the Republic of Ireland. The Attorney-General intervened to say that the principle of banishment had not been accepted since the Middle Ages. "Well, we *are* in the Middle Ages," retorted Wilson bitterly.[1] He was gripped by the familiar mixture of rage, pity and impotence which in the end afflicts every British politician who is concerned with the affairs of Ireland. Almost immediately, a *de facto* truce over Christmas and the New Year temporarily relieved the tension. A group of Irish Church leaders called on Wilson on New Year's Eve – an interminable meeting "with Harold being more generous on time than he ever has to the Cabinet", noted Rees.[2] Whether or not his patience affected the matter, the truce was extended by a fortnight.

Feverish behind-the-scenes negotiations now took place. Wilson agreed to Albert Murray – a former junior minister who was now employed in Number 10 – meeting the Irish politician John O'Connell, so as to try to establish exactly what the IRA wanted in exchange for a permanent ceasefire. As a result of this or, more probably, of formal discussions with the Northern Ireland Office, the truce lasted until the summer, gradually being eroded by murders committed by freelance fanatics on both sides. At the end of the year extra troops and police were drafted into the border areas. The Taioseach wrote to say that he welcomed the move but added: "I also note that you propose soon to dispatch part of the Special Air Services (SAS) to South Armagh. It would, I think, be useful if we could be given at official level some more detailed indications of what you consider the role of this unit will be and particularly under what regulations it will operate."[3] Wilson's reply is not available; probably he evaded the question altogether. The Birmingham bombings and the total defeat of any constructive planning for the future of Ireland had filled him with embittered despair, which the collapse of the latest truce had only deepened. It was one more element in the complex brew which disenchanted him with public life as he began his last three months as Prime Minister.

XXIII

Resignation

1976

It was not only in the last three months that his disenchantment became apparent. One of the points most generally made by those who saw him after his election victories of 1964 and 1966 and then again in 1974 was that in the last period he no longer seemed to be getting fun out of his work. He had achieved his first objective in defeating Heath and recapturing Number 10; he would achieve the second by remaining there for two years and breaking Asquith's record; between those two high points it was merely a question of soldiering on. Even the old delight in intrigue seemed to have faded; he still enjoyed contriving his ingenious reshuffles, but the anger and grief of those who lost their jobs upset him even more than it had done in the past. When he told Barbara Castle that the stress involved gave him stomach pains, he was speaking no more than the truth; he would be physically ill before and after a painful confrontation and for the first time in his life began to sleep badly other than on the very occasional night. Question time in the House of Commons began to prey on his nerves in a way that it had never done in the past. Partly this was because of the practice that had grown up of asking a question of the most innocuous nature – "What plans has the Prime Minister for visiting Sunderland?" – which would be followed by a supplementary on whatever esoteric subject the member fancied. But though this was taxing it would not have worried him in the past. While Heath had been his principal adversary, the adrenaline would still flow more richly on such occasions; with the advent of Mrs Thatcher even that stimulus had gone.

The work was starting to get on top of him. It was not the sudden crises, those he tolerated, even relished; it was the ceaseless grind of routine matters, the pressure of working at a desk where every buck

468

was bound eventually to stop. He listed the official engagements for a single quarter in 1975 – eleven Cabinets, twenty-four Cabinet committees, forty-three other meetings, twenty-eight meetings with industrialists, twenty ministerial speeches, two visits abroad, one visit to Northern Ireland, thirteen other visits at home – and noted ruefully that he had not managed to record a single private or social engagement.[1] At Chequers he hardly found a chance for golf or more than the briefest swim in the pool: partly it was a question of time, it took him longer to do things and there seemed more to do; partly it was because the old zest had gone. He even had to turn down an invitation to the Colchester Oyster Feast, having recently been poisoned on a visit to Paris. "I'm not sure now whether I can risk an oyster again," he minuted sadly, "(certainly not the 4 doz T. Driberg ate when I was there)."[2]

The atmosphere in Number 10 can have done little to cheer him. Marcia Falkender had a sandwich lunch with Benn in October 1975 and complained how awful it was in Downing Street. In the old days she had worked with Gerald Kaufman, now it was Haines and Donoughue, who were feeding Wilson's insecurities. "I have good personal relations with Harold but I'm shut out completely," she complained. Wilson was sometimes on the point of giving up and she was sure that one day he'd resign. "Well, that's a load of rubbish," said Benn, who continued to believe that the Prime Minister would never resign until the moment that he actually did so.[3] When Haines in 1977 published his memoirs of his time at Downing Street, which contained the most bitter and sustained attack on Marcia Falkender,[4] Benn commented sadly on the account of the goings-on at Number 10: "The whole thing is unspeakable and throws a terrible light on the whole Wilson regime; so corrupt and unattractive, really awful. Such a thing could never have happened with Attlee, or Gaitskell, or Jim for that matter."[5]

In Lord Goodman's opinion Marcia Falkender was far from being shut out from the Prime Minister; on the contrary, though she spent less time in the office, her influence in the last six months waxed steadily. She expressed her opinions as forcibly as ever. Early in 1975 it seemed to her that Wilson was being insufficiently attentive to Sigmund Sternberg, failing to put him on the Commercial Development Group or even to consult him about other members. "This is about the fourth or fifth note I have written to you about Sigmund and perhaps one day I actually will get you to consider that he has a point," she wrote indignantly. A month passed, and she had had no satisfaction. "Since you will be unlikely to keep your word, i.e. the note to me that he would get what he wanted in due course – don't you think it would be better just to cast a few bones of recognition for his work in his direction?"[1] She took even less trouble than before to cloak her feelings; at a dinner party she turned on the Queen's private secretary and berated him for having neglected her: "How dare you not take the trouble to get in touch with me, who controls *him*?" she exclaimed, jerking her head towards the Prime Minister.[2]* She took it for granted that her personal problems would have priority over anything else. Lord Goodman was at one point so dismayed by the unnecessary strain that she imposed on the Prime Minister that he told Wilson he could fix her up with a lucrative job elsewhere if that was what he would like. For a moment Wilson's eyes glinted. "Do you really think you could?" he asked, but then after a pause for reflection, "No, it could be worse."[3] It could have been worse. Underneath the ranting and abuse lay affection and total loyalty; Wilson never ceased to value her judgment or to trust her completely. But the impression she made on others was deplorable; his standing in Whitehall was reduced by her behaviour.

Not surprisingly he had increasing recourse to alcohol, though never beyond a mild mistiness in the late evening. Brandy was the only thing that kept him going, he once told Barbara Castle. "Fortunately I have a most intelligent doctor who prescribes it for me. It does something to my metabolism."[4] Joseph Stone, the doctor in question, was wise as well as intelligent; he knew the stresses that politicians were subject to and the palliatives they needed to make them tolerable. But he could never have approved, even if he condoned, the quantities involved. Wilson had got into the habit of fortifying himself with a glass of brandy before any difficult meeting – and difficult meetings were the rule rather than exception at Number 10. His room in the House of Commons contained a large cupboard and when he was being briefed for Prime Minister's question time he would take out a bottle of brandy and drink two or three glasses.[5] Civil servants noted with mild disapproval his habit of sending for a glass of brandy or whisky during ministerial meetings and sipping it alone. In interminable late-night meetings with Lord Goodman he would continuously sip brandy and water.[6] On no one day was the input dangerous, but

---

* It is only fair to say that Lady Falkender's recollection of this incident is decidedly different.

over the years the accumulated damage to his health must have been considerable.

He was a more solitary figure than in the past. Of the two senior politicians who had been closest to him, Crossman and Castle, Crossman was dead and Barbara Castle never recovered the intimacy which she had enjoyed before *In Place of Strife*. When a fierce battle broke out with the British Medical Association (BMA) over Castle's plan to abolish pay-beds in National Health hospitals, Wilson called in Arnold Goodman to act as mediator. He appeared to be gratified rather than distressed when the doctors agreed to deal with Goodman but not the minister, and ruled that negotiations must go ahead. "But who will tell Barbara?" he asked. "I'm not paid danger money," replied Goodman firmly.[1] He still felt close to Castle and would talk to her with a freedom he could not have imagined with Callaghan or Jenkins, but there was always a frisson of distrust. With Kaufman fully occupied with his own career, Marcia Falkender, Haines and Donoughue were the Prime Minister's lines to the world outside Whitehall. It was not exactly claustrophobic, but he needed desperately a politician of comparable stature to himself with whom he could habitually unbend.

Jenkins could have been the man now that Wilson no longer felt his tenure of Number 10 threatened by the Home Secretary. They never established a rapport, however, even as close as that which they had enjoyed in 1968 and 1969. The Prentice affair showed their relationship at its worst. In the reshuffle of June 1975 Wilson, allegedly irritated because during the referendum campaign Prentice had appeared on the same platform as Heath, proposed to move him from Education to Overseas Development and drop him from the Cabinet. Roy Jenkins took this as a personal challenge, since Prentice had become one of his staunchest allies in the Cabinet, and decided that he must resign if Prentice were demoted. He tried to persuade Harold Lever to take the same line, but Lever maintained that no point of principle was involved and that Prentice should never have been in the Cabinet in the first place.[2] Undiscomfited, Jenkins confronted Wilson and an ugly scene followed. Wilson, according to Jenkins, "sat with his head down and poured out a stream of petty venom"; Jenkins, for his part, "retorted with some pretty unforgivable things about the general triviality of his mind and his incapacity to rise to the level of events". In the end the squall passed; Prentice stayed in the Cabinet and Jenkins assured the Prime Minister that it had never been his intention to threaten him. It was not an edifying episode, however: "The heart of the matter was that relations between Wilson and myself had gone over the watershed between constructive tension and debilitating irritation."[1]

The unpleasant aftertaste left by the press's handling of the land deals hung over Number 10 for the whole of Wilson's final administration. Problems arose over the *News of the World* story about Marcia Williams's ennoblement. Haines complained that he had been instructed to issue a categoric denial and had been made to look either a fool or a liar when she was sent to the House of Lords a little later. Wilson countered that the story, which suggested that she was being made a peeress so as to make possible her employment in the government, had been shown to be untrue. The account of what followed as reported in *The Times*, in Wilson's eyes at any rate, suggested "that I had directed the Press Office in the past two years and earlier to put out information which, whether they knew it or not, was the reverse or a prevarication of the truth".[2] The staff of the Press Office decided that this reflected on their professional behaviour and collectively sued for libel. An article in the *Observer* then appeared to imply that this action had been inspired and masterminded by Wilson himself.[3] "The article generally is offensive ..." Wilson wrote indignantly to Goodman. "You know that I did not 'master-mind' the operations. It is not possible for me to direct or incite my staff to issue a libel writ. I would not try to do so, nor would they accept such a direction. The staff of my Press Office came to their own decision without any prompting from me, though they subsequently had my full support."[4]

There were other minor unpleasantnesses that added to the miasma of apprehensive gloom that hung over Downing Street. Lord Brayley, a junior minister whom Wilson had ennobled and appointed to the Ministry of Defence and who was popularly believed to be close to him, resigned in a hurry when he became involved in a financial scandal. John Stonehouse, who had been a senior minister in Wilson's previous government, had been accused of working for the communists, and had not been taken back into office in 1974, caused a still greater furore when he faked his death by drowning while in Miami. One of Wilson's private secretaries, Tom Bridges, took the news into a meeting when Wilson was closeted with his entourage. The Prime Minister puffed on his pipe: "Wonder what his majority is," he remarked. Bridges, who had had a private bet with himself that this would be the immediate response, was able to give the answer off the cuff.[1] Stonehouse eventually re-emerged in Australia and was tried and convicted on eighteen charges of theft and false pretences. It did not redound to the credit of the government in which he had served.

It would be wrong to suggest that life in Downing Street was beset by continual rows, plots and scandals, or that Wilson was deeply depressed or demoralised. He was by nature equable and cheerful, and for most of the time equable and cheerful he remained. He continued to enjoy using Number 10 and Chequers as places where he could entertain friends or attract those whom he found interesting or glamorous. There was still an agreeably eclectic flavour about the guest list for official lunches or dinners: among those invited to meet the Prime Minister of Luxembourg were Henry Moore, Don Revie, Alan Howard and Margaret Drabble.[2] At Chequers one would be more likely to find his allies and financial supporters. One luncheon included Samuel Fisher, Wilfred Brown, Jarvis Astaire, Sigmund Sternberg, Rudy Sternberg, Donald Gosling and similar figures from the business world. It was a satisfaction to Wilson that he could thus repay kindnesses done him in the past. He employed the Honours List to reward personal friends but rarely as a weapon with which to win votes or secure loyalty. When the turbulent Labour member Willie Hamilton, early in 1976, accused him of using this form of patronage to buy back-bench allegiance, he retorted that since March 1974 there had been "no party or political honours as such". The only MPs to have been honoured were Jack Ashley, the junior minister who had conquered total deafness to succeed in his career; Tom Williams, for his work for the Inter-Parliamentary Union; and Peter Kirk for his activities in the Western European Union. Nor were backbenchers' wives or constituency chairmen honoured; any honour to a local politician was given "on the impartial advice of the Department of the Environment in respect of local government services". Wilson could not decide, he said, whether Hamilton was moved more by "animus against the Prime Minister or animus against the Crown".[3] In the House of Commons he told a Tory backbencher that he had altogether conferred only six knighthoods on MPs, compared with fifty-seven in the corresponding period under the previous government.[4]

The knighthood which stirred up the most trouble for Wilson while he was Prime Minister was not granted to one of his supporters from the world of business but conferred on P. G. Wodehouse in the New Year's Honours of 1975. He had carefully considered all the relevant factors, Wilson assured one indignant protester, "but I came to the conclusion that the arguments for the award outweighed those against it, and in particular that the time had come when Wodehouse should be considered to have purged his wartime errors of judgment. They are now over thirty years in the past, and I took the view that they should no longer be held to debar him from receiving official recognition for his work as a writer."[1] Charlie Chaplin was knighted in the same list, and there were complaints that he and Wodehouse had deserted their country and chosen to live outside England. "Though both Chaplin and Wodehouse have done most of their work abroad," replied Wilson, "both have retained their British citizenship and a sense of belonging to Britain, and are generally regarded as being essentially British in their work."[2] Mountbatten was insistent that a further honour should be given to Vera Lynn, the former Forces' Sweetheart. "She is a great favourite of mine and I personally initiated her previous honour," wrote Wilson. He would do what he could. He was as good as his word; later that year she became Dame Vera.[3]

He enjoyed, too, pulling strings to the advantage of causes which he had at heart. He found that the D'Oyly Carte company was in financial trouble and the future of his beloved Gilbert and Sullivan operas was in peril. He attended their centenary celebrations and offered to act as prompter at their performances, without recourse to a book, a task which he would have been well able to perform.[4] More practically, he wrote to the Minister for the Arts to warn that help was likely to be needed from the Arts Council in the near future. "I believe you will agree with me that Gilbert and Sullivan is part of the national heritage, and that as the repository of the performing traditions of the Savoy operas, the D'Oyly Carte Opera Company is an indispensable part of all that Gilbert and Sullivan represents ... It is to my mind unthinkable that it should be allowed to go out of existence for lack of modest financial support."[5] Marcia Falkender, who disliked Gilbert and Sullivan, was nevertheless enlisted in the campaign and secured the powerful support of James Hanson. This was as highbrow as he got. He wrote to the Chancellor of the Exchequer in early 1975 to say that he had supported additional help for the arts but, "If we do not show that we have done something for sport, we shall hear the criticism that we have discriminated against the area which is of greatest interest to the majority, including those among whom our political support is concentrated."[1] He might have added that it was also of greatest interest to him; in his rare intervals of leisure he was far more likely to watch a football or cricket match on television than read a book or listen to music. But he was still always ready to intervene in favour of the Open University. In 1974 he asked the Minister of Education for an extra £2–3 million to keep it going: "It is, I think, one of the greatest achievements of our previous Government. It is vastly popular in this country – I found it always got a good cheer at pre-Election and Election meetings. It is no less of a success story for Britain abroad."[2]

December 1975, Wilson later wrote, was "the most hectic and harrowing month I experienced in nearly eight years as Prime Minister":[3] Chrysler, the row over pay-beds, violence in Northern Ireland, the European summit in Rome, being added to the more traditional financial crisis and all the other day-to-day burdens of government. Underlying it was Wilson's growing conviction that he was the victim of a malign plot to destroy his reputation and bring down his government. Who was responsible, he had at this stage little idea. He suspected that BOSS, the South African Secret Service, was involved; he was not at all sure that some section of the CIA might not also be playing a part; he was reasonably certain that elements of MI5 were doing the donkey work, though at what level he did not know. Wilson was a man who relished mystery. He was a romantic who loved to arrive late at a Cabinet meeting with covert references to long and secret conversations with the White House or the Kremlin. He retained a touching faith in the skills if not the integrity of the intelligence services. He was thus predisposed to scent sabotage or conspiracy where none existed. Roy Jenkins, who as Home Secretary was aware that his Prime Minister was beginning to nourish these suspicions, felt them to be baseless. He knew that MI5 had a low opinion of Wilson but never supposed that they could seriously imagine him to be an agent, witting or unwitting, of the KGB, still less that they might act on these phantasmagoric notions and try to bring him down. Only after "the publication of Peter Wright's tawdry book which nonetheless chimed in with a chorus of other allegations" did he begin to believe that it was not Wilson but elements of the security service who were prey to feverish delusions.[4]

That something nasty was going on seems probable if not certain. That elements of MI5 were involved cannot be proved and probably never could be. When Wright's allegations first surfaced the recently appointed head of MI5, Antony Duff, who as a former Foreign Office official was perfectly ready to suspect the worst about the past activities of his new department, ordered a stringent enquiry. Anyone, retired or still in the service, who might have had cognisance of a plot was interviewed and every relevant document was scrutinised. His unequivocal conclusion was that nobody in MI5 had been involved in the surveillance of Harold Wilson, still less in any operation designed to destabilise his government.[1] The present head of MI5, after long experience in the service, is equally convinced that the bureaucratic machinery of the department would have made it impossible for any significant skullduggery to have taken place, even at the lowest level. In particular it would have been impossible to bug 10 Downing Street without the connivance of the most senior officials and probably the Home Secretary as well.[2]

A reasonable retort would be that such dignitaries would be highly unlikely to reach another conclusion. The fact that they stated no plot existed was not final proof that it did not, and even if they were sincerely convinced that they knew all the facts, this would not prove that they had not been kept in ignorance. The main evidence for the existence of a plot within MI5 – that of Peter Wright – needs however, to put it charitably, to be treated with some caution. On television Wright admitted that his figure of thirty officers in MI5 who "had given their approval to a plot" was exaggerated: "the maximum number was eight or nine. Very often it was only three." When asked: "How many people, when all the talking died down, were still serious in joining you in trying to get rid of Wilson?" he replied, "One, I should say." "Is that part of the book," his interviewer went on, "perhaps an exaggeration of what you recall now?" "I would say it is unreliable," admitted Wright.[3]

The most convincing scenario seems to be that of a vain and disgruntled official bragging in bars, muttering darkly to anyone he thought might prove sympathetic about what could and should be done, and finally inflating his ego and his income by peddling his fantasies to the public. But one cannot rule out the possibility that he, and perhaps other members of MI5, had dealings with foreign intelligence services, or groups of like-minded British citizens, and helped them with advice and information. Even more probably, they tipped off the press, in particular *Private Eye*, about details of Wilson's career which might be used to lend verisimilitude to damaging stories about his communist leanings.[1] It is also conceivable that other British intelligence services may have used some of the substantial funds available to counter communist activities in this misguided enterprise.[2] The evidence of the army intelligence officer, Colin Wallace, supports the view that there was a deliberate campaign to discredit Wilson, though doubts about who, if anyone, Wallace's contacts really represented and to what extent they were confined to Northern Ireland make it hard to assess whether there could have been any serious involvement at a high level in London.[3]

From the point of view of the public perception of Wilson, whatever campaign there may have been achieved remarkably little: the people at large knew nothing of what was being said; the government was not even shaken, let alone destroyed. Within Whitehall wisps of gossip floated about the Prime Minister's financial activities or his involvement with the communist world, but if anyone of any consequence took them seriously he certainly did not make his feeling known at the time nor has he admitted to it subsequently. What is significant for the biographer, however, is that Wilson himself became rattled, demoralised would be too strong a word, but irritated, baffled, and a little apprehensive about what might be going to happen next. One of his colleagues became privy to these fears when he stood next to Wilson in the lavatory at Number 10 and the Prime Minister pointed at the electric light fitting and made an exaggerated gesture of caution, putting his finger to his lips and indicating that confidential talk would be unsafe. After he resigned Wilson was to press his successor to conduct a fuller enquiry into the plot against him. Callaghan ordered a full investigation but could find no evidence of any significant wrongdoing. A sweep was made of Number 10 but not surprisingly it revealed nothing: if there had been any bugging devices they would presumably have been removed with Wilson, and anyway, those who conducted the sweep could have been the ones who placed the bugs.[4] Callaghan concluded that the matter could be taken no further; now, like Jenkins, he wonders whether more might have been going on than he realised at the time.[5]

Lord Hunt, who as Secretary of the Cabinet had direct responsibility over the field of intelligence, became so alarmed by what he felt to be Wilson's paranoiac suspicions of members of MI5 that he persuaded him to meet Michael Hanley, the chief of the security service, and air his suspicions. The meeting seemed to have achieved nothing. It was said that over his last few months in office Wilson would rarely exchange words in the lavatory without first turning on all the taps and was constantly pointing at the ceiling, or the tops of pictures, to indicate that a conversation was being monitored. George Bush, when head of the CIA, once called on Wilson and emerged, shaken, asking: "Is that man mad? He did nothing but complain about being spied on!" He was not mad, but he lived on the fringes of a Kafka-esque world where madness was endemic. If those who are set to catch the spies are spies themselves, who is there left to trust? Outside his immediate entourage, Wilson became less and less ready to trust anyone; the insecurity that he felt added immeasurably to the burdens of office in the last year or so.[1]

Hard facts to support his fears were scarce; are indeed still scarce though much circumstantial evidence has accumulated. The burglaries were the nearest approach to proof. Michael Halls, his private secretary, had been burgled several times; so too had Marcia Falkender. Two girls in the political office had their effects ransacked. Goodman's office was burgled, though no papers of relevance to Wilson were removed; after the office of his accountant was broken into, however, copies of his bank statements were found lying in the street outside. After his resignation Wilson received letters from people in prison complaining that they had been hired to do jobs of which he was the target and had never received their due. They appeared to feel that the decent thing for him to do was to correct the omission. At first Wilson dismissed this series of break-ins as mere coincidence; then he began to think that they might be the work of some unscrupulous opportunist looking for material to sell to the press: "It would be foolish to ignore the possibility that some evil-minded person might have regarded Fleet Street as a potential market for anything he might discover."[2] Only in the later stages of the story did he begin to believe that a systematic campaign designed to discredit him was under way.

A curious episode concerned the International Credit Bank of Geneva. The bank closed its doors on 7 October 1974. A clerk subsequently alleged that Wilson had withdrawn £1,500 from the bank just before the closure, clearly suggesting that the Prime Minister had used confidential information to save himself from a financial loss. The City of London police investigated and found that £1,500 had indeed been deposited, part of a contribution to the running costs of Wilson's office during the period in opposition. It was, however, still there when the bank closed. Who had tipped off the clerk, and why? Odder still, it subsequently appeared that a withdrawal voucher had been prepared for the £1,500 a few days before the closure. Who had prepared it and why had it not been used? Wilson denied all knowledge of it. Various explanations are possible, but an aborted plot to frame the Prime Minister is not the most unlikely. Wilson certainly had no doubt that this was what was involved, and his fears mounted accordingly.[1]

Early in 1976 the long-simmering scandal over Jeremy Thorpe's relationship with Norman Scott became public, with suggestions of conspiracy and incitement to murder. Wilson counted Thorpe as a friend and thought that, as leader of the Liberal Party, he was more sympathetic to Labour than any possible replacement was likely to be. For these reasons alone he would have liked Thorpe to be innocent. Also he was convinced he had found a fellow victim. Barbara Castle noted that "he had got all steamed up about the Jeremy affair," telling all and sundry that it was a plot, set up by the South African government because the Liberals had been active in opposing their policies. "He hinted darkly that he knew all about that sort of thing and had his spies working on it, because he had been the victim of it: the theft of his own confidential papers. Well, he may be right, but I wish he would deal with it coolly, discreetly and silently, as a calculated expression of political principle instead of in this erratic and dramatic Goldfinger way."[2]

Wilson asked Castle for details of a prosecution the Social Services Department had brought against Scott for fraud some time before. Castle obliged, and "Harold's face dropped a bit" when her investigation showed that Thorpe and Scott had enjoyed a much longer and more intimate relationship than the Liberal leader had cared to admit. Since he had committed himself to Thorpe's defence and had attacked the press for hounding an innocent man without due cause, Wilson had reason to feel disconcerted. "He really is an incredible mixture of caution and recklessness," mused Castle. It was recklessness that dictated his answers in the House of Commons on 9 March. At lunch that day he had boasted that he now had conclusive evidence that South African money had been involved in the Thorpe affair: "It's been a great detective exercise, I can tell you. Detective Inspector Falkender has been up to her eyes in it." BOSS had already picked on Wilson but had so far achieved nothing, now they were seeking first to destroy the lesser target. In the House he announced that he had conclusive proof that South African business interests had been involved in the Thorpe affair. It caused quite a stir and promised some relief for the embattled Thorpe: "it's good," the latter told his colleague Cyril Smith. "It will be pushed on to South Africa."[1] It was not, of course. Thorpe's guilt or innocence was in no way affected by the motives of those who had sought to expose him. "Why go overboard for Jeremy?" Castle asked herself. "For the political moral Harold was hinting at was so set about with equivocations that it could not really get home."[2]

Viewed with the advantage of hindsight, many of Wilson's activities over the last year of his prime-ministership seem geared to the needs of life after office. The progress of the British film industry had always been a prime concern of his. It is not in the least surprising that he should address himself to it at this time. Yet it seems reasonable to suppose that, when he envisaged setting up some body which would operate to the permanent advantage of the trade, he had also in mind that it might provide interesting and congenial – if unpaid – work in future years. Certainly the film industry could do with some help. Attendance had slumped from 343 million in 1964 to 142 million in 1973. American investment had largely been withdrawn to finance the huge demands of television in the United States. The trade had various proposals for tax relief, freer use of income from the National Film Fund, the encouragement of foreign productions in the United Kingdom and a levy on the showing of films on television, to which Wilson was generally sympathetic but which he saw might prove unpopular with the Treasury. In July 1975 he set up a working party under the chairmanship of John Terry of the National Film Finance Corporation, with Marcia Falkender on it as his representative, to look into the future needs of the industry and to suggest appropriate remedies.

It was Wilson's conviction that the industry needed a central Film Authority, and with that in mind he insisted that representatives of television as well as cinema should sit on the working party. By the time the working party reported at Number 10 in December 1975 his point of view had prevailed; the proposal was for a single Film Authority. Wilson went as far as he could, and slightly further than he should have, to shape its recommendations. They should put forward their report, he said, without feeling "unduly constrained by considerations of wider political acceptability; this was especially relevant to the proposals concerning personal taxation and VAT."[1] Encouraged by so broad a hint, the working group duly asked for as much as it could hope for and more than it expected. When the matter came up in the House of Commons Wilson was able to announce that the government would act on the two central recommendations in the report: the provision of additional finance and the setting up of a British Film Authority. Up to £5 million would be made available: "a basic fund providing working capital – *not* a subsidy – to enable the industry to set about the task of securing adequate resources from the private sector".[2] Almost certainly he had in mind that by the time the authority started to function he would be available to act as its first chairman. He underestimated the delays involved in the involute operations of bureaucracy. It was the middle of 1976 before an Interim Action Committee was set up to implement the recommendations of the working party and though he became its chairman he had to wait another seven years before a British Screen Advisory Council was established.

There was swifter progress over his negotiations with David Frost for a series on Yorkshire Television with an accompanying book which was at that point to be called *The Prime Ministers*. The principles were thrashed out over dinner in January 1976, Wilson giving no pledge as to when he would be free to do his part but leaving Frost in little doubt that there would not be too long a delay. Within a fortnight the details were falling into place; on behalf of Weidenfeld and Nicolson Robin Denniston chipped in with an offer of £75,000 for the book rights and early in February Frost, through Arnold Goodman, offered £100,000 for all rights, with an additional £50,000 payable if the series were sold to a major American broadcasting outlet. Wilson undertook not to act as host on or to narrate any other television programme for three months after ceasing to be Prime Minister.[3] It was a reasonable though not princely offer, doubly acceptable because it was for work that Wilson would greatly enjoy. To some it seemed degrading that a Prime Minister, while still in office, should haggle over terms for work which he would do when in retirement and for which he could not have hoped to be so handsomely rewarded if he had not been the present tenant of Number 10. It would undoubtedly have been more dignified if Wilson had waited till he was out of office before opening negotiations but he was not a rich man and he wanted to be able to start work as soon as he was free to do so. The terms that he secured were no better than he would have got three months later; indeed he might have stood out for still more generous recompense if he had felt able to reveal just how soon he would be available.

Even the Freedom of the City of London, which was bestowed on him in December 1975, seemed a curious precursor of the committee to enquire into the workings of the City which he was to chair after his resignation. Wilson was delighted by the honour, which he did not feel at all inappropriate to a Labour leader. Indeed, he would have argued that a Labour Prime Minister who was *not* felt worthy to be a Freeman would have failed in his task of uniting the whole community and working to the benefit of every source of the nation's wealth. He prepared a list of personal guests whom he wanted invited to the ceremony and showed it to Haines. Haines queried two names. Of the Israeli Ambassador he said that traditionally the City only invited High Commissioners to these occasions. "O.K. – if they never ask them," Wilson minuted regretfully. Of Arieh Handler, of the International Credit Bank, Haines wondered whether his inclusion might not raise a few eyebrows in the City. "No, he's clean," replied Wilson.[1] It was an attitude that was to cost him much goodwill when the time came for the resignation honours to be published.

That time was fast approaching. The most surprising thing about Harold Wilson's resignation was how much surprise it caused; not among the general public but in those inner circles where anyone who paid attention could have known what to expect. So many people had been told, so many hints dropped, over so long a period, that the secret had been opened as wide as any barn door; yet still when it happened the reaction was stunned incredulity. The main reason for this was a failure to believe that a man as totally wrapped up in politics as Wilson, who had striven so hungrily for office, who had no other interests that he longed to pursue, who was under no immediate challenge in his position, should voluntarily surrender power. Nobody ever had. The only Prime Minister to have resigned in the twentieth century except after electoral defeat, on the insistence of his colleagues or for pressing reason of health, was Stanley Baldwin, and he was sixty-nine years old, tired and very deaf. Wilson was not yet sixty and apparently fit. When he spoke of his intention of retiring, his colleagues laughed understandingly and reflected that they would believe that when they saw it. They had reason to be sceptical; it was indeed extraordinary, so much so that one can almost adopt Roy Jenkins's ingenious explanation – that he had faked his birth certificate and was in fact ten years older, a supposition which would account both for his remarkable precocity and his premature retirement. It was so extraordinary that few could credit it until it happened. But it did happen, and exactly as Wilson said it would.

Wilson believed that, in principle, it was wrong for anyone to hold on to power indefinitely. Gladstone, he wrote disapprovingly, "was totally opposed to resigning. He had come to believe in a doctrine of Divine Right of Prime Ministers. The trouble was that his Cabinet was so mesmerised that they were beginning to believe in it too."[1] His own Cabinet hardly suffered from the same complaint but in 1974 and 1975 there was little sign of any effective challenge to his leadership. His innate pugnacity was such that if there *had* been he might well have felt impelled to hang on so as to prove that he could overcome it; as it was he was in no doubt. After the first election in 1974 he told Haines and Donoughue that they could not expect more than a two-year term under his prime-ministership. That summer while in the Isles of Scilly he said the same to Marcia Falkender. She had heard it all before, accepted that he meant it, but like most others believed that when the time came he would be prevailed on to change his mind.[2]

There was still no indication of exactly what date he had in mind. In August 1975 he suggested to Falkender that the party conference in the late autumn might be a suitable occasion. She persuaded him that such a declaration would disrupt the business of the conference and lead to an unseemly battle for the succession. He then proposed Christmas, but she argued that to choose a public holiday, with a dearth of newspapers, would be a messy way of doing it. Her object was to delay the moment for as long as possible in the hope that something would turn up to make it seem imperative for him to stay on. She could not shift him, though, beyond March 1976, in which month he would be sixty. There were excellent reasons for procrastination if he had sought them: the Queen's Silver Jubilee, a Commonwealth Prime Ministers' conference, the first European summit in London. To renounce the first caused him genuine pain; it was an occasion he would have relished, but he was shrewd enough to see that there would always be something else which, if he allowed it, would change his mind. If it were done when 'tis done, then 'twere well it were done quickly; he took a firm grasp on the dagger and plunged it into his breast.

The dagger did not conclusively go home till September at Balmoral when he told the Queen informally what he intended. After that it would have been difficult to change his mind. It must have been about the same time that Mary pencilled a triumphant "D-Day" against Tuesday, 16 March 1976. For her, at least, it would be an occasion for unequivocal rejoicing. On 10 October he explained the reasons for his resignation to his private secretary, Kenneth Stowe. Stowe, a few days later, passed the news on to the Queen's private secretary, Martin Charteris, who said that the Queen should formally be notified. She was, at the next audience, though no precise date was mentioned until early December. Indeed, even as late as 16 December Stowe was telling Charteris that the announcement might be as early as 25 February. Charteris suggested that the best procedure would be for Wilson to resign as party leader as soon as the announcement was made but to remain as Prime Minister until a successor had been elected.[1]

Now the ripples began to widen out. At a dinner given for various press grandees by Arnold Goodman, Wilson referred to his conversation with the Queen in terms that he intended would be remembered after his resignation had been announced.[2] It was probably from this source that Harold Lever heard the news. He told Callaghan, who was sceptical; even if it was true at the moment, said the Foreign Secretary, there was plenty of time for the Prime Minister to change his mind. No, said Lever, the decision was firm and if Callaghan wanted the succession he should get ready.[3] When Lever told the same story to one or two other carefully selected colleagues, word got back to Wilson of what was happening. Lever was summoned to Number 10 and cross-examined on his sources. He countered by reminding Wilson that he had told him in 1974 that he only meant to stay for two more years. Ah yes, said Wilson, "but since then Northern Ireland has blown up. I can't leave in the middle of that mess." Lever reported this to Callaghan, who said, "I told you so." Not at all, retorted Lever. If it had not been true Wilson would never have bothered to send for him.[4]

Barbara Castle noticed in January that Wilson seemed restive: "His eyes were baggy and he was in one of his 'I'll get the hell out of it' moods (I personally think he is getting ready to chuck things up)." He had given up brandy so as to lose weight and instead was drinking five pints of beer a day. She was told by him in early March that he would be retiring very shortly but got the impression that a date had not yet been fixed and when Alan Watkins, the political columnist, reminded her that a Jubilee was in the offing, she concluded that Wilson would probably stick it out till 1977. Wilson seemed eager to discuss with her who ought to be his successor. Healey, he thought, was anathema to the left; Roy Jenkins too keen on his social life; Benn would only have firm support from "the really vicious group"; Eric Varley was too young; Shore had developed remarkably and was now really very impressive. When Castle remarked that Callaghan, too, would be unacceptable to the left, Wilson made no comment.[1] In fact he had already decided that Callaghan was his favoured successor. Partly this was in a spirit of mischief; it amused him to say that he was making way for an older man: "I suppose Paddy is going to be replaced by an older dog," he remarked to Marcia Falkender.[2] More importantly it was because he believed Callaghan was the best man for the job and, in spite of Barbara Castle's fears, was the only candidate who could hope to keep the party united. Their relationship had been conspicuously good of late. "Happy New Year," Callaghan had written to him on 2 January. "I think 1975 was basically a good year because it marked the beginning of recognition of reality by some important elements in the Party. And it is quite clear that it *is* the Labour Party that has to do the job – no one else can. So don't listen to the prophets of doom – not even to those who want you to retire. I ask you to carry on."[3] Wilson probably took these protestations with a pinch of salt, but the thought was a kind one and he appreciated it.

He did his best to help Callaghan's cause by telling him of his exact plans after a dinner George Weidenfeld gave for him shortly before the resignation. If Healey had had the same amount of warning he would have tempered the bitter attack which he had launched on the left only a few days before zero hour. It is unlikely that it would have affected the eventual result, but Healey's outburst finished any chance he had of picking up enough votes from the soft left to make a fight of it. As it was, he heard of the Prime Minister's decision when standing beside him in the lavatory in 10 Downing Street just before the fateful Cabinet meeting.[1] He thus had a few minutes' start over the other members of the Cabinet; even Peter Shore, Wilson's closest confidant among his colleagues, had been given no warning. Marcia Falkender met Shore as he went into the Cabinet Room and, thinking he would wish to cancel their arrangement to lunch together, asked him what he thought about it all. "About what all?" he asked blankly.[2]

It is still a matter for wonder that Wilson did not change his mind as the chosen date approached. Any time before he had told the Queen he was free to do so; even after the visit to Balmoral he could have found convincing excuses for hanging on. A complex of reasons put him into a frame of mind where the temptation hardly entered his head. One was his health. Wilson himself always stoutly denied that this was a serious factor. Shortly after the announcement of his resignation he declared that he was as fit as he had been twenty years before.

But I know how solicitous my friends can be. $2\frac{1}{2}$ years ago I had a little knee trouble, which was diagnosed as fluid. This gave rise to a slight limp, which was perceived. On the Saturday, the Lord President was telephoned by the representative of an eminent newspaper asking him to confirm that I had had a stroke. As it happened the Lord President knew the exact gravity of my state of health and said, slightly inaccurately, that I had housemaid's knee. But the anxieties and solicitude persisted. Within a few weeks my office had been telephoned as one enquirer after another asked in funereal terms about what they had heard on impeccable evidence, namely two coronaries, three cerebral haemorrhages, leukaemia, lung cancer and, I think, cancer in other parts of the anatomy.[3]

His denial was well founded as far as it went. He did not suffer from leukaemia or lung cancer. But he was not anything like as fit as he had been twenty years before. In 1974 he had suffered a heart flutter brought on by the shock of an aborted landing when returning in an aircraft from Berlin. It did no lasting damage and his doctor, Joseph Stone, described him as "a very tough cookie in medical terms",[4] but it frightened him, and his close associates noticed that from then on he consulted his medical advisers with far greater regularity. He tired more quickly and the psychosomatic stomach pains which he experienced before difficult or stressful meetings became more pronounced. So too did the styes which afflicted him when he was under pressure. In December 1975 Callaghan was so worried by his run-down state that he insisted Wilson cancel a visit to Egypt which he was due to make. Wilson argued the issue but finally succumbed with obvious relief.[1]

Physically this all amounted to little; the most noticeable fact was that he was twelve years older than when he had first become Prime Minister and the difference between forty-eight and sixty is great for anyone. Mentally he was twelve years older too and there the deterioration, though impossible to measure, seems to have been more sharply accentuated. At least one civil servant who had not worked for him before was surprised to find that the famed memory was by no means as sharp as it was said to be; if Wilson quoted a date or a reference at least one figure was likely to be wrong.[2] There were reports of minor lapses, failure to follow a train of thought, confusion of two ideas. In the opinion of one doctor who was well placed to judge the position this may occasionally have amounted to mild confabulation, a condition when the mind blacks out for brief intervals, and the gap in speech is filled by words which superficially fit but in fact are irrelevant to what preceded or followed them. Haines claims that Wilson had lost all capacity for original thought over the last few months and found difficulty in improvising even a routine constituency speech.[3] To Edward Short he seemed a different man in his final year, listless and always very tired. He let one Cabinet committee degenerate into a hopeless tangle in a way that would never have happened in the past.[4]

It would be too much to suggest that he was incapable of performing his duties. Compared with Winston Churchill in the closing stages of his term in office or with Eden at the end of 1956, he was a model of lucidity. But he must have known that he was not the man he was and the knowledge preyed on him. For someone who had prided himself on his quickness of mind, his legendary memory, to slow up, to be at a loss for words or to grope for a statistic was not merely galling, but a blow to his confidence. "He really let me get on with it," says Callaghan of the last twelve months; the cutting edge had gone. He only did things out of a sense of duty.[5]

There were other factors too. Yet another economic crisis was on the way, with the inevitability of further deflation, shaming obeisance to the IMF, more anger from the left. He was desperately worried about inflation yet could see no way of combating it which would not involve recourse to policies at variance with all that he believed desirable. He could not bear to go round the course again, knowing that he had no fresh initiatives to offer, no new tricks to perform. Let Callaghan take up the charge! The possibility of defeat at the next election was very real. Wilson had hated 1970, he had no wish to face humiliation once again. Let Callaghan carry the can! He had had enough.

Mary certainly encouraged him in this attitude; she would indeed have felt betrayed if he had gone back on his resolve to resign. According to Chapman Pincher, Callaghan was asked whether he was not apprehensive lest Wilson had a last-minute change of heart and tried to take back the leadership. "No. Mary wouldn't let him," he replied.[1] Arnold Goodman also believed that Wilson was "absolutely tired and fed up" and that Mary had played an important part in screwing him to the point of resignation.[2] It is noteworthy that among the inner entourage it was only Marcia Falkender who made any serious effort to dissuade him; Haines and Donoughue plainly considered that they felt his decision was the right one. They are both declared enemies of Lady Falkender and it is not surprising that they believe her baleful influence and the turmoil that she created were major factors in inducing Wilson to retire from the field.[3] In fact her absence would probably have been more harmful to Wilson's morale, but it is easy to believe that the squalls of day-to-day life in Downing Street wore the Prime Minister down and made him more ready to give up.

The exact date was kept open till the last moment. At a meeting with Stowe and Haines on 9 March Wilson emphasised that flexibility was essential, "he could not commit himself to a final decision more than twenty-four hours in advance." There were four situations in particular where a sudden crisis might be exacerbated if the Prime Minister were to resign: the Thorpe affair, the sterling exchange rate, Northern Ireland and Rhodesia. Of these the first and last seemed temporarily under control: "he had steadied" Thorpe, Wilson announced optimistically.[4] A balance of payments crisis in early March and a government defeat in the House of Commons on public expenditure made him for a moment doubt whether he should stick to the favoured date of 16 March, but the parliamentary defeat was put right by a vote of confidence and the exchanges settled down. Some people saw a connection between the announcement of the resignation and the decision of Princess Margaret and Lord Snowdon to separate, which was announced in the same week. Wilson, it was suggested, had postponed or advanced his announcement so as to draw the attention of the media from the break-up of the royal marriage. There were discussions between Number 10 and the palace about the way the two decisions should be publicised, but both dates had been fixed independently and well in advance and the fact that they fell more or less together was coincidental.

Wilson's statement to the Cabinet, just after 10.30 a.m. on Tuesday, 16 March, was phlegmatic and characteristically spiced with statistics: he had presided over 472 Cabinets, answered more than 12,000 parliamentary questions, taken the chair at thousands of Cabinet committees. Those not yet in the know were duly confounded: Crosland was "transfixed", Healey "flabbergasted". Joel Barnett came in shortly after Wilson had finished to find "an astonishing scene ... They all seemed dazed."[1] Apart from the amazement, people reacted according to their views of Wilson. Castle found the statement "very movingly worded". Eric Varley passed her a note which read, "It's a very emotional moment." "What's your reaction?" asked Castle. "I think he's wrong," wrote Varley. "I think it will prove how difficult it is to replace him," concluded Castle.[2] Benn for his part found that people were "stunned, but in a curious way, without emotion. Harold is not a man who arouses affection in most people." One of the exceptions was Short who exclaimed, "with visible sorrow – his eyes were filled with tears and his face was red – 'I think this is a deplorable event and I don't know what to say except thank you.'"[3]

If his closest colleagues were thus taken by surprise, it was not to be wondered at that those more distant were incredulous. "I was literally stunned," wrote Hastings Banda. "At sixty, the age of manhood or maturity in politics, when you had at least another twenty years to go, I simply could not get myself to understand why."[4] From a man who would still be very much in charge of his country at the age of eighty-eight such a reaction might have been expected, but many others found it equally hard to understand. "What exactly *was* Harold up to?" mused Barbara Castle. "More than had met the eye, I had no doubt."[5] The conviction that Wilson must be up to something was widespread. One theory, widely held, was that it was a case of *reculer pour mieux sauter*; that he took it for granted that he would be pressed urgently to remain in office or would be called to come back after his successor had met disaster. Silkin "was sure Harold was planning to come back in some way", while Jack Jones admitted that "deep down I had the feeling that he thought he might be called back at some stage."[1] Michael Foot "didn't think Harold was going to retire at all. He said he thought in a few years time there would be a national clamour for him to come back and take charge again."[2] It would be surprising if, as everything crumbled around the unfortunate Callaghan, Wilson had never played with the idea of a desperate party and nation turning to the old master and appealing to him to rescue them. At the time of his resignation, however, such thoughts must have been the most fleeting of phantasmagoria. If he did still hanker after supreme power it is incredible that he should have surrendered it when it was firmly in his grasp, on the off-chance that he might one day be invited to take it back.

A more beguiling scenario has the hard-faced men from MI5 arriving uninvited at Downing Street and telling the Prime Minister that they hold the evidence to cause some fearful scandal – sexual, financial, political, what-you-will – and that they would feel bound to release it unless a resignation were forthcoming within a short space of time. Some people who should have been better informed subscribed to such theories. At dinner with Michael Foot ten days or so before the resignation there was talk of "very strong rumours" that this was about to happen. "Some funny things have evidently been happening," commented Benn. "There is a possibility that some papers which were stolen from Harold's desk may envelop him in some way in a scandal." Three days later he was surmising that Wilson's insistence that the South African intelligence service had played a part in the Thorpe affair might be explained by the fact that he himself was vulnerable and wanted "to establish the principle that the South Africans are trying to destroy British political leaders".[3] Material so melodramatic would be a delight for any biographer. Unfortunately there is not the slightest reason to believe that the security service made any such approach to Wilson or that it would have had anything to charge him with if it had. The fact that Wilson decided to resign at the age of sixty is itself surprising, even astonishing, but there can be no doubt that it was his own decision and taken long before the event.

Between the resignation and the appointment of his successor, Wilson marked time. It was a period pitted with ceremonial occasions of varying solemnity. For Wilson the high spot was on 23 March, when the Queen and Prince Philip came to a farewell dinner at Downing Street. They had done the same for Winston Churchill, but since then the passing of prime ministers had been too painful or too unexpected to allow of such courtesies. For so dedicated a monarchist, to entertain the Queen in what was still his own home provided a peculiar pleasure. He got special satisfaction from the fact that, though the royal car had been ordered for 10.30, the Queen and Prince Philip did not actually leave until a quarter to twelve.[1] After this, the final dinner for the Cabinet was a humdrum affair. Short made "a boring speech", recorded Benn; "of almost painful banality" felt Castle; while Wilson's reply was "even more boring", and delivered in "that curiously toneless and emotionless way he has made a virtue of", according to the same two witnesses.[2] "The time to go is while they are saying why do you go, not why do you stay," pronounced Wilson.[3] Benn relieved the gloom by telling a few funny stories – though Marcia Falkender thought his speech too political – and surprised the party by pulling out a camera and taking photographs.[4] He tried to do the same at Wilson's last Cabinet meeting but was told to put his camera away. "Well, that was it," he reflected when the meeting was over, "and there was Harold sitting with his white hair smoking his pipe and at the end of the Cabinet he got up and we all walked out and not a word was said. He didn't say thanks very much and we didn't say thanks very much. I have never known a man arouse so little emotion – of affection or even of seething hatred. It was just a non-event. Like a civil servant reaching the age of sixty and retiring."[5]

"Uganda will cooperate with your successor whether he is Welsh, Scottish, Irish or English," promised Idi Amin handsomely.[6] Wilson thought that Anglo-Welsh would fill the bill. Though he made a public parade of his neutrality he in fact took little trouble to conceal the fact that he felt Callaghan would and should take his place. When Kissin saw him after his resignation and told him he felt that Healey should be the next Prime Minister, Wilson replied that the party wanted Callaghan and that that was where his support would go.[7] All went to plan. Healey was knocked out in the first ballot and Callaghan won comfortably over Michael Foot in the final round. At the party meeting to announce his victory, Castle noticed with relief, Wilson "got the biggest reception of all, with a standing ovation. I think everyone in the room realised that in his own funny way he had been a big man."[8] Perhaps they did, at that emotional moment, but it was not to last.

XXIV

Retirement

1976–1980

What does a retired Prime Minister do, if his own party is still in power? He *could* continue in office in some less onerous role. Callaghan suggested to Wilson that he might take over from him as Foreign Secretary and asked Marcia Falkender to try to persuade him to accept the offer. He would have been surprised if Wilson had said yes, but not disconcerted; he knew that there were no serious points of difference between them on any of the issues that were likely to cause problems.[1] But the idea, though he appreciated the spirit behind it, held little appeal for Wilson. One way and another, he had been to a plethora of international conferences over the last twelve years, always in a starring role, and he did not relish the prospect of clambering on to the merry-go-round again but in a humbler capacity. Nor did he see any case for becoming Lord President of the Council, Lord Privy Seal or any other grandiose office that carried with it status but no particular responsibilities. If he was not going to run the Cabinet then he was not going to be in it. Much better to make a complete break with the past.

If he had been ejected against his will then there would have been every reason to lead an active life on the back benches, fomenting revolution and sniping at his successor. But Wilson had resigned of his own accord and had given Callaghan's prime ministership his formal blessing. Even if he were to disapprove of any policies of the new government, propriety dictated that he should keep his disquiet to himself for at least a year or two. He was doomed to play a passive role, intervening only to support the ministry whenever it seemed necessary. He could have retired to the Lords and taken on at once the mantle of elder statesman, but though he had every intention of doing this in the long run, at the age of sixty he did not yet feel that it would be wholly appropriate. For a time at least politics were going to play a far smaller part in his life than they ever had in the past. He would concentrate on making some money out of books, films and lectures; and putting on record his own vision of what had happened during the two years of his final administration.

In theory, too, he would be able to see more of his family. He liked the idea, and yet when it came to the point there was not a great deal to be done. Robin was now in his early thirties, working at Oxford or with the Open University. In March 1975, for the only time in his eight years as Prime Minister, Wilson found himself called out of a Cabinet meeting to receive an urgent message from his wife. It was to tell him that he was a grandfather twice over, his daughter-in-law Joy had given birth to twin daughters. From now on he would see much of them at weekends, but the habits of a lifetime are not easily broken. As a father Wilson had been affectionate but remote, as a grandfather he was to be little different. Even if geographically he had been living closer to his children, the psychological distance would not have dwindled. Mary too had made her own life and her own friends, and had built up a considerable reputation with her poetry; her relationship with her husband would not suddenly be transformed because he had rather more time on his hands. Wilson was not cut out to be a family man and his family would not have easily adjusted itself to accommodate him even if he had wanted it to.

The lease of the house in Lord North Street was a short one and, though it later appeared that they had been badly advised, it did not seem in 1976 that they would be able to extend it. It was, anyway, an attractive but inconvenient house, with more stairs than would be desirable if they were going to grow old there. The following year they moved to a first-floor flat in Ashley Gardens, in the shadow of Westminster Cathedral. It was compact, close to the Houses of Parliament and reasonably roomy. Moving there, and organising Grange Farm so as to accommodate his books and papers was time-consuming work, absorbing any energy that was left over from his other pursuits. He was in one way better off than earlier ex-Prime Ministers. In April 1975 it had been arranged that people in that position should have a car and official chauffeur. Benn noted that the drivers in the government car pool were saying: "The crafty bugger must be preparing to get out, and then *he'll* have a car for life."[1] They were not far wrong. The car was a godsend to Wilson. "I don't own a car at all," he told a friend some time later, "indeed I haven't had one since the early seventies, and then it was mostly used by my son."[1] With a secure base in London and the country, an undemanding political routine, various odd jobs in fields of special interest to him, his books and lectures, Wilson could promise himself a pleasantly active and rewarding existence. There were some disagreeable features about his first year in retirement, however. One of them he brought entirely on himself.

The affair of the resignation honours can only be explained by a combination on Wilson's part of naïvety, slackness, obstinacy, generosity, loyalty and that curious streak of recklessness which occasionally marred the even surface of his relentless prudence. He had been criticised in the past for using the honours systems as a means of rewarding old friends and supporters; the elevation of Rudy Sternberg to be first Sir Rudy and then Lord Plurenden had caused particular offence, since it was well known that Sternberg had contributed generously to Wilson's office expenses during the period in opposition. The ripples of disapproval caused by such a gesture, however, were as nothing compared with the indignation caused by the Resignation Honours List. Traditionally, this list provides an outgoing Prime Minister with an opportunity to reward those who had served him while he was in office, from personal secretaries and campaign managers to chauffeurs and door-keepers. It would have been the normal place to have expected a peerage or some other high honour for his political secretary, and though there would always have been enemies ready to attack the award of any distinction to Marcia Falkender, most people would have felt her inclusion in this list unexceptionable. Wilson, however, extended the usual scope of the list to include the names of some of those outside the political circle who had been particularly helpful to him or, as Haines and Donoughue among others believed, to Lady Falkender.

The honours which caused most offence to the purists were peerages for the two show-business magnates, Lew Grade and Bernard Delfont; for Wilson's publisher, George Weidenfeld, with whom it was assumed, in fact incorrectly, that he had a contractual relationship; for Joseph Kagan, manufacturer of the Gannex raincoat; and Professor John Vaizey, whose relationship with the Labour movement was by now tenuous but who was supposed to have been of great help to

Marcia Falkender over her children's education. Among the other names which were to provoke derision were James Hanson, the chairman of Yorkshire Television, which was to broadcast Wilson's series on the Prime Ministers, and Eric Miller, another financier who was said to be close to Marcia Falkender (though she herself maintained that it was Ron Hayward, the General Secretary, who pressed for Miller's inclusion as a generous supporter of the party and Treasurer of the Socialist International). A name which did not figure in the published list but which was supposed to have appeared in earlier drafts was that of Jarvis Astaire, an impresario well known for his interests in bookmaking, greyhound racing and other sporting activities, though also a vigorous fund-raiser for various charities. The information that Astaire was to be included was leaked to the press by someone in Number 10 who was presumably anxious to sabotage the operation; the – theoretically at least – "unknown" informant also reported that the financier James Goldsmith, who in fact received a knighthood, was to become a peer. Goldsmith's relationship with the party was even more remote than that of Vaizey, who at least formally remained a member till 1978. Goldsmith had always shown markedly right-wing views, and though Wilson had met him and admired his business acumen, there had never been any close association between them. According to Haines, after Goldsmith had come to lunch at Number 10, Wilson told a small group of his intimates that Marcia Falkender was to be offered a seat on the board of Goldsmith's company, Cavenham Foods.[1] Lady Falkender contemplated a libel action when she read this accusation in Haines's memoirs, but was crippled by a slipped disc at the time and did not feel equal to the effort.

Haines, Donoughue, Albert Murray and others in Number 10 who felt professionally bound to keep a lower profile argued that if a list of this nature were to appear it would do grave damage to Wilson's reputation and would inevitably give rise to rumours that favours had been received or undue pressure brought to bear. Wilson dismissed their arguments as being trivial. He could not be quite so insouciant when the Political Honours Scrutiny Committee also took exception to the list. According to Lady Summerskill, Labour elder statesman and representative on the committee, she and the Tory member, Lord Crathorne, were appalled by some of the names and told the civil servant present, Sir Stuart Milner-Barry, that they saw objections to at least half of them.[2] How forcibly these views were conveyed to Number 10 is uncertain; Wilson subsequently stated that he was given no reason to suspect that any real objection existed. He must have been aware, however, that the palace shared the doubts of the Scrutiny Committee. It was made clear to him from that quarter that some of the names were felt to be ill-chosen and that it was hoped Wilson would take the opportunity to think again.

He did not think again, or if he did he quickly dismissed any idea that he should make substantial changes. One can conceive several reasons for this determination. In spite of all the voices raised in warning, he still did not believe that there would be any real uproar once the list was published; the matter seemed to him of minimal importance; his nominations were easily defensible; if anyone did object it would be for ignoble motives. By nature singularly tenacious, he disliked going back on something to which he had committed himself. He had convinced himself that the most significant factor behind criticism of the list was anti-Semitism. A high proportion of the personal honours were to Jews. Lady Summerskill would have insisted that this had nothing whatever to do with the objections of the Scrutiny Committee, who were concerned only with the suitability of the names on grounds of politics and public service; no doubt this was true, but in the storm which blew up when the list was published it was not difficult to detect a flavour of racial prejudice which, at least retrospectively, justified some of Wilson's obstinacy.

How far the list was of his own compilation and how far that of Marcia Falkender will never be finally established. In an article in *The Times*, George Hutchinson stated roundly that Wilson's "amanuensis and adviser (one might almost say accomplice) can hardly be exonerated. Lady Falkender has claimed too much influence and responsibility in the past to escape comment and attention now."[1] This attack provoked a furious, 2,000-word counterblast from Marcia Falkender. She complained that the comment on the list had been "sickening", "a sanctimonious protest by an unimaginative element in the Establishment", "unadulterated snobbery" and "much more serious, it has often been covert anti-semitism". It was anyway quite untrue that the list's composition had been her responsibility. It was not the case that she had undue influence over Wilson: "The press have continually claimed that I had it, or claimed that I claimed that I had it. But that does not mean I did. Nor is it true." In the case of the resignation honours, the list was Wilson's "and his alone". She had been consulted about the "Arts and Sports sections", in the same way as Haines and Donoughue had been, but in no other respect was she the author of the list. No one in the Political Office had seen, or had ever seen, an Honours List in its entirety before its publication.[1]

The matter was not allowed to rest there. George Caunt now wrote to *The Times* to claim that this last statement at least was untrue. He claimed to have seen the complete 1970 list on Marcia Falkender's desk eight days before it was published.[2] Haines stated that the original list "was Lady Falkender's, written out in her own hand on the lavender-coloured notepaper she often used. It was that list, with a few deletions and a few additions in the Prime Minister's hand, which the principal private secretary used" to prepare the submission to the Queen.[3] Caunt is dead, Haines holds by his version, amending it only to say that the list was on lilac-coloured paper rather than lavender. He recollects that an earlier, typewritten list of four possible peers had included David Frost. This was one of the names that Wilson evidently deleted.[4] Donoughue in general supports Haines's account. Wilson, he states, knew so little about Goldsmith that only a few weeks before he had asked who he was when he encountered his name on a guest list. Donoughue replied that he was a most capable business man but extremely far to the right politically.[5] Lord Shackleton, who was chairman of the Political Honours Scrutiny Committee from 1976, remembers Wilson rather irritably defending the names put forward. He cannot vouch for the exact words, but recalls Wilson adding something like: "Anyway, it wasn't my list."[6] To all this Lady Falkender retorts that at the time Haines objected only to the "song-and-dance" personalities on the ground that they were too lightweight; that Kagan had been included not at Wilson's wish but on the insistence of Douglas Houghton and Eric Miller at the special request of the General Secretary; that Hanson's honour was in recognition of his rescue of the D'Oyly Carte Opera Company; that neither Frost nor Astaire had ever been on the list (though both had been considered); and that there had been no reaction from the palace. The paper she used was neither lilac nor lavender but pale pink and the only reason the list was in her handwriting was because the principal private secretary quite correctly refused to accept the partly illegible slips of paper which Wilson had given him; she had no access to a typewriter and the need was urgent.[7]

Whatever the division of blame or credit for its compilation, there can be no doubt that Lady Falkender was correct when she said that it was Wilson's list. He himself stated as much: "I still have the original names, substantially as published, written down by myself after consultation with no one else."[1] Even if there was an element of a gallant cover-up in that avowal, the fact remains that he saw the list in draft, amended it, accepted it and must carry the ultimate responsibility for its contents. He paid heavily for his failure to foresee disaster. The press was united in condemnation. Hutchinson, in the article in *The Times* which so offended Lady Falkender, wrote that Wilson's retirement had been "irretrievably damaged. No honours list ... has ever been attended by such farce." Wilson had demeaned his office, injured his party and discredited the system. The *Daily Telegraph* saw it as being "a fitting legacy from an in many ways absurd Prime Minister", while the *Guardian*, rather more pertinently, found it "frankly distressing ... There is the point at which personal patronage has to stop. And there is the point at which straightforward common sense dictates a certain seemly restraint. On both counts, Harold Wilson has strayed into grey territory."[2] That is the gravamen of the charges against Wilson; the resignation honours were not wicked or corrupt, they broke no law and breached no serious principle, but they were silly and ill-judged. Wilson went too far.

From Wilson's point of view they were still more mischievous, since they gave people grounds for darker suspicions and, combined with his apparently sudden resignation, fed the appetite for scandal which lies within even the most respectable of citizens. Benn's reactions, though perhaps more violent than most, were by no means untypical. Even before the list was published he was recounting the rumours in the papers and tut-tutting sorrowfully over the names that had been put forward. "It makes the honours system utterly corrupt." Wilson had "absolutely cooked his goose", he told Joe Ashton. When the list was actually published he wrote that it was:

grubby, disreputable and just told the whole Wilson story in a single episode ... after all he talked about the obscenity of the stock market and the City of London and all his speeches to the Conference about it, that he should pick that particular group of inadequate, buccaneering, sharp shysters for his honours was absolutely disgusting ... We've never had anything quite like this in the Labour Party and it has caused an outcry, quite properly so. It will clearly help to get rid of the honours system. It explains why Wilson was so furious with me in January when he discovered that the National Executive was going to have a look at the honours system ...[3]

The unpleasantness caused by the resignation honours did not tarnish Wilson's delight in the Order of the Garter, which he was awarded in April 1976. Run-of-the-mill knighthoods, whether Gs or Ks, in his eyes were gewgaws, to be handed out to all and sundry without too much thought being given to the worthiness of the recipient. The Most Noble Order of the Garter was something different: it had been founded in 1348, its membership was limited to twenty-four; it united in a tiny elite members of the royal family, ancient aristocrats (ancient, usually, in years as well as lineage) and the most illustrious of meritocrats; it involved flamboyant dressing-up and swaggering at Windsor. It appealed irresistibly to Wilson's romantic impulses and sense of history. According to Callaghan, at an EEC summit meeting when the Italian Prime Minister was delivering a tedious harangue on the international monetary system, Wilson took off his earphones, leaned over and asked: "When I go, Jim, shall I take the Garter, the OM or go to the Lords?" Which would you prefer? asked Callaghan. "I think I'll take the Garter."[1] One of those responsible at the palace claims that he originally asked for the GCVO, another honour which had the attraction of being solely in the monarch's gift but which was felt to be entirely inappropriate. He was hurriedly offered the Garter in case he next requested the Order of Merit, another distinction which did not seem entirely suitable. Whatever the background, he was content with his lot. His enthusiasm for his new role confirmed the suspicions of those purists who suspected that he had never been a socialist at heart. "Today is the day Sir Harold Wilson became a Knight of the Garter at Windsor Castle ... and made a final fool of himself in the presence of the Labour movement," wrote Benn[2] – a harsh judgment, since Attlee before Wilson and Callaghan after him were to accept the same distinction; Attlee with a hereditary earldom added for good measure. His coat of arms was a *pot-pourri* of the interests closest to his heart: the white rose of Yorkshire and the red of Lancashire; the Labour Party emblem of pen and spade; a Trinity House ship; the Bishop Rock Lighthouse to bring in the Isles of Scilly; and the arms of the Abbot of Rievaulx. The motto was peculiarly apposite for a man who throughout his career had gauged so exquisitely the niceties of timing: *Tempus Rerum Imperator* – Time the Ruler of Everything.

The fact that he was now Sir Harold Wilson KG did not in any way discourage those who believed that Harold Wilson KGB, tool of the Soviet secret service, would be a more appropriate appellation.

His resignation, and the failure of subsequent Prime Ministers to investigate with any sustained vigour the "dirty tricks" campaign which he felt had been waged against him, encouraged such suspicions. The resignation of Jeremy Thorpe in May 1976 reinforced Wilson's conviction that South African agents were active in Great Britain and that they had won a notable victory. A fresh public outburst against the machinations of BOSS rekindled the doubts of those who felt he might be preparing for similar trouble himself. "It makes you wonder whether he is the next one for some scandal of a financial kind, linked to the burglary of his papers," surmised Benn darkly. "Very strange, I must say."[1] To describe Wilson's behaviour at this time as paranoid would be too strong since it does now seem probable that there was a firm basis of justification for his belief that some sort of conspiracy had been hatched with a view to destroying his reputation and destabilising his government. His suspicions preyed so bodefully upon his mind, however, that his conduct was not always rational or prudent. In February 1976 he charged his surprised publisher, George Weidenfeld, with a mission to the former American Vice-President, Hubert Humphrey, asking him to establish whether certain people involved in the smear campaign had been working for the CIA. George Bush, the head of the CIA, offered what help he could, but little seems to have emerged from this unpromisingly oblique approach.[2] The most eccentric of his actions came on 12 May 1976, when he summoned a young journalist, Barrie Penrose, to his house in Lord North Street.[3] Penrose arrived with Roger Courtiour as partner, an addition to the party which Wilson accepted without demur. He announced that he wished them to investigate "the forces that are threatening democratic countries like Britain". Elements in MI5 had been spreading stories alleging that he was involved with the Communist Party and that the link was through his political secretary, Marcia Falkender. He recounted all the burglaries that had taken place in banks, solicitors' offices, the houses of secretaries and friends, even the contracts department of Yorkshire Television – each one explicable in isolation but taken together surely evidence of a systematic attempt to gather material for his discrediting? "I see myself as a big fat spider in the corner of the room," he told the startled journalists. "Sometimes I speak when I'm asleep. You should both listen. Occasionally when we meet I might tell you to go to the Charing Cross Road and kick a blind man standing on the corner. That blind man may tell you something, lead you somewhere."

Marcia Falkender supposes that this Buchanesque fantasy must have been intended as an obscure joke; a thesis which Wilson himself endorsed when he wrote to *The Times* to complain of cock and bull stories, written by journalists with limited experience and "little sense of humour".[1] So it probably was: but a man who could joke in such terms to such an audience must surely have himself been thoroughly disturbed. Presumably his hope was that, if Penrose and Courtiour stirred up enough of a fuss, it would be impossible for the government not to set up a Royal Commission to enquire into the reality of Wilson's suspicions.

A menagerie of right-wing figures added their mite to the brew which Wilson and his putative enemies had between themselves concocted. General Sir Walter Walker, founder of a short-lived citizens' army designed to confront the communist menace, told Penrose and Courtiour that "the former Prime Minister, Harold Wilson, was a proven Communist. There was a Communist cell right there in the middle of Downing Street ... He had seen filmed interviews with Harold Wilson on his return from official visits to the Soviet Union. The Labour Premier had been visibly shaking, and Sir Walter felt that was a clear indication that Harold Wilson had been compromised in some way by the KGB."[2] At a luncheon party in the country when Wilson was still Prime Minister Chapman Pincher talked of contacts in MI5 who shared Sir Walter's suspicions. Another guest was Martin Gilbert, the biographer of Churchill, who reported what he had heard to Wilson. Wilson, presumably confusing biographer with subject and grandfather with grandson, told Penrose that the Tory MP, Winston Churchill, had information on the subject. When taxed with this, Churchill denied any special knowledge but suggested that it probably arose from the fact that Wilson had visited the Soviet Union nineteen times. "That does provide the other side with certain opportunities. Have you been able to find out on how many occasions Mrs Williams accompanied him?" The answer, for what it was worth, would have been five.[3]

The celebrated interview between Cecil King and Mountbatten, in which King seemed to be hinting that Mountbatten should head a coup which would evict Wilson and establish a national government, soon figured in Wilson's dossier of horrors. Though it was Mountbatten who first told Wilson of this overture, and showed him the record of the conversation which he had agreed with King's deputy, Hugh

Cudlipp,[1] some hazy impression that the Chief of Defence Staff himself was involved seems to have lingered in Wilson's mind. Solly Zuckerman, who had also been present at the meeting, was accosted by Wilson at a party in Buckingham Palace. Wilson backed Zuckerman against a buffet table, "breathed whisky all over him", and filled him in on the story of the MI5 plot. He dragged in Mountbatten's name and obviously believed he was concerned.[2] What role Mountbatten might have played was left obscure; the trouble with conspiracy theories is that the edges are always blurred and expand continuously, beyond whatever nugget of fact there was at the beginning, to include anyone who might have had even the most tenuous connection with the affair.

No one can doubt that Wilson was distressed by what was going on or by what he thought was going on. He reacted with uncharacteristic capriciousness when the subject was mooted and showed exaggerated sensitivity to anything that he thought might feed the rumours directed against him. In August 1977 he cancelled at short notice a visit to Russia to which he had been looking forward. His main reason, he told the Russian Ambassador, was a report of the visit in the *Daily Telegraph*, headlined "in a very tendentious manner" and giving the impression that one particular firm was paying all his expenses with "more than a hint of corruption or private financial arrangements".[3] Two years before he would have scorned to rearrange his plans on such flimsy grounds. Two years later, too, he might have been more resilient. The obsession did not last. He never ceased to believe that MI5 had worked against him but came to see it in proportion, to accept how insignificant the conspirators had been and how little they had actually achieved. Some time later the lawyer David Hooper wanted to interview him about the plot for the purposes of a book he was writing. "Not aware and at no time was aware of any of those alleged facts," Wilson scribbled on Hooper's letter. "My general view on this rests on the well-known Yorkshire phrase – that there's not one lie in a hundred true."[4]

For a man whose life had not merely centred on but been absorbed by politics for more than thirty years, it is remarkable how far Wilson disappeared from the political scene after his resignation. No one of his stature could wholly vanish. He played a small role in party gatherings, spoke occasionally in the House of Commons, electioneered dutifully in 1979 when the Callaghan government went down to defeat, but his heart was not in it, nor did he pretend it was. He was resolved not to play the part of a back-seat driver, nor would his successor have taken kindly to his doing so. For the first few months Callaghan was punctilious in ringing up the former Prime Minister from time to time to ask how he would have handled any particular problem, but Wilson never deluded himself that his reply was listened to with great deference and little by little the habit died. Every ex-Prime Minister slips into a trough of neglect shortly after he leaves Number 10, reappearing with luck, with reputation refurbished, in a decade or two. Wilson's fall from the public eye was particularly rapid. Partly this was because he chose to concern himself with other matters, partly because the affair of the resignation honours and the wisps of scandal that hung about him diminished the readiness of the younger Labour members to treat him as a revered elder statesman. "I saw Harold wandering around the House and he has absolutely shrunk," commented Benn in April 1976; "it shows that office is something that builds up a man only if he is somebody in his own right. And Wilson isn't."[1] Except for a few old friends and loyalists the party as a whole agreed that Wilson wasn't. He became not a non-person but a person who was half forgotten and largely ignored. In the course of the 1979 election he told a BBC team that was accompanying him that he did not intend to stand again; after Labour's defeat, with the party moving ever further to the left, he wondered whether he would not have done better to call it a day already.[2] With the party in the hands of Michael Foot, his relationship with the leadership became still more remote.

Even before the "winter of discontent" and Callaghan's defeat, Wilson was disenchanted with the performance of the Labour Party. When he visited Roy Jenkins in Brussels in April 1978 he urged the recently appointed President of the European Commission not to lose touch with British politics. "The whole outlook was very bad," he said. "He was filled with dismay. He did not think there was much future for the Government, or indeed the Labour Party. A coalition government would almost certainly be necessary; he would bless it from outside, but not serve."[3] If a coalition *had* been formed and he had been called from retirement to lead it, it is hard to believe he could have refused; service on any other terms he would indeed have resisted. His political life was over and he felt only an occasional tremor of regret. His last years in the House of Commons were clouded by illness but even if they had not been he would have played only the most inconspicuous role.

He was far from under-employed. A few months after his resignation Callaghan asked him to chair a committee to enquire into the workings of financial institutions in the UK, with a wide-ranging remit which allowed him to envisage radical reforms and even the nationalisation of the banks. Wilson had started his public life with a deep distrust for the City establishment. This had been fortified by his battles with Lord Cromer and his conviction that the international bankers had engineered the various sterling crises which had plagued his governments. Gradually, however, he had moved to a more moderate position in which he recognised that the system had its merits. Some of his best friends were bankers. By the time of his retirement he felt that there was more that deserved to be preserved than to be destroyed in the present system. He was delighted to hear that the enquiry was under way, wrote the historian, John Plumb: "800 years of a coral-reef-like growth of privilege and charity which lies behind the City companies will, I suspect, contain some marvellous anomalies and oddities."[1] Eight-hundred-year-old City companies were not as good as the Garter, but they still possessed an appeal which Wilson was romantic enough to respond to and shrewd enough to see held an incalculable but still substantial economic value. Wilson accepted Callaghan's invitation with alacrity and enjoyed the work as much as anything he had done in his life. He had a civil service office with three private secretaries, was fêted endlessly by City magnates, revelled in the statistics, was amused by the personalities and by the oddities which Plumb had predicted he would find, enjoyed particularly the fact that his work was not of the kind that called for instant decisions and that hideous crises were not imminently threatening.

The committee was powerful if cumbersome: four trade unionists; Ralf Dahrendorf, the Director of the London School of Economics; Andrew Graham, Wilson's former policy adviser, and two other academics; Hugh Stephenson from *The Times*; and a selection of City and business dignitaries. The full committee met fifty-five times over a period of almost three years; for Wilson there were, of course, many smaller, peripheral meetings as well and a daunting inflow of paper. In the first year, Wilson revealed in a lecture in the City, the pile of evidence was six feet six inches high, in the second rather more. "I do not have time to read it during the week, but I spend a lot of the weekend reading it, and I have got into the habit, once I have read it, of putting it on the household scales, and it averages something between seven and eight pounds a week."[1] To do the job of chairman conscientiously – and though Wilson was criticised by some for failing to give the committee a lead or push forward its deliberations, no one doubted that he did his homework – would take up any spare time that might be left to him by his other activities.

It was evident from the start that Wilson did not view the committee as being likely to promote radical reform. He stated candidly that that part of the directive which encouraged them to consider what changes were required and to recommend on a possible extension of the public sector was low on the agenda.[2] He did not feel that any serious reconstruction of the City was called for and considered anyway that whatever reforms might be desirable would best be worked out and regulated by the City itself. Priority was given to the question of whether the City was providing the funds that were needed for industrial development; if not why not, were the funds there but misapplied or was a new source of funding needed? The central thrust of the evidence from the Labour Party and the trade unions suggested that the capitalist system was falling down on its task, the banks were not providing the funds to finance economic expansion and had diverted to overseas investment money which could have been better – if not more profitably – spent at home. The banks took the challenge seriously; though, as Keith Middlemas has remarked: "It is fair to conclude that more enthusiasm went into rebutting criticism and in preparing for the Wilson enquiry than into making changes."[3] In the main they found the chairman of the committee to be satisfied with their approach. Wilson considered that the most important task for his committee to undertake was to point the way forward into a world in which the giant pension funds were providing more and more of the money available for investment and thus becoming one of the most significant pieces on the City chessboard. To chart that progress and to point out ways in which it might be modified was the height of his ambitions. Beyond that, his wish above all was to arrive at a consensus and to avoid the kind of dissension that would have followed any attempt to press forward with precise or even general recommendations for reform. These somewhat limited ambitions he achieved most satisfactorily. Nigel Lawson, Tory Financial Secretary at the Treasury by the time the report appeared, described it as "a classic text-book, which will be read for generations to come".[1] Its conclusions, Eric Roll observed, were "broadly conservative ... as far as any possible major changes in the structure of the City were concerned, but, in the process, [it] produced a series of valuable reports, which at the very least form an excellent reference library for students of the subject".[2] It was not what Benn or Foot had hoped for, but if Callaghan or Healey had wanted a bloody revolution in the City they would hardly have put Wilson in charge of the guillotine.

Wilson's work on the City of London enquiry and his writing and lecturing provided a full enough load to fill his time. His main cultural preoccupations were to match his history of the 1964–70 government with a companion volume to cover 1974 to 1976 and to present the films and write the accompanying book for the Yorkshire Television series on the Prime Ministers. Before either of these appeared, however, he had written and published a short study of the office of Prime Minister and its role in Whitehall. *The Governance of Britain*, in his own words, was "an analysis ... as seen by a prime minister of the mainspring of British government, the Cabinet, Cabinet government and the Cabinet Office".[3] "Governance" is a convenient, if slightly pretentious word which can mean either the state of being governed or the state of government. Wilson's subject was the latter. His object, in so far as he had a message to put over, was to stress that the Prime Minister was very much *primus inter pares* and did not possess any of the quasi-dictatorial powers which even commentators as close to the real thing as Richard Crossman had ascribed to the office.

In his preface Wilson proudly stated that not a word of the book had been written before 7 April 1976, two days after he left office: "No prime minister in the 1970s would have the time either to do that or to keep a diary."[4] Given that the book appeared in October of the same year, it was a remarkable achievement both by the author and the publisher. What is perhaps still more remarkable given the haste is that it is both sensible and instructive. William Rodgers called it "a thoughtful and convincing story of how it all happens" and "a valuable contribution to an understanding of the British political system", though he qualified his praise with mild regret that "its high purpose is sometimes vitiated by the intrusion of the politician who wants to leave on record the story of his own success".[5] The author certainly does make frequent appearances in the narrative but Wilson tells the story of his own failures as well as his successes, and though the latter feature more frequently the book as a whole is less vain-glorious than his histories of his administrations. The tone is through-out good-tempered and balanced: "An informal, anecdotal book," Edward Boyle called it, "halfway between a volume of memoirs and a serious treatise."[1]

While Wilson was producing the 80,000 or so words of *The Governance of Britain* he was simultaneously hard at work on *The Prime Ministers* and, in the final stages, on the City of London Enquiry. The filming of *The Prime Ministers* and the demands of the enquiry in particular caused problems, since both involved com-plicated schedules and the participation of many other people. York-shire Television took it for granted that they had a prior claim on Wilson's services and were inclined to be affronted when he was otherwise engaged. Marcia Falkender tried to juggle with the various calls on his time. "As we are not with him when he attends the City meetings it is very difficult to stop him booking things at the time," she explained, "and once everyone round the table has agreed a date between them – which is difficult for them anyway – it is impossible really to alter it."[2] When Wilson did get to the filming sessions he enjoyed them greatly: the subject interested him, he felt that he was good at expounding it, and to be taking part in show business rather than admiring it from the periphery gave him endless satisfaction. In idle moments he would chat with the freelance writer and producer Antony Jay about the oddities of life in Downing Street, conversations which were to bear noble fruit some years later when Jay's scripts for the *Yes, Minister* and *Yes, Prime Minister* series defined for a generation the public's perception of life in the higher reaches of Whitehall.

Inevitably there were problems. Having secured the services of an ex-Prime Minister to present their programmes, Yorkshire Television were anxious to exploit him to the uttermost and to feature his personality and experiences with the same prominence as those of his subjects. Wilson had no wish to remain coyly unobtrusive but was shrewd enough to realise that his critics would be quick to condemn any injudicious hogging of the limelight. For the programme on Churchill, the company asked for a photograph of Wilson while he was in the Prime Minister's wartime secretariat. "I don't know of one," Wilson minuted, "and I don't believe if I had it would improve the programme (especially re: crits that all my chapters are about me)."[1] The problem of whom to invite to the preview party was as perplexing as any. It was suggested that Macmillan would make an appropriate guest of honour. "Just doubtful about Harold Macmillan – tho he probably wdn't come," wrote Wilson. "Suppose he disliked Suez and walked out? He might fall asleep – it's a long programme. Why not Maurice [Macmillan] or Julian Amery?" On the list of potential guests he wrote opposite the name of Lady Gaitskell: "Not against, but might be painful for her." He had few comments on the press list. Against the gossip columnist Nigel Dempster, he wrote, "? but prob yes", and against Richard Ingrams, the editor of *Private Eye*, "I'd say yes, I think"; hardly an enthusiastic welcome but still showing a degree of tolerance.[2]

At last the series began to be shown – the first in November 1977. Tony Benn was among those who saw it. "I watched the first programme of Harold Wilson and David Frost, a couple of real old phonies* ... and it was Wilson on Macmillan. It was so insubstantial, just sort of vague memories and gossip ... I was quite interested because, after all, he has been Prime Minister and seen it from the inside but what you get from watching it is Harold's concept of himself. At the very end, he said that Macmillan had once offered to come back into a national government. I only hope for the sake of the nation *he* never is."[3]

The programmes, and even more the related book,[4] are indeed remarkable for the way they illustrate Wilson's concept of himself.† His work was strikingly free of political dogmatism or even evidence of any strong convictions. Kenneth Morgan found the book "confusing", since "some of his warmest praise goes to Tories, including Pitt, Disraeli, and especially Churchill, with some unexpected nostalgia for the foreign policy of Palmerston".[5] In a letter to an enquirer, Wilson revealed that his greatest heroes from history would be the inventors George and Robert Stephenson, and among politicians Pitt the younger, Peel, Palmerston and Asquith.[6] It is pardonable to feel confused by a pantheon so singularly lacking in any sort of radical afflatus, but students of Wilson would be surprised only by the omission of Baden-Powell. Even in his – very mildly – left-wing youth Wilson never believed that his faction possessed a monopoly of the virtues. By 1977 his dislike of the far left was as strong as that for

---

* A bit hard on Frost, who was thirty-eight at the time.
† See p 163 above.

the most conservative of capitalists and it sometimes seemed that only habit kept him moving through the right lobby in the House of Commons. It is not surprising that the two professional historians who contributed most to his book on the Prime Ministers were Robert Blake and John Plumb, neither of whom is notorious for his left-wing views.

Final Term, his account of the Labour government of 1974–6, appeared in 1979. His book on the 1964–70 government had proved a bad investment from the point of view of the publisher and had done little to stimulate sales of the newspaper which published it. The failure was reflected in the advances offered for this new volume. Denis Hamilton of Times Newspapers offered £30,000 for all rights; reasonably generous by the standards of the day but, allowing for inflation, less than a tenth of what he had paid for the earlier book. The first figure had included an element for the sale of papers, so it is hard to establish a precise relationship between the two, but at least it is clear that Wilson's work was valued far less highly than had been the case a few years before. Wilson's literary agent was dismayed. At one point there had been talk of an advance of £100,000; "quite frankly, I do not consider £30,000 to be adequate for all rights in *Final Term*."[1] There was nothing to be done about it, however; the contractual terms were marginally improved but the essentials of the deal remained the same.

For Wilson the price paid was less important than the fact that he was getting his side of the story on the record; like Churchill he believed that the best way to ensure that history did one justice was to write the history oneself. It cannot be said that he brought to the task a tithe of Churchill's skill or *brio*. *Final Term* is as dull and self-justificatory a book as its predecessor without even the day-by-day breathlessness which gave the former its curious compulsion (and, incidentally, its value to the biographer). It sought to be more impressionistic and succeeded only in being more muddled. Certainly it did not contribute to Wilson's reputation as Prime Minister, probably it diminished it. By the time it was published in 1979 he was anyway already far down into the pit of oblivion. Only time could rescue him; ten *Final Terms* would have made little difference.

He worked on one more book before his illness of 1980 and it meant more to him than any of the others. When he resigned he told Callaghan that he would back the government on every issue but that he would watch its Middle East policy carefully in case it did something that might damage Israel.[1] His devotion to that country did not wane in the years that followed; he had visited it once as Prime Minister, now did so again, and was fêted as a loyal and honoured friend. When Roy Jenkins delivered the Israel Sieff Memorial Lecture in November 1977, he was surprised to find Wilson "huddled in the corner of a row, listening, applauding at the end".[2] Wilson's attendance was not intended as a compliment to Jenkins; he was likely to be present at any occasion which the most eminent of the British friends of Israel might be expected to support. With a £5,000 grant from the Hanson Foundation to help with the research, he embarked on a history and critical examination of the state of Israel. *The Chariot of Israel* was in some ways his best book, certainly the one least affected by the urge to prove himself right. He quoted Blanche Dugdale as saying that Balfour's interest in the Jews "originated in the Old Testament training of his mother, and in his Scottish upbringing".[3] Substitute Yorkshire for Scottish and add the appeal which the prosaic character so often finds in the alien and exotic, and the words could have applied to himself. Balfour was one of the heroes of *The Chariot of Israel*, Bevin the villain. The Labour Foreign Secretary had betrayed the legacy of his Tory predecessor and repeated undertakings by his own party: "Commitments entered into by Lloyd George, Baldwin, Churchill and a generation of Labour Leaders up to 1945 played no part in his policy, except as tiresome undertakings to be got round or, if he was provoked, challenged head on."[4] Under Wilson's leadership, he felt the party had done something to expiate Bevin's sins; there would be no back-sliding so long as he was in a position to prevent it.

XXV

Old Age

1980–1993

In 1980 Harold Wilson became an old man. In the early summer of that year cancer of the bowel was diagnosed and he was taken into St Mark's Hospital in City Road for its removal. The operation lasted four and a half hours; it was successful, but had to be followed five weeks later by another major operation with a third operation later in the year. Even when he was admitted the anaesthetist thought him slow and unresponsive; as a joking tribute the matron had put him into Room Number 10, but he never mentioned it to her (he was treated under the National Health Scheme but given a separate room). His long-term memory remained excellent but he could not remember what he had had for breakfast on the same day.[1] Between the operations and for a few months afterwards he was weak and lethargic, he looked frail and haggard and took more than a year to recover his weight. By the end of November Marcia Falkender was writing that he was feeling a great deal better but "has been ordered by his doctors to take things very easily for a very long time".[2] He was to take things easily for the rest of his life. Elizabeth Longford spent an hour with him in February 1987 and found that he "looked tired but not at all ill; he felt much better since his three operations". Her husband sat next to Wilson at a PLP meeting and found that he had "gained in charm. He was always full of fun and benevolence, but there was too much bombast, which seems to have melted away in suffering."[3]

The meeting must have been one of some significance, since from 1980 Wilson's attendance at any sort of political occasion became increasingly erratic. He confined his interventions in the House of Commons almost entirely to subjects of special interest to him; his last speech, in a debate on higher education, dealt with Bradford

University, of which he had become Chancellor in 1966.[1] When Callaghan resigned as leader in 1980 Wilson rather eccentrically voted for Healey as successor in the first ballot and for Michael Foot in the second: "I suppose this was an existentialist *acte gratuite* – he did not explain," commented Healey drily.[2] By the time Kinnock in his turn replaced Foot, Wilson had left the scene. He had always said that he did not propose to fight another election after Labour's defeat in 1979; he asked his last question in the House of Commons on 4 March 1982 and retired at the general election in June 1983.

That same year he entered the House of Lords. Not everyone was gratified by this transmogrification. Christine Evans of the Yatton and District Labour Party wrote to tell him that his defection had been discussed at a recent meeting of the branch. "In view of your record of dealing with the Lords whilst PM, it was pointed out that you had probably accepted this title to destroy the House of Lords from within. To put members at ease, could you confirm if this is so, and (without giving away any secrets) outline your strategy for such action?" The letter was addressed to Lord Wilson of Huyton. "Ignore," Wilson scribbled. "Hasn't even got name right. 2nd para is such rubbish."[3] The correct title would have been Wilson of Rievaulx, harking back to his Yorkshire ancestry. The choice got him into trouble when in a radio interview with Libby Purves he followed her example in pronouncing the name "Reevo" rather than the more traditional "Rivers". Wilson explained that he had not wished to embarrass his interlocutor by correcting her publicly – he always called it "Rivers" himself.[4]

He took his seat in the Lords in September, sponsored by his two fellow socialist Knights of the Garter, the Lords Longford and Shackleton. It was not till March of the following year that he made his maiden speech – on higher education – and pointed out with some satisfaction that he was in the unusual position of having made two maiden speeches in the same chamber; in 1945 the House of Commons had temporarily taken over the Lords, while their own home was being rebuilt.[5] It cannot be claimed that this was the first of a series of distinguished interventions. Wilson spoke rarely in the House of Lords; in May 1984 he opened and closed a debate on unemployment[6] but a long silence followed and when he resumed speaking it was on matters of trivial import and his contribution was slight and sometimes embarrassingly anecdotal. He continued to attend the House but his appearances became increasingly fitful, escorted always by such stalwart old friends as Marcia Falkender, Peter Lovell-Davis or an avuncular James Callaghan.

In old age his naturally conservative characteristics asserted themselves, sometimes with disconcerting vehemence. In principle he remained faithful to the party, explaining in 1981 that the only reason he did not immediately announce his intention of leaving the House of Commons at the next election was lest people should assume that his action implied "support for Shirley Williams and Co. who ... I do not go along with at all".[1] But though he could never have brought himself formally to defect from Labour, he shared many of the doubts of those who did. In May 1983, in an interview with the *Daily Mail*, he disconcerted his former colleagues by announcing that he saw little hope for their party in the forthcoming election. The traditional Labour voters were in a state of "so much confusion, so much disillusion", that they might well decide to stay at home on polling day. He was worried about Trotskyite infiltration of the Labour Party and Michael Foot's inability or unwillingness to do anything about it. The last straw had been when Foot had appeared on platforms with Militant candidates: "I would not have anything to do with them. I would sling them out on their necks. Their only aim is to wreck the country." Foot's great mistake – and Callaghan's before him – had been to put the party in commission to the unions: "On the whole people don't think much of politicians, but when it comes to leadership they want to know who he or she is."[2]

When this outburst was followed by Tory victory at the election, some suggested that Wilson had been in part responsible. He was unrepentant; if the party could not put itself in order then it did not deserve to win. He greeted the advent of Neil Kinnock with cautious optimism. When, early in 1984, he was rebuked for criticising the leadership, he replied: "I thought that I had in fact said things about Neil which were constructive and complimentary. Indeed, I think he is doing very well, and will grow in the job."[3] Kinnock did not respond in kind, ignoring his former leader with a thoroughness that smacked more of deliberate policy than careless discourtesy. Wilson was hurt and affronted; he knew that he was incapable of playing any significant role in public life but the modicum of flattering attention which is normally bestowed on ex-Prime Ministers would have been enough to satisfy him that the party still held him in esteem. Kinnock did not hold him in esteem and saw no reason to pretend otherwise. To be fair, Wilson had now moved so far to the right in his predilections that anything which drew attention to his existence was liable to cause embarrassment to the party. In mid 1984 he urged Mrs Thatcher to bestow the Order of Merit on Arthur Bryant, describing this eminently unprogressive figure as "a great patriot" and "our greatest historian". Mrs Thatcher replied that she quite agreed, but reminded Wilson that the OM was not given on ministerial advice.[1] In 1987, when the time came to elect a successor to Harold Macmillan as Chancellor of Oxford, an admirer urged Wilson to stand. "I'm not proposing to run," Wilson minuted, "even though I should be the only candidate who was an Oxford don. I would have to spend too much time at meetings, preparing speeches etc. and having to go to dinner at almost all the other colleges. My vote would go to Lord Blake."[2] These comments are curious on two counts; that he denied the status of Oxford don to Robert Blake, former Provost of Queen's, and that he supported the most orthodoxly right-wing of the three candidates. No one would have expected him to vote for Heath but most voters of even moderately left-wing persuasion rallied around the nearest thing to a socialist, the eventual victor, Roy Jenkins.

He made periodic, increasingly fitful, efforts to assert himself and show that he could still play a useful role. Early in 1984 Lord Kissin asked him to make certain representations on his company's behalf on his next visit to Russia. "It would be extremely difficult for me to act in this way, as a former Prime Minister who has had considerable negotiations and contacts with the Soviet Union over very many years," Wilson replied. "I would feel only able to do this if I were acting in an official capacity on behalf of the Company and could so describe myself to the authorities there. I wonder, therefore, whether I can ask you to consider whether or not it might be helpful to you and to your Companies, if I were appointed in some official capacity to your Board so that I might then describe myself in that way when I am in Moscow?"[3] Wilson seems to have thought better of this overture; the draft was never sent and the problem was resolved without Wilson taking on any official link with Kissin's company. Until he left the House of Commons he continued to perform all the duties of a conscientious constituency MP, though he increasingly delegated the leg-work to those more capable of undertaking it. Towards the end of 1982 he took two delegations to call on Keith Joseph, then Secretary of State for Education and Science. He was so impressed by their reception that he wrote to Mrs Thatcher to tell her that, though the delegations had been long-winded and diffuse, Joseph had "listened very patiently and his interventions were right on the ball".[1] It was a generous gesture to a political opponent and one which not many people in his position would have bothered to make.

But with the House of Commons behind him he slipped swiftly from active life. In the years immediately following his resignation as Prime Minister he had done a fair amount of speaking and lecturing, both around the British Isles and in the United States. From 1979 he let himself be handled by a professional organisation and developed what had been little more than a hobby into a useful source of income. But his performances became less proficient; the strain of travel, particularly abroad, began to put an unacceptable burden upon him. He was made to feel foolish on a tour of the United States when his schedule was suddenly altered to include a call on the former President, Jimmy Carter. Wilson became muddled and managed to give the impression that he did not know who Carter was or why he was visiting him. He found it more difficult to adapt to the change in time and would wake in the middle of the night, get up and expect his breakfast to be ready and the car waiting for him. The lecture tours of the United States were abandoned and gradually his speaking engagements at home were also whittled down.

His last book, *Memoirs 1916–64: The Making of a Prime Minister*, was published in 1986, but it was largely a compilation of Brian Connell's with the titular author contributing little beyond a string of anecdotes. It was an amiable and sometimes colourful autobiography, which gave a generally fair if rosy picture of his development, but it added little to the books and articles that had already been produced about him. By the time it appeared his capacity for concentration was limited. He felt himself increasingly out of touch and remote from reality. In April 1988 he was asked to contribute to a programme about the Labour MP, Bessie Braddock. "No, very long ago," he scrawled on the letter.[2] For Wilson in 1988 it seemed that almost everything was very long ago.

In 1991 he was back in hospital again for a hernia operation. He was in a curtained-off section at the end of a public ward, sharing a lavatory with twelve others. "I don't really think I should be here," he said once in a puzzled way. But the nurses appreciated and cosseted him, James Callaghan telephoned to enquire after him, a goodwill message came from the office of the leader of the Labour Party, though only after some prompting from Marcia Falkender. Wilson would hardly have noticed. They were difficult years for Mary Wilson. Having suffered for eight years as the wife of the Prime Minister she now found herself almost entirely preoccupied by his physical welfare. Her greatest relief came when they could retreat to the Isles of Scilly, where everybody knew them and they were taken for granted. But he felt uneasy if cut off from the House of Lords and what he still conceived to be his duties. Patiently he soldiered on through the twilight years, not discontented, happy in his family and his day-to-day pursuits, but ever more remote from the world outside his doors. It was an ironic ending for the man who had once been so much at the centre of affairs, and had made his reputation above all by his quick wits and his prodigious memory.

Those who condemn Wilson most rigorously do so usually on grounds of what he was not, rather than what he was. They judge him by standards which he himself would have deemed irrelevant to a man in his position. The world of politics would be a meaner place if it contained no men or women of passionate principle, no Savonarola intent on castigating the sins of his generation or Shaftesbury resolved to reshape the structure of society; even no Gaitskell or no Thatcher, believing so strongly that they were right that they could stomach compromise only with repugnance. But if politics are to work, if a country is to run efficiently and without constant turmoil, then a *dramatis personae* composed entirely of such zealots would be impossible to accommodate. There is not merely room for, there is a need for the compromiser, the trimmer, the politician who puts first the business of keeping government on the road and views principles with the beady eye of a pragmatist who decides what must be done and only then considers whether it can be modified to serve some long-term end.

Wilson was such a man. This is not to say that he was unprincipled. He believed strongly in social justice. He was resolved that the lot of the poor and under-privileged should be improved; that education and technical training should increase the chances of all citizens to realise their full potential; that the barriers of class should be whittled down and the right of the employer to ride rough-shod over the employed should be curbed and regulated. He was convinced that movement in this direction was more likely under a Labour than a

Conservative government, and that his first duty was therefore to keep Labour in power. If Labour split over some ideological difference, then the Tories would gain or retain power and nothing would be achieved. There *might* be issues of such significance that this result had to be accepted – the reform of the trade unions at one moment seemed to him almost to qualify – but on the whole he doubted whether political suicide could ever be a proper course for the leaders of a great party. So far as nationalisation, Europe or almost any other issue were concerned, the prime consideration was to evolve a policy which would accommodate all but the most irreconcilable of partisans, and so far to blur the controversial points that confrontations could be avoided. As a style of government it lacked either glamour or nobility. In the long term it could sometimes lead to disaster, when unresolved problems festered unseen and then erupted in a form exacerbated by neglect. In the short term it usually worked. A succession of Wilsons as leader would doom any nation to decline; a Wilson from time to time to let the dust settle while the demolition squads of the radicals gather strength for their next enterprise can be positively beneficial.

If a biographer may be forgiven a personal avowal as a brief coda to his narrative, I would say that in Wilson the Prime Minister I found few surprises. I expected him to be more or less as he was, and it was his consistency, his predictability, that were most striking. What *did* impress me far more than I had expected was his extraordinary niceness. All those who worked for him – the civil servants, the secretaries, the chauffeurs, the detectives – are united in praise of his generosity, consideration, lack of pretension, genuine concern for their welfare. He liked people, and wanted them to like him; great men, perhaps, should be indifferent to such considerations, but Wilson laid little claim to grandeur and the weakness, if it were such, was certainly an amiable one.

He treated everyone as they came, would pay more attention to the humblest official who knew his job than to a Cabinet colleague who was badly briefed. He was "the easiest man in the world to work for and with", said George Wigg; always "most agreeable and courteous", Macmillan told Nigel Fisher; "a man of outstanding kindness, charm and generosity", wrote Nabarro; always "understanding and sympathetic", commented Frank Longford. "Almost without exception, staff and civil servants who worked with him spoke of his personal kindness."[1] He was "the nicest Prime Minister we have had since Baldwin", concluded Patrick Cosgrave.[2] One could find many more such judgments. It can fairly be said that Wilson was remote, that he did not pursue friendship beyond the point of superficial affection, that he would rarely if ever have sacrificed an important interest to serve someone to whom he was attached. Attachment, indeed, except to the innermost of his family and entourage, was not a concept that meant much to him. But to be incapable of grand passion or blind loyalty is not to be inhuman. Wilson was cool, certainly, but never cold; his feeling for humanity was generalised but real; he could be a good friend and rarely felt the urge to be an unforgiving enemy.

The comparison with Baldwin – widely different though the two men were in many ways – is one which again and again occurs irresistibly. Speaking of Baldwin after his death, G. M. Trevelyan said that he was "an Englishman indeed; in whom was much guile, never used for low or selfish purposes. In a world of voluble hates, he plotted to make men like, or at least tolerate one another. Therein he had much success, within the shores of this island. He remains the most human and lovable of all the Prime Ministers." A touch of hyperbole can be forgiven the obituarist. Whatever may be true of Baldwin, Wilson certainly from time to time used his guile for purposes which, if not low, were far from lofty. "Likable" would perhaps be a better word than "lovable". But the essence is the same. "Thy Godlike crime was to be kind," wrote Byron of Prometheus,

> To render with thy precepts less,
> The sum of human wretchedness.

There was nothing Titanesque or godlike about Harold Wilson, but it can fairly be said of him that he strove to render less the sum of human wretchedness. He did not always succeed, sometimes he did not seem even to push his efforts to the uttermost, but it was a worthy and consistent goal. For holding to it he can be counted as being on the side of the angels, if never quite a champion in the angelic host.

Notes

Chapter I: The Child and the Boy, 1916–1934

1[1] I am indebted to Mr Ian Anstruther for giving me the benefit of his research into the Wilson family. *See also* Gerard Noel, *Harold Wilson and the "New Britain"*, London, 1964, pp 15–18; and the essay on Harold Wilson's ancestry by C. R. Humphrey-Smith and M. G. Heenan in *Family History* (Institute of Heraldic and Genealogical Studies), vol 3, no 17/18, pp 135–55.

2[1] Harold Wilson, *Memoirs 1916–1964. The Making of a Prime Minister*, London, 1986, p 11.

2[2] Noel, *Wilson*, p 18.

2[3] Leslie Smith, *Harold Wilson. The Authentic Portrait*, London, 1964, p 16.

2[4] Wilson papers, box 2.

3[1] Godfrey Smith, "Notes for a Profile of a Politician", *Sunday Times Colour Magazine*, 9 Feb 1964.

3[2] Wilson papers, box 157.

4[1] Interview with Marjorie Wilson.

4[2] Wilson papers, box 2, Herbert to Harold Wilson, 1 March 1967.

4[3] Taken from Martin Gilbert's forthcoming but (in 1992) unpublished book "In Search of Churchill".

4[4] Interview with Lady Falkender.

5[1] Wilson papers, box 36.

5[2] Wilson, *Memoirs*, p 13.

6[1] Wilson papers, box 157.

6[2] Richard Crossman, *The Diaries of a Cabinet Minister*, vol 2, London, 1976, p 782.

6[3] Kenneth Harris, *Conversations*, London, 1987, p 268.

6[4] *cit.* Leslie Smith, *Wilson*, p 33.

7[1] Harris, *Conversations*, p 267.

7[2] Wilson papers, box 142, Wilson to Gilbert England, 20 Jan 1976.

7[3] Wilson, *Memoirs*, p 9.

7⁴ Interview with Marjorie Wilson; Harold Wilson interview, *Evening Standard*, 12 Sept 1972.

7⁵ *Guardian*, 24 June 1977.

8¹ Harold Wilson, *A Prime Minister on Prime Ministers*, London, 1977, p 127.

8² Noel, *Wilson*, p 18.

9¹ Wilson papers, box 157.

9² Lady Wilson papers, editor of *Meccano Magazine* to Wilson, 17 March, 13 Oct and 29 Nov 1928; and of the *Scout*, 26 June 1928 and 8 Jan 1929.

9³ Wilson, *Memoirs*, p 21.

10¹ Wilson papers, box 4, notes for interview with *Sunday Dispatch*.

10² *Yorkshire Evening Post*, 14 Feb 1963, cit. Andrew Roth, *Sir Harold Wilson. Yorkshire Walter Mitty*, London, 1977, p 57.

10³ cit. Leslie Smith, *Wilson*, p 46.

11¹ George Brown papers, 130. 15, 18 Dec 1963.

11² Roth, *Wilson*, p 58.

12¹ Leslie Smith, *Wilson*, pp 53–5.

12² Wilson, *Memoirs*, p 25.

12³ Noel, *Wilson*, p 28.

12⁴ Leslie Smith, *Wilson*, p 62.

13¹ Dudley Smith, *Harold Wilson. A Critical Biography*, London, 1964, p 21.

13² Interview with Marjorie Wilson.

Chapter II: Oxford, 1934–1939

14¹ Lady Wilson papers, Wilson to family, 13 and 28 Oct 1934.

15¹ Lady Wilson papers, Wilson to family, 13 Oct 1934.

15² Lady Wilson papers, Wilson to family, 2 Dec 1934.

16¹ Interview with Lord Glendevon.

16² Wilson papers, box 157; Lady Wilson papers, Wilson to family, 16 Feb and 20 Oct 1935.

16³ Lady Wilson papers, Wilson to family, 2 June and 10 Nov 1935.

16⁴ Wilson, *Memoirs*, p 38.

16⁵ A. H. Atkins, "Wilson – the Undergraduate I Remember", *Contemporary Review*, Dec 1964, pp 645–7.

16⁶ Lady Wilson papers, Wilson to family, 28 Oct 1934.

16⁷ e.g. Leslie Smith, *Wilson*, p 73.

17¹ Lady Wilson papers, Wilson to Marjorie Wilson, 17 Oct 1934.

17² Wilson papers, box 1, Wilson to G. V. Harries, 5 March 1970.

17³ Lady Wilson papers, Wilson to Marjorie Wilson, 17 Oct 1934.

17⁴ Lady Wilson papers, Wilson to family, 31 Oct 1934.

17⁵ Wilson papers, box 175, Bernard Miles to Wilson, June 1987.

18¹ Lady Wilson papers, Wilson to family, 13 Oct 1934.

18² Lady Wilson papers, Wilson to family, 31 Oct 1934.

18³ Wilson, *Memoirs*, p 35.
18⁴ Lady Wilson papers, Wilson to family, 20 Jan 1935.
18⁵ Paul Foot, *The Politics of Harold Wilson*, London, 1968, p 33.
18⁶ Wilson, *Memoirs*, p 35.
18⁷ Paul Foot, *Wilson*, p. 30.
19¹ Lady Wilson papers, Wilson to family, 3 March 1935.
19² Lady Wilson papers, Wilson to family, 17 Nov 1935.
19³ Lady Wilson papers, Wilson to family, 3 Feb 1935.
19⁴ Lady Wilson papers, Wilson to family, 8 March 1936.
20¹ Lady Wilson papers, Wilson to family, 28 Oct 1934.
20² Lady Wilson papers, Wilson to family, 3 March and 28 April 1935.
20³ Lady Wilson papers, Wilson to family, 13 Oct 1934.
20⁴ Lady Wilson papers, Wilson to family, 30 Jan 1936.
20⁵ Lady Wilson papers, Wilson to family, 19 and 25 May 1935.
21¹ Wilson, *Memoirs*, p 36.
21² Christopher Mayhew, *Time to Explain*, London, 1987, p 27.
21³ Lady Wilson papers, Wilson to family, 8 March 1936.
21⁴ Wilson papers, box 187.
22¹ Austen Morgan, *Harold Wilson*, London, 1992, pp 28-9.
22² Wilson, *Memoirs*, p 29.
23¹ Robert Lusty, *Bound to be Read*, London, 1975, p 285.
24¹ Lady Wilson papers, Wilson to family, 28 Oct 1934 and 16 Feb 1935.
24² *Observer*, 17 Jan 1965.
24³ Leslie Smith, *Wilson*, p 74.
24⁴ Lady Wilson papers, Wilson to family, 4 Feb 1936.
25¹ Letter from Professor Arthur Brown, 28 Aug 1991.
25² A. H. Atkins, "Wilson – the Undergraduate I Remember".
25³ Beveridge papers, V 50, Beveridge to Fosdick, 11 Nov 1937.
25⁴ Wilson, *Memoirs*, p 51.
26¹ Beveridge papers, V 52 (part 2), memorandum of 7 Feb 1940.
26² Beveridge Memorial Lecture delivered to the Institute of Statisticians, 18 Nov 1966.
27¹ Beveridge papers, V 52, 25 Nov 1938.
27² William Beveridge, *Power and Influence*, London, 1953, p 253.
27³ Wilson papers, box 4, article by Hunter Davies.
27⁴ Wilson, *Memoirs*, p 51.
28¹ Wilson, *Memoirs*, p 52.
28² Beveridge papers, V 52 (part 1), Wilson to Beveridge, 13 Dec 1939.
29¹ Wilson papers, box 4, article by Hunter Davies.

Chapter III: The Civil Service, 1940–1945

30¹ Leslie Smith, *Wilson*, p 84.
30² Beveridge papers, draft of chapter 13 of autobiography, VIII, 8.
30³ Wilson, *Memoirs*, p 59.

30⁴ A. Cairncross and N. Watt, *The Economic Section 1939–1961*, London, 1989, pp 14–25.
31¹ Douglas Jay, *Change and Fortune*, London, 1980, p 86.
31² Noel, *Wilson*, p 44.
31³ Wilson, *Memoirs*, p 75.
32¹ PRO POWE 10/216, 18 July 1941.
32² W. H. B. Court, *History of the Second World War. United Kingdom Civil Services (Coal)*, London, HMSO, 1953, p 129.
32³ Wilson's Presidential Address to the Royal Statistical Society, 15 Nov 1972.
33¹ Philip M. Williams, *Hugh Gaitskell*, London, 1979, pp 107–8.
33² Donald MacDougall, *Don and Mandarin*, London, 1987, p 28.
33³ Harris, *Conversations*, p 277.
34¹ Leslie Smith, *Wilson*, p 89.
34² Paul Foot, *Wilson*, p 41.
34³ Lady Wilson papers, Wilson to family, 31 Oct 1943,
35¹ Lady Wilson papers, Wilson to family, 31 Oct 1943.
35² Wilson, *Memoirs*, p 74.
35³ PRO POWE 10/252, 2 Nov 1943.
36¹ Harold Wilson, *New Deal for Coal*, London, 1945.
36² Paul Foot, *Wilson*, pp 44–5.
36³ PRO POWE 10/252.
37¹ Press Association interview released 5 April 1976, *cit.* Roth, *Wilson*, p 47.
37² Peter Hennessy, *Whitehall*, London, 1989, p 104.
37³ Lady Wilson papers, Wilson to family, 31 Oct 1943.
38¹ Peter Hennessy, *Cabinet*, London, 1986, p 15.
38² Wilson papers, box 61, Norman Adamson to Wilson, 29 Oct 1964.
38³ Lady Wilson papers, Wilson to family, 13 Oct 1943.
38⁴ Wilson papers, box 188.
40¹ Paul Foot, *Wilson*, p 149.
40² Wilson, *Memoirs*, p 79.
40³ Roth, *Wilson*, p 75.

Chapter IV: Junior Minister, 1945–1947

41¹ Richard Crossman, *The Diaries of a Cabinet Minister*, vol 1, London, 1975, p 332.
41² Wilson, *Memoirs*, p 9.
41³ Leo Abse, *Private Member*, London, 1973, p 36.
42¹ Henry Kissinger, *The White House Years*, London, 1979, p 92.
42² Lord Wigg, *George Wigg*, London, 1972, p 313.
42³ Richard Crossman, *The Diaries of a Cabinet Minister*, vol 3, London, 1977, p 278.
42⁴ Barbara Castle, *The Castle Diaries 1964–70*, London, 1984, p 297.
43¹ Leslie Smith, *Wilson*, p 147.

43[2] Wigg, *George Wigg*, p 77.

43[3] Richard Marsh, *Off the Rails*, London, 1978, p 40.

43[4] Interview with Michael Stewart.

43[5] Harold Wilson, *Final Term. The Labour Government 1974–1976*, London, 1979, p 121.

43[6] Edward Short, *Whip to Wilson*, London, 1989, p 27.

43[7] Interview with John Freeman.

43[8] Crossman, *Diaries*, vol 1, p 527.

44[1] Tony Benn, *Out of the Wilderness. Diaries 1963–67*, London, 1987 (references to Arrow edition of 1988), p. 85.

44[2] Benn, *Out of the Wilderness*, p 726.

44[3] Peter Kellner and Christopher Hitchens, *Callaghan. The Road to Number Ten*, London, 1976, p 47.

44[4] Anthony Howard and Richard West, *The Making of the Prime Minister*, London, 1965, p 47.

44[5] A parallel also suggested to me by Anthony Howard.

44[6] Interview with Roy Hattersley.

44[7] *The Cecil King Diary, 1965–1970*, London, 1972, p 38.

44[8] Kissinger, *White House Years*, p 92.

44[9] Roth, *Wilson*, p 48.

45[1] Sir Gerald Nabarro, *NAB I*, London, 1969, p 203.

45[2] Frank Longford, *Eleven at No 10*, London, 1984, p 5.

45[3] Wilson papers, box 104.

45[4] Michael Stewart, *Life and Labour*, London, 1980, p 274.

45[5] George Thomas, *Mr Speaker*, London, 1985, p 117.

45[6] Ernest Kay, *Pragmatic Premier*, London, 1967.

45[7] Castle, *Diaries 1964–70*, p 150.

45[8] Interview with Lord Armstrong.

46[1] Crossman, *Diaries*, vol 1, p 230.

46[2] Gordon Walker papers, GNWR 5/11.

46[3] Roy Jenkins, *A Life at the Centre*, London, 1991, p 227.

46[4] e.g. Wilson papers, box 133. Wilson to the editor of the *Northern Echo*, 15 Sept 1983.

47[1] Wilson papers, box 123.

47[2] Frances Donaldson, *A Twentieth Century Life*, London, 1992.

47[3] Interview with with Lord Goodman.

47[4] Marcia Falkender, *Downing Street in Perspective*, London, 1983, p 194.

47[5] Tony Benn, *Against the Tide. Diaries 1973–1976*, London, 1989 (references to Arrow edition of 1990), p 22.

47[6] Interview with Jilly Cooper, *Daily Mail*, 25 Sept 1983.

48[1] Wilson, *Memoirs*, p 82.

48[2] Kenneth Morgan, *Labour in Power, 1945–1951*, Oxford, 1984, p 60.

48[3] Harold Nicolson, *Diaries and Letters 1945–1962*, ed. Nigel Nicolson, London, 1968, p 30.

48[4] Interview with Lord Lever.

48[5] 14 Oct 1944 and 27 July 1945.

49[1] Mayhew, *Time to Explain*, p 86.
49[2] *The Diary of Hugh Gaitskell 1945–1956*, ed. Philip M. Williams, London, 1983, p 7.
49[3] Leslie Smith, *Wilson*, p 100.
49[4] Attlee papers, MS Attlee DEP 18 f 79.
49[5] Wilson, *Memoirs*, p 82.
50[1] Harold Emmerson, *The Ministry of Works*, London, 1956, pp 12–22; cf Noel, *Wilson*, pp 67–9.
50[2] Fred Blackburn, *George Tomlinson*, London, 1954, pp 154–8.
50[3] NA 841 00/3–1147, Gallman to Sec. of State, 11 March 1947.
50[4] Wilson, *Memoirs*, pp 83–6.
50[5] House of Commons, 23 Jan 1946 (*Hansard*, vol 418, col 268).
50[6] NA 841 00/10–944, Gallman to Sec. of State, 9 Oct 1945.
51[1] NA 841 00/9–645, Winant to Sec. of State, 6 Sept 1945.
51[2] Blackburn, *Tomlinson*, p 161.
51[3] House of Commons, 25 March 1946 (*Hansard*, vol 42, cols 140–56).
51[4] House of Commons, 9 Oct 1945 (*Hansard*, vol 414, col 186).
52[1] Wilson, *Memoirs*, p 156.
52[2] *cit.* Crossman, *Diaries*, vol 3, pp 207–8.
52[3] *See* e.g. James Margach, *The Abuse of Power*, London, 1978, p 130.
52[4] Wilson, *Memoirs*, p 89.
53[1] House of Commons, 6 Feb 1947 (*Hansard*, vol 432, col 2002).
53[2] PRO PREM 8/501, 16 Dec 1946.
53[3] Gaitskell, *Diary*, p 22.
53[4] Williams, *Gaitskell*, p 132.
53[5] *The Political Diary of Hugh Dalton 1918–40, 1945–60*, ed. Ben Pimlott, London, 1986, p 373.
53[6] NA 841 01/9–2746, S. D. Berger to Sec. of State, 27 Sept 1946.
54[1] Wilson papers, box 8, Wilson to F. J. Sayer, Aug 1947.
54[2] Roth, *Wilson*, p 89.
54[3] Wilson papers, box 8, Wilson to Dr L. Liepmann, 24 Aug 1945.
55[1] Dudley Smith, *Wilson*, p 23.
55[2] Wilson, *Prime Minister on Prime Ministers*, p 291.
55[3] Falkender, *Downing Street in Perspective*, p 249.
56[1] Dudley Smith, *Wilson*, p 50.
56[2] Article in *Sunday Pictorial*, *cit.* Dudley Smith, *Wilson*, p 54.
56[3] Dalton, *Diary*, p 396.
57[1] For a good exposition of this saga see David Leigh, *The Wilson Plot*, London, 1980, pp 37–52.
57[2] Noel, *Wilson*, p 81.
57[3] Leslie Smith, *Wilson*, p 119.
58[1] PRO FO 371/66328.
58[2] PRO FO 371/66334, 25 July 1947.
58[3] Wilson papers, box 156, G. W. Underdown to Wilson, 9 July 1984.
58[4] Wilson, *Memoirs*, p 95.
58[5] *cit.* Roth, *Wilson*, p 109.
58[6] Attlee papers, MS Attlee DEP 66 ff 78–145.

58[7] Attlee papers, MS Attlee DEP. 67 f 129.
59[1] PRO CAB 128 CM(47).

Chapter V: President of the Board of Trade, 1947–1951

60[1] Noel, *Wilson*, p 85.
60[2] Dudley Smith, *Wilson*, p 62.
60[3] I am indebted to Sir Edward Ford for showing me this extract from Ivor Crosthwaite's unpublished autobiography.
61[1] Attlee papers, DEP. 70 118, Wilson to Attlee, 10 May 1948.
61[2] Interview with Dr Robin Wilson.
61[3] Dudley Smith, *Wilson*, p 97.
62[1] Frank Pakenham, Earl of Longford, *Five Lives*, London, 1963, p 253.
62[2] Gaitskell, *Diary*, p 162.
62[3] Gaitskell, *Diary*, p 62.
62[4] Wilson papers, box 8, Gaitskell to Wilson, 30 Sept 1947.
62[5] Wilson papers, box 8, Laski to Wilson, 30 Sept 1947.
62[6] Wilson papers, box 8, Noel Baker to Wilson, 3 Oct 1947.
62[7] NA 841 00/10–847, Gallman to Sec. of State, 8 Oct 1947.
63[1] Gaitskell, *Diary*, p 35.
63[2] Paul Foot, *Wilson*, p 60.
64[1] PRO CAB 128/10 CM(47), 23 Oct 1947.
64[2] PRO T 229/259, 3 Feb 1949.
64[3] Morgan, *Labour in Power*, p 365.
64[4] PRO CAB 128 15 CM 10(49), 8 Feb 1949.
64[5] PRO CAB 128 13 CM 49(48), 12 July 1948.
65[1] Wilson, *Memoirs*, p 98.
65[2] Lecture to International Fabian Society, 7 Feb 1949.
65[3] PRO CAB 128 15 CM 31(49), 2 May 1949.
66[1] House of Commons, 2 March 1948 (*Hansard*, vol 448, col 219).
67[1] Wilson papers, box 36. Leslie Smith, *Wilson*, p 136. Dudley Smith, *Wilson*, p 85. Paul Foot, *Wilson*, p 117.
67[2] Paul Foot, *Wilson*, p 67.
67[3] Lord Morrison of Lambeth, *Herbert Morrison*, London, 1960, p 325.
67[4] Dalton, *Diary*, p 496.
67[5] PRO CAB 128 15 CM 41(49), 20 June 1949.
68[1] Dudley Smith, *Wilson*, p 79.
68[2] Morrison, *Herbert Morrison*, p 325.
68[3] *Guardian*, 15 Oct 1976.
69[1] *Lancashire and Whitehall: The Diary of Sir Raymond Streat*, ed. Marguerite Dupree, vol II, Manchester, 1987, p 415.
69[2] Dudley Smith, *Wilson*, p 115.
70[1] Goodheart papers, uncatalogued.
71[1] Peter Forster, "J. Arthur Rank and the Shrinking Screen", *Age of Austerity*, ed. Michael Sissons and Philip French, London, 1963, pp 285–7.

71² Wilson papers, box 101, Wilson to Sec. of State for Trade, 23 Feb 1976.
71³ Wilson, *Memoirs*, p 105.
71⁴ PRO CAB 15 CM 22(49), 24 March 1949.
71⁵ Nicholas Davenport, *Memoirs of a City Radical*, London, 1974, p 163.
72¹ NA 841 00/11–2348, State Dept. Office Memo of 23 Nov 1948.
73¹ Attlee papers, DEP. 78, *ff* 261–2.
73² Wilson papers, box 143, Douglas Houghton to Wilson, 17 Feb 1960.
73³ Wilson papers, box 131, Belcher to Wilson, 24 June 1963 and Wilson to Belcher, 25 June 1963.
73⁴ e.g. Leslie Smith, *Wilson*, p 150.
74¹ Jay, *Change and Fortune*, p 187.
74² Gaitskell, *Diary*, p 131.
74³ Jay, *Change and Fortune* p 187; Gaitskell, *Diary*, p 137.
74⁴ Dalton, *Diary*, p 455.
74⁵ Gaitskell, *Diary*, p 137.
75¹ Dalton, *Diary*, p 457.
75² Michael Foot, *Aneurin Bevan. Vol II. 1945–1960*, London, 1973, p 270.
75³ Jay, *Change and Fortune*, p 191.
75⁴ Interview with Lord Jay.
76¹ *The Robert Hall Diaries. 1954–61*, ed. Alec Cairncross, London, 1991, p 83.
76² Jay, *Change and Fortune*, p 187.
76³ Wilson papers, box 157.
76⁴ Interview with Joe Haines.
77¹ Interview with Martin Gilbert.
77² PRO LAB 10/832, Wilson to Isaacs, 13 June 1949; *cf* Morgan, *Labour in Power*, pp 376–7.
77³ *See* Keith Middlemas, *Power, Competition and the State. Vol. 1. Britain in Search of Balance, 1940–61*, London, 1986, pp 181–4, for an excellent account of this *démarche*.
77⁴ PRO PREM 8/11 83, Wilson to Attlee, 17 May 1950.
79¹ Howard, *Making of the Prime Minister*, p 149.
79² Gaitskell, *Diary*, p 155.
79³ Dalton, *Diary*, p 449.
80¹ Mitchell, *Wilson*, p 156.
80² Dalton, *Diary*, p 471.
80³ Dalton, *Diary*, p 466.
80⁴ NA 841 00/2–950, Holmes to Sec. of State, 9 Feb 1950.
81¹ Williams, *Gaitskell*, p 833.
81² Gaitskell, *Diary*, p 216.
81³ Gaitskell, *Diary*, pp 163–4.
82¹ Gaitskell, *Diary*, p 245.
82² Gaitskell, *Diary*, p 247.
82³ PRO CAB 128/15, 1 Aug 1950.
82⁴ PRO CAB 128/19, 25 Jan 1951.
82⁵ Castle, *Diaries*, p 676.

83¹ Wilson papers, box 152, Wilson to Simon Burgess, 3 May 1984.
83² Foot, *Bevan*, vol II, p 294.
83³ Dalton, *Diary*, p 514.
84¹ Interview with John Freeman.
84² PRO CAB 128/19 CM 22(51), 22 March 1951.
84³ Gaitskell, *Diary*, p 242.
84⁴ Dalton, *Diary*, pp 518–19.
84⁵ Bernard Donoughue and G. W. Jones, *Herbert Morrison. Portrait of a Politician*, London, 1973, p 490.
84⁶ CAB 128/19 CM 26(51), 9 April 1951.
84⁷ NA 741 00/4–2051.
84⁸ Dalton, *Diary*, p 524.
84⁹ John Campbell, *Nye Bevan*, London, 1987, pp 234–45.
84¹⁰ NA 741 00/4–2351, Gifford to Sec. of State, 20 April 1951.
85¹ PRO CAB 128 19 CM 26(51), 9 April 1951.
85² Dalton, *Diary*, p 525.
85³ Hugh Dalton, *High Tide and After*, London, 1962, p 369.
85⁴ PRO CAB 128 19 CM 26(51), 9 April 1951.
85⁵ *Patrick Gordon Walker. Political Diaries 1931–1972*, ed. Robert Pearce, London, 1991, p 194.
85⁶ Foot, *Bevan*, vol II, pp 323–4.
85⁷ Interview with John Freeman.
85⁸ Solly Zuckerman, *Monkeys, Men and Missiles*, London, 1988, p 370.
86¹ Francis Williams, *A Prime Minister Remembers*, London, 1961, pp 245–7.
86² Interview with John Freeman.
86³ Woodrow Wyatt, *Confessions of an Optimist*, London, 1985, pp 212–13.
86⁴ Paul Foot, *Wilson*, p 98.
86⁵ Jennie Lee, *My Life with Nye*, London, 1980, p 190.
87¹ Harold Macmillan, *Tides of Fortune*, London, 1969, p 341.
87² House of Commons, 24 April 1951 (*Hansard*, vol 487, cols 228–31).
87³ Emanuel Shinwell, *I've Lived Through It All*, London, 1973, p 207.
88¹ Morrison, *Herbert Morrison*, p 325.

Chapter VI: Opposition Under Attlee, 1951–1953

89¹ Wilson papers, box 157.
90¹ Interview with Peter Meyer.
90² Castle, *Diaries*, p 216.
91¹ *The Back-bench Diaries of Richard Crossman*, ed. Janet Morgan, London, 1981, pp 249–50.
91² Zuckerman, *Monkeys, Men and Missiles*, pp 129–30.
91³ Noel, *Wilson*, p 104.
91⁴ Wilson papers, box 14.
91⁵ Wilson papers, box 28.

92¹ Wilson papers, box 13, Benton to Wilson, 23 Aug 1960.

92² Wilson papers, box 112, Jean Le Roy to Wilson, 6 May 1953.

92³ Wilson papers, box 112, Wilson to Higham, 15 Jan 1954, 23 Jan 1956, 21 Sept 1961.

93¹ *The Times*, 12 Aug 1953.

93² Wilson papers, box 4.

93³ George Caunt diary, November 1955.

94¹ Denis Healey, *The Time of My Life*, London, 1989 (references to Penguin edition), p 368.

95¹ Dalton, *Diary*, p 528.

95² Dudley Smith, *Wilson*, p 135.

96¹ Crossman, *Back-bench Diaries*, p 159.

96² John Campbell, *Nye Bevan*, London, 1987, p 259.

96³ NA 741 00/1–1552, 15 Jan 1952.

96⁴ Peter Clarke, *A Question of Leadership*, London, 1991, p 236.

96⁵ Wilson, *Memoirs*, p 136.

96⁶ Interview with John Freeman.

96⁷ Crossman, *Diaries*, vol 1, p 12.

96⁸ Paul Foot, *Wilson*, p 105.

97¹ Woodrow Wyatt, *What's Left of the Labour Party?*, London, 1977, p 51.

97² NA 741 00/12–1151, reporting conversation of 11 Dec 1951.

97³ NA 741 00/12–1451, report of 14 Dec 1951.

97⁴ Crossman, *Back-bench Diaries*, pp 62–3.

97⁵ Mark Jenkins, *Bevanism. Labour's High Tide*, Nottingham, 1979, p 153.

97⁶ Crossman, *Back-bench Diaries*, p 53.

98¹ Roth, *Wilson*, pp 151 and 162.

98² Crossman, *Back-bench Diaries*, pp 53–4.

98³ Morgan, *Labour in Power*, pp 462–3.

98⁴ *Manchester Guardian*, 10 July 1951.

98⁵ Foot, *Bevan*, vol II, p 352.

99¹ Crossman, *Back-bench Diaries*, pp 159–60.

99² Crossman, *Back-bench Diaries*, p 126.

100¹ A. J. P. Taylor, *Beaverbrook*, London, 1972, p 635.

100² NA 741 00/10–1452, 14 Oct 1952.

100³ Hugh Dalton, *High Tide and After*, London, 1962, p 386.

100⁴ Ian Mikardo, *Back-bencher*, London, 1988, p 152.

100⁵ Jenkins, *Bevanism*, p 161.

101¹ Wilson, *Memoirs*, p 139.

101² Crossman, *Back-bench Diaries*, pp 186–7.

102¹ Crossman, *Back-bench Diaries*, p 217.

102² Crossman, *Diaries*, vol 1, p 12.

103¹ e.g. *Evening Standard*, 15 April 1954.

103² Crossman, *Back-bench Diaries*, p 314.

103³ Mikardo, *Back-bencher*, p 153.

103⁴ Wilson, *Memoirs*, p 141.

104[1] Crossman, *Back-bench Diaries*, p 314.

104[2] *Daily Mail*, 29 April 1954.

104[3] Dalton, *Diary*, p 625.

104[4] Dalton, *Diary*, p 625.

104[5] Lee, *My Life with Nye*, p 202.

104[6] NA 741 00/5–1354, embassy report of 6 May 1954.

105[1] Crossman, *Back-bench Diaries*, p 349.

105[2] 7 May 1954, *cit.* Paul Foot, *Wilson*, p 118.

105[3] Crossman, *Back-bench Diaries*, p 353.

105[4] NA 741 00/11.254, 2 Nov 1954.

105[5] NA 741 00/6–2755, 22 Nov 1954.

105[6] Crossman, *Back-bench Diaries*, p 377.

105[7] Wilson papers, box 60, Jenkins to Wilson, 5 May 1965.

106[1] NA 741 00/3–1455, embassy report of 14 March 1955.

106[2] Crossman, *Back-bench Diaries*, p 402.

106[3] Campbell, *Bevan*, pp 298–9.

106[4] 19 March 1955, *cit.* Noel, *Wilson*, p 170.

107[1] Michael Cockerell, *Live from Number 10*, London, 1988, pp 33–5.

107[2] Wilson, *Memoirs*, p 151.

108[1] Crossman, *Back-bench Diaries*, p 441.

108[2] Emanuel Shinwell, *The Labour Story*, London, 1963, p 199.

108[3] NA 741 00/10–1755, embassy report of 17 Oct 1955.

108[4] Gordon Walker, *Diaries*, p 226.

108[5] Williams, *Gaitskell*, p 361.

109[1] Williams, *Gaitskell*, p 370.

109[2] Wilson papers, box 129, Gaitskell to Wilson, 26 Dec 1953.

Chapter VII: Opposition Under Gaitskell, 1954–1963

110[1] Interview with Gerald Kaufman.

110[2] *Robert Hall Diaries*, p 99.

111[1] Wilson, *Prime Minister on Prime Ministers*, p 308.

111[2] Harold Macmillan, *Riding the Storm*, London, 1971, p 48.

111[3] House of Commons, 18 April 1956 (*Hansard*, vol 551, cols 1014–35).

111[4] Gaitskell, *Diary*, p 448.

112[1] Crossman, *Back-bench Diaries*, pp 762–3.

112[2] House of Commons, 18 July 1961 (*Hansard*, vol 644, cols 1171–88).

112[3] *New Statesman*, 24 March 1961.

112[4] TUC Congress, Blackpool, 1962, *cit.* Geoffrey Goodman, *The Awkward Warrior. Frank Cousins: His Life and Times*, London, 1979, p 327.

112[5] Wilson papers, box 148, Wilson to Mrs Heathcote, 9 Dec 1983.

112[6] Lord Robens, *Ten Year Stint*, London, 1972, p 154.

112[7] Gaitskell, *Diary*, p 410.

113[1] Gaitskell, *Diary*, p 617.

Notes

113² Gaitskell, *Diary*, p 410.
113³ Crossman, *Back-bench Diaries*, p 521.
113⁴ Geoffrey Cox, *See It Happen*, London, 1983, p 78.
113⁵ Harold Wilson, *The Chariot of Israel*, London, 1981, pp 319–20.
113⁶ Wilson papers, box 136, Wilson to L. Rayber, 19 Nov 1956.
114¹ *Robert Hall Diaries*, p 87.
114² Macmillan, *Riding the Storm*, p 418.
114³ *Report of the Tribunal appointed to Inquire into Allegations of Improper Disclosure of Information relating to the Raising of the Bank Rate*, London, HMSO, 1957.
114⁴ House of Commons, 3 Feb 1958 (*Hansard*, vol 581, cols 831–58).
114⁵ Interview with Paul Johnson.
115¹ Crossman, *Back-bench Diaries*, p 662.
115² *Robert Hall Diaries*, p 137.
115³ *Robert Hall Diaries*, p 146.
115⁴ Interview with Lady Falkender.
115⁵ Crossman, *Back-bench Diaries*, p 726.
116¹ Wilson papers, box 129, Gaitskell to Wilson, 16 Sept 1959.
116² Wyatt, *Confessions of an Optimist*, pp 213 and 271.
116³ D. E. Butler and Richard Rose, *The British General Election of 1959*, London, 1960, p 61.
116⁴ Goodman, *Cousins*, p 237.
116⁵ Williams, *Gaitskell*, p 526; cf Crossman, *Back-bench Diaries*, p 795.
116⁶ Interview with Lady Falkender.
117¹ Gordon Walker, *Political Diaries*, p 257.
117² cit. Roth, *Wilson*, p 233.
117³ Wilson, *Prime Minister on Prime Ministers*, pp 200–1.
117⁴ cit. Paul Foot, *Wilson*, p 127.
117⁵ *Daily Mail*, 18 Sept 1959.
117⁶ Crossman, *Back-bench Diaries*, pp 789–91.
118¹ Wilson papers, box 4, folder 1.
118² Wilson papers, box 4, Wilson to John Wilson, 27 Oct 1959.
119¹ Interviews with Joe Haines and Sir Sigmund Sternberg.
119² Crossman, *Back-bench Diaries*, p 581.
120¹ Wigg, *George Wigg*, p 256.
120² Interview with Lord Callaghan.
120³ Margach, *Abuse of Power*, pp 141–2.
120⁴ Interview with Lady Falkender.
121¹ Interview with Lord Callaghan.
121² Interview with Lady Falkender.
122¹ Crossman, *Back-bench Diaries*, p 802.
123¹ Crossman, *Back-bench Diaries*, p 810.
123² Wilson papers, box 143, W. Davies to Wilson, 7 July 1960.
123³ Wilson, *Memoirs*, p 179.
123⁴ Wilson, *Prime Minister on Prime Ministers*, pp 200–1.
123⁵ Harold Wilson, *The Relevance of British Socialism*, London, 1964, p 39.

124[1] Marsh, *Off the Rails*, p 40.
124[2] Paul Foot, *Wilson*, p 126.
124[3] House of Commons, 27 April 1960 (*Hansard*, vol 622, cols 317–30).
124[4] Crossman, *Back-bench Diaries*, pp 837–8, 854.
124[5] Gordon Walker papers, GNWR 1/14, diary for 12 May 1960.
125[1] Gordon Walker papers, GNWR 1/14, diary for 19 May and 2 June 1960.
125[2] *New Left Review*, 3 Oct 1960.
125[3] Shinwell, *I've Lived Through It All*, p 233.
125[4] *Sunday Times*, 9 Oct 1960.
125[5] *Guardian*, 26 Oct 1960.
126[1] Jenkins, *Life at the Centre*, p 132.
126[2] Wilson, *Memoirs*, p 181.
126[3] Interview with Lady Falkender.
126[4] Crossman, *Back-bench Diaries*, pp 880–1.
126[5] Goodman, *Cousins*, p 345.
127[1] Crossman, *Back-bench Diaries*, pp 889–91.
127[2] Kenneth Harris, *Conversations*, London, 1967, p 280.
127[3] Susan Crosland, *Tony Crosland*, London, 1982, p 103.
127[4] Wilson papers, box 139, Wilson to Donald Bruce, 11 Nov 1960.
127[5] Gordon Walker Papers, GNWR 1/14, diary for 30 Dec 1960.
128[1] Williams, *Gaitskell*, p 627 *n*.
128[2] Interview with Lady Falkender.
128[3] Interview with Tony Benn.
128[4] Wilson papers, box 139, letter of 2 Nov 1960.
128[5] House of Commons, 18 April 1961 (*Hansard*, vol 641, cols 976–98).
129[1] *Sunday Telegraph*, 23 April 1961.
129[2] Interview with Lord Jay; cf Jay, *Change and Fortune*, p 278.
129[3] Falkender, *Downing Street in Perspective*, p 219.
129[4] Williams, *Gaitskell*, pp 666–7.
129[5] Paul Foot, *Wilson*, p 132.
130[1] Mayhew, *Time to Explain*, p 177.
130[2] Harold Macmillan, *Pointing the Way*, London, 1972, p 453.
131[1] Interview with Lady Falkender.
131[2] House of Commons, 3 Aug 1961 (*Hansard*, vol 645, cols 1651–70).
131[3] Harold Macmillan, *At the End of the Day*, London, 1973, pp 24–5.
131[4] Crossman, *Back-bench Diaries*, p 952.
132[1] Williams, *Gaitskell*, p 702.
132[2] Williams, *Gaitskell*, p 726.
132[3] Goodman, *Cousins*, p 334.
132[4] Dudley Smith, *Wilson*, p 200.
133[1] Williams, *Gaitskell*, p 740.
133[2] George Caunt diary, 11 Nov 1962.
133[3] George Brown papers, 118. 52, Brandon to Brown, 10 Jan 1963 and 118. 92, Brown to Brandon, undated.
133[4] Howard, *Making of the Prime Minister*, p 11.
134[1] Jenkins, *Life at the Centre*, p 147.

134[2] *The Wilson Years*, BBC series broadcast in 1991, programme 1.
134[3] Wilson papers, box 43.
134[4] Wigg, *George Wigg*, p 256.
135[1] George Brown, *In My Way*, London, 1971, p 83.
135[2] Wilson papers, box 13, Wilson to Benton, 4 March 1963.
135[3] Paul Foot, *Wilson*, p 305.
135[4] Interview with Lady Falkender.
135[5] Thomas, *Mr Speaker*, p 85.
135[6] Benn, *Diaries 1963–67*, p 5.
135[7] Interview with Lord Glenamara.
135[8] Jay, *Change and Fortune*, p 290.
136[1] George Brown papers, 118, 117.
136[2] Robens, *Ten Year Stint*, p 3; Woodrow Wyatt, *Turn Again Westminster*, London, 1973, p 178; interview with Denis Healey; cf Francis Williams, *Nothing So Strange*, London, 1970, p 311 for another view.
136[3] Interview with Lord Jenkins.
136[4] Crossman, *Back-bench Diaries*, p 972.
136[5] Crossman, *Back-bench Diaries*, p 971.
137[1] Stewart, *Life and Labour*, p 122.
137[2] Francis Wheen, *Tom Driberg. His Life and Indiscretions*, London, 1990, p 292.
137[3] Macmillan, *At the End of the Day*, p 396.
137[4] Wilson papers, box 1, Hailsham to Wilson, 16 Feb 1963.

Chapter VIII: Leader of the Opposition, 1963–1964

138[1] Wilson papers, box 13, Wilson to Benton, 4 March 1963.
138[2] Crossman, *Back-bench Diaries*, pp 985–7.
138[3] *See* John Silkin, *Changing Battlefields. The Challenge to the Labour Party*, London, 1987, p 4.
139[1] George Brown papers, 119. 135, Brown to Sydney Jacobson.
139[2] Gordon Walker, *Diaries*, p 278; cf Brown, *In My Way*, p 85.
139[3] Gordon Walker, *Diaries*, p 278.
139[4] Crossman, *Back-bench Diaries*, p 976.
139[5] Gordon Walker, *Diaries*, p 279.
140[1] Wilson, *A Prime Minister on Prime Ministers*, p 200.
140[2] Crossman, *Back-bench Diaries*, pp 985–6.
140[3] Marcia Williams, *Inside No 10*, London, 1972, p 118.
140[4] Jenkins, *Life at the Centre*, p 151.
140[5] Benn, *Out of the Wilderness*, p 13.
140[6] Benn, *Out of the Wilderness*, p 16.
141[1] House of Commons, 16 Jan 1964 (*Hansard*, vol 687, cols 427–52); address to the Press Club in Washington, 1 April 1963 (text in Harold Wilson, *Purpose in Politics. Selected Speeches*, London, 1964, pp 214–15); House of Commons, 31 Jan 1963 (*Hansard*, vol 670, cols 1236–50).

141[2] *Guardian*, 23 Feb 1963.

141[3] Wilson papers, box 153, Bryant to Wilson, 1 Feb 1963.

141[4] Crossman, *Back-bench Diaries*, p 973; cf Harris, *Conversations*, p 274.

142[1] Michael Cockerell, Peter Hennessy and David Walker, *Sources Close to the Prime Minister*, London, 1984, pp 122–3.

142[2] Clarke, *A Question of Leadership*, p 258.

142[3] Robert Harris, *The Making of Neil Kinnock*, London, 1984, p 45.

142[4] Wilson, *A Prime Minister on Prime Ministers*, p 200.

142[5] Interview with Anthony Howard.

143[1] Wilson, *Relevance of British Socialism*, pp 41 and 55.

144[1] Text in Wilson, *Purpose in Politics*, pp 16–28.

144[2] Christopher Booker, *The Neophiliacs*, London, 1969, p 206.

144[3] *Daily Herald*, 2 Oct 1963; *The Times*, 2 Oct 1963.

145[1] Wilson papers, box 131, Ward to Wilson, 1 Nov 1962; Wilson to Ward, 5 Nov 1962.

145[2] Wilson papers, box 131, memo by Wigg of 29 March 1963.

145[3] George Brown papers, 121. 16, Brown to Wilson, 9 April 1963.

145[4] Crossman, *Back-bench Diaries*, p 1005.

146[1] Macmillan, *At the End of the Day*, p 440.

146[2] House of Commons, 17 June 1963 (*Hansard*, vol 679, cols 34–54).

146[3] Wilson papers, box 131, Professor G. Barraclough to Wilson, 14 June 1963; Wilson to Barraclough, 20 June 1963.

146[4] Wilson papers, box 131, Ward to Wilson, 13 June 1963.

146[5] Crossman, *Back-bench Diaries*, p 1001.

147[1] House of Commons, 16 July 1963 (*Hansard*, vol 681, cols 335–6).

147[2] Wilson papers, box 131, Macmillan to Wilson, 16 July 1963; Wilson to Macmillan, 19 July 1963.

147[3] George Brown papers, 119. 144, Brandon to Brown, 19 Feb 1963.

147[4] Goodhart papers, uncatalogued, Goodhart to W. E. Channing, 7 May 1963.

148[1] Text in Wilson, *Purpose in Politics*, pp 214–15.

148[2] A record of this meeting is to be found in Lady Falkender's papers. Text of Oral History Interview between Harold Wilson and Richard Neustadt, 23 March 1964.

148[3] George Brown papers, 121. 36a, Brandon to Brown, 18 April 1963.

149[1] Oral History Interview, *op cit.*, p 51.

149[2] Wilson papers, box 21, Cronin to Wilson, 23 May 1963.

150[1] George Brown papers, 125. 201.

150[2] George Brown papers, 128. 2, Bundy to Brown, 4 Nov 1963.

150[3] Wilson papers, box 13, Benton to Wilson, 27 Sept 1963; Wilson to Benton, 2 Oct 1963.

150[4] Wilson papers, box 43.

150[5] *The Wilson Years*, programme 1.

151[1] Wilson papers, box 183, Wilson to Dr David Lawson, 2 Dec 1963.

151[2] George Brown papers, 128. 19, Brown to David Bruce, 28 Nov 1963.

151[3] George Brown papers, 128. 32 and 110, Brown to Wilson, 29 Nov 1963 and Wilson to Brown, 2 Dec 1963.
151[4] George Brown papers, 134. 86, Brown to Brandon, 10 June 1964.
151[5] Benn, *Out of the Wilderness*, p 97.
152[1] *Daily Telegraph*, 14 March 1964.
152[2] cf Wilfred Beckerman, *The Labour Government's Economic Record: 1964–1970*, London, 1972, p 119.
152[3] Michael Foot, *Harold Wilson. A Pictorial Biography*, Oxford, 1964.
152[4] Interview with Michael Foot.
152[5] Wilson papers, box 2, Maxwell to Wilson, 28 Aug 1964.
153[1] Two excellent accounts of the campaign exist: David Butler and Anthony King's scholarly *The British General Election of 1964* (London, 1965) and Anthony Howard and Richard West's more impressionistic but brilliant *The Making of the Prime Minister* (London, 1965).
153[2] Butler, *General Election of 1964*, p 25.
153[3] Butler, *General Election of 1964*, p 73.
153[4] Cockerell, *Live from Number 10*, p 103.
153[5] Howard, *Making of the Prime Minister*, p 104.
153[6] George Brown papers, 125. 158, Brown to A. L. Williams, undated.
154[1] Kenneth O. Morgan, *Labour People*, Oxford, 1987, p 260.
154[2] Benn, *Out of the Wilderness*, p 26.
154[3] Interview with Lady Falkender.
154[4] Benn, *Out of the Wilderness*, p 75.
154[5] Anthony Howard, *Crossman. The Pursuit of Power*, London, 1990, p 264.
154[6] Lyndon Johnson Library, NSF Country File, UK, vol II, 133, Helms to T. L. Hughes, 12 Oct 1964.
155[1] Benn, *Out of the Wilderness*, p 81.
155[2] Benn, *Out of the Wilderness*, p 146.
155[3] Crossman, *Back-bench Diaries*, p 1013.
155[4] Robert Jenkins, *Tony Benn. A Political Biography*, London, 1980, p 99.
155[5] Nigel Fisher, *Iain Macleod*, London, 1973, pp 205–6.
155[6] Short, *Whip to Wilson*, p 10.
156[1] Butler, *General Election of 1964*, p 131.
156[2] Wheen, *Driberg*, p 99.
156[3] Cockerell, *Live from Number 10*, p 105.
156[4] Cockerell, *Live from Number 10*, p 108.
157[1] Wilson papers, box 181, Normanbrook to Wilson, 23 July 1964; memo by Wilson.
157[2] Cockerell, *Live from Number 10*, p 107.
157[3] Howard, *Crossman*, p 263.
157[4] From Martin Gilbert's as yet (1992) unpublished book, "In Search of Churchill".
158[1] Lyndon Johnson Library, NSF Country File, UK, vol I, 68, report of 14 Sept 1964.

158² George Caunt diary, 6 Oct 1964.
159¹ George Brown papers, 135. 175, Wilson to Brown, 18 Feb 1964.
159² Wilson papers, box 183.
159³ Howard, *Making of the Prime Minister*, pp 163–5.
159⁴ Butler, *General Election of 1964*, p 115.
159⁵ Kay, *Pragmatic Premier*, p 176.
160¹ Lyndon Johnson Library, NSF Country File, UK, vol II, 2, Bruce to State Dept, 15 Oct 1964.
161¹ Wilson papers, boxes 127 and 128.

Chapter IX: The Making of the Government, 1964

162¹ James Griffiths, *Pages from Memory*, London, 1969, p 185.
162² Interview with John Freeman.
162³ Griffiths, *Pages from Memory*, p 187.
162⁴ *The Wilson Years*, programme 2.
163¹ Shinwell, *I've Lived Through It All*, p 248.
163² Jad Adams, *Tony Benn*, London, 1992, pp 240–1.
163³ Wilson, *A Prime Minister on Prime Ministers*, pp 34, 40, 130 and 168.
163⁴ Interview with Sir Oliver Wright.
163⁵ Goodhart papers, Wilson to Goodhart, 29 Oct 1964.
163⁶ Wilson papers, box 58, 18 and 20 Oct 1964.
164¹ Crossman, *Back-bench Diaries*, p 979.
164² Dudley Smith, *Wilson*, p 207.
164³ Wilson papers, box 6.
164⁴ Wigg, *George Wigg*, p 311.
164⁵ Interview with Denis Healey.
164⁶ Kay, *Pragmatic Premier*, p 200.
165¹ Crossman, *Diaries*, vol 1, p 480.
165² Crossman, *Diaries*, vol 1, p 481.
165³ Interview with Dr Robin Wilson.
165⁴ Wilson papers, box 2, Wilson to Herbert Wilson, undated.
165⁵ Interview with Lady Falkender.
165⁶ Wilson papers, box 4, Marjorie Wilson to Wilson.
166¹ Wilson papers, box 2, 13 Feb 1970.
166² Crossman, *Back-bench Diaries*, pp 769 and 867.
166³ Anthony Shrimsley, *The First Hundred Days of Harold Wilson*, London, 1965, p 32.
167¹ Interviews with Lords Jenkins and Goodman.
167² Susan Crosland, *Crosland*, p 161.
167³ Falkender, *Downing Street in Perspective*, p 107.
167⁴ Benn, *Out of the Wilderness*, p 344.
168¹ Unpublished diaries of Tony Benn, vol III, p 506.
169¹ Interview with Graham Ison.

169[2] Frank Pakenham, Earl of Longford, *The Grain of Wheat*, London, 1974, p 28.

169[3] James Margach, *The Anatomy of Power*, London, 1979, p 27.

169[4] Short, *Whip to Wilson*, p 17; interview with Lord Glenamara.

170[1] Harold Wilson, *The Governance of Britain*, London, 1976, p 27.

170[2] Castle, *Diaries 1964–1970*, p 379.

170[3] House of Commons, 23 April 1951 (*Hansard*, vol 487, cols 34–54).

170[4] Benn, *Out of the Wilderness*, p 25.

170[5] Eric Roll, *Crowded Hours*, London, 1985, p 150.

170[6] Jay, *Change and Fortune*, p 295; interview with Lord Jay.

170[7] Hennessy, *Whitehall*, p 187.

170[8] Interview with Lord Callaghan.

171[1] James Callaghan, *Time and Chance*, London, 1987, p 166; interview with Lord Callaghan.

171[2] Jay, *Change and Fortune*, p 295.

171[3] Williams, *Inside Number 10*, p 299.

171[4] A statistic compiled by Clive Ponting, *Breach of Promise*, London, 1989, p 34.

171[5] Interview with Lord Carteris.

171[6] Crossman, *Diaries*, vol 3, p 627.

172[1] Margaret Stewart, *Frank Cousins: A Study*, London, 1968, p 114.

172[2] Jack Jones, *Union Man*, London, 1986, pp 158–9.

172[3] Goodman, *Cousins*, p 398.

173[1] Short, *Whip to Wilson*, p 21.

173[2] Gordon Walker papers, GNWR 1/16, 16 Oct 1964.

173[3] Castle, *Diaries 1964–1970*, p 45.

174[1] House of Commons, 3 Nov 1964 (*Hansard*, vol 701, col 71).

174[2] 6 Nov 1964.

174[3] Short, *Whip to Wilson*, p 69; interview with Lord Glenamara.

174[4] Wilson papers, box 61, Wilson to Fisher, 16 Nov 1964.

174[5] Interview with Lady Falkender.

175[1] Wilson papers, box 49, Banda to Wilson, 23 Oct 1964.

176[1] Zuckerman, *Monkeys, Men and Missiles*, p 369.

176[2] Castle, *Diaries 1964–1970*, p 177 *n*.

176[3] Zuckerman, *Monkeys, Men and Missiles*, p 369.

176[4] Short, *Whip to Wilson*, p 25.

176[5] Simon Hoggart and David Leigh, *Michael Foot: A Portrait*, London, 1981, p 151.

176[6] Interview with Lord Glenamara.

176[7] Short, *Whip to Wilson*, p 27.

176[8] Lyndon Johnson Library, NSF Country File, UK, vol II, 7, embassy to State Department, 19 Oct 1964.

177[1] Crossman, *Diaries*, vol 1, p 70.

177[2] Shinwell, *I've Lived Through It All*, p 238.

177[3] *Ruling Performance. British Governments from Attlee to Thatcher*, ed. Peter Hennessy and Anthony Seldon, Oxford, 1987. David Walker, "The First Wilson Governments", p 191.

177[4] Short, *Whip to Wilson*, p 55.
177[5] Castle, *Diaries 1964–1970*, p 448.
177[6] Short, *Whip to Wilson*, p 39.
177[7] Patrick Gordon Walker, *The Cabinet*, London, 1970, p 40.
178[1] Wilson papers, box 57, Wilson to Helsby, 5 March 1968.
178[2] Short, *Whip to Wilson*, pp 30 and 54.
178[3] Interview with Lord Chalfont.
178[4] Interview with Lord Glenamara.
179[1] Williams, *Inside Number 10*, p 21.
179[2] Jay, *Change and Fortune*, p 208.
179[3] Interviews with Lady Falkender and Gerald Kaufman.
179[4] Interview with Sir Derek Mitchell.
180[1] Short, *Whip to Wilson*, p 173.
180[2] Benn, *Out of the Wilderness*, p 340.
180[3] Wilson papers, box 62, 9 and 10 June 1965.
180[4] "The Apotheosis of the Dilettanti: The Establishment of Mandarins", essay by Balogh in *The Establishment: A Symposium*, ed. Hugh Thomas, London, 1959.
181[1] Wilson papers, box 181, Crossman to Wilson, 19 June 1964.
181[2] Short, *Whip to Wilson*, p 76.
181[3] Wilson papers, box 178.
182[1] Wilson papers, box 121, 19 May 1974.
182[2] Crossman, *Diaries*, vol 2, p 201.
182[3] Interview with Tony Benn.
182[4] Wilson papers, box 13, 22 April 1966.
182[5] Wilson, *Governance of Britain*, p 91.
183[1] Chapman Pincher, *Inside Story*, London, 1978, p 251.
183[2] Interview with Lord Zuckerman.
183[3] Interview with Lord Glenamara.
183[4] Crossman, *Diaries*, vol 1, p 362; Benn, *Out of the Wilderness*, p 319.
183[5] Interview with Peter Shore.
183[6] Interview with Gerald Kaufman.
183[7] Crossman, *Diaries*, vol 1, p 33.
183[8] Cockerell, *Sources Close to the Prime Minister*, p 68.
184[1] Interview with Lord Jenkins.
184[2] Interview with Martin Gilbert.
184[3] Castle, *Diaries 1964–1970*, p 115.
184[4] Peter Hennessy, *Cabinet*, Oxford, 1986, p 20.
184[5] Interview with Lady Falkender.
185[1] Harold Wilson, Jo Grimond and Enoch Powell, *Whitehall and Beyond*, London, 1964, p 18.

Chapter X: The First Administration, 1964–1966

186[1] Anthony Trollope, *The Prime Minister*, vol 1, chapter XXVII.
186[2] Margach, *The Anatomy of Power*, p 5.

187[1] Healey, *The Time of My Life*, p 330.
187[2] Wilson, *A Prime Minister on Prime Ministers*, p 61.
187[3] Marsh, *Off the Rails*, pp 94–5.
187[4] Benn, *Out of the Wilderness*, p 428.
187[5] Wilson papers, box 40, Jenkins to Wilson, 24 Jan 1965.
188[1] 20 March 1976.
188[2] Wilson papers, box 57, Wilson to Helsby, 21 Oct 1964.
188[3] Susan Crosland, *Crosland*, p 205.
188[4] Crossman, *Diaries*, vol 1, p 335.
188[5] Lyndon Johnson Library, NSF Country File, UK, vol II, 158a, Walter Heller to Johnson, 9 Nov 1964.
188[6] Longford, *Eleven at No 10*, p 128.
189[1] Crossman, *Diaries*, vol 2, p 203.
189[2] Healey, *The Time of My Life*, p 330.
189[3] Castle, *Diaries 1964–1970*, p 16.
189[4] Abse, *Private Member*, p 260.
189[5] Jenkins, *Life at the Centre*, pp 224–5.
190[1] Keith Middlemas, *Power, Competition and the State*, vol 2, *Threats to the Postwar Settlement; Britain since 1961–74*, London, 1990, p 110.
190[2] Kellner and Hitchens, *Callaghan*, p 47.
190[3] MacDougall, *Don and Mandarin*, p 152.
190[4] Susan Crosland, *Crosland*, p 135.
190[5] Desmond Donnelly, *Gadarene '68*, London, 1968, p 26; Castle, *Diaries*, p xiii.
190[6] Roll, *Crowded Hours*, p 158; Middlemas, *Threats to the Postwar Settlement*, p 114.
190[7] Interview with Lord O'Brien.
191[1] Phillip Whitehead, *The Writing on the Wall*, London, 1985, p 3.
191[2] Short, *Whip to Wilson*, p 37.
191[3] Lyndon Johnson Library, NSF Country File, UK, vol II, 158a, Heller to Johnson, 9 Nov 1964.
191[4] Lyndon Johnson Library, NSF Country File, UK, vol II, 149, State Dept Research Memo, 23 Oct 1964.
191[5] Wilson papers, box 53, Wilson to Johnson, 19 Nov 1964.
192[1] Samuel Brittan, *Steering the Economy* (revised edition), London, 1969, p 188.
192[2] Crossman, *Diaries*, vol 1, p 116; Jay, *The Wilson Years*, programme 2.
192[3] Wilson papers, box 49, Bustamante to Wilson, 27 Oct 1964.
192[4] Wilson papers, box 53, Wilson to Johnson, 28 Oct 1964.
192[5] Wilson papers, box 53, Gordon Walker to Wilson, 19 Nov 1964.
192[6] Wilson papers, box 57, Wilson to Jay, 28 May 1965.
192[7] Interview with Sir Oliver Wright.
192[8] Wilson papers, box 53, Wilson to Pompidou, 28 Oct 1964.
193[1] Wilson papers, box 54, Wilson to Pompidou, 18 Jan 1965.
192[2] Short, *Whip to Wilson*, pp 23 and 220.

193³ Crossman, *Diaries*, vol 1, pp 53–4.
193⁴ Lyndon Johnson Library, WHCF Name File: Harold Wilson, Schlesinger to Johnson, 25 Nov 1964.
193⁵ Lyndon Johnson Library, NSF Files of McGeorge Bundy, Memos for the Record, 7 Dec 1964.
194¹ Wilson papers, box 53, Wilson to Johnson and Johnson to Wilson, 19 Nov 1964.
194² Harold Wilson, *The Labour Government 1964–1970*, London, 1971, pp 37–8.
194³ Michael Stewart, *The Jekyll and Hyde Years*, London, 1977, p 35.
194⁴ Castle, *Diaries 1964–1970*, p 58.
194⁵ Wilson papers, box 58, Wilson to the Queen, 25 Nov 1964.
194⁶ Cromer papers, DEP 243.69, 22 April 1966.
195¹ *Cecil King Diary, 1965–1970*, p 46.
195² Paul Foot, *Wilson*, p 159.
195³ Lord Rothschild, *Meditations of a Broomstick*, London, 1977, pp 173–4.
195⁴ Harold Wilson, *Purpose in Power. Selected Speeches*, London, 1966, p 21.
196¹ John Whale, *The Half-Shut Eye*, London, 1969.
196² Castle, *Diaries 1964–1970*, pp 3–4.
196³ *See* in particular, Brittan, *Steering the Economy*, p 58.
196⁴ Callaghan, *Time and Chance*, p 184.
197¹ Wilson papers, box 46, Wilson to Helsby, 17 Nov 1964.
197² Wilson papers, box 46, Wilson to Tom Fraser, 21 Nov 1964.
197³ Wilson papers, box 46, Wilson to Bowden, 21 Nov 1964.
197⁴ Wilson papers, box 46, Wilson to Bowden, 25 Jan 1965.
198¹ Martin Gilbert, "In Search of Churchill".
198² Middlemas, *Threats to the Postwar Settlement*, p 93.
199¹ Castle, *Diaries 1964–1970*, p 31.
199² Short, *Whip to Wilson*, p 151.
199³ Wilson, *The Labour Government 1964–1970*, pp 101–2.
199⁴ Wyatt, *Confessions of an Optimist*, p 301.
199⁵ Crossman, *Diaries*, vol 1, p 323.
199⁶ Wyatt, *Confessions of an Optimist*, pp 297–9.
199⁷ Crossman, *Diaries*, vol 1, p 321.
199⁸ Eric Heffer, *The Class Struggle in Parliament*, London, 1973, pp 56–7.
200¹ Goodman, *Cousins*, p 482.
200² Thomas, *Mr Speaker*, p 91.
200³ Crossman, *Diaries*, vol 1, p 282.
201¹ *The Wilson Years*, programme 1.
201² Benn, *Out of the Wilderness*, p 273; Castle, *Diaries 1964–1970*, p 39.
202¹ Wilson papers, box 48, Wilson to John Silkin, 6 June 1966.
202² Wilson papers, box 59, Wilson to Duke of Edinburgh, 7 Jan 1965.
202³ Susan Crosland, *Crosland*, p 172.
202⁴ Wilson papers, box 157.

203[1] Cockerell, *Sources Close to the Prime Minister*, p 123.

203[2] Cockerell, *Live from Number 10*, pp 113–17.

203[3] Wilson papers, box 46.

204[1] Lyndon Johnson Library, NSF Country File, UK, vol III, 116, Martin to Johnson, 30 March 1965.

204[2] Wilson papers, box 54, Wilson to Pearson, 26 April 1954.

204[3] Lyndon Johnson Library, memos to the President, McGeorge Bundy, box 3, vol II, 26a.

204[4] Lyndon Johnson Library, NSF Country File, UK, vol VI, 80a, Bruce to Treasury, 26 July 1965.

205[1] Wilson papers, box 54, Wilson to Johnson, 29 July 1965.

205[2] Lyndon Johnson Library, NSF Country File, UK, box 215.4, Gardner Ackley to Johnson, 29 July 1965.

205[3] Lyndon Johnson Library, NSF Country File, UK, box 215.1, Ball to Johnson, 6 Aug 1965.

205[4] Lyndon Johnson Library, NSF Country File, UK, box 215.14, Bundy to Johnson, 28 July 1965.

205[5] Lyndon Johnson Library, NSF Country File, UK, box 215.12, Bator to Johnson, 29 July 1965.

205[6] Clive Ponting makes an intelligent guess in his *Breach of Promise*, London, 1989, pp 82–4.

206[1] Wilson papers, box 57, Wilson to Brown, 19 Aug 1965.

206[2] Wilson papers, box 14, Wilson to Brown, 6 June 1965.

207[1] Castle, *Diaries 1964–1970*, p 25.

207[2] Cockerell, *Live from Number 10*, p 120.

207[3] James Griffiths, *Pages from Memory*, London, 1969, pp 186–7.

207[4] Wilson papers, box 177.

207[5] Crossman, *Diaries*, vol 1, p 318.

208[1] Lyndon Johnson Library, NSF Country File, UK, box 213, 10 and 17a.

208[2] Lawrence Friedman, *Britain and Nuclear Weapons*, London, 1980, p 32.

208[3] Zuckerman, *Monkeys, Men and Missiles*, pp 373–4.

208[4] Hennessy, *Cabinet*, p 149.

209[1] Lyndon Johnson Library, NSF Country File, UK, box 5, vol 17, 49a, 16 Dec 1965.

209[2] Lyndon Johnson Library, NSF Country File, UK, box 213, Ball to Johnson, 5 Dec 1964.

209[3] Lyndon Johnson Library, memos to the President, McGeorge Bundy, box 2, vol 7, 78, 25 Nov 1964.

209[4] Philip Ziegler, *Mountbatten*, London, 1985, p 597.

209[5] Wilson papers, box 53, Wilson to Brown, 9 Dec 1964.

209[6] Wilson papers, box 50, Kosygin to Wilson, 6 Jan 1965; Wilson to Kosygin, 24 Feb 1965.

210[1] Short, *Whip to Wilson*, p 97.

210[2] Interview with Sir Oliver Wright.

210³ Lyndon Johnson Library, PM Wilson Visit Briefing Book, 32, Sec of State to Johnson, 27 July 1966.
210⁴ Lyndon Johnson Library, NSF Country File, UK, box 213, 10, 2 March 1964.
210⁵ Crossman, *Diaries*, vol 1, p 456.
211¹ Wilson papers, box 50, Lee Kuan Yew to Wilson, 23 Aug 1965.
211² Wilson, *Labour Government 1964–1970*, p 243.
211³ Goodman, *Cousins*, pp 422–3.
212¹ Healey, *Time of My Life*, p 273.
212² Hugh Cudlipp, *Walking on the Water*, London, 1976, p 314; Wilson papers, box 142, Wilson to Cudlipp, 25 March 1976.
212³ Cecil King, *Diary, 1965–1970*, p 30.
212⁴ Cudlipp, *Walking on the Water*, p 291.
212⁵ House of Commons, 29 July 1965 (*Hansard*, vol 717, cols 1186–96).
212⁶ Crossman, *Diaries*, vol 1, p 296.
212⁷ Benn, *Out of the Wilderness*, p 131.
213¹ Jenkins, *Life at the Centre*, p 178.
213² Castle, *Diaries 1964–1970*, p 79.
213³ *The Wilson Years*, programme 2.
213⁴ Short, *Whip to Wilson*, p 204.
214¹ Wilson papers, box 76, Wilson to Helsby, 14 Feb 1966.
214² Interview with Michael Foot.
215¹ Benn, *Out of the Wilderness*, p 390.
215² Castle, *Diaries 1964–1970*, p 34.
215³ Castle, *Diaries 1964–1970*, p 25.
215⁴ Interview with Lady Falkender.
215⁵ Benn, *Out of the Wilderness*, pp 343–4.
216¹ Wilson papers, box 62, Mitchell to D. P. Wratten, 1 Nov 1965.
216² Wilson papers, box 58, Wilson to the Queen, 18 Feb 1966.
216³ Crossman, *Diaries*, vol 1, pp 451–2.
217¹ Castle, *Diaries 1964–1970*, p 105.

Chapter XI: Foreign Affairs, 1964–1966

219¹ Wilson, *A Prime Minister on Prime Ministers*, p 131.
219² Stewart, *Life and Labour*, p 274.
219³ Crossman, *Diaries*, vol 1, p 407; interview with John Freeman.
219⁴ *cit.* Roth, *Wilson*, p 52.
220¹ Interview with John Freeman.
220² Lyndon Johnson Library, NSF Country File, UK, vol V, 36a, Rusk to Johnson, 30 June 1965.
220³ Wilson papers, box 54, Johnson to Wilson, 30 June 1965; box 50, Lal Bahadur to Wilson, 14 July 1965.
220⁴ Wilson papers, box 55, Wilson to Johnson, 12 Dec 1965.
220⁵ Wilson papers, box 54, Wilson to Abdul Rahman, 8 Aug 1965.
220⁶ Wilson papers, box 54, Lee Kuan Yew to Wilson, 21 Aug 1965.

220[7] Wilson papers, box 55, Wilson to Lee Kuan Yew, 30 Aug 1965.

221[1] Lyndon Johnson Library, NSF Trilateral Negotiations and NATO Office of the President File, box 13, note by Jack Valenti of briefing meeting, 16 Dec 1965.

221[2] Lyndon Johnson Library, NSF, memos to the President, Walt Rostow, vol 9, 43, 26 July 1966.

221[3] Lyndon Johnson Library, NSF Country File, UK, box 213, 5 and 5b.

221[4] Wilson, *The Labour Government 1964–1970*, p 48.

222[1] *The Wilson Years*, programme 2.

222[2] Castle, *Diaries 1964–1970*, p xiv.

222[3] Wilson, *The Labour Government 1964–1970*, p 80.

222[4] Castle, *Diaries 1964–1970*, p 13.

222[5] Lyndon Johnson Library, NSF, memos to the President, McGeorge Bundy, vol 8, 1/1, 28 Feb 1965.

223[1] Wilson papers, box 54, Wilson to Stewart, 23 March 1965.

223[2] "Mr Wilson speaks 'frankly and fearlessly' on Vietnam", Bertrand Russell Peace Foundation, London, 1968.

223[3] Lyndon Johnson Library, NSF Country File, UK, vol III, 37, 2 April 1965.

223[4] Wilson papers, box 54, Wilson to Johnson, 12 April 1965.

223[5] Lyndon Johnson Library, NSF, memos to the President, McGeorge Bundy, box 3, vol 9, 109a, 9 March 1965.

224[1] Lyndon Johnson Library, NSF, memos to the President, McGeorge Bundy, box 3, vol 9, 109.

224[2] Lyndon Johnson Library, NSF Country File, UK, vol III, 120, 23 March 1965.

224[3] Lyndon Johnson Library, NSF Country File, UK, box 215, 3c, Rusk to Johnson, 22 March 1965.

224[4] Wilson papers, box 14, Janeway to Kissin, 26 March 1965.

224[5] Wilson papers, box 54, Wilson to Robert Menzies, 26 April 1965.

224[6] Wilson, *The Labour Government 1964–1970*, p 96.

224[7] Lyndon Johnson Library, NSF Country File, UK, vol IV, 22, Bruce to Rusk, 3 June 1965.

225[1] Stewart, *Life and Labour*, p 156.

225[2] Wilson papers, box 50, Nkrumah to Wilson, 23 June 1965.

225[3] Crossman, *Diaries*, vol 1, p 253.

225[4] Castle, *Diaries 1964–1970*, p 40.

225[5] Lyndon Johnson Library, NSF, memos to the President, McGeorge Bundy, box 3, vol II, 38c, 23 June 1965.

226[1] Wilson papers, box 54, Wilson to Johnson, 2 Aug 1965.

226[2] Short, *Whip to Wilson*, p 205.

226[3] Lyndon Johnson papers, Office of the President File, Jack Valenti, memo of 16 Dec 1965.

226[4] Wilson papers, box 55, Wilson to Menzies, 24 Dec 1965.

227[1] Wilson, *The Labour Government 1964–1970*, p 204.

227[2] Wilson papers, box 57, Wilson to Stewart, 1 Feb 1966.

227[3] Wilson papers, box 56, Wilson to Johnson, 9 Feb 1966.

227⁴ Jones, *Union Man*, p 177.

227⁵ Lyndon Johnson Library, NSF Country File, UK, vol VIII, 19, 2 June 1966.

227⁶ Lyndon Johnson Library, NSF, memos to the President, Walt Rostow, box 8, vol 5, 59b.

228¹ Lyndon Johnson Library, NSF, memos to the President, Walt Rostow, box 8, vol 6, 23c.

228² Lyndon Johnson Library, NSF Country File, UK, vol VIII, 12 July 1966.

228³ Lyndon Johnson Library, NSF Country File, UK, vol VIII, 143, 15 July 1966.

228⁴ Wilson papers, box 52, Wilson to Johnson, 26 Feb 1966.

228⁵ Interview with Sir John Morgan.

229¹ Goodman, *Cousins*, pp 492–3.

229² Castle, *Diaries 1964–1970*, p 147.

229³ Lyndon Johnson Library, NSF Country File, UK, box 216, 12, Rostow to Johnson, 28 July 1966.

229⁴ Wilson, *The Labour Government 1964–1970*, pp 264–5.

229⁵ Lyndon Johnson Library, NSF Country File, UK, CO 305, Francis Bator to Johnson, 9 Aug 1966.

230¹ Robert Blake, *A History of Rhodesia*, London, 1977, p 357.

230² Wilson papers, box 49, Smith to Wilson, 17 Oct 1949.

231¹ Castle, *Diaries 1964–1970*, p 46; Wilson, *The Labour Government 1964–1970*, p 25.

231² Crossman, *Diaries*, vol 1, p 37.

231³ Wilson papers, box 49, Nkrumah to Wilson, 27 Oct 1964.

231⁴ Wilson papers, box 49, Smith to Wilson, 10 Nov 1964.

231⁵ Wilson papers, box 53, Wilson to Smith, 17 Nov 1964.

231⁶ Wilson papers, box 53, Wilson to Smith, 27 Nov 1964.

232¹ Wilson papers, box 47, Smith to Wilson, 15 Dec 1964.

232² Wilson papers, box 50, Smith to Wilson, 13 Jan 1965.

232³ Wilson, *The Labour Government 1964–1970*, pp 73–4.

232⁴ Wilson papers, box 54, Wilson to Pearson, 2 April 1965.

232⁵ Wilson papers, box 54, Wilson to Smith, 29 March 1965.

232⁶ Wilson papers, box 50, Nyerere to Wilson, 14 Aug 1965.

233¹ Wilson papers, box 55, Wilson to Stewart, 8 Oct 1965.

233² Wilson papers, box 55, Wilson to Pearson, 9 Oct 1965.

233³ Kenneth Flower, *Serving Secretly: An Intelligence Chief on Record*, London, 1987, p 45.

233⁴ Wilson papers, box 51, Smith to Wilson, 18 Oct 1965.

233⁵ Wilson papers, box 55, Wilson to Nyerere, 21 Oct 1965.

233⁶ Wilson papers, box 51, Pearson to Wilson, 20 Oct 1965.

234¹ Wilson papers, box 55, Wilson to Johnson, 29 Oct 1965.

234² Wilson papers, box 55, Wilson to Brown, 30 Oct 1965.

234³ Wilson, *The Labour Government 1964–1970*, p 159.

234⁴ House of Commons, 1 Nov 1965 (*Hansard*, vol 718, cols 629–48); Benn, *Out of the Wilderness*, p 342.

234⁵ Fisher, *Macleod*, p 273.

235¹ *Cecil King Diary. 1965–1970*, pp 43–5.

235² Lyndon Johnson Library, State Dept – US Embassy London, UK Cables, vol VII, 10/65 – 1/66, 28 Nov 1965.

235³ Healey, *The Time of My Life*, p 332.

235⁴ Wilson papers, box 57, Wilson to Bottomley, 13 Jan 1966.

235⁵ Crossman, *Diaries*, vol 1, p 382; Castle, *Diaries 1964–1970*, p 62.

235⁶ Interview with Martin Gilbert.

236¹ Cromer papers, memorandum on UDI.

236² Cromer papers, memorandum on UDI.

236³ Wilson papers, box 47, Wilson to Brown, 20 Dec 1965.

236⁴ Lyndon Johnson Library, NSF Country File, UK, vol VII, 224a.

236⁵ Castle, *Diaries 1964–1970*, p 90.

236⁶ Lyndon Johnson Library, Office of the President File, box 13, notes taken by Jack Valenti, 16 Dec 1965.

237¹ Wilson papers, box 55, Menzies to Wilson, 9 Dec 1965.

237² Wilson papers, box 51, Bustamante to Wilson, 11 Nov 1965.

237³ Wilson papers, box 51, Kaunda to Wilson, 26 Nov 1965.

237⁴ Lyndon Johnson Library, NSF Country File, UK, vol VII, 30 Dec 1965.

237⁵ Wilson papers, box 57, Wilson to Bottomley, 13 Jan 1966; box 48, Wilson to Cledwyn Hughes, 11 Feb 1966.

237⁶ R. C. Good, *UDI: The International Politics of the Rhodesian Rebellion*, London, 1973, pp 113–15.

237⁷ Tony Benn papers, Supplementary Journal for 1966.

238¹ Wilson papers, box 60, Driberg to Wilson, 15 April 1966 and Wilson to Driberg, 21 April 1966.

238² Wilson papers, box 58, Wilson to the Queen, 14 Sept 1966.

238³ Crossman, *Diaries*, vol 2, pp 29–30.

238⁴ Wilson papers, box 55, Wilson to Gibbs, 13 Nov 1965.

239⁵ Crossman, *Diaries*, vol 2, p 140.

239¹ Castle, *Diaries 1964–1970*, p 194.

239² Lord Elwyn-Jones, *In My Time*, London, 1983, p 212.

239³ Wilson papers, box 56, Wilson to the Pope, 1 Dec 1966.

239⁴ Paul Foot, *Wilson*, p 268.

239⁵ Crossman, *Diaries*, vol 2, p 146.

239⁶ Elwyn-Jones, *In My Time*, p 213.

239⁷ Pakenham, *The Grain of Wheat*, p 52.

240¹ Castle, *Diaries 1964–1970*, p 199.

240² Crossman, *Diaries*, vol 2, p 154.

240³ Benn, *Against the Tide*, p 256.

240⁴ Wilson papers, box 56, Wilson to Johnson, 26 May 1966.

241¹ Wilson papers, box 48, Wilson to Brown, 19 May 1966.

241² Castle, *Diaries 1964–1970*, p 145.

241³ Paul Foot, *Wilson*, p 237.

241⁴ Lyndon Johnson Library, NSF, memos to the President, Walt Rostow, box 8, vol 9. 43, 26 July 1966.

241⁵ Interview with Lord Jay; *Cecil King Diary*, p 67.

241[6] Of 22 Oct 1966.

241[7] Jenkins, *Life at the Centre*, p 190.

241[8] *Cecil King Diary*, p 82.

242[1] Lord O'Neill, *The Autobiography of Terence O'Neill*, London, 1972, p 62.

242[2] O'Neill, *Terence O'Neill*, p 83.

242[3] Wilson papers, box 114, Wilson to Lubbock, 11 Aug 1966.

242[4] Wilson papers, box 54, Wilson to Lemass, 19 Feb 1965.

243[1] Wilson papers, box 50, Lemass to Wilson, 13 March 1965.

Chapter XII: Triumph and Disaster, 1966

244[1] George Caunt diary, *passim*, in particular 7 March 1966.

244[2] Williams, *Inside Number 10*, p 280.

245[1] Crossman, *Diaries*, vol 2, p 506; Benn, *Out of the Wilderness*, p 345.

245[2] Jay, *Change and Fortune*, p 335.

245[3] An excellent account of the electoral campaign is to be found in D. E. Butler and Anthony King's *The British General Election of 1966*, London, 1966.

245[4] *Guardian*, 30 April 1966.

246[1] Crossman, *Diaries*, vol 1, p 483.

246[2] Castle, *Diaries 1964–1970*, p 113.

246[3] Benn, *Out of the Wilderness*, p 397.

246[4] Butler, *The British General Election of 1966*, p 130.

247[1] Cockerell, *Live from Number 10*, p 127.

247[2] Cox, *See It Happen*, pp 179–80.

247[3] Whale, *The Half-Shut Eye*, p 84.

248[1] Callaghan, *Time and Chance*, p 192.

248[2] Cockerell, *Live from Number 10*, p 129.

248[3] Williams, *Inside Number 10*, p 100; interview with Lady Falkender.

248[4] Lyndon Johnson Library, NSF Country File, UK, vol VIII, 64, 17 Feb 1966.

248[5] Interview with Sir Oliver Wright.

249[1] Wilson papers, box 48, Wilson to Bowden, 6 April 1966.

249[2] House of Commons, 28 April 1966 (*Hansard*, vol 727, cols 963–4).

249[3] Crossman, *Diaries*, vol 1, p 495.

249[4] Gordon Walker papers, 1/16, Wilson to Gordon Walker, 4 April 1966.

249[5] Interview with Lord Thomson.

250[1] Wilson papers, box 67, Callaghan to Wilson, 5 April 1966.

250[2] Gordon Walker, *Diaries*, p 307.

250[3] Castle, *Diaries 1964–1970*, p 135.

251[1] Crossman, *Diaries*, vol 1, p 538.

251[2] Interview with Lady Falkender.

251[3] *The Wilson Years*, programme 3.

252[1] Castle, *Diaries 1964–1970*, p 135; Crossman, *Diaries*, vol 1, p 554; Benn, *Out of the Wilderness*, pp 436 and 439.

252² Goodman, *Cousins*, p 485.

252³ Stewart, *Cousins*, pp 140–3.

252⁴ Stewart, *Cousins*, pp 143–4.

253¹ Benn, *Against the Tide*, p 510; Benn, unpublished diary, 29 Jan 1976.

253² Lady Falkender's papers, "Harold Wilson's Views on Economic Crisis of July/August 1966".

253³ Jay, *Change and Fortune*, p 346.

253⁴ "Wilson's Views on Economic Crisis", *op. cit.*

253⁵ Castle, *Diaries 1964–1970*, pp 147–8.

253⁶ e.g. Ponting, *Breach of Promise*, p 56.

254¹ Lyndon Johnson Library, NSF, memos to the President, Walt Rostow, box 8, vol 8, 6, 14 July 1966.

254² "Wilson's Views on Economic Crisis", *op. cit.*

254³ George Caunt diary.

255¹ Castle, *Diaries 1964–1970*, p 147.

255² Crossman, *Diaries*, vol 1, p 577.

255³ Wilson papers, box 67, Brown to Wilson, 20 July 1966.

255⁴ Callaghan, *Time and Chance*, p 200.

256¹ Wilson papers, box 56, Wilson to Indira Gandhi, 3 Aug 1966.

256² Lyndon Johnson Library, NSF, memos to the President, Walt Rostow, box 8, vol 9, 43, 26 July 1966.

256³ Castle, *Diaries 1964–1970*, p 152; *Cecil King Diary*, p 80; Crossman, *Diaries*, vol 1, p 581.

256⁴ Lyndon Johnson Library, NSF Country File, UK, box 216, PM, Wilson Visit Briefing Book, 52, 27 July 1966.

257¹ Crossman, *Diaries*, vol 1, p 587.

257² Crossman, *Diaries*, vol 1, p 591.

257³ Wilson, *The Labour Government 1964–1970*, p 256.

257⁴ Castle, *Diaries 1964–1970*, pp 145 and 172.

257⁵ Interview with Lord Goodman.

257⁶ Benn, *Out of the Wilderness*, pp 466 and 472.

257⁷ *Cecil King Diary*, p 101.

258¹ Benn, *Out of the Wilderness*, p 475.

258² Benn, unpublished diary, 12 Sept 1966.

258³ Castle, *Diaries 1964–1970*, p 147.

258⁴ Crossman, *Diaries*, vol 2, p 87.

258⁵ Jenkins, *Life at the Centre*, p 197.

259¹ "Wilson's Views on Economic Crisis", *op. cit.*

259² Shinwell, *I've Lived Through It All*, p 243.

259³ Wilson, *The Labour Government 1964–1970*, p 273.

260¹ Wilson papers, box 177, Williams to Wilson, Sept 1966.

260² Castle, *Diaries 1964–1970*, p 165.

260³ "Wilson's Views on Economic Crisis", *op. cit.*

260⁴ Callaghan, *Time and Chance*, pp 202–3.

261¹ Crossman, *Diaries*, vol 2, p 22.

261² Cudlipp, *Walking on the Water*, p 296.

261³ Lyndon Johnson Library, NSF Country File, UK, box 216, 15, 14 Oct 1966.

Chapter XIII: The Road to Devaluation, 1967

262¹ Crossman, *Diaries*, vol 2, p 729.
262² Crossman, *Diaries*, vol 2, p 718.
262³ Susan Crosland, *Crosland*, p 184.
263¹ Interview with Graham Ison.
263² Wilson papers, box 132, Wilson to Rees-Mogg, 9 March 1970.
263³ Castle, *Diaries 1964–1970*, p 115.
263⁴ *The Life and Times of Private Eye. 1961–1971*, Harmondsworth, 1971, p 18.
263⁵ Wilson papers, box 39, 14 Dec 1966.
263⁶ Wilson papers, box 39, 6 Jan 1970.
264¹ Wilson papers, box 2, Marcia Williams to Herbert Wilson, 12 March 1970.
264² Crossman, *Diaries*, vol 3, p 711.
264³ Stewart, *Life and Labour*, p 209.
264⁴ Crossman, *Diaries*, vol 2, p 439.
264⁵ Wilson papers, box 38, 22 Nov 1967.
265¹ Wilson papers, box 62, 20 Jan 1967.
265² Crossman, *Diaries*, vol 2, p 304.
265³ Short, *Whip to Wilson*, p 248.
265⁴ Crossman, *Diaries*, vol 3, p 373.
266¹ Wilson papers, box 134, Wilson to W. W. Hamilton, 30 April 1974.
266² Tony Benn, *Office Without Power. Diaries 1968–1972*, London, 1988 (references to Arrow Books edition, 1989), p 255.
266³ e.g. Crossman, *Diaries*, vol 2, p 88; Marsh, *Off the Rails*, p 114.
266⁴ Crossman, *Diaries*, vol 2, p 297.
267¹ Margach, *Abuse of Power*, pp 6 and 146.
267² Castle, *Diaries 1964–1970*, p 254.
267³ Interviews with Lord Goodman, David Astor and Nora Beloff.
267⁴ House of Commons, 21 Feb 1967 (*Hansard*, vol 741, cols 1432–3). For the fullest account of the matter see Peter Hedley and Cyril Aynsley, *The D-Notice Affair*, London, 1967.
268¹ Cmnd 3312.
268² House of Lords, 6 July 1967 (*Hansard*, vol 284, cols 776).
268³ Castle, *Diaries 1964–1970*, p 268.
268⁴ Wilson, *Labour Government 1964–1970*, pp 373–4.
268⁵ Wilson papers, box 76, Wilson to Lloyd-Hughes, undated.
269¹ Pincher, *Inside Story*, p 245.
269² Crossman, *Diaries*, vol 3, p 388; Benn, *Office Without Power*, p 236.
269³ Robert Jenkins, *Benn*, p 144.
269⁴ Cockerell, *Live from Number 10*, p 133.
269⁵ Lusty, *Bound to be Read*, p 253.

269[6] Wilson papers, box 57, Wilson to Short, 19 March 1968.
270[1] Wilson papers, box 130, Wilson to Hill, 4 Feb 1969.
270[2] Cockerell, *Live from Number 10*, p 140; Lord Hill, *Behind the Scenes*, London, 1974, pp 99–101.
270[3] Cockerell, *Live from Number 10*, p 151.
270[4] Interview with Lady Falkender.
270[5] Wilson papers, box 57, Wilson to Gardiner, 29 Jan 1967.
271[1] Jay, *Change and Fortune*, pp 378–9.
271[2] Gordon Walker, *The Cabinet*, pp 33–4; interview with Lord Jenkins.
271[3] Wilson papers, box 177, Castle to Wilson and Crossman to Wilson, 11 Sept 1967.
271[4] Marsh, *Off the Rails*, p 89.
271[5] Gordon Walker, *The Cabinet*, p 110.
272[1] Wilson papers, box 77, Wigg to Wilson, 10 March 1967.
272[2] Interview with Paul Johnson.
272[3] Castle, *Diaries 1964–1970*, p 261.
272[4] Tony Benn papers, supplementary journal for 1966.
272[5] Crossman, *Diaries*, vol 2, p 159.
272[6] Interview with Denis Healey; Crossman, *Diaries*, vol 3, p 378.
274[1] Lady Falkender papers, Wilson's Memo on Devaluation Crisis, dictated 2–17 Nov 1967.
274[2] Crossman, *Diaries*, vol 2, pp 779–81; Hennessy, *Whitehall*, p 262.
274[3] Peter Jenkins, *The Battle of Downing Street*, London, 1970, p 95.
274[4] Crossman, *Diaries*, vol 2, p 260.
274[5] Interview with Lord Owen.
274[6] Crossman, *Diaries*, vol 2, p 243.
274[7] Lyndon Johnson Library, NSF Country File, UK, box 216, Briefing Book 2/67.12a.
275[1] Crossman, *Diaries*, vol 2, p 287.
275[2] Crossman, *Diaries*, vol 2, p 262.
275[3] Benn, *Out of the Wilderness*, p 490; Castle, *Diaries 1964–1970*, p 232; Wigg, *George Wigg*, p 343.
275[4] Wilson papers, box 177, Crossman to Wilson, 5 March 1967.
276[1] Wilson papers, box 119, Norfolk to Wilson, 19 Oct 1967 and Wilson to Norfolk, 31 Oct 1967.
276[2] Emrys Hughes, *Sydney Silverman*, London, 1969, pp 195–8.
276[3] Crossman, *Diaries*, vol 2, p 392.
276[4] Hoggart, *Foot*, p 157.
276[5] John Campbell, *Roy Jenkins*, London, 1983, p 102.
276[6] Crossman, *Diaries*, vol 2, p 445.
277[1] Wilson papers, box 38, 13 June 1967.
278[1] Wilson papers, box 57, Wilson to Trend, 10 April 1967.
278[2] Wilson papers, box 57, Wilson to Stewart, 30 Aug 1967.
278[3] Castle, *Diaries 1964–1970*, p 283.
278[4] Lady Falkender papers, Wilson's Memo on Devaluation Crisis.
279[1] Interview with Graham Ison.
279[2] Crossman, *Diaries*, vol 2, pp 461–2.

279³ Castle, *Diaries 1964–1970*, p 290.
279⁴ Wilson papers, box 69, Wilson to Pearson, 4 Sept 1967.
279⁵ *Cecil King Diary, 1965–1970*, p 141.
279⁶ Brittan, *Steering the Economy*, p 58.
280¹ Goodman, *Cousins*, p 540.
280² Crosland, *Tony Crosland*, p 185.
280³ Crossman, *Diaries*, vol 2, p 576.
281¹ The substance of this and, unless otherwise indicated, the next few paragraphs comes from Wilson's Memo on Devaluation Crisis in Lady Falkender's papers.
281² Lyndon Baines Johnson, *The Vantage Point*, London, 1972, p 315.
282¹ e.g. the *Spectator*, 24 Nov 1967.
282² Castle, *Diaries 1964–1970*, p 325.
282³ *Cecil King Diary, 1965–1970*, p 157.
283¹ Benn, *Out of the Wilderness*, p 513.
283² Castle, *Diaries 1964–1970*, p 329.
283³ Callaghan, *Time and Chance*, p 223.
283⁴ Jenkins, *Life at the Centre*, p 215.
283⁵ Interview with Lady Falkender.
283⁶ Jenkins, *Life at the Centre*, p 215.
283⁷ Castle, *Diaries 1964–1970*, p 333.
283⁸ Campbell, *Jenkins*, p 111.
283⁹ Crossman, *Diaries*, vol 2, p 639.
284¹ Interview with Lady Falkender.
284² Falkender, *Downing Street in Perspective*, p 229.
284³ Jenkins, *Life at the Centre*, pp 259–60.
284⁴ Wilson papers, box 69, Wilson to Johnson, 17 Nov 1967.
284⁵ Paul Foot, *Wilson*, pp 194–5.
285¹ Healey, *The Time of My Life*, p 273.
285² Benn, *Office Without Power*, p 13.
285³ Wilson papers, box 72, Johnson to Wilson, 14 Jan 1968.
285⁴ Wilson papers, box 72, Wilson to Johnson, 15 Jan 1968.
286¹ Margach, *The Abuse of Power*, p 178.
286² Phillip Whitehead, *The Writing on the Wall*, London, 1985, p 11.
286³ Wilson papers, box 2, Williams to Herbert Wilson, 23 Nov 1967.

Chapter XIV: Strains Within the Cabinet, 1968

287¹ Castle, *Diaries 1964–1970*, p 465.
287² Crossman, *Diaries*, vol 2, p 477.
288¹ Silkin, *Changing Battlefields*, pp 78–9.
288² Castle, *Diaries 1964–1970*, p 336.
288³ Wilson papers, box 69, 13 Dec 1967.
288⁴ Healey, *The Time of My Life*, p 336.
289¹ Healey, *The Time of My Life*, pp 335–6.
289² Gordon Walker, *Diaries*, p 317.

289³ Gordon Walker, *Diaries*, p 318.
290¹ Wilson papers, box 67, Brown to Wilson, 18 Dec 1967.
290² Wilson papers, box 67, Wilson to Brown, 18 Dec 1967.
290³ Crossman, *Diaries*, vol 2, p 626.
290⁴ Wilson, *The Labour Government 1964–1970*, p 493; Castle, *Diaries 1964–1970*, p 370.
290⁵ Benn, *Office Without Power*, p 33.
290⁶ The speech is quoted extensively in Wilson, *The Labour Government 1964–1970*, pp 525–8.
291¹ Wilson papers, box 119, Wilson to Osborne, 14 Aug 1967.
291² Lyndon Johnson Library, NSF, NS Council History, box 53, Tab 60a, Johnson to Wilson, 15 March 1968.
291³ Brown, *In My Way*, pp 175–8.
292¹ Lady Falkender papers, Wilson's Memo on Gold Crisis of March 1968, dictated 14 March 1968.
292² Marsh, *Off the Rails*, pp 119–21.
292³ Wilson's Memo on Gold Crisis.
292⁴ Brown, *In My Way*, p 178.
292⁵ Wilson's Memo on Gold Crisis.
292⁶ Castle, *Diaries 1964–1970*, p 403; Crossman, *Diaries*, vol 2, p 714.
293¹ Castle, *Diaries 1964–1970*, p 417.
293² Marsh, *Off the Rails*, pp 122–4.
293³ Wilson papers, box 67, Healey to Wilson, 1 April 1968.
293⁴ Castle, *Diaries 1964–1970*, pp 417 and 430.
293⁵ Gordon Walker, *Diaries*, p 321.
294¹ Wilson papers, box 57, Wilson to Jenkins, 9 May 1968.
294² Cudlipp, *Walking on the Water*, p 371.
294³ Crossman, *Diaries*, vol 3, p 58.
294⁴ Wilson papers, box 2, Williams to Marjorie Wilson, 15 May 1968.
294⁵ Lyndon Johnson Library, NSC Meetings File, box 2, vol V, Tab 69 and Bruce to Sec. of State, 5 June 1968.
295¹ Mayhew, *Time to Explain*, p 181.
295² Gordon Walker, *Diaries*, pp 322–3.
295³ Interview with Roy Hattersley.
295⁴ Gordon Walker, *Diaries*, p 323.
295⁵ Mayhew, *Time to Explain*, pp 184–5.
296¹ Brown, *In My Way*, pp 194–5.
296² Wilson papers, box 42, Wilson's record of NEC subcommittee meeting of 15 July 1968.
297¹ Crossman, *Diaries*, vol 3, p 166.
297² *Financial Times*, 2 Oct 1968.
297³ Goodman, *Cousins*, p 560.
298¹ Wilson, *The Labour Government 1964–1970*, p 583; Jenkins, *Life at the Centre*, p 264; Crossman, *Diaries*, vol 3, p 272.
298² The rumours were summarised in the *Sunday Times* "Insight" column of 8 Dec 1968.

Chapter XV: In Place of Strife, 1969

299[1] David Butler and Michael Pinto-Duschinsky, *The British General Election of 1970*, London, 1971, p 38. The fullest account of the affair is to be found in Peter Jenkins's admirable *The Battle of Downing Street*, London, 1970.

300[1] Heffer, *The Class Struggle*, p 103.

301[1] Castle, *Diaries 1964–1970*, p 566.

301[2] Marsh, *Off the Rails*, p 139; interview with Lord Marsh.

301[3] Interview with Lord Callaghan.

302[1] Interview with Lord Lever.

302[2] Davenport, *Memoirs of a City Radical*, p 221.

303[1] Heffer, *The Class Struggle*, p 126.

303[2] Castle, *Diaries 1964–1970*, pp 625–6.

303[3] Wilson papers, box 74, Wilson to Peart and Peart to Wilson, 31 March 1969.

303[4] Wilson papers, box 67, Callaghan to Wilson, 2 April 1969.

303[5] Castle, *Diaries 1964–1970*, p 631.

304[1] Crossman, *Diaries*, vol 3, p 435.

304[2] Goodman, *Cousins*, p 580.

304[3] Jones, *Union Man*, p 203.

304[4] Wilson papers, box 148, Wilson to Castle, 14 April 1969.

304[5] Silkin, *Changing Battlefields*, p 79.

305[1] Abse, *Private Member*, p 152.

305[2] Heffer, *The Class Struggle*, p 128.

305[3] Crossman, *Diaries*, vol 3, p 463; Castle, *Diaries 1964–1970*, pp 640–1.

305[4] Castle, *Diaries 1964–1970*, p 642.

305[5] Wilson papers, box 61, Boothby to Wilson, 26 April 1969.

306[1] Crossman, *Diaries*, vol 3, p 470.

306[2] Mayhew, *Time to Explain*, p 185.

306[3] Gordon Walker, *Diaries*, p 325.

306[4] Callaghan, *Time and Chance*, p 275.

306[5] Frank Pakenham, Earl of Longford, *Diary of a Year*, London, 1982, p 154.

307[1] Harris, *Making of Neil Kinnock*, p 46.

307[2] *cit.* Heffer, *The Class Struggle*, p 130.

307[3] Benn, *Office Without Power*, p 166.

307[4] Crossman, *Diaries*, vol 3, p 480; Healey, *The Time of My Life*, p 341.

307[5] Jay, *Change and Fortune*, p 440.

307[6] Crossman, *Diaries*, vol 3, p 481.

308[1] Castle, *Diaries 1964–1970*, pp 657–8 and 661.

308[2] Jones, *Union Man*, pp 203–4.

309[1] Wilson papers, box 67, Ennals to Wilson, 6 June 1969.

309[2] Castle, *Diaries 1964–1970*, pp 668–9.

309[3] Interview with Joe Haines.

310¹ Crossman, *Diaries*, vol 3, p 519; Castle, *Diaries 1964–1970*, p 673; Benn, *Office Without Power*, p 187.
310² Wilson papers, box 74, Wilson to Healey, 18 June 1969.
310³ Castle, *Diaries 1964–1970*, pp 676–9; Wilson, *The Labour Government 1964–1970*, p 661.
310⁴ *The Cecil King Diary, 1970–1974*, London, 1975, p 133.
310⁵ Benn, *Office Without Power*, p 187.
311¹ Howard, *Crossman*, pp 292–4.
311² Castle, *Diaries 1964–1970*, p 679.
311³ Healey, *The Time of My Life*, p 341.
311⁴ Wilson papers, box 73, Lee Kuan Yew to Wilson, 10 May 1959.
312¹ Peter Jenkins, *Battle of Downing Street*, p 167.
312² Jenkins, *Life at the Centre*, p 291.
312³ Susan Crosland, *Crosland*, p 204.
312⁴ Brown, *In My Way*, pp 198–9.
312⁵ Castle, *Diaries 1964–1970*, p 706.
312⁶ Goodman, *Cousins*, p 589.
313¹ Castle, *Diaries 1964–1970*, p 747.
313² Benn, *Office Without Power*, p 237.
314¹ Crossman, *Diaries*, vol 3, pp 725–6.
314² Crossman, *Diaries*, vol 3, p 107.
315¹ Wilson, *The Labour Government 1964–1970*, p 540.
315² Wilson papers, box 45, Wilson to John Staniforth, 12 April 1970.
315³ Crossman, *Diaries*, vol 3, p 906.
316¹ Crossman, *Diaries*, vol 3, p 799.
316² Interview with John Freeman.
317¹ For a well-argued presentation of the Wilson government's achievements, see Kenneth O. Morgan, *Labour People*, Oxford, 1987, pp 252–3.
317² Jenkins, *Life at the Centre*, p 299.

Chapter XVI: Foreign Affairs, 1967–1970

318¹ Wilson papers, box 130, Wilson to Hattersley, 1 Dec 1969.
318² Lyndon Johnson Library, NSF Country File, UK, vol VIII, 1978, 257A.
319¹ Wilson papers, box 119, Wilson to Sandys, 24 July 1967.
319² Castle, *Diaries 1964–1970*, p 282.
319³ Wilson papers, box 68, Vorster to Wilson, 28 Oct 1967.
319⁴ Interview with Lady Falkender. For a well-argued if slightly tendentious analysis of the oil embargo, *see* Ponting, *Breach of Promise*, pp 249–56 and also Martin Bailey's *Oilgate: The Sanctions Scandal*, London, 1979, pp 200–14.
320¹ Wilson papers, box 122, Wilson to Gibbs, 29 March 1968.
320² Castle, *Diaries 1964–1970*, p 392.
320³ Wilson papers, box 72, Wilson to Gorton, 27 March 1968.
321¹ Wilson papers, box 57, Wilson to Stewart, 13 Sept 1968.

321[2] Wilson papers, box 72, Wilson to Johnson, 7 Oct 1968.

321[3] Crossman, *Diaries*, vol 3, p 216.

321[4] Wilson papers, box 72, Stewart to Wilson, 8 Oct 1968.

321[5] Wilson papers, box 72, Kaunda to Wilson, 8 Oct 1968.

321[6] Wilson papers, box 72, Wilson to Jenkins, 14 Oct 1968.

321[7] Greenwood papers, Bodleian Library, uncatalogued, 1st tier, shelf 1.

322[1] Wilson papers, box 72, Wilson to Stewart, 13 oct 1968.

322[2] Wilson papers, box 67, Williams to Wilson, 4 Nov 1968; Prentice to Wilson, 24 Oct 1968.

322[3] Interview with Sir Richard Faber.

322[4] Williams, *Inside Number 10*, p 272.

322[5] Wilson papers, box 72, Thomson to Wilson, 11 Nov 1968.

322[6] Wilson papers, box 72, Wilson to Kaunda, 23 Oct 1968.

323[1] Wilson papers, box 72, Thomson to Wilson and Wilson to Thomson, 6 Nov 1968.

323[2] Wilson papers, box 125, Wilson to Judd, 23 Dec 1968.

323[3] Wilson papers, box 72, Wilson to Pearson *et al.*, 2 July 1968.

324[1] Crossman, *Diaries*, vol 3, p 326.

324[2] Interview with John Freeman.

324[3] "Mr Wilson speaks 'frankly and fearlessly' on Vietnam", Bertrand Russell Peace Foundation, 1968.

324[4] Wilson papers, box 69, Wilson to Johnson, 7 Feb 1967.

325[1] *The Secret Diplomacy of the Vietnam War. The Negotiating Volumes of the Pentagon Papers*, ed. George C. Herring, Austin, Texas, 1983.

325[2] Lyndon Johnson Library, Oral History Collection, interviews with Chester Cooper, AC 74 – 2000.

325[3] Wilson papers, box 69, Wilson to Johnson, 12 Feb 1967.

325[4] Wilson papers, box 69, Johnson to Wilson, 12 Feb 1967.

326[1] Lyndon Johnson Library, Oral History Collection, *op. cit.*

326[2] Crossman, *Diaries*, vol 2, p 237.

326[3] *Sunday Times*, 16 May 1971.

326[4] Wilson papers, box 57, Wilson to Brown, 15 March 1967.

326[5] Kissinger, *White House Years*, p 43.

326[6] Benn, *Out of the Wilderness*, p 501.

326[7] Wilson papers, box 72, Johnson to Wilson, 6 Oct 1967.

327[1] Lady Falkender papers, Wilson's Memo on Devaluation Crisis.

327[2] Interview with Winston Churchill; Castle, *Diaries 1964–1970*, p 374.

327[3] Wilson papers, box 72, Wilson to Johnson, 13 Feb 1968.

328[1] Interview with John Freeman; Kissinger, *White House Years*, p 95.

328[2] Kissinger, *White House Years*, pp 59 and 92.

328[3] Wilson papers, box 73, Nixon to Wilson, 5 March 1969.

328[4] Interview with John Freeman.

328[5] Wilson papers, box 74, Nixon to Wilson, 3 Feb 1969.

328[6] Williams, *Inside Number 10*, p 279.

329[1] Kissinger, *White House Years*, p 91.

329[2] Castle, *Diaries 1964–1970*, p 763.

329[3] Lyndon Johnson Library, NSF, Trilateral Negotiations and NATO

1966–67, Book 1, Tab 5c, Johnson to Wilson, 26 Aug 1966.

329⁴ Lyndon Johnson Library, WH Central File, Confidential File, FO 4–1, FO3–2–1.

329⁵ Wyatt, *Turn Again Westminster*, p 157.

330¹ Wilson papers, box 69, Wilson to Holt, 20 April 1967.

330² Wilson papers, box 69, Holt to Wilson, 21 April 1967.

330³ Lyndon Johnson Library, Country File, UK, box 216, visit of PM Harold Wilson 6/2/67, 22.

330⁴ Lyndon Johnson Library, Country File, UK, box 216, visit of PM Harold Wilson 6/2/67, 53d.

330⁵ Wilson papers, box 69, Johnson to Wilson, 6 July 1967.

331¹ Wilson papers, box 69, Holt to Wilson, 13 July 1967.

331² Wilson papers, box 72, Thomson to Wilson, 8 Jan and 12 Jan 1968.

331³ Wilson papers, box 72, Brown to Wilson, 11 Jan 1968.

331⁴ Wilson papers, box 72, Johnson to Wilson, 12 Jan 1968.

331⁵ Castle, *Diaries 1964–1970*, p 215.

332¹ Whitehead, *The Writing on the Wall*, p 9.

332² Lyndon Johnson Library, NSF Trilateral Negotiations, Book 1, Tab 33a, Johnson to Wilson, 15 Nov 1966.

332³ Interview with Sir Michael Palliser.

332⁴ Jay, *Change and Fortune*, pp 365–7.

332⁵ Marsh, *Off the Rails*, p 96.

333¹ Jay, *Change and Fortune*, p 370.

333² Donnelly, *Gadarene '68*, p 89.

333³ Crossman, *Diaries*, vol 2, p 465.

333⁴ Wilson, *The Labour Government 1964–1970*, p 368.

333⁵ Donnelly, *Gadarene '68*, p 90.

333⁶ Jay, *Change and Fortune*, p 371.

334¹ Wilson papers, box 57, Wilson to Trend, 5 March 1967.

334² *Cecil King Diary, 1965–1970*, p 124.

334³ Castle, *Diaries 1964–1970*, p 215.

334⁴ Donnelly, *Gadarene '68*, p 91.

334⁵ Lyndon Johnson Library, "Secret Administrative History of the State Department", chapter 3, Europe, section C.

335¹ Castle, *Diaries 1964–1970*, p 244.

335² Wilson papers, box 69, Wilson to Brown, 20 April 1967.

335³ Gordon Walker, *Diaries*, p 313.

335⁴ Martin Gilbert, "In Search of Churchill".

335⁵ Wilson papers, box 69, Wilson to Brown, 21 June 1967.

336¹ Wilson papers, box 167, transcript of 12 July 1977.

336² Crossman, *Diaries*, vol 2, p 392.

336³ Wilson papers, box 122, Wilson to Kennett, 31 Jan 1968.

337¹ Wilson papers, box 74, Stewart to Wilson, 6 Feb 1969; Wilson to Stewart, 12 Feb 1969.

337² Wilson, *The Labour Government 1964–1970*, pp 611–12.

337³ Crossman, *Diaries*, vol 3, p 379.

337⁴ Wilson papers, box 57, 30 Oct 1969.

337[5] Crossman, *Diaries*, vol 3, p 719.
337[6] Interview with Lord Thomson.
338[1] House of Commons, 25 Feb 1970 (*Hansard*, vol 796, cols 1324–37).
338[2] Wilson papers, box 68, Gowon to Wilson, 31 May 1967.
338[3] Wilson, *The Labour Government 1964–1970*, p 557.
339[1] Wilson papers, box 72, Wilson to Gowon, 5 April 1968; Gowon to Wilson, 16 April 1968.
339[2] Wilson papers, box 72, Wilson to Stewart, 6 Dec 1968.
339[3] Wilson papers, box 72, Wilson to Stewart, 6 Dec 1968.
339[4] Castle, *Diaries 1964–1970*, p 628.
340[1] Wilson papers, box 75, Wilson to Nixon, 17 Jan 1970.
340[2] Crossman, *Diaries*, vol 3, p 779.
340[3] Interview with Lady Falkender.
341[1] Mayhew, *Time to Explain*, p 159.
341[2] Wilson papers, box 177.
341[3] Wilson, *The Chariot of Israel*, p 331.
341[4] Castle, *Diaries 1964–1970*, pp 257–8; Gordon Walker, *Diaries*, p 314.
342[1] *Abba Eban. An Autobiography*, London, 1978, pp 345–6.
342[2] Wilson papers, box 69, Wilson to Pearson, 25 May 1967.
342[3] Wilson papers, box 69, Wilson to Kosygin, 28 May 1967.
342[4] Wilson papers, box 69, Wilson to Brown, 3 June 1967.
342[5] Lyndon Johnson Library, NSF Histories, vol 1, Tabs 21–30, 24 May 1967.
342[6] Patrick Gordon Walker, *The Cabinet*, London, 1970, pp 138–52.
342[7] *Daily Mail*, 9 April 1970.
342[8] Wilson, *The Labour Government 1964–1970*, p 401.
343[1] Morgan, *Wilson*, p 307.
343[2] Interview with Lord Marsh.
343[3] Crossman, *Diaries*, vol 3, p 423.
343[4] Interview with Lord Chalfont; Wilson papers, box 72, Wilson to Stewart, 6 Dec 1968.
344[1] Wilson papers, box 57, Wilson to Brown, 28 April 1967.
344[2] Crossman, *Diaries*, vol 3, p 347.
345[1] Wilson papers, box 72, Wilson to O'Neill, 19 Nov 1968; O'Neill to Wilson, 6 Dec 1968.
345[2] Information from Nigel Hamilton.
345[3] *Cecil King Diary*, p 253.
345[4] James Callaghan, *A House Divided*, London, 1973, p 99.

Chapter XVII: Electoral Defeat, 1970

346[1] Castle, *Diaries 1964–1970*, p 758.
347[1] Wilson, *Governance of Britain*, p 38.
347[2] Interview with Joe Haines.
347[3] Joe Haines, *The Politics of Power*, London, 1977, p 170.

347[4] Castle, *Diaries 1964–1970*, p 769; Benn, *Office Without Power*, p 249.

347[5] Interview with Joe Haines.

347[6] Crossman, *Diaries*, vol 3, p 893.

348[1] *The Wilson Years*, programme 3.

348[2] Crossman, *Diaries*, vol 3, pp 920–1.

348[3] Wilson papers, box 75, Wilson to Nixon, 17 May 1970.

348[4] Kissinger, *White House Years*, p 932.

348[5] David Butler and Michael Pinto-Duschinsky, *The British General Election of 1970*, London, 1971, p xii.

348[6] Crossman, *Diaries*, vol 3, pp 914–15.

349[1] Castle, *Diaries 1964–1970*, p 802.

349[2] Butler, *The British General Election of 1970*, p 146.

349[3] Haines, *Politics of Power*, p 170.

349[4] Interview with William Camp.

349[5] Cockerell, *Live from Number 10*, p 156.

349[6] Wyatt, *Confessions of an Optimist*, pp 314–15.

350[1] Abse, *Private Member*, p 46.

350[2] *The Wilson Years*, programme 3.

350[3] Wilson papers, box 1, Hiller to Wilson, 4 Nov 1970.

350[4] Jones, *Union Man*, pp 220–1.

350[5] Butler, *The British General Election of 1970*, p 2 *n.*

350[6] Castle, *Diaries 1964–1970*, p 800.

350[7] Interview with William Camp.

351[1] Interview with Lord Lovell-Davis.

351[2] Benn, *Against the Tide*, p 92.

352[1] Interview with Graham Ison.

353[1] Hill, *Behind the Screen*, p 157.

353[2] Wilson papers, box 83.

353[3] Interview with Graham Ison.

353[4] Interview with Lady Falkender.

353[5] Silkin, *Changing Battlefields*, p 12.

353[6] e.g. Interview with William Camp.

354[1] Williams, *Inside Number 10*, p 2; Falkender, *Downing Street in Perspective*, p 14.

354[2] Interview with Joe Haines.

354[3] Jenkins, *Life at the Centre*, p 304.

354[4] Benn, *Office Without Power*, p 296.

Chapter XVIII: Adjusting to Opposition, 1970–1971

355[1] Crossman, *Diaries*, vol 2, p 36.

356[1] George Caunt diary, 23 June and 1 Aug 1970.

356[2] *Cecil King Diary, 1970–1974*, p 88.

356[3] Wilson papers, box 21, 8 Dec 1970 and 24 July 1970.

357[1] Williams, *Inside Number 10*, p 7.

357² *Cecil King Diary, 1970–1974*, p 24.
357³ Interview with Lady Falkender.
358¹ Wilson papers, box 38, 23 Feb 1972.
359¹ Wilson papers, box 5, Wilson to Goodman Derrick, 11 Nov 1971.
360¹ George Caunt diary, 16 Oct 1970.
360² Haines, *Politics of Power*, p 176.
360³ *Cecil King Diary, 1970–1974*, p 60.
361¹ *Cecil King Diary, 1970–1974*, pp 62–3.
361² Gilbert, "In Search of Churchill".
361³ Wilson papers, box 85, Trend to Wilson, 1 Oct 1970.
361⁴ Wilson papers, box 41, Wilson to Robert Simpson, 10 Sept 1971.
362¹ Gilbert papers, record of meeting of 16 March 1971.
362² *Cecil King Diary, 1970–1974*, p 125.
362³ *New Statesman*, 30 July 1971.
362⁴ *The Times*, 26 July 1971.
362⁵ *Chicago Sunday Times*, 28 Nov 1971.
362⁶ *Financial Times*, 29 July 1971.
363¹ *Cecil King Diary, 1970–1974*, p 160.
363² Wilson papers, box 112, Wilson to Higham, 2 Aug 1971.
364¹ Jenkins, *Life at the Centre*, pp 309–10.
364² *The Wilson Years*, programme 4.
364³ Haines, *Politics of Power*, p 175; interview with Joe Haines.
364⁴ Interview with Lady Falkender.
364⁵ George Caunt diary, 16 July 1970.
364⁶ George Caunt diary, 31 Dec 1970.
365¹ Benn, *Against the Tide*, p 25.
365² "The Secretariat of the Leader of H.M. Opposition and the Labour Party", Report by Hesketh, Hardy, Hirshfield and Co, copy in Gilbert papers.
365³ Interview with Lord Goodman.
366¹ Wilson papers, box 89.
367¹ Wilson papers, box 18, 6 Nov 1973.
368¹ Castle, *Diaries 1964–1970*, pp 74–5.
368² Greenwood papers, uncatalogued, memo of 8 Aug 1972.
368³ Cockerell, *Live from Number 10*, p 177.
369¹ Hill, *Behind the Screen*, p 182.
369² Wilson papers, box 83.
370¹ Hill, *Behind the Screen*, p 190.

Chapter XIX: Opposition, 1970–1974

371¹ Abse, *Private Member*, p 46.
371² Wilson papers, box 88, Houghton to Wilson, 29 June 1970.
372¹ Benn, *Office Without Power*, pp 299–300.
372² Falkender, *Downing Street in Perspective*, p 15; interview with Joe Haines.

372³ Falkender, *Downing Street in Perspective*, p 45.
372⁴ *Cecil King Diary, 1970–1974*, pp 62 and 84.
372⁵ *Cecil King Diary, 1970–1974*, p 62.
372⁶ Benn, *Office Without Power*, p 328; *Cecil King Diary, 1970–1974*, p 89.
373¹ Benn, *Office Without Power*, pp 336–7.
373² Wilson papers, box 94, Berkeley to Wilson, 22 Aug 1970; Wilson to Berkeley, undated.
373³ *Cecil King Diary, 1970–1974*, p 126.
373⁴ Interview with Tony Benn.
374¹ Benn, *Office Without Power*, pp 328 and 360.
374² Benn, *Office Without Power*, pp 328 and 352.
374³ Haines, *Politics of Power*, p 174.
374⁴ Benn, *Office Without Power*, p 352.
374⁵ Wilson papers, box 41, Crossman to Wilson, Aug 1971.
375¹ Wigg, *George Wigg*, p 152.
375² Benn, *Office Without Power*, p 391.
375³ Wilson papers, box 88, Judd to Wilson, 19 April 1971.
375⁴ Wilson papers, box 37, Williams to Wilson, 22 June and 15 Sept 1971.
375⁵ Wilson papers, box 88, Judd to Wilson, 6 Nov 1970.
375⁶ *Cecil King Diary, 1970–1974*, p 83.
376¹ Wilson papers, box 40, Joseph to Wilson, 22 May 1972; Wilson to Joseph, 18 July 1972.
376² Wilson papers, box 83, Mellish to Wilson, 10 Nov 1970; Wilson to Mellish, 11 Nov 1970.
377¹ Heffer, *Class Struggle*, pp 224–5.
377² Cockerell, *Live from Number 10*, p 184.
377³ Benn, *Office Without Power*, p 408.
377⁴ Robert Jenkins, *Benn*, p 158; Benn, *Office Without Power*, p 408.
378¹ Callaghan, *A House Divided*, p 175; Wilson, *Final Term*, p 68; Haines, *Politics of Power*, p 123.
378² House of Commons, 25 November 1971 (*Hansard*, vol 826, cols 1571–93).
378³ Callaghan, *A House Divided*, p 176.
378⁴ Benn, *Office Without Power*, p 387.
379¹ Wilson papers, box 87.
379² Wilson papers, box 87, Wilson to O'Brien, April 1972.
379³ Haines, *Politics of Power*, p 128.
379⁴ Conor Cruse O'Brien, *States of Ireland*, London, 1972, p 286.
380¹ Wilson papers, box 87, Faulkner to Wilson, 14 March 1972; Wilson to Faulkner, 17 March 1972.
280² Wilson papers, box 86.
380³ Wilson papers, box 87, McIldoon to Wilson, 15 March 1972.
380⁴ Interview with Lord Thomson.
381¹ Robert Jenkins, *Benn*, p 175.
382¹ Philip Goodhart, *Full-Hearted Consent*, London, 1976, p 12.
382² Campbell, *Jenkins*, p 143.

382[3] Jenkins, *Life at the Centre*, pp 318–19.

382[4] Benn, *Office Without Power*, p 336.

382[5] Wilson papers, box 84.

382[6] Jenkins, *Life at the Centre*, p 317.

382[7] Benn, *Office Without Power*, p 343.

383[1] Interview with Lord Owen.

383[2] *Cecil King Diary, 1970–1974*, p 121.

383[3] Wilson papers, box 37, Wilson to Brandt, 26 July 1971.

383[4] Jenkins, *Life at the Centre*, p 320.

383[5] Benn, *Office Without Power*, p 356; Barbara Castle, *The Castle Diaries 1974–1976*, London, 1990, pp 12–13.

384[1] Campbell, *Jenkins*, p 141.

384[2] Gordon Walker, *Diaries*, p 326.

384[3] Wilson papers, box 41, Wilson to Mellish, 7 Oct 1971.

385[1] Benn, *Office Without Power*, p 379.

385[2] Benn, *Office Without Power*, p 382.

385[3] House of Commons, 28 Oct 1971 (*Hansard*, vol 823, cols 2080–106).

385[4] Wilson papers, box 85, Wilson to Heath, 13 Jan 1972.

385[5] Jenkins, *Life at the Centre*, p 346.

386[1] Jenkins, *Life at the Centre*, p 349.

386[2] Wilson papers, box 89, Jenkins to Wilson, 10 April 1972; Williams to Wilson, 10 April 1972.

386[3] Wilson papers, box 37, Behrendt to Wilson, 1 Feb 1972.

387[1] Benn, *Office Without Power*, p 428.

387[2] Healey, *The Time of My Life*, p 359.

387[3] Wilson papers, box 37, Wilson to Brandt, 14 Dec 1972.

387[4] Healey, *The Time of My Life*, p 360.

388[1] Callaghan, *Time and Chance*, p 290.

388[2] Interview with Martin Gilbert.

388[3] Wilson papers, box 18, Sternberg to Wilson, 12 Nov 1973.

388[4] Wilson papers, box 85, Wilson to Heath, 10 Oct 1973; Heath to Wilson, 12 Oct 1973.

389[1] Wilson, *Chariot of Israel*, p 367.

389[2] Wilson papers, box 86, Kerr to Wilson, 17 Oct 1973.

389[3] House of Commons, 18 Oct 1973 (*Hansard*, vol 861, cols 427–42).

389[4] Wilson papers, box 88, Wilson to Faulds, 10 Dec 1973.

389[5] Wilson papers, box 95, Wilson to Sadat, 7 March 1974.

390[1] Wilson papers, box 83, Dunn to Wilson, 27 April 1972.

390[2] Wilson papers, box 83.

390[3] Benn, *Office Without Power*, p 428.

391[1] 30 June 1972.

391[2] *Political Quarterly*, vol 43, no 4, Oct–Dec 1972, p 381.

391[3] Wilson papers, box 45, Wilson to Soviet Ambassador, 6 July 1972.

391[4] Harris, *Neil Kinnock*, p 71.

392[1] Edmund Dell, *A Hard Pounding*, Oxford, 1991, p 15.

392[2] Castle, *Diaries 1974–1976*, pp 37–8.

393[1] Keith Middlemas, *Politics in Industrial Society*, London, 1979, p 446.

393² Wilson papers, box 45, Wilson to Sternberg, 28 Nov 1973.
393³ Castle, *Diaries 1974–1976*, p 418.
394¹ Benn, *Against the Tide*, p 38.
394² Whitehead, *Writing on the Wall*, p 122.
394³ Benn, *Against the Tide*, p 42.
394⁴ Wilson papers, box 85, Mikardo to Hayward, 12 July 1973.
394⁵ Benn, *Against the Tide*, p 58.
395¹ Benn, *Against the Tide*, p 64.
395² Kellner, *Callaghan*, p 122.
396¹ Mikardo, *Back-bencher*, pp 187–9.
396² Benn, *Against the Tide*, p 55.
396³ Wilson papers, box 39, Wilson to Hetherington, 27 Feb 1973.
397¹ Greenwood papers, uncatalogued, 1st tier, shelf 1, diary, late Nov 1973.
397² Benn, *Against the Tide*, p 75.
397³ Joe Gormley, *Battled Cherub*, London, 1982, pp 133–4.
398¹ Gormley, *Battled Cherub*, p 135.
398² Wilson papers, box 179, Wilson to Heath, 23 Nov 1973; Heath to Wilson, 27 Nov 1973.
398³ Benn, *Against the Tide*, p 80.
398⁴ Castle, *Diaries 1974–1976*, p 27.
399¹ Benn, *Office Without Power*, p 318.

Chapter XX: The Two Elections, 1974

401¹ Benn, *Against the Tide*, p 97.
401² Haines, *Politics of Power*, p 187.
401³ Wilson papers, box 135, Wilson to Arthur Haigh, 8 Dec 1974.
401⁴ As with every other election, I have drawn heavily on the work of David Butler and his various partners, in this case: David Butler and Michael Kavanagh, *The British General Election of February 1974*, London, 1974.
402¹ Bernard Donoughue, *Prime Minister. The Conduct of Policy under Harold Wilson and James Callaghan*, London, 1987, p 40.
402² Benn, *Against the Tide*, p 94.
402³ Castle, *Diaries 1974–1976*, p 29.
403¹ Kellner, *Callaghan*, p 123; Benn, *Against the Tide*, p 101.
403² Tony Benn, unpublished diary, 29 Jan 1976.
404¹ Butler, *British General Election of February 1974*, p 82.
404² Benn, *Against the Tide*, pp 105–9.
404³ *Cecil King Diary, 1970–1974*, p 345.
404⁴ Cockerell, *Live from Number 10*, p 198.
404⁵ Falkender, *Downing Street in Perspective*, pp 52–3; Cockerell, *Live from Number 10*, p 197; Benn, *Against the Tide*, pp 108–9.
405¹ Donoughue, *Prime Minister*, p 45.
405² *The Wilson Years*, programme 4.

405³ Jenkins, *Life at the Centre*, p 368.
406¹ Benn, *Against the Tide*, p 105.
406² Falkender, *Downing Street in Perspective*, p 69.
407¹ Falkender, *Downing Street in Perspective*, p 80.
407² Jenkins, *Life at the Centre*, p 370.
408¹ Castle, *Diaries 1974–1976*, pp 32–3.
408² Castle, *Diaries 1974–1976*, p 108.
409¹ Cockerell, *Live from Number 10*, p 207.
409² Margach, *Abuse of Power*, p 6.
409³ *Observer*, 20 Feb 1977.
409⁴ Interview with Martin Gilbert.
410¹ Falkender papers, Wilson to Williams, 18 May 1974.
410² Benn, *Against the Tide*, p 160.
410³ Pincher, *Inside Story*, p 259.
410⁴ Castle, *Diaries 1974–1976*, p 153.
410⁵ Wilson papers, box 134, Wilson to Heath, 9 May 1974.
410⁶ Benn, *Against the Tide*, p 137.
411¹ Howard, *Crossman*, p 317.
411² Wilson, *Governance of Britain*, p 27.
411³ Jenkins, *Life at the Centre*, p 374.
411⁴ Donoughue, *Prime Minister*, p 48.
412¹ Jones, *Union Man*, p 281.
412² Castle, *Diaries 1974–1976*, p 37.
412³ Castle, *Diaries 1974–1976*, p 168.
412⁴ Donoughue, *Prime Minister*, p 50.
412⁵ Joel Barnett, *Inside the Treasury*, London, 1982, p 3.
412⁶ Interview with Lord Owen.
412⁷ Healey, *The Time of My Life*, p 389.
412⁸ *Labour Party 1974 Report*, p 141.
413¹ Castle, *Diaries 1974–1976*, p 36.
413² Castle, *Diaries 1974–1976*, p 37.
413³ Castle, *Diaries 1974–1976*, p 158.
413⁴ Wilson, *Final Term*, p 14.
413⁵ Falkender, *Downing Street in Perspective*, p 131.
413⁶ Benn, *Against the Tide*, p 122.
414¹ Interview with Lord Charteris.
414² Interviews with Lords Hunt, Armstrong and Bridges.
414³ Benn, *Against the Tide*, p 120.
415¹ Wilson papers, box 121, Hayward to editor, *Daily Mail*, 25 April 1974.
415² Hennessy, *Whitehall*, pp 244–5.
415³ Lord Rothschild, *Random Variables*, London, 1984, p 20.
416¹ Hennessy, *Cabinet*, p 173.
416² Donoughue, *Prime Minister*, p 50.
416³ Wilson papers, box 108, Wilson to Healey, 23 April 1974.
417¹ Wilson papers, box 95, transcript of conversation of 23 Aug 1974.
417² Wilson papers, box 134, Wilson to Knox, 5 June 1974.

418[1] Wilson papers, box 134, Wilson to Ramsey, 6 May 1974.
418[2] Wilson papers, box 135, Wilson to Coggan, 12 Aug 1974.
418[3] Wilson papers, box 135, Wilson to Priestley, 3 Sept 1974.
418[4] Wilson papers, box 108, 8 July 1974.
418[5] Wilson papers, box 100, Robin Butler to Noreen Bovill (Dept of the Environment).
419[1] Wilson papers, box 83, Chalfont to Wilson, 20 Sept 1974.
419[2] Castle, *Diaries 1974–1976*, pp 96–7.
419[3] Wilson papers, box 96, Wilson to Ford, 18 Sept 1974.
420[1] Butler, *British General Election of October 1974*, p 291.
420[2] Wilson papers, box 135, Wilson to Arthur Haigh, 8 Dec 1974.
420[3] Butler, *British General Election of October 1974*, p 13.
420[4] Haines, *Politics of Power*, p 213.
421[1] *Daily Telegraph*, obituary of Edward Brown.
421[2] Benn, *Against the Tide*, pp 226 and 244.
421[3] Wilson papers, box 135, Wilson to Lee Kuan Yew, 21 Oct 1974.

Chapter XXI: Britain and Europe, 1974–1975

422[1] Benn, *Against the Tide*, p 192.
423[1] Vernon Bogdanor, *The People and the Party System*, Cambridge, 1981, p 41.
423[2] Benn, *Against the Tide*, p 116.
423[3] Wilson, *Final Term*, p 54.
423[4] Silkin, *Changing Battlefields*, p 187.
423[5] Callaghan, *Time and Chance*, p 300.
423[6] Benn, *Against the Tide*, p 140.
424[1] Castle, *Diaries 1974–1976*, p 109.
424[2] Benn, *Against the Tide*, p 184.
424[3] Interview with Lord Lever.
424[4] Castle, *Diaries 1974–1976*, p 155.
424[5] Wilson papers, box 108, Wilson to Callaghan, 18 June 1974.
424[6] Wilson papers, box 108, Wilson to Benn, 4 July 1974.
424[7] Benn, *Against the Tide*, p 192.
425[1] Benn, *Against the Tide*, p 277.
425[2] Wilson papers, box 96, Wilson to Schmidt, 5 Dec 1974.
426[1] Text in Wilson, *Final Term*, Appendix III.
426[2] Castle, *Diaries 1974–1976*, p 248.
426[3] Benn, *Against the Tide*, p 283.
426[4] Benn papers, general, Foot to Wilson, 27 Nov 1974; Wilson to Foot, 24 Dec 1974.
427[1] Interview with Michael Foot.
427[2] Wilson papers, box 137, Wilson to Benn, 6 Jan 1975.
427[3] Castle, *Diaries 1974–1976*, p 289; Benn, *Against the Tide*, p 305.
428[1] Interview with Sir Michael Butler.
428[2] Jenkins, *Life at the Centre*, p 494.

429¹ Wilson papers, box 97, Wilson to Schmidt, 24 March 1975.
429² Goodhart, *Full-Hearted Consent*, p 132.
429³ House of Commons, 7 April 1975 (*Hansard*, vol 889, cols 821–38).
430¹ 8 April 1975.
430² Hennessy, *Cabinet*, p 87.
430³ Benn, *Against the Tide*, p 361.
430⁴ Wilson papers, box 101, Wilson to Jenkins, 28 May 1975.
430⁵ Jenkins, *Life at the Centre*, pp 410–11.
430⁶ Wilson papers, box 101, Wilson to Jenkins, 28 and 29 May 1975.
431¹ Interview with Michael Foot.
431² Benn, *Against the Tide*, pp 352–5.
431³ Jay, *Change and Fortune*, p 484.
432¹ Castle, *Diaries 1974–1976*, p 379.
432² Wilson papers, box 101, Wilson to Callaghan, undated.
433¹ 6 June 1975.
433² Phillip Whitehead, *The Writing on the Wall*, London, 1985, p 139.
433³ Interview with Lord Jenkins.
433⁴ Interview with Lady Falkender.
434¹ House of Commons, 4 Dec 1975 (*Hansard*, vol 901, cols 1931–43).
434² Wilson papers, box 142, Wilson to Aitken, 3 March 1976.

Chapter XXII: The Last Administration, 1975–1976

435¹ Castle, *Diaries 1974–1976*, p 357.
435² Wilson papers, box 108, Wilson to Benn, 26 March 1974.
436¹ Wilson papers, box 43, Meinertzhagen to Charles Villiers, 29 March 1974.
436² Benn, unpublished diary, 10 Feb 1976.
436³ Benn, *Against the Tide*, p 278.
436⁴ Interview with Winston Churchill.
436⁵ Wilson papers, box 101, Wilson to Castle, 1 Dec 1975.
436⁶ Benn, *Against the Tide*, p 421.
437¹ Tony Benn papers, PM's Personal Minute M 52/W/74 of 14 May 1974.
437² Tony Benn papers.
437³ Benn, *Against the Tide*, p 156.
437⁴ Benn, *Against the Tide*, p 175.
437⁵ Benn, *Against the Tide*, pp 176–9.
438¹ Edmund Dell, *A Hard Pounding*, Oxford, 1991, pp 91–6.
438² Benn, *Against the Tide*, p 194.
438³ Benn, *Against the Tide*, p 197.
438⁴ Benn, *Against the Tide*, p 212.
438⁵ Benn, *Against the Tide*, p 214.
438⁶ Whitehead, *Writing on the Wall*, p 131.
438⁷ 30 Oct 1974.

439¹ Castle, *Diaries 1974–1976*, p 206; Wilson papers, box 108, Wilson to Benn etc, 31 Oct 1974.
439² Benn, *Against the Tide*, p 257.
439³ Wilson papers, box 108, Wilson to Hart, 5 Nov 1974.
439⁴ Castle, *Diaries 1974–1976*, p 239.
439⁵ Benn, *Against the Tide*, p 275.
439⁶ Benn, *Against the Tide*, p 285.
440¹ Castle, *Diaries 1974–1976*, p 371.
440² Benn, *Against the Tide*, p 388.
440³ Castle, *Diaries 1974–1976*, p 409.
440⁴ Susan Crosland, *Crosland*, p 293.
441¹ Robert Jenkins, *Benn*, p 224.
441² Benn, *Against the Tide*, p 385.
441³ Cockerell, *Sources Close to the Prime Minister*, p 127.
441⁴ Benn, *Against the Tide*, p 375.
441⁵ Benn, *Against the Tide*, pp 389–90.
441⁶ Falkender, *Downing Street in Perspective*, p 210.
441⁷ Benn, *Against the Tide*, pp 375–6.
442¹ Castle, *Diaries 1974–1976*, p 413.
442² Wilson papers, box 104, Mellish to Wilson, 17 Dec 1974.
442³ Benn, *Against the Tide*, p 285.
442⁴ Castle, *Diaries 1974–1976*, p 283.
443¹ Wilson papers, box 108, Wilson to Shepherd, 20 Nov 1974.
443² Healey, *The Time of My Life*, p 394; Haines, *Politics of Power*, p 43.
443³ *Ruling Performance*, Whitehead, "The Labour Governments, 1974–1979", p 251.
444¹ Keith Middlemas, *Power, Competition and the State, vol 3. The End of the Postwar Era. Britain since 1974*, London, 1991, p 55.
444² Dell, *Hard Pounding*, p 174.
444³ Dell, *Hard Pounding*, p 156.
445¹ Castle, *Diaries 1974–1976*, p 428.
445² Benn, *Against the Tide*, p 405.
445³ Wilson papers, box 138, Wilson to Healey, 27 June 1975.
446¹ Healey, *The Time of My Life*, pp 394–5.
446² Dell, *Hard Pounding*, pp 160–6.
446³ Haines, *Politics of Power*, p 57.
446⁴ Interview with Lord Hunt of Tanworth.
446⁵ Donoughue, *Prime Minister*, p 67.
447¹ Donoughue, *Prime Minister*, p 68.
447² Wilson, *Final Term*, p 115.
447³ Wilson, *Final Term*, p 116.
447⁴ Interview with Joe Haines.
447⁵ Interview with Lady Falkender.
448¹ Benn, *Against the Tide*, p 430.
448² Wilson papers, box 138, Wilson to Goodhew, 23 June 1975.
449¹ Joel Barnett, *Inside the Treasury*, London, 1982, pp 80–2.
449² Castle, *Diaries 1974–1976*, p 463.

449³ House of Commons, 23 July 1975 (*Hansard*, vol 896, col 648).

449⁴ Mikardo, *Back-bencher*, p 198.

449⁵ Benn papers, Wilson to Benn, Personal Minute M/5/76, Feb 1976.

449⁶ Benn papers, Wilson to Benn, Personal Minute M/31/76, 8 March 1976.

450¹ Sandelson papers, Wilson to Sandelson, 21 July 1975.

450² Harris, *Kinnock*, p 81.

451¹ Benn, *Against the Tide*, pp 488 and 523.

451² Jenkins, *Life at the Centre*, p 394.

451³ Interview with Denis Healey.

451⁴ Cockerell, *Live from Number 10*, p 206.

452¹ Wilson papers, box 96, Idi Amin to Wilson, 11 Oct 1974.

452² Dell, *Hard Pounding*, pp 50–1.

452³ Wilson papers, box 100, Robert Armstrong to R. A. Custis, 25 Oct 1974.

453¹ Wilson papers, box 140, Wilson to Moonman, 3 Oct 1975.

453² Benn, unpublished diary, 21 Jan 1976.

453³ Wilson, *Final Term*, pp 212–13.

453⁴ Wilson papers, box 104, evidence to Committee of Privy Councillors on Ministerial Memoirs, 1 July 1975.

453⁵ Hugo Young, *The Crossman Affair*, London, 1976, p 95.

454¹ Hennessy, *Cabinet*, p 178.

454² Young, *Crossman Affair*, p 43.

454³ Wilson papers, box 104, evidence to Committee on Ministerial Memoirs.

455¹ House of Commons, 6 Feb 1975 (*Hansard*, vol 885, cols 1554–6).

455² Wilson papers, box 104, Aldington to Wilson, 7 Feb 1975; Heath to Wilson, 6 Feb 1975.

455³ Castle, *Diaries 1974–1976*, p 309.

455⁴ Castle, *Diaries 1974–1976*, pp 314–15.

456¹ Wilson papers, box 138, Wilson to Lawson, 20 May 1975.

456² Wilson papers, box 109, Lawson to Wilson, 17 March 1976.

456³ Dell, *Hard Pounding*, pp 134–5.

457¹ Wilson papers, box 102, Armstrong to Hutton, 15 Jan 1975.

457² Mikardo, *Back-bencher*, pp 195–9.

458¹ Benn, *Against the Tide*, p 460.

458² Barnett, *Inside the Treasury*, p 73.

459¹ Wilson, *Final Term*, p 198.

459² Wilson papers, box 96, Wilson to Ford, 31 Oct 1974.

459³ Wilson papers, box 96, Ford to Wilson, 13 Nov 1974.

459⁴ Wilson papers, box 96, Wilson to Ford, 20 Nov 1974.

460¹ Wilson papers, box 96, Wilson to Whitlam, 27 Nov 1974.

460² Interview with Lord Owen.

460³ Benn, *Against the Tide*, pp 267–8.

460⁴ *Ruling Performance*, ed. Hennessy, p 253.

460⁵ Benn, *Against the Tide*, p 269.

461¹ Healey, *Time of My Life*, p 313.

461² Wilson papers, box 80, Wilson to Nixon, 9 Aug 1974.
461³ Falkender, *Downing Street in Perspective*, pp 174–5.
461⁴ Castle, *Diaries 1974–1976*, p 305.
461⁵ Castle, *Diaries 1974–1976*, p 313.
462¹ Wilson, *Final Term*, p 160.
462² Interview with Lord Bridges.
462³ Wilson papers, box 96, Wilson to Ford, 14 Aug 1974.
463¹ Wilson papers, box 135, Wilson to Constantine, 16 Dec 1974.
463² Wilson papers, box 96, Sadat to Wilson, 13 March 1974.
463³ Wilson, *Chariot of Israel*, p 375.
463⁴ Wilson, *Chariot of Israel*, p 376.
464¹ Wilson papers, box 102, P. R. H. Wright to R. N. Dales, 19 June 1975.
464² Wilson papers, box 97, Wilson to Ford, 22 Dec 1975.
464³ Wilson papers, box 102, P. R. H. Wright to S. J. Barrett, April 1975.
465¹ Wilson papers, box 97, Wilson to Giscard, 6 Nov 1975.
465² Wilson, *Final Term*, p 161.
465³ Wilson papers, box 96, Manley to Wilson, 7 May 1975.
466¹ Wilson papers, box 96, Cosgrave to Wilson, 21 March 1974; Wilson to Cosgrave, 28 March 1974.
466² Wilson, *Final Term*, pp 76–7.
466³ Donoughue, *Prime Minister*, p 130.
466⁴ Benn, *Against the Tide*, p 162.
466⁵ Wilson papers, box 111, Caradon to Wilson, 29 May 1974; Wilson to Caradon, 31 May 1974.
466⁶ Donoughue, *Prime Minister*, p 128.
467¹ Benn, *Against the Tide*, p 273.
467² Rees, *Northern Ireland*, p 159.
467³ Wilson papers, box 99, Cosgrave to Wilson, 7 Jan 1966.

Chapter XXIII: Resignation, 1976

469¹ Wilson, *Governance of Britain*, p 85.
469² Wilson papers, box 148, 28 Jan 1975.
469³ Benn, *Against the Tide*, p 534.
469⁴ Haines, *Politics of Power, see*, in particular, pp 157–69.
469⁵ Benn, unpublished diary, 7 Feb 1977.
470¹ Wilson papers, box 20, 27 Jan and 28 Feb 1975.
470² Interview with Lord Charteris.
470³ Interview with Lord Goodman.
470⁴ Castle, *Diaries 1964–1970*, p 79.
470⁵ Interview with Joe Haines.
470⁶ Interview with Lord Goodman.
471¹ Interview with Lord Goodman.
471² Interview with Lord Lever.
472¹ Jenkins, *Life at the Centre*, p 425.
472² Wilson papers, box 142, Wilson to Goodman, 1 March 1976.

Notes

472³ Article by Michael Davie, *Observer*, 21 March 1976.
472⁴ Wilson papers, box 142, Wilson to Goodman, 24 March 1976.
473¹ Interview with Lord Bridges.
473² *The Castle Diaries 1964–1976*, London, 1990, p 728.
473³ Wilson papers, box 142, Wilson to John Watkinson, 5 Feb 1976.
473⁴ House of Commons, 12 Feb 1976 (*Hansard*, vol 905, col 612).
474¹ Wilson papers, box 137, Wilson to David Stoddart, 16 Jan 1975.
474² Wilson papers, box 137, Wilson to Bruce Douglas-Mann, 22 Jan 1975.
474³ Wilson papers, box 137, Wilson to Mountbatten, 20 Feb 1975.
474⁴ Wilson, *Memoirs*, p 26.
474⁵ Wilson papers, box 101, Wilson to Hugh Jenkins, 27 March 1975.
475¹ Wilson papers, box 137, Wilson to Healey, 24 Feb 1975.
475² Wilson papers, box 137, Wilson to Prentice, undated.
475³ Wilson, *Final Term*, p 200.
475⁴ Jenkins, *Life at the Centre*, p 384.
476¹ Interview with Sir Antony Duff.
476² Interview with Mrs Stella Rimington.
476³ *Panorama*, October 1988.
477¹ Patrick Marnham, *Private Eye Story*, London, 1982, p 155.
477² The questions have been exhaustively considered in, *inter alia*, David Leigh's *The Wilson Plot* (*op. cit.*) and Stephen Dorrill and Robin Ramsay's *Smear! Wilson and the Secret State*, London, 1991. Though perforce making bricks with a sometimes exiguous amount of straw, both books amass a great deal of interesting and relevant material and deserve to be taken seriously.
477³ Paul Foot, *Who Framed Collin Wallace?*, London, 1989.
477⁴ House of Commons, 6 May 1987 (*Hansard*, 6th series, col 115, col 724).
477⁵ Interview with Lord Callaghan.
478¹ Interview with Lord Hunt of Tanworth.
478² Wilson's evidence to Royal Commission on Press, submitted April 1977, *The Times*, 14 May 1977.
479¹ Wilson papers, box 80.
479² Castle, *Diaries 1974–1976*, pp 640–1.
480¹ Cyril Smith, *Big Cyril*, London, 1977, p 194.
480² Castle, *Diaries 1974–1976*, pp 642, 648 and 677–9.
481¹ Wilson papers, box 117.
481² House of Commons, 29 March 1976 (*Hansard*, vol 908, cols 333–4).
481³ Wilson papers, box 167.
482¹ Wilson papers, box 7.
483¹ Wilson, *A Prime Minister on Prime Ministers*, p 126.
483² Falkender, *Downing Street in Perspective*, pp 3–4.
484¹ Wilson papers, box 109, memo by Kenneth Stowe; interview with Lord Charteris.
484² Wilson, *Final Term*, p 229.
484³ Callaghan, *Time and Chance*, p 386.
484⁴ Interview with Lord Lever.

485[1] Castle, *Diaries 1974–1976*, pp 628–9, 672 and 674.
485[2] Benn, *Against the Tide*, p 542.
485[3] Wilson papers, box 109, Callaghan to Wilson, 2 Jan 1976.
486[1] Healey, *Time of My Life*, p 446.
486[2] Interview with Lady Falkender.
486[3] Wilson papers, box 109.
486[4] Margach, *Anatomy of Power*, pp 42–3.
487[1] Interview with Lord Callaghan.
487[2] Interview with Lord Bridges.
487[3] Interview with Joe Haines.
487[4] Interview with Lord Glenamara.
487[5] Interview with Lord Callaghan.
488[1] Pincher, *Inside Story*, p 363.
488[2] Castle, *Diaries 1974–1976*, p 695.
488[3] Interviews with Joe Haines and Lord Donoughue.
488[4] Wilson papers, box 109, record of meeting.
489[1] Susan Crosland, *Crosland*, p 311; Healey, *Time of My Life*, p 446; Barnett, *Inside the Treasury*, p 84.
489[2] Castle, *Diaries 1974–1976*, pp 689–91.
489[3] Benn, *Against the Tide*, p 535.
489[4] Wilson papers, box 109, Banda to Wilson, 22 March 1976.
489[5] Castle, *Diaries 1974–1976*, p 690.
490[1] Castle, *Diaries 1974–1976*, p 735; Jones, *Union Man*, p 304.
490[2] Benn, *Against the Tide*, p 542.
490[3] Benn, *Against the Tide*, pp 527 and 528.
491[1] Wilson, *Final Term*, p 236.
491[2] Benn, *Against the Tide*, p 542; Castle, *Diaries 1974–1976*, p 699.
491[3] Castle, *Diaries 1974–1976*, p 699.
491[4] Falkender, *Downing Street in Perspective*, p 9.
491[5] Benn, unpublished diary, 5 April 1976.
491[6] Wilson papers, box 109, Idi Amin to Wilson, 17 March 1976.
491[7] Interview with Lord Kissin.
491[8] Castle, *Diaries 1974–1976*, p 718.

Chapter XXIV: Retirement, 1976–1980

492[1] Interviews with Lord Callaghan and Lady Falkender.
493[1] Benn, *Against the Tide*, p 369.
494[1] Wilson papers, box 154, Wilson to Mrs V. Herbert, 25 April 1984.
495[1] Haines, *Politics of Power*, p 156.
496[1] Letter from Lady Summerskill to *The Times*, 27 May 1977.
496[2] *The Times*, 29 May 1976.
497[1] *The Times*, 31 May 1976.
497[2] *The Times*, 2 June 1976.
497[3] Haines, *Politics of Power*, p 153.
497[4] Interview with Joe Haines.

497⁵ Interview with Lord Donoughue.
497⁶ Interview with Lord Shackleton.
497⁷ Interview with Lady Falkender.
498¹ *The Times*, 3 June 1976.
498² *Daily Telegraph*, 26 May 1976; *Guardian*, 26 May 1976.
498³ Benn, unpublished diaries, 23, 24 and 27 May 1976.
499¹ Benn, *Against the Tide*, pp 624–5.
499² Benn, unpublished diary, 14 June 1976.
500¹ Benn, *Against the Tide*, p 565.
500² Interview with Lord Weidenfeld.
500³ The account of this episode is set out in Barrie Penrose and Roger Courtiour's *The Pencourt File*, London, 1978. Wilson has never challenged their account of the conversations that took place between them.
501¹ Interview with Lady Falkender; *The Times*, 2 Feb 1977.
501² Penrose, *Pencourt File*, p 246.
501³ Penrose, *Pencourt File*, p 233; Pincher, *Inside Story*, pp 43–5; interview with Winston Churchill.
502¹ Ziegler, *Mountbatten*, p 661.
502² Interview with Lord Zuckerman.
502³ Wilson papers, box 115, Wilson to Semenov, 31 Aug 1977.
502⁴ Wilson papers, box 160, 14 July 1986.
503¹ Benn, *Against the Tide*, p 557.
503² Wilson papers, box 164, Wilson to Sean Hughes, 4 Feb 1981.
503³ Roy Jenkins, *European Diary 1977–1981*, London, 1989, p 243.
504¹ Wilson papers, box 172, Plumb to Wilson, 12 Oct 1976.
505¹ "The City Enquiry – Its Progress to Date", The City Association Accounting Lecture, London, 1979, pp 8–9.
505² *Ibid*, p 1.
505³ Middlemas, *Power, Competition and the State*, vol 3, pp 67–8.
506¹ House of Commons, 23 Jan 1978 (*Hansard*, vol 997, col 595).
506² Roll, *Crowded Hours*, p 208.
506³ Wilson, *Governance of Britain*, p x.
506⁴ Wilson, *Governance of Britain*, p xi.
506⁵ *Hampstead and Highgate Express*, 22 Oct 1976.
507¹ *Yorkshire Post*, 21 Oct 1976.
507² Wilson papers, box 167, Falkender to Barbara Twigg.
508¹ Wilson papers, box 167, 27 Nov 1977.
508² Wilson papers, box 167.
508³ Benn, unpublished diary, 5 Nov 1977.
508⁴ Wilson, *A Prime Minister on Prime Ministers*, pp 34, 126, 40, 131 and 168.
508⁵ Morgan, *Labour People*, p 259.
508⁶ Wilson papers, box 158, Wilson to Kirsty Todd, 7 Feb 1985.
509¹ Wilson papers, box 162, Jacqueline Korn to Falkender, 26 July 1979.
510¹ Interview with Lord Callaghan.
510² Jenkins, *European Diary*, p 177.

510[3] Wilson, *Chariot of Israel*, p 34.
510[4] Wilson, *Chariot of Israel*, p 127.

Chapter XXV: Old Age, 1980–1993

511[1] Interview with Dr Leon Kaufman.
511[2] Wilson papers, box 165, Falkender to Richard Stone, 21 Nov 1980.
511[3] Pakenham, *Diary of a Year*, p 43.
512[1] House of Commons, July 1981 (*Hansard*, 6th series, vol 8, cols 471–3).
512[2] Healey, *Time of My Life*, p 478.
512[3] Wilson papers, box 126, 13 Sept 1983.
512[4] Wilson papers, box 152, Wilson to T. A. Elmer, 14 March 1984.
512[5] House of Lords, 14 March 1984 (*Hansard*, HL, vol 449, col 762).
512[6] House of Lords, 9 May 1984 (*Hansard*, HL, vol 451, cols 923–8).
513[1] Wilson papers, box 164, Wilson to Sean Hughes, 4 Feb 1981.
513[2] 28 May 1983.
513[3] Wilson papers, box 154, Wilson to G. Hodgkin, 21 Jan 1984.
514[1] Wilson papers, box 152, Wilson to Thatcher, undated; Thatcher to Wilson, 27 April 1984.
514[2] Wilson papers, box 173, John Kentleton to Wilson, 2 Feb 1987.
514[3] Wilson papers, box 154.
515[1] Wilson papers, box 163, Wilson to Thatcher, 8 Nov 1982.
515[2] Wilson papers, box 112.
518[1] Wigg, *George Wigg*, p 341; Wilson papers, box 109, Fisher to Wilson, 22 March 1976; Nabarro, *NAB 1*, p 203; Longford, *Grain of Wheat*, p 87.
518[2] *Spectator*, 20 March 1976.

Bibliographical Note

Lord Wilson's archive will eventually be deposited in the Bodleian Library but at the moment of writing it is to be found in some 200 boxes in a basement near Baker Street. The papers have been arranged according to subject and period but have not been catalogued. I numbered each box as I read it, and quote that number in my reference notes. This notation is unlikely to be of much use to future researchers but I hope that the details I give for each document will make it relatively easy to trace once the archive is in its permanent home.

In addition to the main archive – which includes all Lord Wilson's official prime-ministerial papers from Downing Street – some related papers remain in the possession of Lady Wilson and the Baroness Falkender. I have referred to these as Lady Wilson's papers and Lady Falkender's papers.

The next most important collection of manuscripts is probably that in the Lyndon Johnson Library in Austin, Texas – in particular the dispatches of the American Ambassador, David Bruce. The National Archives in Washington also contain much interesting material about Wilson's early career. The Public Record Office in London has not yet released any of the papers relating to Wilson's period as Prime Minister but contains much material relating to his time as a junior minister and President of the Board of Trade.

Other manuscript collections of value include the Attlee papers (Bodleian), the Tony Benn papers, including unpublished portions of his diary (Tony Benn), the George-Brown papers (Bodleian), the Beveridge papers (British Library of Political and Economic Science), the diary of George Caunt (*Sunday Times*), the Cromer papers (Baring Brothers), the Martin Gilbert papers (Martin Gilbert), the Arthur Goodhart papers (Bodleian), the Patrick Gordon Walker papers

(Churchill College), the Greenwood papers (Bodleian), the Joe Haines papers (Joe Haines), the Sandelson papers (Neville Sandelson), the Zuckerman papers (Solly Zuckerman).

To list again all the books cited in the notes would seem superfluous but a brief mention of those works exclusively or substantially devoted to Harold Wilson might be of use. Lord Wilson has written extensively about his own career, most notably in *The Labour Government 1964–1970* (London, 1971) and *Final Term. The Labour Government 1974–1976* (London, 1979). His earlier life was covered in *Memoirs 1916–1964. The Making of the Prime Minister* (London, 1986) but this was a slight and largely ghosted work. Others of his books in which he figures prominently are *The Governance of Britain* (London, 1976), *A Prime Minister on Prime Ministers* (London, 1977) and *The Chariot of Israel* (London, 1981).

A crop of short biographies were written about the time of his becoming leader of the opposition and then Prime Minister: Gerard Noel, *Harold Wilson and the "New Britain"* (London, 1964); Leslie Smith, *Harold Wilson: The Authentic Portrait* (London, 1964) and Dudley Smith, *Harold Wilson: A Critical Biography* (London, 1964). Michael Foot's *Harold Wilson: A Pictorial Biography* (London, 1964) is what its title suggests. Ernest Kay's adulatory *Pragmatic Premier* (London, 1967) was briskly followed by Paul Foot's hostile *The Politics of Harold Wilson* (London, 1968). Andrew Roth's *Sir Harold Wilson: Yorkshire Walter Mitty* (London, 1977) perished prematurely as a result of a libel action. A period of quiet was ended with Austen Morgan's *Harold Wilson* and Ben Pimlott's *Harold Wilson* (both London, 1992).

Other books dealing predominantly with Wilson include Bernard Donoughue, *Prime Minister. The Conduct of Policy under Harold Wilson and James Callaghan* (London, 1987); Stephen Dorrill and Robin Ramsay, *Smear! Wilson and the Secret State* (London, 1991); Joe Haines, *The Politics of Power* (London, 1977); Anthony Howard and Richard West, *The Making of the Prime Minister* (London, 1965); David Leigh, *The Wilson Plot* (London, 1988); Barrie Penrose and Roger Courtiour, *The Pencourt File* (London, 1978); Edward Short, *Whip to Wilson* (London, 1989); Marcia Williams, *Inside Number 10* (London, 1972) and (as Marcia Falkender) *Downing Street in Perspective* (London, 1983).

Index

Index

Index

Index

Index

Index

Index

Index

Index

Index

Index

Wilson, (James) Harold (Baron Wilson of
Rievaulx)—*cont*
devaluation 73–5; Jewish
sympathies 76, 340–1; wins Huyton
seat 79–80; and Gaitskell's promotion
to Chancellor 81–2; relations with
Gaitskell 81, 102, 105, 108–9, 115–
16; on German rearmament 82–3, 101;
1951 resignation 82–8; as business
consultant 90–2, 118; US lecture
tours 92, 150, 515; writings 92–3,
359–63, 372, 506–9, 515; generosity to
parents 93; 1951 election success 95;
political stance 95–7; supports
monarchy 96–7, 215; chairs Keep-Left
Group 97–8; and control of
Treasury 99; succeeds Bevan on
Shadow Cabinet 103–5; on nuclear
weapons and unilateralism 105–6,
124–5; party TV appearance 106–7;
1955 election victory 107; 1955 report
on party organisation 107–8, 121,
450; congratulates Gaitskell as party
leader 108–9; as shadow
Chancellor 110–12; cultivates sense of
humour 110–11; relations with
Macmillan 110–11, 145, 147;
economic policy 111–12; on Suez
crisis 113–14; 1957 bank rate
accusations 114–15; in 1959
election 116–17; and abolition of
party's nationalisation clause 117,
123, 140, 142; relations with Marcia
Falkender 118–22, 158, rivalry with
Gaitskell 122, 126–9, 181–2; and
Bevan's death 123; as shadow Foreign
Secretary 129–30; views on EEC
membership 130–2, 141, 192, 240–2,
331–8, 380–91, 422–8, 432–3; success
at 1962 party conference 132; Brown
defeats in deputy leadership
election 132–3; and Gaitskell's death
and succession 133–7; elected party
leader 137, 138; forms Shadow
Cabinet 139; eschews social life 141,
167, 272; relations with media and
press 141–2, 156, 162, 202–3, 247,
266–70, 350, 352–3, 420–1, 456–7;
belief in science and technology 142–
4; on Profumo affair 145–6; visits
Kennedy 145, 147–9; visits
Khrushchev 149–50; Michael Foot
eulogises 152; campaigns in 1964
election 153–60; speech writing 155;
mistrusts BBC 156–7, 203, 247, 269–
70, 352–3, 368; 1964 premiership and
government 161, 162–3, 169–78; on
former Prime Ministers 162–3, 507–9;
earnings 166; drinking habits 166,
470, 485; dress 166; eating 167;
creates DEA 170–1; outburst over
Gordon Walker's defeat at
Smethwick 174; reorganisation of
Downing Street 181, 414–15; circle of
advisers 182–5; administrative

style 186–9, 196–8; amiability and
kindliness 187–8, 196, 517–18;
vainglory 188; economic measures and
trade deficit 189–90, 192–5; resists
devaluation 190–1; first legislative
programme and reforms 193, 198–
202, 204–6, 217; rejects Tory coalition
proposal 195; at 1965 party
conference 195; defers election 196;
and Churchill's death 197; and steel
nationalisation 198–9; and Open
University 201; plans 1966
election 206–7, 216–17; and defence
commitments 206, 207–11, 275, 284–
5, 329–30, 459–61; 1965 government
reshuffle 212–14; on
patronage 213–14; relations with
unions 216–17; negotiations over
Rhodesia 218–19, 229–39, 318–20,
321–4; and Vietnam 218, 221–9, 324–
7, 329; in Salisbury 233–4;
calmness 244; in 1966 election 244–
8; and Labour majority 248–9; 1966
reshuffle and reforms 249–51, 259–
60; and seamen's strike 251–2;
announces 1966 economies 255–6;
appearance 256; relish for Downing
Street life 262–4; Driberg's obituary
leaked 263; and D-Notice
affair 267–9; and conduct of Cabinet
meetings 270–4, 292; succession
question 272, 373–4; relations with
PLP 274–7, 305–6; political judgment
and integrity 277–8; 1967 Cabinet
reshuffle 278–9; and 1967 economic
crisis and devaluation 280–4, 286; and
arms to South Africa 287–91; 1968
reshuffle 293; plots to depose 294–
6; popularity falls 299; and industrial
legislation (*In Place of Strife*) 299–
312, 376; party hostility to 305–7;
rebukes Scanlon 308; dispute with
Cabinet 310–11; and intelligence
services 313, 475–8, 490, 500–1;
achievements 316–17; declares
intention to resign 317, 408–9;
relations with Nixon 328–9; tour of
European capitals 332–6; and
Nigerian civil war 338–40; and 1967
Middle East war 340–2; and Northern
Ireland 344–5, 378–80, 465–7; 1970
election defeat 346–54, 355–6;
homes 358; financial support 358–
60, 363, 365–6, 368–9; Commons
office 363–4; honours lists 366, 367–
8, 410, 449, 473–4, 482, 494–8;
incorruptibility 366–7; KG 367, 499;
and *Yesterday's Men* broadcast 368–
70; 1970 confirmation as leader 371–
3; and Tory legislation on unions 376–
7; and EEC referendum 381–2, 422–
33, 440; interest in Israel 387–9; and
South Africa 388; conciliates
unions 391–2; leadership
criticised 390–1, 396–7; denounces

Index